Course	INTRO TO BUSINESS WRITING
Course Number	**W232**
	Smiljka Cubelic
	Indiana University-South Bend
	ENGLISH

ISBN-10: 1121581862   ISBN-13: 9781121581869

Contents

Credits

CHAPTER 1

Succeeding in Business Communication

Chapter Outline

NEWSWORTHY COMMUNICATION

A Communication Recovery from Disaster

In 2009 and 2010 the Toyota Motor Corporation recalled more than 8 million cars and trucks after highly publicized incidents of accelerator pedal failure. In chilling accidents replayed on news reports and the Internet, Toyota accelerator pedals became stuck, causing serious—and sometimes fatal—crashes.

Toyota, the world's largest automaker, had built its business on customer trust and loyalty by providing consistent quality in its cars. But now, in addition to the financial costs of the pedal recalls and the government investigations, the company faced a public relations disaster: customers no longer trusted Toyota to provide safe vehicles.

The company responded with a carefully designed communication campaign to restore customer trust in the Toyota brand. On February 2, 2010, Jim Lentz, Toyota's president and chief operating officer in the United States, sent a letter to all Toyota customers with a personal apology and a commitment to correct the problems. This letter kicked off a publicity campaign of personal and open letters, newspaper and magazine advertisements, and television commercials that all focused on how Toyota was taking responsibility and improving its operations.

"For Toyota, good communication helped the company recover from the costly and embarrassing recalls."

Every company relies on communication with its customers to build trust. When crises hit, as in the case of Toyota's recalls, communication becomes even more important. The quality of written and spoken messages could make the difference between a company's failure and recovery after a crisis. In the late 1990s, Ford Motor Company and the Firestone Tire and Rubber Company were investigated for a series of rollover accidents involving blown-out tires. After first denying the problems and then blaming each other, both companies took years to recover from the crisis—they were still dealing with recalls and complaints in 2006, more than six years after the initial problems.

By contrast, Toyota's straightforward apology and aggressive communication in many forms of media helped restore its image quickly. In fact, by December 2010, Toyota announced that it had "regained the number one spot as the most-considered automobile brand among new-car shoppers." For Toyota, good communication helped the company recover from the costly and embarrassing recalls.

Source: Toyota, "2010 Year-End Progress Report: Major Changes Help Toyota Put Even More Focus on Its Customers," news release, December 20, 2010, http://www.toyota.com/about/news/corporate/2010/12/21-1-Progress.html; and Jim Lentz, "Open Letter to Toyota Customers," Toyota, February 2, 2010, http://www.toyota.com/recall/v2/pdf/ToyotaCustomerLetter.pdf.

4 Part 1 The Building Blocks of Effective Messages

Learning Objectives

After studying this chapter, you will know

LO 1-1 Why you need to be able to communicate well.

LO 1-2 What the costs of communication are.

LO 1-3 What the costs of poor communication are.

LO 1-4 What role conventions play in business communication.

LO 1-5 How to solve business communication problems.

Communication Is Key to Pay

How can you make more money at your job?

The number one way, according to the *Wall Street Journal*, is to "listen to your boss." Specifically, do the work your boss wants done, follow directions, work hard, and let your boss know what you have accomplished. Employees who follow this method collect raises at a rate of 9.9%, while average performers receive 3.6% and poor performers get 1.3%, according to one survey.

Just as important is to make sure you ask your manager to define expectations. Don't assume you know what your manager wants. Make sure you understand what your manager considers an outstanding performance in your position.

Adapted from Perri Capell, "10 Ways to Get the Most Pay out of Your Job," *Wall Street Journal*, September 18, 2006, R1.

The amount of business communication is staggering. The U.S. Postal Service processed 177 billion pieces of mail in 2009, most of which were business communications. Merchants send American consumers 20 billion catalogs annually, through the mail and e-mail. When you consider that most of your business communications are electronic or oral, you can start to imagine the staggering number of business communications that people compose, hear, and read. As one small piece of that, the head of Best Buy says his company handles more than 1.5 billion customer interactions annually. The Radicati Group, a technology market research firm, projects that 294 billion e-mail messages were sent daily in 2010, of which 89.1% were spam.[1]

Business depends on communication. People must communicate to plan products and services; hire, train, and motivate workers; coordinate manufacturing and delivery; persuade customers to buy; and bill them for the sale. Indeed, for many businesses and nonprofit and government organizations, the "product" is information or services rather than something tangible. Information and services are created and delivered by communication. In every organization, communication is the way people get work done.

Communication takes many forms: face-to-face or phone conversations, informal meetings, presentations, e-mail messages, letters, memos, reports, blogs, tweets, text messaging, and websites. All of these methods are forms of **verbal communication,** or communication that uses words. **Nonverbal communication** does not use words. Pictures, computer graphics, and company logos are nonverbal. Interpersonal nonverbal signals include how people sit at meetings, how large offices are, and how long someone keeps a visitor waiting.

COMMUNICATION ABILITY = PROMOTABILITY **LO 1-1**

Even in your first job, you'll communicate. You'll listen to instructions; you'll ask questions; you may solve problems with other workers in teams. Even "entry-level" jobs require high-level skills in reasoning, mathematics, and communicating. As a result, communication ability consistently ranks first among the qualities that employers look for in college graduates.[2] Warren Buffet told Columbia Business School students that they could increase their value 50% by learning communication skills, and that many of them did not yet have those skills.[3]

As more people compete for fewer jobs, the ones who will build successful careers are those who can communicate well with customers and colleagues. Robert O. Best, Chief Information Officer of UNUMProvident, an insurance corporation, cautions, "You used to be able to get away with being a technical nerd. . . . Those days are over."[4]

The National Commission on Writing surveyed 120 major corporations, employing nearly 8 million workers. Almost 70% of respondents said that at least two-thirds of their employees have specific writing responsibilities included in their position descriptions. These writing responsibilities include:

- E-mail (100% of employees)
- Presentations with visuals, such as PowerPoint slides (100%)
- Memos and correspondence (70%)
- Formal reports (62%)
- Technical reports (59%)

Respondents also noted that communication functions were least likely to be outsourced.[5]

Because communication skills are so important, good communicators earn more. Research has shown that among people with two- or four-year degrees, workers in the top 20% of writing ability earn, on average, more than three times as much as workers whose writing falls into the worst 20%.[6] Jeffrey Gitomer, business consultant and author of best-selling business books, says there are three secrets to getting known in the business world; all of them are communication skills: writing, e-zining (he reaches over 130,000 subscribers each week), and speaking. He states, "Writing leads to wealth."[7]

In spite of the frequency of on-the-job writing and the importance of overall communication skills, employers do not find college students well skilled in writing. A survey of employers conducted on behalf of the Association of American Colleges and Universities found that writing was one of the weakest skills of college graduates.[8] In another large survey, respondents noted that a lack of "effective business communication skills appears to be a major stumbling block among new [job] entrants—even at the college level. Spelling errors, improper use of grammar, and the misuse of words were common in written reports, PowerPoint presentations, and e-mail messages."[9]

"I'LL NEVER HAVE TO WRITE BECAUSE . . ."

Some students think that an administrative assistant will do their writing, that they can use form letters if they do have to write, that only technical skills matter, or that they'll call or text rather than write. Each of these claims is fundamentally flawed.

Claim 1:   An administrative assistant will do all my writing.

Reality: Because of automation and restructuring, job responsibilities in offices have changed. Today, many offices do not have typing pools. Most secretaries have become administrative assistants with their own complex tasks such as training, research, and database management for several managers. Managers are likely to take care of their own writing, data entry, and phone calls.

Claim 2:   I'll use form letters or templates when I need to write.

Reality: A form letter is designed to cover only routine situations, many of which are computerized or outsourced, Also, the higher you rise, the more frequently you'll face situations that aren't routine, that demand creative solutions.

Claim 3:   I'm being hired as an accountant, not a writer.

Reality: Almost every entry-level professional or managerial job requires you to write e-mail messages, speak to small groups, write documents, and present your work for annual reviews. People who do these things well are likely to be promoted beyond the entry level. Employees in jobs as diverse as firefighters, security professionals, and construction project managers are all being told to polish their writing and speaking skills.[10]

Claim 4:   I'll just pick up the phone.

Put It in Writing

Raymond Dreyfack credits his writing skills for his successful career at Faberge Perfumes. As he worked in supervisory and management jobs, he kept his eye open for opportunities to solve problems and improve performance. Then, when he had an idea, he wrote a memo to his boss.

Why a memo? The written format forced Dreyfack to organize his initial idea clearly and concisely. Editing memos trained Dreyfack to consider whether his messages reflected the reader's interests and viewpoints. The written format also gave Dreyfack's boss time to consider the idea and reflect on its merits. (If you spring an idea on your boss in the hallway, he or she might find it easier to blurt out a *no* than to give the idea fair consideration.)

Adapted from Raymond Dreyfack, "The Write Way to Jump-Start Your Career," *Supervision* 65, no. 4 (April 2004): 13–15.

6

Part 1   The Building Blocks of Effective Messages

Reality: Important phone calls require follow-up letters, memos, or e-mail messages. People in organizations put things in writing to make themselves visible, to create a record, to convey complex data, to make things convenient for the reader, to save money, and to convey their own messages more effectively. "If it isn't in writing, it didn't happen" is a maxim at many companies. Writing is an essential way to record agreements, to make yourself visible, and to let your accomplishments be known.

COMMUNICATING ON THE JOB

Communication—oral, nonverbal, and written—goes to both internal and external audiences. **Internal audiences** are other people in the same organization: subordinates, superiors, peers. **External audiences** are people outside the organization: customers, suppliers, distributors, unions, stockholders, potential employees, trade associations, special interest groups, government agencies, the press, and the general public.

People in organizations produce a large variety of documents. Figures 1.1 and 1.2 list a few of the specific documents produced at Ryerson, a company that fabricates and sells steel, aluminum, other metals, and plastics to a wide variety of industrial clients and has sales offices across the United States, Canada, and China.

All of the documents in Figures 1.1 and 1.2 have one or more of the three basic purposes of organizational writing: to inform, to request or persuade, and to build goodwill. In fact, most messages have multiple purposes. When you answer a question, for instance, you're informing, but you also want to build goodwill by suggesting that you're competent and perceptive and that your answer is correct and complete.

THE COST OF COMMUNICATION   LO 1-2

Writing costs money. The annual Social Security statements cost $70 million a year to mail, even with huge economies of scale.[11] The cost does not include employee time in the writing and processing, a major expense.

Business communication involves paper documents, electronic communications, and most of all, interpersonal abilities.

Figure 1.1 Internal Documents Produced in One Organization

Document	Description of document	Purpose(s) of document
Transmittal	Memo accompanying document, telling why it's being forwarded to the receiver	Inform; persuade reader to read document; build image and goodwill
Monthly or quarterly report	Report summarizing profitability, productivity, and problems during period. Used to plan activity for next month or quarter	Inform; build image and goodwill (report is accurate, complete; writer understands company)
Policy and procedure bulletin	Statement of company policies and instructions (e.g., how to enter orders, how to run fire drills)	Inform; build image and goodwill (procedures are reasonable)
Request to deviate from policy and procedure bulletin	Persuasive memo arguing that another approach is better for a specific situation than the standard approach	Persuade; build image and goodwill (request is reasonable; writer seeks good of company)
Performance appraisal	Evaluation of an employee's performance	Inform; persuade employee to improve
Memo of congratulations	Congratulations to employees who have won awards, been promoted	Build goodwill

Document cycling processes also increase costs. In many organizations, all external documents must be approved before they go out. A major document may **cycle** from writer to superior to writer to another superior to writer again 10 or more times before final approval. Longer documents can involve large teams of people and take months to write.

Large organizations handle so much paper that even small changes to their communication practices amount to millions of dollars. Through better use of technology, InterContinental Hotels Group cut communications costs by $2.6 million in two years. Xerox Global Services Europe touts contractual annual savings of up to 1 million Euros for organizations with 4,000 or more employees who switch to its printing services.[12]

Figure 1.2 External Documents Produced in One Organization

Document	Description of document	Purpose(s) of document
Quotation	Letter giving price for a specific product or service	Inform; build goodwill (price is reasonable)
Claims adjustment	Letter granting or denying customer request to be given credit for defective goods	Inform; build goodwill
Job description	Description of qualifications and duties of job. Used for performance appraisals, salaries, and hiring	Inform; persuade good candidates to apply; build goodwill (job duties match level, pay)
10-K report	Report filed with the Securities and Exchange Commission detailing financial information	Inform
Annual report	Report to stockholders summarizing financial information for year	Inform; persuade stockholders to retain stock and others to buy; build goodwill (company is a good corporate citizen)
Thank-you letter	Letter to suppliers, customers, or other people who have helped individuals or the company	Build goodwill

8

Hurricane Katrina Storms Communication Lines

Hurricane Katrina caused massive destruction to the Gulf Coast. During the storm, communication failures among local, state, and federal officials left their own harm.

The main communication problems included these issues:

- Lack of communication among responding organizations: FEMA claimed it was days before they knew about the thousands of people in the New Orleans Convention Center.

- Incompatible communication systems: The lack of coordination and communication caused by these systems put even more lives at risk by delaying assistance where it was most needed. Some rescuers in helicopters were unable to communicate with rescuers in boats. Some units of the National Guard actually used runners to communicate.

- Inconsistent messages: State and local agency teams received conflicting messages which led to confusion.

The massive communication problems led to an entire chapter on communication in the U.S. House of Representatives report on the Hurricane Katrina disaster.

Adapted from U.S. House of Representatives, *A Failure of Initiative: Final Report of the Select Bipartisan Committee to Investigate the Preparation for and Response to Hurricane Katrina*, 109th Cong., 2d sess. (Washington, DC, February 15, 2006), http://www.gpoaccess.gov/katrina report/mainreport.pdf.

Communication failures increased the damage caused by Hurricane Katrina.

Good communication is worth every minute it takes and every penny it costs. A study of 335 U.S. and Canadian companies with an average of 13,000 employees each and median annual revenues of $1.8 billion found that those companies who best communicated with their employees enjoyed "greater employee engagement and commitment, higher retention and productivity, and—ultimately—better financial performance. . . .

- They boasted a 19.4% higher market premium (the degree to which the company's market value exceeds the cost of its assets).

- They were 4.5 times more likely to report high levels of employee engagement.

- They were 20% more likely to report lower turnover rates."[13]

Another significant cost of communication is e-mail storage. In addition to the exponential increase in frequency, e-mails are also growing in size. Furthermore, many of them come with attachments. And businesses are storing much of this huge load on their servers. But the cost of the hardware is only some of the storage cost; a larger cost is administering and maintaining the archives. These costs include downtime when storage systems crash and time spent retrieving lost or corrupted messages.[14]

COSTS OF POOR COMMUNICATION LO 1-3

Poor communication can cost billions of dollars. We all can think of examples.

- Hurricane Katrina caused billions of dollars of damage—damage that was worsened by horrendous miscommunications between federal, state, and private relief organizations (see the sidebar "Hurricane Katrina Storms Communication Lines " on this page.).

- The space industry has had billion-dollar mistakes—mistakes where miscommunications were major contributing factors as confirmed by official government investigations (see sidebars on pages 9 and 12).

- Ford and Bridgestone Firestone's failure to coordinate the design of the Ford Explorer and its tires cost them billions of dollars. In hindsight, people agree the mistakes could have been prevented if the different teams involved had communicated more effectively with each other.[15]

- Internal and external communication problems have contributed greatly to delays in Boeing's 787 Dreamliner, delays which have cost Boeing billions in penalties and have caused some customers to switch their orders to Airbus.[16]
- From figures provided by the members of the Business Roundtable, the National Commission on Writing calculated the annual private sector costs of writing training at $3.1 billion.[17] These figures do not include the retail and wholesale trade businesses.
- Even part of the subprime mortgage collapse, which helped spark a global recession, has been connected to poor communication. Documents supposedly explaining some of the riskier investments were so convoluted that even most experts could not understand them. Goldman Sachs paid a $550 million fine to settle allegations that it misled investors in mortgage bonds.[18]

Costs of poor communication are not just financial. People died in the rollovers of Ford Explorers, noted above. In the aftermath of Hurricane Katrina, inaccurate media reports of looting convinced some residents to stay to protect their property instead of evacuating; false reports of shootings at helicopters resulted in some states refusing to send trained emergency workers. According to the presidential commission, inadequate communication among British Petroleum, Halliburton, and Transocean, as well as within their own companies, was a contributing factor in BP's massive oil spill, which caused so much damage, as well as fatalities, in the Gulf of Mexico.[19]

Not all communication costs are so dramatic, however. When communication isn't as good as it could be, you and your organization pay a price in wasted time, wasted effort, lost goodwill, and legal problems.

Wasted Time

Bad writing takes longer to read as we struggle to understand what we're reading. How quickly we can do this is determined by the difficulty of the subject matter and by the document's organization and writing style.

Second, bad writing may need to be rewritten. Poorly written documents frequently cycle to other people for help.

Third, ineffective communication may obscure ideas so that discussions and decisions are needlessly drawn out.

Business Communication Lessons from Mars

The *Mars Climate Orbiter* spacecraft lost contact with NASA mission control just after it arrived at Mars. A subsequent investigation revealed that the main problem was a minor software programming error caused by communication errors.

Like many business projects, the *Mars Climate Orbiter* involved a wide range of people in a range of locations. The programmers who wrote the software that controlled the spacecraft's engines worked in Great Britain, and used metric measurements in their calculations, while the engineers who made the satellite's engines worked in the United States, and used English measurements. Both teams assumed that they were using the same measurement standards, neither team made any attempt to check, and no one else caught the error. With that failure, NASA lost a $125 million satellite and years of effort, while gaining a major public embarrassment.

Adapted from NASA MCO Mission Failure Mishap Investigation Board, *Mars Climate Orbiter Mishap Investigation Board Phase I Report*, November 10, 1999, ftp://ftp.hq.nasa.gov/pub/pao/reports/1999/MCO_report.pdf.

When the *Mars Climate Orbiter* spacecraft crashed as a result of poor communication, the United States lost a $125 million satellite and years of effort.

10

Poor Customer Service Becomes Costly

A customer called AOL to cancel his service. The phone call lasted 21 minutes, including automated answering, waiting in a queue, and a five-minute conversation with a customer service representative. During the conversation, the customer service representative refused to comply with the customer's request to close his account despite 21 requests to "cancel" his service and approximately 9 "I-don't-need-it, I-don't-want-it, and I-don't-use-it" statements. To express his dissatisfaction, the customer posted the recorded conversation on the Web as a digital "documentary," which was heard by 300,000 visitors and highlighted on the *Today* show on NBC. Following the post, an AOL executive vice president e-mailed employees notifying them of the post and warning them that any of their customer interactions could be similarly posted. In addition, because of similar earlier violations, AOL agreed to pay a fine of $1.25 million and to use a third-party verification system.

Another customer service incident occurred when a customer welcomed a Comcast technician into his home to replace a faulty modem. When the technician called the central office, he was placed on hold and proceeded to fall asleep on the couch after an hour of waiting. In response, the customer recorded a short documentary, "A Comcast Technician Sleeping on My Couch" and posted it to YouTube where 500,000 viewers watched the customer service blunder.

Adapted from Randall Stross, "AOL Said, 'If You Leave Me I'll Do Something Crazy,'" *New York Times*, July 2, 2006, E3.

Fourth, unclear or incomplete messages may require the receiver to gather more information and some receivers may not bother to do so; they may make a wrong decision or refuse to act.

Wasted Efforts

Ineffective messages don't get results. A receiver who has to guess what the sender means may guess wrong. A reader who finds a letter or memo unconvincing or insulting simply won't do what the message asks.

One company sent out past-due bills with the following language:

> Per our conversation, enclosed are two copies of the above-mentioned invoice. Please review and advise. Sincerely, . . .

The company wanted money, not advice, but it didn't say so. The company had to write third and fourth reminders. It waited for its money, lost interest on it—and kept writing letters.

Lost Goodwill

Whatever the literal content of the words, every letter, e-mail, or report serves either to build or to undermine the image the reader has of the writer.

Part of building a good image is taking the time to write correctly. Even organizations that have adopted casual dress still expect writing to appear professional and to be free from typos and grammatical errors.

Messages can also create a poor image because of poor audience analysis and inappropriate style. The form letter printed in Figure 1.3 failed because it was stuffy and selfish. The comments in red show specific problems with the letter.

- **The language is stiff and legalistic.**   Note the sexist "Gentlemen:" and obsolete "Please be advised," "herein," and "expedite."
- **The tone is selfish.**   The letter is written from the writer's point of view; there are no benefits for the reader. (The writer says there are, but without a shred of evidence, the claim isn't convincing.)
- **The main point is buried** in the middle of the long first paragraph. The middle is the least emphatic part of a paragraph.
- **The request is vague.**   How many references does the supplier want? Are only vendor references OK, or would other credit references, like banks, work too? Is the name of the reference enough, or is it necessary also to specify the line of credit, the average balance, the current balance, the years credit has been established, or other information? What "additional financial information" does the supplier want? Annual reports? Bank balance? Tax returns? The request sounds like an invasion of privacy, not a reasonable business practice.
- **Words are misused** (*herein for therein*), suggesting either an ignorant writer or one who doesn't care enough about the subject and the reader to use the right word.

You will learn more about tone in Chapter 3 and language in Chapter 5.

Legal Problems

Poor communication choices can lead to legal problems for individuals and organizations. The news is full of examples. Domino's pizza, which promised to deliver pizza to your door in 30 minutes, dropped that promise after a lawsuit, involving an accident with a Domino's delivery person, claimed that the

Figure 1.3   A Form Letter That Annoyed Customers

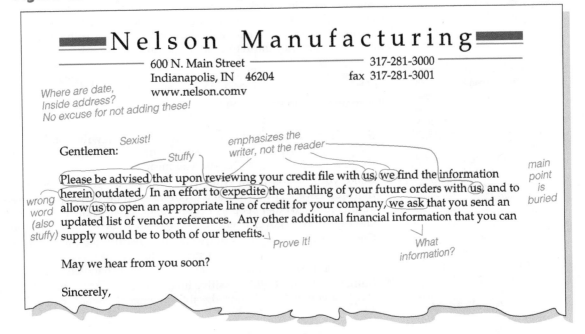

pledge led to accidents. Domino's settled for a sum in the seven-figure range, but dropped the promise because the company feared other lawsuits.[20]

Individual communications can also have legal consequences. Steamy text messages revealed an affair between Detroit mayor Kwame Kilpatrick and one of his aides; both the messages and the affair contradicted testimony the mayor had given under oath. Consequences included loss of office, jail time, and a $1 million fine.

US Representative Mark Foley resigned after his instant messages to House pages were published. E-mails have helped bring about the fall of many executives, including

- Senior Enron executives
- Boeing CEO Harry Stonecipher
- Credit Suisse First Boston banker Frank Quattrone
- Hewlett-Packard Chairperson Patricia Dunn
- Walmart Vice Presidents Julie Roehm and Sean Womack
- South Carolina Governor Mark Sanford

One San Francisco law firm says that 70% of their routine evidence now comes from e-mails.[21]

In particular, letters, memos, e-mails, and instant messages create legal obligations for organizations. When a lawsuit is filed against an organization, the lawyers for the plaintiffs have the right to subpoena documents written by employees of the organization. These documents may then be used as evidence, for instance, that an employer fired an employee without adequate notice or that a company knew about a safety defect but did nothing to correct it.

These documents may also be used as evidence in contexts the writer did not intend. This means that a careless writer can create obligations that the organization does not mean to assume. For instance, a letter from a manager

Columbia Disaster Communication Failures

In 2003, the *Columbia* space shuttle disintegrated on re-entry, resulting in the deaths of all seven crew members. The independent research team investigating the disaster found communication problems to be the root cause of the accident. The researchers concluded that organizational barriers prevented effective communication of critical safety information and restrained communication of professionals.

The report identified the following communication problems:

- Communication flow between managers and subordinates: Managers did not heed the concerns of the engineers regarding debris impacts on the shuttle. Throughout the project, communication did not flow effectively up to or down from program managers.

- Circulation of information among teams: Although engineers were concerned about landing problems and therefore conducted experiments on landing procedures, the concerns were not relayed to managers or to system and technology experts who could have addressed the concerns.

- Communication sources: Managers received a large amount of their information from informal channels, which blocked relevant opinions and conclusions from engineers.

Adapted from Columbia Accident Investigation Board, *Report of Columbia Accident Investigation Board, Volume I*, August 2003, http://www.nasa.gov/columbia/home/CAIB_Vol1.html.

telling a scout troop they may not visit a factory floor because it is too dangerous could be used in a worker's compensation suit.[22]

Careful writers and speakers think about the larger social context in which their words may appear. What might those words mean to other people in the field? What might they mean to a judge and jury?

BENEFITS OF IMPROVING COMMUNICATION

Better communication helps you to

- **Save time.**   Eliminate the time now taken to rewrite badly written materials. Reduce reading time, since comprehension is easier. Reduce the time taken asking, "What did you mean?"
- **Make your efforts more effective.**   Increase the number of requests that are answered positively and promptly—on the first request. Present your points—to other people in your organization; to clients, customers, and suppliers; to government agencies; to the public—more forcefully.
- **Communicate your points more clearly.**   Reduce the misunderstandings that occur when the audience has to supply missing or unclear information. Make the issues clear, so they can be handled.
- **Build goodwill.**   Build a positive image of your organization. Build an image of yourself as a knowledgeable, intelligent, capable person.

CRITERIA FOR EFFECTIVE MESSAGES

Good business and administrative communication meets five basic criteria: it's clear, complete, and correct; it saves the audience's time; and it builds goodwill.

- **It's clear.**   The meaning the audience gets is the meaning the communicator intended. The audience doesn't have to guess.
- **It's complete.**   All of the audience questions are answered. The audience has enough information to evaluate the message and act on it.
- **It's correct.**   All of the information in the message is accurate. The message is free from errors in spelling, grammar, word choice, and sentence structure.
- **It saves the audience's time.**   The style, organization, and visual or aural impact of the message help the audience read or hear, understand, and act on the information as quickly as possible.
- **It builds goodwill.**   The message presents a positive image of the communicator and his or her organization. It treats the receiver as a person, not a number. It cements a good relationship between the communicator and the receiver.

Whether a message meets these five criteria depends on the interactions among the communicator, the audience, the purposes of the message, and the situation. No single set of words will work in all possible situations.

USING TECHNOLOGY FOR COMMUNICATION

In this technological age, different forms of media are encompassing all parts of life. For instance, in 2010, the average American spent 158 hours a month watching television, accounting for approximately half their leisure time.

They also spent 25 hours a month using the Internet, which has become the third most popular news platform, behind only local and national television news. The Internet is now ahead of radio and national and local print newspapers as a news source. However, the greatest use of Internet time is for social networking. Personal e-mail has fallen out of second place to be replaced by gaming.[23]

Technology has even gripped the highest office in the country. President Obama battled with U.S. intelligence agencies to keep his BlackBerry when he took office; he is the first president in the history of our country to use e-mail while in office.

If the highest office in the land demands technology, the business world is no exception. When it comes to technology, business continually embraces all forms that help increase productivity and save money. Almost all office employees are expected to know how to navigate through the web and to use word processing, e-mail, spreadsheet, database, and presentation software. Newer forms of technology, especially social media such as Facebook, Twitter, and texting, are also becoming prominent in business offices. Chapter 9 will discuss communication technologies in more detail.

FOLLOWING CONVENTIONS LO 1-4

Conventions are widely accepted practices you routinely encounter. For example, you wouldn't write an analytical report to your boss who only wanted a "yes" or "no" on whether you could make the scheduled meeting with potential clients. You would send the more appropriate and conventional response—an e-mail.

Similarly, common business communications have conventions. These conventions help people recognize, produce, and interpret different kinds of communications. Each chapter in this textbook presents conventions of traditional business documents. For example, Chapter 13 discusses conventions of job application letters, Chapter 11 highlights conventions of persuasive messages, and Chapter 19 talks about conventions of delivering oral presentations.

Conventions change over time. Consider how the conventions governing movies and television have changed just during your lifetime, allowing more explicit sex and violence. Similarly, conventions change in business. Paper memos have mostly given way to e-mails, and some e-mails are being replaced by text messaging.

The key to using conventions effectively, in spite of their changing nature, is to remember that they always need to fit the rhetorical situation—they always need to be adjusted for the particular audience, context, and purpose. For instance, Chapter 10 provides guidelines on constructing negative messages. However, you will need to adapt these guidelines based on the way your organization presents their negative messages. Some organizations will use a more formal tone than others; some present negative news bluntly, while others ease into it more gently.

Since every organization will be unique in the conventions they follow, the information presented in this text will provide a basic understanding of common elements for particular genres. You will always need to adjust the basics for your particular needs.

The best way to learn conventions in a particular workplace is to see what other workers are doing. How do they communicate with each other? Do their practices change when they communicate with superiors? What kinds of letters and memos do they send? How much do they e-mail? What tone is preferred? Close observation will help your communications fit in with the conventions of your employer.

14   Part 1   The Building Blocks of Effective Messages

UNDERSTANDING AND ANALYZING BUSINESS COMMUNICATION SITUATIONS

The best communicators are conscious of the context in which they communicate; they're aware of options.

Ask yourself the following questions:

- **What's at stake—to whom?** Think not only about your own needs but also about the concerns your boss and your audience will have. Your message will be most effective if you think of the entire organizational context—and the larger context of shareholders, customers, and regulators. When the stakes are high, you'll need to take into account people's feelings as well as objective facts.

- **Should you send a message?** Sometimes, especially when you're new on the job, silence is the most tactful response. But be alert for opportunities to learn, to influence, to make your case.

- **What channel should you use?** Paper documents and presentations are formal and give you considerable control over the message. E-mail, texting, tweeting, phone calls, and stopping by someone's office are less formal. Oral channels are better for group decision making, allow misunderstandings to be cleared up more quickly, and seem more personal. Sometimes you may need more than one message, in more than one channel.

- **What should you say?** Content for a message may not be obvious. How detailed should you be? Should you repeat information that the audience already knows? The answers will depend on the kind of message, your purposes, audiences, and the corporate culture. And you'll have to figure these things out for yourself, without detailed instructions.

- **How should you say it?** How you arrange your ideas—what comes first, second, and last—and the words you use shape the audience's response to what you say.

HOW TO SOLVE BUSINESS COMMUNICATION PROBLEMS LO 1-5

When you're faced with a business communication problem, you need to develop a solution that will both solve the organization's problem and meet the psychological needs of the people involved. The strategies in this section will help you solve the problems in this book. Almost all of these strategies can also be applied to problems you encounter on the job. Use this process to create good messages:

- Gather knowledge and brainstorm solutions.
- Answer the five questions for analysis in Figure 1.4.
- Organize your information to fit your audiences, your purposes, and the context.
- Make your document visually inviting.
- Revise your draft to create a friendly, businesslike, positive style.
- Edit your draft for standard spelling, punctuation, and grammar; double-check names and numbers.
- Use the response you get to plan future messages.

Figure 1.4 Questions for Analysis

1. Who is (are) your audience(s)?
2. What are your purposes in communicating?
3. What information must your message include?
4. How can you build support for your position? What reasons or benefits will your audience find convincing?
5. What aspects of the total situation may be relevant?

Gather Knowledge and Brainstorm Solutions.

Problem solving usually starts by gathering knowledge. What are the facts? What can you infer from the information you're given? What additional information might be helpful? Where could you get it? What emotional complexities are involved? This information will usually start to suggest some solutions, and you should brainstorm other solutions. In all but the very simplest problems, there are multiple possible solutions. The first one you think of may not be best. Consciously develop several solutions. Then measure them against your audience and purposes: Which solution is likely to work best?

You will learn more about gathering knowledge in Chapter 15 and more about brainstorming in Chapter 8.

Answer the Five Questions for Analysis.

The five questions in Figure 1.4 help you analyze your audience(s), purpose(s), and the organizational context.

1. **Who is (are) your audience(s)?**

   What audience characteristics are relevant for this particular message? If you are writing or speaking to more than one person, how do the people in your audience differ? How much does your audience know about your topic? How will they respond to your message? What objections might they have?

   Some characteristics of your audience will be irrelevant; focus on ones that matter *for this message*. Whenever you address several people or a group, try to identify the economic, cultural, or situational differences that may affect how various subgroups may respond to what you have to say. For a more complete audience analysis, see the questions in Chapter 2.

2. **What are your purposes in communicating?**

   What must this message do to meet the organization's needs? What must it do to meet your own needs? What do you want your audience to do? To think or feel? List all your purposes, major and minor.

   Even in a simple message, you may have several related purposes: to announce a new policy, to make the audience aware of the policy's provisions and requirements, and to have them feel that the policy is a good one, that the organization cares about its employees, and that you are a competent communicator and manager.

3. **What information must your message include?**

   Make a list of the points that must be included; check your draft to make sure you include them all. To include information without emphasizing it, put it in the middle of a paragraph or document and present it as briefly as possible.

4. **How can you build support for your position? What reasons or benefits will your audience find convincing?**

   Brainstorm to develop reasons for your decision, the logic behind your argument, and possible benefits to the audience if they do as you ask. Reasons and audience benefits do not have to be monetary. Making the

Just a Deadline; No Directions

School assignments are spelled out, sometimes even in writing. In the workplace, workers are less likely to get details about what a document should include. The transition can be disorienting. One intern reported, "I was less prepared than I thought. . . . I was so used to professors basically telling you what they want from you that I expected to be, if not taught, then told, what exactly it was that they wanted these brochures to accomplish. . . . They have not taken the time to discuss it—they just put things on my desk with only a short note telling me when they needed it done. No directions or comments were included."

Intern's quotation from Chris M. Anson and L. Lee Forsberg, "Moving Beyond the Academic Community," *Written Communication* 7, no. 3 (April 1990): 211.

Classroom versus Workplace Contexts

Professors Aviva Freedman and Christine Adam found in a research study that students have to relearn ways to acquire basic knowledge when trying to mesh with their employer's organization once they enter the workforce.

School is structured to help students learn. On the other hand, the workplace is structured to get results, not help the learner/new employee. New college graduate hires frequently don't understand the context of communications. For example, new employees have to figure out which co-workers are trustworthy and can be a guide while not pushing away others.

Moreover, the roles of participants in each situation are different. While school settings have an instructor as the voice of authority, workplace settings are comprised of people with varying degrees of relevant and useful knowledge.

What has been your experience with internships? Have you noticed other ways in which workplace settings differ from classroom expectations?

Adapted from Aviva Freedman and Christine Adam, "Learning to Write Professionally: 'Situated Learning' and the Transition from University to Professional Discourse," *Journal of Business and Technical Communication* 10, no. 4 (October 1996): 395–427.

audience's job easier or more pleasant is a good benefit. In an informative or persuasive message, identify multiple audience benefits. In your message, use those that you can develop most easily and effectively.

Be sure the benefits are adapted to your audience. Many people do not identify closely with their organizations; the fact that the organization benefits from a policy will help the individual only if the saving or profit is passed directly on to the employees. Instead, savings and profits are often eaten up by returns to stockholders, bonuses to executives, and investments in plants and equipment or in research and development.

5. **What aspects of the total situation may be relevant?**

Should you consider the economy? The time of year? Morale in the organization? Any special circumstances? The organization may be prosperous or going through hard times; it may have just been reorganized or may be stable. All these different situations will affect what you say and how you say it.

Think about the news, the economy, the weather. Think about the general business and regulatory climate, especially as it affects the organization specified in the problem. Use the real world as much as possible. Think about interest rates, business conditions, and the economy. Is the industry in which the problem is set doing well? Is the government agency in which the problem is set enjoying general support? Think about the time of year. If it's fall when you write, is your business in a seasonal slowdown after a busy summer? Gearing up for the Christmas shopping rush? Or going along at a steady pace unaffected by seasons?

To answer these questions, draw on your experience, your courses, and your common sense. Read the *Wall Street Journal* or look at a company's website. Sometimes you may even want to phone a local business person to get information.

Organize Your Information to Fit Your Audiences, Your Purposes, and the Situation.

You'll learn different psychological patterns of organization in Chapters 9 through 11. For now, remember these three basic principles:

- Put good news first.
- In general, put the main point or question first. In the subject line or first paragraph, make it clear that you're writing about something that is important to the reader.
- Disregard the above point and approach the subject indirectly when you must persuade a reluctant audience.

Make Your Document Visually Inviting.

A well-designed document is easier to read and builds goodwill. To make a document visually attractive

- Use subject lines to orient the reader quickly.
- Use headings to group related ideas.
- Use lists and indented sections to emphasize subpoints and examples.
- Number points that must be followed in sequence.
- Use short paragraphs—usually eight typed lines or fewer.

If you plan these design elements before you begin composing, you'll save time and the final document will probably be better.

The best medium for a document depends on how it will be used. For example, a document that will be updated frequently may need to be on a website so the reader can easily obtain the most current information. Chapters 6 and 16 will provide more information on the design of documents and visuals.

Revise Your Draft to Create a Friendly, Businesslike, Positive Style.

In addition to being an organizational member or a consumer, your reader has feelings just as you do. Writing that keeps the reader in mind uses **you-attitude** (see Chapter 3). Read your message as if you were in your reader's shoes. How would you feel if *you* received it?

Good business and administrative writing is both friendly and businesslike. If you're too stiff, you put extra distance between your reader and yourself. If you try to be too chummy, you'll sound unprofessional. When you write to strangers, use simple, everyday words and make your message as personal and friendly as possible. When you write to friends, remember that your message may be read by people you've never even heard of: avoid slang, clichés, and "in" jokes.

Sometimes you must mention limitations, drawbacks, or other negative elements, but don't dwell on them. People will respond better to you and your organization if you seem confident. Expect success, not failure. If you don't believe that what you're writing about is a good idea, why should they?

You emphasize the positive when you

- Put positive information first, give it more space, or set it off visually in an indented list.
- Eliminate negative words whenever possible.
- Focus on what is possible, not what is impossible.

Edit Your Draft for Standard English; Double-Check Names and Numbers.

Business people care about correctness in spelling, grammar, and punctuation. If your grasp of mechanics is fuzzy, if standard English is not your native dialect, or if English is not your native language, you'll need to memorize rules and perhaps find a good book or a tutor to help you. Even software spelling and grammar checkers require the writer to make decisions. If you know how to write correctly but rarely take the time to do so, now is the time to begin to edit and proofread to eliminate careless errors. Correctness in usage, punctuation, and grammar is covered in Appendix B.

Always proofread your document before you send it out. Double-check the reader's name, any numbers, and the first and last paragraphs. Chapter 5 will provide more tips on revising and editing communication.

Use the Response You Get to Plan Future Messages.

Evaluate the **feedback,** or response, you get. The real test of any message is "Did you get what you wanted, when you wanted it?" If the answer is *no*, then the message has failed—even if the grammar is perfect, the words elegant, the approach creative, the document stunningly attractive. If the message fails, you need to find out why.

Succeeding against the Odds

I developed my communication skills as a technique of survival. I was born in poverty and spent two years on the welfare rolls, and I learned early that I had to communicate or die. And so I talked my way out of poverty—I communicated my way to the top. . . .

I read and re-read books on self-improvement, success and communication. The most important lesson I learned from these books is what I call "other focusing." This means, among other things, that if we want to communicate with employees, managers, and even competitors we must ask ourselves not what we want but what they want.

This rule made me a millionaire. For the only way I got to where I am today was by persuading thousands of blacks and whites, some of whom were very prejudiced, that the only way they could get what they wanted was by helping me get what I wanted. All the law and prophecy of communication theory can be found in that formula.

John H. Johnson, owner and publisher of *Ebony* magazine, quoted in Gloria Gordon, "EXCEL Award Winner John H. Johnson Communicates Success," *IABC Communication World* 6, no. 6 (May 1989): 18–19.

Analyze your successes, too. You want to know *why* your message worked. There has to be a reason, and if you can find what it is, you'll be more successful more often.

HOW TO USE THIS BOOK

This book has many aids to help you learn the material.

- Chapter outlines, learning objectives, and headings all provide previews of the contents. They can give you hooks on which to hang the information you are reading.
- Examples of written documents provide illustrations of effective and ineffective communications. Comments in red ink highlight problems; those in blue ink note effective practices.
- Terminology is defined in the glossary at the end of the book.
- Sidebars provide workplace examples of ideas discussed in the text. They are categorized for you by the icons that appear beside them. A gold star with any icon signifies a classic example.
  - On-the-job examples have briefcase icons.
  - Ethics and legal examples have gavel icons.
  - Websites have an @ sign.
  - Technology examples have smartphone icons.
  - International examples have globe icons.
  - Fun examples have balloon icons.
- Chapter summaries at the end of each chapter, and review questions at the beginning of each set of chapter exercises, help you review the chapters for retention.

SUMMARY OF KEY POINTS

- Communication helps organizations and the people in them achieve their goals. The ability to write and speak well becomes increasingly important as you rise in an organization.
- People put things in writing to create a record, to convey complex data, to make things convenient for the reader, to save money, and to convey their own messages more effectively.
- Internal documents go to people inside the organization. External documents go to audiences outside: clients, customers, suppliers, stockholders, the government, the media, and the general public.
- The three basic purposes of business and administrative communication are to inform, to request or persuade, and to build goodwill. Most messages have more than one purpose.
- Poor writing wastes time, wastes effort, and jeopardizes goodwill.
- Good business and administrative writing meets five basic criteria: it's clear, complete, and correct; it saves the reader's time; and it builds goodwill.
- To evaluate a specific document, we must know the interactions among the writer, the reader(s), the purposes of the message, and the context. No single set of words will work for all readers in all situations.
- Common business communications have conventions, as do organizations. Business communicators need to know how to adjust conventions to fit a particular audience, context, and purpose.

- To understand business communication situations, ask the following questions:
  - What's at stake—to whom?
  - Should you send a message?
  - What channel should you use?
  - What should you say?
  - How should you say it?
- The following process helps create effective messages:
  - Gather knowledge and brainstorm solutions.
  - Answer the analysis questions in Figure 1.4.
  - Organize your information to fit your audiences, your purposes, and the context.
  - Make your document visually inviting.
  - Revise your draft to create a friendly, businesslike, positive style.
  - Edit your draft for standard English; double-check names and numbers.
  - Use the response you get to plan future messages.

CHAPTER 1   # Exercises and Problems

Go to www.mhhe.com/locker10e for additional Exercises and Problems.

1.1   Reviewing the Chapter

1. Why do you need to be able to communicate well? (LO 1-1)
2. What are some myths about workplace communication? What is the reality for each myth? (LO 1-1)
3. What are the costs of communication? (LO 1-2)
4. What are the costs of poor communication? (LO 1-3)
5. What role do conventions play in business communication? (LO 1-4)
6. What are the components of a good problem-solving method for business communication opportunities? (LO 1-5)

1.2   Assessing Your Punctuation and Grammar Skills

To help you see where you need to improve in grammar and punctuation, take the Diagnostic Test, B.1, Appendix B.

1.3   Letters for Discussion—Landscape Plants

Your nursery sells plants not only in your store but also by mail order. Today you've received a letter from Pat Sykes, complaining that the plants (in a $572 order) did not arrive in a satisfactory condition. "All of them were dry and wilted. One came out by the roots when I took it out of the box. Please send me a replacement shipment immediately."

The following letters are possible approaches to answering this complaint. How well does each message meet the needs of the reader, the writer, and the organization? Is the message clear, complete, and correct? Does it save the reader's time? Does it build goodwill?

1.

Dear Sir:

I checked to see what could have caused the defective shipment you received. After ruling out problems in transit, I discovered that your order was packed by a new worker who didn't understand the need to water plants thoroughly before they are shipped. We have fired the worker, so you can be assured that this will not happen again.

Although it will cost our company several hundred dollars, we will send you a replacement shipment.

Let me know if the new shipment arrives safely. We trust that you will not complain again.

2.   Dear Pat:

Sorry we screwed up that order. Sending plants across country is a risky business. Some of them just can't take the strain. (Some days I can't take the strain myself!) We'll send you some more plants sometime next week and we'll credit your account for $372.

3.   Dear Mr. Smith:

I'm sorry you aren't happy with your plants, but it isn't our fault. The box clearly says, "Open and water immediately." If you had done that, the plants would have been fine. And anybody who is going to buy plants should know that a little care is needed. If you pull by the leaves, you will pull the roots out. Since you don't know how to handle plants, I'm sending you a copy of our brochure, "How to Care for Your Plants." Please read it carefully so that you will know how to avoid disappointment in the future.

We look forward to your future orders.

4.   Dear Ms. Sykes:

Your letter of the 5th has come to the attention of the undersigned.

According to your letter, your invoice #47420 arrived in an unsatisfactory condition. Please be advised that it is our policy to make adjustments as per the Terms and Conditions listed on the reverse side of our Acknowledgment of Order. If you will read that document, you will find the following:

> ". . . if you intend to assert any claim against us on this account, you shall make an exception on your receipt to the carrier and shall, within 30 days after the receipt of any such goods, furnish us detailed written information as to any damage."

Your letter of the 5th does not describe the alleged damage in sufficient detail. Furthermore, the delivery receipt contains no indication of any exception. If you expect to receive an adjustment, you must comply with our terms and see that the necessary documents reach the undersigned by the close of the business day on the 20th of the month.

5.   Dear Pat Sykes:

You'll get a replacement shipment of the perennials you ordered next week.

Your plants are watered carefully before shipment and packed in specially designed cardboard containers. But if the weather is unusually warm, or if the truck is delayed, small root balls may dry out. Perhaps this happened with your plants. Plants with small root balls are easier to transplant, so they do better in your yard.

The violas, digitalis, aquilegias, and hostas you ordered are long-blooming perennials that will get even prettier each year. Enjoy your garden!

1.4 Online Messages for Discussion—Responding to Rumors

The Acme Corporation has been planning to acquire Best Products, and Acme employees are worried about how the acquisition will affect them. Ed Zeplin, Acme's human resource manager, has been visiting the Acme chat sites and sees a dramatic rise in the number of messages spreading rumors about layoffs. Most of the rumors are false.

The following messages are possible responses that Ed can post to the chat sides. How well does each message meet the needs of the reader, the writer, and the organization? Is the message clear, complete, and correct? Does it save the reader's time? Does it build goodwill?

1.

It Will Be Great!
Author: L. Ed Zeplin, HR
Date: Tuesday, May 23

I am happy to tell you that the HR news is good. Two months ago, the CEO told me about the merger, and I have been preparing a human resource plan ever since.

I want you to know about this because morale has been bad, and it shouldn't be. You really should wait for the official announcements, and you'll see that the staffing needs will remain strong. My department has been under a lot of pressure, but if you'll be patient, we'll explain everything—the staffing, the compensation.

Our plan should be ready by Monday, and then if you have any questions, just contact your HR rep.

2.

HR Staffing
Author: HR Boss
Date: Tuesday, May 23

The rumors are false. Just ask anyone in HR. There will be no layoffs.

3.

Don't Believe the Rumors
Author: lezeplin@acme.com
Date: Tuesday, May 23

Acme has 475 employees, and Best Products has 132 employees. Our human resource plan for next year calls for 625 employees. If you do the math, you can see that there will be no layoffs. Rather, we will be hiring 18 employees. Of course, as we consolidate operations with Best, there will be some redeployments. However, our plan indicates that we will be able to retain our current staff. All employees are valued at Acme, as our current benefits package testifies.

Our HR plan is based on the best analytic techniques and a business forecast by a top consulting firm. If you're an employee, you should review our business plan, at the Our Goals page on Acme's intranet. Everyone should read Acme's mission statement on our home page, www.acme.com/homepage.html.

4.

Layoff Rumors Do Acme a Disservice
Author: Zeplin in HR
Date: Tuesday, 23 May

If you come here to get your company information, you aren't getting the straight story. The people posting to this discussion board are spreading false rumors, not the truth. If you want to know the truth about Acme, ask the people who have access to the information.

As HR manager, I can assure you we won't be laying off employees after the merger with Best Products. I'm the one who approves the staffing plan, so I should know. If people would ask me, instead of reading the negative, whining lies at this site, they would know the facts, too.

If people really cared about job security, they would be working and exceeding their goals, rather than wasting their time in rumor-mongering on message boards. Hard work: that's the key to success!

5.

The True Story about Lay-Offs
Author: lezeplin@acme.com
Date: Tuesday, 23 May

Whenever there is a merger or acquisition, rumors fly. It's human nature to turn to rumors when a situation seems uncertain. The case of Acme acquiring Best Products is no exception, so I'm not surprised to see rumors about layoffs posted on this message board.

Have no fear! I am working closely with our CEO and with the CEO and human resource manager at Best Products, and we all agree that our current staff is a valuable asset to Acme, to Best, and to our combined companies in the future. We have no plans to lay off any of our valued people. I will continue monitoring this message board and will post messages as I am able to disclose more details about our staffing plans. In the meantime, employees should watch for official information in the company newsletter and on our intranet.

We care about our people! If employees ever have questions about our plans and policies, they should contact me directly.

L. Ed Zeplin, HR Manager

1.5   Discussing Communication Barriers

With a small group, discuss some of the communication barriers you have witnessed in the workplace or classroom. What confuses audiences? What upsets them? What creates ill will? What causes loss of interest? Try to pinpoint exactly how the communication broke down. How closely do the problems you've identified coincide with the content from Chapter 1?

1.6   Identifying Poor Communicators

Almost everyone has come in contact with someone who is a poor communicator. With a small group, discuss some of your experiences with poor communicators either in the workplace or in the classroom. Why was the communicator ineffective? What would have made communication clearer? After your discussion, develop a list of poor communication traits and what can be done to overcome them.

1.7   Discussing Wiio's Laws

Reread the list of Wiio's laws in the sidebar on page 14. With a small group, discuss examples of those laws you have witnessed in
a. The workplace
b. The classroom
c. The news media
d. Social networking sites

1.8   Identifying Changing Conventions

This chapter talks about the need to be aware of conventions and how they shift with time. What are some changing classroom communication conventions you have observed in your classes? What are some changing communication conventions you have observed at your workplace, or those of your family and friends? With a small group, discuss your examples.

1.9   Understanding the Role of Communication in Your Organization

Interview your work supervisor to learn about the kinds and purposes of communication in your organization. Your questions could include the following:
- What kinds of communication (e.g., memos, e-mail, presentations) are most important in this organization?
- What communications do you create? Are they designed to inform, to persuade, to build goodwill—or to do a combination?
- What communications do you receive? Are they designed to inform, to persuade, to build goodwill—or to do a combination?
- Who are your most important audiences within the organization?
- Who are your most important external audiences?
- What are the challenges of communicating in this organization?
- What kinds of documents and presentations does the organization prefer?

As your instructor directs,
a. Share your results with a small group of students.
b. Present your results in a memo to your instructor.
c. Join with a group of students to make a group presentation to the class.
d. Post your results online to the class.

1.10   Introducing Yourself to Your Instructor

Write a memo (at least 1½ pages long) introducing yourself to your instructor. Include the following topics:

Background: Where did you grow up? What have you done in terms of school, extracurricular activities, jobs, and family life?

Interests: What are you interested in? What do you like to do? What do you like to think about and talk about?

Academics: What courses have you liked the best in school? Why? What life skills have you gained? How do you hope to use them? What do you hope to gain from this course?

Achievements: What achievements have given you the greatest personal satisfaction? List at least five.

Include things that gave *you* a real sense of accomplishment and pride, whether or not they're the sort of thing you'd list on a résumé.

Goals: What do you hope to accomplish this term? Where would you like to be professionally and personally five years from now?

Use complete memo format with appropriate headings. (See Appendix A for examples of memo format.) Use a conversational writing style; check your draft to polish the style and edit for mechanical and grammatical correctness. A good memo will enable your instructor to see you as an individual. Use specific details to make your memo vivid and interesting. Remember that one of your purposes is to interest your reader!

1.11   Introducing Yourself to Your Collaborative Writing Group

Write a memo (at least 1½ pages long) introducing yourself to the other students in your collaborative writing group. Include the following topics:

Background: What is your major? What special areas of knowledge do you have? What have you done in terms of school, extracurricular activities, jobs, and family life?

Previous experience in groups: What groups have you worked in before? Are you usually a leader, a follower, or a bit of both? Are you interested in a quality product? In maintaining harmony in the group? In working efficiently? What do you like most about working in groups? What do you like least?

Work and composing style: Do you like to talk out ideas while they're in a rough stage or work them out on paper before you discuss them? Would you rather have a complete outline before you start writing or just a general idea? Do you want to have a detailed schedule of everything that has to be done and who will do it, or would you rather "go with the flow"? Do you work best under pressure, or do you want to have assignments ready well before the due date?

Areas of expertise: What can you contribute to the group in terms of knowledge and skills? Are you good at brainstorming ideas? Researching? Designing charts? Writing? Editing? Word processing? Managing the flow of work? Maintaining group cohesion?

Goals for collaborative assignments: What do you hope to accomplish this term? Where does this course fit into your priorities?

Use complete memo format with appropriate headings. (See Appendix A for examples of memo format.) Use a conversational writing style; edit your final draft for mechanical and grammatical correctness. A good memo will enable others in your group to see you as an individual. Use details to make your memo vivid and interesting. Remember that one of your purposes is to make your readers look forward to working with you!

1.12 Describing Your Experiences in and Goals for Writing

Write a memo (at least 1½ pages long) to your instructor describing the experiences you've had writing and what you'd like to learn about writing during this course.

Answer several of the following questions:

- What memories do you have of writing? What made writing fun or frightening in the past?
- What have you been taught about writing? List the topics, rules, and advice you remember.
- What kinds of writing have you done in school? How long have the papers been?
- How has your school writing been evaluated? Did the instructor mark or comment on mechanics and grammar? Style? Organization? Logic? Content? Audience analysis and adaptation? Have you gotten extended comments on your papers? Have instructors in different classes had the same standards, or have you changed aspects of your writing for different classes?

- What voluntary writing have you done—journals, poems, stories, essays? Has this writing been just for you, or has some of it been shared or published?
- Have you ever written on a job or in a student or volunteer organization? Have you ever edited other people's writing? What have these experiences led you to think about real-world writing?
- What do you see as your current strengths and weaknesses in writing skills? What skills do you think you'll need in the future? What kinds of writing do you expect to do after you graduate?

Use complete memo format with appropriate headings. (See Appendix A for examples of memo format.) Use a conversational writing style; edit your final draft for mechanical and grammatical correctness.

CHAPTER

2

Adapting Your Message to Your Audience

Chapter Outline

NEWSWORTHY COMMUNICATION

Audiences Change with Time

Every year in late January, the president of the United States gives the State of the Union address to one of the largest and most diverse audiences of any communication. Congress, the news media, foreign leaders and diplomats, students, and members of the American public from all walks of life watch, listen, or read the president's comments each year.

Traditionally, the president uses the State of the Union to recount his successes and to spell out his political goals for the coming year. In 2010, President Barack Obama outlined ambitious plans for health care reform, economic recovery, and an increased focus on education and green energy initiatives. He focused much of his speech on the challenges faced by the people of America and the steps he and his Democratic party were taking to help.

In 2011, however, the president faced a different audience. Even though many of the *people* listening were the same, the *situation* and the *attitudes* had changed. In spite of President Obama's success with his goals during 2010, many Americans were dissatisfied. Riding a wave of discontent with the government, conservative Republicans had gained control of

"His tone and presentation reflected the changed audience he faced— one more divided than the one he addressed in 2010."

the House of Representatives in the November elections and gained several seats in the Senate. Throughout the election, the tenor of political discourse had become increasingly pointed and divisive.

President Obama responded to his audience with a different kind of State of the Union—one that still outlined ambitious plans, but focused more on bipartisan efforts to achieve them. His tone was more conciliatory and more focused on uniting the parties in Congress under his leadership, but his core messages remained the same: improving health care, rebuilding the economy, strengthening education, and expanding green energy initiatives. His tone and presentation reflected the changed audience he faced—one more divided than the one he addressed in 2010.

The ability to adjust your message to your audience is one key to effective communication. While President Obama addressed a complex audience of millions, most communications have very small, specific audiences—real people with real situations and real concerns. Learning to adjust to your audience will provide you with an excellent foundation for any kind of communication.

Sources: Barak Obama, "Remarks by the President in State of the Union Address," January 28, 2010, transcript, The White House, Office of the Press Secretary, http://www.whitehouse.gov/the-press-office/remarks-president-state-union-address; Barak Obama, "Remarks by the President in State of the Union Address," January 25, 2011, transcript, The White House, Office of the Press Secretary, http://www.whitehouse.gov/the-press-office/2011/01/25/remarks-president-state-union-address.

Learning Objectives

After studying this chapter, you will know

LO 2-1 Ways to analyze different kinds of audiences.

      a. Individuals

      b. Groups

      c. Organizations

LO 2-2 How to choose channels to reach your audience.

LO 2-3 How to analyze your audience and adapt your message to it.

LO 2-4 How to identify and develop audience benefits.

Knowing who you're talking to is fundamental to the success of any message. You need to identify your audiences, understand their motivations, and know how to reach them.

IDENTIFYING YOUR AUDIENCES

The first step in analyzing your audience is to decide who your audience is. Organizational messages have multiple audiences:

1. A **gatekeeper** has the power to stop your message instead of sending it on to other audiences. The gatekeeper therefore controls whether your message even gets to the primary audience. Sometimes the supervisor who assigns the message is the gatekeeper; sometimes the gatekeeper is higher in the organization. In some cases, gatekeepers may exist outside the organization.

2. The **primary audience** decides whether to accept your recommendations or acts on the basis of your message. You must reach the primary audience to fulfill your purposes in any message.

3. The **secondary audience** may be asked to comment on your message or to implement your ideas after they've been approved. Secondary audiences also include lawyers who may use your message—perhaps years later—as evidence of your organization's culture and practices.

4. An **auxiliary audience** may encounter your message but will not have to interact with it. This audience includes the "read-only" people.

5. A **watchdog audience,** though it does not have the power to stop the message and will not act directly on it, has political, social, or economic power. The watchdog pays close attention to the transaction between you and the primary audience and may base future actions on its evaluation of your message.

As the following examples show, one person can be part of two audiences. Frequently, a supervisor is both the primary audience and the gatekeeper.

Dawn is an assistant account executive in an ad agency. Her boss asks her to write a proposal for a marketing plan for a new product the agency's client is introducing. Her **primary audience** is the executive committee of the client company, who will decide whether to adopt the plan. The **secondary audience** includes the marketing staff of the client company, who will be asked for comments on the plan, as well as the artists, writers, and media buyers who will carry out details of the plan if it is adopted. Her boss, who must approve the plan before it is submitted to the client, is the **gatekeeper.** Her office colleagues who read her plan are her **auxiliary audience.**

Joe works in the information technology department of a large financial institution. He must write a memo explaining a major software change. His boss is the **gatekeeper;** the software users in various departments are the **primary audience.** The **secondary audience** includes the tech people who will be helping the primary audience install and adjust to the new software. The **auxiliary audience** includes department program assistants who forward the memo to appropriate people in each department. A **watchdog audience** is the board of directors.

WAYS TO ANALYZE YOUR AUDIENCE   LO 2-1

The most important tools in audience analysis are common sense and empathy. **Empathy** is the ability to put yourself in someone else's shoes, to feel with that person. Use what you know about people and about organizations to predict likely responses.

Analyzing Individuals

When you write or speak to people in your own organization and in other organizations you work closely with, you may be able to analyze your audience as individuals. You may already know them, or can probably get additional information easily. You may learn that one manager may dislike phone calls, so you will know to write your request in an e-mail. Another manager may have a reputation for denying requests made on a Friday, so you will know to get yours in earlier.

A useful schema for analyzing people is the **Myers-Briggs Type Indicator.**® This instrument uses four pairs of dichotomies to identify ways that people differ.[1] One of these dichotomies is well known: Extroversion-Introversion, measuring how individuals prefer to focus their attention and get energy. Extroverted types are energized by interacting with other people. Introverted types get their energy from within.

The other three dichotomies in Myers-Briggs® typology are Sensing-Intuition, Thinking-Feeling, and Judging-Perceiving. The Sensing-Intuition dichotomy measures the way an individual prefers to take in information. Sensing types gather information through their senses, preferring what is real and tangible. Intuitive types prefer to gather information by looking at the big picture, focusing on the relationships and connections between facts.

The Thinking-Feeling dichotomy measures the way an individual makes decisions. Thinking types prefer to use thinking in decision making to consider the logical consequences of a choice or action. Feeling types make decisions based on the impact to people, considering what is important to them and to others involved.

The Judging-Perceiving dichotomy measures how individuals orient themselves to the external world. Judging types like to live in a planned, orderly way, seeking closure. Perceiving types prefer to live in a flexible, spontaneous way, enjoying possibilities.

The descriptors on each of the scales' dichotomies represent a preference, just as we have a preference for using either our right or our left hand to write. If necessary, we can use the opposite style, but we have less practice in it and use it less easily.

You can find your own personality type by taking the Myers-Briggs Type Indicator® instrument at your college's counseling center or student services office. Some businesses administer the Myers-Briggs Type Indicator® instrument to all employees to assist with team building and/or personal growth and development.

Reading Levels

One of the most relevant demographic measures for writers is the literacy level of your audience. Unfortunately, even in advanced economies you have to ask how well your audience can read and put information to use. In the United States, the answer may be "not very well."

The National Assessment of Adult Literacy (NAAL), conducted by the US Department of Education, found that 14% of adults had difficulty reading well enough to follow simple instructions (such as when to take medication), 12% struggled to use simple forms (deciding where to sign their name on a form), and 22% had trouble working with numbers (simple addition tasks). NAAL also found that 5% of adults were nonliterate—their language skills weren't strong enough to participate in the assessment.

Overall, that translates into 30 million adults in the United States with "below basic" reading and comprehension levels, and another 63 million with only "basic" literacy levels. For business writers, this poses a challenge. When composing a message for a broad audience of employees or customers, you may have to use short sentences, simple words, and clarifying graphics. What other techniques might you use to ensure that audiences with lower literacy levels can understand and use your message?

Adapted from Mark Kutner, Elizabeth Greenberg, and Justin Baer, "National Assessment of Adult Literacy (NAAL): A First Look at the Literacy of America's Adults in the 21st Century," American Institutes for Research, National Center for Education Statistics, U.S. Department of Education, 2006, http://nces.ed.gov/NAAL/PDF/2006470.PDF.

Figure 2.1   Using Personalities in Communication

If your audience is	Use this strategy	Because
Extraverting	Try out ideas orally.	Extraverts like to develop ideas by talking; they are energized by people.
Introverting	Communicate in writing so the audience can think about your message before responding.	Introverts like to think before they communicate. Written messages give them their thinking time.
Sensing	Present all of the needed facts, and get them right. Present your reasoning step by step. Stress practicalities.	Sensing people are good at facts, and expect others to be, also. They trust their own experience more than someone else's account.
Intuiting	Focus on the big picture and underlying patterns first. Save details for later. Use metaphors and analogies in explanations. Stress innovation.	Intuitive people like new possibilities and innovation; they enjoy problem solving and creative endeavors. They can be impatient with details, routine, and repetition.
Thinking	Use logic and principles of consistency and fairness rather than emotion or personal circumstances.	Thinking people make decisions based on logic and abstract principles. They are often uncomfortable with emotion or personal revelations.
Feeling	Stress positives. Show how your ideas value the people needs of the organization. Use tactful language.	Feeling people care about other people and their feelings. They are empathetic and desire harmony.
Judging	Make your communications very organized. Provide all needed information. Follow company procedures. Schedule work in advance; provide time frames for various tasks.	Judging people are eager to make decisions, so they may not seek out additional information. They prefer a structured, orderly work life.
Perceiving	Provide alternatives. Ask for action or a decision by a specific date.	Perceiving people like to gather lots of information before making decisions, and they like to keep all options open as long as possible.

Source: People Types and Tiger Stripes, 4e 2009 Gordon Lawrence. Used with permission. CAPT, Inc.

As Figure 2.1 suggests, you'll be most persuasive if you play to your audience's strengths. Indeed, many of the general principles of business communication appeal to the types most common among managers. Putting the main point up front satisfies the needs of judging types, and some 75% of US managers are judging. Giving logical reasons satisfies the needs of the nearly 80% of U.S. managers who are thinking types.[2]

Analyzing Members of Groups

In many organizational situations, you'll analyze your audience not as individuals but as members of a group: "taxpayers who must be notified that they owe more income tax," "customers who use our accounting services," or "employees with small children." Focus on what group members have in common. Although generalizations won't be true for all members of the group, generalization is necessary when you must appeal to a large group of people with one message. In some cases, no research is necessary: It's easy to guess the attitudes of people who must be told they owe more taxes. In other cases, databases may yield useful information. In still other cases, you may want to do original research.

Databases enable you to map demographic and psychographic profiles of customers or employees. **Demographic characteristics** are measurable features that can be counted objectively: age, sex, race, religion, education level, income, and so on.

Sometimes demographic information is irrelevant; sometimes it's important. Does education matter? Well, the fact that the reader has a degree from

Group membership sometimes gives clues about your audience.

One Huge Audience

Baby boomers number 76 million and account for about half of total U.S. consumer spending. They are expected to spend an additional $50 billion over the next decade. So businesses are subtly beginning to accommodate the needs of this major audience.

Subtle is a key word: boomers do not like to be reminded that they are aging. For instance, many boomers dislike having people talk slowly to them, so ADT Security Services trains new operators to talk quickly and get to the point. CVS stores have installed carpeting to reduce slipping. Arm & Hammer sharpened the color contrast on its cat litter packaging and increased font size 20%.

Euphemisms abound. ADT's medical-alert systems are now "companion services"; bathroom-fixture manufacturer Kohler has "belay" bars instead of grab bars for showers; and Kimberly-Clark's Depends are sometimes labeled as underwear. Small packages of Depends look like underwear and hang on hooks rather than being stacked on shelves like diapers.

Adapted from Ellen Byron, "How to Market to an Aging Boomer: Flattery, Suberfuge, and Euphemism," *Wall Street Journal*, February 5, 2011, A1.

Eastern State rather than from Harvard may not matter, but how much the reader knows about accounting may. Does family structure matter? Sometimes. Some hotels and resorts offer family packages that include baby-sitting, multiple bedrooms, and children's activities.

Age certainly matters. Mutual funds are aiming for young investors by lowering the minimum investment to less than the cost of an iPod, and simplifying choices.[3]

One aspect of age that gets much press is the differences between generations in the office. Many older people believe younger workers have a sense of entitlement, that they expect great opportunities and perks without working for them. On the other hand, many younger workers see their older colleagues as rigid and hostile. Figure 2.2 shows some of the frequently mentioned age differences. While awareness of generational differences may help in some communication situations, such lists are also a good place to attach mental warnings against stereotypes. Plenty of baby boomers also like frequent positive feedback, and almost everyone likes a chance to make a difference.

For most companies, income is a major demographic characteristic. In 2011, Walmart quietly returned to its "everyday low prices" after experimenting with low-priced sale products balanced by slightly higher prices elsewhere. The new pricing had not appealed to Walmart's financially strapped customers. The chain also returned shotguns and rifles to the shelves of many of its stores in an attempt to attract more male customers.[4]

Location is yet another major demographic characteristic. You can probably think of many differences between regional audiences, or urban/rural audiences, in the United States. See Chapter 7 for more information on cross-cultural audiences.

Psychographic characteristics are qualitative rather than quantitative: values, beliefs, goals, and lifestyles. Knowing what your audience finds important allows you to choose information and benefits that the audience will find persuasive. The Choice and Gaylord hotel groups use semantic analysis software on their customer satisfaction surveys. Results can be connected to specific hotels, departments, shifts, employees, and rooms, allowing managers to track trends and respond to problems. Digital marketing companies are combining consumers' web surfing records with personal off-line data from sources such as the Census Bureau, consumer research firms such as Nielsen,

    Part 1   The Building Blocks of Effective Messages

Chinese Internet Companies

Chinese Internet companies are besting their American counterparts for Chinese users, and part of the reason is that they analyze their audience and give them what they want.

- Baidu's Internet search dominates Google's. One reason is that early on, Baidu's search bar was longer and wider than Google's, an important difference because Chinese characters are more complex than English letters, and the larger bar makes them clearer.

- Tencent Holdings popularized instant messaging in China by pairing it with blogging and online gaming, both highly popular in China. Now it has a bigger market value than Yahoo.

- Alibaba e-commerce site Taobao added instant messaging to allow buyers and sellers to haggle over prices, just as business is done off-line in China. eBay couldn't compete and closed its website in China.

Adapted from Loretta Chao, "Something Borrowed . . . ," *Wall Street Journal*, November 16, 2009, R4.

Figure 2.2   Some Generational Differences in the Office

	Baby Boomers	Generation X and Millenials
Birth Dates	Between 1946 and 1964	1964 and on
Work ethic	Long hours in office	Productivity counts, not hours at office
Values	Hard work; consistency; hierarchy; clearly defined roles; serious about work	Work–life balance; flexibility; autonomy, informality; variety of challenges; the workplace can be fun
Preferred channels	Face-to-face, e-mail	Texting, social networks
Motivators	Duty to company	Why a task is important; what's in it for them
Communication style	Through channels and hierarchy; accept annual evaluation	Freely offer opinions, both laterally and upward; want great amounts of attention and praise; want faster feedback
Decorum	Follow basic business decorum	May need to be reminded about basic business decorum

Sources: Ron Alsop, "The 'Trophy Kids' Go to Work," *Wall Street Journal*, October 21, 2008, D1, D4; and Piper Fogg, "When Generations Collide," *Chronicle of Higher Education*, July 18, 2008, B18.

credit card and shopping histories, and real estate and motor vehicle records. The combined data allow marketers to reach narrowly defined audiences, especially convenient for cable TV ads.[5]

Analyzing the Organizational Culture and the Discourse Community

Be sensitive to the culture in which your audiences work and the discourse community of which they are a part. **Organizational culture** is a set of values, attitudes, and philosophies. An organization's culture is revealed verbally in the organization's myths, stories, and heroes, as well as in documents such as employee manuals. It is revealed nonverbally through means such as dress codes, behavior standards, or the allocation of space, money, and power. A **discourse community** is a group of people who share assumptions about what channels, formats, and styles to use for communication, what topics to discuss and how to discuss them, and what constitutes evidence.

In an organization that values equality and individualism, you can write directly to the CEO and address him or her as a colleague. In other companies, you'd be expected to follow a chain of command. Some organizations prize short messages; some expect long, thorough documents. Messages that are consistent with the organization's culture have a greater chance of succeeding.

You can begin to analyze an organization's culture by asking the following questions:

- Is the organization tall or flat? Are there lots of levels between the CEO and the lowest worker, or only a few?
- How do people get ahead? Are the organization's rewards based on seniority, education, being well-liked, saving money, or serving customers? Are rewards available only to a few top people, or is everyone expected to succeed?

Some companies are beginning to accept visible body art and long hair in traditional workplace cultures.

- Does the organization value diversity or homogeneity? Does it value independence and creativity or being a team player and following orders?
- What stories do people tell? Who are the organization's heroes and villains?
- How important are friendship and sociability? To what extent do workers agree on goals, and how intently do they pursue them?
- How formal are behavior, language, and dress?
- What does the work space look like? Do employees work in offices, cubicles, or large rooms?
- What are the organization's goals? Making money? Serving customers and clients? Advancing knowledge? Contributing to the community?

To analyze an organization's discourse community, ask the following questions:

- What media, formats, and styles are preferred for communication?
- What do people talk about? What topics are not discussed?
- What kind of and how much evidence is needed to be convincing?

CHOOSING CHANNELS TO REACH YOUR AUDIENCE LO 2-2

A communication **channel** is the means by which you convey your message. Communication channels vary in speed, accuracy of transmission, cost, number of messages carried, number of people reached, efficiency, and ability to

A Channel Pro

Virgin Atlantic Airlines (VAA) uses multiple channels to support its branding as a fun, innovative, honest, caring, and value-offering airline.

- The most-read portion of its Facebook page contains travel tips from crew members, communication that comes across as honest and caring.

- Its website contains a "rapid response" link to Twitter and Facebook for up-to-date communications during crises.

- Its Vtravelled site allows customers to exchange travel information and advice.

- Its Facebook Flight Status app was a first for any airline, as was its iPhone app, Flight Tracker, which includes real-time aircraft positions.

- In response to suggestions from its online community, it launched an airport taxi-sharing service.

VAA's head of e-business says, "Twitter is no more than a sound bite. Facebook can be an article. The website is for in-depth detail. They all need to signpost each other."

Adapted from Patrick Barwise and Sean Meehan, "The One Thing You Must Get Right When Building a Brand," *Harvard Business Review* 88, no. 12 (December 2010): 83–84.

promote goodwill. Depending on the audience, your purposes, and the situation, one channel may be better than another.

A written message makes it easier to

- Present extensive or complex data.
- Present many specific details.
- Minimize undesirable emotions.
- Track details and agreements.

Oral messages make it easier to

- Use emotion to help persuade the audience.
- Focus the audience's attention on specific points.
- Resolve conflicts and build consensus.
- Modify plans.
- Get immediate action or response.

Choosing the right channel can be tricky sometimes. Even in the office, you will have to decide if your message will be more effective as an e-mail, text message, phone call, visit, or sticky note posted on a colleague's computer. In nonstandard situations, choosing a channel can be challenging. If you are the head of a small, nonprofit literacy agency which helps adults learn to read, how do you reach your clients? You cannot afford TV ads, and they cannot read print channels such as flyers. If you are a safety officer for a manufacturer, how do you send out product recall notifications? How many people file the

M&M candies offer a sweet communication channel to organizations.

contact-information cards when they purchase an item? If you are the benefits manager in a large manufacturing plant, how will you get information about your new benefits plan out to the thousand people on the floor? They don't use computers at work and may not have computer access at home.

Businesses are becoming ever more savvy about using the array of channels. Ad money has been moving out of print and TV channels and into online advertising, which totaled $25 billion in 2010. Of those billions, $2 billion were spent on social media sites, Facebook in particular.[6]

Businesses use Twitter, YouTube, and Flickr to highlight new products and services. Many companies have interactive websites and forums where customers can get product information and chat about products; Amazon is the prime example. Diaper companies are giving perks to "mommy" bloggers to talk about their products; car companies are using strong social media influencers to post their opinions online.[7] Nonprofits advertise events, connect with volunteers, and schedule volunteer service on their Facebook pages. And all that social network chatter can now be mined by software which performs semantic analyses providing feedback to advertisers about both products and audiences.

Even traditional paper channels are moving online. Publishers are making their travel books into e-books and cell phone apps. Newspapers are expanding from print to blogs, podcasts, and chatrooms. In fact, Warren Buffet himself warned the *Washington Post*, on whose board he served, that the paper-only model would no longer work.[8] In 2010, 41% of Americans got their national and international news from the Internet, surpassing newspapers (40%) for the first time, and online advertising surpassed print newspaper advertising for the first time.[9]

The big three TV network newscasts are facing similar problems. According to the Pew Research Center, network evening news audiences have been on a downward trend for three decades. Staffers have been cut, as have bureaus and offices. Audience median age is now over 50.[10] In response to declining viewership, networks are posting news in online stories and videos, as well as blogs.

Trolling for Plaintiffs

Law firms are spending millions to develop their online presence—and to get new clients. And this online spending is replacing more traditional spending for yellow pages, TV, and radio ads.

Many of these online sites look like community forums or news boards. They are publicized on forums such as Facebook and Twitter. Many firms, knowing that people generally trust material they find in electronic searches far more than they trust ads, are also adding content so that their sites appear early in a Google search.

The marketing officer for one such law firm told the *Wall Street Journal* that people reaching the firm through social media were twice as likely to become clients as those who made contact through television or print.

Adapted from Nathan Koppel, "Using Social Networking as Legal Tool: Law Firms Say They Are Turning to the Web to Develop Evidence for Suits and Market Themselves to Potential Clients," *Wall Street Journal*, June 15, 2010, B4.

Heartlanders   American Classics   Surburban Pioneers

Multi-Culti Mosaic   Young Digerati   Young Influentials

Greenbelt Sports   Blue-Chip Blues   Close-In Couples

Market research firm Claritas, Inc., combines demographic and psychographic data to identify 66 lifestyle segments, including "Young Digerati" (tech-savvy young adults), "Close-In Couples" (older, African-American couples), and "Blue-Chip Blues" (young families with well-paying blue-collar jobs). PRIZM is a trademark or registered trademark of The Nielsen Company (US), LLC.

Is It the Black Abyss for the White Pages?

White pages may become a relic as more and more telecommunication companies cease to print paper copies.

As land lines steadily decrease, more and more people rely solely on their cell phones, whose numbers usually are not in the white pages. Furthermore, those cell phones store frequently used numbers. For numbers not in their cell phones, most consumers now check the Internet.

Telecommunication companies tout the change as an environmentally friendly one. Verizon notes a savings of 17,000 tons of paper annually by switching to Internet listings in its 12-state area of operation.

Adapted from Michael Felberbaum, "It's Looking Dark for White Pages of Phone Books," *Des Moines Register*, November 12, 2010, 1A.

Creative uses of channels are appearing everywhere (for more on electronic channels, see Chapters 4 and 9):

- Intel is using electronic billboards in New York's Penn Station to promote its Smart TV technology. People with the appropriate mobile app will be personally greeted by the signs.[11]
- Popular bands such as Phish have developed their own apps, with features such as remixing tools and games, for their fans.[12]
- Toy maker Mattel is using Facebook, Twitter, and a series of eight webisodes to celebrate the 50th birthday of Barbie's boyfriend Ken. The webisodes allow Mattel to extend the audience to teenagers and adults who have an emotional tie with the toy and may be collectors.[13]
- Dunkin' Donuts quickie contest for people to submit pictures of themselves drinking iced coffee in the winter generated 140 submissions and 3.9 million product plugs through posts and status updates.[14]
- Digital book store Wowio is selling ads on e-books readers download from its site.[15]
- Bill Cosby recorded a hip-hop album to help carry his message of education and self-respect to new audiences. To sell its cleaning products, Clorox put out an album, "The Blue Sky Project: A Clorox Charity Collection." Companies such as Procter & Gamble and Allstate also offer full-length versions of tunes used in their ads. In regions such as the United Kingdom and Asia, original songs featured in ads often become quite popular.[16]
- Vienna, Austria, raised money for the main public library with a phone sex hotline. Pay by the minute and you got to hear a famous Austrian actress reading passages from the library's collection of erotic fiction from the 18th through 20th centuries.[17]

Creative channels abound. Ads are appearing on hotel shower curtains, the bellies of pregnant women, airport luggage conveyor belts, grocery checkout conveyors, sidewalks, and toilet stall doors. Ads inside subway tunnels appear to be in motion as trains ride by. One company prints ads on cardboard shirt hangers which are distributed free to cleaners. The hangers are touted as a good way to reach male consumers.[18]

As consumers become ever more savvy about ways to ignore advertising, one channel that has received publicity is the vivistitial: ads that take advantage of more receptive times in consumers' lives. One much talked about example is the elevator ad. Captivate offers video programming, such as news headlines and weather, in elevators. The programming is not intrusive: screens are not huge and the video does not have sound. Recall of Captivate ads is two to four times higher than that of TV ads.[19]

USING AUDIENCE ANALYSIS TO ADAPT YOUR MESSAGE   LO 2-3

Zeroing in on the right audience with the right message is frequently a formula for success. If you know your audience well and if you use words well, much of your audience analysis and adaptation will be unconscious. If you don't know your audience or if the message is very important, take the time to analyze your audience formally and to revise your message with your analysis in mind. The questions in Figure 2.3 will help guide a careful analysis.

Figure 2.3   Analyzing Your Audience

These questions will help you analyze your audience:

1. How will the audience initially react to the message?
2. How much information does the audience need?
3. What obstacles must you overcome?
4. What positive aspects can you emphasize?
5. What are the audience's expectations about the appropriate language, content, and organization of messages?
6. How will the audience use the document?

As you answer these questions for a specific audience, think about the organizational culture in which the person works. At every point, your audience's reaction is affected not only by his or her personal feelings and preferences but also by the political environment of the organization, the economy, and current events.

1. How Will the Audience Initially React to the Message?

a. Will the audience see this message as important?   Audiences will read and act on messages they see as important to their own careers; they may ignore messages that seem unimportant to them.

When the audience may see your message as unimportant, you need to

- Use a subject line or first paragraph that shows your reader this message is important and relevant.
- Make the action as easy as possible.
- Suggest a realistic deadline for action.
- Keep the message as short as possible.

A Zappos Channel

[According to Tony Hsieh, founder and CEO of Zappos, the popular Internet footwear business], "There's a lot of buzz these days about 'social media' and 'integration marketing.' As unsexy and low-tech as it may sound, our belief is that the telephone is one of the best branding devices out there. You have the customer's undivided attention for five to ten minutes, and if you get the interaction right, what we've found is that the customer remembers the experience for a very long time and tells his or her friends about it.

. . .

"At Zappos, we don't measure call times (our longest phone call was almost six hours long!). . . . We don't have scripts because we trust our employees to use their best judgment when dealing with each and every customer. . . . We're trying to build a lifelong relationship with each customer one phone call at a time."

Quoted from Tony Hsieh, *Delivering Happiness: A Path to Profits, Passion, and Purpose* (New York: Business Plus, 2010), 143–45. With permission from Central Grand Publishing.

STONE SOUP   *BY JAN ELIOT*

38   Part 1   The Building Blocks of Effective Messages

Customer Analysis

According to Harvey Mackay, author of the business bestseller *Swim with the Sharks without Being Eaten Alive*, the Golden Rule of sales is Know Your Customer. Your customers are not companies, but rather the individuals at companies who decide whether or not to buy your goods or services. To analyze these buyers, he has developed a 66-question customer profile, the Mackay 66.

The profile includes questions about such topics as the individual's education, spouse, children, politics, religion, activities, hobbies, vacations, cars, personality, personal goals, and business goals. In addition to typical questions you might expect, such as employment record, the profile also asks about

- Status symbols in office.
- Sensitive items to be avoided.
- Subjects arousing strong feelings.
- Favorite conversation topics.

Mackay uses the information in these profiles to meet the needs of his customers. (He says he also guards it with his life, because he knows how sensitive it is.)

Adapted from Harvey Mackay, "Knowing Your Customer Is Key," *Des Moines Register*, November 29, 2010, 6E.

b. How will the fact that the message is from you affect the audience's reaction? The audience's experience with you and your organization shapes the way they respond to this new message. Someone who thinks well of you and your organization will be prepared to receive your message favorably; someone who thinks poorly of you and the organization will be quick to find fault with what you say and the way you say it.

When your audience has negative feelings about your organization, your position, or you personally, you need to

- Make a special effort to avoid phrases that could seem condescending, arrogant, rude, hostile, or uncaring.
- Use positive emphasis (Chapter 3) to counteract the natural tendency to sound defensive.
- Develop logic and benefits fully.

2. How Much Information Does the Audience Need?

a. How much does the audience already know about this subject? It's easy to overestimate the knowledge an audience has. People outside your own immediate unit may not really know what it is you do. Even people who once worked in your unit may have forgotten specific details now that their daily work is in management. People outside your organization won't know how *your* organization does things.

When some of your information is new to the audience, you need to

- Make a special effort to be clear. Define terms, explain concepts, use examples, avoid acronyms.
- Link new information to old information that the audience already knows.
- Use paragraphs and headings to break up new information into related chunks so that the information is easier to digest.
- Test a draft of your document with your reader or a subset of your intended audience to see whether the audience can understand and use what you've written.

b. Does the audience's knowledge need to be updated or corrected? Our personal experience guides our expectations and actions, but sometimes needs to be corrected. If you're trying to change someone's understanding of something, you need to

- Acknowledge the audience's initial understanding early in the message.
- Use examples, statistics, or other evidence to show the need for the change, or to show that the audience's experience is not universal.
- Allow the audience to save face by suggesting that changed circumstances call for new attitudes or action.

c. What aspects of the subject does the audience need to be aware of to appreciate your points?   When the audience must think of background or old information to appreciate your points, you can

- Preface information with "As you know" or "As you may remember" to avoid suggesting that you think the audience does not know what you're saying.
- Put old or obvious information in a subordinate clause.

3. What Obstacles Must You Overcome?

a. Is your audience opposed to what you have to say?   People who have already made up their minds are highly resistant to change. When the audience will oppose what you have to say, you need to

- Start your message with any areas of agreement or common ground that you share with your audience.
- Make a special effort to be clear and unambiguous. Points that might be clear to a neutral audience can be misinterpreted by someone opposed to the message.
- Make a special effort to avoid statements that will anger the audience.
- Limit your statement or request to the smallest possible area. If parts of your message could be delivered later, postpone them.
- Show that your solution is the best solution currently available, even though it isn't perfect.

b. Will it be easy for the audience to do as you ask?   Everyone has a set of ideas and habits and a mental self-image. If we're asked to do something that violates any of those, we first have to be persuaded to change our attitudes or habits or self-image—a change we're reluctant to make.

When your request is time-consuming, complicated, or physically or psychologically difficult, you need to

- Make the action as easy as possible.
- Break down complex actions into a list, so the audience can check off each step as it is completed. This list will also help ensure complete responses.
- Show that what you ask is consistent with some aspect of what the audience believes.
- Show how the audience (not just you or your organization) will benefit when the action is completed.

4. What Positive Aspects Can You Emphasize?

a. From the audience's point of view, what are the benefits of your message?   Benefits help persuade the audience that your ideas are good ones. Make the most of the good points inherent in the message you want to convey.

- Put good news first.
- Use audience benefits that go beyond the basic good news.

Tiny Marketing

In its goal of attracting 1 billion additional consumers, Procter & Gamble is adding new marketing techniques to its arsenal. Since most of these potential customers are poor women in developing countries who buy single-use packets of products such as shampoo, soap, and detergent, P&G is packaging its products in small portions. The small packages also please the tiny mom-and-pop stores, many just kiosks or closet-sized stores, which serve these customers. These stores aggregated are P&G's largest customer, larger even than Wal-Mart. To attract owners, P&G employs local agents who tidy and price P&G in-store products, distribute promotional items, and stock shelves—sparing owners trips to distributors.

P&G is also developing special products just for these markets. One example is feminine hygiene products. Because many customers lack the money and privacy to change pads frequently, P&G developed a low-priced, extra-absorbent pad, which is now the leading product in Mexico.

What unique marketing practices have you noticed in other countries?

Adapted from Ellen Byron, "P&G's Global Target: Shelves of Tiny Stores: It Woos Poor Women Buying Single Portions; Mexico's 'Hot Zones,'" *Wall Street Journal*, July 16, 2007, A1.

Customer Service Channels

"If you think the privacy of your medical information has been compromised, you can file a complaint with the Office for Civil Rights. A brochure distributed by this office tells people they can call and 'ask for a civil-rights or privacy-complaint form.'

"But you can't really ask for anything, because when you call the number, you can't get a person on the line.

"An automated voice thanks you for calling and then breaks the news:

"'We're sorry, a staff person is not able to receive your call. This number is not able to receive messages.'

"Callers are directed to a website to file a complaint. Twice. And if you don't have a computer, . . . [t]he voice tells you . . . 'most local libraries have computers available that residents can use to access the Internet at no extra cost.'"*

Is this an ethical way to distribute information? What groups of people does this channel discriminate against? Do you know of other organizations that communicate only through the web?

*Quoted from "Not Exactly a Model for Customer Service," *Des Moines Register*, August 23, 2008, 14A.

b. What experiences, interests, goals, and values do you share with the audience? A sense of solidarity with someone can be an even more powerful reason to agree than the content of the message itself. When everyone in your audience shares the same experiences, interests, goals, and values, you can

- Consider using a vivid anecdote to remind the audience of what you share. The details of the anecdote should be interesting or new; otherwise, you may seem to be lecturing the audience.
- Use a salutation and close that remind the audience of their membership in this formal or informal group.

5. What Are the Audience's Expectations about the Appropriate Language, Content, and Organization of Messages?

a. What style of writing does the audience prefer? Good writers adapt their style to suit the reader's preferences. A reader who sees contractions as too informal needs a different style from one who sees traditional business writing as too stuffy. As you write,

- Use what you know about your reader to choose a more or less formal, more or less friendly style.
- Use the reader's first name in the salutation only if both of you are comfortable with a first-name basis.

b. Are there hot buttons or "red flag" words that may create an immediate negative response? You don't have time to convince the audience that a term is broader or more neutral than his or her understanding. When you need agreement or approval, you should

- Avoid terms that carry emotional charges for many people: for example, *criminal, un-American, feminist, fundamentalist, liberal.*
- Use your previous experience with individuals to replace any terms that have particular negative meanings for them.

c. How much detail does the audience want? A message that does not give the audience the amount of or kind of detail they want may fail. Sometimes you can ask your audience how much detail they want. When you write to people you do not know well, you can

- Provide all the detail they need to understand and act on your message.
- Group chunks of information under headings so that readers can go directly to the parts of the message they find most interesting and relevant.
- Be sure that a shorter-than-usual document covers the essential points; be sure that a longer-than-usual document is free from wordiness and repetition.

d. Does the audience prefer a direct or indirect organization? Individual personality or cultural background may lead someone to prefer a particular kind of structure. You'll be more effective if you use the structure and organization your audience prefers.

6. How Will the Audience Use the Document?

a. Under what physical conditions will the audience use the document?   Reading a document in a quiet office calls for no special care. But suppose the audience will be reading your message on the train commuting home, or on a ladder as he or she attempts to follow instructions. Then the physical preparation of the document can make it easier or harder to use.

When the reader will use your document outside an office,

- Use lots of white space.
- Make the document small enough to hold in one hand.
- Number items so the reader can find his or her place after an interruption.

b. Will the audience use the document as a general reference? As a specific guide?   Understanding how your audience will use the document will enable you to choose the best pattern of organization and the best level of detail.

If the document will serve as a general reference,

- Use a specific subject line to aid in filing and retrieval. If the document is online, consider using several keywords to make it easy to find the document in a database search program.
- Use headings within the document so that readers can skim it.
- Give the office as well as the person to contact so that the reader can get in touch with the appropriate person some time from now.
- Spell out details that may be obvious now but might be forgotten in a year.

If the document will be a detailed guide or contain instructions,

- Check to be sure that all the steps are in chronological order.
- Number steps so that readers can easily see which steps they've completed.
- Group steps into five to seven categories if there are many individual steps.
- Put any warnings at the beginning of the document; then repeat them just before the specific step to which they apply.

Audience Is Not a Mystery for Her

Every year, mystery writer Mary Higgins Clark sells 3.7 million copies of her books; in fact, she has sold over 100 million copies in the United States alone.

Perhaps the biggest factor in her success is her careful audience analysis; she gives her audience what they want. In her case, this means intelligent women in danger who unravel sinister plots and often help engineer their own escapes. Her heroines tend to be self-made professionals.

Because her novels are always "G-rated" (no cursing, no living together before marriage, no explicit depictions of violence), they are a favorite of mother–daughter book clubs and sell heavily for Mother's Day, the third biggest book-selling holiday of the year (Father's Day and Christmas are bigger).

Adapted from Alexandra Alter, "The Case of the Best-Selling Author: How a Former Pan-Am Stewardess Has Stayed at the Top of the Publishing Game Since 1975," *Wall Street Journal*, March 25, 2011, D1.

AUDIENCE ANALYSIS WORKS

Audience analysis is a powerful tool. Amazon.com tracks users' online histories to make suggestions on items they might like. Nintendo believes that much of its success is extending its concept of audience. An important part of its audience is hard-core gamers, a very vocal group—they love to blog. But if Nintendo listened just to them, they would be the only audience Nintendo had. Instead, Nintendo extended its audience by creating the Wii, a new system that the hard-core gamers had not imagined and one that is collecting new users who never imagined owning a system at all.[20] With the introduction of Wii Fit, Nintendo is expanding its audience to more women and even senior citizens.

Best Buy uses its extensive customer feedback to tweak its private-label electronics. The company noticed, for instance, that many portable DVD players

Audience Analysis at the Front Line

Some major businesses are sending their executives out to the front lines for a day or more to increase awareness of both clients' and employees' needs. Such stints are bringing changes to the front lines. A Loews executive who served as a bellhop, pool attendant, and housekeeper at a Florida hotel sweated so much in his polyester uniform that he had both the style and material of the uniforms altered. Executives at DaVita, a firm that runs kidney dialysis centers, learn that patient needs must come first, even before company paperwork.

Other companies which send executives out to be low-level workers include Walt Disney, Continental Airlines, Sysco, and Amazon.com.

What do you think executives learn on the front lines at these companies? Can you think of other companies that would benefit from similar programs for their executives?

Adapted from Joann S. Lublin, "Top Brass Try Life in the Trenches: To Promote Understanding, Firms Require Executives to Perform Entry-Level Jobs," *Wall Street Journal*, June 25, 2007, B1, B3.

The U.S. Census Bureau prepared over 100 posters, similar to this one, to reach various segments of its audience.

Source: "Posters," U.S. Census Bureau: United States Census 2010, http://2010.census.gov/partners/materials/posters-materials.php.

were purchased for young children. So they developed a spill-resistant model with rubberized edges that became a top seller.[21]

Tesco PLC, Britain's largest retailer, signs up customers for its Clubcard. The card gives customers discounts, and it gives Tesco audience data. When Tesco added Asian herbs and ethnic foods in Indian and Pakistani neighborhoods, the data showed the products were also popular with affluent white customers, so Tesco expanded its roll-out. When customers buy diapers the first time, they get coupons for usual baby products such as wipes and toys. They also get coupons for beer, because the data show that new fathers buy more beer.[22]

AUDIENCE BENEFITS LO 2-4

Use your analysis of your audience to create effective **audience benefits,** advantages that the audience gets by using your services, buying your products, following your policies, or adopting your ideas. In informative messages, benefits give reasons to comply with the information you announce and suggest that the information is good. In persuasive messages, benefits give reasons to act and help overcome audience resistance. Negative messages do not use benefits.

Characteristics of Good Audience Benefits

Good benefits meet four criteria. Each of these criteria suggests a technique for writing good benefits.

1. Adapt benefits to the audience. When you write to different audiences, you may need to stress different benefits. Suppose that you manufacture a product and want to persuade dealers to carry it. The features you may cite in ads directed toward customers—stylish colors, sleek lines, convenience, durability, good price—won't convince dealers. Shelf space is at a premium, and no dealer carries all the models of all the brands available for any given product. Why should the dealer stock your product? To be persuasive, talk about the features that are benefits from the dealer's point of view: turnover, profit margin, the national advertising campaign that will build customer awareness and interest, the special store displays you offer that will draw attention to the product.

2. Stress intrinsic as well as extrinsic motivators. **Intrinsic motivators** come automatically from using a product or doing something. **Extrinsic motivators** are "added on." Someone in power decides to give them; they do not necessarily come from using the product or doing the action. Figure 2.4 gives examples of extrinsic and intrinsic motivators for three activities.

Intrinsic motivators or benefits are better than extrinsic motivators for two reasons:

- There just aren't enough extrinsic motivators for everything you want people to do. You can't give a prize to every customer every time he or she places an order or every subordinate who does what he or she is supposed to do.
- Research shows that extrinsic motivators may actually make people *less* satisfied with the products they buy or the procedures they follow.

In a groundbreaking study of professional employees, Frederick Herzberg found that the things people said they liked about their jobs were all intrinsic motivators—pride in achievement, an enjoyment of the work itself, responsibility. Extrinsic motivators—pay, company policy—were sometimes mentioned as things people disliked, but they were never cited as things that motivated or satisfied them. People who made a lot of money still did not mention salary as a good point about the job or the organization.[23]

Steak 'n Shake restaurant chain wanted to find out what motivated its employees to do their best at work. The company learned that what employees want more than money is respect and the feeling that management listens to them and values their input.[24]

3. Prove benefits with clear logic and explain them in adequate detail. An audience benefit is a claim or assertion that the audience will benefit if they do something. Convincing the audience, therefore, involves two steps: making sure that the benefit really will occur, and explaining it to the audience.

Witness.org: Sharing Evidence of Human Rights Abuses

"For the past 16 years Witness has provided video cameras to carefully selected activists and community leaders in more than 100 countries. The group has amassed one of the largest existing collections of human-rights-abuse footage and has shown its videos to policy makers and human-rights groups around the world."

The graphic and disturbing nature of these videos make them difficult to distribute to public forums (such as YouTube), where user guidelines prevent anyone from sharing violent or sexually explicit material. Instead, Witness created their own version of YouTube—http://hub.witness.org/—where anyone can submit video clips of human rights abuses, and anyone can log in and view the evidence.

Witness' video evidence has led to war crimes prosecutions and put pressure on governments to change their policies.

How does Witness' approach demonstrate a keen understanding of audience analysis? What "audience benefits" does their website address? What ethical concerns might there be about publishing graphic video evidence on a public website?

Quoted and adapted from David Kushner, "In Your Eyes: Peter Gabriel's Human-Rights Group Embraces Social Media. A YouTube for Unseen Atrocities," *Fast Company,* November 2008, 80–2.

Figure 2.4 Extrinsic and Intrinsic Motivators

Activity	Extrinsic motivator	Intrinsic motivator
Making a sale	Getting a commission	Pleasure in convincing someone; pride in using your talents to think of a strategy and execute it
Turning in a suggestion to a company suggestion system	Getting a monetary reward when the suggestion is implemented	Solving a problem at work; making the work environment a little more pleasant
Writing a report that solves an organizational problem	Getting praise, a good performance appraisal, and maybe a raise	Pleasure in having an effect on an organization; pride in using your skills to solve problems; solving the problem itself

If the logic behind a claimed benefit is faulty or inaccurate, there's no way to make that particular benefit convincing. Revise the benefit to make it logical.

Faulty logic:	Moving your account information into Excel will save you time.
Analysis:	If you have not used Excel before, in the short run it will probably take you longer to work with your account information using Excel. You may have been pretty good with your old system!
Revised benefit:	Moving your account information into Excel will allow you to prepare your monthly budget pages with a few clicks of a button.

If the logic is sound, making that logic evident to the audience is a matter of providing enough evidence and showing how the evidence proves the claim that there will be a benefit. Always provide enough detail to be vivid and concrete. You'll need more detail in the following situations:

- The audience may not have thought of the benefit before.
- The benefit depends on the difference between the long run and the short run.
- The audience will be hard to persuade, and you need detail to make the benefit vivid and emotionally convincing.

The apparel industry, which is actively seeking a middle-aged and baby boomer audience, is using details to attract them. Slacks may offer slimming panels, and jeans may offer stretch waists and room for padded hips and thighs. Tops may cover upper arms. The potential market is huge. Women over 35 bought over half the annual $100 billion spent on women's apparel purchases.[25]

Until recently, Islamic women who wanted to go swimming had a problem. To meet their customers' needs, the Australian company Ahiida now makes hooded full-bodied bathing suits, called Burqinis, for Muslim women who wish to go swimming while still maintaining the Islamic customs of full body coverage.

Source: Lisa Miller, "Belief Watch: Surf's Up!" *Newsweek,* January 29, 2007, 15.

4. Phrase benefits in you-attitude.   If benefits aren't worded with you-attitude (Chapter 3), they'll sound selfish and won't be as effective as they could be. It doesn't matter how you phrase benefits while you're brainstorming and developing them, but in your final draft, check to be sure that you've used you-attitude.

Lacks you-attitude: We have the lowest prices in town.

You-attitude: At Havlichek Cars, you get the best deal in town.

Ways to Identify and Develop Audience Benefits

Brainstorm lots of benefits—perhaps twice as many as you'll need. Then you can choose the ones that are most effective for your audience, or that you can develop most easily. The first benefit you think of may not be the best.

Sometimes benefits will be easy to think of and to explain. When they are harder to identify or to develop, use the following steps to identify and then develop good benefits.

1. Identify the needs, wants, and feelings that may motivate your audience.   All of us have basic needs, and most of us supplement those needs with possessions or intangibles we want. We need enough food to satisfy nutritional needs, but we may want our diet to make us look sexy. We need basic shelter, but we may want our homes to be cozy, luxurious, or green. And our needs and wants are strongly influenced by our feelings. We may feel safer in a more expensive car, even though research does not show that car as being safer than cheaper models.

2. Identify the objective features of your product or policy that could meet the needs you've identified.   Sometimes just listing the audience's needs makes it obvious which feature meets a given need. Sometimes several features together meet the need. Try to think of all of them.

Suppose that you want to persuade people to come to the restaurant you manage. It's true that everybody needs to eat, but telling people they can satisfy their hunger needs won't persuade them to come to your restaurant rather than going somewhere else or eating at home. Depending on what features your restaurant offered, you could appeal to one or more of the following subgroups:

Subgroup	Features to meet the subgroup's needs
People who work outside the home	A quick lunch; a relaxing place to take clients or colleagues
Parents with small children	High chairs, children's menus, and toys to keep the kids entertained while they wait for their order
People who eat out a lot	Variety both in food and in decor
People on tight budgets	Economical food; a place where they don't need to tip (cafeteria or fast food)
People on special diets	Low-sodium and low-carb dishes; vegetarian food; kosher food
People to whom eating out is part of an evening's entertainment	Music or a floor show; elegant surroundings; reservations so they can get to a show or event after dinner; late hours so they can come to dinner after a show or game

No Substitute for Face Time

In the face of globalization and remote video feeds that simultaneously connect workers and clients all around the world, face-to-face meetings are still critical in global business. Culturally, the world is still incredibly diverse, and to make global coalitions, such as launching a Coca-Cola bottling plant in Albania a few years ago, meeting the right people in person was crucial for Coke's CEO.

Another example is MTV in the center of Islamic nations. Would it be possible to enter MTV into the Arabian market without offending the religious institutions of this region? Not without many carefully planned, face-to-face meetings. The chief of MTV Networks International managed to accomplish the establishment of MTV Arabia by convincing the mayor of Mecca that the new station would provide educational opportunities and would not show skin.

Collaborative technologies such as videoconferencing may be convenient and less expensive than frequent flying, but technology simply cannot take the place of physically sitting down with a colleague or client to solve problems and form alliances.

Adapted from Tom Lowry et al., "It's All About the Face-to-Face," *BusinessWeek*, January 28, 2008, 48–51.

Whenever you're communicating with customers or clients about features that are not unique to your organization, it's wise to present both benefits of the features themselves and benefits of dealing with your company. If you talk about the benefits of the new healthy choices in children's menus but don't mention your own revised menu, people may go somewhere else!

3. Show how the audience can meet their needs with the features of the policy or product.   Features alone rarely motivate people. Instead, link the feature to the audience's needs—and provide details to make the benefit vivid.

Weak:	You get quick service.
Better:	If you only have an hour for lunch, try our Business Buffet. Within minutes, you can choose from a variety of main dishes, vegetables, and a make-your-own-sandwich-and-salad bar. You'll have a lunch that's as light or filling as you want, with time to enjoy it—and still be back to the office on time.

AUDIENCE BENEFITS WORK

Appropriate audience benefits work so well that organizations spend much time and money identifying them and then developing them.

- Procter & Gamble increased the market share of Gain detergent, and saw annual sales of over a billion dollars, by focusing on a benefit their audience considered important: the scent.[26]
- Hotels study which benefits are worth the money, and which are not. Holiday Inn keeps restaurants and bars in all their hotels, even though they are not money makers, but does not have bellhops. Staybridge Suites cleans less often but has "Sundowner receptions" which give guests a free meal and a chance to socialize.[27]
- *The Daily Sun*, a South African tabloid, is gaining market share, when other newspapers are losing it, by focusing on stories—soccer, sex, soap operas, local witches, supernatural events like evil flying tortoises—its audience wants to read. This audience, primarily newly enfranchised black Africans, has given the paper an audited paid circulation of over a half million.[28]
- Many companies offer their employees health benefits, an arrangement that benefits both the company and employee. Meredith Corporation, publisher of magazines such as *Better Homes and Gardens*, *Family Circle*, and *Parents*, pays for employee health screenings. Employees who accept the offer get $300 off their health insurance cost; Meredith gets a decrease in corporate health care costs.[29]
- Companies branching out into servicing their products find that they are more successful if they offer benefits in addition to cost saving. One truck company offers its customers fleet-management services, including monitoring fuel consumption and showing drivers how to increase their gas mileage. This service in turn helps its customers appeal to environmentally concerned clients such as government agencies.[30]

Remember that audience benefits must be appropriate for the audience before they work. Tylenol tried a new ad campaign that said, "We put our love into Tylenol." Upset customers who remembered the Tylenol cyanide poisonings wrote in saying they didn't want anyone putting anything into their Tylenol.[31]

THE McPLAYBOOK

Now That's Fast Food

To pump up business 24/7, McDonald's has sped up its new-product introductions. Here's its secret recipe:

Make it easy to eat

McDonald's does more than half its business at drive-through windows. That means it needs snacks and meals that can be held in one hand while the other is on the steering wheel.

Make it easy to prepare

McDonald's restaurant crews turn over entirely within a year, on average. To maintain consistency amid this churn, tasks must be simple to learn and repeat.

Make it quick

It's called fast food for a reason. McDonald's tests all new products for cooking times so customers don't have to wait even a second longer than absolutely necessary.

Make what the customers want

McDonald's prowls the market for new products and then spends months in carefully monitored field tests to ensure that people will buy its new concoctions.

McDonald's plans menu items to meet the needs and expectations of customers, employees, and franchise owners.

Source: From Michael Arndt, "Special Report: McDonald's," Reprinted from the February 5, 2007 issue of *BusinessWeek*. Used with permission of Bloomberg L. P. Copyright © 2011. All rights reserved.

Sometimes it is hard to know what your audience wants. A classic example is "feature creep" in electronic goods. Unfortunately, consumers seem to want lots of features in their electronics when they buy them, but then become frustrated trying to use them and return the devices. In the United States, product returns cost $100 billion.[32] Research has shown that over half the wares are in complete working order; consumers just cannot operate them.[33]

WRITING OR SPEAKING TO MULTIPLE AUDIENCES WITH DIFFERENT NEEDS

Many business and administrative messages go not to a single person but to a larger audience. When the members of your audience share the same interests and the same level of knowledge, you can use the principles outlined above for individual readers or for members of homogeneous groups. But often different members of the audience have different needs.

Researcher Rachel Spilka has shown that talking to readers both inside and outside the organization helped corporate engineers adapt their documents successfully. Talking to readers and reviewers helped writers involve readers in the planning process, understand the social and political relationships among readers, and negotiate conflicts orally rather than depending solely on the document. These writers were then able to think about content as well as about organization and style, appeal to common grounds (such as reducing waste or increasing productivity) that multiple readers shared, and reduce the number of revisions needed before documents were approved.[34]

When it is not possible to meet everyone's needs, meet the needs of gatekeepers and decision makers first.

Localizing Incentive Programs

Incentive programs are employee benefits aimed to reward good work performances. Globalization has complicated such programs, because what works in one country may not work in another.

In the United States, top performers might be rewarded with an expensive luxury item such as a watch. In China or India, a moped might be more appropriate.

Travel awards may also differ. US employees generally prefer unstructured, leisurely vacations, such as those offered by beach resorts. Europeans tend to prefer more adventurous trips, perhaps including a strenuous mountain hike or rafting trip. Many Chinese prefer highly structured tours with carefully planned itineraries.

Religion can also be a factor. Many U.S. employees would appreciate a trip to Las Vegas, with a complimentary bottle of champagne in their room. But many religious people in the Middle East or Asia would not want the gambling or the alcohol.

What are some employee incentives you can name that would be appropriate in one country but not another? What are some ways large firms can work with these differences?

Adapted from Irwin Speizer, "Good Intentions, Lost in Translation," *Workforce Management*, November 21, 2005, http://www.workforce.com/archive/feature/benefits-compensations/good-intentions-lost-translation/index.php.

As you write for multiple audiences, consider these strategies:

Content and number of details

- Provide an overview or executive summary for readers who want just the main points.
- In the body of the document, provide enough detail for decision makers and for anyone else who could veto your proposal.
- If the decision makers don't need details that other audiences will want, provide those details in appendices—statistical tabulations, earlier reports, and so forth.

Organization

- Use headings and a table of contents so readers can turn to the portions that interest them.
- Organize your message based on the decision makers' attitudes toward it.

Level of formality

- Avoid personal pronouns. *You* ceases to have a specific meaning when several different audiences use a document.
- If both internal and external audiences will use a document, use a slightly more formal style than you would in an internal document.
- Use a more formal style when you write to international audiences.

Technical level

- In the body of the document, assume the degree of knowledge that decision makers will have.
- Put background and explanatory information under separate headings. Then readers can use the headings and the table of contents to read or skip these sections, as their knowledge dictates.
- If decision makers will have more knowledge than other audiences, provide a glossary of terms. Early in the document, let readers know that the glossary exists.

SUMMARY OF KEY POINTS

- The **primary audience** will make a decision or act on the basis of your message. The **secondary audience** may be asked by the primary audience to comment on your message or to implement your ideas after they've been approved. The **auxiliary audience** encounters the message but does not have to interact with it. A **gatekeeper** controls whether the message gets to the primary audience. A **watchdog audience** has political, social, or economic power and may base future actions on its evaluation of your message.
- A communication channel is the means by which you convey your message to your audience.
- The following questions provide a framework for audience analysis:
  1. What will the audience's initial reaction be to the message?
  2. How much information does the audience need?

3. What obstacles must you overcome?

4. What positive aspects can you emphasize?

5. What expectations does the audience have about the appropriate language, contents, and organization of messages?

6. How will the audience use the document?

■ **Audience benefits** are advantages that the audience gets by using your services, buying your products, following your policies, or adopting your ideas. Benefits can exist for policies and ideas as well as for goods and services.

■ Good benefits are adapted to the audience, based on **intrinsic** rather than **extrinsic motivators,** supported by clear logic, explained in adequate detail, and phrased in you-attitude. Extrinsic benefits simply aren't available to reward every desired behavior; further, they reduce the satisfaction in doing something for its own sake.

■ To create audience benefits,

1. Identify the feelings, fears, and needs that may motivate your audience.

2. Identify the features of your product or policy that could meet the needs you've identified.

3. Show how the audience can meet their needs with the features of the policy or product.

■ When you write to multiple audiences, use the primary audience to determine level of detail, organization, level of formality, and use of technical terms and theory.

| CHAPTER 2 | Exercises and Problems | *Go to www.mhhe.com/locker10e for additional Exercises and Problems. |

2.1   Reviewing the Chapter

1. Who are the five different audiences your message may need to address? (LO 2-1)

2. What are some characteristics to consider when analyzing individuals? (LO 2-1)

3. What are some characteristics to consider when analyzing groups? (LO 2-1)

4. What are some questions to consider when analyzing organizational culture? (LO 2-1)

5. What is a discourse community? Why will discourse communities be important in your career? (LO 2-1)

6. What are standard business communication channels? (LO 2-2)

7. What kinds of electronic channels seem most useful to you? Why? (LO 2-2)

8. What are considerations to keep in mind when selecting channels? (LO 2-2)

9. What are 12 questions to ask when analyzing your audience? (LO 2-3)

10. What are four characteristics of good audience benefits? (LO 2-4)

11. What are three ways to identify and develop audience benefits? (LO 2-4)

12. What are considerations to keep in mind when addressing multiple audiences? (LO 2-3)

2.2   Reviewing Grammar

Good audience analysis requires careful use of pronouns. Review your skills with pronoun usage by doing grammar exercise B.5, Appendix B.

2.3   Identifying Audiences

In each of the following situations, label the audiences as gatekeeper, primary, secondary, auxiliary, or watchdog audiences (all audiences may not be in each scenario):

1. Kent, Carol, and Jose are planning to start a website design business. However, before they can get started, they need money. They have developed a business plan and are getting ready to seek funds from financial institutions for starting their small business.

2. Barbara's boss asked her to write a direct mail letter to potential customers about the advantages of becoming a preferred member of their agency's travel club. The letter will go to all customers of the agency who are over 65 years old.

3. Paul works for the mayor's office in a big city. As part of a citywide cost-cutting measure, a blue-ribbon panel has recommended requiring employees who work more than 40 hours in a week to take compensatory time off rather than being paid overtime. The only exceptions will be the police and fire departments. The mayor asks Paul to prepare a proposal for the city council, which will vote on whether to implement the change. Before they vote, council members will hear from (1) citizens, who will have an opportunity to read the proposal and communicate their opinions to the city council; (2) mayors' offices in other cities, who may be asked about their experiences; (3) union representatives, who may be concerned about the reduction in income that will occur if the proposal is implemented; (4) department heads, whose ability to schedule work might be limited if the proposal passes; and (5) the blue-ribbon panel and good-government lobbying groups. Council members come up for reelection in six months.

4. Sharon, Steven's boss at Bigster Corporation, has asked him to write an e-mail for everyone in her division, informing them of HR's new mandatory training sessions on new government regulations affecting Bigster's services.

2.4   Analyzing Multiple Audiences

Like most major corporations, the U.S. Census Bureau has multiple, conflicting audiences, among them the president, Congress, press, state governments, citizens (both as providers and users of data), statisticians, and researchers.

- For the bureau, who might serve as gatekeeper, primary, secondary, auxiliary, and watchdog audiences?
- What kinds of conflicting goals might these audiences have?

- What would be appropriate benefits for each type of audience?
- What kinds of categories might the bureau create for its largest audience (citizens)?
- How do some of the posters at the website below differ for different audiences?: "Posters," U.S. Census Bureau: United States Census 2010, http://2010.census.gov/partners/materials/posters-materials.php.

2.5   Choosing a Channel to Reach a Specific Audience

Suppose your organization wants to target a product, service, or program for each of the following audiences. What would be the best channel(s) to reach that group in your city? To what extent would that channel reach all group members?

a. Stay-at-home mothers
b. Vegetarians
c. Full-time students at a university
d. Part-time students at a community college
e. Non-English speakers
f. People who use hearing aids
g. Parents whose children play softball or baseball
h. Attorneys
i. Female owners of small businesses
j. Pet owners

2.6   Identifying and Developing Audience Benefits

Listed here are several things an organization might like its employees to do:

1. Use less paper.
2. Attend a brown-bag lunch to discuss ways to improve products or services.
3. Become more physically fit.
4. Volunteer for community organizations.
5. Write fewer e-mails.
6. Attend mandatory training about new government regulations affecting the business.

As your instructor directs,

a. Identify the motives or needs that might be met by each of the activities.

b. Take each need or motive and develop it as an audience benefit in a full paragraph. Use additional paragraphs for the other needs met by the activity. Remember to use you-attitude!

2.7   Identifying Objections and Audience Benefits

Think of an organization you know something about, and answer the following questions for it:

a. Your organization is thinking about developing a knowledge management system that requires workers to input their knowledge and experience in their job functions into the organizational database. What benefits could the knowledge management system offer your organization? What drawbacks are there? Who would be the easiest to convince? Who would be the hardest?

b. New telephone software would efficiently replace your organization's long-standing human phone operator who has been a perennial welcoming voice to incoming callers. What objections might people in your organization have to replacing the operator? What benefits might your organization receive? Who would be easiest to convince? Who would be the hardest?

c. Your organization is thinking of outsourcing one of its primary products to a manufacturer in another country where the product can be made more cost-efficiently. What fears or objections might people have? What benefits might your organization receive? Who would be the easiest to convince? Who would be hardest?

As your instructor directs,

a. Share your answers orally with a small group of students.

b. Present your answers in an oral presentation to the class.

c. Write a paragraph developing the best audience benefit you identified. Remember to use you-attitude.

2.8   Analyzing Benefits for Multiple Audiences

The U.S. Census Bureau lists these benefits from cooperating with the census:

> "Census information affects the numbers of seats your state occupies in the U.S. House of Representatives. And people from many walks of life use census data to advocate for causes, rescue disaster victims, prevent diseases, research markets, locate pools of skilled workers and more.
>
> "When you do the math, it's easy to see what an accurate count of residents can do for your community. Better infrastructure. More services. A brighter tomorrow for everyone. In fact, the information the census collects helps to determine how more than $400 billion dollars of federal funding each year is spent on infrastructure and services like:
>
> ■ Hospitals
> ■ Job training centers
> ■ Schools
> ■ Senior centers
> ■ Bridges, tunnels and other public works projects
> ■ Emergency services"

How well do these benefits meet the four characteristics of good audience benefits discussed in this chapter?

Quoted from "Why It's Important," U.S. Census Bureau: United States Census 2010, accessed May 8, 2010, http://2010 .census.gov/2010census/about/why-important.php.

2.9   Addressing Your Audience's Need for Information

"Tell me about yourself."

This may be the most popular opening question of job interviews, but it's also a question that you'll encounter in nearly any social situation when you meet someone new. Although the question may be the same, the answer you give will change based upon the rhetorical situation: the audience, purpose, and context of the question.

For each of the following situations in a–g, ask yourself these questions to help create a good response:

- How will the audience react to your answer? Will the audience see the message as important? What information will you need to include in your answer to keep their attention?

- How will the audience use your answer? Why is the audience asking the question? What information is relevant to the audience and what information can you leave out?

- How much information does the audience need? What information do they already know about you? What level of detail do they need?

- What are the audience's expectations about your answer? What are the appropriate word choices and

tone for your answer? What topics should you avoid (at least for now)?

- What are the physical conditions that will affect your answer? Where are you (e.g., Are you outside, in a noisy room, on the phone)? How much time do you have to give your response?

Write your response to the statement "Tell me about yourself." Assume that the question is being asked by

a. A recruiter at a career fair in your university's auditorium.

b. A recruiter in a job interview in a small interview or conference room.

c. An attractive male or female at a popular weekend nightspot.

d. Your instructor on the first day of class.

e. Your new roommate on your first day in the dormitory.

f. A new co-worker on your first day at a new job.

g. A new co-worker on your first day volunteering at your local food pantry.

2.10   Analyzing Individuals

Read about the Myers-Briggs Type Indicator on page 29. On the web, take one of the free tests similar to the Myers-Briggs. Read about your personality type and consider how accurate the description may be. Print your results.

As your instructor directs,

- Share your results orally with a small group of students and discuss how accurately the Type Indicator describes you. Identify some of the differences among your personality types and consider how the differences would affect efforts to collaborate on projects.

- Identify other students in the classroom with the same combination of personality traits. Create a brief oral presentation to the class that describes your Type Indicator and explains how the pros and cons of your personality will affect group dynamics in collaborative work.

- Write a brief memo to your instructor describing your results, assessing how well the results reflect your personality, and suggesting how your personality traits might affect your work in class and in the workplace.

2.11   Getting Customer Feedback

Smart businesses want to know what their customers and clients are saying about their products and services. Many websites can help them do so.

Check some of the common sites for customer comments. Here is a list to get you started:

http://www.amazon.com
http://www.angieslist.com
http://getsatisfaction.com
http://www.my3cents.com
http://www.ratepoint.com
http://www.suggestionbox.com

http://www.thesqueakywheel.com
http://www.yelp.com
What does each site do?
What are good features of each site?
What are drawbacks?

As your instructor directs,

a. Discuss your findings in a memo to your instructor.

b. Share your findings in small groups.

c. As a group, make a presentation to your classmates.

2.12   Identifying International Audience Benefits

Reread the sidebar on page 39 explaining how Procter & Gamble is marketing its products in developing countries. In small groups, discuss different marketing practices you have become aware of in other countries. How do these practices benefit consumers? How do they benefit store owners?

As your instructor directs,

a. Post your findings electronically to share with the class.

b. Present your findings in a memo to your instructor.

c. Present your findings in an oral presentation to the class.

2.13   Evaluating a New Channel

To combat software piracy, Microsoft tried an unusual communication channel. A new software update turned screens black on computers using pirated software; the update also posted a message to switch to legitimate software copies. The update did not prevent people from using their machines, and they could manually change their wallpaper back to its previous design. But the black screen returned every 60 minutes. Microsoft said there was little protest except in China, where ironically the software piracy problem is greatest.

In small groups, discuss this practice.

■ What do you think of this channel?

■ Is it ethical?

■ Will it help or hurt Microsoft profits in China?

■ How do you think receivers of the black screen react?

As your instructor directs,

a. Post your findings electronically to share with the class.

b. Present your findings in a memo to your instructor.

c. Present your findings in an oral presentation to the class.

Source: Loretta Chao and Juliet Ye, "Microsoft Tactic Raises Hackles in China: In Antipiracy Move, Software Update Turns Screens Black and Urges Users to Buy Legal Windows Copies," *Wall Street Journal*, October 23, 2008, B4.

2.14   Discussing Ethics

a. What do you think about the practice among some companies of giving perks such as free samples to bloggers to discuss their products? Does your opinion change according to the expense of the perk (free tissues vs. tablet computers, for instance)? How can you tell if bloggers have been influenced by the companies whose products they discuss?

b. What do you think about the practice of law firms using social media to find plaintiffs (see sidebar on page 35)? Is it any worse to use social media than print or TV ads? Why? Look at some of the sites provided by law firms. Try http://www.oil-rig-explosions.com/, http://www.consumerwarningnetwork.com/; http://www.sokolovelaw.com/legal-help/dangerous-drugs/birth-control; http://westwoodscammed.me/. How persuasive is the content?

c. What do you think about the practice of tracking consumers' Internet surfing and selling the information to marketers? Does the tracking seem more intrusive when it is combined with off-line records such as shopping and credit card records?

d. What do you think about the practice of companies asking their employees to take health screenings and then giving them hundreds of dollars off their health insurance if they do so? What benefits do you see for employees? Drawbacks? Is this just a way to penalize employees who refuse by making them pay more for health insurance?

2.15   Banking on Multiple Audiences

Bruce Murphy, an executive at KeyBank, is working on a new problem: how to extend banking services to a new audience—people who use banks intermittently or not at all. It is a large group, estimated at 73 million people. Together, they spend an estimated $11 billion in fees at places such as check-cashing outlets, money-wire companies, and paycheck lenders (companies offering cash advances on future paychecks).

However, they are a tough audience. Many of them have a deep distrust of banks or believe banks will not serve them. Murphy also faced another tough audience: bank managers who feared attracting forgeries and other bad checks and thus losing money. One manager actually said, "Are you crazy? These are the very people we're trying to keep out of the bank!"

To attract the new customers, KeyBank cashes payroll and government checks for a 1.5% fee, well below the 2.44% which is average for check-cashing outlets. The bank also started offering free financial education classes. In fact, the bank even has a program to help people with a history of bounced checks to clear their records by paying restitution and taking the financial education class.

The program is growing, both among check-cashing clients and branches offering the services, to the satisfaction of both audiences.

- What are some other businesses that could expand services to underserved populations?
- What services would they offer?
- What problems would they encounter?
- What audience appeals could they use to attract clients or customers?

Source: Adapted from Ann Carrns, "Banks Court a New Client: The Low-Income Earner: KeyCorp Experiments with Check Cashing," *Wall Street Journal*, March 16, 2007, A1, A14.

2.16   Announcing a New Employee Benefit

Your company has decided to pay employees for doing charity work. Employees can spend one hour working with a charitable or nonprofit group for every 40 hours they work. As Vice President of Human Resources, you need to announce this new program.

Pick a specific organization you know something about, and answer the following questions about it:

1. What proportion of the employees are already involved in volunteer work?
2. Is community service or "giving back" consistent with the organization's corporate mission?
3. Some employees won't be able or won't want to participate. What is the benefit for them in working for a company that has such a program?

4. Will promoting community participation help the organization attract and retain workers?

As your instructor directs,

a. Present your answers in an oral presentation to the class.
b. Present your answers in a memo to your instructor.
c. Share your answers with a small group of students and write a joint memo reporting the similarities and differences you found.

2.17   Announcing a Tuition Reimbursement Program

Assume that your organization is considering reimbursing workers for tuition and fees for job-related courses. As Director of Education and Training, you will present to company executives a review of pros and cons for the program. To prepare, you have composed a list of questions you know they may have. Pick a specific organization that you know something about, and answer the following questions about it.

1. What do people do on the job? What courses or degrees could help them do their current jobs even better?
2. How much education do people already have? How do they feel about formal schooling?
3. How busy are employees? Will most have time to take classes and study in addition to working 40 hours a week (or more)?
4. Is it realistic to think that people who get more education would get higher salaries? Or is money for increases limited? Is it reasonable to think that most

people could be promoted? Or does the organization have many more low-level than high-level jobs?
5. How much loyalty do employees have to this particular organization? Is it "just a job," or do they care about the welfare of the organization?
6. How competitive is the job market? How easy is it for the organization to find and retain qualified employees?
7. Is knowledge needed to do the job changing, or is knowledge learned 5 or 10 years ago still up-to-date?
8. How competitive is the economic market? Is this company doing well financially? Can its customers or clients easily go somewhere else? Is it a government agency dependent on tax dollars for funding? What about the current situation makes this an especially good time to hone the skills of the employees you have?
9. Do you support the program? Why or why not?

2.18   Crafting a Memo for a Particular Audience

Your supervisor at a fitness center wants to increase the organization's membership and has asked you to write a letter to the three primary population segments in your town: retirees, college students, and working professionals with families. Using the following fitness benefits

your supervisor gave you to help you get started, write a version of a letter targeted at each of the three audiences.
- Become a member with no sign-up fees.
- Attend free nutrition classes to help with weight control and optimal fitness.

- Attend any of our many fitness classes, scheduled for your convenience.
- Enjoy the new indoor/outdoor pool with lap lanes and zero-gravity entrance.
- Use the large selection of free-weights and exercise machines.

- Lose weight and feel your healthiest with a personal trainer, who will guide you toward your fitness goals.

Remember these benefits were just to get you started; you are expected to come up with more on your own.

2.19 Analyzing Your Co-Workers

What do your co-workers do? What hassles and challenges do they face? To what extent do their lives outside work affect their responses to work situations? What do your co-workers value? What are their pet peeves? How committed are they to organizational goals? How satisfying do they find their jobs? Are the people you work with quite similar to each other, or do they differ from each other? How?

As your instructor directs,

a. Share your answers orally with a small group of students.

b. Present your answers in an oral presentation to the class.

c. Present your answers in a memo to your instructor.

d. Share your answers with a small group of students and write a joint memo reporting the similarities and differences you found.

2.20 Analyzing the Audiences of Noncommercial Web Pages

Analyze the implied audiences of two web pages of two noncommercial organizations with the same purpose (combating hunger, improving health, influencing the political process, etc.). You could pick the home pages of the national organization and a local affiliate, or the home pages of two separate organizations working toward the same general goal.

Answer the following questions:

- Do the pages work equally well for surfers and for people who have reached the page deliberately?
- Possible audiences include current and potential volunteers, donors, clients, and employees. Do the pages provide material for each audience? Is the material useful? Complete? Up-to-date? Does new material encourage people to return?

- What assumptions about audiences do content and visuals suggest?
- Can you think of ways that the pages could better serve their audiences?

As your instructor directs,

a. Share your results orally with a small group of students.

b. Present your results orally to the class.

c. Present your results in a memo to your instructor. Attach copies of the home pages.

d. Share your results with a small group of students, and write a joint memo reporting the similarities and differences you found.

e. Post your results in an e-mail message to the class. Provide links to the two web pages.

2.21 Analyzing a Discourse Community

Analyze the way a group you are part of uses language. Possible groups include

- Work teams.
- Sports teams.
- Sororities, fraternities, and other social groups.
- Churches, mosques, synagogues, and temples.
- Geographic or ethnic groups.
- Groups of friends.

Questions to ask include the following:

- What specialized terms might not be known to outsiders?
- What topics do members talk or write about? What topics are considered unimportant or improper?
- What channels do members use to convey messages?
- What forms of language do members use to build goodwill? to demonstrate competence or superiority?

- What strategies or kinds of proof are convincing to members?
- What formats, conventions, or rules do members expect messages to follow?
- What are some nonverbal ways members communicate?

As your instructor directs,

a. Share your results orally with a small group of students.

b. Present your results in an oral presentation to the class.

c. Present your results in a memo to your instructor.

d. Share your results with a small group of students, and write a joint memo reporting the similarities and differences you found.

CHAPTER

3

Building Goodwill

Chapter Outline

NEWSWORTHY COMMUNICATION

Restoring Goodwill at Delta

Traveling by air can be a frustrating experience. High prices, extra fees, delays, and cancellations can leave a customer feeling frazzled and angry. After a year in which it had the highest number of customer complaints, Delta Air Lines is trying to change its image by sending all 11,000 flight agents back to training.

In day-long seminars, agents learn how to respond to customer complaints and worries with a positive attitude and a focus on improving the customer's experience. The seminars include these key points:

■ *Be positive.* The agents are taught to smile and express appreciation for the customers' business, especially when the customers are unhappy or when there are problems.

■ *Be honest.* If a passenger is late and going to miss her flight, the agents learn to tell her immediately and offer to help rebook, rather than encouraging her to rush through the airport.

■ *Recognize the customer's feelings.* Empathizing with a frustrated customer can make the difference between a bad experience and a good

> *"Agents learn how to respond to customer complaints and worries with a positive attitude and a focus on improving the customer's experience."*

experience. Agents may not be able to solve all customers' complaints, but by acknowledging frustration they show that they care and are attempting to help.

■ *Don't apologize for the rules.* Baggage fees and other expenses have become part of the flying experience. Agents should stick to the facts, rather than saying they agree with angry customers. Michael Hazelton, a facilitator for the training classes, said, "You may think you are bonding with the customer by agreeing the fees are horrible, but the customer thinks, 'This person just threw his company under the bus.'"

■ *Don't place blame.* Customers know when they've made poor decisions, such as arriving late or not allowing enough time to get through airport security. Agents should work to help the customers and solve problems as much as possible.

Of course, better customer service can't solve every problem with flying. But at Delta Air Lines, they believe that an increased focus on the customer will improve peoples' impressions of the flying experience.

Source: Scott McCartney, "Delta Sends Its 11,000 Agents to Charm School," *Wall Street Journal,* February 3, 2011, D3.

Learning Objectives

After studying this chapter, you will know how to

LO 3-1   Create you-attitude.

LO 3-2   Create positive emphasis.

LO 3-3   Improve tone in business communications.

LO 3-4   Reduce bias in business communications.

Goodwill smooths the challenges of business and administration. Companies have long been aware that treating customers well pays off in more sales and higher profits.

- Amazon's corporate mission says "We seek to be Earth's most customer centric company for three primary customer sets: consumer customers, seller customers and developer customers." Jeff Bezos, Amazon's founder and CEO, has a video on YouTube entitled "Everything I Know." It has three points: obsess over customers, invent on behalf of customers, and think long term, because doing so allows you to serve customers better.[1]
- Tony Hsieh built Zappos around customer service, including a service attitude for their vendors.
- Linda Thaler and Robin Koval built the Kaplan Thaler Group into an advertising agency with nearly $1 billion in billings using goodwill, you-attitude, and positive tone.[2]
- A study by Vanderbilt University found that a portfolio of companies whose ACSI (American Consumer Satisfaction Index) scores were above the national average far outperformed the market. Over a 10-year period, the portfolio gained 212%; the Standard & Poor 500-stock index rose 105% over the same period.[3]

Goodwill is important internally as well as externally. More and more organizations are realizing that treating employees well is financially wise as well as ethically sound. Happy employees create less staff turnover, thus reducing hiring and training costs. A University of Pennsylvania study of 3,000 companies found that investing 10% of revenue on capital improvement boosted company productivity 3.9%, but spending the money on employees increased productivity 8.5%, or more than twice as much.[4]

You-attitude, positive emphasis, and bias-free language are three ways to help build goodwill. Messages that show **you-attitude** use the audience's point of view, not the writer's or speaker's. **Positive emphasis** means focusing on the positive rather than the negative aspects of a situation. **Bias-free language** does not discriminate against people on the basis of sex, physical condition, race, ethnicity, age, or any other category. All three help you achieve your purposes and make your messages friendlier, more persuasive, more professional, and more humane. They suggest that you care not just about money but also about the needs and interests of your customers, employees, and fellow citizens.

YOU-ATTITUDE   LO 3-1

Putting what you want to say in you-attitude is a crucial step both in thinking about your audience's needs and in communicating your concern to your audience.

How to Create You-Attitude

You-attitude is a style of communication that looks at things from the audience's point of view, emphasizing what the audience wants to know, respecting the audience's intelligence, and protecting the audience's ego.

To apply you-attitude on a sentence level, use the following techniques:

1. **Talk about the audience, not about yourself.**
2. **Refer to the customer's request or order specifically.**
3. **Don't talk about feelings, except to congratulate or offer sympathy.**
4. **In positive situations, use *you* more often than *I*. Use *we* when it includes the audience.**
5. **In negative situations, avoid the word *you*. Protect the audience's ego. Use passive verbs and impersonal expressions to avoid assigning blame.**

Revisions for you-attitude do not change the basic meaning of the sentence. However, revising for you-attitude often makes sentences longer because the revision is more specific and has more information. Long sentences need not be wordy. **Wordiness** means having more words than the meaning requires. We can add information and still keep the writing concise.

1. Talk about the audience, not about yourself. Your audience wants to know how they benefit or are affected. When you provide this information, you make your message more complete and more interesting.

Lacks you-attitude: We have negotiated an agreement with Apex Rent-a-Car that gives you a discount on rental cars.

You-attitude: As a Sunstrand employee, you can now get a 20% discount when you rent a car from Apex.

2. Refer to the customer's request or order specifically. Refer to the customer's request, order, or policy specifically, not as a generic *your order* or *your policy*. If your customer is an individual or a small business, it's friendly to specify the content of the order. If you're dealing with a company with which you do a great deal of business, give the invoice or purchase order number.

Lacks you-attitude: Your order . . .

You-attitude
(to individual):   The desk chair you ordered . . .

You-attitude
(to a large store):   Your invoice #783329 . . .

3. Don't talk about feelings, except to congratulate or offer sympathy. In most business situations, your feelings are irrelevant and should be omitted.

Lacks you-attitude: We are happy to extend you a credit line of $10,000.

You-attitude: You can now charge up to $10,000 on your American Express card.

It *is* appropriate to talk about your own emotions in a message of congratulations or condolence.

You-attitude: Congratulations on your promotion to district manager! I was really pleased to read about it.

Customer Service Becoming Popular with Businesses

More companies are improving customer service to increase both sales and market share.

Walgreens is training pharmacists to work more closely with patients with chronic illnesses such as diabetes. Pharmacists are replacing their normal 3- to 5-minute meetings with regular 20- to 45-minute patient meetings to help them manage their disease.

American Express is training call-center agents to focus on building customer loyalty rather than processing the call quickly.

Even Comcast, which has had well-publicized problems with customer service, is giving its 24,000 call-center agents additional training.

Adapted from Dana Mattioli, "Customer Service as a Growth Engine," *Wall Street Journal*, June 7, 2010, B6.

Exercising Empathy for Employees and Customers

Although the concept of happy employees leading to happy customers is not new, it is experiencing a resurgence in many different industries. For example, call centers are allowing seasoned employees to work at home while a grocery chain is giving employees a profit-sharing plan that rewards them for excellent customer service.

Companies are finding creative ways to help employees identify with customers. USAA, an insurance agency for the military, provides new employees with MREs (meals ready to eat) during orientation so they will better understand the lifestyle of the members they serve.

Cabela's, an outdoor outfitter, encourages employees to use products they sell by loaning items free of charge in exchange for writing reviews on a company system. The loans are good perks for employees, and they help staff understand the issues customers may have with the products.

At Four Seasons Hotels, employees receive free overnight stays and meals at the hotel for themselves and a guest. They gain a customer's perspective on the hotel, but they also grade the hotel on various services.

The companies exercising empathy for employees and customers believe their customer service helps set them apart from other organizations.

Adapted from Jena McGregor, "Customer Service Champs," *Business-Week*, March 5, 2007, 52.

Don't talk about your audience's feelings, either. It's distancing to have others tell us how we feel—especially if they are wrong.

Lacks you-attitude:	You'll be happy to hear that Open Grip Walkway Channels meet OSHA requirements.
You-attitude:	Open Grip Walkway Channels meet OSHA requirements.

Maybe the audience expects that anything you sell would meet government regulations (OSHA—the Occupational Safety and Health Administration—is a federal agency). The audience may even be disappointed if they expected higher standards. Simply explain the situation or describe a product's features; don't predict the audience's response.

When you have good news, simply give the good news.

Lacks you-attitude:	You'll be happy to hear that your scholarship has been renewed.
You-attitude:	Congratulations! Your scholarship has been renewed.

4. In positive situations, use *you* more often than *I*. Use *we* when it includes the audience.   Talk about the audience, not you or your company.

Lacks you-attitude:	We provide health insurance to all employees.
You-attitude:	You receive health insurance as a full-time Procter & Gamble employee.

Most readers are tolerant of the word *I* in e-mail messages, which seem like conversation. But edit paper documents to use *I* rarely if at all. *I* suggests that you're concerned about personal issues, not about the organization's problems, needs, and opportunities. *We* works well when it includes the reader. Avoid *we* if it excludes the reader (as it would in a letter to a customer or supplier or as it might in a memo about what *we* in management want *you* to do).

5. In negative situations, avoid the word *you*. Protect your audience's ego. Use passive verbs and impersonal expressions to avoid assigning blame.   When you report bad news or limitations, use a noun for a group of which your audience is a part instead of *you* so people don't feel that they're singled out for bad news.

Lacks you-attitude:	You must get approval from the director before you publish any articles or memoirs based on your work in the agency.
You-attitude:	Agency personnel must get approval from the director to publish any articles or memoirs based on their work at the agency.

Use passive verbs and impersonal expressions to avoid blaming people. **Passive verbs** describe the action performed on something, without necessarily saying who did it. (See Chapter 5 for a full discussion of passive verbs.) In most cases, active verbs are better. But when your audience is at fault, passive verbs may be useful to avoid assigning blame.

Impersonal expressions omit people and talk only about things. Normally, communication is most lively when it's about people—and most interesting to audiences when it's about them. When you have to report a mistake or bad news, however, you can protect your audience's ego by using an impersonal expression, one in which things, not people, do the acting.

Lacks you-attitude:	You made no allowance for inflation in your estimate.
You-attitude (passive):	No allowance for inflation has been made in this estimate.
You-attitude (impersonal):	This estimate makes no allowance for inflation.

Hallmark is producing a new line of cards for common situations such as depression or chemotherapy. For example, "Get Well Soon," is not appropriate for someone who is battling cancer. Hallmark has changed the tone of their Journey's Collection to reflect the needs of their dual audiences—buyers and receivers of cards.

Source: David Twiddy, "Hallmark Tackles Real-Life Situations," *Chicago Tribune*, February 19, 2007, sec. Business.

> **You-Attitude with International Audiences**
>
> When you communicate with international audiences, look at the world from their point of view.
>
> The United States is in the middle of most of the maps sold in the United States. It isn't in the middle of maps sold elsewhere in the world.
>
> The United States clings to a measurement system that has been abandoned by most of the world. When you write for international audiences, use the metric system.
>
> Even pronouns and direction words need attention. *We* may not feel inclusive to readers with different assumptions and backgrounds. *Here* won't mean the same thing to a reader in Bonn as it does to one in Boulder.

A purist might say that impersonal expressions are illogical: An estimate, for example, is inanimate and can't "make" anything. In the pragmatic world of business writing, however, impersonal expressions help you convey criticism tactfully.

You-Attitude beyond the Sentence Level

Good messages apply you-attitude beyond the sentence level by using content and organization as well as style to build goodwill.

To create goodwill with content,

- Be complete. When you have lots of information to give, consider putting some details in an appendix, which may be read later.
- Anticipate and answer questions your audience is likely to have.
- Show why information your audience didn't ask for is important.
- Show your audience how the subject of your message affects them.

Figure 3.1   A Letter Lacking You-Attitude

SIMMONS STRUCTURAL STEEL
450 INDUSTRIAL PARK
CLEVELAND, OH 44120
(216) 555-4670
FAX: (216) 555-4672

December 11, 2012

Ms. Carol McFarland
Rollins Equipment Corporation
18438 East Night Hawk Way
Phoenix, AZ 85043-7800

Dear Ms. McFarland:

Not you-attitude

Legalistic

We are now ready to issue a check to Rollins Equipment in the amount of
$14,207.02. To receive said check, you will deliver to me a release of the
mechanic's liens in the amount of $14,207.02.   *Sounds dictatorial*

Lacks you-attitude

Focuses on negative

Before we can release the check, we must be satisfied that the release is in the
proper form. We must insist that we be provided with a stamped original of the
lien indicating the document number in the appropriate district court where it
is filed. Also, either the release must be executed by an officer of Rollins
Equipment, or we must be provided with a letter from an officer of Rollins
Equipment authorizing another individual to execute the release.   *Hard to read, remember*

Please contact the undersigned so that an appointment can be scheduled for
this transaction.   *Jargon*

Sincerely,

Kelly J. Pickett

Kelly J. Pickett

To organize information to build goodwill,

- Put information your audience is most interested in first.
- Arrange information to meet your audience's needs, not yours.
- Use headings and lists so readers can find key points quickly.

Consider the letter in Figure 3.1. As the red marginal notes indicate, many
individual sentences in this letter lack you-attitude. Fixing individual sentences could improve the letter. However, it really needs to be totally rewritten.

Figure 3.2 shows a possible revision of this letter. The revision is clearer, easier to read, and friendlier.

POSITIVE EMPHASIS LO 3-2

Some negatives are necessary. When you have bad news to give—announcements of layoffs, product defects and recalls, price increases—straightforward negatives build credibility. (See Chapter 10 on how to present bad news.) Sometimes negatives are needed to make people take a problem

Figure 3.2   A Letter Revised to Improve You-Attitude

SIMMONS STRUCTURAL STEEL

450 INDUSTRIAL PARK
CLEVELAND, OH 44120
(216) 555-4670
FAX: (216) 555-4672

December 11, 2012

Ms. Carol McFarland
Rollins Equipment Corporation
18438 East Night Hawk Way
Phoenix, AZ 85043-7800

Dear Ms. McFarland:

Let's clear up the lien in the Allen contract.   *Starts with main point from the reader's point of view*

Focuses on what reader gets

Rollins will receive a check for $14,207.02 when you give us a release for the mechanic's lien of $14,207.02. To assure us that the release is in the proper form,

   1. Give us a stamped original of the lien indicating the document's district court number, and   *List makes it easy to see that reader needs to do two things—and that the second can be done in two ways.*

   2. Either
     a. Have an officer of Rollins Equipment sign the release
       or
     b. Give us a letter from a Rollins officer authorizing someone else to sign the release.

Please call me to tell me which way is best for you.   *Emphasizes reader's choice*

Sincerely,

Kelly J. Pickett

Kelly J. Pickett   *Extension number makes it easy for reader to phone.*
Extension 5318

Defining Allowable Negatives

The Des Moines *Register* issued the following standards for contributors to its electronic forum:

"[The Des Moines *Register*'s] new updated standards make the distinction between offensive opinion and offensive approach.

We will remove comments including these types of specific information or language:

- Libel. In general terms, that means a comment that includes a false statement of fact that actually harms a person's reputation (as opposed to insulting or offending them).
- Sexually explicit or crude sexual comments about someone.
- Threatening statements or statements that suggest violent acts against someone.
- Crude comments about a child.
- Swearing or obscenity.
- Derogatory phrases to define a group of people.
- Nasty name-calling (language such as "moron" and "white trash").

But we will allow opinions some will find offensive.

We will allow conversation that is simply strident in tone.

We will allow criticism of public officials.

We will allow criticism of people who are subjects of stories.

We will allow opinions that some may find offensive about tough social issues around race and sexual orientation, as long as they don't include the kind of specific language I just described."

Quoted from Carolyn Washburn, "Inviting Robust Conversation, but Spelling Out a Few Rules," *Des Moines Sunday Register*, April 15, 2007.

seriously. In some messages, such as disciplinary notices and negative performance appraisals, one of your purposes is to make the problem clear. Even here, avoid insults or attacks on your audience's integrity or sanity.

Sometimes negatives create a "reverse psychology" that makes people look favorably at your product. German power tool manufacturer Stihl advertises that its chain saws and other tools are *not* sold by chains like Lowe's or Home Depot. Instead, the company emphasizes that its products are sold through independent retailers. While the campaign risks offending potential customers by implying that shopping at big box stores means that they don't appreciate quality, Stihl insists that its high-end products are worth the prices that are charged by specialty stores.[5]

But in most situations, it's better to be positive. Researchers have found that businesspeople responded more positively to positive than to negative language and were more likely to say they would act on a positively worded request.[6] In ground-breaking research for Met Life, Martin Seligman found that optimistic salespeople sold 37% more insurance than pessimistic colleagues. As a result, Met Life began hiring optimists even when they failed to meet the company's other criteria. These "unqualified" optimists outsold pessimists 21% in their first year and 57% in the next.[7]

Positive emphasis is a way of looking at things. Is the bottle half empty or half full? You can create positive emphasis with the words, information, organization, and layout you choose. "Part-time" may be a negative phrase for someone seeking full-time employment, but it may also be a positive phrase for college students seeking limited work hours while they pursue their education. It may become even more positive if connected with flexible hours.

How to Create Positive Emphasis

Create positive emphasis by using the following techniques:

1. Avoid negative words and words with negative connotations.
2. Beware of hidden negatives.
3. Focus on what the audience can do rather than on limitations.
4. Justify negative information by giving a reason or linking it to an audience benefit.
5. Put the negative information in the middle and present it compactly.

Choose the technique that produces the clearest, most accurate communication.

1. Avoid negative words and words with negative connotations. Figure 3.3 lists some common negative words. If you find one of these words in a draft, try to substitute a more positive word. When you must use a negative, use the *least negative* term that will convey your meaning.

The following examples show how to replace negative words with positive words.

Negative:	We have failed to finish taking inventory.
Better:	We haven't finished taking inventory.
Still better:	We will be finished taking inventory Friday.
Negative:	If you can't understand this explanation, feel free to call me.
Better:	If you have further questions, just call me.
Still better:	Omit the sentence.

Figure 3.3   Negative Words to Avoid

afraid	impossible	**Some dis- words:**	**Many un- words:**
anxious	lacking	disapprove	unclear
avoid	loss	dishonest	unfair
bad	neglect	dissatisfied	unfortunate
careless	never		unfortunately
damage	no		unpleasant
delay	not	**Many in- words:**	unreasonable
delinquent	objection	inadequate	unreliable
deny	problem	incomplete	unsure
difficulty	reject	inconvenient	
eliminate	sorry	insincere	
error	terrible	injury	
except	trivial		
fail	trouble		
fault	wait	**Some mis- words:**	
fear	weakness	misfortune	
hesitate	worry	missing	
ignorant	wrong	mistake	
ignore			

Omit double negatives.

Negative:	Never fail to back up your documents.
Better:	Always back up your documents.

When you must use a negative term, use the least negative word that is accurate.

Negative:	Your balance of $835 is delinquent.
Better:	Your balance of $835 is past due.

Getting rid of negatives has the added benefit of making what you write easier to understand. Sentences with three or more negatives are very hard to understand.[8]

2. Beware of hidden negatives.   Some words are not negative in themselves but become negative in context. *But* and *however* indicate a shift, so, after a positive statement, they are negative. *I hope* and *I trust that* suggest that you aren't sure. *Patience* may sound like a virtue, but it is a necessary virtue only when things are slow. Even positives about a service or product may backfire if they suggest that in the past the service or product was bad.

Negative:	I hope this is the information you wanted. [Implication: I'm not sure.]
Better:	Enclosed is a brochure about road repairs scheduled for 2012.
Still better:	The brochure contains a list of all roads and bridges scheduled for repair during 2012, specific dates when work will start, and alternate routes.
Negative:	Please be patient as we switch to the automated system. [Implication: You can expect problems.]
Better:	If you have questions during our transition to the automated system, call Melissa Morgan.
Still better:	You'll be able to get information instantly about any house on the market when the automated system is in place. If you have questions during the transition, call Melissa Morgan.
Negative:	Now Crispy Crunch tastes better. [Implication: it used to taste terrible.]
Better:	Now Crispy Crunch tastes even better.

Truly Friendly Skies

United pilot Denny Flanagan goes out of his way to create goodwill with his passengers and customers. He takes pictures of pets in cargo compartments and shows their owners that the pets are safely onboard. He phones the parents of unaccompanied minors to keep them up-to-date on delays. He hands out his business cards to all passengers, and the lucky ones with his signature on the back get free books, wine, or discount coupons. When his flights are delayed or diverted, he tries to find snacks like McDonald's hamburgers for his passengers. Before some of his delayed flights he is in the passenger lounge using his cellphone to help passengers with their connections. . . .

Captain Flanagan says, "I just treat everyone like it's the first flight they've ever flown. . . . The customer deserves a good travel experience."

One of those customers noted, "If other folks in the airline industry had the same attitude, it would go a long way to mitigating some of the negative stuff that has come about in the last four or five years."

Truth Can Be Spoken in Different Ways

"One Iranian told a fable of an ancient king who had an ominous dream. In the dream the king saw himself aged and afflicted, with decaying and falling teeth. Calling together his court astrologers for an interpretation, the shaken king heard the first say, "Your Majesty, I regret to tell you that the interpretation must be bad. The dream means that you will die within a year." In a rage the king threw the brash astrologer out of his court and turned to the second man.

The second astrologer said, "Your Majesty, it is good news, the very best. It means that all your programs and projects will live on after you, and all your sons and daughters will survive you." The king, who was old and knew he might die soon, nevertheless was pleased with this interpretation and richly rewarded the astrologer."

Quoted from John P. Fieg and John G. Blair, *There Is a Difference: 12 Intercultural Perspectives* (Washington, DC: Meridian House International, 1975), 83.

Removing negatives does not mean being arrogant or pushy.

Negative:	I hope that you are satisfied enough to place future orders.
Arrogant:	I look forward to receiving all of your future business.
Better:	Whenever you need computer chips, a call to Mercury is all it takes for fast service.

When you eliminate negative words, be sure to maintain accuracy. Words that are exact opposites will usually not be accurate. Instead, use specifics to be both positive and accurate.

Negative:	The exercycle is not guaranteed for life.
Not true:	The exercycle is guaranteed for life.
True:	The exercycle is guaranteed for 10 years.

Legal phrases also have negative connotations for most readers and should be avoided whenever possible.

3. Focus on what the audience can do rather than on limitations.   When there are limits, or some options are closed, focus on the alternatives that remain.

Negative:	We will not allow you to charge more than $5,000 on your VISA account.
Better:	You can charge $5,000 on your new VISA card.
or:	Your new VISA card gives you $5,000 in credit that you can use at thousands of stores nationwide.

As you focus on what will happen, check for **you-attitude.** In the last example, "We will allow you to charge $5,000" would be positive, but it lacks you-attitude.

When you have a benefit and a requirement the audience must meet to get the benefit, the sentence is usually more positive if you put the benefit first.

| Negative: | You will not qualify for the student membership rate of $55 a year unless you are a full-time student. |
| Better: | You get all the benefits of membership for only $55 a year if you're a full-time student. |

4. Justify negative information by giving a reason or linking it to an audience benefit.   A reason can help your audience see that the information is necessary; a benefit can suggest that the negative aspect is outweighed by positive factors. Be careful, however, to make the logic behind your reason clear and to leave no loopholes.

| Negative: | We cannot sell individual pastel sets. |
| Loophole: | To keep down packaging costs and to help you save on shipping and handling costs, we sell pastel sets in packages of 12. |

Suppose the customer says, "I'll pay the extra shipping and handling. Send me six." If you truly sell only in packages of 12, you need to say so:

| Better: | To keep down packaging costs and to help customers save on shipping and handling costs, we sell pastel sets only in packages of 12. |

If you link the negative element to a benefit, be sure it is a benefit your audience will acknowledge. Avoid telling people that you're doing things "for their own good." They may have a different notion of what their own good is. You may think you're doing customers a favor by limiting their credit so they don't get in over their heads and go bankrupt. They may think they'd

Some stores might say, "Put books you don't want here." But bookseller Joseph-Beth in Lexington, KY, uses positive emphasis.

Four Ways to Say "Yes" Instead of "No"

"'Yes, I want to help.'
Even if you have to say no personally, there is usually an alternative yes. By helping to solve someone's problem—say, by referring them to someone who might be able to help them—you keep the positive energy in motion.

'Yes, you can do better.'
Rather than say, "This is terrible," it's a lot more motivating to say, "You do such terrific work. I'm not sure this is up to your caliber."

'Yes, I see you.'
It only takes a minute to send a thank-you note or respond to an unsolicited résumé.

'Yes, your talents lie elsewhere.'
Warren Buffet says that he's never fired anyone. He has just helped them to find the right job."

Quoted from Linda Kaplan Thaler and Robin Koval, *The Power of Nice: How to Conquer the Business World with Kindness* (New York: Currency, 2006), 84–87.

be better off with more credit so they could expand in hopes of making more sales and more profits.

5. Put the negative information in the middle and present it compactly.   Put negatives at the beginning or end only if you want to emphasize the negative. To deemphasize a written negative, put it in the middle of a paragraph rather than in the first or last sentence and in the middle of the message rather than in the first or last paragraphs.

When a letter or memo runs several pages, remember that the bottom of the first page is also a position of emphasis, even if it is in the middle of a paragraph, because of the extra white space of the bottom margin. (The first page gets more attention because it is on top and the reader's eye may catch lines of the message even when he or she isn't consciously reading it; the tops and bottoms of subsequent pages don't get this extra attention.) If possible, avoid placing negative information at the bottom of the first page.

Giving a topic lots of space emphasizes it. Therefore, you can de-emphasize negative information by giving it as little space as possible. Give negative information only once in your message. Don't list negatives with bulleted or numbered lists. These lists take space and emphasize material.

How to Check Positive Emphasis

All five of the strategies listed above help create positive emphasis. However, you should always check to see that the positive emphasis is appropriate, sincere, and realistic.

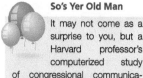

So's Yer Old Man

It may not come as a surprise to you, but a Harvard professor's computerized study of congressional communications reveals that 27% of the time members of Congress are taunting each other.

The three categories the study expected to find were well-known to political scientists: claiming credit, taking a position, and "advertising" someone or something to get one's name out there. That members of Congress also spend a quarter of their time taunting each other came as a surprise. Taunting was most common among members with a relatively safe position.

Adapted from David A. Fahrenthold, "27% of Communication by Members of Congress Is Taunting, Professor Concludes," *Washington Post*, April 6, 2011, http://www.washingtonpost.com/politics/27percent-of-communication-by-members-of-congress-is-taunting-professor-concludes/2011/04/06/AF1no2qC_story.html.

As you read at the beginning of this section, positive emphasis is not always **appropriate.** Some bad news is so serious that presenting it with positive tone is insensitive, if not unethical. Layoffs, salary cuts, and product defects are all topics in this category.

Some positive emphasis is so overdone that it no longer seems **sincere.** The used-car sales rep selling a rusting auto is one stereotype of insincerity. A more common example for most business people is the employee who gushes praise through gritted teeth over your promotion. Most of us have experienced something similar, and we know how easy it is to see through the insincerity.

Positive emphasis can also be so overdone that it clouds the reality of the situation. If your company has two finalists for a sales award, and only one award, the loser does not have second place, which implies a second award. On the other hand, if all sales reps win the same award, top performers will feel unappreciated. Too much praise can also make mediocre employees think they are doing great. Keep your communications **realistic.**

Restraint can help make positive emphasis more effective. Conductor Otto Klemperer was known for not praising his orchestra. One day, pleased with a particularly good rehearsal, he spoke a brusque "good." His stunned musicians broke into spontaneous applause. Klemperer rapped his baton on his music stand to silence them and said, "Not *that* good."[9]

TONE, POWER, AND POLITENESS LO 3-3

Tone is the implied attitude of the communicator toward the audience. If the words of a document seem condescending or rude, tone is a problem. Norms for politeness are cultural and generational; they also vary from office to office.

Tone is tricky because it interacts with context and power. Language that is acceptable within one group may be unacceptable if used by someone outside the group. Words that might seem friendly from a superior to a subordinate may seem uppity if used by the subordinate to the superior. Similarly, words that may be neutral among peers may be seen as negative if sent by a superior to subordinate.

Paul Goward, the former police chief of Winter Haven, Florida, discovered this lesson about the connection between power and tone. Goward sent an e-mail to about 80 employees asking "Are You a Jelly Belly?" In the e-mail, he provided 10 reasons why his employees should be in better shape; the reasons ranged from health risks to department image. The e-mail added, "If you are unfit, do yourself and everyone else a favor. . . . See a professional about a proper diet. . . . Stop making excuses. . . . We didn't hire you unfit and we don't want you working unfit." The e-mail so offended employees that Goward was forced to resign.[10]

Using the proper tone with employees can have huge economic impact for a business. A Litigation Trends Survey, based on reports from 310 in-house counsel, found employee lawsuits to be the top litigation concern of corporate lawyers. Disgruntled employees are suing more than ever before, and disputes over wages or hours frequently can be brought as class actions, making them even more expensive.[11]

The desirable tone for business writing is businesslike but not stiff, friendly but not phony, confident but not arrogant, polite but not groveling. Several guidelines will help you achieve the tone you want.

Use Courtesy Titles for People You Don't Know Well

Most U.S. organizations use first names for everyone, whatever their age or rank. But many people don't like being called by their first names by people they don't know or by someone much younger. When you talk or write to people outside your organization, use first names only if you've established a personal relationship. If you don't know someone well, use a courtesy title (see *pages 71–72* for more on courtesy titles):

Dear Mr. Reynolds:
Dear Ms. Lee:

Be Aware of the Power Implications of the Words You Use

"Thank you for your cooperation" is generous coming from a superior to a subordinate; it's not appropriate in a message to your superior. Different ways of asking for action carry different levels of politeness.[12]

Order: (lowest politeness)	Turn in your time card by Monday.
Polite order: (midlevel politeness)	Please turn in your time card by Monday.
Indirect request: (higher politeness)	Time cards should be turned in by Monday.
Question: (highest politeness)	Would you be able to turn in your time card by Monday?

Higher levels of politeness may be unclear. In some cases, a question may seem like a request for information to which it's acceptable to answer, "No, I can't." In other cases, it will be an order, simply phrased in polite terms.

You need more politeness if you're asking for something that will inconvenience the audience and help you more than the person who does the action. Generally, you need less politeness when you're asking for something small, routine, or to the audience's benefit. Some discourse communities, however, prefer that even small requests be made politely.

Lower politeness:	To start the scheduling process, please describe your availability for meetings during the second week of the month.
Higher politeness:	Could you let me know what times you'd be free for a meeting the second week of the month?

Attempts To Create a Unisex Pronoun

For more than 150 years, people have attempted to coin a unisex pronoun. None of the attempts has been successful.

Date	he or she	his or her	him or her
1850	ne	nis	nim
1884	le	lis	lim
1938	se	sim	sis
1970	ve	vis	ver
1977	e	e's	em
1988	ala	alis	alum

Adapted from Dennis E. Baron, "The Epicene Pronoun: Word That Failed," *American Speech* 56 (1981): 83–97; and Ellen Graham, "Business Bulletin," *Wall Street Journal*, December 29, 1988, A1.

REDUCING BIAS IN BUSINESS COMMUNICATION   LO 3-4

According to the U.S. Census Bureau, the United States now has more women than men, and more women than men are attending college and attaining postsecondary degrees. The Hispanic population is the fastest growing in the country; it numbered 50.5 million in the 2010 census. Four states (California, Hawaii, New Mexico, and Texas) plus the District of Columbia have a "majority–minority" population, where more than 50% are part of a minority group. The number of people 65 and older is also growing; that population now numbers over 40 million, and 6.5 million of them are still in the workforce.[13] These figures highlight the growing diversity of the workplace and the need to communicate with appropriate language.

Bias-free language is language that does not discriminate against people on the basis of sex, physical condition, race, ethnicity, age, religion or any other category. It includes all audience members, helps to sustain goodwill, is fair and friendly, and complies with the law.

Check to be sure that your language is bias-free. Doing so is ethical; it can also avoid major problems and lawsuits.

- Josef Ackermann, chief executive of Deutsche Bank, was mocked in the international news when he said at a news conference that including women on the bank's all-male executive board would make it "more colorful and prettier too." The publicity added to mistrust of the bank at an awkward time when it was lobbying to dissuade German policy makers from imposing restrictions.[14]

- Conservative advice expert Dr. Laura Schlessinger resigned abruptly from her syndicated radio show after a controversy arising from her multiple use of a racial epithet while talking to an African American caller.

- Famous radio personality Don Imus was fired by CBS after making racist comments about the Rutgers University women's basketball team.

Making Language Nonsexist

Nonsexist language treats both sexes neutrally. Check to be sure that your messages are free from sexism in four areas: job titles, courtesy titles and names, pronouns, and other words and phrases.

Job titles   Use neutral titles which do not imply that a job is held only by men or only by women. Many job titles are already neutral: *accountant, banker, doctor, engineer, inspector, manager, nurse, pilot, secretary, technician,* to name a few. Other titles reflect gender stereotypes and need to be changed.

Instead of	Use
Businessman	A specific title: executive, accountant, department head, owner of a small business, men and women in business, businessperson
Chairman	Chair, chairperson, moderator
Fireman	Firefighter
Foreman	Supervisor
Mailman	Mail Carrier
Salesman	Salesperson, sales representative
Waitress	Server
Woman lawyer	Lawyer
Workman	Worker, employee. Or use a specific title: crane operator, bricklayer, etc.

Courtesy titles and names   E-mails to people you know normally do not use courtesy titles. However, letters, memos, and e-mails to people with whom you have a more formal relationship require courtesy titles in the salutation *unless* you're on a first-name basis with your reader. (See Appendix A for examples of memo and letter formats.)

When you know your reader's name and gender, use courtesy titles that do not indicate marital status: *Mr.* for men and *Ms.* for women. *Ms.* is particularly useful when you do not know what a woman's marital status is. However, even when you happen to know that a woman is married or single, **you still use Ms.** unless know that she prefers another title. There are, however, two exceptions:

1. If the woman has a professional title, use that title if you would use it for a man.

   Dr. Kristen Sorenson is our new company physician.

   The Rev. Elizabeth Townsley gave the invocation.

2. If the woman prefers to be addressed as *Mrs.* or *Miss*, use the title she pre-fers rather than Ms. (You-attitude takes precedence over nonsexist lan-guage: address the reader as she—or he—prefers to be addressed.) To find out if a woman prefers a traditional title,

- Check the signature block in previous correspondence. If a woman types her name as *(Miss) Elaine Anderson* or *(Mrs.) Kay Royster*, use the title she designates.
- Notice the title a woman uses in introducing herself on the phone. If she says, "This is Robin Stine," use Ms. when you write to her. If she says, "I'm Mrs. Stine," use the title she specifies.
- When you're writing job letters or crucial correspondence, call the company and ask the receptionist which title your reader prefers.

In addition to using parallel courtesy titles, use parallel forms for names.

Not Parallel	Parallel
Members of the committee will be Mr. Jones, Mr. Yacone, and Lisa.	Members of the committee will be Mr. Jones, Mr. Yacone, and Ms. Melton.
	or
	Members of the committee will be Irving, Ted, and Lisa.

When you know your reader's name but not the gender, either

- Call the company and ask the receptionist, or
- Use the reader's full name in the salutation:

   Dear Chris Crowell:

   Dear J. C. Meath:

72

Booming Business

As the 78 million U.S. baby boomers age, more and more companies are making products with adaptations for physical infirmities:

■ Appliance control panels with adjustable typefaces and color combinations.

■ Ovens, dishwashers, and washer/dryer sets mounted higher so people have to bend over less.

■ Sink fixtures with levers instead of knobs, for hands with limited mobility.

■ Cellphones with large keys and large numbers on the screen.

Nissan and Ford Motor Companies fit their design engineers with special body suits that mimic aging bodies. The suits have an expanded waist, limited mobility in key joints, and goggles that mimic the effect of cataracts.

Marketing these new features requires a delicate touch, because no one likes to be reminded that their body is failing.

Reproduced with permission of Dow Jones & Company, Inc. via Copyright Clearance Center.

When you know neither the reader's name nor gender, you have three options:

■ Omit the salutation and use a subject line in its place. (See Figure A.4, Simplified Format.)
  SUBJECT: RECOMMENDATION FOR BEN WANDELL
■ Use the reader's position or job title:
  Dear Loan Officer:
  Dear Registrar:
■ Use a general group to which your reader belongs:
  Dear Investor:
  Dear Admissions Committee:

Pronouns   When you refer to a specific person, use the appropriate gender pronouns:

In his speech, John Jones said that . . .

In her speech, Judy Jones said that . . .

When you are referring not to a specific person but to anyone who may be in a given job or position, traditional gender pronouns are sexist.

Sexist: a. Each supervisor must certify that the time sheet for his department is correct.

Sexist: b. When the nurse fills out the accident report form, she should send one copy to the Central Division Office.

Business communication uses four ways to eliminate sexist generic pronouns: use plurals, use second-person *you*, revise the sentence to omit the pronoun, or use pronoun pairs. Whenever you have a choice of two or more ways to make a phrase or sentence nonsexist, choose the alternative that is the smoothest and least conspicuous.

The following examples use these methods to revise sentences *a* and *b* above.

1. Use plural nouns and pronouns.

   Nonsexist: a. Supervisors must certify that the time sheets for their departments are correct.

   Note: When you use plural nouns and pronouns, other words in the sentence may need to be made plural too. In the example above, plural supervisors have plural time sheets and departments.

   Avoid mixing singular nouns and plural pronouns.

   Nonsexist but lacks agreement: b. When the nurse fills out the accident report, they should send one copy to the Central Division Office.

   Since *nurse* is singular, it is incorrect to use the plural *they* to refer to it. The resulting lack of agreement is acceptable orally but is not yet acceptable in writing. Instead, use one of the other ways to make the sentence nonsexist.

2. Use *you*.

   Nonsexist: a. You must certify that the time sheet for your department is correct.

   Nonsexist: b. When you fill out an accident report form, send one copy to the Central Division Office.

   You is particularly good for instructions and statements of the responsibilities of someone in a given position.

3. Substitute an article (*a*, *an*, or *the*) for the pronoun, or revise the sentence so that the pronoun is unnecessary.

Nonsexist: a. The supervisor must certify that the time sheet for the department is correct.

Nonsexist: b. The nurse will

    1. Fill out the accident report form.

    2. Send one copy of the form to the Central Division Office.

4. When you must focus on the action of an individual, use pronoun pairs.

Nonsexist: a. The supervisor must certify that the time sheet for his or her department is correct.

Nonsexist: b. When the nurse fills out the accident report form, he or she should send one copy to the Central Division Office.

Other words and phrases If you find any terms similar to those in the first column in Figure 3.4 in your messages or your company's documents, replace them with terms similar to those in the second column.

Not every word containing *man* is sexist. For example, *manager* is not sexist. The word comes from the Latin *manus* meaning *hand*; it has nothing to do with maleness.

Avoid terms that assume that everyone is married or is heterosexual.

Biased: You and your husband or wife are cordially invited to the reception.

Better: You and your guest are cordially invited to the reception.

Making Language Nonracist and Nonageist

Language is **nonracist** and **nonageist** when it treats all races and ages fairly, avoiding negative stereotypes of any group. Use the following guidelines to check for bias in documents you write or edit.

Give someone's race or age only if it is relevant to your story. When you do mention these characteristics, give them for everyone in your story—not just the non-Caucasian, non-young-to-middle-aged adults you mention.

Figure 3.4 Getting Rid of Sexist Terms and Phrases

Instead of	Use	Because
The girl at the front desk	The woman's name or job title: "Ms. Browning," "Rosa," "the receptionist"	Call female employees *women* just as you call male employees *men*. When you talk about a specific woman, use her name, just as you use a man's name to talk about a specific man.
The ladies on our staff	The women on our staff	Use parallel terms for males and females. Therefore, use *ladies* only if you refer to the males on your staff as *gentlemen*. Few businesses do, since social distinctions are rarely at issue.
Manpower Manhours Manning	Personnel Hours or worker hours Staffing	The power in business today comes from both women and men.
Managers and their wives	Managers and their guests	Managers may be female; not everyone is married.

New Technology Access for People with Visual and Hearing Impairments

In October 2010, President Obama signed into law a bill aimed at making technologies that are staples of life more accessible. The law mandates

- Easier Internet connections on smart phones.
- Audible descriptions of action on TV.
- Captions for dialogue on TV.
- TV remotes with buttons or switches for easier access to closed captioning.
- Equipment compatible with hearing aids for Internet phone calls.

Adapted from "Bill Will Improve Technology Access for Blind, Deaf," *Des Moines Register*, October 9, 2010, 3A.

Organizations are making their business sites more accommodating to people with disabilities.

Refer to a group by the term it prefers. As preferences change, change your usage. Fifty years ago, *Negro* was preferred as a more dignified term than *colored* for African Americans. As times changed, *Black* and *African American* replaced it. Gallup polls show that the majority of black Americans (about 60%) have no preference between the two terms. However, among those who do care, polls show a slight trend toward African American.[15]

Oriental has now been replaced by *Asian*.

The term *Latino* is the most acceptable group term to refer to Mexican Americans, Cuban Americans, Puerto Ricans, Dominicans, Brazilianos, and other people with Central and Latin American backgrounds. (*Latina* is the term for an individual woman.) Better still is to refer to the precise group. The differences among various Latino groups are at least as great as the differences among Italian Americans, Irish Americans, Armenian Americans, and others descended from various European groups.

Baby boomers, older people, and *mature customers* are more generally accepted terms than *Senior Citizens* or *Golden Agers*.

Avoid terms that suggest that competent people are unusual. The statement "She is an intelligent purple woman" suggests that the writer expects most purple women to be stupid. "He is an asset to his race" suggests that excellence in the race is rare. "He is a spry 70-year-old" suggests that the writer is amazed that anyone that old can still move.

Talking about People with Disabilities and Diseases

A disability is a physical, mental, sensory, or emotional impairment that interferes with the major tasks of daily living. According to the U.S. Census Bureau, 19% of Americans currently have a disability; of those, about 48% who were 21–64 and had a "nonsevere disability" were employed full-time.[16] The number of people with disabilities will rise as the population ages.

To keep trained workers, more and more companies are making accommodations for disabilties. Companies such as Sylvania, American Express, and

General Motors are offering accommodations such as telecommuting, flexible hours, workshift changes, and assignment changes.[17]

When talking about people with disabilities, use **people-first language** to focus on the person, not the condition. People-first language names the person first, then adds the condition. Use it instead of the traditional noun phrases that imply the condition defines the person. In 2010, President Obama signed Rosa's Law, which replaces "mentally retarded" with "an individual with an intellectual disability," in most federal statutes.[18]

Instead of	Use	Because
The mentally retarded	People with an intellectual disability	The condition does not define the person or his or her potential.
Cancer patients	People being treated for cancer	

Avoid negative terms, unless the audience prefers them. You-attitude takes precedence over positive emphasis: use the term a group prefers. People who lost their hearing as infants, children, or young adults often prefer to be called *deaf*, or *Deaf* in recognition of Deafness as a culture. But people who lose their hearing as older adults often prefer to be called *hard of hearing*, even when their hearing loss is just as great as that of someone who identifies him- or herself as part of the Deaf culture.

Using the right term requires keeping up with changing preferences. If your target audience is smaller than the whole group, use the term preferred by that audience, even if the group as a whole prefers another term.

Some negative terms, however, are never appropriate. Negative terms such as *afflicted*, *suffering from*, and *struck down* also suggest an outdated view of any illness as a sign of divine punishment.

Instead of	Use	Because
Confined to a wheelchair	Uses a wheelchair	Wheelchairs enable people to escape confinement.
AIDS victim	Person with AIDS	Someone can have a disease without being victimized by it.
Abnormal	Atypical	People with disabilities are atypical but not necessarily abnormal.

Choosing Bias-Free Photos and Illustrations

When you produce a document with photographs or illustrations, check the visuals for possible bias. Do they show people of both sexes and all races? Is there a sprinkling of various kinds of people (younger and older, people using wheelchairs, etc.)? It's OK to have individual pictures that have just one sex or one race; the photos as a whole do not need to show exactly 50% men and 50% women. But the general impression should suggest that diversity is welcome and normal.

Check relationships and authority figures as well as numbers. If all the men appear in business suits and the women in maids' uniforms, the pictures are sexist even if an equal number of men and women are pictured. If the only nonwhites pictured are factory workers, the photos support racism even when an equal number of people from each race are shown.

R-E-S-P-E-C-T

"Most major airlines and hotel chains provide disability training to employees. . . . I recognize when someone has been trained—to offer me a Braille menu, use my name when addressing me, or take a moment to orient me to a new environment. What I appreciate even more, though, is . . . simple, common courtesy.

"I don't care how many pages in an employee manual somewhere are devoted to . . . the dos and don'ts of interacting with someone who is deaf, blind, or mentally retarded. Among hundreds of experiences in airports and hotels, the one distinction that separates the (mostly) pleasing from the (occasionally) painful in my encounters has been the honest friendliness and respect with which I have or have not been treated.

"Ask me where I'd like to sit, whether I need help getting there, and what other kinds of help I need.

"Please, assume that I know more about my disability than anyone else ever could.

"Respect me as you do any other customer who is paying for the same service, and have the grace to apologize if something does go wrong.

"Too many companies, it seems to me, are busy shaking in their boots over the imagined high cost of accommodating people with disabilities when, in many instances, a good old-fashioned refresher course in manners would cover most bases."

Quoted from Deborah Kendrick, "Disabled Resent Being Patronized," *Columbus Dispatch*, July 21, 1996, 3B. Reprinted with permission.

SUMMARY OF KEY POINTS

- **You-attitude** is a style of communication that looks at things from the audience's point of view, emphasizing what the audience wants to know, respecting the audience's intelligence, and protecting the audience's ego.

  1. Talk about the audience, not about yourself.
  2. Refer to the audience's request or order specifically.
  3. Don't talk about feelings except to congratulate or offer sympathy.
  4. In positive situations, use *you* more often than *I*. Use *we* when it includes the audience.
  5. In negative situations, avoid the word *you*. Protect the audience's ego. Use passive verbs and impersonal expressions to avoid assigning blame.

- Apply you-attitude beyond the sentence level by using organization and content as well as style to build goodwill.

- **Positive emphasis** means focusing on the positive rather than the negative aspects of a situation. To create positive emphasis

  1. Avoid negative words and words with negative connotations.
  2. Beware of hidden negatives.
  3. Focus on what the audience can do rather than on limitations.
  4. Justify negative information by giving a reason or linking it to an audience benefit.
  5. Put the negative information in the middle and present it compactly.

- Check to see that your positive emphasis is appropriate, sincere, and clear.

- The desirable tone for business communication is businesslike but not stiff, friendly but not phony, confident but not arrogant, polite but not groveling.

- Bias-free language is fair and friendly; it complies with the law. It includes all members of your audience; it helps sustain goodwill.

- Check to be sure that your language is nonsexist, nonracist, and nonageist.

- Communication should be free from sexism in four areas: job titles, courtesy titles and names, pronouns, and other words and phrases.

- *Ms.* is the nonsexist courtesy title for women. Whether or not you know a woman's marital status, use *Ms. unless* the woman has a professional title or unless you know that she prefers a traditional title.

- Four ways to make pronouns nonsexist are to use plurals, to use *you*, to revise the sentence to omit the pronoun, and to use pronoun pairs.

- When you talk about people with disabilities or diseases, use the term they prefer.

- When you produce newsletters or other documents with photos and illustrations, picture a sampling of the whole population, not just part of it.

CHAPTER 3   Exercises and Problems   *Go to www.mhhe.com/locker10e for additional Exercises and Problems.*

3.1   Reviewing the Chapter

1. What are five ways to create you-attitude? (LO 3-1)
2. What are five ways to create positive emphasis? (LO 3-2)
3. How can you improve the tone of business messages? (LO 3-3)

4. What are different categories to keep in mind when you are trying to reduce bias in business messages? (LO 3-4)
5. What techniques can you use when you are trying to reduce bias in business messages? (LO 3-4)

3.2   Evaluating the Ethics of Positive Emphasis

The first term in each pair is negative; the second is a positive term that is sometimes substituted for it. Which of the positive terms seem ethical? Which seem unethical? Briefly explain your choices.

cost	investment	nervousness	adrenaline
second mortgage	home equity loan	problem	challenge
tax	user fee	price increase	price change
		for-profit hospital	tax-paying hospital
		used car	pre-owned car
		credit card fees	usage charges

3.3   Eliminating Negative Words and Words with Negative Connotations

Revise each of the following sentences to replace negative words with positive ones. Be sure to keep the meaning of the original sentence.

1. You will lose customer goodwill if you are slow in handling returns and issuing refunds.
2. Do not put any paper in this box that is not recyclable.
3. When you write a report, do not make claims that you cannot support with evidence.
4. Don't drop in without an appointment. Your counselor or case worker may be unavailable.
5. I am anxious to discuss my qualifications in an interview.

3.4   Focusing on the Positive

Revise each of the following sentences to focus on the options that remain, not those that are closed off.

1. Scholarship applications that arrive December 1 or later cannot be processed.
2. You cannot use flextime unless you have the consent of your supervisor.
3. As a first-year employee, you are not eligible for dental insurance.
4. I will be out of the country October 25 to November 10 and will not be able to meet with you then.
5. You will not get your first magazine for at least four weeks.

3.5   Identifying Hidden Negatives

Identify the hidden negatives in the following sentences and revise to eliminate them. In some cases, you may need to add information to revise the sentence effectively.

1. The seminar will help you become a better manager.
2. Thank you for the confidence you have shown in us by ordering one of our products. It will be shipped to you soon.
3. This publication is designed to explain how your company can start a recycling program.
4. I hope you find the information in this brochure beneficial to you and a valuable reference as you plan your move.
5. In thinking about your role in our group, I remember two occasions where you contributed something.
6. [In job letter] This job in customer service is so good for me; I am so ready to take on responsibility.

3.6   Improving You-Attitude and Positive Emphasis

Revise these sentences to improve you-attitude and positive emphasis. Eliminate any awkward phrasing. In some cases, you may need to add information to revise the sentence effectively.

1. You'll be happy to learn that the cost of tuition will not rise next year.
2. Although I was only an intern and didn't actually make presentations to major clients, I was required to prepare PowerPoint slides for the meetings and to answer some of the clients' questions.
3. At DiYanni Homes we have more than 30 plans that we will personalize just for you.

4. Please notify HR of your bank change as soon as possible to prevent a disruption of your direct deposit.

5. I'm sorry you were worried. You did not miss the deadline for signing up for a flexible medical spending account.

6. We are in the process of upgrading our website. Please bear with us.

7. You will be happy to hear that our cellphone plan does not charge you for incoming calls.

8. The employee discount may only be used for purchases for your own use or for gifts; you may not buy items for resale. To prevent any abuse of the discount privilege, you may be asked to justify your purchase.

9. I apologize for my delay in answering your inquiry. The problem was that I had to check with our suppliers to see whether we could provide the item in the quantity you say you want. We can.

10. If you mailed a check with your order, as you claim, we failed to receive it.

11. This job sounds perfect for me.

3.7   Eliminating Biased Language

Explain the source of bias in each of the following, and revise to remove the bias.

1. We recommend hiring Jim Ryan and Elizabeth Shuman. Both were very successful summer interns. Jim drafted the report on using rap music in ads, and Elizabeth really improved the looks of the office.

2. All sales associates and their wives are invited to the picnic.

3. Although he is blind, Mr. Morin is an excellent group leader.

4. Unlike many blacks, Yvonne has extensive experience designing web pages.

5. Chris Renker
   Pacific Perspectives
   6300 West Corondad Blvd.
   Los Angles, CA
   Gentlemen:

6. Enrique Torres has very good people skills for a man.

7. *Parenting 2012* shows you how to persuade your husband to do his share of child care chores.

8. Mr. Paez, Mr. O'Connor, and Tonya will represent our office at the convention.

9. Sue Corcoran celebrates her 50th birthday today. Stop by her cubicle at noon to get a piece of cake and to help us sing "The Old Grey Mare Just Ain't What She Used to Be."

10. Because older customers tend to be really picky, we will need to give a lot of details in our ads.

3.8   Analyzing You-Attitude

Your book gives some examples of occasions when you-attitude is inappropriate. What are some other examples? Why are they inappropriate? How would you fix them?

3.9   Analyzing Positive Tone

LaQuinta ran a series of ads using cartoons, like the one on this page, featuring people making the best of disasters. You can see the whole series at this website: http://www.lq.com/lq/brightside/index.jsp.

What do you think of these ads? Does the use of negatives help or hinder them? What overall impression of LaQuinta do the ads leave with you?

wake up on the bright side

"WELL ... LOOKS LIKE MY LAPTOP'S FRIED. BUT WHAT A FANTASTIC OPPORTUNITY FOR A LITTLE VENTRILOQUISM."

For reservations, visit LQ.com

LA QUINTA
INNS & SUITES

Reprinted with permission.

3.10   Analyzing Goodwill

A recent study by a law professor shows that credit card companies make offers to people fresh out of bankruptcy. In the study of 341 families, almost 100% received credit card offers within a year after completing bankruptcy proceedings, and 87% of those offers mentioned the bankruptcy proceedings. In fact, 20% of the offers came from companies the family had owed before the bankruptcy.

In small groups, discuss whether you think this practice is ethical. Why or why not? What reasons exist for not offering new credit to people who have just gone through bankruptcy? Why might such people need new credit cards?

Adapted from Marie Beaudette, "Study: Credit Card Offers Flood Once-Bankrupt Consumers," *Des Moines Register*, August 10, 2007, 6D.

3.11   Analyzing Ethics

[Female lawyers and their female corporate clients recently had a "shoe event" at a Manhattan boutique to network.]

"Such women-only networking events are proliferating at law firms and an array of other companies, including [accounting, investing, and industrial companies]. There are spa retreats, conferences at resorts, evenings at art galleries and cooking demonstrations, all organized by women who want to network and socialize with clients in their own way—at least some of the time.

"The top brass at such companies support the events for several reasons, most notably, they help to boost the bottom line. . . .

"Still, holding women-only networking events raises some complicated issues. Are these single-sex events just as exclusionary as the traditional spectator sports events and steak-and-cigar dinners have been for men? What about women who have male clients and vice versa?"

How do you feel about women-only events? Are they ethical?

Quoted from Carol Hymowitz, "High Power and High Heels: Companies Move beyond Sports, Steak and Scotch to Cultivate New Clients," *Wall Street Journal*, March 26, 2007, B1.

3.12   Analyzing a Form Letter

Analyze the following form letter.
  Is it a goodwill message?
  Where does it show you-attitude? Where does it need more you-attitude?

Evaluate the use of positive tone.
What is your overall impression of the letter?

Debbie Harrington
1436 Gooden Road
Lincoln, NE 54367

THE FOLLOWING INFORMATION IS TIME SENSITIVE; PLEASE REVIEW CAREFULLY

James Honda of Lincoln has partnered with Automobile Resellers, Inc., to replenish drastically reduced vehicle inventories. James Honda of Lincoln is in need of a number of high-demand pre-owned vehicles and records indicate that you may own one of these vehicles. Your 2007 Honda Civic has been classified as a high-demand vehicle. The purpose of this letter is to request the opportunity to BUY BACK your vehicle for perhaps more than you thought possible.

Bring this letter for admittance to this event. Simply present it to a dealership representative who will assist you in this BUY BACK process. Also, you may have won up to $20,000. To see if your claim number is a guaranteed cash prize winner, simply visit James Honda of Lincoln on the event date and claim your prize.

During this exciting event, James Honda of Lincoln has agreed to aggressively price its entire inventory of new and pre-owned cars, trucks, vans, and sport utilities. With rates as low as 0% and rebates up to $5,000, we are confident that you can upgrade your 2007 Honda Civic and in many cases reduce your current monthly payment with little out-of-pocket expense.

Due to the nature of this event it will not be advertised to the general public. Your status as a customer as well as your possession of a high-demand vehicle entitles you to attend this exciting event.

Appointments are recommended due to the anticipated response of this event. To schedule an appointment or if you are unable to attend on the below event date, please contact James Honda of Lincoln toll-free at 800.123.4567.

EVENT DATE:
Saturday, Nov 21st—9:00 a.m. to 6:00 p.m.

EVENT SITE:
JAMES HONDA OF LINCOLN
220 Kitty Hawk
Lincoln, NE 54367

As your instructor directs,

- Share your findings orally with a small group of students.
- Share your findings orally with the class.
- Post your findings in an e-mail to the class.
- Summarize your findings in a memo to your instructor.

3.13   Revising a Form Letter

Revise this form letter to improve positive tone and you-attitude (and to catch spelling and punctuation errors):

Dear customer,

We wish you a Happy New Year from Happy Catalog. Its been awhile since we heard from you. We have a special offer to welcome you back.

Our customers are the focus of what we do. All of our efforts center on exceeding our customer expectations.

Happy Catalog stands behind everything we sell, as we have since 1986. We will provide you with even better service, tailored to meet you needs and guaranteed to offer more of the helpful, unique and hard to find merchandise we're known for. Whether you choose to shop by phone, mail, or e-mail us, we promise to continually improve our process to better serve you. If you have been disappointed in any way, please accept our sincerest apology.

We have a special offer, exclusively for you, to welcome you back. When you use the enclosed coupon, you'll save 20% on any order, regardless of order size. Hurry, this offer will expire the beginning of February.

Welcome back! Thank you for your business.

Sincerly,
I. M. President
Happy Catalog.

3.14 Advising a Hasty Subordinate

Three days ago, one of your subordinates forwarded to everyone in the office a bit of e-mail humor he'd received from a friend. Titled "You know you're Southern when . . . ," the message poked fun at Southern speech, attitudes, and lifestyles. Today you get this message from your subordinate:

> Subject: Should I Apologize?
>
> I'm getting flamed left and right because of the Southern message. I thought it was funny, but some people just can't take a joke. So far I've tried not to respond to the flames, figuring that would just make things worse. But now I'm wondering if I should apologize. What do you think?

Answer the message.

3.15 Responding to a Complaint

You're Director of Corporate Communications; the employee newsletter is produced by your office. Today you get this e-mail message from Caroline Huber:

> Subject: Complaint about Sexist Language
>
> The article about the "Help Desk" says that Martina Luna and I "are the key customer service representatives 'manning' the desk." I don't MAN anything! I WORK.

Respond to Caroline. And send a message to your staff, reminding them to edit newsletter stories as well as external documents to replace biased language.

3.16 Exploring the Positive Effects of Negative Messages

In 2004, Gap Inc. (Gap, Old Navy, and Banana Republic) released a social responsibility report that acknowledged wage, health, and safety violations in many of its overseas factories. Rather than hiding this information, Gap chose to go public and address the problem. In 2006, Ford Motor Company released a series of online documentaries about the company's turnaround efforts which included a film about the company stock receiving a "sell" rating from industry analysts.

Find an example of a company that has shared its problems and its plans to solve those problems with the public. What went wrong? How did the company respond? How did the company report the problem?

Can you find the current status of the company and its recovery?

As your instructor directs,

a. Share your findings orally with a small group of students.

b. Post your findings in an e-mail to the class.

c. Summarize your findings in a memo to your instructor.

d. Join with a group of students to create a written report summarizing negative corporate news.

Adapted from Cheryl Dahl, "Gap's New Look: The See-Through," *Fast Company*, September 2004, 69–70.

3.17 Evaluating Bias in Visuals

Evaluate the portrayals of people in one of the following:

- Ads in one issue of a business magazine
- A company's annual report
- A company's web page

Do the visuals show people of both sexes and all races? Is there a sprinkling of people of various ages and physical conditions? What do the visuals suggest about who has power?

As your instructor directs,

a. Share your findings orally with a small group of students.

b. Post your findings in an e-mail to the class.

c. Summarize your findings in a memo to your instructor.

d. Present your findings in an oral presentation to the class.

e. Join with a small group of students to create a written report.

3.18   Revising a Memo for Positive Tone

Revise the following memo to improve positive tone.

TO: All Staff

SUBJECT: Decorating Your Work Area

With the arrival of the holiday season, employees who wish to decorate their work areas should do so only with great caution. Don't do something stupid that might burn down the entire office. If you wish to decorate, don't forget the following guidelines:

1. If using decorative lights, don't place them in obstructive places.
2. Do not overload your workstation with decorations that will interfere with your daily duties.
3. Don't forget to turn off and/or unplug all lights at the end of your workday.
4. Do not use hot lights; they can burn your countertop so it is imperative that everyone take care in selecting your lights.
5. Do not use decorations which will offend people of other religions.
6. Absolutely no candles are allowed.

Don't forget these guidelines, and we'll have a great holiday season. Thank you for your cooperation.

3.19   Dealing with Negative Clients

An executive at one of your largest client companies is known for his negative attitude. He is feared for his sharp tongue and scathing attacks, and he bullies everyone. Everyone you know, including yourself, is afraid of him. Unfortunately, he is also the one who decides whether or not you get your annual contract. Your contract is up for renewal, and you have some new services you think his company would like.

In small groups, discuss at least four ways to handle Mr. Bully. Write up your two best to share with the whole class. Also write up the reasons you think these two approaches will work. Share your two approaches with the whole class, as a short oral presentation or online.

As a class, select the two best approaches from those offered by the small groups. Discuss your criteria for selection and rejection.

3.20   Writing Business Thank-You Notes

Some businesses make a practice of sending goodwill messages to some of their customers.

Pick a business you patronize that might logically send some thank-you notes. Write a suitable note and design a tasteful visual for it. In a separate document, write a memo to your instructor explaining your design and content decisions.

Questions you might want to consider:

■ Who is your audience? Will you write to everyone? Will you target big spenders? Trend setters? People who might become long-term customers? How will you identify your categories?

■ What tone did you select? What words and phrases help produce that tone? What words and phrases did you avoid? What diction choices did you make to convey sincerity?

■ What content did you choose? Why? What content choices did you discard?

■ What design features did you choose? Why? What design features did you discard?

3.21   Evaluating You-Attitude and Positive Emphasis in University Websites

As they plan their college visits, many students begin by visiting university websites. Imagine you are a high school senior and a prospective student. Go to the "Prospective Students" part of your school's website and read about housing, course offerings, and student life. Evaluate the information you find for you-attitude and positive emphasis. Compare the text for prospective students with the text on several sites targeted for current students. Does the tone change? In what ways? What information increases or decreases you-attitude?

Now visit the website of another university. Review the same type of information for prospective students and compare it to that of your own school. Which school does a better job? Why?

As your instructor directs,

- Share your findings orally with a small group of students.
- Share your findings orally with the class.
- Post your findings in an e-mail to the class.
- Summarize your findings in a memo to your instructor.

3.22   Evaluating You-Attitude and Positive Emphasis at IRS

The IRS has a page called "Where's My Refund?" In 2007, the page read like this:

"Where's My Refund?"

"You filed your tax return and you're expecting a refund. You have just one question and you want the answer now—*Where's My Refund?*"

"Whether you split your refund among several accounts, opted for direct deposit to one account or asked IRS to mail you a check, you can track your refund through this secure Web site. You can get refund information even if you filed just to request the telephone excise tax refund."

"To get to your personal refund information, be ready to enter your:"

- Social Security Number (or IRS Individual Taxpayer Identification Number)
- Filing status (Single, Married Filing Joint Return, Married Filing Separate Return, Head of Household, or Qualifying Widow(er))
- Exact refund amount shown on your return

"If you don't receive your refund within 28 days from the original IRS mailing date shown on *Where's My Refund?*, you can start a refund trace online."

If *Where's My Refund?* shows that IRS was unable to deliver your refund, you can change your address online.

"*Where's My Refund?* will prompt you when these features are available for your situation. "

"Okay now, *Where's My Re-fund?*"

Now read their current "Where's My Refund" page on their website. What changes have they made? Which version has more you-attitude and positive emphasis? Which version do you like better? Why? Write your answers in a memo to your instructor or classmates.

Quoted from "Where's My Refund?" U.S. Department of the Treasury, updated April 6, 2011, http://www.irs.gov/individuals/article/0,,id=96596,00.html.

3.23   Designing for People with Disabilities

Reread the sidebar on page 75. In small groups discuss these questions:

- What are some other products you can think of that could be redesigned for easier use by people with disabilities?
- What themes would you use to advertise these products? Remember that no one likes to be reminded that they are losing physical capacities.
- What are some changes companies should make to their advertising and product information for easier access by people with disabilities?

As your instructor directs, in small groups

- Summarize your discussion in a memo for your instructor.
- Summarize your discussion in a memo for your class list serve.
- Prepare a short presentation for your classmates.

3.24   Revising a "Goodwill Disaster"

Li, an intern at All-Weather, a window manufacturer, has been asked to write a letter to a recent young customer asking him if some new engineers can tour his gallery to see the products in use. Here is his draft:

> Dear Mr. Mason,
> Executive Director,
> Iconic Art Gallery, St. Paul, MN
>
> You must be glad that you chose All-Weather's energy efficient bow windows, horizontal sliders, and fiberglass doors for your art gallery. As everyone who is anyone knows, we offer the finest quality wood, vinyl, aluminum, steel, and fiberglass composite windows and doors you can find in the US of A. As you also know, our customer service representatives are ready to assist you 24/7 (and more!) with any installation or maintenance needs you may have (even if it's your responsibility or fault, I might add). After doing so much for an important customer such as you, we have a small favor to ask of you, which we're sure you will not deny us. We just hired some new engineers who will join our manufacturing division to continue to make the fine products that we make. Unfortunately, they have never seen how our finished products look outside or inside actual homes or offices. (On a personal note, I confess I don't know what they can learn from one visit to a home or an office.) Our VP (Manufacturing), an asset to All-Weather, says that we should send these engineers out on a field visit. And he should know, shouldn't he, being the VP and all? That is why I'm writing to you (the pleasure is mine, though).
>
> These fresh minds need exposure to actual conditions in actual markets. We think that if they visit your art gallery, they will see how our products are helping you get results your art gallery could never dream of before. If you don't believe me, take a peek inside your exhibits room, whose space seems to have expanded thanks to our bow window that you have installed. I myself remember what a cramped-looking room it was before. No, I'm not asking you to share your admission fees with us, though free exhibition tickets wouldn't hurt (I'm kidding, sir). Also, you should perhaps buy more windows and doors from us (and attract more visitors as a result!). Also, don't forget to mention us favorably to your patrons.
>
> Oh, and by the way, will you please let us know the day and time suitable to you when we might send those engineers to your art gallery? Our orientation program begins in three weeks time. Looking forward to your prompt acceptance of our request (with or without free exhibition tickets).
>
> Sincerely,
> Li

Li was trying for a breezy tone which he thought appropriate for a young art gallery owner but obviously went overboard.

Based on your reading of Chapter 3, complete the following tasks:

- List problems in Li's draft.
- Prepare another list of changes that would improve the draft. Be specific in your suggestions. For instance, it's insufficient to say "more you-attitude" or "more politeness." Point to places in the draft where these strategies might be useful. Also, rephrase relevant sentences or paragraphs for more you-attitude or more politeness, whichever is the case.
- What is the primary purpose of the letter? The secondary purpose?
- Revise the draft.

CHAPTER

4

Navigating the Business Communication Environment

Chapter Outline

NEWSWORTHY COMMUNICATION

A Refreshingly Ethical Project

One of the best-known corporate social responsibility efforts is Pepsi's Refresh Project, launched in February 2010.

In its first year, the Refresh Project promised $20 million in donations to organizations and individuals who submitted "refreshing ideas that change the world." Competition for grants, especially in the $250,000 category, was high, with community, health, and religious organizations forming alliances and dominating voting by encouraging supporters to vote up to the maximum allowed under contest rules. Such competition shut out many smaller, grassroots organizations that couldn't muster the same kind of support among voters.

Despite initial complaints of unfair competition, Pepsi Refresh Project reported 12,642 idea submissions and over 76 million votes. The project awarded $6.4 million in grants to arts and health organizations, and provided funds that helped improve 26 playgrounds and start 47 organizations.

To even the field for the second year of Project Refresh, Pepsi revised voting procedures. Additionally, Pepsi eliminated the $250,000 grant category, but offered twice as many grants of $50,000 or less, which are sought by smaller groups. Jill Beraud, chief marketing officer for PepsiCo Beverages America, explained that the changes were meant to make the competition for Project Refresh grants more democratic.

While some analysts worry that Pepsi is spending too much on promoting an image of social responsibility and not enough on marketing its major brands, PepsiCo remains committed to Project Refresh and plans to expand the initiative to China and Latin America. According to PepsiCo Chairman and Chief Executive Indra K. Nooyi, companies must find ways to make their brands stand apart from other brands in their same market, and social responsibility is one way to do that. As she explained at an industry conference in December 2010, "It's a matter of, 'What does this brand stand for in terms of doing something positive in the world?"

> *"What does this brand stand for in terms of doing something positive in the world?"*

Source: Valerie Bauerlein, "Pepsi Hits 'Refresh' on Donor Project," *Wall Street Journal,* January 31, 2011, B4.

Learning Objectives

After studying this chapter, you will know

LO 4-1   Why ethics is so important in business communication.

LO 4-2   How corporate culture impacts the business environment.

LO 4-3   How to improve interpersonal communication.

LO 4-4   How to use your time more efficiently.

LO 4-5   What the trends in business communication are.

Dilbert May Get You Fired

Catfish Bend Casinos in Burlington, Iowa, fired a seven-year employee for placing a Dilbert cartoon on a company bulletin board. The employee posted the cartoon after the company announced the casino was closing and 170 workers would probably be laid off.

The Dilbert cartoon called decision makers "drunken lemurs" and said they had time but no talent.

The employee, who was identified from security tapes, thought the comic was humorous and might cheer up some of his colleagues. Managers found it insulting misconduct. They then tried to block his unemployment benefits, but the judge sided with the employee, calling the posting "a good-faith error in judgment."

Adapted from Clark Kauffman, "Bosses Check Video, Fire Man Who Put up Comic," *Des Moines Register*, December 19, 2007, 1A, 10A.

In addition to adapting to audiences and building goodwill, business communications are heavily influenced by the environments in which they are created and interpreted. Part of this environment is shaped by national culture, such as the growing concern about business ethics, and part is shaped by corporate culture. Part is shaped by individual behaviors, such as those involved in interpersonal communication. A final part is shaped by widespread trends—trends such as globalization or the green movement. Technology and information overload, which are perhaps the largest of these trends, are discussed extensively in Chapter 9, along with effective ways to deal with them.

ETHICS   LO 4-1

With the official recognition of a serious worldwide recession in the fall of 2008, along with the subprime mortgage debacle, ethics concerns have become a major part of the business environment. Financial giants such as AIG, Bear Sterns, Lehman Brothers, Merrill Lynch, Wachovia, and Washington Mutual had to be bailed out or went bankrupt. Banks, corporate officials, and rating agencies all were accused of unethical behavior. The SEC charged Goldman Sachs with fraud on securities linked to subprime mortgages; the firm settled out of court for over half a billion dollars.

Even drug companies were not immune. Glaxo pleaded guilty to charges that it knowingly sold adulterated drugs, including the antidepressant Paxil, and paid fines of $750 million. Pfizer paid $2.3 billion for promoting drugs for unauthorized uses.[1]

Billionaires fell as well. Bernie Madoff was sentenced to prison in what may have been the biggest Ponzi scheme in history, one that defrauded thousands of investors of billions of dollars. Hedge-fund manager Raj Rajaratnam was convicted of securities fraud and conspiracy in the biggest insider-trading case to that time.[2]

The Ethics Resource Center, America's oldest nonprofit organization devoted to ethical practice, reported in its 2009 *National Business Ethics Survey*®, that 49% of employees surveyed personally witnessed unethical or illegal behavior; 37% of those witnesses did not report it. The most frequent misconducts were company resource abuse, abusive behavior, lying to employees, e-mail or Internet abuse, conflicts of interest, discrimination, lying to stakeholders, employee benefit violations, health or safety violations, employee privacy breach, improper hiring practices, and falsifying time or expenses.[3]

Some common reasons for not reporting ethical misconduct are

- It's standard practice here.
- It's not a big deal.
- It's not my responsibility (a particularly common reason for junior employees).
- I want to be loyal to my colleagues/manager/company (stated negatively, this reason is "fear of consequences").[4]

On the other side of the coin, positive ethical efforts are also getting attention. The United Nations Global Compact, the world's largest corporate effort for global citizenship, focuses on human rights, labor, environment, and anticorruption measures. More than 5,300 businesses in 130 countries participate.[5] The Clinton Global Initiative has brought together 150 heads of state, 18 Nobel laureates, and hundreds of CEOs, who collectively have committed $63 billion. This money has already impacted the lives of 300 million people in 180 countries.[6]

The United States has its own efforts:

- Bill and Melinda Gates' foundation received double attention when Warren Buffett announced his transfer of billions of dollars to it. The three philanthropists have attracted still more attention with their efforts to convince other billionaires to pledge the majority of their wealth to philanthropy. The list of those who have made the pledge is posted at givingpledge.org; it included 69 pledgers in Spring 2011.
- Google, the "Don't Be Evil" company, has invested over $100 million in Google.org to use "Google's strengths in information and technology to build products and advocate for policies that address global challenges."[7]
- Robin Hood, a venture philanthropy, "robs" the rich (its board members cover all costs, so 100% of money donated goes to fund programs) to help the poor in New York City.[8]

Social entrepreneurs, backed by social investors like Bill Gates, are extending the reach of philanthropy. Grameen Bank founder Muhammad Yunus won the 2006 Nobel Peace Prize for his work with microfinance. The bank says it has brought 68% of its 8.3 million clients out of extreme poverty. Social Finance is launching Social Impact Bonds (SiB). SiBs help social enterprises acquire the sustainable revenues they need to succeed. Financial returns for investors are based on improved social outcomes.[9]

Business ethics includes far more than corporate greed, international pacts, and philanthropy, of course. Much of business ethics involves routine practices, and many of these practices involve communication. How can we make our contracts with our clients and suppliers easier to understand? How can we best communicate with our employees? How much should our hospital disclose about infection rates?

Many basic, daily communication decisions involve an ethics component. Am I including all the information my audience needs? Am I expressing it in ways they will understand? Am I putting it in a format that helps my audience grasp it quickly? Am I including information for all segments of my audience? Am I taking information from other sources accurately? Am I acknowledging my sources? Figure 4.1 lists some of the web resources that deal with business ethics.

Figure 4.2 elaborates on ethical components of communication. As it suggests, language, graphics, and document design—basic parts of any

Definitely Not Full Disclosure

"A prominent spine surgeon and researcher at the University of Wisconsin received $19 million in payment over five years from Medtronic Inc., one of the country's largest makers of spinal devices. . . ."

"The surgeon . . . received the payments while helping Medtronic develop and promote a number of spinal products. Medtronic's $19 million in payments . . . went 'greatly' beyond what was evident in disclosures he made to the university. . . .

'[During those five years, the surgeon] told the university that he received $20,000 or more from Medtronic. . . .' The disclosures conform to school policies, which currently don't require researchers to specify amounts received above $20,000. . . .

"Charles Rosen, a University of California, Irvine, spinal surgeon who is also president of the Association for Medical Ethics, said the Wisconsin disclosure policy is similar to that of many universities and medical societies. He said those policies are insufficient. . . ."

" 'When you are advocating devices or procedures, it can't be said this is a private matter and that no one should know how much this company is paying me,' he said. 'It should be very public. People should know.' "

Quoted from David Armstrong and Thomas M. Burton, "Medtronic Paid This Researcher More Than $20,000—Much More," *Wall Street Journal*, January 16, 2009. Copyright © 2009 by Dow Jones & Company, Inc. Reproduced with permission of Dow Jones & Company, Inc. via Copyright Clearance Center.

No Illegal Downloads in France

France became one of the first countries to enforce an antipiracy law against Internet scofflaws. It is going after all illegal downloaders of copyrighted film and music, regardless of where the material was made.

The law was passed after heavy lobbying from involved industries, who claim that illegal downloads cost the French music industry €700 million ($978 million) annually.

Offenders receive two warnings, first by e-mail and then by registered letter. A third offense can lead to legal proceedings plus a one-year Internet blackout for the offender.

Adapted from Max Colchester, "All Eyes on France as Officials Enforce New Antipiracy Law," *Wall Street Journal*, November 27, 2010, B1.

Figure 4.1   Business Ethics Resources on the Web

- **Business Ethics Resources on the Internet**
  http://www.ethicsweb.ca/resources/business
- **Defense Industry Initiative on Business Ethics and Conduct**
  http://dii.org
- **DePaul University's Institute for Business and Professional Ethics**
  http://commerce.depaul.edu/ethics
- **Ethics Resource Center**
  http://www.ethics.org
- **E-Business Ethics**
  http://www.e-businessethics.com
- **Various Codes of Conduct**
  http://www.ethicsweb.ca/resources/business/codes.html

business document—can be ethical or manipulative. Persuading and gaining compliance—activities at the heart of business and organizational life—can be done with respect or contempt for customers, co-workers, and subordinates.

In these days of instant communication, you, like the organization in which you work, must always act in an ethical manner. Consequences for not doing so are becoming more common as disgruntled colleagues/employees now have ample means for whistleblowing. Of course, there are also positive reasons for ethical behavior. In addition to moral reasons, there are business ones. As the Ethics Resource Center notes, customers and employees are attracted

Figure 4.2   Ethical Issues in Business Communications

Manner of conveying the message	Qualities of the message	Larger organizational context of the message
• Is the language audience-friendly? Does it respect the audience? • Do the words balance the organization's right to present its best case with its responsibility to present its message honestly? • Do graphics help the audience understand? Or are graphics used to distract or confuse? • Does the design of the document make reading easy? Does document design attempt to make readers skip key points?	• Is the message an ethical one that is honest and sensitive to all stakeholders? • Have interested parties been able to provide input? • Does the audience get all the information it needs to make a good decision or is information withheld? • Is information communicated so the audience can grasp it or are data "dumped" without any context? • Are the arguments logical? Are they supported with adequate evidence? • Are the emotional appeals used fairly? Do they supplement logic rather than substitute for it? • Does the organizational pattern lead the audience without undue manipulation?	• How does the organization treat its employees? How do employees treat each other? • How sensitive is the organization to stakeholders such as the people who live near its factories, stores, or offices and to the general public? • Does the organization support employees' efforts to be honest, fair, and ethical? • Do the organization's actions in making products, buying supplies, and marketing goods and services stand up to ethical scrutiny? • Is the organization a good corporate citizen, helpful rather than harmful to the community in which it exists? • Are the organization's products or services a good use of scarce resources?

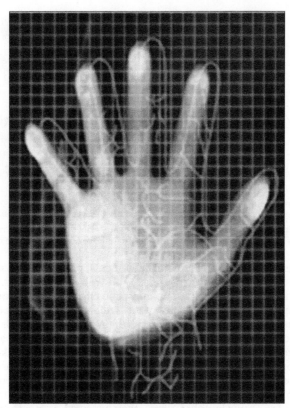

GMAT is now using palm vein scans to eliminate hired test takers. See sidebar on this page.

Business School Ethics

GMAT test scores were canceled for applicants who allegedly supplied or accessed exam questions posted on a website. Business schools were notified that these students had prepared improperly for the exam, and the Graduate Management Admission Council, which oversees the exam, obtained a court order to shut down the site, believed to be maintained in China.

The council also announced that it will be requiring GMAT test takers to take a palm vein scan, an infrared picture of the blood vessels in their hands. This new security measure is a new attempt to wipe out proxies—hired brains that take the test for an applicant.

The efforts to cheat continue in business school. Donald McCabe, a Rutgers University professor of management who has studied academic dishonesty for two decades, says that students in business schools cheat more than other students. His findings are backed up by a Duke University study which found that 56% of master's students in business administration cheat, again the highest rate among graduate students.

Adapted from John Hechinger, "Schools Cancel GMAT Scores," *Wall Street Journal*, September 11, 2008, D6; and "The Ethical Mind: A Conversation with Psychologist Howard Gardner," *Harvard Business Review*, March 2007, 51–56.

to ethical businesses. Rosabeth Moss Kanter, a professor at Harvard Business School, argues in her book, *Supercorp: How Vanguard Companies Create Innovation, Profits, Growth, and Social Good,* that companies desiring to do good have a competitive advantage. In fact, a benevolent viewpoint provides a wider view of society and thus awareness of new opportunities for growth and innovation by solving the problems of unmet needs.

Tony Hsieh, the founder and CEO of Zappos, offers this useful ethics guideline:

> As a guiding principle in life for anything I do, I try to ask myself, *What would happen if everyone in the world acted in the same way? What would the world look like? What would the net effect be on the overall happiness in the world?* [Hsieh's italics]
>
> This thought experiment has been useful to me when thinking about whether to share how we do things at Zappos, or whether to get upset at the waitress who accidentally got my order wrong, or whether to hold the door open for a stranger who's a slightly inconvenient distance away.
>
> The same questions are just as important for deciding what not to do, even if not doing anything is the default choice.[10]

CORPORATE CULTURE LO 4-2

Another strong influence on the business environment is corporate culture (see Chapter 2 for ways to analyze corporate culture). Corporate cultures vary widely. They range from formal—with individual offices, jackets, and hierarchical lines of command—to informal, with open office space, casual attire, and flat organizational structures. Characteristics of popular corporate

Part 1   The Building Blocks of Effective Messages

Rule 34: Don't Plagiarize

"Do not plagiarize" should have been included in *Unwritten Rules of Management,* the book by William Swanson, CEO of Raytheon. In 2004, Raytheon gave employees free copies of the book, which contained 33 rules. The book quickly became widely read by professionals and executives because of its humorous approach. However, an engineer at Hewlett-Packard discovered that 13 of the rules had been previously published by W. J. King in his 1944 bestseller, *The Unwritten Laws of Engineering.* Further findings uncovered that the additional rules were obtained from Defense Secretary Rumsfeld and humor editorial writer Dave Barry.

Swanson apologized for the mistake, which, he states, began when he asked employees to create a presentation from a file. The presentation was a great hit, which led to the creation of the 33 rules—one for each year he worked for Raytheon. Unfortunately, the rules were not original and the sources were not properly cited.

How can you avoid plagiarism?

Adapted from Lisa Takeuchi Cullen, "Rule No. 1: Don't Copy," *Time,* May 15, 2006, 41.

Thoughtful Perks

Some companies have unique perks:

- On-site laundry pickup and delivery
- Café lunch delivery at desks
- Professional home cleaning
- Two weeks fully paid leave to work for green nonprofits
- Up to $5,000 and an extra week off for vacations abroad
- Charge card to use in a nearby restaurant

Adapted from "10 Perks We Love," *Inc.,* June 2010, 94.

Some employees use exercise balls as desk chairs. The balls require employees to use core muscles to maintain posture. Employees say they are also fun because they can bounce.

cultures include flexible work arrangements, profit sharing, information sharing, good training, health insurance, and wellness programs.

Both large and small companies get cited for their corporate cultures. Google is known for company gyms, well-stocked snack rooms, restaurants, and casual work attire. Dealer.com offers subsidized meals at its café, with organic and locally grown food, wellness seminars on exercise and stress management, chair massages, bike rentals, tennis and basketball courts, fitness center, and half-price ski passes. The company supports its sports teams, including softball, volleyball, soccer, bowling, and dragon-boat racing.[11]

Two companies in the same field may have very different cultures. When Procter & Gamble bought Gillette, they expected a smooth marriage between the world's number one toothbrush, Oral-B, and the world's number two toothpaste, Crest. But cultural differences caused problems. Gillette employees found P&G's culture rigid, its decision making slow. Gillette employees also had to learn P&G's famous acronyms, such as CIB (consumer is boss) and FMOT (first moment of truth, when consumers notice the product). P&G people sent memos, Gillette people called meetings.[12]

Wise companies also use effective corporate cultures to retain hourly workers. Hotels lose two-thirds of their hourly workers annually, according to hotel survey firm Market Metrix. Each departure costs midrange hotels about $5,000 in lost productivity, recruiting, and training. But Joie de Vivre Hospitality has a turnover rate that is half the industry average. The CEO attributes the low rate to a corporate culture that listens to employees, enacts some of their suggestions, and tries to make work fun. In addition to awards, the company sponsors parties, annual retreats, and regularly scheduled dinners. It also offers free classes on subjects such as Microsoft Excel and English as a second language.[13]

Corporate culture is at the heart of the customer service focus at Zappos, the Internet footwear retailer. The company nurtures a touch of weirdness to make work more fun. That same touch of weirdness also encourages innovation. To increase serendipitous interactions, all employees enter and exit through the reception area. Logging in to the company computer requires completing the short multiple-choice test to name the randomly selected employee whose picture is displayed.[14] Tours of corporate offices are always unique, because teams are always changing their décor:

> You might find a popcorn machine or a coffee machine dressed up as a robot in our lobby. As you passed through different departments, you might find an aisle of cowbells . . . , a makeshift bowling alley . . . , employees dressed up as pirates,

employees karaokeing, a nap room, a petting zoo, or a hot dog social. You might see a parade pass by because one of our departments decided that it was the perfect day to celebrate Oktoberfest.[15]

INTERPERSONAL COMMUNICATION LO 4-3

Within the corporate environment, some people are more likely to be successful than others, and one major reason for the variation is interpersonal communication skill. Much important communication takes place in hallways, at the coffee machine, and in break rooms. Successful professionals communicate well with different categories of people—co-workers, bosses, clients—in a variety of settings. To do so, they cultivate skills in diverse areas such as listening, conversation, nonverbal communication, and networking. They also practice skills in conflict resolution and teamwork (see Chapter 8 for a discussion of these latter two skills).

These skills are part of what Daniel Goleman has widely popularized as Emotional Intelligence in his books on the subject. He presents much evidence to show that while intelligence and expertise are necessary to climb to the top in organizations, once at the top emotional intelligence, not IQ, predicts the star leaders.[16]

Listening

Listening is crucial to building trust. However, listening on the job may be more difficult than listening in classes. Many classroom lectures are well organized, with signposts and repetition of key points to help hearers follow. But conversations usually wander. A key point about when a report is due may be sandwiched in among statements about other due dates for other projects. Finally, in a classroom you're listening primarily for information. In interchanges with friends and co-workers, you need to listen for feelings, too. Feelings such as being rejected or overworked need to be dealt with as they arise. But you can't deal with a feeling unless you are aware of it.

Listening errors also can result from being distracted by your own emotional response, especially when the topic is controversial. Listeners have to be aware of their emotional responses so that they can clarify the speaker's intent and also allow time for cooling off, if necessary. A "you" attitude is as helpful for listening as it is for writing. Listening is more effective if the listener focuses more on understanding than on formulating a reply. Thinking about your own response too often causes you to miss important information.

Some listening errors also happen because the hearer wasn't paying enough attention to a key point. Be aware of points you need to know and listen for them.

Inattention and emotions can cause listeners to misinterpret a speaker. To reduce listening errors caused by misinterpretation,

- Paraphrase what the speaker has said, giving him or her a chance to correct your understanding.
- At the end of the conversation, check your understanding with the other person. Especially check who does what next.
- After the conversation, write down key points that affect deadlines or how work will be evaluated. Sometimes these key points need to be confirmed in an e-mail.
- Don't ignore instructions you think are unnecessary. Before you do something else, check with the order giver to see if there is a reason for the instruction.

Warren Buffett on Ethics

In a 2008 letter to Berkshire directors, Warren Buffett says this about ethics:

"We *must* continue to measure every act against not only what is legal but also what we would be happy to have written about on the front page of a national newspaper in an article written by an unfriendly but intelligent reporter."

"Sometimes your associates will say 'Everybody else is doing it.' This rationale is almost always a bad one if it is the main justification for a business action. It is totally unacceptable when evaluating a moral decision. Whenever somebody offers that phrase as a rationale, in effect they are saying that they can't come up with a *good* reason. If anyone offers this explanation, tell them to try using it with a reporter or a judge and see how far it gets them."

". . . It's very likely that if a given course of action evokes hesitation *per se*, it's too close to the line and should be abandoned. There's plenty of money to be made in the center of the court. If it's questionable whether some action is close to the line, just assume it is outside and forget it."

The material is copyrighted and used with permission of the author.

94   Part 1   The Building Blocks of Effective Messages

Small Companies, Large Hearts

Some small companies are building philanthropy into their business models. Hook & Ladder Brewing Company donates a portion of all sales to local burned firefighters and other burn survivors. ColorMe Company, which produces arts and crafts materials for children, gives 10% of earnings to children's charities. Toms shoes gives a pair of new shoes to a child in need for every pair of shoes purchased from them.

Charitable contributions like these help attract and keep customers and employees and set such companies apart from their competitors.

What do you think of such philanthropic business models? What potential problems do such models have? Do you think the benefits will outweigh the pitfalls?

Adapted from "H&L History," Hook & Ladder Brewing Company, accessed May 26, 2011, http://www.hookand ladderbeer.com/Public/Content .aspx; "Homepage," ColorMe Company, accessed May 26, 2011, http:// www.colormecompany.com/; "Official Store," TOMS Company, accessed May 26, 2011, http://www.toms.com/.

- Consider the other person's background and experiences. Why is this point important to the speaker? What might he or she mean by it?

Listening to people is an indication that you're taking them seriously. **Acknowledgment responses**—nods, *uh huhs*, smiles, frowns—help carry the message that you're listening. However, remember that listening responses vary in different cultures.

In **active listening**, receivers actively demonstrate that they've understood a speaker by feeding back the literal meaning, the emotional content, or both. These strategies create active responses:

- Paraphrase the content. Feed back the meaning in your own words.
- Identify the feelings you think you hear.
- Ask for information or clarification.
- Offer to help. ("What can I do to help?")

When dealing with problems, instead of acknowledging what the other person says, many of us immediately respond in a way that analyzes or attempts to solve or dismiss the problem. People with problems need first of all to know that we hear that they're having a rough time. Figure 4.3 lists some of the responses that block communication. Ordering and threatening both tell the other person that the speaker doesn't want to hear what he or she has to say. Preaching attacks the other person. Minimizing the problem suggests the other person's concern is misplaced. It can even attack the other person's competency by suggesting that other people are coping just fine with bigger problems. Even advising shuts off discussion. Giving a quick answer minimizes the pain the person feels and puts him or her down for not seeing (what is to us) the obvious answer. Even if it is a good answer from an objective point of view, the other person may not be ready to hear it. And too often, the off-the-top-of-the-head solution doesn't address the real problem.

Active listening takes time and energy. Even people who are skilled active listeners can't do it all the time. Active listening can reduce the conflict that

Figure 4.3   Blocking Responses versus Active Listening

Blocking response	Possible active response
Ordering, threatening "I don't care how you do it. Just get that report on my desk by Friday."	**Paraphrasing content** "You're saying that you don't have time to finish the report by Friday."
Preaching, criticizing "You should know better than to air the department's problems in a general meeting."	**Mirroring feelings** "It sounds like the department's problems really bother you."
Minimizing the problem "You think *that's* bad. You should see what *I* have to do this week."	**Asking for information or clarification** "What parts of the problem seem most difficult to solve?"
Advising "Well, why don't you try listing everything you have to do and seeing which items are most important?"	**Offering to help solve the problem together** "Is there anything I could do that would help?"

Source: These responses that block communication are based on a list in Thomas Gordon and Judith Gordon Sands, *P.E.T. in Action* (New York: Wyden, 1976), 117–18.

results from miscommunication, but it alone cannot reduce the conflict that comes when two people want apparently inconsistent things or when one person wants to change someone else.

Conversational Style

Deborah Tannen, a linguist who specializes in gender discourse, uses the term **conversational style** to denote our conversational patterns and the meaning we give to them: the way we show interest, politeness, appropriateness.[17] Your answers to the following questions reveal your own conversational style:

- How long a pause tells you that it's your turn to speak?
- Do you see interruption as rude? or do you say things while other people are still talking to show that you're interested and to encourage them to say more?
- Do you show interest by asking lots of questions? or do you see questions as intrusive and wait for people to volunteer whatever they have to say?

Tannen concludes that the following features characterize her own conversational style:

Fast rate of speech.

Fast rate of turn-taking.

Persistence—if a turn is not acknowledged, try again.

Preference for personal stories.

Tolerance of, preference for simultaneous speech.

Abrupt topic shifting.

Different conversational styles are not necessarily good or bad, but people with different conversational styles may feel uncomfortable without knowing why. A subordinate who talks quickly may be frustrated by a boss who speaks slowly. People who talk more slowly may feel shut out of a conversation with people who talk more quickly. Someone who has learned to make requests directly ("Please pass the salt") may be annoyed by someone who uses indirect requests ("This casserole needs some salt").

In the workplace, conflicts may arise because of differences in conversational style. If people see direct questions as criticizing or accusing, they may see an ordinary question ("Will that report be ready Friday?") as a criticism of their progress. One supervisor might mean the question simply as a request for information. Another supervisor might use the question to mean "I want that report Friday."

Researchers Daniel N. Maltz and Ruth A. Borker believe that differences in conversational style (Figure 4.4) may be responsible for the miscommunication that often occurs in **male–female conversations.** Certainly conversational style is not the same for all men and for all women, but research has found several common patterns in the U.S. cultures studied so far.[18] For example, researchers have found that women are much more likely to nod and to say *yes* or *mm hmm* than men are.[19] Maltz and Borker hypothesize that to women, these symbols mean simply "I'm listening; go on." Men, on the other hand, may decode these symbols as "I agree" or at least "I follow what you're saying so far." A man who receives nods and *mms* from a woman may feel that she is inconsistent and unpredictable if she then disagrees with him. A woman may feel that a man who doesn't provide any feedback isn't listening to her.

Encyclopedia of Ethical Failure

"[Stephen] Epstein, the director of the Pentagon's Standards of Conduct Office, is mounting an ethical cleansing offensive from inside the corridors of power. His weapon of choice is the 'Encyclopedia of Ethical Failure,' a hit parade he publishes on the Internet to regale bureaucrats with tales of shenanigans and shockingly bad judgment that have shot down the careers of fellow public servants across government.

"Take the case of the Customs . . . officer who landed a government helicopter on his daughter's grade-school playground: Despite having a supervisor's ill-considered clearance to fly there, . . . the officer was fired for misusing government property. . . .

"Mr. Epstein combs through the press, legal records and internal government investigation reports for material. . . . He often finds humor in the missteps. Two Veterans Affairs bureaucrats were charged with overbilling the government and receiving kickbacks from a supplier. 'The product? . . . Red tape.'"

Figure 4.4   Different Conversational Styles

	Debating	Relating
Interpretation of questions	See questions as requests for information.	See questions as way to keep a conversation flowing.
Relation of new comment to what last speaker said	Do not require new comment to relate explicitly to last speaker's comment. Ignoring previous comment is one strategy for taking control.	Expect new comments to acknowledge the last speaker's comment and relate directly to it.
View of aggressiveness	See aggressiveness as one way to organize the flow of conversation.	See aggressiveness as directed at audience personally, as negative, and as disruptive to a conversation.
How topics are defined and changed	Tend to define topics narrowly and shift topics abruptly. Interpret statements about side issues as effort to change the topic.	Tend to define topics gradually, progressively. Interpret statements about side issues as effort to shape, expand, or limit the topic.
Response to someone who shares a problem	Offer advice, solutions.	Offer solidarity, reassurance. Share troubles to establish sense of community.

Sources: Based on Daniel N. Maltz and Ruth A. Borker, "A Cultural Approach to Male-Female Miscommunication," *Language and Social Identity*, ed. John J. Gumperz (Cambridge: Cambridge University Press, 1982), 213; and Deborah Tannen, *Talking from 9 to 5: Women and Men in the Workplace: Language, Sex and Power* (New York: William Morrow, 1995).

Interpersonal Skills for Doctors

The risk of being sued for medical malpractice lies not so much with training, credentials, or even the number of mistakes made. Rather, it depends on doctors' interpersonal skills. Again and again, patients in malpractice suits say they were rushed, ignored, or treated like objects. A study of surgeons showed that those who had never been sued

- Made orienting comments at visits, so patients knew what was going to happen and when it was best to ask questions.
- Practiced active listening ("Tell me more about that").
- Laughed and were funny during visits.

The difference was all in how they talked to their patients; there was no difference in amount or quality of information.

Adapted from Malcolm Gladwell, *Blink: The Power of Thinking without Thinking* (New York: Back Bay Books, 2007), 40–43.

Research has also shown that in our culture men tend to interrupt more than women; women tend to wait for a pause in the discussion before speaking. When former Secretary of State Madeleine Albright was asked to give advice to professional women hoping to rise in the ranks, she replied, "Learn to interrupt."[20]

Nonverbal Communication

Nonverbal communication—communication that doesn't use words—takes place all the time. Smiles, frowns, who sits where at a meeting, the size of an office, how long someone keeps a visitor waiting—all these communicate pleasure or anger, friendliness or distance, power and status.

Researchers have begun to study a category of nonverbal communication called **social signals**—tone of voice, gestures, proximity to others, facial expressions—as keys to business success. Researchers can study these signals in individuals and then predict accurately who will win raises or business plan contests. The more successful people are more energetic and positive. They do talk more, but they also listen more, drawing other people out.[21]

Most of the time we are no more conscious of interpreting nonverbal signals than we are conscious of breathing. Yet nonverbal signals can be misinterpreted just as easily as can verbal symbols (words). And the misunderstandings can be harder to clear up because people may not be aware of the nonverbal cues that led them to assume that they aren't liked, respected, or approved.

Learning about nonverbal language can help us project the image we want to present and make us more aware of the signals we are interpreting. However, even within a single culture, a nonverbal symbol may have more than one meaning.

In the business world, two sets of nonverbal signals are particularly important: spatial cues and body language.

Spatial Cues In the United States, the size, placement, and privacy of one's office connotes status. Large corner offices have the highest status. An individual office with a door that closes connotes more status than a desk in a common area. Windows also may matter. An office with a window may connote more status than one without.

People who don't know each other well may feel more comfortable with each other if a piece of furniture separates them. For example, a group may work better sitting around a table than just sitting in a circle. Desks can be used as barricades to protect oneself from other people.

Body Language Our body language communicates to other people much about our feelings. Our facial expressions, eye contact, gestures, posture, and body positions all telegraph information about us. In the United States, **open body positions** include leaning forward with uncrossed arms and legs, with the arms away from the body. **Closed** or **defensive body positions** include leaning back, sometimes with both hands behind the head, arms and legs crossed or close together, or hands in pockets. As the labels imply, open positions suggest that people are accepting and open to new ideas. Closed positions suggest that people are physically or psychologically uncomfortable, that they are defending themselves and shutting other people out.

People who cross their arms or legs often claim that they do so only because the position is more comfortable. But notice your own body the next time you're in a perfectly comfortable discussion with a good friend. You'll probably find that you naturally assume open body positions. The fact that so many people in organizational settings adopt closed positions may indicate that many people feel at least slightly uncomfortable in school and on the job.

Some nonverbal communications appear to be made and interpreted unconsciously by many people. Researchers at MIT are showing that when we get excited about something, we have more nervous energy. Another such signal is fluency, or consistency. Consistency in motions (such as in surgery) or

Liar Detection

Although not infallible, these are signs of lying:

Body language: Physical cues such as sweating and fidgeting may be telling.

Details: False stories often lack details. Pushing for details increases chances the liar may slip up.

Unpleasantness: Liars are less cooperative, pleasant, and friendly than truth tellers. They also make more negative statements and complaints.

Eye contact: Failure to make eye contact is often a sign of lying.

Stress signs: Dilated pupils and a rise in voice pitch may be present.

Pauses: Most liars will have pauses in their stories as they make them up.

Inconsistencies: Ask suspected liars to repeat their stories; listen for inconsistencies.

Adapted from Elisabeth Eaves, "Ten Ways to Tell if Someone Is Lying to You," *Forbes,* July 22, 2010, http://www.forbes.com/2006/11/02/tech-cx_ee_technology_liar_slide.html.

(a)   (b)

(a) (left) "THE REAL THING: A real smile involves the whole face, not just the mouth. While muscles pull the corners of the mouth up (1), an involuntary nerve causes the upper eyefold (2) to relax."

(b) (right) "THE SOCIAL SMILE: When faking, the lips are pulled straight across (3). Though this creates cheek folds (4) similar to those of a real smile, the lack of eye crinkles (5) is a dead giveaway."

Quoted from Andy Raskin, "A Face Any Business Can Trust," Business 2.0 4, no. 11 (December 2003): 60.

98   **Part 1**   The Building Blocks of Effective Messages

Are Interruptions Impolite?

In the dominant U.S. culture, interrupting can seem impolite, especially if a lower-status person interrupts a superior.

Simulated negotiations have measured the interruptions by businesspeople in 10 countries. The following list is ordered by decreasing numbers of interruptions:

Korea
Germany
France
China
Brazil
Russia
Taiwan
Japan
United Kingdom
United States

This list does not mean that U.S. businesspeople are more polite, but rather that how people show politeness differs from culture to culture. Chinese and Italians (who also interrupt frequently) use interruptions to offer help, jointly construct a conversation, and show eagerness to do business—all of which are polite.

Based on Jan M. Ulijn and Xiangling Li, "Is Interrupting Impolite? Some Temporal Aspects of Turn-Taking in Chinese-Western and Other Intercultural Encounters," *Text* 15, no. 4 (1995): 600, 621.

Body language can give big clues about our attitude to office visitors.

tone (speech) tells us who is expert, or at least well practiced. Such signals are hard to fake, which may explain their influence.[22]

Body language is complicated by the fact that nonverbal signs may have more than one meaning. A frown may signal displeasure or concentration. A stiff posture that usually means your co-worker is upset may today just be a sign of sore back muscles.

Misunderstandings are even more common when people communicate with people from other cultures or other countries. Knowing something about other cultures may help you realize that a subordinate who doesn't meet your eye may be showing respect rather than dishonesty. But it's impossible to memorize every meaning that every nonverbal sign has in every culture. And in a multicultural workforce, you may not know whether someone retains the meanings of his or her ancestors or has adopted the dominant U.S. meanings. The best solution is to ask for clarification.

Networking

A much underappreciated skill in the business environment is **networking,** the ability to connect with many different kinds of people. Most of us can relate to the people in our immediate work group, although even there differences in ability to connect impact performance. But true networking is creating connections with still more people. It involves creating connections before they are needed, creating diverse connections in widely spread areas, knowing which people to turn to when you need additional expertise, knowing people outside the company.

Good networkers know who will help them cut through red tape, who can find an emergency supplier, who will take on extra work in a crisis. Informal conversations, about yesterday's game and Li's photography exhibit as well as what's happening at work, connect them with the **grapevine,** an informal source of company information. Participation in civic, school, religious, and professional organizations connects them to a larger environment. They attend conferences, trade shows, fundraisers, and community events. They use social networking sites such as LinkedIn (see Chapter 9 for more on electronic networks).

Networking becomes even more important as you climb the corporate ladder. Good managers interact with their employees continually, not just when they need something. They listen to lunchroom conversations; they chat with employees over coffee.

Much research shows that networking is crucial to job success. In *Emotional Intelligence,* Daniel Goleman tells of research in a division at Bell Labs to determine what made the star performers in the division. Everyone in the division had a high academic IQ, which meant that IQ was not a good predictor of job productivity (although academic knowledge and IQ are good predictors of success on earlier career ladder rungs). But networking skill was a good predictor. The stars put effort into developing their network, and they cultivated relationships in that network *before* they were needed.[23]

Goleman identifies three different kinds of workplace networks: conversational (who talks to whom), expertise (who can be turned to for advice), and trust (who can be trusted with sensitive information like gripes). Unsurprisingly, the stars of an organization are often heavily networked in all three varieties.[24]

Good networkers share certain interpersonal communication behaviors. They adapt their behavior and attitude to the people around them. They subtly mirror the postures, behaviors, and emotional states of people near them. They share some personal and emotional information about themselves, a sharing that helps build trust. They capitalize on the benefits of physical proximity—trading some phone calls for actual office visits, attending both informal and formal gatherings. One study showed that people with these skills penetrated the center of their workplace network in just 18 months; people lacking in these skills took 13 years.[25]

TIME MANAGEMENT LO 4-4

As your work environment becomes more complex, with multiple networks, responsibilities, and projects, good time management becomes crucial. Although much time management advice sounds like common sense, it is amazing the number of people who do not follow it.

Techniques

Probably the most important time management technique is to prioritize the demands on your time, and make sure you spend the majority of your time on the most important demands. If your career success depends on producing reports, news articles, and press releases about company business, then that is what you need to spend the majority of your time doing.

Randy Pausch, in his highly popular video and book *The Last Lecture,* makes this point about prioritizing most eloquently. His lecture is a moving reminder to make time for friends and family. His colleagues noted that he would regularly tell his students they could always make more money later, but they could never make more time.[26]

In *The 7 Habits of Highly Effective People,* Stephen Covey presents a useful time management matrix which sorts activities by urgency and importance; see Figure 4.5. Obviously we should focus our time on important, urgent activities, but Covey also advises putting significant time into quadrant II, important but nonurgent activities, which he calls the heart of effective management. Quadrant II activities include networking, planning, and preparing.[27]

Authoritative Body Language

Carol Kinsey Goman, author of *The Silent Language of Leaders: How Body Language Can Help—or Hurt—How You Lead,* offers these tips to increase your image of authority:

- Keep your head straight up. Head tilts show concern or interest for individuals, but may be processed as submission signals in power situations.

- Expand your space. Stand tall, spread your elbows a little, widen your stance, and spread your materials on the table at the next meeting. Authority is demonstrated through height and space.

- Use the tonal arc, in which your voice rises in pitch through a sentence but drops back down at the end. Ending on a higher pitch often indicates uncertainty or a need for approval.

- Look serious when the subject is serious. Smiles are frequently inappropriate in power situations.

- Do not nod to express listening or engagement; nodding undercuts authority.

- Minimize movements, especially gestures.

- Have a firm handshake.

Adapted from Carol Kinsey Goman, "10 Common Body Language Traps for Women in the Workplace," *On Leadership* (blog), *Washington Post,* May 2, 2011, http://www.washingtonpost.com/blogs/on-leadership/post/10-common-body-language-traps-for-women-in-the-workplace/2011/03/03/AFI0GFbF_blog.html.

Gossip Networking

Although it has a tarnished reputation, gossip can benefit both individuals and organizations, research shows. Gossiping is a form of networking. According to Joe Labianca, a professor at the University of Kentucky's Center for Research on Social Networks in Business, the more workers gossip, the better their understanding of the work environment and the higher their peers rate their influence. Gossip disseminates valuable information about workers, such as who doesn't do their share or who is impossible to work with.

And guess what? Managers gossip, too. In fact, they may have more "gossip partners" than nonmanagers.

Adapted from Giuseppe Labianca, "It's Not 'Unprofessional' to Gossip at Work," *Harvard Business Review*, (September 2010): 29.

Figure 4.5 Stephen Covey's Time Management Matrix. Covey advises putting significant time into quadrant II.

	Urgent	Not Urgent
Important	I ACTIVITIES: Crises Pressing problems Deadline-driven projects	II ACTIVITIES: Prevention, PC activities Relationship building Recognizing new opportunities Planning, recreation
Not Important	III ACTIVITIES: Interruptions, some calls Some mail, some reports Some meetings Proximate, pressing matters Popular activities	IV ACTIVITIES: Trivia, busy work Some mail Some phone calls Time wasters Pleasant activities

Source: Stephen R. Covey, *The 7 Habits of Highly Effective People: Restoring the Character* (New York: Free Press, 2004), 150–54. Reprinted with permission of the author.

These are some other common tips for time management:

- Keep lists—both daily and long term. Prioritize items on your list.
- Ask yourself where you want to be in three or five years and work accordingly.
- Do large, important tasks first, and then fill in around them with smaller tasks.
- Break large tasks into small ones. Remember that you do not always have to work sequentially. If you have been putting off a report because you cannot decide how to write its introduction, start with the conclusions or some other part that is easy for you to write.
- Find blocks of time: put your phone on answering machine, ignore e-mail, avoid the break room, move discretionary meetings. Put these blocks at your most productive time; save e-mail and meetings for less productive times.
- Avoid time sinks: some people, long phone conversations, constant e-mail checks.
- Decide at the end of today's work session what you will do in tomorrow's session, and set yourself up to do it. Find the necessary file; look up the specifications for that proposal.
- At end of week, evaluate what you didn't get done. Should you have done it for promotion, goodwill, ethics?

Multitasking

Many workers believe they can manage some of their time crunch problems by multitasking. Unfortunately, decades of research on the subject show that this is a false belief. It is particularly false when long-term learning or communication tasks are involved.[28] Just think of all the e-mails that get sent to unintended audiences while the writer is multitasking, or all the phone calls for which the caller, busy multitasking, forgets who is being called or why in the short time between dialing and pickup.

Research shows that when we think we are multitasking, we are really switching back and forth between tasks. And there is always a start-up delay involved in returning to a previous task, no matter how brief the delay. These delays may make it faster to do the tasks sequentially, in which case we will probably do them better, too. In fact, some research shows it can take up to 50% longer to multitask.[29] Other research shows that multitasking hurts overall attention and memory, even when not multitasking.[30]

When we return to a task following an interruption—either from someone else, like a phone call, or from ourselves, like a visit to FaceBook—it may take us close to half an hour to get back into the original task.[31] Sometimes, we do not get back to the task correctly. Pilots who are interrupted in their preflight checklist may miss an item when they return to it. One crash, in which 153 people died, has been blamed on an error resulting from such an interruption.[32]

TRENDS IN BUSINESS COMMUNICATION LO 4-5

Both business and business communication are constantly changing. One of the biggest changes for most people is the shift to electronic communications. This all-encompassing trend is the subject of Chapter 9. Related to this shift are trends in data security and electronic privacy. Other trends are customer service, work/family balance, environmental concern, globalization and outsourcing, diversity, teamwork, job flexibility, innovation and entrepreneurship. As this list of trends suggests, rapid change itself is another major trend in the business environment.

Data Security

As business communication becomes increasingly electronic, concerns about data theft mushroom. Just as individuals take steps—like not providing important identification numbers by e-mail—to prevent identity theft, organizations take steps to protect their data. The need for them to do so becomes always more urgent as hackers continue to produce more sophisticated software. In 2011, Sony reported the theft of names, birthdates, and possibly credit card numbers for 77 million people.[33]

Not all the lost data comes from hackers. Lost or stolen laptops and smart phones containing sensitive data also add to the problem. Flash drives, because of their small size, are an even bigger problem. Corporate security measures include bans on personal electronic devices. Some companies are even disabling extra USB connections to ensure employees cannot attach these devices. Others are performing random checks of laptops to look for unauthorized or unsecured files and using scans of fingerprints, eyes, or faces to limit and track access to specific computers.[34]

Data security problems affect individuals, too. When hackers get names and e-mail addresses, they can send **phishing messages,** e-mails that try to lure receivers to send sensitive information. When hackers can connect the names and addresses to actual firms the readers use, such as banks and stores, the phishing e-mails look so official that even executives and professionals are convinced to respond.

Electronic Privacy

As organizations respond to growing security concerns, their efforts often encroach on workers' privacy. Organizations are monitoring many different kinds

As the Old Song Says, "I Got Rhythm"

One of the newest electronic security methods is keystroke authentication. It turns out that your typing pattern, the pressure of your fingers on the keys and your typing speed, is unique. It allows you to prove electronically that you are who you say you are.

Keystroke patterning has a long history. The military began using it over a hundred years ago to identify individual senders of Morse code by their tapping rhythms. As the location of those senders shifted, military trackers got data on enemy movements.

Currently, the biggest users of keystroke patterning are banks and credit unions, who are employing it in addition to standard password authentication. Since identity theft has become such a major problem, banks and credit unions are under a federal mandate to use stronger authentication measures to protect online customers.

Adapted from Kathleen Kingsbury, "Telltale Fingertips: With Biometrics, How You Type Can Allow Websites to Know Who You Are—Or Aren't," *Time Bonus Section,* January 2007, A10.

Identity theft is such a growing concern that some companies make it the main focus of their business.

of electronic interactions. According to a survey by the American Management Association of 304 companies,

- 73% store and review e-mail.
- 66% monitor Internet usage.
- 65% block inappropriate websites.
- 48% use video surveillance.
- 45% record time spent on phone and numbers dialed.
- 43% store and review computer files.[35]

The same study also showed that 45% track keystrokes (and time spent at the computer). Because of findings from such monitoring, some companies are blocking access to particular websites, especially Facebook, YouTube, sports and online shopping sites. Many organizations claim that heavy usage of these sites slows down company communications such as file transfers and e-mail. In 2009, Senator Chuck Grassley called for a halt of funds to the National Science Foundation after a report was released that found that some employees spent up to 20% of their workday looking at porn instead of reviewing grant proposals.[36]

Other surveillance techniques use GPS (global positioning system) chips to monitor locations of company vehicles, as well as arrival and departure times at job sites. EZ-Pass, the electronic toll collection system, records are being used in courts as proof of infidelity. Workers may tell their spouses they are in a meeting, but EZ-Pass has a record of where and when their vehicle entered or exited that day.[37] Cellphones and computers give approximate location signals that are accurate enough to help law enforcement officials locate suspects.

The division between corporate data security and personal privacy has become increasingly complex and blurry. Corporate surveillance does not necessarily stop when employees leave their offices or cars. It can continue to the company parking areas and even employees' homes. Companies such as Google, Delta Air Lines, and even Burger King have fired workers for content on their personal blogs. Although many workers believe their blogs are protected by the first amendment, the truth is that in most states, companies can fire employees for almost any reason except discrimination.[38]

A survey by the American Management Association found that over a quarter of companies fired employees for e-mail misuse.[39] New technologies make it increasingly easy for companies—and lawyers—to track employees. "E-discovery" software can aid searchers in sorting millions of documents and e-mails in just days to find relevant ones for court cases. They go far beyond finding specific words and terms. In some of the best, if you search for "dog," you will also find documents with "man's best friends" and even the notion of "walk." Other programs can find concepts rather than just key words. Still others look at activities—who did what when, who talked to whom—to extract patterns. They find anomalies, such as switching media from e-mail to phone or a face-to-face communication, or when a document is edited an unusual number of times by unusual people.[40]

Other media are also connected with privacy issues. Some Twitter users have found the hard way that their messages are not private. Paul Chambers lost his job and was convicted of threatening to blow up an airport after sending a joking tweet to his friends.[41] Detroit mayor Kwame Kilpatrick was charged with perjury and forced to resign after text messages he sent were used against him by prosecutors. Embarrassing photos of hapless individuals pepper the web. Employees have also been fired for posting on their personal Facebook site disparaging comments about their employers. And even "old" technology can threaten privacy. Illinois Governor Blagojevich was impeached on the bases of taped phone conversations.

Although more individuals are starting to sue over their firings, and a few are winning, the legal scale is still weighted in favor of employers. In 2010 the Supreme Court ruled that searches on work equipment are reasonable and not a violation of Fourth Amendment rights.

Someone's Watching

The anonymous life exists no more, if it ever did. Now private incidents are constantly being publicized on the Internet. New sites are constantly springing up that allow ordinary citizens to post blogs, comments, pictures, or videos about faux pas ranging from bad driving to leaving doggie droppings. Anyone, from your next door neighbor to the guy sitting next to you on the bus while you are loudly talking on your cellphone, can report a complaint about your social infraction on these websites.

For example, a North Carolina driver found himself accused of reckless driving. Unfortunately, the posting doesn't stop there; readers added the driver's full name and cellphone number. Other "violators" have had home address, occupation, and employer's name posted.

Check out some of these sites:
Platewire.com
Mybikelane.com
Litterbutt.com
Rudepeople.com

How would you feel if one of your actions were deemed obnoxious enough to show up on one of these websites? Do you think the self-policing of these types of websites can really make a difference?

Adapted from Jennifer Saranow, "The Snoop Next Door: Bad Parking, Loud Talking—No Transgression Is Too Trivial to Document Online," *Wall Street Journal*, January 12, 2007, W1.

Some companies are seeking to help individuals protect their privacy by offering services that delete messages and documents from multiple phones at a set time. Users can set an expiration time for their messages, which will be used to delete the messages from their own phones, the recipients' phones, and the messaging service's computer servers.[42] Other companies, for example, allow users to choose what kinds of ads they will see or to opt out altogether. Companies like Microsoft and Mozilla are beginning to include do-not-track features in their popular Internet browsers, to keep advertisers and others from monitoring online habits.[43]

In 2009, the Federal Trade Commission endorsed industry self-regulation to protect consumer privacy. Websites and companies that collect consumer data such as searches performed and websites visited are to (1) clearly notify consumers that they do so, (2) provide an easy way to opt out, (3) protect the data, and (4) limit its retention, but breaches of these guidelines continue to occur.[44]

A highly publicized study by the *Wall Street Journal* of the 50 most popular websites in the United States found that those sites installed 3,180 tracking files on the test computer. Twelve sites, including Dictionary.com, Comcast.net, and MSN.com, installed over 100 tracking tools each. Some tracking files could track sensitive health and financial data; other files could transmit keystrokes; still other files could reattach trackers that a person deleted. Apps on smart phones are performing similar trackings.[45]

Customer Service

One effect of the recession was to push more businesses into focusing on their customer service. Amazon, for instance, is well-known for its mission to be "Earth's most customer centric company." But it is far from alone. Customer satisfaction is increasingly important for all businesses; in fact, it is a leading indicator of financial success.[46] Companies with higher scores on the American Customer Satisfaction Index (ACSI) tend to see better sales and stock performance than do companies with lower scores.[47] In an age where unhappy customers can share their experiences with thousands of web users, focusing on customer satisfaction is vital.

Improving customer service doesn't always mean spending extra money. Companies are learning to cross-train employees, so they can fill in where needed. Other companies are giving extra attention to their best customers to keep them loyal. Walgreens is training its pharmacists to work more closely with patients with chronic illnesses such as diabetes.[48] A tried and true way of improving customer service is increasing the oral communication skills of sales reps and customer service agents.

Work/Family Balance

In addition to improving customer satisfaction, businesses are also focusing on their own employees. To reduce turnover, and increase employee satisfaction, companies are trying to be more family friendly by proving flextime, telecommuting, time off for family needs, and extended career breaks for caregiving. The balance of work and family is becoming such a popular topic that the *Wall Street Journal* now runs a regular column called "Work and Family."

At Cisco, 95% of employees take advantage of flextime, and 90% do some of their work off-site (the average is two days a week). Mothers of young

Many organizations promote virtual offices, which allow employees to work from home.

Santa Letters

Even letters to Santa Claus reflect the wider business environment.

During good times, children tend to ask for everything they see. But tougher economic times are reflected in children's letters. The letters talk of grim topics such as lost jobs and homes. They plead for basic necessities—rent money for mom, diapers for the baby, socks and warm clothing for everyone.

The Chicago main post office alone receives over 12,000 letters to Santa. Employees and volunteers sort them by gender and family size, then put them in the lobby where customers can select a child to help. Hundreds do so.

Adapted from Stacy St. Clair, "Letters to Santa Reflect Reality of Grim Economy: Kids' Requests for Toys Are Replaced with Wishes for Pajamas—or Rent Money for Their Parents," *Des Moines Register*, December 11, 2008, 3A.

children can take extended leave of up to two years, including one with full benefits. Cisco also offers job sharing and some positions that work full-time from home. Microsoft offers in-home sick care for sick children, as well as local centers for mildly ill children.[49]

At times, employees find ways other than physical presence to demonstrate their commitment and enthusiasm for organizational goals. Thanks to technology advances, employees can use laptops, e-mail, or cellphones to do work at any time, including weekends and evenings. The downside of this trend is that sometimes work and family life are not so much balanced as blurred. For instance, many employers are giving portable media players to workers for training courses, language lessons, and general organizational announcements to hear on their own time. Some employees are also expected to conduct business 24-hours a day because of different time zones of workplaces. The flexibility of employees is necessary in an age of downsizing and globalization, but it means that families are being impacted.

Dilbert's company, the one of cartoon fame, no longer uses the phrase work/family balance; instead, it uses "'work-life integration' so it's easier to make you work when you would prefer being with loved ones."[50]

Environmental Concern

As global warming becomes an issue of increasing concern, more and more companies are trying to soften their environmental impact. They do so for a variety of reasons in addition to environmental concerns. Sometimes such awareness saves money; sometimes executives hope it will create favorable publicity for the company. However, many marketing experts say that green advertising is now just standard operating procedure.[51] Environmental activist groups such as Greenpeace and Friends of the Earth go even further. These groups have sharply and publicly criticized some large companies for exaggerating their commitment to the environment. One study claims that 95% of the "green" products it examined made claims that were lies, unsupported by proof, or couched in meaningless language ("all-natural").[52]

Fortune's 2007 list of the 20 most admired companies was organized around environmental awareness. The top companies on it owed a significant part of their growth to strategies and products aimed at helping the environment.

Walmart is boosting its purchase of local, small-farmer grown produce, both domestically and internationally. GE has spent more than $5 billion in research and development for its ecomagination initiative; it has committed itself to an additional $10 billion by 2015. Revenues from its energy-efficient and environmentally sound products and services crossed $18 billion in 2009, almost two times the company average.[53]

Globalization and Outsourcing

In the global economy, importing and exporting are just a start. More and more companies have offices and factories around the world:

- McDonald's serves food in over 119 countries on six continents.[54]
- 3M operates in over 65 countries; 65% of its sales are international.[55]
- UPS serves over 220 countries and territories.[56]
- Coca-Cola sells its beverages in over 200 countries.[57]
- Walmart has 4,600 stores outside the continental United States, including ones in Central America, South America, China, India, and Japan.[58]

Alternate energy has become a leading environmental issue, bringing both business and good publicity to some companies.

McDonald's now serves food in China.

The site of the store, factory, or office may not be the site of all the jobs. A data center in Washington can support many workers in India as businesses are outsourcing domestically and globally. **Outsourcing** means going outside the company for products and services that once were produced by the company's employees. Companies can outsource technology services, customer service, tax services, legal services, accounting services, benefit communications, manufacturing, and marketing. Outsourcing is often a win–win solution: the company saves money or gets better service, and the outsourcers make a profit. In *The World Is Flat*, Thomas Friedman says "the accountant who wants to stay in business in America will be the one who focuses on designing creative, complex strategies. . . . It means having quality-time discussions with clients."[59] He sees the work of the future as customization, innovation, service, and problem solving.[60]

All the challenges of communicating in one culture and country increase exponentially when people communicate across cultures and countries. Succeeding in a global market requires **intercultural competence,** the ability to communicate sensitively with people from other cultures and countries, based on an understanding of cultural differences. To learn more about international communication, see Chapter 7.

Diversity

Women, people of color, and immigrants have always been part of the U.S. workforce. But for most of this country's history, they were relegated to clerical, domestic, or menial jobs. Now, U.S. businesses realize that barriers to promotion hurt the bottom line as well as individuals. Success depends on using the brains and commitment as well as the hands and muscles of every worker.

In the last decade, we have also become aware of other sources of diversity beyond those of gender, race, and country of origin: age, religion, class,

Team Communication Saves Lives

Communication break-downs during patient transfers between units or person-nel shifts are the largest source of medical error. The hospital accred-itation board is now requiring hos-pitals to establish standards for transfer communications. To help hospitals, the Institute for Health-care Improvement is working with hospitals on a communication rubric known as SBAR:

- Situation: describe briefly, get attention.
- Background: offer enough to provide context for the problem.
- Assessment: your assess-ment of overall condition.
- Recommendation: your spe-cific recommendations.

Kaiser Permanente, the large health care organization, pio-neered using the model, which helps doctors and nurses convey the most critical information in just 60 seconds. The model increases communication between doctors who don't want nurses' opinions and nurses who are reluctant to provide their opinions.

One Kaiser physician adminis-trator says, "In almost all serious avoidable episodes of patient harm, communication failure plays a central role. . . . By teach-ing caregivers new models of 'structured communication',. . . we can make sure that we are all in the same movie."

Adapted from Laura Landro, "Hospi-tals Combat Errors at the 'Hand-Off': New Procedures Aim to Reduce Mis-cues as Nurses and Doctors Transfer Patients to Next Shift," *Wall Street Journal*, June 28, 2006, D1, D2.

regional differences, sexual orientation, and physical disabilities are now areas of diversity. Helping each worker reach his or her potential requires more flexibility from managers as well as more knowledge about intercultural communication. And it's crucial to help workers from different backgrounds understand each other—especially in today's global economy. To learn more about diversity and the workforce, read Chapter 7.

Teamwork

More and more companies are getting work done through teams. Teamwork brings together people's varying strengths and talents to solve problems and make decisions. Often, teams are cross-functional (drawing from different jobs or functions) or cross-cultural (including people from different nations or cultural groups served by the company).

Teams, including cross-functional teams, helped Sarasota Memorial Hospital resolve major problems with customer and employee satisfaction. For example, team members from the emergency room recorded every step in the process from pulling into the parking lot through decisions about patient care, and then they eliminated unnecessary steps. The ER team worked with the laboratory staff to improve the process of getting test results. At Michelin, the French tire maker, teams bring together people from the United States and Europe. According to the company's chemical purchasing manager for Europe, the exchange between the two continents helps employees on both sides of the Atlantic understand each other's per-spectives and needs.[61]

Increasing emphasis on teamwork is a major reason given by organizations such as AT&T, Intel, Hewlett-Packard, and the U.S. Interior Department for calling telecommuting workers back to the office.[62] To learn more about work-ing in teams, see Chapter 8.

Job Flexibility

In traditional jobs, people did what they were told to do. But today, jobs that are routine can readily be done in other countries at lower cost. Many U.S. jobs have already been subject to such "offshoring," and more are sure to follow. The work that remains in the United States is more likely to be complex work requiring innovation, flexibility, and adaptation to new learning.

Today's workers do whatever needs to be done, based on the needs of cus-tomers, colleagues, and anyone else who depends on their work. They help team members finish individual work; they assist office mates with pressing deadlines. They are resourceful: they know how to find information and solu-tion ideas. They work extra hours when the task demands it. They are ready to change positions and even locations when asked to do so. They need new skill sets even when they don't change jobs.

At Sarasota Memorial Hospital, food service workers do more than bring food to patients; they open containers, resolve problems with meals, help patients read their menus, and adjust orders to meet patients' preferences. This attentiveness not only serves the patients; it is part of a team-spirited approach to patient care that in this case frees nurses to do other work.[63] The experience at Sarasota Memorial is backed up by research suggesting that the most effective workers don't see work as assigned tasks. Instead, they define their own goals based on the needs of customers and clients.[64]

Your parents may have worked for the same company all their lives. You may do that, too, but you have to be prepared to job-hunt throughout your career. That means continuing to learn—keeping up with new technologies, new economic and political realities, new ways of interacting with people.

Innovation and Entrepreneurship

As global competition increases, and industrial milieus change ever more quickly, innovation becomes more and more important. *Fortune*'s 2008 list of most admired companies was organized around innovation. Apple, at the top of the list, also got the top marks for innovation.

Many companies rely on all employees for suggestions. A classic article in the *Harvard Business Review* made famous the examples of 3M (where researchers can spend 15% of their time on ideas that don't need management approval), Thermo Electron (where managers can "spin out" promising new businesses), and Xerox (where employees write business proposals competing for corporate funds to develop new technologies).[65] 3M also sends 9,000 employees, in 35 countries, into customers' workplaces to work beside people there and to note problems the company can solve. American Express established a $50 million innovation fund to finance employees' ideas.[66] Google is famous for its 20% rule: technical employees can spend about 20% of their time on projects outside their main job, and even their managers cannot remove that free margin.[67]

The spirit of innovation is inspiring some workers to start their own businesses. The U.S. Census Bureau counted 21.4 million nonemployer businesses (self-employed workers without employees) in 2008.[68] In fact, these businesses are the majority of all U.S. businesses. These entrepreneurs have to handle all the communication in the business: hiring, training, motivating, and evaluating employees; responding to customer complaints; drafting surveys; writing business plans; making presentations to venture capitalists; and marketing the product or service.

Rapid Rate of Change

As any employee who has watched his or her job shift can testify, change—even change for the better—is stressful. Even when change promises improvements, people have to work to learn new skills, new habits, and new attitudes.

Rapid change means that no college course or executive MBA program can teach you everything you need to know for the rest of your working life. You'll need to stay abreast of professional changes by reading trade journals as well as professional websites and blogs, participating in professional Listservs, and attending professional events. Take advantage of your company's training courses and materials; volunteer for jobs that will help you gain new skills and knowledge. Pay particular attention to your communication skills; they become even more important as you advance up your career ladder. A survey of 1,400 financial executives found that 75% considered oral, written, and interpersonal skills even more important for finance professionals now than they were just a few years ago.[69]

The skills you polish along the way can stand you in good stead for the rest of your life: critical thinking, computer savvy, problem solving, and the ability to write, speak, and work well with other people are vital in most jobs. It's almost a cliché, but it is still true: the most important knowledge you gain in college is how to learn.

World-Class Innovation

Ideo, the world-famous design consulting firm, has over 1,000 patents and 346 design awards. Their message to the world is that creativity is not a burst of inspiration but rather a teachable process—understand, observe, brainstorm, prototype—that can be incorporated into businesses of all sizes.

One of their clients, the giant health care provider Kaiser Permanente, now has its own innovation center that follows the Ideo way. That center tackled the all-too-common problem of medication errors, errors that harm more than 1.5 million people in the United States alone. A team shadowed doctors, nurses, and pharmacists as they prescribed, administered, and filled medications. They made videos; they kept journals. And they discovered that interruptions were the cause of most errors. So the team brainstormed solutions, including "Leave Me Alone!" aprons and red "Do Not Cross!" lines in front of medication stations. The program has reduced interruptions by 50%.

Adapted from Linda Tischler, "A Designer Takes On His Biggest Challenge Ever," *Fast Company*, February 2009, 78–83, 101.

SUMMARY OF KEY POINTS

- The economic news continues to create concern over lapses in business ethics. On the other hand, positive ethical efforts are also increasing.
- Corporate cultures range from informal to formal and impact such widely diverse areas as worker performance and sales.

■ Interpersonal communication includes such areas as listening, conversational style, body language, and networking. Its importance in career success is receiving new recognition.

■ Time management skills are also crucial to job success. Probably the most important time management technique is to prioritize the demands on your time, and make sure you spend the majority of your time on the most important demands.

■ Decades of research on multitasking show that it does not increase job performance and may actually hinder it.

■ Eleven trends in business, government, and nonprofit organizations affect business and administrative communication: data security, electronic privacy, customer service, work/family balance, environmental concern, globalization and outsourcing, diversity, teamwork, job flexibility, innovation and entrepreneurship, and rapid change.

CHAPTER 4   Exercises and Problems

Go to www.mhhe.com/locker/10e for additional Exercises and Problems.

4.1   Reviewing the Chapter

1. What are some positive ethical efforts that are getting attention? (LO 4-1)

2. What are some ethical components of communication? (LO 4-1)

3. What are some elements of corporate culture? How do they affect business? (LO 4-2)

4. What are some ways to improve interpersonal communication? (LO 4-3)

5. What are some communication signals you might receive from specific body language cues? (LO 4-3)

6. What are some ways to manage your time more efficiently? (LO 4-4)

7. What are 11 trends in business communication? What do these trends mean for you? (LO 4-5)

8. What are some electronic privacy issues that could affect you at your workplace? (LO 4-5)

4.2   Protecting Privacy Online

As companies demand ever-more accurate audiences to whom they can pitch their products and services, the debate over online tracking vs. privacy continues.

Working in small groups, discuss some of the challenges you see to protecting your privacy on the Internet.

■ Should companies be allowed to track your online activity? Is it OK if they notify you they are tracking you? Do you like targeted placement ads, similar to Google's recommendations for you? Where do you find a balance between allowing Internet sites to use your information to provide better service and protecting your privacy?

■ Are employers justified in monitoring employees' e-mail, Twitter, and Internet usage on company machines?

■ Are employers justified in monitoring employees' Facebook accounts? Do you think it is fair when employees get fired for comments they post on their Facebook site?

■ What do you think of companies like Google tracking searches to produce sites like Google Flu Trends, which shows where people are getting sick during flu season?

4.3   Following Trends in Business Communication

Pick three of the trends discussed in this chapter and explain how they have impacted business communications in an organization where you—or a friend or family member—have worked.

As your instructor directs,

a. Share your information in small groups.

b. Present your group findings to your classmates.

c. Post your information online for your classmates.

4.4 Applying Ethics Guidelines

Reread the ethics guidelines by Warren Buffett (sidebar on page 93) and Tony Hsieh (end of Ethics section). In small groups, apply them to some business ethics situations currently in the news.

- How would the situations be handled by Buffett? Hsieh?

- Do you approve of those solutions?
- Do you find one statement more helpful than the other? Why?

4.5 Making Ethical Choices

Indicate whether you consider each of the following actions ethical, unethical, or a gray area. Which of the actions would you do? Which would you feel uncomfortable doing? Which would you refuse to do?

Discuss your answers with a small group of classmates. In what ways did knowing you would share with a group change your answers?

1. Taking home office supplies (e.g., pens, markers, calculators, etc.) for personal use.
2. Inflating your evaluation of a subordinate because you know that only people ranked *excellent* will get pay raises.
3. Making personal long-distance calls on the company phone.
4. Updating your Facebook page and visiting the pages of friends during business hours.
5. Writing a feasibility report about a new product and de-emphasizing test results that show it could cause cancer.
6. Coming in to the office in the evening to use the company's computer for personal projects.

7. Designing an ad campaign for a cigarette brand.
8. Working as an accountant for a company that makes or advertises cigarettes.
9. Working as a manager in a company that exploits its nonunionized hourly workers.
10. Writing copy for a company's annual report hiding or minimizing the fact that the company pollutes the environment.
11. "Padding" your expense account by putting on it charges you did not pay for.
12. Telling a job candidate that the company "usually" grants cost-of-living raises every six months, even though you know that the company is losing money and plans to cancel cost-of-living raises for the next year.
13. Laughing at the racist or sexist jokes a client makes, even though you find them offensive.
14. Reading the *Wall Street Journal* on company time.

4.6 Analyzing Business Ethics

New Oriental Education & Technology Group offers Chinese students intensive courses to prepare for SAT, GRE, and TOEFL exams. The object of the courses is to enable their students to achieve scores that will get them into American colleges and universities. The courses provide traditional prep help, such as cramming vocabulary words, but they also offer more controversial techniques.

- They avail themselves of websites where students download the test questions they remember immediately after the exam. Since the tests do recycle some questions to ensure score consistency over time, they can prep students for actual exam questions.
- They provide tricks (e.g., females in the test passages are always smarter than males) that help students choose correct answers just by looking at the choices, without understanding the passages.

- Since many of their students are good at math, they recommend that five minutes into the math section, their students should flip back to the reading and finish it. Flipping is prohibited, but this timing helps students escape the attention of the proctors, who look for it at the beginning and end of each test section.
- They help students prepare essays and speeches on topics—such as biographies of famous Americans, that can be memorized and adapted to many situations, thus avoiding extemporaneous performances.

The upside of their efforts is that many of their students do fulfill dreams of getting into American schools. The downside is that many of these same students have such poor English skills that they cannot understand the lectures or participate in class discussions. Nor can they write class papers without help. Unfortunately, they score so well that they even sometimes test out of the transitional programs many schools have to help students with shaky English skills.

Is New Oriental an ethical business?

What would Warren Buffett say (see pg. 93)?

What would Tony Hsieh say (see end of Ethics section)?

What are New Oriental's effects on its students?

Why do American schools accept these students?

What could be done to make the situation more ethical?

Source: Daniel Golden, "U.S. College Test Prep in China Is: [sic]" *Bloomberg Businessweek,* May 9, 2011, 58–63.

4.7   Analyzing Philanthropic Websites

Working in small groups, go to the websites of some of the large philanthropic organizations such as the Gates Foundation, Google.org, or the Clinton Global Initiative. What commonalities do you see? Which aspects do you like best? If you were a rich multibillionaire who was going to leave a billion dollars to a philanthropy, which one would you choose? Why? Write your findings and answers to these questions in a memo to share with your class.

4.8   Analyzing Pro Bono Work

Pro bono legal work, free legal work for those in need, has long been a law tradition. But now some elite firms are so eager for pro bono work—to boost their image or ranking, to get high-profile cases, and to attract top law students—that they are paying for it.

- What do you think of organizations that charge law firms to do pro bono work?

- What do you think of law firms that do pro bono work just to boost their image or ranking? Does their motivation matter?
- When law firms pay to work on high-profile cases, what happens to welfare cases, landlord–tenant disputes, or divorce cases among poorer couples?

Discuss your answers in small groups.

4.9   Analyzing a Letter

Dr. Joseph Biederman, Professor of Psychiatry at Harvard Medical School and Chief of Clinical and Research Programs in Pediatric Psychopharmacology and Adult ADHD, wrote a letter to the editor of the *Wall Street Journal* that appeared December 19, 2008, on page A16. The letter reputes the claim that he had a significant relationship with pharmaceutical manufacturers. Find the letter in your library's electronic copy of the *Wall Street Journal.* (In ProQuest, the letter is listed under the title "I was Doing the Right Thing." Authors of letters to the editor are listed as Anonymous in ProQuest.)

For a memo to your instructor, analyze the letter.

- What was your first impression?
- Is the letter convincing to you?
- What part makes you most sympathetic to the doctor?
- Is there any part that works against the doctor?
- Who are the audiences?
- What is the purpose of the letter?

After you analyze the letter as it is, look up some articles about Dr. Biederman. Three that appeared in the *Wall Street Journal,* including the one referenced in the letter, are

- David Armstrong, "Harvard Researchers Fail To Report Drug Payments," *Wall Street Journal,* June 9, 2008, A2.
- David Armstrong and Alicia Mundy, "J&J Emails Raise Issues of Risperdal Promotion," *Wall Street Journal,* November 25, 2008, B1.
- Jennifer Levitz, "Drug Researcher Agrees to Curb Role," *Wall Street Journal,* December 31, 2008, B3.

Do these articles change your opinion of the letter? Why?

Include both parts of your analysis, of the letter itself and the impact of the articles, in a memo to your instructor.

4.10   Analyzing Corporate Culture

Some businesses are deciding not to hire people with visible body art. Do you think such policies are allowable expressions of corporate culture, or are they a form of discrimination? Discuss your answers in small groups.

4.11   Analyzing Corporate Culture

Go to *Fortune*'s 100 Best Companies to Work For website: http://money.cnn.com/magazines/fortune/bestcompanies/2011/full_list/.

Look up six companies you find interesting. What are unique features of their corporate culture? What features seem to be common with many companies? Which features did you find particularly appealing? Write up your findings in a memo for your instructor.

4.12   Analyzing Customer Service

Go to a business on campus or in your community where you can observe customer service for a half hour. Make sure you observe at least three different kinds of service.

- Where did you go? Why?
- What categories of service did you observe?
- What examples of good service did you see?

- What examples of service that could be improved did you see? How would you improve it?
- If you were the manager of the business, what changes would you make to impact customer service?

Write up your findings in a memo to your instructor.

4.13   Analyzing Nonverbal Communication

Choose one of your courses and make notes on nonverbal communications you see in the classroom.

- What are some dominant traits you see among the students?
- What are some interesting behaviors you see in individual students?
- Does the nonverbal communication differ from the beginning and end of the class?

- What are nonverbal communications from the instructor?
- Overall, what does the nonverbal communication in the classroom tell you about student learning in that class?

Write up your findings in a memo to your instructor.

4.14   Analyzing Body Language

Go to a location such as your campus or city library where you can watch people at work and rest. Spend a half hour observing examples of body language around you. Make sure your half hour includes examples of at least one group at work, individuals at work, and individuals relaxing.

- What were some interesting examples of body language you noted?
- What were some common features of body language?

- Did you see any unique body language?
- Could you make assumptions about group relations based on the body language you saw exhibited by members of the group?
- How did the body language of individuals who were relaxing differ from that of the group members?

Write up your findings in a memo for your instructor.

4.15   Analyzing Your Time Management

For two days, write down exactly how you spend your time. Be specific. Don't just say "two hours studying." Instead, note how long you spent on each item of study (e.g., 15 min. reviewing underlinings in sociology chapter, 20 min. reviewing class notes, an hour and 20 min. reading accounting chapter). Include time spent on items such as grooming, eating, talking with friends (both in person and on phone), texting, watching television, and sleeping.

Now analyze your time record. Does anything surprise you? How much time did you spend studying?

Is it enough? Did you spend more time studying your most important subjects? Your hardest subjects? Did you spend time on projects that are due later in the term? Did you spend time on health-related items? Do you see items on which you spent too much time? Too little time? Did you spend any time on items that would fit in Covey's quadrant II (see page 100)?

As your instructor directs,

a.   Share your findings in small groups.

b.   Write up your findings in a memo for your instructor.

4.16   Analyzing the Business Environment Where You Work

In a memo to your instructor, describe and analyze the business environment at an organization where you have worked. Use this chapter as a guide for content. What

aspects of the environment did you like? Dislike? What aspects helped your job performance? What aspects hindered your job performance?

4.17   Participating in a Networking Event

In this exercise, you are going to participate in a networking event, an abbreviated "talk and walk."

To prepare for the event,

- Prepare business cards for yourself, using a computer application of your choice.
- Prepare a list of people in your class that you would like to meet (give a visual description if you do not know their names).
- Prepare a list of questions you would like to have answered.
- Collect materials to use for taking notes during the event.

During the event, you will have six three-minute sessions to talk with a fellow student. Your instructor will time the sessions and tell you when to change people.

After the event, analyze what you have learned. Here are some questions to get you started:

- Who was the most interesting? Why?
- Who did you like the most? Why?
- Who would you most like to have on a team in this class? Why?
- Did you meet anyone who might become a professional contact? Explain.
- What lessons did you learn about networking?

As your instructor directs,

- Share your analyses in small groups; then prepare an informal oral report for the class.
- Write up your analysis in a memo to your teacher.
- Write up your analysis in a memo to post on your class website.

CHAPTER

11

CHAPTER

Crafting Persuasive Messages

Chapter Outline

NEWSWORTHY COMMUNICATION

Bet You Watch This Safety Video

Most airline passengers ignore the pre-flight safety presentation, where the flight crew details important procedures in case of emergency. Even though the information is vital, the presentation is standard and routine.

New Zealand's national airline is uniquely persuading its passengers to watch the safety presentation: the company filmed its safety video with the crew members

"New Zealand's national airline is uniquely persuading its passengers to watch the safety presentation."

wearing nothing but skin-painted uniforms. The saucy video uses safety equipment to protect the actors' privacy. The safety video is complemented by television commercials for the airline that feature a new slogan: "At Air New Zealand, our fares have nothing to hide."

New Zealand's approach got plenty of attention. In the first four days after its release, it had more than 1 million views on YouTube.

Source: Adapted from "New Zealand Safety Video Bares Painted Plane Crew," *Des Moines Register*, July 4, 2009, 4A.

Learning Objectives

After studying this chapter, you will know how to

LO 11-1   Analyze a persuasive situation.

LO 11-2   Identify basic persuasive strategies.

LO 11-3   Write persuasive direct requests.

LO 11-4   Write persuasive problem-solving messages.

LO 11-5   Write sales and fund-raising messages.

LO 11-6   Use rational and emotional appeals to support persuasive messages.

Persuasion is almost universal in good business communications. If you are giving people information, you are persuading them to consider it good information, or to remember it, or even to use it. If you are giving people negative news, you are trying to persuade them to accept it. If you work for a company, you are a "sales representative" for it. Your job depends on its success.

Some messages, however, seem more obviously persuasive to us than others. Employees try to persuade their supervisors to institute flex hours or casual Fridays; supervisors try to persuade workers to keep more accurate records, thus reducing time spent correcting errors; or to follow healthier lifestyles, thus reducing health benefit costs. You may find yourself persuading your colleagues to accept your ideas, your staff to work overtime on a rush project, and your boss to give you a raise.

Whether you're selling safety equipment or ideas, effective persuasion is based on accurate logic, effective emotional appeal, and credibility or trust. Reasons have to be ones the audience finds important; emotional appeal is based on values the audience cares about; credibility depends on your character and reputation.

Persuasive messages include requests, proposals and recommendations, sales and fund-raising messages, job application letters, and efforts to change people's behavior, such as collection letters, criticisms or performance appraisals where you want the subordinate to improve behavior, and public-service ads designed to reduce drunk driving, drug use, and so on. Reports are persuasive messages if they recommend action.

This chapter gives general guidelines for persuasive messages. Chapter 17 discusses proposals; reports are the subject of Chapter 18. Chapter 13 covers job application letters.

All persuasive messages have several purposes:

Primary purpose:
- To have the audience act or change beliefs.

Secondary purposes:
- To build a good image of the communicator.
- To build a good image of the communicator's organization.
- To cement a good relationship between the communicator and audience.
- To overcome any objections that might prevent or delay action.
- To reduce or eliminate future communication on the same subject so the message doesn't create more work for the communicator.

ANALYZING PERSUASIVE SITUATIONS LO 11-1

Choose a persuasive strategy based on your answers to five questions. Use these questions to analyze persuasive situations:

1. What do you want people to do?
2. What objections, if any, will the audience have?
3. How strong is your case?
4. What kind of persuasion is best for the situation?
5. What kind of persuasion is best for the organization and the culture?

1. What Do You Want People to Do?

Identify the specific action you want and the person who has the power to do it. If your goal requires several steps, specify what you want your audience to do *now*. For instance, your immediate goal may be to have people come to a meeting or let you make a presentation, even though your long-term goal is a major sale or a change in policy.

2. What Objections, If Any, Will the Audience Have?

If you're asking for something that requires little time, money, or physical effort and for an action that's part of the person's regular duties, the audience is likely to have few objections.

Often, however, that is not the case, and you'll encounter some resistance. People may be busy and have what they feel are more important things to do. They may have other uses for their time and money. To be persuasive, you need to show your audience that your proposal meets their needs; you need to overcome any objections.

The easiest way to learn about objections your audience may have is to ask. Particularly when you want to persuade people in your own organization or

Giving Water

Without access to clean water, many people in Africa and Asia struggle with disease and unsanitary conditions. Scott Harrison has made it his mission to provide clean water to as many people as possible. Through his organization, called charity: water, he has given access to clean water to nearly 1 million people, with the help of thousands of individual donors. The organization's success depends on its successful marketing, which is built on three principles:

1. *All money from new donors goes directly into providing water.* Harrison asks only his top supporters to cover administrative costs.

2. *Donors can track their donation's impact.* The organization lets donors name wells and see their location on Google Earth.

3. *Use social media and new media.* Harrison's organization has raised over a million dollars through Twitter and other Internet media. Entertaining web videos and creative social media campaigns garner extensive support.

So far, charity: water has raised over 10 million dollars; it is continuing to gain support from around the world.

Adapted from Nicholas D. Kristof, "Clean, Sexy Water," *New York Times*, July 11, 2009, http://www.nytimes.com/2009/07/12/opinion/12kristof.html.

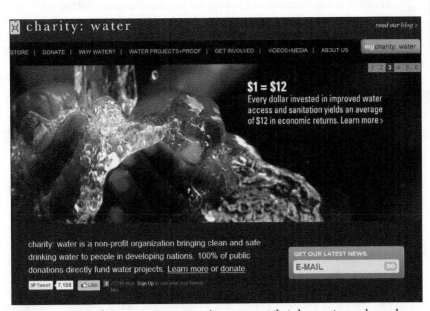

Charity: water's website presents a persuasive argument that clean water can be made available for millions of people.

316   Part 3   Basic Business Messages

Men's Health

Real men don't ask for directions and they certainly don't go to the doctor. These old stereotypes may have some truth in them. One study found that only 57% of men have visited the doctor in the past year, while 74% of women have. The federal government's Agency for Healthcare Research and Quality is trying to persuade more men to get health care with a series of humorous newspaper and television ads.

The ads, which can be viewed online at www.ahrq.gov/healthymen/, use dark humor to show how timely medical care can prevent serious diseases and early death. In one ad, a real estate broker tells a family they will have many happy years in their new home, but then turns to the father and tells him that he will die in three years from a preventable disease. She adds that it could have been detected early with a simple test, but he didn't get the test.

Other ads in the series feature men participating in weddings, graduations, and other family activities wearing hospital gowns. The messages, entitled "Real Men Wear Gowns," encourage men to get regular checkups and testing to benefit them and their families.

Adapted from Laura Landro, "New Ads Try to Shock Men into Going to See the Doctor," *Wall Street Journal*, June 15, 2010, D3.

your own town, talk to knowledgeable people. Phrase your questions nondefensively, in a way that doesn't lock people into taking a stand on an issue: "What concerns would you have about a proposal to do *x?*" "Who makes a decision about *y?*" "What do you like best about [the supplier or practice you want to change]?" Ask follow-up questions to be sure you understand: "Would you be likely to stay with your current supplier if you could get a lower price from someone else? Why?"

People are likely to be most aware of and willing to share objective concerns such as time and money. They will be less willing to tell you that their real objection is emotional. People have a **vested interest** in something if they benefit directly from keeping things as they are. People who are in power have a vested interest in retaining the system that gives them their power. Someone who designed a system has a vested interest in protecting that system from criticism. To admit that the system has faults is to admit that the designer made mistakes. In such cases, you'll need to probe to find out what the real reasons are.

Whether your audience is inside or outside your organization, they will find it easier to say *yes* when you ask for something that is consistent with the person's self-image.

3. How Strong Is Your Case?

The strength of your case is based on three aspects of persuasion: argument, credibility, and emotional appeal.

Argument refers to the reasons or logic you offer. Sometimes you may be able to prove conclusively that your solution is best. Sometimes your reasons may not be as strong, the benefits may not be as certain, and obstacles may be difficult or impossible to overcome. For example, suppose that you wanted to persuade your organization to offer a tuition reimbursement plan for employees. You'd have a strong argument if you could show that tuition reimbursement would improve the performance of marginal workers or that reimbursement would be an attractive recruiting tool in a tight job market. However, if dozens of fully qualified workers apply for every opening you have, your argument would be weaker. The program might be nice for workers, but you'd have a hard job proving that it would help the company.

Some arguments are weakened by common errors known as logical **fallacies.** These are some common types of logical fallacies:[1]

- *Hasty generalization.* Making general assumptions based on limited evidence. "Most of my friends agree that the new law is a bad idea. Americans do not support this law."
- *False cause.* Assuming that because one event follows another, the first event caused the second. "In the 1990s farmers increased their production of corn for ethanol. Soon after, more Americans began using ethanol fuel in their cars."
- *Weak analogy.* Making comparisons that don't work. "Outlawing guns because they kill people is like outlawing cars because they kill people."
- *Appeal to authority.* Quoting from a famous person who is not really an expert. "Hollywood actor Joe Gardner says this hand mixer is the best on the market today."
- *Appeal to popularity.* Arguing that because many people believe something, it is true. "Thousands of Americans doubt the reality of climate change, so climate change must not be happening."

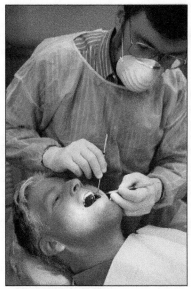

As the recession affected professionals, even dentists increased their sales messages—using e-mails, phone calls, and tweets in addition to their postcard reminders—to persuade their patients to keep coming for dental appointments.

Source: Maureen Scarpelli, "Dentists Step Up Marketing as Patients Skip Their Visits," *Wall Street Journal*, August 11, 2009, B5.

- *Appeal to ignorance.* Using lack of evidence to support the conclusion. "There's nothing wrong in the plant; all the monitors are in the safety zone."
- *False dichotomy.* Setting up the situation to look like there are only two choices. "If you are not with us, you are against us."

Credibility is the audience's response to you as the source of the message. Credibility in the workplace has three sources: expertise, image, and relationships.[2] Citing experts can make your argument more credible. In some organizations, workers build credibility by getting assigned to high-profile teams. You build credibility by your track record. The more reliable you've been in the past, the more likely people are to trust you now.

We are also more likely to trust people we know. That's one reason that new CEOs make a point of visiting as many branch offices as they can. Building a relationship with someone—even if the relationship is based on an outside interest, like sports or children—makes it easier for that person to see you as an individual and to trust you.

When you don't yet have the credibility that comes from being an expert or being powerful, build credibility by the language and strategy you use:

- **Be factual.** Don't exaggerate. If you can test your idea ahead of time, do so, and report the results. Facts about your test are more convincing than opinions about your idea.
- **Be specific.** If you say "X is better," show in detail *how* it is better. Show the audience exactly where the savings or other benefits come from so that it's clear that the proposal really is as good as you say it is.
- **Be reliable.** If you suspect that a project will take longer to complete, cost more money, or be less effective than you originally thought, tell your audience *immediately*. Negotiate a new schedule that you can meet.

Emotional appeal means making the audience *want* to do what you ask. People don't make decisions—even business decisions—based on logic alone. As John Kotter and Holger Rathgeber, authors of the popular business book *Our Iceberg Is Melting*, found, "feelings often trump thinking."[3] Jonah Lehrer, author of *How We Decide*, goes a step further. He offers research that shows people make better decisions—ones that satisfy them better—about large purchases such as a couch when they followed their emotions: "The process of thinking requires feeling, for feelings are what let us understand all the information that we can't directly comprehend. Reason without emotion is impotent."[4]

De Tijd, a Belgian business newspaper, won a European Marketing Council award for its emotional appeal to get human resource managers to use its pension brochure. Every manager who published a job ad in the newspaper received a handwritten letter from Cyriel, age 84, applying for the position. The message on the last page of Cyriel's application read, "Save your employees from having to do like Cyriel: to look for a job when they retire. Offer your employees our brochure." Sales of the brochure increased 24%.[5]

4. What Kind of Persuasion Is Best for the Situation?

Different kinds of people require different kinds of persuasion. What works for your boss may not work for your colleague. But even the same person may require different kinds of persuasion in different situations. Many people who make rational decisions at work do not do so at home, where they may decide to smoke and overeat even though they know smoking and obesity contribute to many deaths.

For years, companies have based their persuasion techniques on the idea that money is most people's primary motivator. And sometimes it is, of course. How many people buy an extra item to reach the $25 amount for free shipping at Amazon? But research in the last decade has shown that people are also motivated by other factors, including competition and community perceptions. Utility companies, for example, have found that people are more likely to conserve energy if they see how their use compares to their neighbors' use. And patients are more likely to take their medications regularly if there is a system to notify doctors or family members when they do. These factors, derived from behavioral economics, open up new ways to persuade people to act.[6]

Even when money is the motivator, companies are beginning to use it differently, especially when trying to persuade their employees to lead healthier lives. Many of these new techniques stem from **behavioral economics,** a branch of economics that uses insights from sociology and psychology. It finds that people often behave irrationally, although still predictably, and not in their own best interests. Techniques include lotteries and short-term financial incentives. Employees who enroll in weight-loss or smoking-cessation programs and stick with them might be eligible for a daily lottery (people tend to give greater weight to the small probability of a lottery than to the much larger probability of long-term health improvements from a healthier lifestyle) or a regular series of payments (people tend to value short-term benefits over long-term health improvements). Capitalizing on the well-known aversion to loss, companies are also asking employees in such programs to put a dollar or two each day into the program. Employees who meet their goals get their money back plus matching funds.[7]

In *Drive: The Surprising Truth about What Motivates Us,* Daniel Pink summarizes decades of research that shows many businesses are using the wrong kinds of persuasion on their employees who do knowledge work,

work that demands sophisticated understanding, flexible problem solving, and creativity. According to this research, once basic levels of financial fairness are reached, "carrot" motivators, such as financial ones, do not work for employees who are expected to be innovative. In fact, carrot motivators will actually decrease innovation; they turn creative work into drudgery.

"Stick" motivators, in the form of ill-chosen goals, are also harmful and can lead to unethical and illegal behavior. Managers hit short-term goals to get performance bonuses, even when they know the short-term goals will cause long-term problems. Sears set sales quotas on its auto repair personnel, who then made national news by overcharging and performing unnecessary repairs. Mortgage issuers offered financial incentives for new mortgages, which got offered to people who could not afford them, leading to a worldwide recession.

So what does motivate knowledge workers? Pink says it is three drives: "our deep-seated desire to direct our own lives, to expend and expand our abilities, and to live a life of purpose."[8]

5. What Kind of Persuasion Is Best for the Organization and the Culture?

A strategy that works in one organization may not work somewhere else. One **corporate culture** may value no-holds-barred aggressiveness. In another organization with different cultural values, an employee who used a hard-sell strategy for a request would antagonize people.

Organizational culture (see Chapter 2) isn't written down; it's learned by imitation and observation. What style do high-level people in your organization use to persuade? When you show a draft to your boss, are you told to tone down your statements or to make them stronger? Role models and advice are two ways organizations communicate their culture to newcomers.

Different kinds of persuasion also work for different **social cultures.** In North Carolina, police are using a new combination to persuade drug dealers to shut down. The combination includes iron-clad cases against the dealers, but also pressure from loved ones—mothers, grandmothers, mentors—along with a second chance. Texas used a famous antilitter campaign based on the slogan "Don't Mess with Texas." Research showed the typical Texas litterer was 18–35, male, a pickup driver, and a lover of sports and country music. He did not respond to authority (Don't litter) or cute owls (Give a hoot; don't pollute). Instead, the campaign aimed to convince this target audience that people like him did not pollute. Ads featured Texan athletes and musicians making the point that Texans don't litter. The campaign was enormously successful: during its first five years, Texas roadside litter decreased 72% and roadside cans 81%.[9] The campaign is still going 25 years later.[10]

What counts for "evidence" also varies by culture. In general, people count a scientist as an expert only when that scientist agrees with a position held by most of those who share their cultural values. This remains true even if the scientist got a degree from a major university, is on the faculty at another major university, and is a member of the National Academy of Sciences.[11]

Different **native cultures** also have different preferences for gaining compliance. In one study, students who were native speakers of American English judged direct statements ("Do this"; "I want you to do this") clearer and more effective than questions ("Could you do this?") or hints ("This is needed"). Students who were native speakers of Korean, in contrast, judged direct statements to be *least* effective. In the Korean culture, the clearer a request is, the

Parrot Persuasion

The tiny island of St. Lucia in the Caribbean is the only home of the St. Lucia Parrot, a beautiful blue, green, and red bird which was on the brink of extinction; only 100 of the parrots remained in the wild.

St. Lucia's forestry department hired Paul Butler, a new college grad, to head an effort to preserve the parrot. Butler faced an enormous task. The St. Lucia Parrot had few legal protections, and the citizens of the island didn't seem to care.

Armed with a tiny budget and a passion for the project, Butler embarked on a public relations campaign to convince St. Lucians that their parrot was special and should be protected. He arranged for puppet shows, T-shirts, and bumper stickers. He had volunteers in parrot costumes visit local schools. He even convinced a phone company to make calling cards with the lovely parrot next to the not-so-lovely bald eagle.

St. Lucia's forestry department was happy with his campaign: the St. Lucia Parrot population has improved to between 600 and 700 birds.

Adapted from Chip Heath and Dan Heath, *Switch: How to Change Things When Change Is Hard* (New York: Broadway Books, 2010), 149–51.

Selling Education

At the end of every year, college football teams in the United States participate in highly anticipated title contests and bowl games. As part of each televised event, the two universities whose teams are playing in the games are given 30-second advertising spots during halftime.

What do the universities do with their time? A *Wall Street Journal* study of 112 university commercials found that most are an odd mixture of messages: academics, the arts, athletics, and scientific achievements, all trying to appeal to high school students, their parents, alumni, and taxpayers. The study found that with so many audiences and confused messages, most of the ads were unsuccessful. A few, however, stood out.

- Some ads used famous alumni, like Jon Hamm (Missouri) or Tom Brokaw (Iowa), to talk about their schools.

- Rice University used historical footage of John F. Kennedy delivering his famous speech at the Rice campus about putting a man on the moon.

- Minnesota delivered an ad focused on the research of professor Massoud Amin, who is developing a better power grid.

The most successful ads showed an understanding of their audience and focused on a single, clear message.

Adapted from Darren Everson, "Those Halftime College Ads: A Review," *Wall Street Journal*, November 19, 2010, D12.

ruder and therefore less effective it is.[12] Another study notes that communicators from countries such as China, Japan, and Korea prefer to establish personal relationships before they address business issues. They also show modesty and humility, debasing their egos in favor of collective relationships and disdaining personal profit.[13]

Researchers are studying the sale of counterfeit drugs, which is a huge business, both in the United States and abroad. They have found that the quality of the fakes matters only in the United States; people in other countries are willing to accept a price–quality trade-off. United States citizens harbor ill will toward big drug companies; people in other countries do not. United States citizens consider the consumption of counterfeit drugs unethical; people in China and Russia do not.

So what should drug companies do? In countries placing a low priority on drug quality, companies can highlight the dangers of such drugs, including the contaminants that are common in them. In cultures lacking ethical concerns, drug companies can stress social concerns. Diluted malaria drugs, for instance, can help the parasite causing the disease to develop drug resistance.[14]

CHOOSING A PERSUASIVE STRATEGY   LO 11-2

If your organization prefers a specific approach, use it. If your organization has no preference, or if you do not know your audience's preference, use the following guidelines to help you choose a strategy. These guidelines work in many cases but not all.

- Use the **direct request pattern** when
  - The audience will do as you ask without any resistance.
  - You need responses only from people who will find it easy to do as you ask.
  - The audience may not read all of the message.
- Use the **problem-solving pattern** when the audience may resist doing as you ask and you expect logic to be more important than emotion in the decision.
- Use the **sales pattern** when the audience may resist doing as you ask and you expect emotion to be more important than logic in the decision.

 WARNING: You always need to consider your audience and situation before choosing your persuasive strategy.

WHY THREATS ARE LESS EFFECTIVE THAN PERSUASION

Sometimes people think they will be able to mandate change by ordering or threatening subordinates. Real managers disagree. Research shows that managers use threats only for obligatory duties such as coming to work on time. For more creative duties—like being part of a team or thinking of ways to save the company money—good managers persuade. Persuasion not only keeps the lines of communication open, it fosters better working relationships and makes future discussions go more smoothly.[15]

Threats are even less effective in trying to persuade people whose salaries you don't pay.

A **threat** is a statement—explicit or implied—that someone will be punished if he or she does (or doesn't do) something. Various reasons explain why threats don't work:

1. **Threats don't produce permanent change.** Many people obey the speed limit only when a marked police car is in sight.
2. **Threats won't necessarily produce the action you want.** If you punish whistleblowers, you may stop hearing about problems you could be solving—hardly the response you'd want!
3. **Threats may make people abandon an action—even in situations where it would be appropriate.** Criticizing workers for chatting with each other may reduce their overall collaboration.
4. **Threats produce tension.** People who feel threatened put their energies into ego defense rather than into productive work.
5. **People dislike and avoid anyone who threatens them.** A supervisor who is disliked will find it harder to enlist cooperation and support on the next issue that arises.
6. **Threats can provoke counteraggression.** Getting back at a boss can run the gamut from complaints to work slowdowns to sabotage.

In *The Tipping Point*, Malcolm Gladwell describes classic fear experiments conducted at Yale University. The point of the experiments was to get students to go to the health center for tetanus shots. Students were given high-fear or low-fear versions of booklets explaining why they should get the shots. The high-fear booklet included gruesome pictures and text; the low-fear booklet did not. As you might predict, more of the students reading the high-fear booklet said they would get the shots than those reading the low-fear version. But only 3% of students in either group actually did so. However, one small change upped the percentage to 28% (evenly spread across both groups). That change was including a campus map with the health center circled and the times shots were available listed. The map shifted the persuasion from abstract material about the dangers of tetanus to practical, personal advice.[16]

MAKING PERSUASIVE DIRECT REQUESTS LO 11-3

When you expect quick agreement, you can generally save your audience's time by presenting the request directly (see Figure 11.1). Also use the direct request pattern for busy people who do not read all the messages they receive and in organizations whose cultures favor putting the request first.

This pattern is also frequently used to persuade in dire situations. In 2008, at the height of the United States' financial crisis, Ben Bernanke and Henry Paulson, then treasury secretary, bluntly asked Congress for $700 billion to rescue the banks and prevent a deep, prolonged recession.[17]

Making Ethics Training Fun

BearingPoint, a management and technology consulting firm, has taken a different approach to its ethics training.

Russ Berland, BearingPoint's chief compliance officer, faced the problem of reworking the company's ethics and compliance program from a rarely used legal manual into a regularly consulted solution to ethics problems. After interviewing associates from around the country, he found that many of them had experienced ethical dilemmas, and their stories were interesting and compelling.

Berland and his associates then came up with a brilliant idea: instead of simply reworking the manual, they decided to put the drama of real-life situations on television. They hired a director and filmed 10 episodes in a weekend, with the plan to release one episode each Monday. Using the format of NBC's hit sitcom *The Office*, the episodes talked about sticky ethics subjects with comic exaggeration.

The series was an instant hit. Employees not only watched the videos, they responded to them, talked about them, and searched for the next episodes before they were released. With humor and heart, BearingPoint helped persuade employees to "take" their ethics training.

Adapted from Dan Heath and Chip Heath, "The Power of Razzle-Dazzle," *Fast Company*, December 2009/January 2010, 69–70; BearingPoint's ethics videos are online at http://fastcompany.com/aggrieva.

Figure 11.1 How to Organize a Persuasive Direct Request

1. **Consider asking immediately for the information or service you want.** Delay the request if it seems too abrupt or if you have several purposes in the message.

2. **Give your audience all the information they will need to act on your request.** Number your questions or set them off with bullets so readers can check to see that all have been answered.

3. **Ask for the action you want.** Do you want a check? A replacement? A catalog? Answers to your questions? If you need an answer by a certain time, say so. If possible, show why the time limit is necessary.

In written direct requests, put the request, the topic of the request, or a question in the subject line.

> Subject: Request for Updated Software
>
> My copy of HomeNet does not accept the nicknames for Gmail accounts.

> Subject: Status of Account #3548-003
>
> Please get me the following information about account #3548-003.

> Subject: Do We Need an Additional Training Session in October?
>
> The two training sessions scheduled for October will each accommodate 20 people. Last month, you said that 57 new staff accountants had been hired. Should we schedule an additional training session in October? Or can the new hires wait until the next regularly scheduled session in February?

Figure 11.2 illustrates a direct request. Note that a direct request does not contain benefits and does not need to overcome objections: it simply asks for what is needed.

Figure 11.2   A Direct Request

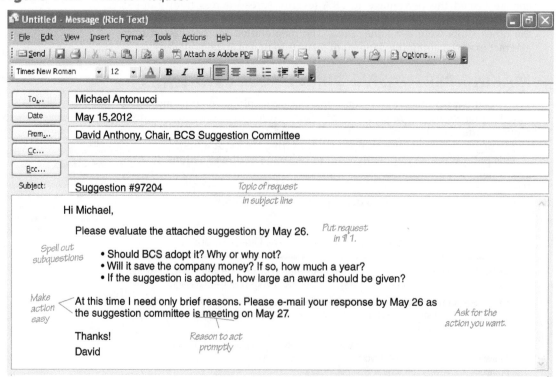

Direct requests should be clear. Don't make people guess what you want.

Indirect request: Is there a newer version of the 2003 *Chicago Manual of Style?*

Direct request: If there is a newer version of the 2003 *Chicago Manual of Style*, please send it to me.

In a claim, a message asking for correction or compensation for goods or services, explain the circumstances so that the reader knows what happened. Be sure to include all the relevant details: date of purchase, model or invoice number, and so on.

In more complicated direct requests, anticipate possible responses. Suppose you're asking for information about equipment meeting certain specifications. Explain which criteria are most important so that the reader can recommend an alternative if no single product meets all your needs. You may also want to tell the reader what your price constraints are and ask whether the item is in stock or must be special-ordered.

During the recession, the Campaign for a Commercial-Free Childhood urged parents to write to toy manufacturers asking them to suspend advertising toys to children during the holiday season. The CCFC offered parents a sample letter, one which put the request in the first sentence. Anticipating strong reactions from toy manufacturers, the CCFC pointed out that it is wrong to make children expect toys that their parents cannot afford. The letter offered the alternative of advertising the toys to parents, who of course buy the toys, rather than to children. (See Exercise 11.26 for more details and the text of the sample letter.)[18]

WRITING PERSUASIVE PROBLEM-SOLVING MESSAGES LO 11-4

Generally, you will use an indirect approach and the problem-solving pattern of organization (see Figure 11.3) when you expect resistance from your audience but can show that doing what you want will solve a problem you and your audience share. This pattern allows you to disarm opposition by showing all the reasons in favor of your position before you give your audience a chance to say *no*. As always, you need to analyze your audience and situation before you choose this approach to ensure it is a good one for the occasion.

Figure 11.3   How to Organize a Persuasive Problem-Solving Message

1. **Catch the audience's interest by mentioning a common ground.** Show that your message will be interesting or beneficial. You may want to catch attention with a negative (which you will go on to show can be solved).

2. **Define the problem you both share (which your request will solve).** Present the problem objectively: don't assign blame or mention personalities. Be specific about the cost in money, time, lost goodwill, and so on. You have to convince people that *something* has to be done before you can convince them that your solution is the best one.

3. **Explain the solution to the problem.** If you know that the audience will favor another solution, start with that solution and show why it won't work before you present your solution.

   Present your solution without using the words *I* or *my*. Don't let personalities enter the picture; don't let the audience think they should say *no* just because you've had other requests accepted recently.

4. **Show that any negative elements (cost, time, etc.) are outweighed by the advantages.**

5. **Summarize any additional benefits of the solution.** The main benefit—solving the problem—can be presented briefly since you described the problem in detail. However, if there are any additional benefits, mention them.

6. **Ask for the action you want.** Often your audience will authorize or approve something; other people will implement the action. Give your audience a reason to act promptly, perhaps offering a new benefit. ("By buying now, we can avoid the next quarter's price hikes.")

324   **Part 3**   Basic Business Messages

Figure 11.4   A Problem-Solving Persuasive Message

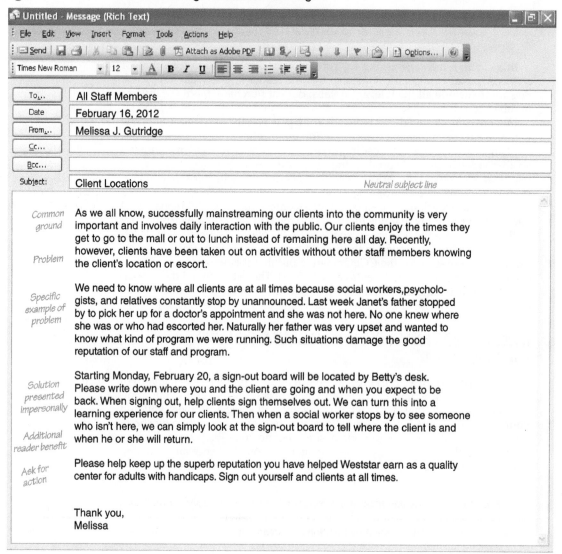

The message in Figure 11.4 uses the problem-solving pattern of organization. Benefits can be brief in this kind of message since the biggest benefit comes from solving the problem.

Subject Lines for Problem-Solving Messages

When you have a reluctant audience, putting the request in the subject line just gets a quick *no* before you've had a chance to give all your arguments. One option is to use a neutral subject line. In the following example, the first is the most neutral. The remaining two increasingly reveal the writer's preference.

Subject: A Proposal to Change the Formula for Calculating Retirees' Benefits

Subject: Arguments for Expanding the Marysville Plant

Subject: Why Cassano's Should Close Its West Side Store

Another option is to use common ground or a benefit—something that shows the audience that this message will help them.

> **Subject: Reducing Energy Costs in the Louisville Office**
>
> Energy costs in our Louisville office have risen 12% in the last three years, even though the cost of gas has remained constant and the cost of electricity has risen only 5%.

Although your first paragraph may be negative in a problem-solving message, your subject line should be neutral or positive.

Developing a Common Ground

A common ground avoids the me-against-you of some persuasive situations and suggests that both you and your audience have a mutual interest in solving the problems you face. To find a common ground, we analyze the audience; understand their biases, objections, and needs; and identify with them to find common goals. This analysis could be carried out in a cold, manipulative way. It should, however, be based on a respect for and sensitivity to the audience's position.

Audiences are highly sensitive to manipulation. No matter how much you disagree with your audience, respect their intelligence. Try to understand why they believe or do something and why they may object to your position. If you can understand your audiences' initial positions, you'll be more effective—and you won't alienate your audience by talking down to them.

The best common grounds are specific. Often a negative—a problem the audience will want to solve—makes a good common ground.

Vague common ground:	We all want this plant to be profitable.
Improved specific common ground:	We forfeited a possible $1,860,000 in profits last month due to a 17% drop in productivity.

In your common ground, emphasize the parts of your proposal that fit with what your audience already does or believes. Some HMOs are trying to improve patients' health (and cut the costs of providing care for them) by reaching out to individual patients and persuading them to take medications, get needed tests, and manage chronic conditions. Often, they first have to overcome patients' belief that HMOs want to limit their access to care. They do so by emphasizing the patients' needs and health.

Use audience analysis to evaluate possible common grounds. Suppose you want to install a system to play background music in a factory. To persuade management to pay for the system, a possible common ground would be increasing productivity. However, to persuade the union to pay for the system, you'd need a different common ground. Workers would see productivity as a way to get them to do more work for the same pay. A better common ground would be that the music would make the factory environment more pleasant.

Dealing with Objections

If you know that your audience will hear other points of view, or if your audience's initial position is negative, you have to deal with their objections to persuade them. The stronger the objection is, the earlier in your message you should deal with it.

That Personal Touch

Selling a home in a crowded market can be difficult. Real estate brokers and homeowners often need to turn to unconventional methods to help their homes stand out. One Atlanta broker, Rhonda Duffy, asks her clients to include a personal touch in selling their homes: Each homeowner writes a personal letter to potential buyers.

While the letters do review the important facts about the home, they accomplish much more. Through the letters, homeowners can paint a picture of the best features and intangible benefits of the home. The letters show that real people have lived in the home and have been happy there. These personal letters can make a big impact on buyers, most of whom are not just investing in property, but are looking for a lifestyle. The letters also make the homes memorable. Duffy explains, "It's 'the letter house' instead of 'the green carpet house.'"

Adapted from Amy Hoak, "Desperate Times, Desperate Measures," *Wall Street Journal*, December 13, 2010, R10.

The best way to deal with an objection is to eliminate it. When hail damaged mail-order apples just before harvest, the orchard owner inserted a note in each crate being shipped:

> Note the hail marks which have caused minor skin blemishes in some of these apples. They are proof of their growth at a high mountain altitude where the sudden chills from hailstorms help firm the flesh, develop the natural sugars, and give these apples their incomparable flavor.

No one asked for a refund; in fact, some customers requested the hail-marked apples the next year.[19]

If an objection is false and is based on misinformation, give the response to the objection without naming the objection. (Repeating the objection gives it extra emphasis.) In a brochure, you can present responses with a "question/answer" format.

When objections have already been voiced, you may want to name the objection so that your audience realizes that you are responding to that specific objection. However, to avoid solidifying the opposition, don't attribute the objection to your audience. Instead, use a less personal attribution: "Some people wonder . . ."; "Some citizens are afraid that. . . ."

If real objections remain, try one or more of the following strategies to counter objections:

1. Specify how much time and/or money is required—it may not be as much as the audience fears.

> Distributing flyers to each house or apartment in your neighborhood will probably take two afternoons.

2. Put the time and/or money in the context of the benefits they bring.

> The additional $252,500 will (1) allow the Essex Shelter to remain open 24 rather than 16 hours a day, (2) pay for three social workers to help men find work and homes, and (3) keep the Neighborhood Bank open, so that men don't have to cash Social Security checks in bars and so that they can save for the $800 deposit they need to rent an apartment.

3. Show that money spent now will save money in the long run.

> By buying a $1,000 safety product, we can avoid $5,000 in OSHA fines.

4. Show that doing as you ask will benefit some group or cause the audience supports, even though the action may not help the audience directly. This is the strategy used in fund-raising letters.

> By being a Big Brother or a Big Sister, you'll give a child the adult attention he or she needs to become a well-adjusted, productive adult.

5. Show the audience that the sacrifice is necessary to achieve a larger, more important goal to which they are committed.

> These changes will mean more work for all of us. But we've got to cut our costs 25% to keep the plant open and to keep our jobs.

Chapter 11   Crafting Persuasive Messages

327

The Central Asia Institute uses positive images and language to show how financial contributions help promote world peace by building schools in Asian countries. See https://www.ikat.org/

6. Show that the advantages as a group outnumber or outweigh the disadvantages as a group.

> None of the locations is perfect. But the Backbay location gives us the most advantages and the fewest disadvantages.

Use the following steps when you face major objections:

1. **Find out why your audience members resist what you want them to do.** Sit down one-on-one with people and listen. Don't try to persuade them; just try to understand.
2. **Try to find a win–win solution.** People will be much more readily persuaded if they see benefits for themselves. Sometimes your original proposal may have benefits that the audience had not thought of, and explaining the benefits will help. Sometimes you'll need to modify your original proposal to find a solution that solves the real problem and meets everyone's needs.
3. **Let your audience save face.** Don't ask people to admit that they have been wrong all along. If possible, admit that the behavior may have been appropriate in the past. Whether you can do that or not, always show how changed circumstances or new data call for new action.
4. **Ask for something small.** When you face great resistance, you won't get everything at once. Ask for a month's trial. Ask for one step that will move toward your larger goal. For example, if your ultimate goal is to eliminate prejudice in your organization, a step toward that goal might be to convince managers to make a special effort for one month to recognize the contributions of women or members of minorities in group meetings.
5. **Present your arguments from your audience's point of view.** Offer benefits that help the audience, not just you. Take special care to avoid words that attack or belittle your audience. Present yourself as someone helping your audience achieve their goals, not someone criticizing or giving orders from above.

Hard Tests for Persuasion

How do you get your employees to agree to be tested for AIDS? This was a huge concern for SABMiller, a South African brewer who faced losing about 15% of its workforce within three years. Their first step was to hire an outside testing firm to allay fears that a positive HIV test would become company gossip or hurt careers. Participants also joined raffles for free radios and TVs. The company paid for anti-retroviral treatment for infected employees.

How do you get employees to leave their jobs? France Telecom's need for a major workforce reduction inspired them to be creative. In addition to traditional means such as early retirement plans and retirement bonuses, they developed a program to shift people to public sector jobs at other institutions. They also helped employees start their own businesses, offering assistance with writing business plans, applying for loans, and purchasing equipment. They paid for consultations with business people and new educational courses.

What other hard tests for businesses can you identify? What persuasive solutions can you imagine?

Adapted from William Echikson and Adam Coher, "SABMiller's AIDS Test Program Gets Results: Effort Benefits Business, Saves Employee Lives; Building Confidence Is Key," *Wall Street Journal*, August 18, 2006, A7; and Leila Abboud, "At France Telecom, Battle to Cut Jobs Breeds Odd Tactics: Company Offers Money, Advice on Starting New Business if Employees Will Leave," *Wall Street Journal*, August 14, 2006, A1.

From Full Time to Part Time

Many employees dream about working fewer hours or even cutting back to part-time work. But managers agree that most employees ask their boss the wrong way. Too often employees focus on why *they* want part-time work; managers want to hear about advantages and disadvantages for the company.

You might use these persuasive arguments to convince your employer to let you work fewer hours:

- Demonstrate that you understand and appreciate corporate policies on part-time work.

- Stress that your dedication to your work won't fade when you start working fewer hours.

- Agree to be reached outside the office if your colleagues need you.

- Present a plan detailing how the rest of your work will get done.

- Suggest a trial period to show your plan will work.

- Above all, treat the situation as a persuasive message: develop a common ground with your employer, anticipate objections, and suggest solutions.

Adapted from Erin White, "Build a Case before Asking to Work Less," *Wall Street Journal*, October 24, 2006, B7.

Organizational changes work best when the audience buys into the solution. And that happens most easily when they themselves find it. Management can encourage employees to identify problems and possible solutions. If that is not possible because of time, sensitive information, or organizational cultural constraints, a good second alternative is to fully explain to employees how the decision for organizational change was made, the reasons behind the change, what alternatives were considered, and why they were rejected. A study of over 100 employers found that workers who received such explanations were more than twice as likely to support the decision as those workers who did not.[20]

Offering a Reason for the Audience to Act Promptly

The longer people delay, the less likely they are to carry through with the action they had decided to take. In addition, you want a fast response so you can go ahead with your own plans.

Request action by a specific date. Try to give people at least a week or two: they have other things to do besides respond to your requests. Set deadlines in the middle of the month, if possible. If you say, "Please return this by March 1," people will think, "I don't need to do this till March." Ask for the response by February 28 instead. Similarly, a deadline of Friday, 5 pm, will frequently be seen as Monday morning. If such a shift causes you problems, if you were going to work over the weekend, set a Thursday deadline. If you can use a response even after the deadline, say so. Otherwise, people who can't make the deadline may not respond at all.

Your audience may ignore deadlines that seem arbitrary. Show why you need a quick response:

- **Show that the time limit is real.** Perhaps you need information quickly to use it in a report that has a due date. Perhaps a decision must be made by a certain date to catch the start of the school year, the Christmas selling season, or an election campaign. Perhaps you need to be ready for a visit from out-of-town or international colleagues.

- **Show that acting now will save time or money.** If business is slow and your industry isn't doing well, then your company needs to act now (to economize, to better serve customers) in order to be competitive. If business is booming and everyone is making a profit, then your company needs to act now to get its fair share of the available profits.

- **Show the cost of delaying action.** Will labor or material costs be higher in the future? Will delay mean more money spent on repairing something that will still need to be replaced?

Building Emotional Appeal

Emotional appeal helps make people care. Stories and psychological description are effective ways of building emotional appeal.

Even when you need to provide statistics or numbers to convince the careful reader that your anecdote is a representative example, **telling a story** first makes your message more persuasive. In *Made to Stick*, Chip and Dan Heath report on research done at Carnegie Mellon supporting the value of stories. After a survey (completing the survey for money ensured all participants had cash for the real experiment), participants received an envelope with a letter requesting they donate to Save the Children. Researchers tested two letters: one was full of grim statistics about starving Africans. The other letter told the story of seven-year-old Rokia. Participants receiving the Rokia letter gave more

Emotional appeals can be intense. The Save Darfur campaign used this ad to raise awareness of horrifying brutality and genocide. Do you think this graphic of a half-buried hand works to solicit support for this cause? Or is the emotional appeal too intense?

than twice as much money as those receiving the statistics letter. A third group received a letter with both sets of information: the story and the statistics. This group gave a little more than the statistics group, but far less than the group that had the story alone. The researchers theorized that the statistics put people in an analytical frame of mind which canceled the emotional effect of the story.[21]

As with other appeals, the **emotional appeal** should focus on the audience. To customers who had fallen behind with their payments, a credit card company sent not the expected stern collection notice but a hand-addressed, hand-signed greeting card. The front of the card pictured a stream running through a forest. The text inside noted that sometimes life takes unexpected turns and asked people to call the company to find a collaborative solution. When people called the 800 number, they got credit counseling and help in creating a payment plan. Instead of having to write off bad debts, the company received payments—and created goodwill.[22]

In his marketing book *Buyology,* marketing guru Martin Lindstrom points out that advertisers deliberately create somatic markers, icons that associate the advertised goods with some value you admire. Car tires pretty much look the same, but if you head for Michelin instead of Goodyear, you may be responding to carefully crafted somatic markers. The cute baby once used in their ads translates into safety for your child. The plump Michelin man suggests the protective padding of good tires and thus sturdy durability. The high-end Michelin travel and food guides bring an association of top-of-the line quality.[23]

330   **Part 3** Basic Business Messages

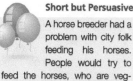

Emotional appeal is often used in public service announcements. Here the AdCouncil uses the emotional appeal of the young child to underscore Tyler's need for help.

Sometimes emotional appeals go too far and alienate audiences. Germany's Federal Constitutional Court ruled that a PETA ad campaign was an offense against human dignity and not protected by freedom of speech laws. The campaign compared factory farms and animal slaughterhouses to Jewish concentration camps and the Holocaust.[24]

Sense impressions—what the reader sees, hears, smells, tastes, feels—evoke a strong emotional response. **Psychological description** means creating a scenario rich with sense impressions so readers can picture themselves using your product or service and enjoying its benefits. The flyer for a university's food services in Figure 11.5 gets your gastric juices flowing.

You can also use psychological description to describe the problem your product, service, or solution will ease. Psychological description works best early in the message to catch readers' attention.

> Because our smokers take their breaks on the front patio, clients visiting our office frequently pass through a haze of acrid smoke—as well as through a group of employees who are obviously not working.

Putting It All Together

The Campaign for a Commercial-Free Childhood sent a letter to toy manufacturers direct from the CCFC, in addition to the letters from parents discussed in the Making Persuasive Direct Requests section earlier in this chapter. The

Figure 11.5 Using Psychological Description to Develop Benefits

You-attitude psychological description

The Colonial Room

When you dine in the Illini Union Colonial Room, it's easy to imagine yourself a guest in a fine Virginian mansion. Light from the gleaming chandeliers reflects from a hand-carved mirror hanging over the dark, polished buffet. Here you can dine in quiet elegance amid furnishings adapted from 18th century Williamsburg and the Georgian homes of the James River Valley in Virginia.

Perhaps you'd like a dinner of stuffed rainbow trout. Or the pork fricassee. The menu features a variety of complete meals which are changed daily, as well as the regular a la carte service. Whatever your choice, you'll enjoy an evening of fine dining at very reasonable prices.

The Illini Union Colonial Room is located on the northeast corner of the first floor. Dinners are served Monday through Friday from 5:30 to 7:30 p.m. Please call 333-0690 for reservations, and enjoy the flavor of the Colonies tonight.

Visual details

Details appeal to sight, taste, smell

Emphasis on reader's choice— Not every reader will want the same thing

The Cafeteria

In the Illini Union Cafeteria, you start out with an empty tray and silverware. Then comes the food, several yards of it, all yours for the choosing. By the time you've finished, your empty tray has become a delicious meal.

In the morning, the warm aroma of breakfast fills the air. Feast your eyes and then your appetite on the array of eggs, bacon, pancakes, toast, sausage, rolls, juices, and coffee . . . They're all waiting to wake you up with good taste. Have a hearty breakfast or make it quick and tasty. The warm, freshly baked sweet rolls and coffeecakes practically beg to be smothered in butter and savored with a cup of hot coffee.

By 11 a.m. the breakfast menu has made way for lunch. Here come the plump Reuben sandwiches and the toasty grilled cheese. Soups and salads make their appearance. A variety of vegetables are dressed up to entice you and several main dishes lead the luncheon parade. Any number of complete meals can take shape as you move along.

What? Back for dinner? Well, no wonder! The Cafeteria sets out a wide selection of entrees and side dishes. Veal parmigiana steams for your attention but the roast beef right next to it is rough competition. Tomorrow the fried chicken might be up for selection. Choose the dinner combination that best fits your appetite and your pocket.

The newly remodeled Cafeteria is on the ground floor and is open for breakfast from 7 to 11 a.m. Monday through Saturday and 8 to 11 a.m. on Sunday. Lunch is served from 11 a.m. to 1:15 p.m. Monday through Saturday and 11 a.m. to 2 p.m. on Sunday. Dinner is served from 4:45 to 7 p.m. Monday through Friday.

A meal in a restaurant is expensive. A meal at home is a chore. But a meal at the Cafeteria combines good food and reasonable prices to make dining a pleasure.

organization's letter, which was two pages, used most of the elements discussed in this section of the chapter in its quest to stop holiday toy advertising to children.

Although major secondary purposes of the CCFC's letter were avoiding either disappointing children at the holidays or forcing parents to buy toys they could ill afford, the CCFC could not use these purposes as common grounds with toy manufacturers, who might see their own sales as a much greater goal. Therefore they highlighted a different way to sell toys:

> We understand the need to create awareness of your products. We urge you to do that by advertising directly to parents.

332

The letter anticipated many objections from toy manufacturers. To counter claims that parents did not need to cut back on toy buying, the CCFC cited information gathered by the Associated Press. To counter claims that advertising directly to children does not lead to toy requests and hence family stress, the CCFC referred to a review of research in the academic journal *Applied Developmental Psychology.* To counter claims that the toy industry was cutting back on ads to children, they referred to media figures.

The letter also used emotional appeals:

> As you know, children are more vulnerable to advertising than adults. Seductive advertising designed explicitly to exploit their vulnerabilities will create unrealistic expectations in kids too young to understand the economic crises and will make parenting in these uncertain times even more difficult.

The fast approach of the holiday sales push provided the reason for prompt action. For more details about this campaign, including the full text of CCFC's letter and some responses from toy manufacturers, see Exercise 11.26.[25]

TONE IN PERSUASIVE MESSAGES

The best phrasing for tone depends on your relationship to the your audience. When you ask for action from people who report directly to you, polite orders ("Please get me the Ervin file") and questions ("Do we have the third-quarter numbers yet?") will work. When you need action from co-workers, superiors, or people outside the organization, you need to be more polite.

How you ask for action affects whether you build or destroy positive relationships with other employees, customers, and suppliers. Avoiding messages that sound parental or preachy is often a matter of tone. Adding "Please" is a nice touch. Tone will also be better when you give reasons for your request or reasons to act promptly.

Parental:	Everyone is expected to comply with these regulations. I'm sure you can see that they are commonsense rules needed for our business.
Better:	Even on casual days, visitors expect us to be professional. So please leave the gym clothes at home!

Writing to superiors is trickier. You may want to tone down your request by using subjunctive verbs and explicit disclaimers that show you aren't taking a *yes* for granted.

Arrogant:	Based on this evidence, I expect you to give me a new computer.
Better:	If department funds permit, I would like a new computer.

Passive verbs and jargon sound stuffy. Use active imperatives—perhaps with "Please" to create a friendlier tone.

Stuffy:	It is requested that you approve the above-mentioned action.
Better:	Please authorize us to create a new subscription letter.

It can be particularly tricky to control tone in e-mail messages, which tend to sound less friendly than paper documents or conversations. For important requests, compose your message offline and revise it carefully before you send it.

Major requests that require great effort or changes in values, culture, or lifestyles should not be made in e-mail messages.

Undercutting Persuasion to Be Ethical

Companies and executives spend time and money to persuade employees to be ethical in their actions. But even the best managers may not see unethical behavior. The *Harvard Business Review* listed five reasons why:

1. Ill-Conceived Goals: If goals are expressed in the wrong way (like a goal for a number of billable hours), they may encourage employees to lie or cheat in order to achieve them.

2. Motivated Blindness: Managers may overlook their employees' unethical choices if those choices benefit the managers' interests.

3. Indirect Blindness: Managers may not hold their employees accountable for unethical behavior by contractors or other third parties.

4. The Slippery Slope: Managers may miss unethical behavior when it develops slowly over time.

5. Overvaluing Outcomes: If the employees are meeting the right outcomes, managers may ignore the unethical behavior.

To ensure ethical practice, companies and executives must find ways around these barriers.

Adapted from Max H. Bazerman and Ann E. Tenbrusel, "Ethical Breakdowns," *Harvard Business Review* 89, no.4 (April 2011): 58–65.

VARIETIES OF PERSUASIVE MESSAGES

Performance appraisals and letters of recommendation are two important kinds of persuasive messages.

Performance Appraisals

Good supervisors give their employees regular feedback on their performances. The feedback may range from a brief "Good job!" to a hefty bonus. Blanchard and Johnson's *One Minute Manager* is a popular business guide for brief but effective performance feedback.

Performance appraisals have a tarnished reputation. Employees may not want to be honest with their supervisor about their need for improvement or training. A supervisor who praises an employee may need to reward that person. On the other hand, a supervisor who criticizes a poor performance may then need to explain why this person wasn't managed more effectively. Supervisors of Army Major Nidal Hasan, who killed 13 at Fort Hood, praised him in performance appraisals, even though they knew he was often late for work, disappeared when on call, saw few patients, and pushed his religious views on those around him.[26]

Critics also complain about vague criteria and feedback, or stock phrases. They note that "not a team player" is being used to eliminate the need to give high achievers well-deserved promotions. Even widely touted techniques such as 360-degree feedback (anonymous input from supervisors, peers, and subordinates) have their critics. Some companies are suspending this form of appraisal because of conflicting input with vague support.[27]

Companies are recognizing the need to lavish more praise on their workers, especially younger ones. Land's End and Bank of America hired consultants to teach their supervisors how to compliment workers. The Scooter Store Inc. hired a "celebrations assistant," whose duties included handing out 100–500 celebration balloons and tossing 25 pounds of confetti—per week. (The celebrations assistant became averse to confetti, so her praise came in the form of text messaging.) Such companies see the praise as a way to maintain work quality and keep good workers.[28]

Performance appraisal documents are more formal ways by which supervisors evaluate, or appraise, the performance of their subordinates. In most organizations, employees have access to their appraisals; sometimes they must sign the document to show that they've read it. The superior normally meets with the subordinate to discuss the appraisal.

As a subordinate, you should prepare for the appraisal interview by listing your achievements and goals. What have you accomplished during the appraisal period? What supporting details will you need? Where do you want to be in a year or five years? What training and experience do you need to reach your goals? If you need training, advice, or support from the organization to improve, the appraisal interview is a good time to ask for this help. As you prepare, choose the persuasive strategy that will best present your work.

Appraisals need to both protect the organization and motivate the employee. Sometimes these two purposes conflict. Most of us will see a candid appraisal as negative; we need praise and reassurance to believe that we're valued and can do better. But the praise that motivates someone to improve can come back to haunt the company if the person does not eventually do acceptable work. An organization is in trouble if it tries to fire someone whose evaluations never mention mistakes.

Put Positive Emphasis in Performance Appraisals

Positive emotional appeal is a great tool for performance reviews and other "management moments" where you need to give motivating feedback to a co-worker, teammate, or employee.

Julia Stewart, the chair and CEO of the restaurant company DineEquity, describes how she uses positive emotional appeals when she gives feedback to employees. "I'd go behind the counter, get on the food prep line, and catch an employee doing something right. I'd say, 'Great job—that's the perfect way to portion that taco' and then turn to the next person down the line and ask, 'Did you see how well this was done?' Or I'd stand in the middle of the kitchen and half-shout, 'Who did the walk-in here today?' There would be silence, and then someone would confess, 'I did.' And I'd compliment him on the job and ask the people in the kitchen to gather around so they could see what had gone right and what could be done even better the next time."

This type of positive emphasis is a great persuasive tool: your audience associates your feedback with the positive emotional feeling of being praised, which makes them more likely to view your recommendations as positive and act on them.

Adapted from Daisy Wademan Dowling, "DineEquity Chairman and CEO Julia A. Stewart on Leaders as Teachers," *Harvard Business Review* 87, no. 3 (March 2009): 29.

When you are writing performance appraisals that need to document areas for improvement, avoid labels (*wrong, bad*) and inferences. Instead, cite specific observations that describe behavior.

Inference:	Sam is an alcoholic.
Vague observation:	Sam calls in sick a lot. Subordinates complain about his behavior.
Specific observation:	Sam called in sick a total of 12 days in the last two months. After a business lunch with a customer last week, Sam was walking unsteadily. Two of his subordinates have said that they would prefer not to make sales trips with him because they find his behavior embarrassing.

Sam might be an alcoholic. He might also be having a reaction to a physician-prescribed drug; he might have a mental illness; he might be showing symptoms of a physical illness other than alcoholism. A supervisor who jumps to conclusions creates ill will, closes the door to solving the problem, and may provide grounds for legal action against the organization.

Be specific in an appraisal.

Too vague:	Sue does not manage her time as well as she could.
Specific:	Sue's first three weekly sales reports have been three, two, and four days late, respectively; the last weekly sales report for the month is not yet in.

Without specifics, Sue won't know that her boss objects to late reports. She may think that she is being criticized for spending too much time on sales calls or for not working 80 hours a week. Without specifics, she might change the wrong things in a futile effort to please her boss.

It is also important that specifics be included in performance appraisals for good employees to help them continue to shine and also to receive their well-deserved raises and promotions.

Appraisals are more useful to subordinates if they make clear which areas are most important and contain specific recommendations for improvement. No one can improve 17 weaknesses at once. Which two should the employee work on this month? Is getting in reports on time more important than increasing sales?

Phrase goals in specific, concrete terms. The subordinate may think that "considerable progress toward completing" a report may mean that the project should be 15% finished. The boss may think that "considerable progress" means 50% or 85% of the total work.

Sometimes a performance appraisal reflects mostly the month or week right before the appraisal, even though it is supposed to cover six months or a year. Many managers record specific observations of subordinates' behavior two or three times a month. These notes jog the memory so that the appraisal doesn't focus unduly on recent behavior.

A recent trend in performance appraisals is attempting to make them objective. Instead of being subjectively evaluated on intangible qualities like "works well with others," employees are monitored on how well they meet quantifiable goals. Nurses might be ranked on items such as low infection rates and high patient-satisfaction scores. Technical support personnel might be ranked on number of projects completed on time and customer-satisfaction scores.[29] If you will be evaluated by the numbers, try to have a say in setting your goals so you are not judged on items to which you only indirectly contribute. Make sure your goals stay updated so you are not judged on goals which are no longer a priority for your position or your efforts on new goals are not being measured.

Figure 11.6 shows a performance appraisal for a member of a collaborative business communication student group.

Figure 11.6   A Performance Appraisal

February 13, 2012

To: Barbara Buchanan

From: Brittany Papper *BAP*

Subject line indicates that memo is a performance appraisal

Subject: Your Performance Thus Far in Our Collaborative Group

Overall evaluation

You have been a big asset to our group. Overall, our communications group has been one of the best groups I have ever worked with, and I think that only minor improvements are needed to make our group even better.

These headings would need to be changed in a negative performance appraisal.

Strengths

Specific observations provide dates, details of performance

You demonstrated flexibility and compatibility at our last meeting before we turned in our proposal on February 9 by offering to type the proposal since I had to study for an exam in one of my other classes. I really appreciated this because I definitely did not have the time to do it. I will definitely remember this if you are ever too busy with your other classes and cannot type the final report.

Another positive critical incident occurred February 2. We had discussed researching the topic of sexual discrimination in hiring and promotion at Midstate Insurance. As we read more about what we had to do, we became uneasy about reporting the information from our source who works at Midstate. I called you later that evening to talk about changing our topic to a less personal one. You were very understanding and said that you agreed that the original topic was a touchy one. You offered suggestions for other topics and had a positive attitude about the adjustment. Your suggestions ended my worries and made me realize that you are a positive and supportive person.

Other strengths

Your ideas are a strength that you definitely contribute to our group. You're good at brainstorming ideas, yet you're willing to go with whatever the group decides. That's a nice combination of creativity and flexibility.

Areas for Improvement

Two minor improvements could make you an even better member.

Specific recommendations for improvement

The first improvement is to be more punctual to meetings. On February 2 and February 5 you were about 10 minutes late. This makes the meetings last longer. Your ideas are valuable to the group, and the sooner you arrive the sooner we can share in your suggestions.   *Positive cast to suggestion*

Specific behavior to be changed

The second suggestion is one we all need to work on. We need to keep our meetings positive and productive. I think that our negative attitudes were worst at our first group meeting February 3. We spent about half an hour complaining about all the work we had to do and about our busy schedules in other classes. In the future if this happens, maybe you could offer some positive things about the assignment to get the group motivated again.

Overall Compatibility

Positive, forward-looking ending

I feel that this group has gotten along very well together. You have been very flexible in finding times to meet and have always been willing to do your share of the work. I have never had this kind of luck with a group in the past and you have been a welcome breath of fresh air. I don't hate doing group projects any more!

336   **Part 3**   Basic Business Messages

Letters of Recommendation

You may write letters of recommendation when you want to recommend someone for an award or for a job. Letters of recommendation must be specific. General positives that are not backed up with specific examples and evidence are seen as weak recommendations. Letters of recommendation that focus on minor points also suggest that the person is weak.

Either in the first or the last paragraph, summarize your overall evaluation of the person. Early in the letter, perhaps in the first paragraph, show how well and how long you've known the person. In the middle of the letter, offer specific details about the person's performance. At the end of the letter, indicate whether you would be willing to rehire the person and repeat your overall evaluation. Figure A.3 in Appendix A shows a sample letter of recommendation.

Although experts are divided on whether you should include negatives, the trend is moving away from doing so. Negatives can create legal liabilities, and many readers feel that any negative weakens the letter. Other people feel that presenting but not emphasizing honest negatives makes the letter more convincing. In either case, you must ensure that your recommendation is honest and accurate.

In many discourse communities, the words "Call me if you need more information" in a letter of recommendation mean "I have negative information that I am unwilling to put on paper. Call me and I'll tell you what I really think."

In an effort to protect themselves against lawsuits, some companies state only how long they employed someone and the position that person held. Such bare-bones letters have themselves been the target of lawsuits when employers did not reveal relevant negatives.

SALES AND FUND-RAISING MESSAGES   LO 11-5

Sales and fund-raising messages are a special category of persuasive messages. They are known as **direct marketing** because they ask for an order, inquiry, or contribution directly from the audience. Direct marketing which includes printed (direct mail), verbal (telemarketing), and electronic (e-mails, social media, websites, infomercials) channels, is a $300 billion industry.[30]

This section focuses on two common channels of direct marketing: sales and fund-raising letters. Large organizations hire professionals to write their direct marketing materials. If you own your own business, you can save money by doing your firm's own direct marketing. If you are active in a local group that needs to raise money, writing the fund-raising letter yourself is likely to be the only way your group can afford to use direct mail. If you can write an equally effective e-mail message, you can significantly cut the costs of a marketing campaign or supplement the success of your direct mail with direct e-mail.

The principles in this chapter will help you write solid, serviceable letters and e-mails that will build your business and help fund your group.

Sales, fund-raising, and promotional messages have multiple purposes:

Primary purpose:
   To have the reader act (order the product, send a donation).

Secondary purpose:
   To build a good image of the writer's organization (to strengthen the commitment of readers who act, and make readers who do not act more likely to respond positively next time).

Organizing a Sales or Fund-Raising Message

Use the sales persuasion pattern to organize your message (see Figure 11.7).

Opener The opener of your message gives you a chance to motivate your audience to read the rest of the message.

A good opener will make readers want to read the message and provide a reasonable transition to the body of the message. A very successful subscription letter for *Psychology Today* started out,

> Do you still close the bathroom door when there's no one in the house?

The question was both intriguing in itself and a good transition into the content of *Psychology Today*: practical psychology applied to the quirks and questions we come across in everyday life.

It's essential that the opener not only get attention but also be something that can be linked logically to the body of the message. A sales letter started,

> Can You Use $50 This Week?

Certainly that gets attention. But the letter only offered the reader the chance to save $50 on a product. Readers may feel disappointed or even cheated when they learn that instead of getting $50, they have to spend money to save $50.

To brainstorm possible openers, use the four basic modes: questions, narration, startling statements, and quotations.

1. Questions

> Dear Subscriber,
>
> **ARE YOU NUTS?** Your subscription to PC Gamer is about to expire!
> **No reviews. No strategies. No tips.**
> *No PC Gamer. Are you willing to suffer the consequences?*

This letter urging the reader to renew *PC Gamer* is written under a large banner question: Do you want to get eaten alive? The letter goes on to remind its audience, mostly young males, of the magazine's gaming reviews, early previews, exclusive demo discs, and "awesome array of new cheats for the latest games"—all hot buttons for computer gaming fans.

Good questions are interesting enough that the audience want the answers, so they read the letter.

Poor question: Do you want to make extra money?

Better question: How *much* extra money do you want to make next year?

A series of questions can be an effective opener. Answer the questions in the body of the letter.

Figure 11.7 How to Organize a Sales or Fund-Raising Message

1. Open by catching the audience's attention.
2. In the body, provide reasons and details.
3. End by telling the audience what to do and providing a reason to act promptly.

Persuading to Save

In the past several decades, the percentage of income Americans save has decreased dramatically. Until the early 1980s, Americans saved nearly 10% of their income. In 2009, however, we saved a paltry 0.9%. Some banks are trying to encourage their customers to save regularly by some unusual methods.

Eight credit unions in Michigan started a program called "Save to Win." This strange cross between a savings program and a lottery taps into many Americans' love of gambling. Customers who put at least $25 into a one-year CD receive an entry into a monthly drawing for $400 and an annual jackpot for $100,000. The CDs are insured, but pay slightly less than the conventional rate. The program is working, and some of the winners are putting their winnings directly into savings accounts.

Adapted from Jason Zweig, "Using the Lottery Effect to Make People Save," *Wall Street Journal*, July 18, 2009, B1.

338   Part 3   Basic Business Messages

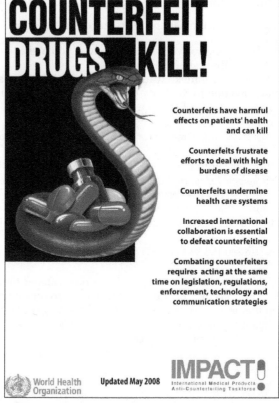

This World Health Organization poster juxtaposes lifesaving medicines with a deadly cobra in a visual "startling statement."

2. Narration, stories, anecdotes

Dear Reader:

She hoisted herself up noiselessly so as not to disturb the rattlesnakes snoozing there in the sun.

To her left, the high desert of New Mexico. Indian country. To her right, the rock carvings she had photographed the day before. Stick people. Primitive animals.

Up ahead, three sandstone slabs stood stacked against the face of the cliff. In their shadow, another carving. A spiral consisting of rings. Curious, the young woman drew closer. Instinctively, she glanced at her watch. It was almost noon. Then just at that moment, a most unusual thing happened.

Suddenly, as if out of nowhere, an eerie dagger of light appeared to stab at the topmost ring of the spiral. It next began to plunge downward—shimmering, laser-like.

It pierced the eighth ring. The seventh. The sixth. It punctured the innermost and last. Then just as suddenly as it had appeared, the dagger of light was gone. The young woman glanced at her watch again. Exactly twelve minutes had elapsed.

Coincidence? Accident? Fluke? No. What she may have stumbled across that midsummer morning three years ago is an ancient solar calendar. . . .

This subscription letter for *Science84* argues that it reports interesting and significant discoveries in all fields of science—all in far more detail than do other media. The opener both builds suspense so that the reader reads the subscription letter and suggests that the magazine will be as interesting as the letter and as easy to read.

3. Startling statements

> Dear Membership Candidate:
>
> I'm writing to offer you a job.
> It's not a permanent job, understand. You'll be working for only as much time as you find it rewarding and fun.
> It's not even a paying job. On the contrary, it will cost *you* money.

This fund-raising letter from Earthwatch invites readers to participate in its expeditions, subscribe to its journal, and donate to its programs. Earthwatch's volunteers help scientists and scholars dig for ruins, count bighorns, and monitor changes in water; they can work as long as they like; they pay their own (tax-deductible) expenses.

Variations of this mode include special opportunities, twists, and challenges.

4. Quotations

> "I never tell my partner that my ankle is sore or my back hurts. You can't give in to pain and still perform."
>
> —Jill Murphy
> Soloist

The series of which this letter is a part sells season tickets to the Atlanta Ballet by focusing on the people who work to create the season. Each letter quotes a different member of the company. The opening quote is used on the envelope over a picture of the ballerina and as an opener for the letter. The letters encourage readers to see the artists as individuals, to appreciate their hard work, and to share their excitement about each performance.

Body   The body of the message provides the logical and emotional links that move the audience from their first flicker of interest to the action that is wanted. A good body answers the audience's questions, overcomes their objections, and involves them emotionally.

All this takes space. One of the industry truisms is "The more you tell, the more you sell." Tests show that longer letters bring in more new customers or new donors than do shorter letters. A four-page letter is considered ideal for mailings to new customers or donors.

Can short letters work? Yes, when you're writing to old customers or when the mailing is supported by other media. E-mail direct mail is also short—generally just one screen. The Direct Marketing Association says a postcard is the mailing most likely to be read.[31] The shortest message on record may be the two-word postcard that a fishing lake resort sent its customers: "They're biting!"

Fraud Victims

Financial scams and fraud cost Americans billions of dollars each year. According to studies of scammers, the victims of fraud aren't the uneducated or naïve. Most victims are well-educated, middle-aged men who have an excellent understanding of finances. So why are they falling prey to scammers? The studies offer these reasons:

- **Overconfidence.** Because of their education and experience in investing, most victims trust their own judgment without consulting experts for advice.

- **Pure motives.** Many victims are taken in because they want to provide an inheritance for their children or grandchildren. The motivation to help may encourage the victims to make unwise decisions.

- **Emotional reactions.** In one experiment during the Christmas season, the Better Business Bureau and a local television station in Idaho set up a fake bell ringer with a plastic Halloween bucket. Even though he had no identifying signs, shoppers automatically gave him money while he rang his bell.

- **Pro/con lists.** Research has shown that when people attempt to make lists of positives and negatives about a decision, whichever side they focus on first has the greatest impact on their choice.

Adapted from Karen Blumenthal, "Fraud Doesn't Always Happen to Someone Else," *Wall Street Journal*, August 12, 2009, D1.

Content for the body of the message can include

- Information the audience will find useful even if they do not buy or give.
- Stories about how the product was developed or what the organization has done.
- Stories about people who have used the product or who need the organization's help.
- Word pictures of people enjoying the benefits offered.

Because consumers are more likely to choose or favor the familiar, linking your sales message to the things people do or use every day is a good way to increase your message's perceived importance. Of course, that requires that you do a good job of audience analysis up front. Stanford University researchers showed that children given chicken nuggets and French fries preferred the taste of the food in McDonald's packaging, even though all the food came from the same source. The familiarity effect works on adults, too. In another study, adults tasting the same peanut butter from three different jars preferred the spread from the jar with a name brand label.[32]

Costs are generally mentioned near the end of the body and are connected to specific benefits. Sometimes costs are broken down to monthly, weekly, or daily amounts: "For less than the cost of a cup of coffee a day, you can help see that Eren is no longer hungry."

Action Close   The action close in the message must do four things:

1. **Tell the audience what to do:** Specify the action you want. Avoid *if* ("If you'd like to try . . .") and *why not* ("Why not send in a check?"). They lack positive emphasis and encourage your audience to say *no*.
2. **Make the action sound easy:** "Fill in the information on the reply card and mail it today." If you provide an envelope and pay postage, say so.
3. **Offer a reason for acting promptly.** People who think they are convinced but wait to act are less likely to buy or contribute. Reasons for acting promptly are easy to identify when a product is seasonal or there is a genuine limit on the offer—time limit, price rise scheduled, limited supply, and so on. Sometimes you can offer a premium or a discount if your audience acts quickly. When these conditions do not exist, remind readers that the sooner they get the product, the sooner they can benefit from it; the sooner they contribute funds, the sooner their dollars can go to work to solve the problem.
4. **End with a positive picture** of the audience enjoying the product (in a sales message) or of the audience's money working to solve the problem (in a fund-raising message). The last sentence should never be a selfish request for money.

The action close can also remind people of central selling points, and mention when the customer will get the product.

Using a P.S.   In a direct mail letter or e-mail, the postscript, or P.S., occupies a position of emphasis by being the final part of the message. Direct mail often uses a deliberate P.S. after the signature block. It may restate the central selling point or some other point the letter makes, preferably in different words so that it won't sound repetitive when the reader reads the letter through from start to finish.

The Master Salesman

Dale Carnegie was an unsuccessful businessman, a failed actor, and an undistinguished author of western novels when he began teaching public speaking at a Harlem YMCA in 1912. His course in public speaking eventually turned into a self-help business empire, built on his still-popular book, *How to Win Friends and Influence People*, published in 1936.

Carnegie's *How to Win Friends* remains one of the most influential business books of all time. Warren Buffett has based his career on the principles in the book, and Lee Iacocca says it changed his life.

What is it about the book that makes it so powerful? In 30 simple principles, Carnegie lays out a course of self-improvement, based on self-confidence and powerful public speaking, that ties directly into business success. His ideas weren't new when he wrote the book, and they are certainly not new now. Carnegie once said, however, "I present, reiterate, and glorify the obvious—because the obvious is what people need to be told."

Adapted from Dan Winters, "The Best Salesman in Business," *Fortune*, May 3, 2010, 202–4.

Here are four of the many kinds of effective P.S.'s.
Reason to act promptly:

> P.S.   Once I finish the limited harvest, that's it! I do not store any SpringSweet Onions for late orders. I will ship all orders on a first-come, first-served basis and when they are gone they are gone. Drop your order in the mail today . . . or give me a call toll free at 800-531-7470! (In Texas: 800-292-5437)

Sales letter for Frank Lewis Alamo Fruit

Description of a premium the reader receives for giving:

> P.S.   And . . . we'll be pleased to send you—as a new member—the exquisite, full-color Sierra Club Wilderness Calendar. It's our gift . . . absolutely FREE to you . . . to show our thanks for your membership at this critical time.

Fund-raising letter for Sierra Club

Reference to another part of the package:

> P.S.   Photographs may be better than words, but they still don't do justice to this model. Please keep in mind as you review the enclosed brochure that your SSJ will look even better when you can see it firsthand in your own home.

Sales letter for the Danbury Mint's model of the Duesenberg SSJ

Restatement of central selling point:

> P.S.   It is not easy to be a hungry child in the Third World. If your parents' crops fail or if your parents cannot find work, there are no food stamps . . . no free government-provided cafeteria lunches.
>   Millions of hungry schoolchildren will be depending on CARE this fall. Your gift today will ensure that we will be there—that CARE won't let them down.

Fund-raising letter for CARE

Strategy in Sales Messages and Fund-Raising Appeals

In both sales messages and fund-raising appeals, the basic strategy is to help your audience see themselves using your products/services or participating in the goals of your charity. Too often, communicators stress the new features of their gadgets, rather than picturing the audience using it, or the statistics about their cause, rather than stories about people helping that cause.

Sales Messages   The basic strategy in sales messages is satisfying a need. Your message must remind people of the need your product meets, prove that the product will satisfy that need, show why your product is better than similar products, and make people *want* to have the product. Use psychological description (p. 330) to show people how the product will help them. Details about how the product is made can carry the message of quality. Testimonials from other buyers can help persuade people that the product works. In fact, sales trainer and best-seller business author Jeffrey Gitomer cites customer testimonials as one of the best ways to overcome price resistance.[33]

Generally, the price is not mentioned until the last fourth of the message, after the content makes the audience *want* the product.

Tempest in a Water Glass

Everyone needs water, so how much persuasion does it take to sell it? As the *Wall Street Journal* reported, there's a lot of persuasion involved in the water business—and some controversy as well.

Bottled water is big business in France: French citizens consume 145 liters per person per year, compared to 85 liters a year for Americans. When the public water companies that serve Paris ran advertisements promoting tap water over bottled with the slogan "Which brand delivers excellent water to your house all year round?" the major bottled water companies responded in kind. Their ad featured a toilet bowl and the catchphrase "I don't drink the water I use to flush."

Think about the persuasive techniques involved in the two ad campaigns. What psychological descriptions of their target audience do the ads employ? How do you think the Parisian Water Works ought to respond to the bottled water ads?

Adapted from David Gauthier-Villars, "Water Fight in France Takes a Dirty Turn," *Wall Street Journal*, February 1, 2007, B7.

Combining Charity with Marketing

When Crate & Barrel, the upscale furniture retailer, set out to support education with donations, they didn't just give money to needy schools. Instead, they sent out coupons in their mailers, inviting their customers to use the DonorsChoose website to decide how and where Crate & Barrel would donate its money.

The response? Customers loved the program. Not only did the coupons inspire a higher rate of customer involvement—11% of the coupons were redeemed, compared to 2% in a normal mass mailing—but the coupons also improved customers' perceptions of the company: 75% of the customers who used the DonorsChoose coupons said they now considered Crate & Barrel a company with a positive attitude toward the community, while 82% said they'd be more likely to buy the company's products in the future.

Think about the nonprofit organizations that you support: how might they convince local businesses to try the same approach?

Adapted from Emily Steel, "Novel Program Blends Charity and Marketing," *Wall Street Journal*, December 20, 2006, B1, B5.

You can make the price more palatable with the following techniques:

- **Link the price to the benefit the product provides.** "Your piece of history is just $39.95."
- **Link the price to benefits your company offers.** "You can reach our customer service agents 24/7."
- **Show how much the product costs each day, each week, or each month.** "You can have all this for less than the cost of a cup of coffee a day." Make sure that the amount seems small and that you've convinced people that they'll use this product sufficiently.
- **Allow customers to charge sales or pay in installments.** Your bookkeeping costs will rise, and some sales may be uncollectible, but the total number of sales will increase.

Fund-Raising Appeals   In a fund-raising appeal, the basic emotional strategy is **vicarious participation**. By donating money, people participate vicariously in work they are not able to do personally. This strategy affects the pronouns you use. Throughout the appeal, use *we* to talk about your group. However, at the end, talk about what *you* the audience will be doing. End positively, with a picture of the audience's dollars helping to solve the problem.

Fund-raising appeals require some extra strategy. To achieve both your primary and secondary purposes, you must give a great deal of information. This information (1) helps to persuade people; (2) gives supporters evidence to use in conversations with others; and (3) gives people who are not yet supporters evidence that may make them see the group as worthwhile, even if they do not give money now.

In your close, in addition to asking for money, suggest other ways people can help: doing volunteer work, scheduling a meeting on the subject, writing letters to Congress or the leaders of other countries, and so on. By suggesting other ways to participate, you not only involve your audience but also avoid one of the traps of fund-raising appeals: sounding as though you are interested in your audience only for the money they can give.

Deciding How Much to Ask For   Most messages to new donors suggest a range of amounts, from $50 or $100 (for employed people) up to perhaps double what you *really* expect to get from a single donor. A second strategy is to ask for a small, set amount that nearly everyone can afford ($15 or $25).

One of the several reasons people give for not contributing is that a gift of $25 or $100 seems too small to matter. It's not. Small gifts are important both in themselves and to establish a habit of giving. The American Heart Association recently determined that first-time donors responding to direct mail give an average of $21.84 and give $40.62 over a lifetime. But multiplied by the 7.6 million donors who respond to the AHA's mailings, the total giving is large. Also, over $20 million of the money that the AHA receives from estate settlements after a person's death comes from people who have a relationship as direct-mail donors.[34]

You can increase the size of gifts by using the following techniques:

- **Link the gift to what it will buy.** Tell how much money it costs to buy a brick, a hymnal, or a stained glass window for a church; a book or journal subscription for a college library; a meal for a hungry child. Linking amounts to specific gifts helps the audience feel involved and often motivates them to give more: instead of saying, "I'll write a check for $25," the person may say, "I'd like to give a ———" and write a check to cover it.

- **Offer a premium for giving.** Public TV and radio stations have used this ploy with great success, offering books, CDs, DVDs, umbrellas, and carryall bags for gifts at a certain level. The best premiums are things that people both want and will use or display, so that the organization will get further publicity when other people see the premium.
- **Ask for a monthly pledge.** People on modest budgets could give $15 or $25 a month; more prosperous people could give $100 a month or more. These repeat gifts not only bring in more money than the donors could give in a single check but also become part of the base of loyal supporters, which is essential to the continued success of any organization that raises funds.

Annual appeals to past donors often use the amount of the last donation as the lowest suggested gift, with other gifts 25%, 50%, or even 100% higher.

Always send a thank-you message to people who respond to your appeal, whatever the size of their gifts. By telling about the group's recent work, a thank-you message can help reinforce donors' commitment to your cause.

Logical Proof in Fund-Raising Messages   The body of a fund-raising message must prove that (1) the problem deserves attention, (2) the problem can be solved or at least alleviated, (3) your organization is helping to solve or alleviate it, (4) private funds are needed, and (5) your organization will use the funds wisely.

1. The problem deserves attention.   No one can support every cause. Show why your audience should care about solving this problem.

If your problem is life-threatening, give some statistics: Tell how many people are killed in the United States every year by drunk drivers, or how many children in the world go to bed hungry every night. Also tell about one individual who is affected.

If your problem is not life-threatening, show that the problem threatens some goal or principle your audience find important. For example, a fundraising letter to boosters of a high school swim team showed that team members' chances of setting records were reduced because timers relied on stopwatches. The letter showed that automatic timing equipment was accurate and produced faster times, since the timer's reaction time was no longer included in the time recorded.

2. The problem can be solved or alleviated.   People will not give money if they see the problem as hopeless—why throw money away? Sometimes you can reason by analogy. Cures have been found for other deadly diseases, so it's reasonable to hope that research can find a cure for cancer and AIDS. Sometimes you can show that short-term or partial solutions exist. For example, UNICEF shows how simple changes—oral rehydration, immunization, and breast feeding—could save the lives of millions of children. These solutions don't affect the underlying causes of poverty, but they do keep children alive while we work on long-term solutions.

3. Your organization is helping to solve or alleviate the problem.   Prove that your organization is effective. Be specific. Talk about your successes in the past. Your past success helps readers believe that you can accomplish your goals.

Donating to Operating Expenses?

Wouldn't you want to make sure that your charitable donations went to support worthwhile causes, rather than overhead expenses within a nonprofit organization? Many people do, and so look for nonprofits that either limit their spending on overhead or can guarantee that gifts will go toward specific programs, not overhead.

However, even nonprofit organizations have bills to pay. As the *Wall Street Journal* reports, some nonprofits are challenged with the tasks of soliciting donations while convincing donors that money spent on overhead is still money well spent. One solution? Some nonprofits ask for donations specifically to cover their operating expenses by asking for money to support their teams or their business plans.

Philanthropy advisers suggest that donors also consider how effectively the charity uses its money. Some organizations that spend 70% of their funds on their core mission do a better job than those who spend 80%.

The very best way to judge a charity? Be one of their volunteers.

How would asking for a donation to pay for a nonprofit's overhead be different than asking for donations to support a worthy cause? What persuasive strategies could you use to make that request?

Adapted from Rachel Emma Silverman and Sally Beatty, "Save the Children (but Pay the Bills, Too)," *Wall Street Journal*, December 26, 2006, D1, D2.

www.habitat.org

Habitat for Humanity's website provides information for potential and current donors, volunteers, and clients.

Enclosures In Fund-Raising Letters

Fund-raising letters sometimes use inexpensive enclosures to add interest and help carry the message.

Brochures are inexpensive, particularly if you photocopy them. Mailings to alumni have included "Why I Teach at Earlham" (featuring three professors) and letters from students who have received scholarships.

Seeds don't cost much. Mailings from both Care and the New Forests Fund include four or five seeds of the leucaena, a subtropical tree that can grow 20 feet in a year. Its leaves feed cattle; its wood provides firewood or building materials; its roots reduce soil erosion. (Indeed, the enclosure easily becomes the theme for the letter.)

Reprints of newspaper or magazine articles about the organization or the problem it is working to solve add interest and credibility. Pictures of people the organization is helping build emotional appeal.

Major campaigns may budget for enclosures: pictures of buildings, CDs of oral history interviews, and maps of areas served.

These are some of the specifics that the charity:water website gives about its efforts:

> Our Progress So Far: 3,962 projects funded. 1,794,983 people will get clean water. 19 countries, 25 local partners.[35]

4. Private funds are needed to accomplish your group's goals.   We all have the tendency to think that taxes, or foundations, or church collections yield enough to pay for medical research or basic human aid. If your group does get some tax or foundation money, show why more money is needed. If the organization helps people who might be expected to pay for the service, show why they cannot pay, or why they cannot pay enough to cover the full cost. If some of the funds have been raised by the people who will benefit, make that clear.

5. Your organization will use the funds wisely.   Prove that the money goes to the cause, not just to the cost of fund-raising. This point is becoming increasingly important as stories become more common of "charities" that give little money to their mission. One study of 80 professional fund-raisers serving over 500 charities found the median percentage of proceeds going to the charity was 24%; only five charities received more than 75%. In fact, one fund-raising company charged charities more money than the company raised.[36]

Emotional Appeal in Fund-Raising Messages   Emotional appeal is needed to make people pull out their checkbooks. How strong should emotional appeal be? A mild appeal is unlikely to sway anyone who is not already committed, but your audience will feel manipulated by appeals they find too strong and reject them. Audience analysis may help you decide how much emotional appeal to use. If you don't know your audience well, use the strongest emotional appeal *you* feel comfortable with.

Emotional appeal is created by specifics. It is hard to care about, or even to imagine, a million people; it is easier to care about one specific person. Details and quotes help us see that person as real. Sensory details also help people connect to a cause. Covenant House, an organization that takes in homeless youth, does both. They provide vivid pictures both of children arriving at their door and of individuals who have turned their lives around. They also use relevant sensory details: a child crawling into bed on a cold night, feeling warm and safe under soft blankets, versus a girl crawling into a cardboard box on the street to try to stay warm on a cold night.[37]

Sample Fund-Raising Letter   The letter from UNICEF (Figure 11.8) seeks aid for people in Darfur. It stresses the enormity of the problem—"4.7 million people," "millions of families," "millions of children"—and what UNICEF has already done to help them. It moves on to the specific need for "additional emergency supplies of therapeutic nutritional supplements," and shows them to be life-saving aids. It applies specifics to donations: $25 will buy 49 packets. The close continues the sense of urgency, while the P.S. reemphasizes the good that has already been done with the nutritional packets.

Writing Style

Direct mail is the one kind of business writing where elegance and beauty of language matter; in every other kind, elegance is welcome but efficiency is all that finally counts. Direct mail imitates the word choice and rhythm of conversation. The best sales, fund-raising, and promotional writing is closer to the language of poetry than to that of academia: it shimmers with images, it echoes with sound, it vibrates with energy.

Figure 11.8   A Fund-Raising Letter

CHILDREN ARE STARVING IN DARFUR

Emotional appeal in headline

Will you help rush 49 packets of ready-to-eat therapeutic nutritional supplement to save malnourished children in Darfur?

Dear Dr. Kienzler,

In spite of intense world pressure and the sustained work of UNICEF, the humanitarian crisis in Darfur continues to worsen. Continued violence has affected 4.7 million people - half of them children - with refugee camps filled to capacity.

Letter opens with startling statement about enormity of problem

Hundreds of thousand of lives have been lost, and the exodus of millions of families has torn this country apart. UNICEF has been coordinating relief for the world's largest refugee relocation effort, establishing and maintaining emergency shipments of food, clean water, and medical supplies.

Pragraph shows what UNICEF has been doing

The recent suspension of humanitarian aid organizations by the government of Sudan has left UNICEF as the only remaining major source of emergency support for millions of children struggling to survive in Darfur. Today, UNICEF supports 260 primary health facilities and mobile clinics . . . has trained and deployed nearly 1,000 community healthy workers . . . and has been the primary source of vaccines, cold chain equipment, and operational staff for polio and measles immunization campaigns.

Fund raising letters may use format features such as underlining and ellipses

UNICEF also directly maintains over 100 therapeutic and supplementary feeding centers. But with millions of children and no readily available source of food, and tens of thousands of children already suffering from severe malnutrition, UNICEF needs to provide additional emergency supplies of therapeutic nutritional supplements.

The specially formulated high-protein, high-energy paste revives children with remarkable results and can reverse the most severe effects of malnutrition. Your gift today of $25 can supply 49 packets - and just three of these packets daily can help a malnourished child recover with minimal adverse health effects.

Sentence shows situation is not hopeless

Shows impact of reasonable individual gift

Every minute counts. Please act now.

Need for immediate action

Sincerely,
Caryl M. Stren

Caryl M. Stren
President & CEO

P. S. By providing nutritional supplies and other assistance, UNICEF successfully treated over 53,000 malnourished children in Darfur last year, saving them from almost-certain death. Please send a generous gift today to continue these vital efforts.

Reiteration of successful effort

Source: Reprinted with permission from the U.S. Fund for UNICEF.

346   **Part 3**   Basic Business Messages

Adapted from Louise Lee, "Catalogs, Catalogs, Everywhere," *Business-Week*, December 4, 2006, 32–34.

The Changing Role of Catalogs

If sales from mass-mailer catalogs have been declining in recent years, replaced by e-commerce sales through websites, isn't it time to retire paper catalogs? Not necessarily: catalogs are still one way for companies to build customer interest and persuade customers to make purchases—even if those purchases are online.

Catalogs can be an integral part of a company's marketing plan:

- Instead of showing a company's entire stock, a good catalog will save space (and costs!) by listing a representative sampling. The idea is to attract the widest possible range of customers, with the widest possible interests.

- Good catalogs increase customer involvement with the products, either by providing them with a shopping experience "in hand" or by directing them to an interactive website.

Think about the catalogs that you receive in the mail. How do you use them? What would you need to see in a catalog to convince you to visit its website or a physical store?

Catalogs are still an excellent way for companies to build customer interest and persuade customers to buy—even if the sales are made at the company's website.

Many of the things that make writing vivid and entertaining *add* words because they add specifics or evoke an emotional response. Individual sentences should flow smoothly. The passage as a whole may be fun to read precisely because of the details and images that "could have been left out."

Make Your Writing Interesting   If the style is long-winded and boring, the reader will stop reading. Eliminating wordiness is crucial. You've already seen ways to tighten your writing in Chapter 5. Direct mail goes further, breaking some of the rules of grammar. In the following examples, note how sentence fragments and ellipses (spaced dots) are used in parallel structure to move the reader along:

> Dear Member-elect:
>
> If you still believe that there are nine planets in our solar system . . . that wine doesn't breathe . . . and that you'd recognize a Neanderthal man on sight if one sat next to you on the bus . . . check your score. There aren't. It does. You wouldn't.

Subscription letter for *Natural History*

Use Psychological Description   Psychological description (p. 330) means describing your product or service with vivid sensory details. In a sales letter, you can use psychological description to create a scenario so readers can picture themselves using your product or service and enjoying its benefits. You can also use psychological description to describe the problem your product or service will solve.

A *Bon Appétit* subscription letter used psychological description in its opener and in the P.S., creating a frame for the sales letter:

> Dear Reader:
>
> First, fill a pitcher with ice.
> Now pour in a bottle of ordinary red wine, a quarter cup of brandy, and a small bottle of Club soda.
> Sweeten to taste with a quarter to half cup of sugar, garnish with slices of apple, lemon, and orange. . . .

> . . . then *move your chair to a warm, sunny spot.* You've just made yourself Sangria—one of the great glories of Spain, and the perfect thing to sit back with and sip while you consider this invitation. . . .
>
> . . .
>
> P.S. One more thing before you finish your Sangria. . . .

It's hard to imagine any reader really stopping to follow the recipe before finishing the letter, but the scenario is so vivid that one can imagine the sunshine even on a cold, gray day.

Make Your Letter Sound Like a Letter, Not an Ad   Maintain the image of one person writing to one other person that is the foundation of all letters. Use an informal style with short words and sentences, and even slang.

You can also create a **persona**—the character who allegedly writes the letter—to make the letter interesting and keep us reading. Use the rhythms of speech, vivid images, and conversational words to create the effect that the author is a "character."

The following opening creates a persona who fits the product:

> Dear Friend:
>
> There's no use trying. I've tried and tried to tell people about my fish. But I wasn't rigged out to be a letter writer, and I can't do it. I can close-haul a sail with the best of them. I know how to pick out the best fish of the catch, I know just which fish will make the tastiest mouthfuls, but I'll never learn the knack of writing a letter that will tell people why my kind of fish—fresh-caught prime-grades, right off the fishing boats with the deep-sea tang still in it—is lots better than the ordinary store kind.

Sales letter, Frank Davis Fish Company

This letter, with its "Aw, shucks, I can't sell" persona, with language designed to make you see an unassuming fisherman ("rigged out," "close-haul"), was written by a professional advertiser.[38]

SOLVING A SAMPLE PROBLEM

Little things add up to big issues, especially where workplace quality of life is at stake.

Problem

FirstWest Insurance's regional office has 300 employees, all working the same 8-to-5 shift. Many of them schedule their lunch break during the noon hour, and that's where the problem started: there was only one microwave in the canteen. People had to wait up to 30 minutes to heat their lunches. As Director of Human Resources, you implemented lunch shifts to break the gridlock. That program failed: people were used to their schedules and resisted the change. In your second attempt, you convinced FirstWest's Operations Vice President to approve a purchase order for a second microwave oven.

Now there's a new problem: fish. FirstWest recently recruited five new employees. They're from the Philippines, and fish is a prominent part of their diet. Each afternoon, they take lunch together and reheat their meals—often containing fish—and each afternoon, the air conditioning system in your closed-air building sends the aroma of spiced fish wafting through the whole office.

348   Part 3   Basic Business Messages

Face-to-face Persuasion

When you present your persuasive messages in a spoken, face-to-face format, remember that your interpersonal interactions are an important part of your message. A recent study of successful retail salespeople identified some strong techniques you can use when you're speaking persuasively:

- Use their name. People respond well when you show that you care enough about them to use their name.

- Show your Interest. Build goodwill and rapport by asking about, noticing, and remembering details about your audience's history and preferences.

- Identify mutual interests. Turn your persuasive pitch into a conversation by inviting stories from your audience and sharing your own in return.

- Be polite and honest. Many people react to persuasive messages by being on guard against potential dishonesty. Demonstrate your respect for your audience by backing up your claims with evidence: show them, don't tell them, and invite them to judge for themselves.

- Give—and seek—information. Take the pressure off your persuasive message by changing it into an informative message instead of sales. Build rapport by inviting your audience to share their knowledge with you.

Adapted from Dwayne D. Gremler and Kevin P. Gwinner, "Rapport-Building Behaviors Used by Retail Employees," *Journal of Retailing* 84, no. 3 (2008): 308–24.

Other employees have complained bitterly about the "foul odor." You've spoken to the new employees, and while they're embarrassed by the complaints, they see no reason to change. After all, they're just as disgusted by the smell of cooking beef: why haven't you asked the American employees not to reheat hamburger? And having just purchased a second oven, you know that management won't pay $1,000 for a new microwave with a filter system that will eliminate the odors. It's time to set a microwave-use policy.

Analysis of the Problem

Use the problem analysis questions in the first chapter to think through the problem.

1. Who is (are) your audience(s)?

   You'll be addressing all of the employees at this location. That's a broad audience, but they have certain characteristics in common, at least regarding this topic. They're all on a similar lunch schedule, and many of them use the canteen and the microwaves. They've also responded poorly to a previous attempt to change their lunch habits.

   Many members of your audience won't see this as their problem: only the new employees are doing something objectionable. The new employees will react poorly to being singled out.

2. What are your purposes in writing?

   To help eliminate cooking odors. To solve a minor issue before it begins to impact morale.

3. What information must your message include?

   The effects of the present situation. The available options and their costs (in money, and also in time, effort, and responsibility).

4. How can you build support for your position? What reasons or benefits will your audience find convincing?

   Improving the workplace environment—and eliminating a minor but persistent irritation—should improve morale. While expensive solutions exist, this is a matter that can, and should, be solved with cooperative behaviors.

5. What aspects of the total situation may be relevant?

   This issue is a minor one, and it may be difficult to get people to take it seriously. The easy solution—mandating what the new employees are allowed to bring for lunch—is discriminatory. For budgetary reasons, company management will not invest in a third (and much more expensive) microwave for the canteen.

Discussion of the Sample Solutions

The solution shown in Figure 11.9 is unacceptable. By formatting the communication as a notice designed to be posted in the canteen, the author invites the audience to publicly embarrass their co-workers: a form of threat. The subject line displays the author's biases in a way that discourages further discussion on the topic and eliminates the possibility of a broader consensus for any solution to the problem. The author uses emotional appeals to place blame on a small segment of the audience, but the lack of logical observations or arguments (and the presence of clip art and emoticons) undermines the author's seriousness. The demand to stop cooking food with strong smells is vague: does this include pizza? popcorn? The author concludes with a threat, again eliminating the possibility of consensus-based actions.

Figure 11.9 An Unacceptable Solution to the Sample Problem

ATTENTION!!!!

DON'T BRING DISGUSTING LUNCHES!!

Negative, biased subject line and clip art

Negative diction

Some of you (you KNOW!!! who you are) have been bringing in <u>foul-smelling</u> food and cooking it in the microwave at lunch. We've all smelled the result. It's not fair that everyone has to put up with your <u>stink</u>.

I'm writing to tell everyone that this is the END. As of today, no one is allowed to cook any food with a <u>strong smell</u> in the canteen microwave ovens. *Vague diction*

Threatens

The microwaves are a privilege and not a right. If you people continue to abuse company property, the microwaves will be removed from the canteen for good. ☹ *Don't use emoticons in serious communications*

Thank you in advance for your cooperation in this matter.

Close does not sound sincere after threat

Clip art not appropriate for this serious communication

✓ **Checklist** | Checklist for Direct Requests

- ☐ If the message is a memo, does the subject line indicate the request? Is the subject line specific enough to differentiate this message from others on the same subject?
- ☐ Does the first paragraph summarize the request or the specific topic of the message?
- ☐ Does the message give all of the relevant information? Is there enough detail?
- ☐ Does the message answer questions or overcome objections that readers may have without introducing unnecessary negatives?
- ☐ Does the closing tell the reader exactly what to do? Does it give a deadline if one exists and a reason for acting promptly?

Originality in a direct request may come from

- ☐ Good lists and visual impact.
- ☐ Thinking about readers and giving details that answer their questions, overcome any objections, and make it easier for them to do as you ask.
- ☐ Adding details that show you're thinking about a specific organization and the specific people in that organization.

The second solution, shown in Figure 11.10, is a more effective persuasive message. The author recognizes that this persuasive situation centers on good-will, and begins with a neutral subject line (as a more directed subject could

---

The "Default" Choice Is Yes

Have you ever been presented with an online form that had response boxes prechecked for you? One way to sidestep your customers' objections is to provide them with default responses: choices they can make that encourage an easy, objection-free response. Here are some common types of defaults:

- **Benign** default choices give customers a range of responses that you've chosen for them: you present a sample of the best or most likely responses ("Press one for English, para Espanol oprima numero dos").

- **Persistent** default choices use the customer's last response to the same situation as their current response (such as a billing form which assumes that your billing address is the same as your mailing address).

- **Smart** default choices use what you know about past customer behavior to suggest current choices that they're likely to agree with (such as retailer websites that offer a list of other products you may be interested in based on what you've selected already).

- **Forced** defaults are selections your customers must make in order to access a product or service (such as the licensing agreement for most software packages).

These defaults offer quick, convenient ways to encourage customers to respond in predictable ways. They can also allow you to constrain your customers' choices. What ethical concerns do you need to consider before you use defaults in your persuasive messages?

Adapted from Daniel G. Goldstein et al., "Nudge Your Customers toward Better Choices," *Harvard Business Review* 86, no. 12 (December 2008): 99–105.

350   Part 3   Basic Business Messages

Figure 11.10   A Good Solution to the Sample Problem

Date: November 15, 2012

To: FirstWest Grand Harbor Co-Workers

From: Arnold M. Morgan, Human Resources Director **AMM**

Subject: Canteen Microwave Policies   *Neutral subject line*

Creates common ground

We all notice when someone uses the microwaves in the first-floor canteen to reheat strong-smelling food. These odors are distracting—whether they're the scent of burned popcorn, a fish lunch, or fresh-baked brownies—and none of us need any extra distractions in our busy days! Let's work together to "clear the air."

Cause of problem

How is it that we all smell food cooking in the first-floor canteen? Our building has a closed-air ventilation system: it's good for the environment and it saves on heating and cooling costs by recirculating air throughout the building. It also circulates any odors in the air. That's why we can smell food from the first-floor canteen down in the basement archives and up in the third-floor conference rooms: we're all sharing the same air.

We're all sharing the same microwaves, too. Due to popular demand, we recently purchased a second microwave to relieve crowding at lunchtime. We've looked into purchasing a third microwave—an odor-eliminating, air-filtration microwave—but that would cost $1,000, plus $20/month for filters. That seems expensive, especially since there are simple things each of us can do to reduce problems with odors.

Easy solutions to problem

- **Use containers with lids** when you heat up your food. Not only will this help contain any odors, it will reduce the mess in the microwaves.

- **Clean up any mess you make** when you cook. If you cook something with a strong odor—or something that spatters!—take a minute when you're done and wipe the oven down with a damp paper towel.

- **Stay with your food** while it's cooking. When food overcooks or burns, it smells more strongly, so watching your food and removing it from the oven before it overcooks is the easiest way to avoid creating a distracting smell.

We work together as a team every day to serve our customers and succeed as an organization. Please take a little time to use the microwaves responsibly, and help us make sure that the only smell in our workplace is success!

ends on positive note

detract from goodwill). The opening paragraph creates common ground by describing the problem in terms of group experience, rather than by assigning blame. It includes fish odors in with pleasant odors (brownies) and suggests that the memo's purpose is to propose a consensus-based solution.

The problem is spelled out in detail, balancing the emotional, goodwill-centered problem with rational arguments based on process and cost. The solution is presented as small, easily accommodated, changes. The memo ends by linking cooperation with the audience benefit of group participation and identity.

✓ *Checklist* **Checklist for Problem-Solving Persuasive Messages**

☐ If the message is a memo, does the subject line indicate the writer's purpose or offer a benefit? Does the subject line avoid making the request?

☐ Does the first sentence interest the audience?

☐ Is the problem presented as a joint problem both communicator and audience have an interest in solving, rather than as something the audience is being asked to do for the communicator?

☐ Does the message give all of the relevant information? Is there enough detail?

☐ Does the message overcome objections that the audience may have?

☐ Does the message avoid phrases that sound dictatorial, condescending, or arrogant?

☐ Does the closing tell the audience exactly what to do? Does it give a deadline if one exists and a reason for acting promptly?

Originality in a problem-solving persuasive message may come from

☐ A good subject line and common ground.

☐ A clear and convincing description of the problem.

☐ Thinking about the audience and giving details that answer their questions, overcome objections, and make it easier for them to do as you ask.

☐ Adding details that show you're thinking about a specific organization and the specific people in that organization.

Ethics and Direct Mail

Deception in direct mail is all too easy to find.

Some mailers have sent "checks" to readers. But the "check" can only be applied toward the purchase of the item the letter is selling.

Some mailings now have yellow Post-it notes with "handwritten" notes signed with initials or a first name only—to suggest that the mailing is from a personal friend.

One letter offers a "free" membership "valued at $675" (note the passive—who's doing the valuing?) but charges—up front—$157 for "maintenance fees."

Such deception has no place in well-written direct mail.

SUMMARY OF KEY POINTS

- The primary purpose in a persuasive message is to have the audience act or change beliefs. Secondary purposes are to overcome any objections that might prevent or delay action, to build a good image of the communicator and the communicator's organization, to cement a good relationship between the communicator and audience, and to reduce or eliminate future communication on the same subject.

- **Credibility** is the audience's response to you as the source of the message. You can build credibility by being factual, specific, and reliable.

- You always need to consider your audience and situation before choosing your persuasive strategy. In general,
  - Use the **direct request pattern** when the audience will do as you ask without any resistance. Also use the direct request pattern for busy readers in your own organization who do not read all the messages they receive. See Figure 11.1.
  - Use the **problem-solving pattern** when the audience may resist doing what you ask and you expect logic to be more important than emotion in the decision. See Figure 11.3.
  - Use the **sales pattern** when the audience may resist doing as you ask and you expect emotion to be more important than logic in the decision. See Figure 11.10.

- Use one or more of the following strategies to counter objections that you cannot eliminate:
  - Specify how much time and/or money is required.
  - Put the time and/or money in the context of the benefits they bring.
  - Show that money spent now will save money in the long run.
  - Show that doing as you ask will benefit some group the audience identifies with or some cause the audience supports.

Get Involved

Getting involved with nonprofit work is a great opportunity to give back to your community while developing your professional and communication skills. Here are some online resources to get you started:

- http://www1.networkfor good.org/
- http://www.change.org/
- http://www.dosomething.org/
- http://firstgiving.org/
- http://www.donorschoose.org/
- http://www.kiva.org/
- http://www.opportunity.org/
- http://www.accion.org/
- http://www.jumo.com/

- Show the audience that the sacrifice is necessary to achieve a larger, more important goal to which they are committed.
    - Show that the advantages as a group outnumber or outweigh the disadvantages as a group.
    - Turn the disadvantage into an opportunity.
- Threats don't produce permanent change. They won't necessarily produce the action you want, they may make people abandon an action entirely (even in situations where abandoning would not be appropriate), and they produce tension. People dislike and avoid anyone who threatens them. Threats can provoke counteraggression.
- To encourage people to act promptly, set a deadline. Show that the time limit is real, that acting now will save time or money, or that delaying action will cost more.
- Build emotional appeal with stories and psychological description.
- Performance appraisals should cite specific observations, not inferences. They should contain specific suggestions for improvement and identify the two or three areas that the worker should emphasize in the next month or quarter.
- Letters of recommendation must be specific and tell how well and how long you've known the person.
- A good opener makes readers want to read persuasion messages and provides a reasonable transition to the body of the message. Four modes for openers are questions, narration, startling statements, and quotations. A good body answers the audience's questions, overcomes their objections, and involves them emotionally. A good action close tells people what to do, makes the action sound easy, gives them a reason for acting promptly, and ends with a benefit or a picture of their contribution helping to solve the problem.
- In a fund-raising appeal, the basic strategy is vicarious participation. By donating money, people participate vicariously in work they are not able to do personally.
- The primary purpose in a fund-raising appeal is to get money. An important secondary purpose is to build support for the cause so that people who are not persuaded to give will still have favorable attitudes toward the group and will be sympathetic when they hear about it again.

CHAPTER 11   Exercises and Problems

*Go to www.mhhe.com/locker10e for additional Exercises and Problems.

11.1   Reviewing the Chapter

1. What are four questions you should answer when analyzing persuasive situations? Which question do you think is the most important? Why? (LO 11-1)
2. What are three basic persuasive strategies? In what kinds of situations is each preferred? (LO 11-2)
3. Why aren't threats effective persuasion tools? (LO 11-2)
4. How do you start the body of persuasive direct requests? Why? (LO 11-3)
5. How do you organize persuasive problem-solving messages? (LO 11-4)
6. How do you develop a common ground with your audience? (LO 11-4)
7. What are 10 ways to deal with objections? (LO 11-4 and LO 11-6)
8. What are ways to build emotional appeal? (LO 11-4 and LO 11-6)
9. What are four good beginnings for sales and fund-raising messages? (LO 11-5)
10. What are ways to de-emphasize costs or donation requests? (LO 11-5)
11. What kinds of rational evidence should you use to support your persuasion? (LO 11-6)
12. What kinds of emotional appeals should you use to support your persuasion? (LO 11-6)

11.2   Reviewing Grammar

Persuasion uses lots of pronouns. Correct the sentences in Exercise B.4, Appendix B, to practice making pronouns agree with their nouns, as well as practicing subject–verb agreement.

11.3   Writing Psychological Description

For one or more of the following groups, write two or three paragraphs of psychological description that could be used in a brochure, news release, or direct mail message directed to members of that group.

1. Having a personal trainer.

   Audiences: Professional athletes
                       Busy managers
                       Someone trying to lose weight
                       Someone making a major lifestyle change after a heart attack

2. Volunteering time to a local charity event (you pick the charity) as part of a team from your workplace.

   Audiences: Your workplace colleagues
                       Your boss
                       Finance department
                       PR department

3. Using vending machines newly installed in school cafeterias and stocked with healthful snacks, such as yogurt, raisins, carrots with dip, and all-natural juices.

   Audiences: High school students
                       Parents
                       High school faculty

4. Attending a fantasy sports camp (you pick the sport), playing with and against retired players who provide coaching and advice.

5. Attending a health spa where clients get low-fat and low-carb meals, massages, beauty treatments, and guidance in nutrition and exercise.

Hints:

- For this assignment, you can combine benefits or programs as if a single source offered them all.
- Add specific details about particular sports, activities, and so on, as material for your description.
- Be sure to use vivid details and sense impressions.
- Phrase your benefits with you-attitude.

11.4   Evaluating Subject Lines

Evaluate the following subject lines. Is one subject line in each group clearly best? Or does the "best" line depend on company culture, whether the message is a paper memo or an e-mail message, or on some other factor?

1. Subject: Request
   Subject: Why I Need a New Computer
   Subject: Increasing My Productivity

2. Subject: Who Wants Extra Hours?
   Subject: Holiday Work Schedule
   Subject: Working Extra Hours During the Holiday Season

3. Subject: Student Mentors
   Subject: Can You Be an E-Mail Mentor?
   Subject: Volunteers Needed

4. Subject: More Wine and Cheese
   Subject: Today's Reception for Japanese Visitors
   Subject: Reminder

5. Subject: Reducing Absenteeism
   Subject: Opening a Day Care Center for Sick Children of Employees
   Subject: Why We Need Expanded Day Care Facilities

11.5   Evaluating P.S.'s

Evaluate the following P.S.'s. Will they motivate readers to read the whole messages if readers turn to them first? Do they create a strong ending for those who have already read the message?

1. P.S. It only takes <u>one</u> night's stay in a hotel you read about here, <u>one</u> discounted flight, <u>one</u> budget-priced cruise, or <u>one</u> low-cost car rental to make mailing back your Subscription Certificate well worth it.

   P.P.S. About your free gift! Your risk-free subscription to CONSUMER REPORTS TRAVEL LETTER comes with a remarkable 314-page book as a FREE GIFT.

2. P.S. Help spread the tolerance message by using your personalized address labels on all your correspondence. And remember, you will receive a free *Teaching Tolerance* magazine right after your tax-deductible contribution arrives.

3. P.S. Every day brings more requests like that of Mr. Agyrey-Kwakey—for our "miracle seeds." And it's urgent that we respond to the emergency in Malaysia and Indonesia by replanting those forests destroyed by fire. Please send your gift today and become a partner with us in these innovative projects around the world.

4. P.S. Even as you read this letter, a donated load of food waits for the ticket that will move it to America's hungry. Please give today!

11.6   Choosing a Persuasive Approach

For each of the following situations requiring a persuasive message, choose the persuasive approach that you feel would work best. Explain your reasoning; then give a short list of the types of information you'd use to persuade your audience.

1. Asking for an extension on a project.
2. Requesting a job interview.
3. Requesting a free trial of a service.
4. Inviting customers to a store opening.
5. Reporting a co-worker's poor work performance.
6. Asking your supervisor to reconsider a poor performance review.
7. Requesting a new office computer.
8. Requesting time off during your company's busy season.

As your instructor directs,

a. Write a memo, letter, or e-mail that addresses one of the situations in this exercise, drawing on details from your personal experiences. (You might address a real problem that you've faced.)

b. Write a memo to your instructor listing the choices you've made and justifying your approach.

11.7   Identifying Observations

Susan has taken the following notes about her group's meetings. Which of the following are specific observations that she could use in a performance appraisal of group members? If she had it to do over again, what kinds of details would turn the inferences into observations?

1. Feb. 22: Today was very frustrating. Sam was totally out of it—I wonder if he's on something. Jim was dictatorial. I argued, but nobody backed me up. Masayo might just as well have stayed home. We didn't get anything done. Two hours, totally wasted.

2. February 24: Jim seems to be making a real effort to be less domineering. Today he asked Sam and me for our opinions before proposing his own. And he noticed that Masayo wasn't talking much and brought her into the conversation. She suggested some good ideas.

3. February 28: Today's meeting was OK. I thought Masayo wasn't really focusing on the work at hand. She needs to work on communicating her ideas to others. Sam was doing some active listening, but he needs to work at being on time. Jim was involved in the project. He has strong leadership skills. There were some tense moments, but we got a lot done, and we all contributed. I got to say what I wanted to say, and the group decided to use my idea for the report.

4. March 5: This week most of us had midterms, and Masayo had an out-of-town gymnastics trip. We couldn't find a time to meet. So we did stuff by e-mail. Sam and Jim found some great stuff at the library and on the web. Jim created a tentative schedule that he sent to all of us and then revised. I wrote up a draft of the description of the problem. Then Masayo and I put everything together. I sent my draft to her; she suggested revisions (in full caps so I could find them in the e-mail message). Then I sent the message to everyone. Masayo and Jim both suggested changes, which I made before we handed the draft in.

5. March 15: We were revising the proposal, using Prof. Jones's comments. When we thought we were basically done, Masayo noticed that we had not responded to all of the specific comments about our introductory paragraph. We then went back and thought of some examples to use. This made our proposal better and more complete.

As your instructor directs,

a. Based on Susan's notes, write a performance appraisal memo addressed to Prof. Jones. For each group member, including Susan, note specific areas of good performance and make specific suggestions for improvement.

b. Write a memo to your instructor describing the process you used to make your recommendations. Be sure to identify each of the observations you used to provide specific details, and each of the inferences that needed more information.

11.8   Revising a Form Memo

You've been hired as a staff accountant; one of your major duties will be processing expense reimbursements. Going through the files, you find this form memo:

> Subject: Reimbursements
>
> Enclosed are either receipts that we could not match with the items in your request for reimbursement or a list of items for which we found no receipts or both. Please be advised that the Accounting Department issues reimbursement checks only with full documentation. You cannot be reimbursed until you give us a receipt for each item for which you desire reimbursement. We must ask that you provide this information. This process may be easier if you use the Expense Report Form, which is available online.
>
> Thank you for your attention to this matter. Please do not hesitate to contact us with questions.

You know this memo is horrible. Employees have to use the Expense Report Form; it is not optional. In addition to wordiness, a total lack of positive emphasis and you-attitude, and a vague subject line, the document design and organization of information bury the request.

Create a new memo that could be sent to people who do not provide all the documentation they need in order to be reimbursed.

11.9   Creating Persuasive Videos

As they try to undo the harm from YouTube drinking videos starring their institutions, school officials are making their own YouTube videos. Some, such as deans lecturing on course offerings, are ludicrously bad. Other videos are slick promotional films. Still others, such as videos of classes, are somewhere in between.

Some schools are sponsoring contests to persuade students to create videos showing what they like about the school. One humorous one showed a student in a three-piece suit dancing across campus to "It's Raining Men." The student creator said he wanted a school where people dance around and have a good time.

What would you put in a video to convince students—and parents who foot the bills—to consider your school? Share your ideas in small groups.

Source: Susan Kinzie, "Colleges Putting Their Own Spin on YouTube," *Washington Post,* May 12, 2008, A01.

11.10   Creating Alternative Activities

You are residence director at Expensive Private University. Enrollment at your school has been declining because of repeated publicity about excessive drinking among the students. Last year 23 were treated for alcohol poisoning at the local hospital, and one died.

You have been ordered by the president of EPU to develop alcohol-free activities for the campus and ways to persuade students to participate. She wants your plans by the end of June so EPU can work on implementing them for the next academic year. Write the memo to her detailing your plans. Write a second memo to your instructor explaining your persuasive strategies.

Hints:

- Who are your audiences?
- Do they share any common ground?
- What objections will your audiences have?
- What are some ways you can deal with those objections?
- What pitfalls do you need to avoid?

11.11   Evaluating Persuasion Strategies

In June 2009, the Lorillard Tobacco Company responded to new legislation regulating the tobacco industry with a full-page ad in the *Wall Street Journal*. With a classmate or in a small group, evaluate the ad to pick out its persuasion strategies. Use the following questions in your evaluation:

- What audience is this message intended to reach?
- What strategies does the message use in its introduction and conclusion?
- What persuasion strategies does the message use?

- Which phrases are designed to create emotion in readers?
- How does the corporate author of the message affect how you perceive the persuasive arguments? How would your perceptions change if this same message were written by a government watchdog group? an antitobacco group?

Write a memo to your instructor with your evaluation of the ad.

FDA—Tobacco Regulation: Truth and Consequences

As the Family Smoking Prevention and Tobacco Control Act (H.R.1256/S.982)—which mandates that the Food and Drug Administration (FDA) regulate the tobacco industry—moves through the U.S. Senate, this is a critical time for lawmakers and all Americans to take a closer look at the major flaws in this legislation, and consider the serious consequences that could result.

The FDA Is the Wrong Agency

Putting the FDA in charge of an inherently dangerous product is inconsistent with the agency's mission to ensure the safety and efficacy of our nation's food, drugs, biologics, and medical devices. With the legacy of recent food and drug contaminations still reverberating, the FDA is an agency that is already overwhelmed in its mission to protect Americans. A March 2009 poll by the American Society for Quality (ASQ) reveals that Americans are losing confidence in the FDA's "Gold Standard" ability to protect the nation's food and drug supply. The survey found 61 percent of U.S. adults feel the food recall process in only fair or poor, while 73 percent of adults say they are as equally concerned about food safety as the war on terror.

A Boost to the Black Market

History clearly demonstrates that when consumer choice is thwarted by government policy, whether through exorbitant taxes, regulatory burdens, or outright bans, black markets arise to take advantage of the situation. This legislation will increase the price of tobacco products in order to pay for FDA regulation, which will only make it more lucrative and attractive for those who want to illegally profit (and likely deprive the federal and state governments of billions of dollars in taxes as a result) from this regulatory effort. And with huge profits—and low penalties for arrest and conviction—illicit cigarette trafficking now has begun to rival drug trafficking as a funding choice for terrorist groups. A congressional investigation led by Rep. Peter King (R-NY), ranking member of the House Homeland Security Committee, in April 2008 found that cigarette smugglers with ties to terrorist groups are acquiring millions of dollars from illegal cigarette sales and funneling the cash to organizations such as al Qaeda and Hezbollah.

Prohibition in Disguise

We believe the proponents of these new regulations would like nothing more than to outlaw smoking completely in our society. This bill is but a first big step in that direction, allowing the FDA to mandate changes to cigarettes as we know them and prevent new, potentially safer products from entering the marketplace. Should we let the FDA prohibit smoking or demand that the American people and those they elect to make such important decisions be the final arbiter of this issue?

A Blow to Safer Products

The regulations in this legislation would also require that the FDA approve any new tobacco product that claims to lessen the risk from smoking before it can be marketed. However, the standard that such new product must meet—that it is appropriate for the protection of the public health, determined with respect to the risks and benefits to the population as a whole, including users and non-users of the tobacco product—may well be impossible to meet, thereby assuring that no safer products ever come to market. Indeed, this bill will stifle the innovation that may provide promising hope for safer, less harmful tobacco products.

With respect to these specific issues, we urge the Senate to thoroughly review the current legislation and find an effective and different regulatory solution.

Lorillard Tobacco Company

Source: Lorillard Tobacco Company, "FDA-Tobacco Regulation: Truth and Consequences," advertisement, *Wall Street Journal,* June 3, 2009, A7.

11.12   Asking for More Time and/or Resources

Today, this message from your boss shows up in your e-mail inbox:

> Subject: Want Climate Report
>
> This request has come down from the CEO. I'm delegating it to you. See me a couple of days before the board meeting—the 4th of next month—so we can go over your presentation.
>
> I want a report on the climate for underrepresented groups in our organization. A presentation at the last board of directors' meeting showed that while we do a good job of hiring women and minorities, few of them rise to the top. The directors suspect that our climate may not be supportive and want information on it. Please prepare a presentation for the next meeting. You'll have 15 minutes.

Making a presentation to the company's board of directors can really help your career. But preparing a good presentation and report will take time. You can look at exit reports filed by Human Resources when people leave the company, but you'll also need to interview people—lots of people. And you're already working 60 hours a week on three major projects, one of which is behind schedule. Can one of the projects wait? Can someone else take one of the projects? Can you get some help? Should you do just enough to get by? Ask your boss for advice—in a way that makes you look like a committed employee, not a shirker.

11.13   Persuading Employees Not to Share Files

Your computer network has been experiencing slowdowns, and an investigation has uncovered the reason. A number of employees have been using the system to download and share songs and vacation photos. You are concerned because the bulky files clog the network, and downloading files opens the network to computer viruses and worms. In addition, management does not want employees to spend work time and resources on personal matters. Finally, free downloads of songs are often illegal, and management is worried that a recording firm might sue the company for failing to prevent employees from violating its copyrights.

As director of Management Information Systems (MIS), you want to persuade employees to stop sharing files unrelated to work. You are launching a policy of regularly scanning the system for violations, but you prefer that employees voluntarily use the system properly. Violations are hard to detect, and increasing scanning in an effort to achieve system security is likely to cause resentment as an intrusion into employees' privacy.

Write an e-mail message to all employees, urging them to refrain from downloading and sharing personal files.

11.14   Not Doing What the Boss Asked

Today, you get this e-mail message:

> To: All Unit Managers
>
> Subject: Cutting Costs
>
> Please submit five ideas for cutting costs in your unit. I will choose the best ideas and implement them immediately.

You think your boss's strategy is wrong. Cutting costs will be easier if people buy into the decision rather than being handed orders. Instead of gathering ideas by e-mail, the boss should call a meeting so that people can brainstorm, teaching each other why specific strategies will or won't be easy for their units to implement.

Reply to your boss's e-mail request. Instead of suggesting specific ways to cut costs, persuade the boss to have a meeting where everyone can have input and be part of the decision.

11.15   Handling a Sticky Recommendation

As a supervisor in a state agency, you have a dilemma. You received this e-mail message today:

> From: John Inoye, Director of Personnel, Department of Taxation
>
> Subject: Need Recommendation for Peggy Chafez
>
> Peggy Chafez has applied for a position in the Department of Taxation. On the basis of her application and interview, she is the leading candidate. However, before I offer the job to her, I need a letter of recommendation from her current supervisor.
>
> Could you please let me have your evaluation within a week? We want to fill the position as quickly as possible.

Peggy has worked in your office for 10 years. She designed, writes, and edits a monthly statewide newsletter that your office puts out; she designed and maintains the department website. Her designs are creative; she's a very hard worker; she seems to know a lot about computers.

However, Peggy is in many ways an unsatisfactory staff member. Her standards are so high that most people find her intimidating. Some find her abrasive. People have complained to you that she's only interested in her own work; she seems to resent requests to help other people with projects. And yet both the newsletter and the web page are projects that need frequent interaction. She's out of the office a lot. Some of that is required by her job (she takes the newsletters to the post office, for example), but some people don't like the fact that she's out of the office so much. They also complain that she doesn't return voice-mail and e-mail messages.

You think managing your office would be a lot smoother if Peggy weren't there. You can't fire her: state employees' jobs are secure once they get past the initial six-month probationary period. Because of budget constraints, you can hire new employees only if vacancies are created by resignations. You feel that it would be pretty easy to find someone better.

If you recommend that John Inoye hire Peggy, you will be able to hire someone you want. If you recommend that John hire someone else, you may be stuck with Peggy for a long time.

As your instructor directs,

a. Write an e-mail message to John Inoye.

b. Write a memo to your instructor listing the choices you've made and justifying your approach.

Hints:

■ Polarization may make this dilemma more difficult than it needs to be. What are your options? Consciously look for more than two.

■ Is it possible to select facts or to use connotations so that you are truthful but still encourage John to hire Peggy? Is it ethical? Is it certain that John would find Peggy's work as unsatisfactory as you do? If you write a strong recommendation and Peggy doesn't do well at the new job, will your credibility suffer? Why is your credibility important?

11.16   Persuading Tenants to Follow the Rules

As resident manager of a large apartment complex, you receive free rent in return for collecting rents, doing simple maintenance, and enforcing the complex's rules. You find the following notice in the files:

> Some of you are failing to keep any kind of standard of sanitation code, resulting in the unnecessary cost on our part to hire exterminators to rid the building of roaches.
>
> Our leases state breach of contract in the event that you are not observing your responsibility to keep your apartment clean.
>
> We are in the process of making arrangements for an extermination company to rid those apartments that are experiencing problems. Get in touch with the manager no later than 10 pm Monday to make arrangements for your apartment to be sprayed. It is a fast, odorless operation. You are also required to put your garbage in plastic bags. Do not put loose garbage or garbage in paper bags in the dumpster, as this leads to rodent or roach problems.
>
> Should we in the course of providing extermination service to the building find that your apartment is a source of roaches, then you will be held liable for the cost incurred to rid your apartment of them.

The message is horrible. The notice lacks you-attitude, and it seems to threaten anyone who asks to have his or her apartment sprayed.

The annual spraying scheduled for your complex is coming up. Under the lease, you have the right to enter apartments once a year to spray. However, for spraying to be fully effective, residents must empty the cabinets, remove kitchen drawers, and put all food in the refrigerator. People and pets need to leave the apartment for about 15 minutes while the exterminator sprays.

Tell residents about the spraying. Persuade them to prepare their apartments to get the most benefit from it, and persuade them to dispose of food waste quickly and properly so that the bugs don't come back.

Hints:

■ What objections may people have to having their apartments sprayed for bugs?

■ Why don't people already take garbage out promptly and wrap it in plastic? How can you persuade them to change their behavior?

■ Analyze your audience. Are most tenants students, working people, or retirees? What tone would be most effective for this group?

11.17   Asking an Instructor for a Letter of Recommendation

You're ready for the job market, transfer to a four-year college, or graduate school, and you need letters of recommendation.

As your instructor directs,

a. Assume that you've orally asked an instructor for a recommendation, and he or she has agreed to write one, but asks, "Why don't you write up something to remind me of what you've done in the class? Tell me what else you've done, too. And tell me what they're looking for. Be sure to tell me when the letter needs to be in and to whom it goes." Write the e-mail.

b. Assume that you've been unable to talk with the instructor whose recommendation you want. When you call, no one answers the phone; you stopped by once and no one was in. Write asking for a letter of recommendation.

c. Assume that the instructor is no longer on campus. Write him or her asking for a recommendation.

Hints:

- Be detailed about what the organization is seeking and the points you'd like the instructor to mention.
- How well will this instructor remember you? How much detail about your performance in his or her class do you need to provide?

- Specify the name and address of the person to whom the letter should be written; specify when the letter is due.

11.18   Writing a Performance Appraisal for a Member of a Collaborative Group

During your collaborative writing group meetings, keep a log of events. Record specific observations of both effective and ineffective things that group members do. Then evaluate the performance of the other members of your group. (If there are two or more other people, write a separate appraisal for each of them.)

In your first paragraph, summarize your evaluation. Then in the body of your memo, give the specific details that led to your evaluation by answering the following questions:

- What specifically did the person do in terms of the task? Brainstorm ideas? Analyze the information? Draft the text? Suggest revisions in parts drafted by others? Format the document or create visuals? Revise? Edit? Proofread? (In most cases, several people will have done each of these activities together. Don't overstate what any one person did.) What was the quality of the person's work?
- What did the person contribute to the group process? Did he or she help schedule the work? Raise

or resolve conflicts? Make other group members feel valued and included? Promote group cohesion? What roles did the person play in the group?

Support your generalizations with specific observations. The more observations you have and the more detailed they are, the better your appraisal will be.

As your instructor directs,

a. Write a midterm performance appraisal for one or more members of your collaborative group. In each appraisal, identify the two or three things the person should try to improve during the second half of the term.

b. Write a performance appraisal for one or more members of your collaborative group at the end of the term. Identify and justify the grade you think each person should receive for the portion of the grade based on group process.

c. Give a copy of your appraisal to the person about whom it is written.

11.19   Writing a Self-Assessment for a Performance Review

Your company privileges good communication skills. In fact, during their second year, all employees are sent to a four-month communication course. As part of your annual review, you must prepare a self-assessment that includes your assessment of your progress in the

communication course. Assume that your business communication course is the company's communication course and prepare the communications part of your self-assessment. The company expects this portion to be a page long.

11.20   Evaluating Sales and Fund-Raising Messages

Collect the sales and fund-raising messages that come to you, your co-workers, landlord, neighbors, or family. Use the following questions to evaluate each message:

- What mode does the opener use? Is it related to the rest of the message? How good is the opener?
- What central selling point or common ground does the message use?
- What kinds of proof does the message use? Is the logic valid? What questions or objections are not answered?
- How does the message create emotional appeal?

- Is the style effective?
- Does the close tell people what to do, make action easy, give a reason for acting promptly, and end with a positive picture?
- Does the message use a P.S.? How good is it?
- Is the message visually attractive? Why or why not?
- What other items besides the letter or e-mail are in the package?

As your instructor directs,

a. Share your analysis of one or more messages with a small group of your classmates.

b. Analyze one message in a presentation to the class. Make a copy of the message to use as a visual aid in your presentation.

c. Analyze one message in a memo to your instructor. Provide a copy of the message along with your memo.

d. With several other students, write a group memo or report analyzing one part of the message

(e.g., openers) or one kind of letter (e.g., political messages, organizations fighting hunger, etc.). Use at least 10 messages for your analysis if you look at only one part; use at least 6 messages if you analyze one kind of message. Provide copies as an appendix to your report.

11.21 Writing a Fund-Raising Appeal

Write a 2½- to 4-page letter to raise money from *new donors* for an organization you support. You must use a real organization, but it does not actually have to be conducting a fund-raising drive now. Assume that your letter would have a reply card and postage-paid envelope. You do NOT have to write these, but DO refer to them in your letter.

Options for organizations include

- Tax-deductible charitable organizations—religious organizations; hospitals; groups working to feed, clothe, and house poor people.

- Lobbying groups—Mothers Against Drunk Driving, the National Abortion Rights Action League, the

National Rifle Association, groups working against nuclear weapons, etc.

- Groups raising money to fight a disease or fund research.

- Colleges trying to raise money for endowments, buildings, scholarships, faculty salaries.

For this assignment, you may also use groups which do not regularly have fund-raising drives but which may have special needs. Perhaps a school needs new uniforms for its band. Perhaps a sorority or fraternity house needs repairs, remodeling, or expansion.

11.22 Asking to Telecommute

You need to relocate to another city, where the company you work for does not have a branch office. You would prefer to remain working at this company, so telecommuting would be an ideal situation. Write a proposal in memo format to persuade your employer to allow you to work from a remote location.

Hints:

- Establish common ground: you want to stay, and many firms would rather allow an employee to telecommute than risk losing a valued team member.

- Point out potential benefits to your employer: you may save the company money on office resources, extend their usual business hours, or provide customer service to a remote location.

- Provide for oversight: outline a framework for evaluating your performance and participating on team projects, and perhaps offer a trial period.

11.23 Calling in a Favor

Last month, your co-worker Mike asked you for a favor: he needed to take an afternoon off to look after one of his children, but he didn't have any vacation or leave time left. Your supervisor had authorized him to take the time off as long as he could get someone else to cover his client meetings for him. You agreed, and spent the day covering for him.

Now you're in the same position: you need to take a morning off, and your supervisor wants you to convince someone to cover for you. You'll be missing a conference call with a client that cannot be rescheduled, and which will take an hour. Mike is the obvious choice—he knows the client, and he owes you a favor—but you know that he's very busy and might object to taking on more work.

Write a short memo or e-mail to Mike asking him to return the favor and cover for you.

Hints:

- Your informal relationship with Mike allows you to exchange favors. It also means that you can use more informal language and tone in your e-mail. (Not too informal, though: any e-mail can be forwarded.)

- Be sure to build common ground and goodwill as part of your opening.

- Mike may object to taking on more work. What other objections might he raise? Be sure to address those objections in your e-mail.

11.24 Creating a Healthy Snackfood Counter

You work in a friendly environment where people like to bring in treats to share with their co-workers. They do it so often that there's an area in your workplace that people jokingly call "Snackfood Counter," lined with donuts, candy, chips, pretzels, soda, and other not-too-healthy fare.

Write a memo, suitable for distributing to a wide audience at your workplace, to convince your co-workers to make the switch to healthy snacks. Build common ground, offset any negatives with benefits, and provide concrete suggestions for future actions. Be sure to build and maintain goodwill: people contribute to Snackfood Counter to be friendly, and may interpret your request as a complaint.

11.25 Recostuming Happy Halloween

Your team has been put in charge of organizing your company's Halloween event. Employees may come to work dressed in a costume. During the lunch hour, you'll hold a costume contest with prizes for the most original costumes (and a prize for the department or team with the highest rate of participation), followed by a party for your staff members. Last year's party was a big hit: about 30% of your employees dressed up, and you anticipate that the number will be higher this year.

However, last year there were a number of (moderately) racy and (somewhat) tasteless costumes, and some complaints about those costumes. The team who organized last year's Halloween ignored those complaints "because we're all adults here, and we can all take a joke." Well, this year, we *won't* all be adults: your company is also sponsoring a trick-or-treat event for kids from 10 local foster homes. Immediately following the costume contest and lunch, there will be dozens of (supervised) kids, ages 2–8, going office-to-office for candy. Your Human Resources department has provided the candy and treats, but it's up to you to make sure that the costume contest is kid-friendly.

As your instructor directs:

- Write a memo, suitable for distributing to all staff, which establishes guidelines for participating in the costume contest and persuades your co-workers to comply.
- Create a sign, suitable for posting in the common areas of your workplace, that establishes your costume guidelines and invites your co-workers to participate in the event.

Hints:

- Adults are more likely to comply with a policy decision when they understand the rationale behind that decision. Be sure to communicate your decision process as well as your guidelines.
- Choose a persuasive message format, create common ground and goodwill, and use creativity in both your language and your visual design.

11.26 Campaigning against Holiday Toy Ads

Discussions on pages 323 and 330 outlined the campaign of CCFC (Campaign for a Commercial-Free Childhood) against holiday toy ads directed at children.

This is the sample letter to toy manufacturers from parents suggested by CCFC:

I am writing to urge you to suspend all advertising to children this holiday season. With the global economic crisis intensifying, many families will have to scale back their holiday shopping this year. It's wrong to create unrealistic expectations in children or to foment family stress by encouraging kids to lobby for gifts that their parents may not be able to afford.

I understand the need to create awareness of your products. I urge you to do that by advertising directly to parents instead of enlisting children as lobbyists for their holiday gifts. Since it's parents, not children, who can truly understand their family's financial situation in these difficult times, it is more important than ever that you respect their authority as gatekeepers. Please target parents instead of children with your holiday advertising.

Source: "Tell Toy Companies: Target Parents, Not Kids, with Holiday Ads," Campaign for a Commercial-Free Childhood, Judge Baker Children's Center, accessed June 30, 2011, http://salsa.democracyinaction.org/o/621/t/6914/campaign.jsp?campaign_KEY=26139

This is the letter to toy manufacturers from the CCFC:

CAMPAIGN FOR A COMMERCIAL-FREE CHILDHOOD

Campaign for a Commercial-Free Childhood
c/o Judge Baker Children's Center
53 Parker Hill Avenue, Boston, MA 02120-3225
Phone: 617-278-4172• Fax: 617-232-7343
Email: CCFC@JBCC.Harvard.edu
Website: www.commercialfreechildhood.org

PLEASE NOTE: This letter was sent to 24 companies, not just Mattel. A complete list can be found at: www.commercialfreechildhood.org/actions/holidaymarketers.htm

October 27, 2008

Mr. Robert Eckert
Chief Executive Officer, Mattel
333 Continental Boulevard
El Segundo, CA 90245

CCFC
STEERING COMMITTEE:

Enola Aird, JD

Kathy Bowman, EdS

Nancy Carlsson-Paige, EdD

Allen Kanner, PhD

Tim Kasser, PhD

Joe Kelly

Velma LaPoint, PhD

Diane Levin, PhD

Karen Lewis

Alex Molnar, PhD

Alvin F. Poussaint, MD

Michele Simon, JD, MPH

Dear Mr. Eckert:

As families struggle to cope with the global economic crisis, we are writing to urge you to suspend all holiday marketing aimed at children. With fears of a recession or even a depression intensifying, Americans routinely list the economy as their number one concern. There is little doubt that many parents will have to scale back their holiday purchases significantly and experts predict that parents will spend less money on toys and gifts for children this holiday season. [1] Under normal circumstances it is unfair to bypass parents and target children directly with marketing, but with an uncertain future and budgets tighter than ever, it is particularly egregious to foment family conflict by advertising toys and games directly to kids that their parents may not be able to afford.

Research demonstrates that children's exposure to advertising is linked to the things they ask their parents to buy and family stress. [2] Using advertising to encourage children to nag for products may be good for sales, but it creates considerable family conflict. Even in normal times, buying holiday gifts causes financial strain for many families. A 2005 poll found that approximately one-third of Americans took more than three months to pay off their holiday credit card debt and 14% carried credit card debt into the next holiday season. [3]

Early reports indicate that spending on advertising to children will not reflect the current economic downturn. To date, spending forecasts for forth quarter television advertising on children's television have not been affected. [4] If parents are cutting their purchases back this holiday season while commercial pressures on children remain at record levels, the burden on families will be tremendous.

As you know, children are more vulnerable to advertising than adults. Seductive advertising designed explicitly to exploit their vulnerabilities will create unrealistic expectations in kids too young to understand the economic crises and will make parenting in these uncertain times even more difficult. **We understand the need to create awareness of your products. We urge you to do that by advertising directly to parents instead of enlisting children as lobbyists for their holiday gifts.** Since it's parents, not children, who can truly understand their family's financial situation in these difficult times, it is more important than ever that you respect their authority as gatekeepers: Target parents instead of children this holiday season.

Please note that we are sending this letter to CEO's of all the leading toy and game manufacturers and will be happy to offer public praise for any company that puts America's families first by suspending their holiday advertising to children. We would also welcome the opportunity to discuss this matter with you further.

Sincerely,

Susan Linn, Ed.D.

[1] Anderson, M. (2008, Oct 8). Holiday spending on toys expected to be less. *The Associated Press.* Accessed October 17, 2008 from http://www.thenewstribune.com/1031/v-lite/story/502479.html.
[2] Buijen, M. & Valkenburg (2003). The effects of television advertising on materialism, parent–child conflict, and unhappiness: A review of research. *Applied Developmental Psychology,* 24, 437–456.
[3] Center for a New American Dream (2005). Hot Holiday Gift for Kids This Year? — A Piggy Bank, Say Fed Up Americans. Accessed October 17, 2008 from http://www.newdream.org/holiday/poll05.php.
[4] Freidman, W. (2008, Oct 13). So Far, Kids' TV Saved from Ad Hits. *MediaPost's Media Daily News.* Accessed October 17, 2008 from http://www.mediapost.com/publications/?fa=Articles.showArticle&art_aid=92573.

Source: Reprinted with permission of Judge Baker Children's Center, Boston, MA.

364   **Part 3**   Basic Business Messages

This is the response from the TIA (Toy Industry Association):

Toy Industry Association's Statement

The Toy Industry Association notes with interest, but begs to disagree with, the Campaign for a Commercial-Free Childhood's suggestion that marketing of toys be focused this year on parents and not on children.

We believe parents should know what their children want and are perfectly capable of deciding, as they have always done, how to fit satisfaction of those desires into the family budget. Children are a vital part of the gift selection process and should not be removed from it.

We offer several thoughts to guide families through the gift buying process:

- Children have their own ideas about what appeals to them and parents are not necessarily going to know, without their children's input, if a new toy is going to excite them. We have faith in parents' ability to hear from their children what they would like and then make a decision as to what, and how much, to give them.
- In fact, most parents and grandparents appreciate knowing which items are on their child's wish lists before they go out to purchase a gift for them, as it makes shopping easier. If children are not aware of what is new and available, how will they be able to tell their families what their preferences are?
- Parents do a pretty good job of budgeting and making purchase decisions. While there is certainly greater economic disturbance going on now, families have always faced different levels of economic well-being and have managed to tailor their spending to their means.

Toy Industry Association, Inc.

Source: Reprinted with permission of Judge Baker Children's Center, Boston, MA.

This is the statement on the website of the TIA:

TIA Statement on Marketing to Children

TIA Position Statement for Holiday Season 2008

The Toy Industry Association and its members are proud of the toys and games we produce and their role in play, which is an important, life-shaping experience in the growth of a child. We believe it is appropriate to market toys and games both to children and to their parents, so long as it is done responsibly.

Ultimately, TIA and its members understand that a parent or primary caregiver knows his or her child best. Our research confirms that parents agree that they should be involved in all aspects of their child's life, including the child's television viewing, computer time, and purchasing decisions.

The toy industry believes firmly in self-regulation and is committed to follow best practices in marketing to our consumers, as reflected in various national codes and industry guidelines. These include the Children's Advertising Review Unit of the Council of Better Business Bureaus (of which TIA is a long-standing member) in the United States and the codes of the International Chamber of Commerce and local self-regulatory codes internationally. We are actively involved with various self-regulatory organizations in continually reviewing and improving those guidelines as needed.

Children are the reason our industry exists. We are parents ourselves and we treat all children with the same care and respect.

Source: Industry Statements, from http://www.toyassociation.org/AM/Template.cfm?Section=Industry_Statements&TEMPLATE=/CM/HTMLDisplay.cfm&CONTENTID=1474 (accessed April 5, 2009).

In small groups, discuss these four documents. Here are some questions to get you started:

1. Do the openers grab your attention? Why or why not?
2. What persuasive strategies do they use?
3. What arguments do they use? How do they build credibility?
4. What common ground do they use?
5. What emotional appeals do they use?
6. How do they deal with objections?
7. What are the differences between the TIA response to CCFC and the TIA's statement on its own website?
8. Do the documents convince you? Why or why not? Which document is the most persuasive?
9. How could these documents be improved?

As your instructor directs,

a. As a group, share your analyses with the class in a five-minute presentation.
b. Prepare three documents for your instructor.
   - Write a detailed analysis of one of the documents.
   - On the basis of that analysis, rewrite the document.
   - Write a memo explaining the changes you made and why you kept some of the original document (if you did).

Newsworthy Communication

Changing Channels

Channels for job documents are changing so rapidly that newspapers and business magazines are running articles on the subject. In 2010, *Fortune* ran an eight-page story on LinkedIn, "How LinkedIn Will Fire Up Your Career." Calling it Facebook for grownups, *Fortune* says that LinkedIn is the only social site that matters for careers.

The numbers for LinkedIn are impressive. The site has over 60 million profiles and more than a half million groups—based on companies, schools, and

> *"Fortune says that LinkedIn is the only social site that matters for careers."*

affinities—you can join to help you make connections. You can attach your résumé, pack your profile with key words that make you easy to find, connect to your blog and Twitter account, and invite colleagues to comment on your work (and approve all comments before they appear on your profile).

Your profile will be in good company. The average member is college-educated and makes $107,000. Every *Fortune* 500 company is represented.

You do have your profile there, right?

Source: Jessi Hempel, "How LinkedIn Will Fire Up Your Career," *Fortune,* April 2010, 74–82.

Learning Objectives

After studying this chapter, you will know how to

LO 12-1   Prepare a detailed time line for your job search.

LO 12-2   Prepare a résumé that makes you look attractive to employers.

LO 12-3   Deal with common difficulties that arise during job searches.

LO 12-4   Handle the online portion of job searches.

LO 12-5   Keep your résumé honest.

You will probably change jobs many times during your career. Although no longitudinal study has ever been completed, the U.S. Bureau of Labor Statistics has started one, the National Longitudinal Survey of Youth. It shows that the average person born in the latter years of the baby boom held an average of 11 jobs from age 18 to age 44. In fact, 25% of them have held 15 jobs or more. Even in middle age, when job changing slows down, 68% of jobs ended in fewer than five years. This means that you should keep your résumé up to date.[1]

A **résumé** is a persuasive summary of your qualifications for a job with a specific employer. If you're on the job market, having a résumé is a basic step in the job hunt. When you're employed, having an up-to-date résumé makes it easier to take advantage of opportunities that may come up for even better jobs. If you're several years away from job hunting, preparing a résumé now will help you become more conscious of what to do in the next two or three years to make yourself an attractive candidate.

This chapter covers paper and electronic résumés. Job application letters (sometimes called cover letters) are discussed in Chapter 13. Chapter 14 discusses interviews and communications after the interview. All three chapters focus on job hunting in the United States. Conventions, expectations, and criteria differ from culture to culture: different norms apply in different countries.

All job communications should be tailored to your unique qualifications and the specifications of the job you want. Adopt the wording or layout of an example if it's relevant to your own situation, but don't be locked into the forms in this book. You've got different strengths; your résumé will be different, too.

A TIME LINE FOR JOB HUNTING   LO 12-1

Many employers consider the way you do your job hunt to be evidence of the way you will work for them. Therefore, you should start preparing yourself several years ahead of your formal applications.

Informal preparation for job hunting should start soon after you arrive on campus. Check out the services of your college placement and advising offices. Join extracurricular organizations on campus and in the community to increase your knowledge and provide a network for learning about jobs. Find a job that gives you experience. Note which courses you like—and why you like them. If you like thinking and learning about a subject, you're more likely to enjoy a job in that field. Select course projects and paper topics that will help you prepare for a job—and look good on your résumé.

Once you have selected a major, start reading job ads, particularly those posted on your professional organization's website. What kinds of jobs are available? Do you need to change your course selections to better fit them? What kinds of extras are employers seeking? Do they want communication skills? Extra statistics courses? International experience? Learn this information early while you still have time to add to the knowledge and skill sets you are acquiring. Attend job seminars and job fairs. Join your professional association and its listserv.

Formal preparation for job hunting should begin a full year *before you begin interviewing*. Enroll for the services of your campus placement office. Ask friends who are on the job market about their experiences in interviews; find out what kinds of job offers they get. Check into the possibility of getting an internship or a co-op job that will give you relevant experience before you interview.

The year you interview, register with your Placement Office early. An active job search takes significant chunks of time, so plan accordingly. If you plan to graduate in the spring, prepare your résumé and plan your interview strategy early in the fall. Initial campus interviews occur from October to February for May or June graduation. In January or February, write to any organization you'd like to work for that hasn't interviewed on campus. From February to April, you're likely to visit one or more offices for a second interview.

Try to have a job offer lined up *before* you get the degree. People who don't need jobs immediately are more confident in interviews and usually get better job offers. If you have to job-hunt after graduation, plan to spend at least 30 hours a week on your job search. The time will pay off in a better job that you find more quickly.

EVALUATING YOUR STRENGTHS AND INTERESTS

A self-assessment is the first step in producing a good résumé. Each person could do several jobs happily. Richard Bolles, a nationally recognized expert in career advising for over a third of a century and author of the *What Color Is Your Parachute* books, says most people who don't find a job they like fail because they lack information about themselves.[2] Personality and aptitude tests can tell you some of your strengths, but you should still answer for yourself questions like these:

- What skills and strengths do you have?
- What achievements have given you the most satisfaction? *Why* did you enjoy them? What jobs would offer these kinds of satisfactions?
- What work conditions do you like? Would you rather have firm deadlines or a flexible schedule? Do you prefer working independently or with other people? Do you prefer specific instructions and standards for evaluation or freedom and uncertainty? How comfortable are you with pressure? How much challenge do you want?
- What kind of work/life balance do you want? Are you willing to take work home? To work weekends? To travel? How important is money to you? Prestige? Time to spend with family and friends?
- How fast do you want to move up? Are you willing to pay your dues for several years before you are promoted?
- Where do you want to live? What features in terms of weather, geography, cultural and social life do you see as ideal?
- Is it important to you that your work achieve certain purposes or values, or do you see work as just a way to make a living? Are an organization's culture and ethical standards important to you? If so, what values will you look for?

What Employers Want, I

You can increase your odds of getting an interview by understanding what hiring managers are thinking while they evaluate your résumé. The following are questions managers ask themselves:

Can this applicant fill the needs of the company? Your résumé should stress all of your most relevant skills and experience which match the position opening. Rather than submitting a generic résumé for every position you apply for, create a customized résumé based on your review of the job opening.

Will this applicant stay with the company long term? Managers seek employees who are most likely to stay with a company long term because the hiring process is long, difficult, and costly. The cost of replacing an employee averages $13,355 according to a study conducted by the Employment Policy Foundation. To avoid costly turnover, managers look at your résumé to see if you have a stable work history.

Will this applicant be professional? Your résumé represents your ability to communicate. Unfortunately, managers will eliminate résumés for the slightest problems since they may receive hundreds of résumés for one position. Make sure your résumé is easy to follow and does not contain typos or grammatical mistakes.

Adapted from Robert Half International, "What Employers Think When They Read Your Résumé," CareerBuilder, September, 23, 2008, http://www.careerbuilder.com/Article/CB-427-Resumes-Cover-Letters-What-Employers-Think-When-They-Read-Your-R%C3%A9sum%C3%A9/.

370   Part 4   The Job Hunt

What Employers Want, II

Careerbuilder.com asked hiring managers what the top five attributes are when they hire new graduates.

1. **Relevant experience:** Managers look for a candidate's ability to make his/her job experience relevant to the company—and find this ability lacking. Most managers say they view volunteer activities as relevant experience.

2. **Professionalism during the interview:** Managers want to see candidates who dress professionally, who have researched the company, and who are prepared to answer standard interview questions.

3. **Fit within the company culture:** Managers want candidates whose personalities and work styles fit well.

4. **Education:** Managers consider the school, degree, major, GPA, and relevant courses.

5. **Enthusiasm:** Managers want candidates who are clearly interested in the job and show the energy they would bring to their work.

Adapted from Laura Morsch, "Five Must-Haves for New Grads," Experience, Inc., accessed April 3, 2011, http://tribe.experience.com/alumnus/article?channel_id=career_management&source_page=additional_articles&article_id=article_1156346148348.

Once you know what is most important to you, check to see what businesses are looking for (see Figure 12.4). Then analyze the job market to see where you could find what you want. Each possibility will require somewhat different training and course selection, underscoring the need for you to begin considering your job search process early in your college career.

USING THE INTERNET IN YOUR JOB SEARCH

The Internet is a crucial tool for job seekers as well as employers.

Probably the most common use of the Internet for job candidates is to search for openings (see Figure 12.1). In addition to popular job boards like Monster and CareerBuilder job candidates typically search for jobs posted on organizations' Facebook pages, LinkedIn sites, and Twitter (TwitJobSearch.com). They also check electronic listings in local newspapers and professional societies. However, you do need to be careful when responding to online ads. Some of them turn out to be pitches from career or financial services firms, or even phishing ads—ploys from identity thieves seeking your personal information.

Phishing ads often look like real postings; many have company names and logos nearly identical to those of real employers. People behind phishing ads may even e-mail job candidates to build up trust. Privacy experts caution job candidates to be particularly careful with job postings that lack details about the hiring company or job description, and ads that list a large salary range.[3]

In addition to searching for ads, every job candidate should check the Internet for information about writing résumés and application letters, researching specific companies and jobs, and preparing for interviews. Many comprehensive sites give detailed information that will help you produce more effective documents and be a better-prepared job candidate.

As you search the Web, remember that not all sites are current and accurate. In particular, be careful of .com sites: some are good, others are not. Check your school's career site for help. Check the sites of other schools: Stanford, Berkeley, and Columbia have particularly excellent career sites. And even good sources can have advice that is bad for you. Figure 12.2 lists some of the best sites.

A relatively new use of the Internet for job searchers is online job fairs. At online fairs, you can browse through virtual booths, leave your résumé at promising ones, and sometimes even apply on the spot, all without leaving your home. Other advantages of online job fairs are their wide geographic and 24-hour access.

Figure 12.1   Job Listings on the Web

Job Sites	
America's Job Bank www.jobbankinfo.org	**Monster.com** www.monster.com
CareerBuilder.com www.careerbuilder.com	**MonsterTrak** http://college.monster.com
Careers.org www.careers.org	
EmploymentGuide.com www.employmentguide.com	Job listings from the *Chicago Tribune, Detroit News, Los Angeles Times, Miami Herald, Philadelphia Inquirer, San Jose Mercury News,* and other city newspaper's websites.
Federal Jobs Career Central www.fedjobs.com	
Indeed.com www.indeed.com	

Figure 12.2   Comprehensive Web Job Sites Covering the Entire Job Search Process

About.com (Part of New York Times Company)
  http://jobsearch.about.com
	Monster.com
	  www.monster.com

Campus Career Center
  www.campuscareercenter.com
	MonsterCollege
	  http://college.monster.com/?wtime_
	  n=monstertrak

CareerBuilder
  www.careerbuilder.com
	OWL (Purdue Online Writing Lab)
	  http://owl.english.purdue.edu

Career Rookie
  www.careerrookie.com
	Quintessential Careers
	  www.quintcareers.com

College Central
  www.collegecentral.com
	The Riley Guide
	  www.rileyguide.com

College Grad Job Hunter
  www.collegegrad.com
	Spherion Career Center
	  www.spherion.com/corporate/ret-
	  registered.jsp

The Five O'Clock Club
  www.fiveoclockclub.com
	wetfeet
	  www.wetfeet.com/undergrad

JobHuntersBible.com (Dick Bolles)
  www.jobhuntersbible.com
	Vault
	  www.vault.com

As you do all this research for your job hunt, you will probably begin to find conflicting advice. When evaluating suggestions, consider the age of the advice; what was true five years ago may not be true today, because the job search process is changing so. Also consider your industry; general advice that works for most may not work for your industry. Above all, consider what advice helps you present yourself as favorably as possible.

PERSONAL BRANDING

A specialized use of the Internet is for **personal branding**, a popular term for marketing yourself, including job searching. It covers an expectation that you will use various options, from the traditional résumé and cover letter to social media, to market your expertise. According to one recent survey, 83% of employers use social media to find new employees. Of those, 89% use LinkedIn, 28% use Facebook, and 14% use Twitter.[4] As has always been true of job searches, you will use these tools to show your value (what do you offer employers?) and quality (why should they hire you instead of other candidates?). These are some of the most popular tools:

- **LinkedIn:**   This site allows you to include useful information beyond your résumé, and, unlike your web page, it has a powerful search engine behind it.

- **Personal web page:**   Your web page allows you to connect to examples of your professional work.

- **Blogs:**   A blog in particular can contribute to your professional image if it focuses on your professional specialty and current issues in your field. However, keeping a blog up to date is time-consuming work during an already stressful period.

Rebranding Yourself

Whether you are looking to advance in your career or to change careers entirely, you may need to do some personal rebranding. *Rebranding* is the effort you make to change other people's perceptions about who you are and what you do well. But it is not always an easy process. Here are five tips to help you with your rebranding:

1. **Set your goals.** Who do you want to be? What skills will you need to get there?

2. **Define your points of difference.** What makes you special? How can your differences help you be noticed and connected with your new brand?

3. **Develop a narrative.** How do your past experiences and skills strengthen your new career?

4. **Reintroduce yourself.** How will you tell your friends and co-workers about your new brand?

5. **Prove your worth.** How can you show that you will be a contributing member of your new field?

These five steps will help you on your path to a new personal brand.

Adapted from Dorie Clark, "Reinventing Your Personal Brand," *Harvard Business Review*, 89, no. 3 (2011): 78–81.

372   **Part 4**   The Job Hunt

Digital Dirt

Do you wonder if your employer can find out if you committed a crime, experienced financial difficulties, really attended college, or received a driving ticket? According to a survey of executive recruiters by ExecuNet, an executive job-search and networking organization, 75% of recruiters use search engines to uncover information about job candidates.

Prospective employers can use employment screening services to obtain records from private, state and federal agencies. Employers also check social networking sites such as Facebook, and Google names to find blogs and personal websites.

Remember that nothing on the Web is private. Do not post or write anything on the Internet that you do not want a prospective employer to see—starting today.

How can you clean up your reputation online?

- Google yourself. If you find something you would rather your prospective employer did not see, contact the website and ask for it to be removed.

- Clean up your Facebook or personal website. Remove any pictures that may not present a professional image or may be misunderstood by an outsider, especially pictures showing you drinking or dressed inappropriately.

- Cover negative information by increasing your positive online presence, including creating a professional web page with many links to your accomplishments.

Adapted from Jared Flesher, "How to Clean up Your Digital Dirt before It Trashes Your Job Search," *Wall Street Journal*, January 12, 2006, http://online.wsj.com/article/C60112FLESHER.html.

- **Facebook:** Keep content professional. Avoid inappropriate language and all content involving alcohol, other drugs, and incomplete attire. Remember that Facebook has a history of making personal information public.
- **Twitter:** Share useful information such as thoughtful comments about news in your field as you work to build up your Twitter network. Aim for quality, not numbers. Also, follow companies you would like to work for.
- **Professional forums:** Participate thoughtfully: doing so enables people to recognize your name favorably when your application arrives.
- **Cover letter:** Still an excellent tool for personal branding. It gives you more room to provide supporting details about your value and quality.

> ⚠ **WARNING:** Select your tools carefully; you probably do not have time to use successfully all the tools on this list. Stay professional in all venues; avoid negative comments about people, your school, and your employers. In addition to content, writing (grammar, coherence, style, logic, spelling) will be judged by potential employers. The list of candidates rejected after a basic web search grows daily.

NETWORKING

Many experts now consider networking to be THE most important factor in finding a job. It is important for entry-level work, and becomes even more crucial as you advance in your career.

Networking starts with people you know—friends, family, friends of your parents, classmates, teammates, gym mates, colleagues—and quickly expands to electronic contacts in the social media noted above. Let people know you are looking for a job, and what your job assets are. Use social media to emphasize your field knowledge and accomplishments. Join your school's alumni association to find alumni in businesses that interest you.

The secret to successful networking is reciprocity. Too many people network just for themselves, and they quickly gain a "one-way" reputation that hurts further networking. Good networkers work for a "two-way" reputation; to earn it, they look for ways to reciprocate. They help their contacts make fruitful connections. They share useful information and tips. Successful networks are not just for finding jobs: they are vital for career success.

A CAUTION ABOUT BLOGS, SOCIAL NETWORKING SITES, AND INTERNET TRACKING

Most employers routinely Google job candidates, and many report they are totally turned off by what they find—especially on personal blogs and web pages and social networking sites such as Facebook. If you have a personal blog, web page, or other electronic presence, check sites carefully before you go on the job market.

- Remove any unprofessional material such as pictures of you at your computer with a beer in your hand or descriptions of your last party.
- Remove negative comments about current or past employers and teachers. People who spread dirt in one context will probably do so in others, and no one wants to hire such people.

- Remove political and social rants. While thoughtful, supported opinions can show both education and logic, emotional or extreme statements will turn off most employers.
- Remove any personal information that will embarrass you on the job. If you blog about romance novels, but don't want to be teased about your choice in literature on your new job, make ruthless cuts on your blog.
- Remove inappropriate material posted by friends, relatives, and colleagues.
- Check your blog for writing aptitude. Many employers will consider your blog an extended writing sample. If yours is full of grammatical and spelling errors, obviously you are not a good writer.

Even if you take your blog off-line while you are job searching, employers may still find it in cached data on search engines. The best advice is to plan ahead and post nothing unprofessional on the web.

⚠️ **WARNING:** According to a 2010 report on research commissioned by Microsoft, a quarter or more of recruiters also check photo- and video-sharing sites, gaming sites, virtual world sites, and classifieds and auction sites such as Craigslist, Amazon, and eBay.[5]

USING AN INTERNSHIP AS A JOB HUNTING TOOL

Internships are becoming increasingly important as ways to find out about professions, employers, and jobs. Many companies use their internships to find full-time employees. GE, for example, makes about 80% of its new-graduate hires from students who held summer internships with the company; in 2010 PricewaterhouseCoopers offered a full-time job to 90% of its eligible summer interns. A *Wall Street Journal* survey of college recruiters found 25% reporting that more than 50% of their new-graduate hires came from their intern pools. The National Association of Colleges and Employers found in its 2010 survey of internships that 57% of interns became full-time hires (see Figure 12.3). In fact, some industry experts are predicting that within the next few years intern recruiting will largely replace entry-level recruiting.[6]

Figure 12.3   Percentage of Interns Offered Full-Time Jobs

Industry	Percentage
Entertainment/media	85
Oil and gas extraction	81
Construction	80
Accounting	75
Food and beverage	71
Retail	70
Finance/insurance/real estate	67
Engineering	67
Computer and electronics	64
Chemical/pharmaceutical	61

Source: Joe Walker, "Getting Creative to Land an Internship," *Wall Street Journal*, June 8, 2010, D7.

Even if your internship does not lead to a full-time job, it can still give you valuable insight into the profession, as well as contacts you can use in your job search. An increasingly important side benefit is the work you do in your internship, which can become some of the best items in your professional portfolio.

HOW EMPLOYERS USE RÉSUMÉS LO 12-2

Understanding how employers use résumés will help you create a résumé that works for you.

1. **Employers use résumés to decide whom to interview.** See Figure 12.4. (The major exceptions are on-campus interviews, where the campus placement office has policies that determine who meets with the interviewer.) Since résumés are used to screen out applicants, omit anything that may create a negative impression.

2. **Résumés are scanned or skimmed.** At many companies, résumés are scanned electronically. Only résumés that match key words are skimmed by a human being. A human may give a résumé 10 to 30 seconds before deciding to keep or toss it. You must design your résumé to pass both the "scan test" and the "skim test" by emphasizing crucial qualifications.

3. **Employers assume that your letter and résumé represent your best work.** Neatness, accuracy, and freedom from typographical errors are essential. Spelling errors will probably cost you your chance at a job, so proofread carefully.

4. **After an employer has chosen an applicant, he or she submits the applicant's résumé to people in the organization who must approve the appointment.** These people may have different backgrounds and areas of expertise. Spell out acronyms. Explain awards, Greek-letter honor societies, unusual job titles, or organizations that may be unfamiliar to the reader.

Figure 12.4 Employers Want Colleges to Place More Emphasis on These Skills

Skill	Percent
Effective communication, both oral and written	89
Critical thinking and analytical reasoning	81
Application of knowledge to the work world, through internships and other hands-on experiences	79
Ability to analyze and solve complex problems	75
Teamwork	71
Innovation and creativity	70
Understanding of basic concepts and new developments in science and technology	70
Ability to locate, organize, and evaluate information from multiple sources	68
Understanding of global contexts and developments	67
Ability to work with numbers and understand statistics	63

Source: Hart Research Associates, *Raising the Bar: Employers' Views on College Learning in the Wake of the Economic Downturn: A Survey among Employers Conducted on Behalf of the Association of American Colleges and Universities,* January 20, 2010, http://www.aacu.org/leap/documents/2009_EmployerSurvey.pdf.

GUIDELINES FOR RÉSUMÉS

Writing a résumé is not an exact science. What makes your friend look good does not necessarily help you. If your skills are in great demand, you can violate every guideline here and still get a good job. But when you must compete against many applicants, these guidelines will help you look as good on paper as you are in person.

Length

A one-page résumé is sufficient, but do fill the page. Less than a full page suggests that you do not have very much to say for yourself.

If you have more good material than will fit on one page, use a second page. A common myth is that all résumés must fit on one page. According to surveys conducted by international staffing firm Accountemps of executives at the 1,000 largest companies in this country, approval of the two-page résumé is increasing *if* candidates have sufficient good material that relates to the posted job.[7] An experiment that mailed one- or two-page résumés to recruiters at major accounting firms showed that even readers who said they preferred short résumés were more likely to want to interview the candidate with the longer résumé.[8] The longer résumé gives managers a better picture of how you will fit in.

If you do use more than one page, the second page should have at least 10 to 12 lines. Use a second sheet of paper; do not print on the back of the first page. Leave less important information for the second page. Put your name and "Page 2" on the page. If the pages are separated, you want the reader to know whom the qualifications belong to and that the second page is not your whole résumé.

Emphasis

Emphasize the things you've done that (a) are most relevant to the position for which you're applying, (b) show your superiority to other applicants, and (c) are recent (in the last three to five years). Whatever your age at the time you write a résumé, you want to suggest that you are now the best you've ever been.

Show that you're qualified by giving relevant details on course projects, activities, and jobs where you've done similar work. Be brief about low-level jobs that simply show dependability. To prove that you're the best candidate for the job, emphasize items that set you apart from other applicants: promotions, honors, achievements, experience with computers or other relevant equipment, foreign languages, and so on.

You can emphasize material by putting it at the top or the bottom of a page, by giving it more space, and by setting it off with white space. The beginning and end—of a document, a page, a list—are positions of emphasis. When you have a choice (e.g., in a list of job duties), put less important material in the middle, not at the end, to avoid the impression of "fading out." You can also emphasize material by presenting it in a vertical list, by using informative headings, and by providing details. Headings that name skills listed in the job ad, or skills important for the job (e.g., Managerial Experience) also provide emphasis and help set you apart from the crowd.

Details

Details provide evidence to support your claims, convince the reader, and separate you from other applicants. Numbers make good details. Tell how many people you trained or supervised, how much money you budgeted or saved. Describe the interesting aspects of the job you did.

Increasing Expectations for Employees

A survey conducted for the Association of American Colleges and Universities found that employers really are expecting more of their employees. You are not just imagining the change. Compared to past expectations, 88% to 91% expected employees to

- Take on more responsibilities.
- Use a broader skills set.
- Coordinate more with other departments.
- Acquire more learning and skills.
- Deal with more complex challenges.

How does your résumé reflect these new realities?

Adapted from Hart Research Associates, *Raising the Bar: Employers' Views on College Learning in the Wake of the Economic Downturn: A Survey among Employers Conducted on Behalf of the Association of American Colleges and Universities*, January 20, 2010, http://www.aacu.org/leap/documents/2009_EmployerSurvey.pdf.

Too vague:	Sales Manager, *The Daily Collegian*, University Park, PA, 2010–2012. Supervised staff; promoted ad sales.
Good details:	Sales Manager, *The Daily Collegian*, University Park, PA, 2010–2012. Supervised 22-member sales staff; helped recruit, interview, and select staff; assigned duties and scheduled work; recommended best performers for promotion. Motivated staff to increase paid ad inches 10% over previous year's sales.

Omit details that add nothing to a title, that are less impressive than the title alone, or that suggest a faulty sense of priorities (e.g., listing hours per week spent filing). Either use strong details or just give the office or job title without any details.

Writing Style

Without sacrificing content, be as concise as possible.

Wordy:	Member, Meat Judging Team, 2008–09
	Member, Meat Judging Team, 2009–10
	Member, Meat Judging Team, 2010–11
	Captain, Meat Judging Team, 2011–12
Tight:	Meat Judging Team, 2008–12; Captain 2011–12
Wordy:	Performed foundation load calculations
Tight:	Calculated foundation loads

Résumés normally use phrases and sentence fragments. Complete sentences are acceptable if they are the briefest way to present information. To save space and to avoid sounding arrogant, never use *I* in a résumé. *Me* and *my* are acceptable if they are unavoidable or if using them reduces wordiness.

Verbs or gerunds (the *ing* form of verbs) create a more dynamic image of you than do nouns, so use them on résumés that will be read by people instead of scanning programs. In the following revisions of job responsibilities, nouns, verbs, and gerunds are in bold type:

Nouns:	Chair, Income Tax Assistance Committee, Winnipeg, MB, 2011–2012. Responsibilities: **recruitment** of volunteers; flyer **design, writing,** and **distribution** for **promotion** of program; **speeches** to various community groups and nursing homes to advertise the service.
Verbs:	Chair, Income Tax Assistance Committee, Winnipeg, MB, 2011–2012. **Recruited** volunteers for the program. **Designed, wrote,** and **distributed** a flyer to promote the program; **spoke** to various community groups and nursing homes to advertise the service.
Gerunds:	Chair, Income Tax Assistance Committee, Winnipeg, MB, 2011–2012. Responsibilities included **recruiting** volunteers for the program; **designing, writing,** and **distributing** a flyer to promote the program; and **speaking** to various community groups and nursing homes to advertise the service.

Note that the items in the list must be in parallel structure (p. 135).

> **WARNING:** All spelling and grammar should be perfect. If they are not your strong suits, pay an editor. In these days of massive responses to job postings, don't give recruiters an easy elimination of your résumé through careless errors. Remember that spell checks will not catch all errors, as all those store "mangers" will tell you.

Key Words

Now that electronic résumé scans are common, all résumés, but particularly electronic résumés, need to use **key words**—words and phrases the employer will have the computer seek. Key words are frequently nouns or noun phrases: database management, product upgrades, cost compilation/analysis. However, they can also be adjectives such as *responsible*. Key words are frequently the objects of all those action verbs you are using in your résumé; conducted *publicity campaigns*, wrote weekly division *newsletter*.

Key words may include

- Software program names such as Excel.
- Job titles.
- Types of degrees.
- College or company names.
- Job-specific skills, buzzwords, and jargon.
- Professional organizations (spell out the name and then follow it with its abbreviation in parentheses to increase the number of matches).
- Honor societies (spell out Greek letters).
- Personality traits, such as creativity, dependability, team player.
- Area codes (for geographic narrowing of searches).

To find the key words you need in your job search, look through job ads and employer job sites for common terminology. If many ads mention "communication skills," your résumé should too.

Some key words are widely popular. A survey of over 3,000 hirers conducted for CareerBuilder reported these key words as ones searched for most often:[9]

- Problem-solving and decision-making skills (50%)
- Oral and written communications (44%)
- Customer service or retention (34%)
- Performance and productivity improvement (32%)
- Leadership (30%)
- Technology (27%)
- Team-building (26%)
- Project management (20%)
- Bilingual (14%)

In addition to using popular key words, you should double-check to make certain your résumé uses the language of the particular job ad to which you are responding. If the ad uses "software engineers" instead of "computer programmers," then your résumé should also use "software engineers." If the ad talks about "collaboration," you will use that word instead of "teamwork" when you discuss your group work experience.

Use key words liberally in your Summary of Qualifications section. However, to get an interview, your résumé will usually need to put key words into a context proving you have the skills or knowledge. This means that key words will also have to appear in the rest of your résumé, too. Since you will not know exactly what key words are desired, it makes sense to use some synonyms and similar terms: *manager* and *management*, *Excel* and *spreadsheets*, *creative* and *creativity*.

Layout and Design

The layout and design of your résumé will be vital to catch the eye of the employer who is spending only 10 seconds on each document.

 WARNING: Do not use résumé templates that come with word-processing software. Many employers see so many résumés from these templates that they learn to recognize—and discount—them.

Almost certainly, you can create a better résumé by adapting a basic style you like to your own unique qualifications. Experiment with layout, fonts, and spacing to get an attractive résumé. Consider creating a letterhead that you use for both your résumé and your application letter.

Decide what are your best selling points and promote them early. Since most résumés will be put into electronic formats (discussed later in chapter), make sure the first screen of information about you is strong, tempting readers to look further.

One of the major decisions you will make is how to treat your **headings**. Do you want them on the left margin, with text immediately below them, as in Figure 12.5? Do you want them alone in the left column, with text in a column to the right, as in Figure 12.7? Generally, people with more text on their résumés use the first option. Putting headings in their own column on the left takes space and thus helps spread a thinner list of accomplishments over the page. But be careful not to make the heading column too wide, or it will make your résumé look unbalanced and empty.

Work with **fonts**, bullets, and spacing to highlight your information. Do be careful, however, not to make your résumé look "busy" by using too many fonts. Generally three fonts should be the top limit, and you should avoid unusual fonts. Keep fonts readable by using at least 10-point type for large fonts such as Arial and 11-point for smaller fonts such as Times New Roman. Use enough white space to group items and make your résumé easy to read, but not so much that you look as if you're padding.

Use **color** sparingly, if at all. Colored text and shaded boxes can prevent accurate scanning. Similarly, white 8½- by 11-inch paper is standard, but do use a good-quality paper.

All of these guidelines are much more flexible for people in creative fields such as advertising and design.

KINDS OF RÉSUMÉS

Two basic categories of résumés are chronological and skills. A **chronological résumé** summarizes what you did in a time line (starting with the most recent events, and going backward in **reverse chronology**). It emphasizes degrees, job titles, and dates. It is the traditional résumé format. Figures 12.5 and 12.8 show chronological résumés.

Use a chronological résumé when

- Your education and experience are a logical preparation for the position for which you're applying.
- You have impressive job titles, offices, or honors.

A **skills résumé**, also called a functional résumé, emphasizes the skills you've used, rather than the job in which you used them or the date of the experience. Figure 12.7 shows a skills résumés. Use a skills résumé when

Figure 12.5   A Community College Chronological Résumé to Use for Career Fairs and Internships

Lee Cheng
chengl@eccc.edu

Vary font sizes. Use larger size for name and main headings.

Campus Address
1524 Main Street
New Brunswick, NJ 08901
732-403-5718

Using both addresses ensures continuous contact information.

Permanent Address
2526 Prairie Lane
Middlesex, NJ 00846
732-404-7793

Education
East Coast Community College
AA in Financial Management, June 2012
GPA: 3.0/4.0 *Give your grade average if it's 3.0 or higher.*

Summary of Qualifications

Use key words employers might seek.

- Self-motivated, detail-minded, results-oriented
- Consistently successful track record in sales
- Effectively developed and operated entrepreneurial business

List 3–7 qualifications.

Sales Experience
Financial Sales Representative, ABC Inc., New Brunswick, NJ, February 2011–present
- Establish client base
- Develop investment strategy plans for clients
- Research and recommend specific investments

Other Experience
Entrepreneur, A-Plus T-Shirt Company, Middlesex, NJ, September 2008–January 2011

One way to handle self-employment.

- Created a saleable product (graphic T-shirts)
- Secured financial support
- Located a manufacturer
- Supervised production
- Sold T-shirts to high school students
- Realized a substantial profit to pay for college expenses

Cook, Hamburger Shack, Seaside Heights, NJ, Summers 2007–2008
- Learned sales strategies
- Ensured customer satisfaction
- Collaborated with a team of 25

Collector and Repair Worker, ACN, Inc., Middlesex, NJ, Summer 2005–2006
- Collected and counted approximately $10,000 a day *Specify large sums of money.*
- Assisted technicians with troubleshooting and repairing coin mechanisms

Other Skills
Computer: Word, Excel, InDesign, WordPress, Outlook
Language: Fluent in Spanish *Many employers appreciate a second language.*

What Happens to Your Résumé?

Each year, technology giant Siemens Global hires more than 10,000 employees out of over 780,000 applicants. One civil engineering position had 187 applications, but only three made it through to the face-to-face interview. How does Siemens find the right people? CNNMoney found four key steps:

1. Hire internally. Like many corporations, Siemens advertises positions both internally and externally, but hires 40% of open positions from inside the company.

2. Use the web. Siemens posts jobs on Monster and Career-Builder. Recruiters also use LinkedIn both to eliminate candidates and to recruit people who may not be looking for a job.

3. Use computers to scan applications and find applicants who match job requirements.

4. Conduct initial interviews by phone. Only after applicants pass this step can they be sent on to the hiring manager.

For large corporations, using technology and recruiters to screen applicants is vital to finding the right people for jobs.

Adapted from Tami Luhby, "The Secret Life of a Résumé," CNNMoney, May 18, 2011, http://money.cnn.com/fdcp?unique=1305728467379.

- Your education and experience are not the usual route to the position for which you're applying.
- You're changing fields.
- You want to combine experience from paid jobs, activities, volunteer work, and courses to show the extent of your experience in administration, finance, public speaking, and so on.

The two kinds differ in what information is included and how that information is organized. You may assume that the advice in this chapter applies to both kinds of résumés unless there is an explicit statement that the two kinds of résumés would handle a category differently.

WHAT TO INCLUDE IN A RÉSUMÉ

Although the résumé is a factual document, its purpose is to persuade. In a job application form or an application for graduate or professional school, you answer every question even if the answer is not to your credit. In a résumé, you cannot lie, but you can omit some information that does not work in your favor.

Résumés commonly contain the following information. The categories marked with an asterisk are essential.

- Name and Contact Information*
- Career Objective
- Summary of Qualifications
- Education*
- Honors and Awards
- Experience*
- Other skills
- Activities
- Portfolio

You may choose other titles for these categories and add categories that are relevant for your qualifications, such as computer skills or foreign languages.

Education and Experience always stand as separate categories, even if you have only one item under each head. Combine other headings so that you have at least two long or three short items under each heading. For example, if you're in one honor society and two social clubs, and on one athletic team, combine them all under Activities and Honors.

If you have more than seven items under a heading, consider using subheadings. For example, a student who had a great many activities might divide them into Campus Activities and Community Service.

Put your strongest categories near the top and at the bottom of the first page. If you have impressive work experience, you might want to put that category first and Education second.

Name and Contact Information

Use your full **name,** even if everyone calls you by a nickname. You may use an initial rather than spelling out your first or middle name. Put your name in big type.

If you use only one **address,** consider centering it under your name. If you use two addresses (office and home, campus and permanent, until_____ / after_____) set them up side by side to balance the page visually. Use either

A résumé is your most important document at career fairs.

post office (two-letter, full caps, no period) abbreviations for the state or spell out the state name, but do be consistent throughout your résumé.

Urbana, IL 61801

Wheaton, Illinois 60187

Give a complete **phone number,** including the area code. Some job candidates give both home and cellphone numbers. Do provide a phone number where you can be reached during the day. Employers usually call during business hours to schedule interviews and make job offers. Do not give lab or dorm phone numbers unless you are sure someone there will take an accurate message for you at all times. Also, be sure that all answering machines have a professional-sounding message.

If you have a **web page,** and you are sure it looks professional (both content and writing), you may wish to include its URL. Be sure your web page does not reveal personal information—such as marital status, ethnicity, religious beliefs, or political stance—that could work against you. Be particularly careful of photographs.

Provide an **e-mail address.** Some job candidates set up a new e-mail address just for job hunting. Your e-mail address should look professional; avoid sexy, childish, or illicit addresses. List your **LinkedIn** site, if you have one.

Career Objective

Career objective statements should sound like the job descriptions an employer might use in a job listing. Keep your statement brief—two lines at most. Tell what you want to do, what level of responsibility you want to hold. The best career objectives are targeted to a specific job at a specific company.

Ineffective career objective: To offer a company my excellent academic foundation in hospital technology and my outstanding skills in oral and written communication

382   Part 4   The Job Hunt

Better career objective: Hospital and medical sales for Rand Medical requiring experience with state-of-the-art equipment

Good career objectives are hard to write. If you talk about entry-level work, you won't sound ambitious; if you talk about where you hope to be in 5 or 10 years, you won't sound as though you're willing to do entry-level work. When you're applying for a job that is a natural outgrowth of your education and experience, you may omit this category and specify the job you want in your cover letter.

Often you can avoid writing a career objective statement by putting the job title or field under your name:

Joan Larson Ooyen	Terence Edward Garvey	David R. Lunde
Marketing	Technical Writer	Corporate Fitness Director

Note that you can use the field you're in even if you're a new college graduate. To use a job title, you should have some relevant work experience.

If you use a separate heading for a career objective, put it immediately after your contact information, before the first major heading (see Figure 12.7). The résumé in Figure 12.5 does not use a Career Objective because it is being used for various jobs offered at a career fair. If you were particularly interested in several jobs there, you would make targeted résumés for those companies. More and more experts are advising that objectives be clarified in the cover letter rather than wasting valuable space at the top of the résumé.

Summary of Qualifications

A section summarizing the candidate's qualifications seems to have first appeared with scannable résumés, where its key words helped increase the number of matches a résumé produced. But the section proved useful for human readers as well and now is a standard part of many résumés. The best summaries show your knowledge of the specialized terminology of your field and offer specific, quantifiable achievements.

Weak: Staff accountant

Better: Experience with accounts payable, accounts receivable, audits, and month end closings. Prepared monthly financial reports.

Weak: Presentation skills

Better: Gave 20 individual and 7 team presentations to groups ranging from 5 to 100 people.

Some career advisers believe a summary is too repetitious of other sections on a one-page résumé. They believe the space is better used by listing your achievements that set you apart from other candidates.

Education

Education can be your first major category if you've just earned (or are about to earn) a degree, if you have a degree that is essential or desirable for the position you're seeking, or if you can present the information briefly. Put your Education section later if you need all of page 1 for another category or if you lack a degree that other applicants may have (see Figure 12.7).

Under Education, provide information about your undergraduate and graduate degrees, including the location of institutions and the year you received or expect your degree, if these dates are within the last 10 years.

Use the same format for all schools. List your degrees in reverse chronological order (most recent first).

> Master of Accounting Science, May 2012, Arizona State University, Tempe, AZ
> Bachelor of Arts in Finance, May 2010, New Mexico State University, Las Cruces, NM

> BS in Industrial Engineering, May 2012, Iowa State University, Ames, IA
> AS in Business Administration, May 2010, Des Moines Area Community College, Ankeny, IA

When you're getting a four-year degree, include community college only if it will interest employers, such as by showing an area of expertise different from that of your major. You may want to include your minor, emphasis, or concentration and any graduate courses you have taken. Include study abroad, even if you didn't earn college credits. If you got a certificate for international study, give the name and explain the significance of the certificate. Highlight proficiency in foreign or computer languages by using a separate category.

To punctuate your degrees, do not space between letters and periods:

A.S. in Office Administration

B.S. in Accounting

Ed.D. in Business Education

Current usage also permits you to omit the periods (BS, MBA), but be consistent with the usage you choose.

Professional certifications can be listed under Education or in a separate category.

If your GPA is good and you graduated recently, include it. If your GPA is under 3.0 on a 4.0 scale, use words rather than numbers: "B– average." If your GPA isn't impressive, calculate your average in your major and your average for your last 60 hours. If these are higher than your overall GPA, consider using them. The National Association of Colleges and Employers, in its Job Outlook 2010 survey, found that 75% of employers do screen job applicants by GPA.[10] If you leave your GPA off your résumé, most employers will automatically assume that it is below a 3.0. If yours is, you will need to rely on internships, work experience, and skills acquired in activities to make yourself an attractive job candidate.

After giving the basic information (degree, field of study, date, school, city, state) about your degree, you may wish to list courses, using short descriptive titles rather than course numbers. Use a subhead like "Courses Related to Major" or "Courses Related to Financial Management" that will allow you to list all the courses (including psychology, speech, and business communication) that will help you in the job for which you're applying. Don't say "Relevant Courses," as that implies your other courses were irrelevant.

> Bachelor of Science in Management, May 2012, Illinois State University, Normal, IL
> GPA: 3.8/4.0
>
> Courses Related to Management:
>
> | | |
> |---|---|
> | Personnel Administration | Business Decision Making |
> | Finance | International Business |
> | Management I and II | Marketing |
> | Accounting I and II | Legal Environment of Business |
> | Business Report Writing | Business Speaking |

Listing courses is an unobtrusive way to fill a page. You may also want to list courses or the number of hours in various subjects if you've taken an unusual combination of courses that uniquely qualify you for the position for which you're applying.

384   Part 4   The Job Hunt

The Value of "Soft Skills"

What are MBA programs teaching? Soft skills—lessons in teamwork, leadership, and communication. Specifically, students are working on listening, teamwork, interpersonal communication, presentations, and sensitivity to others. Why? Businesses are requesting MBA graduates with strong soft skills because they believe these students will be employees who can lead, communicate, and negotiate.

In response, schools such as the Stanford Graduate School of Business are requiring all first-year students to take personality tests, participate in teamwork exercises, and examine their people skills. At Tuck, professors designed a program which places students in teams of five to work together throughout their program.

Recruiters note that job candidates need to present their soft skills in language appropriate for the particular job they are seeking.

Adapted from Phred Dvorak, "M.B.A. Programs Hone 'Soft Skills,'" *Wall Street Journal*, February 12, 2007, B3; and Dana Mattioli, "Hard Sell on 'Soft' Skills Can Primp a Résumé: Experience with Facebook, Class Project, Juggling Activities Can Impress Employers," *Wall Street Journal*, May 15, 2007, B6.

> BS in Marketing, May 2012, California State University at Northridge
>   30 hours in marketing
>   15 hours in Spanish
>   9 hours in Chicano studies

If your course list is similar to that of others in your major, you should use the space for material that better shows your uniqueness. In that case, another way to fill the page is to include a Projects section, in which you highlight some course projects relevant to the jobs you are seeking.

As you advance in your career, your education section will shrink until finally it probably will include only your degrees and educational institutions.

Honors and Awards

It's nice to have an Honors and Awards section, but not everyone can do so. If you have fewer than three and therefore cannot justify a separate heading, consider a heading Honors and Activities to get that important word in a position of emphasis.

Include the following kinds of entries in this category:

- Academic honor societies. Specify the nature of Greek-letter honor societies (i.e., journalism honorary) so the reader doesn't think they're just social clubs.
- Fellowships and scholarships, including honorary scholarships for which you received no money and fellowships you could not hold because you received another fellowship at the same time.
- Awards given by professional societies.
- Major awards given by civic groups.
- Varsity letters; selection to all-state or all-America teams; finishes in state, national, or Olympic meets. (These could also go under Activities but may look more impressive under Honors. Put them under one category or the other—not both.)

Identify honor societies ("national journalism honorary," "campus honorary for top 2% of business majors") for readers who are not in your discipline. If your fellowships or scholarships are particularly selective or remunerative, give supporting details:

Clyde Jones Scholarship: four-year award covering tuition, fees, room, and board.
Marilyn Terpstra Scholarship: $25,000 annually for four years.
Heemsly Fellowship: 50 awarded nationally each year to top Information Science juniors.

Be careful of listing Dean's List for only one or two semesters. Such a listing reminds readers that in these days of grade inflation you were off the list many more times than you were on it. Omit honors like "Miss Congeniality" or "Muscle Man Star" that work against the professional image you want your résumé to create.

As a new college graduate, try to put Honors on page 1. In a skills résumé, put Honors on page 1 if they're major (e.g., Phi Beta Kappa, Phi Kappa Phi). Otherwise, save them until page 2—Experience will probably take the whole first page.

Experience

You may use other headings if they work better: Work Experience, Summer and Part-Time Jobs, Military Experience, Marketing Experience. In a skills résumé, headings such as "Marketing Experience" allow you to include accomplishments from activities and course projects. Headings that reflect skills mentioned in the job ad are particularly effective.

What to include   Under this section in a chronological résumé, include the following information for each job you list: position or job title, organization, city and state (no zip code), dates of employment for jobs held during the last 10 to 15 years, and other details, such as full- or part-time status, job duties, special responsibilities, or the fact that you started at an entry-level position and were promoted. Use strong verbs such as the ones in Figure 12.6 to brainstorm what you've done. Try to give supporting details for highly valued attributes such as communication skills and leadership experience. Include any internships and co-ops you have had. Also, include unpaid jobs and self-employment if they provided relevant skills (e.g., supervising people, budgeting, planning, persuading). Experience information for skills résumés is discussed on page 387.

Normally, go back as far as the summer after high school. Include earlier jobs if you started working someplace before graduating from high school but continued working there after graduation, or if the job is pertinent to the one you are applying for. If you worked full-time after high school, make that clear.

The details you give about your experience are some of the most vital information on your résumé. As you provide these details, use bulleted lists (easy to read) rather than paragraphs which are harder to read and may be skipped over. Remember that items in lists need to have parallel structure; see page 135 for a refresher. Focus on results rather than duties; employers are far more interested in what you accomplished than in what you had to do. Use numbers to support your results wherever possible:

Supervised crew of 15

Managed $120,000 budget; decreased expenses by 19%.

Wrote monthly electronic newsletter; increased hits by 12%.

Emphasize accomplishments that involve money, customers, teamwork, leadership, computer skills, and communication.

Altruism and Jobs

Weak economies send more graduates to investigate working for social causes. And many of these grads find they like making a difference.

Teach for America, the nonprofit that trains top college grads for teaching in poverty school districts, saw applications jump 42% in 2009. The Peace Corps had 16% more applications.

All of these opportunities provide experience and leadership skills valuable on the job market. They also provide strong networks of successful alumni.

Increased competition for these positions means that applicants should highlight business experience, language skills (especially Spanish and French), and volunteer experience.

Will you make a difference?

Adapted from Kyle Stock, "Jobless Professionals Yearn to Do Good: Nonprofits See a Flood of Applications with Business and Legal Know-How," *Wall Street Journal*, June 9, 2009, D6.

Figure 12.6   Action Verbs for Résumés

analyzed	directed	led	reviewed
budgeted	earned	managed	revised
built	edited	motivated	saved
chaired	established	negotiated	scheduled
coached	evaluated	observed	simplified
collected	examined	organized	sold
conducted	helped	persuaded	solved
coordinated	hired	planned	spoke
counseled	improved	presented	started
created	increased	produced	supervised
demonstrated	interviewed	recruited	trained
designed	introduced	reported	translated
developed	investigated	researched	wrote

386   Part 4   The Job Hunt

I Do Good Work

[Create an "I Do Good Work" folder to] back up your claims of top performance with solid evidence.

Before you leave the office this Friday, write down five things you—not necessarily others—believe you did well this week, even if they represent common tasks. Perhaps you returned all phone calls, leaving no loose ends to tie at the end of the week. Or maybe the details you provide in your sales reports enabled you to find additional product fits for the client. Any letters from happy customers or e-mails thanking you for solving a problem should go right in your folder. . . .

Tuck that list away and continue this weekly exercise for the entire month. At the end of the month, narrow the four or five lists to 10 accomplishments that stand out to you. At the end of the year, review the 120 items and cull them to 25. Formalize the language that describes those 25 achievements and print them out in an organized manner . . . along with your references.

"When someone asks, 'What do you bring to this organization?' you won't merely reply, 'I'm good with people,' you'll hand that sales manager or HR person proof," says professional trainer Carol Price.

Quoted from Julie Sturgeon, "All About You," *Selling Power*, September 2000, 57.

Use past tense verbs for jobs you held in the past, and present tense verbs for jobs you still have. Do not list minor duties such as distributing mail or filing documents. If your duties were completely routine, say, at your summer job at McDonald's, do not list them. If the jobs you held in the past were low-level ones, present them briefly or combine them:

> 2008–2012 Part-time and full-time jobs to finance education

If as an undergraduate you've earned a substantial portion of your college expenses with jobs and scholarship, say so in a separate statement under either Experience or Education. (Graduate students are expected to support themselves.)

> These jobs paid 40% of my college expenses.

> Paid for 65% of expenses with jobs, scholarships, and loans.

Paying for school expenses just with loans is generally not considered noteworthy.

Formats for setting up Experience   There are two basic ways to set up the Experience section of your résumé. In **indented format**, items that are logically equivalent begin at the same space, with carryover lines indented. Indented format emphasizes job titles. It provides work information in this order:

Job title, name of organization, city, state, dates. Other information.

> Experience
> **Engineering Assistant,** Sohio Chemical Company, Lima, Ohio, Summers 2011 and 2012.
> • Tested wastewater effluents for compliance with Federal EPA standards
> • Helped chemists design a test to analyze groundwater quality and seepage around landfills
> • Presented weekly oral and written progress reports to Director of Research and Development
> **Animal Caretaker,** Animalcare, Worthington, Ohio, Summers 2008–2010.

Two-margin or **block format** frequently can be used to emphasize *when* you worked, if you've held only low-level jobs. Don't use two-margin format if your work history has gaps.

> EXPERIENCE
> | | |
> |---|---|
> | Summers, 2010–12 | Repair worker, Bryant Heating and Cooling, Providence, RI |
> | 2010–11 | Library Clerk, Boston University Library, Boston, MA. Part-time during school year |
> | 2008–10 | Food Service Worker, Boston University, Boston, MA. Part-time during school year |
> | Summer, 2009 | Delivery person, Domino's Pizza, Providence, RI |

The left column can also emphasize steadily increasing job titles.

Experience at Gene Elton, Miami, Florida
Intern
Computer Programmer
Systems Analyst

The right column would list duties and dates.

Use a hyphen to join inclusive dates:

March-August, 2012 (or write out March to August, 2012)
2009–2012 or 2009–12

If you use numbers for dates, do not space before or after the slash:

10/10–5/11

Skills résumés   Skills résumés stress the skills you have acquired rather than specific jobs you have held. They show employers that you do have the desired skill set even if you lack the traditional employment background. They allow you to include skills acquired from activities and course projects in addition to jobs. On the other hand, they are also a clue to employers that you do lack that traditional background, or that you have gaps in your job history, so you will need to make your skill set convincing.

In a skills résumé, the heading of your main section usually changes from "Experience" to "Skills." Within the section, the subheadings will be replaced with the skills used in the job you are applying for, rather than the title or the dates of the jobs you've held (as in a chronological résumé). For entries under each skill, combine experience from paid jobs, unpaid work, classes, activities, and community service.

Use headings that reflect the jargon of the job for which you're applying: *logistics* rather than *planning* for a technical job; *procurement* rather than *purchasing* for a job with the military. Figure 12.7 shows a skills résumé for someone who is changing fields.

A job description can give you ideas for headings. Possible headings and subheadings for skills résumés include

Administration	**Communication**
Budgeting	Editing
Coordinating	Fund-Raising
Evaluating	Interviewing
Implementing	Negotiating
Negotiating	Persuading
Planning	Presenting
Supervising	Writing

Many jobs require a mix of skills. Try to include the skills that you know will be needed in the job you want. You need at least three subheadings in a skills résumé; six or seven is not uncommon. Give enough detail under each subheading so the reader will know what you did. Put the most important category from the reader's point of view first.

In a skills résumé, list your paid jobs under Work History or Employment Record near the end of the résumé (see Figure 12.7). List only job title, employer, city, state, and dates. Omit details that you have already used under Skills.

Other Skills

You may want a brief section in a chronological résumé where you highlight skills not apparent in your work history. These skills may include items such as foreign languages or programming languages. You might want to list software you have used or training on expensive equipment (electron microscopes, NMR machines). As always on your résumé, be completely honest: "two years of high school German," or "elementary speaking knowledge of Spanish." Any knowledge of a foreign language is a plus. It means that a company desiring a second language in its employees would not have to start from scratch in training you. Figure 12.8 lists skills in its Qualifications section.

Job Skills Checklist

Having trouble identifying your skills? OWL, Purdue's Online Writing Lab, has an excellent list to help get you going. Connect the skills you identify to experiences in your life that demonstrate the skills; then put the best material into your résumé and cover letter. See this website: http://owl.english.purdue.edu/owl/resource/626/1/.

Figure 12.7   A Skills Résumé for Someone Changing Fields

Molly Schooner
www.ukansas.edu/~Schooner88/home.htm

If you have a professional web page, include its URL.

266 Van Buren Drive
Lawrence, KS 66044
schoonerm@ukansas.edu
785-897-1534 (home)
785-842-4242 (cell)

Objective
To contribute my enthusiasm for writing as a Technical Writer at PDF Productions

Job objective includes the position and name of the company.

Skills

Largest section on skills résumé; allows you to combine experiences from work and class.

Computer
- Designed a web page using Dreamweaver
  www.lawrenceanimalshelter.com
- Used a variety of Macintosh and PC platform programs and languages:

Aspects(online discussion forum)	Adobe Professional
Dreamweaver CS5	HTML
PageMaker	Java Script
XML	Photoshop CS5

Specify computer programs you know well.

Design and Writing

Use parallel structure for bulleted lists.

- Designed a quarterly newsletter for local animal shelter
- Developed professional brochures
- Wrote a variety of professional documents: letters, memos, and reports
- Edited internal documents and promotional materials
- Proofread seven student research papers as a tutor

Organization and Administration
- Coordinated program schedules
- Developed work schedules for five employees
- Led a 10-member team in planning and implementing sorority philanthropy program
- Created cataloging system for specimens
- Ordered and handled supplies, including live specimens

Employment History

Condensed to make room for skills.

Technical Writer, Lawrence Animal Shelter, Lawrence, KS, 2010–present
Undergraduate Lab Assistant, Department of Biology,
     University of Kansas, Lawrence, KS, 2010–present
Tutor, University of Kansas, Lawrence, KS, 2009–2010

Uses reverse chronology.

Education
Bachelor of Arts, May 2012
University of Kansas, Lawrence, KS
Major: Animal Ecology
Minor: Chemistry
GPA: 3.4/4.0

Give minor when it can be helpful.

Honors

End with strong items at the bottom of your page, a position of emphasis.

Phi Kappa Phi Honor Society
Alpha Lambda Delta Honor Society, Ecology Honorary
Dean's List, 2007 – present
Raymond Hamilton Scholarship, 2010–2011
     ($5,000 to a top ecology student in Kansas)

Explain honors your reader may not know.

Figure 12.8   A One-Page Chronological Résumé

Jeff Moeller

831.503.4692
51 Willow Street
San José, CA 95112
jmoeller@csmb.edu

*Use job title
and company name in
Career Objective.*

Career Objective
To bring my attention to detail and love for computer/video games to Telltale Games as a Game Designer

Qualifications
- Experienced in JavaScript, Lua, and Python
- Intermediate proficiency with Visual Studio; high proficiency with Source Safe
- Excellent communication, interpersonal, and collaboration skills
- Advanced knowledge of computers
- Love of video games

*Highlights
qualifications
specific to the job.*

Education
California State University—Monterey Bay
August 2008–May 2012 (expected)
Bachelor of Science in Computer Science and Information Technology

*Keeps Education
section simple to
emphasize
experience.*

Experience
Online Marketing Consultant—Self–Employed
October 2009–present

*Lists job titles
on separate lines.*

- Manage multiple-client Google Adwords accounts
- Install web software and implement designs for fast turnarounds
- Interface with clients using Basecamp

Editor-in-Chief—Point Network LLC
June 2007–present

*Use present tense verbs
when you are doing the job now.*

- Write and edit for several LucasArts-related gaming news websites
- Design and code websites using Wordpress
- Manage and administrate the LucasForums.com community

Online Marketing Assistant—Hayfield Group
May 2010–August 2010; May 2010–August 2011

*Use past tense for
jobs that are over.*

- Managed all client Google Adwords accounts
- Assisted in or managed planning and executing PPC and SEO campaigns
- Coded the company website and integrated the Drupal CMS
- Prepared website analytics reports using Google Analytics and other analytics suites

Community Manager—Praise Entertainment, Inc.
April 2009–September 2011
- Managed the community at AdminFusion.com, a website geared toward online forum owners
- Organized and ran a monthly contest for community members

*Close with strong
section.*

Honors and Activities
- Member of the gaming press for E3 2010 and 2011
- Member of second place team in 2011 National STEM Video Game challenge
  (see demo, "Parrot Villa" at www.STEMChallenge.gov/2011_winners)

*Include activities that employer
might value.*

What to Know about Job References

Many job reference myths exist that may undermine your job search:

Myth: I don't have to mention a job that didn't work out, especially if I worked there only a short while.

Fact: Employers check jobs through Social Security, and they will believe the worst of omissions.

Myth: Companies are not legally allowed to give damaging information about applicants.

Fact: Although many companies have formal policies of providing only bare-bones data, many employees within those organizations still engage in providing additional, negative information about applicants. Voice tone, or mentioning that you may not be eligible for rehire, may speak volumes.

Myth: References do not matter once you are hired.

Fact: References may still be checked after you are hired and can be used for grounds for termination.

Myth: References are not needed after you have a job.

Fact: Stay in contact with your references. You never know when you may want to change jobs.

Activities

Employers may be interested in your activities if you're a new college graduate because they can demonstrate leadership roles, management abilities, and social skills as well as the ability to juggle a schedule. If you've worked for several years after college or have an advanced degree (MBA, JD), you can omit Activities and include Professional Activities and Affiliations or Community and Public Service. If you went straight from college to graduate school but have an unusually strong record demonstrating relevant skills, include this category even if all the entries are from your undergraduate days.

Include the following kinds of items under Activities:

- Volunteer work. Include important committees, leadership roles, communication activities, and financial and personnel responsibilities.
- Membership in organized student activities. Include important subcommittees, leadership roles. Include minor offices only if they're directly related to the job for which you're applying or if they show growing responsibility (you held a minor office one year, a bigger office the following year). Include so-called major offices (e.g., vice president) even if you did very little. Provide descriptive details if (but only if) they help the reader realize how much you did and the importance of your work, or if they demonstrate usable job skills.
- Membership in professional associations. Many of them have special low membership fees for students, so you should join one or more.
- Participation in varsity, intramural, or independent athletics. However, don't list so many sports that you appear not to have had adequate time to study.
- Social clubs, if you held a major leadership role or if social skills are important for the job for which you're applying.

As you list activities, add details that will be relevant for your job. Did you handle a six-figure budget for your Greek organization? Plan all the road trips for your soccer club? Coordinate all the publicity for the campus blood drive? Design the posters for homecoming? Major leadership, financial, and creative roles and accomplishments may look more impressive if they're listed under Experience instead of under Activities.

Portfolio

If you have samples of your work available, you may want to end your résumé by stating "Portfolio (or writing samples) available on request." or by giving the URL for your work.

REFERENCES

References are generally no longer included on résumés. Nor do you say "References Available on Request," since no job applicant is going to refuse to supply references. However, you will probably be asked for references at some point in your application process, so it is wise to be prepared.

You will need at least three, usually no more than five, never more than six. As a college student or a new graduate, include at least one professor and at least one employer or adviser—someone who can comment on your work habits and leadership skills. If you're changing jobs, include your current superior. For a skills résumé, choose references who can testify to your abilities in the most important skills areas. Omit personal or character references, who cannot talk about your work. Don't use relatives, friends, or roommates, even if you've worked for them, because everyone will believe they are biased in your favor.

Always ask permission to use the person as a reference. Doing so is not only polite, but ensures the person will remember you when contacted. Instead of the vague "May I list you as a reference?" use, "Can you speak specifically about my work?" Jog the person's memory by taking along copies of work you did for him or her and a copy of your current résumé. Tell the person what qualifications a specific employer is seeking. Keep your list of references up-to-date. If it's been a year or more since you asked someone, ask again—and tell the person about your recent achievements.

On your list of references, provide name, title or position, organization, city, state, phone number, and e-mail for each of your references. If their connection to you is not clear, add an identifying line (former academic adviser; former supervisor at Careltons) so they do not look like personal references. You could also give the full mailing address if you think people are more likely to write than to call. Use courtesy titles (*Dr., Mr., Ms.*) for all or for none. By convention, all faculty with the rank of assistant professor or above may be called *Professor.*

References that the reader knows are by far the most impressive. In fact, employers may ask about you among people they already know: a former classmate may now work for them; a professor in your major department may consult for them. Through these routes, employers can get references about you even in companies whose formal human resources policy provides only dates of employment. Therefore, you should be well thought of by as many people as possible.

Some employers are also checking contacts on social networking sites such as LinkedIn and Facebook to find people who may know you. When you are on the job market, you may want to consider adjusting your privacy settings so that your contacts are visible to only a select few. On sites without such adjustments, you need to be careful with your contact list. Remember that Facebook has a history of making personal information public.

Include the name and address of your placement office if you have written recommendations on file there; that contact information will be all you need.

WHAT NOT TO INCLUDE IN A RÉSUMÉ

Certain items do not belong on résumés used in the United States (standards differ in other countries). These include age, ethnicity, marital status, number of children, and health. Photographs also do not belong on résumés unless you are applying for jobs such as entertainment positions. Although interested parties can frequently find your picture on Facebook, for instance, pictures have long been excluded because of their ability to enable discrimination. For safety reasons, résumés should never include your Social Security number.

Including these kinds of information shows you have not researched the job-hunting process. Since many employers take your performance on the job hunt as an indication of the quality of work you will do for them, résumé lapses indicate that you may not be the best employee.

Since résumés are used to eliminate a large pool of job candidates down to the handful that will be interviewed, do not include controversial activities or associations. This category generally includes work for specific religious or political groups. (If the work is significant, you can include it generically: Wrote campaign publicity for state senator candidate.)

High school facts are generally omitted once you are a junior in college unless you have good reasons for keeping them. These reasons might include showing you have local connections or showing skill in a needed area not covered by college activities (perhaps you are applying for coaching jobs where a

Résumé Checklist

Does the résumé have a good, easy-to-read layout?

Does it include your name, address, city, state, zip code, phone number, and e-mail address at the top of the page?

Does it use bullets or bold to highlight key elements?

Does it list information in order of relevance to the position?

Does it give specifics, not generalities, about your experience?

Did you double check the spelling, grammar and punctuation?

Does it use action verbs to describe your job duties?

Is your résumé truthful?

Is it tailored for a specific employer?

Does a 10-second reading reveal the basics about you?

Does the résumé warrant an interview, if you were an employer?

How does your résumé rate?

Adapted from UC Berkeley Career Center, "Résumé and Letter Writing: Résumé Checklist," in *Job and Internship Guide 2010–2011*, accessed April 3, 2011, http://career.berkeley.edu/Guide/ResumeLetterWriting.pdf.

variety of team sports will help you, and you played basketball in high school and volleyball in college). The fact that you have good high school activities but few if any college activities is not a good reason. In this case, listing high school activities will show you are on a downward trend at a very early age!

Do not pad your résumé with trivial items; they are easily recognized as padding and they devalue the worth of your other items. For instance, except under the most unusual circumstances, graduate students should not list grants for travel to conferences as honors, since such travel grants are ubiquitous. Some community groups, especially religious organizations, list all college graduates in their group-specific "honorary." Since everyone who graduates will belong, these are not considered honors.

As you advance in your career, you will continually cut information from earlier stages of your life, as well as from outside activities, to focus on your recent career achievements.

DEALING WITH DIFFICULTIES LO 12-3

Some job hunters face special problems. This section gives advice for six common problems.

"I Don't Have Any Experience."

If you have a year or more before you job hunt, you can get experience in several ways:

- Take a fast-food job—and keep it. If you do well, you'll be promoted to a supervisor within a year. Use every opportunity to learn about the management and financial aspects of the business.
- Sign on with agencies that handle temporary workers. As an added bonus, some of these jobs become permanent.
- Join a volunteer organization that interests you. If you work hard, you'll quickly get an opportunity to do more: manage a budget, write fund-raising materials, and supervise other volunteers.
- Freelance. Design brochures, create web pages, do tax returns for small businesses. Use your skills—for free, if you have to at first.
- Write. Create a portfolio of ads, instructions, or whatever documents are relevant for the field you want to enter. Ask a professional—an instructor, a local business person, someone from a professional organization—to critique them.

If you're on the job market now, think carefully about what you've really done. Complete sentences using the action verbs in Figure 12.6. Think about what you've done in courses, in volunteer work, in unpaid activities. Especially focus on skills in problem solving, critical thinking, teamwork, and communication. Solving a problem for a hypothetical firm in an accounting class, thinking critically about a report problem in business communication, working with a group in a marketing class, and communicating with people at the senior center where you volunteer are experience, even if no one paid you.

"All My Experience Is in My Family's Business."

In your résumé, simply list the company you worked for. For a reference, instead of a family member, list a supervisor, client, or vendor who can talk about your work. Since the reader may wonder whether "Jim Clarke" is any relation to the owner of

"Clarke Construction Company," be ready to answer interview questions about why you're looking at other companies. Prepare an answer that stresses the broader opportunities you seek but doesn't criticize your family or the family business.

"I Want to Change Fields."

Have a good reason for choosing the field in which you're looking for work. "I want a change" or "I need to get out of a bad situation" does not convince an employer that you know what you're doing.

Think about how your experience relates to the job you want. Sam wants a new career as a pharmaceutical sales representative. He has sold woodstoves, served subpoenas, and worked on an oil rig. A chronological résumé makes his work history look directionless. But a skills résumé could focus on persuasive ability (selling stoves), initiative and persistence (serving subpoenas), and technical knowledge (courses in biology and chemistry).

Learn about the skills needed in the job you want: learn the buzzwords of the industry. Figure 12.7 shows a skills résumé of someone changing fields from animal ecology to technical writing. Her reason for changing could be that she found she enjoyed the writing duties of her jobs more than she enjoyed the ecology field work.

"I've Been Out of the Job Market for a While."

You need to prove to a potential employer that you're up-to-date and motivated:

- Create a portfolio of your work to show what you can do for the employer.
- Do freelance work.
- Be active in professional organizations. Attend meetings.
- Look for volunteer work where you can use and expand relevant work skills.
- Attend local networking events.
- Read the journals and trade publications of your field.
- Learn the software that professionals use in your field.
- Be up-to-date with electronic skills such as IMing, text messaging, and computer searching.
- Take professional training to expand your skill set.

Employment counselors advise that you not leave a gap on your résumé; such a gap makes employers speculate about disasters such as nervous breakdowns or jail time. They suggest you matter-of-factly list an honorable title such as Parent or Caregiver; do not apologize. Better yet is to fill in the gap with substantial volunteer experience. Heading a $75,000 fund-raising drive for a new playground looks good for almost any employer. A side benefit of volunteer work, in addition to new career skills, is networking. Boards of directors and agency executives are frequently well-connected members of the community.

"I Was Laid Off."

In times of large layoffs, this is not an overwhelming obstacle. You do not need to point out the layoff in your application materials; the end date of your last employment will make the point for you. Instead, use your documents to highlight your strengths.

Should I Create a Video Résumé?

What is a video résumé?

Job hunters post short videos as part of their job applications through services such as YouTube, Google video, and video résumé sites.

Who uses video résumés?

Anyone can. Currently, most video résumés are produced by applicants interested in entertainment and media, but job seekers in other industries are starting to use video postings.

What are the benefits to employers?

Employers get an opportunity to screen applicants before asking for an interview. This may save an employer from conducting an interview.

Are there risks?

Yes, discrimination on the basis of sex, age, and ethnicity.

If you decide to create a video posting, you may want to consider these tips for your video résumé:

1. Be brief and concise. Remember that employers generally spend less than 30 seconds per résumé. Don't expect them to spend longer on your video.

2. Be prepared. Avoid reading a script. You should be conversational and natural in your presentation.

3. Tailor the video to the specific employer and position.

4. Be professional. Post a video that is clear, audible, and free from background noise.

394   Part 4   The Job Hunt

Do be prepared to be asked about the layoff in an interview. Why were you laid off when other employees were retained? It helps if you can truthfully give a neutral explanation: the accounting work was outsourced; our entire lab was closed; the company laid off everyone who had worked fewer than five years. Be sure you do not express bitterness or self-pity; neither emotion will help you get your new job. On the other hand, do not be overly grateful for an interview; such excess shows a lack of self-confidence. Be sure to show you are keeping yourself current by doing some of the items in the bulleted list in the previous section.

"I Was Fired."

First, deal with the emotional baggage. You need to reduce negative feelings to a manageable level before you're ready to job-hunt.

Second, take responsibility for your role in the termination.

Third, try to learn from the experience. You'll be a much more attractive job candidate if you can show that you've learned from the experience—whether your lesson is improved work habits or that you need to choose a job where you can do work you can point to with pride.

Fourth, collect evidence showing that earlier in your career you were a good worker. This evidence could include references from earlier employers, good performance evaluations, and a portfolio of good work.

Some common strategies may also give you some help for references. You should check with the Human Resources Department to understand the company's reference policy. Some companies now give no references other than verification of job title and work dates. Others do not give references for employees who worked only a short time.[11] Another option is to ask someone other than your former boss for a reference. Could you ask a supplier or vendor? A different department head?

A different tactic is suggested by Phil Elder, an interviewer for an insurance company. He suggests calling the person who fired you and saying something like this: "Look, I know you weren't pleased with the job I did at _____. I'm applying for a job at _____ now and the personnel director may call you to ask about me. Would you be willing to give me the chance to get this job so that I can try to do things right this time?" All but the hardest of heart, says Elder, will give you one more chance. You won't get a glowing reference, but neither will the statement be so damning that no one is willing to hire you.[12]

Above all, be honest. Do not lie about your termination at an interview or on a job application. The application usually requires you to sign a statement that the information you are providing is true and that false statements can be grounds for dismissal.

ELECTRONIC RÉSUMÉS   LO 12-4

In addition to a paper résumé for job fairs, interviews, and potential contacts, you will need electronic versions of your résumé. With a few exceptions noted below, these résumés will have the same content but will be formatted differently so they can be "read" by both software and humans.

Sending Your Résumé Electronically

Many employers are asking to have résumés posted on their organizations' websites. When doing so, be sure you follow their directions exactly. You may also be asked by some employers to send your résumé by e-mail.

Beware of Spam Filters

Employers are using filters to keep out spam and damaging computer viruses. Unfortunately, legitimate e-mails, including résumés, are also getting blocked. Applicants who send résumés with an e-mail may be rejected by spam filters for various reasons such as "foul" language (B.S.) or overused phrases (*responsible for* or *duties included*).

What can you do to avoid spam filters?

- Avoid acronyms or titles that may be considered "foul" language.
- Watch overusing words or phrases.
- Avoid words like *free, extend, unbelievable, opportunity, trial, mortgage.*
- Avoid using unusual colors.
- Be careful of using all capitals, exclamation points, or dollar amounts in subject lines.

What preventative steps can you take to avoid being caught by spam filters?

- Set your personal spam filter to high; then send your résumé to your own e-mail account
- Send your résumé to a spam checker.

Adapted from Michael Trust, "How to Stop Your Résumé from Becoming Spam," Careerealism, October 11, 2010, http://www.careerealism.com/stop-resume-spam.

Here are some basic guidelines of e-mail job-hunting etiquette:

- Don't use your current employer's e-mail system for your job search. You'll leave potential employers with the impression that you spend company time on writing résumés and other nonwork-related activities.
- Set up a free, Internet-based e-mail account using services such as Hotmail, Gmail, or Yahoo! to manage correspondence related to your job hunt.
- Avoid using silly or cryptic e-mail addresses. Instead of bubbles@aol.com, opt for something business-like: yourname@yahoo.com.
- Write a simple subject line that makes a good first impression: Résumé—Kate Sanchez. A good subject line will improve the chances that your résumé is actually read, since e-mail from unknown senders is often deleted without being opened. If you are responding to an ad, use the job title or job code listed.
- Before sending your résumé into cyberspace, test to see how it will look when it comes out on the other end. E-mail it to yourself and a friend, then critique and fix it.
- Send only one résumé, even if the firm has more than one position for which you qualify. Most recruiters have negative reactions to multiple résumés.
- Experts differ on whether candidates should phone to follow up. Phoning once to be sure your résumé arrived is probably fine.

It's important to heed the specific directions of employers that you are e-mailing. Many do not want attachments because of viruses. While a few may want a Microsoft Word or PDF attachment of your résumé, others may specify that you paste your résumé directly into the body of your e-mail message.

If you are sending your résumé in the text of an e-mail,

- Start all lines at the left margin.
- Do not use bold, underlining, bullets, tabs, or unusual fonts. Instead use keys such as asterisks.
- You can also put some headings in all capital letters, but use this device sparingly.
- To avoid awkward line breaks for your readers, shorten line lengths to 65 characters and spaces.

Play Safe

Before posting your job application online, you should verify the site is safe. Here are some criteria:

1. **Have you heard of the site?** If not, be careful. Look for online reviews of the site.

2. **Does it ask you to register before you can search for jobs?** This is a big red flag. Try a different site.

3. **Does it have a comprehensive privacy policy?** Read the policy to see if they sell or rent your information. Putting up your job packet on a nonprivate forum could affect your identity in the future. Do not assume the site is protected if it has a privacy seal.

4. **Can you limit access to your personal contact information?** Identity theft is a growing problem. Good sites allow you to protect personal contact information.

5. **Does it let you delete your résumé after you get a job?** Safe websites should allow you to delete your documents or make them inactive while you are not conducting a job search. You don't want your new boss to think you are still on the job market for an even better position.

Adapted from Susan Joyce, "15 Critical Criteria for Choosing the Best Job Site for You," NETability, Inc., accessed April 3, 2011. http://www.job-hunt.org/choosing.shtml.

Your résumé will look plain to you, but the employers receiving it are used to the look of in-text résumés.

If you are sending your résumé as an attachment, name the document appropriately: Smith Robyn Résumé.docx. Never name it Résumé.docx; you do not want it to get lost in a long directory of documents.

With your résumé include a brief cover letter that will make the receiver want to look at your résumé. In it, mention the types of files you've included. (See Figure 13.8.) Remember, it takes only an instant for readers to delete your e-mail. Do not give them reasons to trash your résumé.

Some people confuse electronic and scannable résumés. The former are résumés you send in or attached to an e-mail. The latter are paper résumés specially formatted for older software. Software programs have greatly improved recently and most can now scan regular résumés posted on websites. However, if you are asked to send a scannable résumé, guidelines for creating one are in Appendix D.

Posting Your Résumé on the Web

You will probably want to post your résumé online. Be selective when you do: stick with well-known sites for safety reasons. Choose one or two of the large popular sites such as Monster or CareerBuilder. Also choose one or two smaller sites, preferably ones specific to your desired occupation or location. A well-chosen niche site can show employers that you know your field. Studies are still showing that about 25% of external hires are made through job boards.[13]

Many responsible career sites recommend that you should not succumb to **résumé blasting**—posting your résumé widely on the web. Many employers consider such blasting to be akin to spam and they respond negatively to job candidates who do it.

If the websites you choose have you place your information into their résumé form, cut and paste from your résumé to avoid typos. Do not use résumé templates unless you are asked to do so; they will rarely present you as well as the layout you have designed for yourself.

For safety reasons, use your e-mail address as contact information instead of your address and phone number. Make sure your e-mail address looks professional; you should not be HotLips@Yahoo.com. To foil identity thieves, some web consultants also recommend that you remove all dates from your résumé, and that you replace employer names with generic descriptions (statewide information technology company). Identity thieves can take information directly from online résumés, or they can call employers and, claiming to be conducting background checks, get additional information.

Since many databases sort résumés by submission date, renew your résumé by making small changes to it at least every two weeks. If you don't get any response to your résumé after a month or two, post it on a different site.

If you post your résumé on your personal website, be sure that all the links go to professional-looking pages, such as documents you have created. Now is not the time to link to pictures of you partying. Also, make sure the first screen includes a current job objective and Summary of Qualifications. One study found that résumés on personal websites were particularly useful for self-employed workers, for whom they attracted clients.[14]

When you have your new job, remove your résumé from all sites. Your new employer will probably take a dim view of finding your résumé on job sites and it is virtually impossible to block your online résumé from people at your current place of employment.

HONESTY [LO 12-5]

Be absolutely honest on your résumé—and in the rest of your job search. Just ask Marilee Jones, former Dean of Admissions at Massachusetts Institute of Technology (MIT). In 1979, when she applied for an admissions job at MIT, her résumé listed bachelor's and master's degrees from Rensselaer Polytechnic Institute. In reality, she attended there only one year as a part-time student. By 1997, when she was promoted to the deanship, she did not have the courage to correct her résumé. In April 2007, she was forced to resign, even though she was a nationally recognized leader in admissions, after an anonymous tip.[15]

Most businesses now conduct some kind of background check on job applicants. Even graduate schools, particularly business schools, are checking applicants.[16] A survey of over 3,000 hirers conducted for CareerBuilder reported that 49% had caught lies on résumés.

Background checks on job candidates can include a credit check, legal and criminal records, complete employment history, and academic credentials. Such checks turn up some incredible whoppers. Résumés have been found using someone else's photo, listing degrees from nonexistent schools, listing fake Mensa memberships, and even claiming a false connection to the Kennedy clan.[17]

You can omit some material on your résumé, because obviously you cannot include everything about your life to date. For instance, it's still ethical to omit a low GPA, although most employers will assume it is very low indeed to be omitted. But what you do include must be absolutely honest.

Some of the most frequent inaccuracies on résumés are inflated job titles and incorrect dates of employment. While these data are easy to fudge, they are also easy to catch in background checks. It is also possible that some of these particular inaccuracies come from careless records kept by job candidates. Do you remember the exact job title of that first job you held as a sophomore in high school? Keep careful records of your employment history!

If employers do an employment history check, and many do, they will have a complete work history for you. They will be able to spot inaccurate company names and work dates. If you left a company off your résumé, they may wonder why; some may assume your performance at that company was not satisfactory.

Other areas where résumés are commonly inaccurate are

- Degrees: many people conveniently forget they were a few hours short of a degree.
- GPAs: inflating one's grade point seems to be a big temptation.
- Honors: people list memberships in fake honoraries, or fake memberships in real honoraries.
- Fake employers.
- Job duties: many people inflate them.
- Salary increases.
- Fake addresses: people create these to have the "local" advantage.
- Fake contact information for references: this information frequently leads to family members or friends who will give fake referrals.
- Technical abilities.
- Language proficiency.

All dishonesty on a résumé is dangerous, keeping you from being hired if discovered early, and causing you to be fired if discovered later. However, the last two bullets listed above are particular dangerous because your chances are good of being asked at an interview to demonstrate your listed proficiencies.

Résumé Lies Lead to Termination

Listed below are high-level professionals who learned the hard way that eventually employers will discover discrepancies on résumés.

- Dave Edmondson, former chief executive of RadioShack, resigned after lying about having a college degree.
- George O'Leary, former Notre Dame football coach, resigned over inaccuracies in both his academic and athletic backgrounds.
- Jeffrey Papows, former CEO of Lotus Corporation, quit over discrepancies in his military and educational record.
- Kenneth Lonchar, CFO of Veritas software, resigned over inaccuracies in his academic background.

Have you checked your résumé to make sure you have not inflated your credentials?

Adapted from Rachel Zupek, "Infamous Résumé Lies," Career-Builder, July 7, 2010, http://msn.careerbuilder.com/Article/MSN-1154-Cover-Letters-Resumes-Infamous-R%C3%A9sum%C3%A9-Lies.

SUMMARY OF KEY POINTS

The Cost of a Typo

Typos can cost you a job. Many employers say they will not consider résumés with spelling mistakes or typographical errors.

Why? Employers consider your job documents to be examples of your finest work. If you are careless on them, they assume you will be even more careless in the work you do for them.

Spell check is not enough. Too many "mangers" (managers) with great ability "to to" attend to detail are seeking work in the "pubic area" (public arena). You get the point. Proofread your documents carefully. Get your friends and family to proof them also, but remember, no one cares as much about your documents as you do. If English is not your first language, or your strong suit, consider paying for a professional editor. The success of your career starts with these documents.

- Informal preparation for job hunting should start soon after you arrive on campus. Formal preparation for job hunting should begin a full year before you begin interviewing. The year you interview, register with your placement office early.
- Personal branding and networking, particularly through social media such as LinkedIn, are now an important part of job searching.
- Employers skim résumés to decide whom to interview. Employers assume that the letter and résumé represent your best work.
- Emphasize information that is relevant to the job you want, is recent (last three years), and shows your superiority to other applicants.
- To emphasize key points, put them in headings, list them vertically, and provide details.
- Résumés use sentence fragments punctuated like complete sentences. Items in the résumé must be concise and parallel. Verbs and gerunds create a dynamic image of you.
- A **chronological résumé** summarizes what you did in a time line (starting with the most recent events, and going backward in **reverse chronology**). It emphasizes degrees, job titles, and dates. Use a chronological résumé when
  - Your education and experience are a logical preparation for the position for which you're applying.
  - You have impressive job titles, offices, or honors.
- A **skills résumé** emphasizes the skills you've used, rather than the job in which or the date when you used them. Use a skills résumé when
  - Your education and experience are not the usual route to the position for which you're applying.
  - You're changing fields.
  - You want to combine experience from paid jobs, activities, volunteer work, and courses to show the extent of your experience in administration, finance, speaking, etc.
  - Your recent work history may create the wrong impression (e.g., it has gaps, shows a demotion, shows job-hopping, etc.).
- Résumés contain the applicant's contact information, education, and experience. Career objectives, summary of qualifications, honors and awards, other skills, activities, and a portfolio reference may also be included.
- Many résumés are now sent electronically and are posted on the Internet or the organization's website.
- Remove any unprofessional material from your personal web page, blog, and social networking sites.
- Always be completely honest in your résumé and job search.

CHAPTER 12	**Exercises and Problems**	*Go to www.mhhe.com/locker10e for additional Exercises and Problems.*

12.1   Reviewing the Chapter

1. What should you do soon after starting college to prepare for your job search? (LO 12-1)
2. What should you do a full year before your job search? (LO 12-1)
3. How can you use writing components such as emphasis and details to help set yourself apart from other candidates? (LO 12-2)

4. What are factors you should consider when preparing your contact information? (LO 12-2)
5. Why are career objectives hard to write? (LO 12-2)
6. What are key words? How do you use them in your summary of qualifications? In electronic résumés? (LO 12-2)
7. What kinds of details make your experience look most attractive to potential employers? (LO 12-2)
8. How can activities help make you look attractive to potential employers? (LO 12-2)
9. What can you do to help get the best references possible? (LO 12-2)
10. Pick one of the common problems job hunters may face and explain how you would deal with it if it happened to you during your career. (LO 12-3)
11. What are some basic guidelines of e-mail job-hunting etiquette? (LO 12-4)
12. What safety precautions do you need to take when you post your résumé online? (LO 12-4)
13. What roles are blogs and Facebook pages playing in the job search? (LO 12-4)
14. Why is it more important now than ever before to be completely honest on your résumé? (LO 12-5)

12.2 Reviewing Grammar

Most résumés use lists, and items in lists need to have parallel structure. Polish your knowledge of parallel structure by revising the sentences in Exercise B.7, Appendix B.

12.3 Analyzing Your Accomplishments

List the 10 achievements that give you the most personal satisfaction. These could be things that other people wouldn't notice. They can be accomplishments you've achieved recently or things you did years ago.
   Answer the following questions for each accomplishment:
1. What skills or knowledge did you use?
2. What personal traits did you exhibit?
3. What about this accomplishment makes it personally satisfying to you?

As your instructor directs,
a. Share your answers with a small group of other students.
b. Summarize your answers in a memo to your instructor.
c. Present your answers orally to the class.

12.4 Remembering What You've Done

Use the following list to jog your memory about what you've done. For each item, give three or four details as well as a general statement.
   Describe a time when you
1. Used facts and figures to gain agreement on an important point.
2. Identified a problem that a group or organization faced and developed a plan for solving the problem.
3. Made a presentation or a speech to a group.
4. Won the goodwill of people whose continued support was necessary for the success of some long-term project or activity.
5. Interested other people in something that was important to you and persuaded them to take the actions you wanted.
6. Helped a group deal constructively with conflict.
7. Demonstrated creativity.
8. Took a project from start to finish.
9. Created an opportunity for yourself in a job or volunteer position.
10. Used good judgment and logic in solving a problem.

As your instructor directs,
a. Identify which job(s) each detail is relevant for.
b. Identify which details would work well on a résumé.
c. Identify which details, further developed, would work well in a job letter.

12.5 Developing Action Statements

Use 10 of the verbs from Figure 12.6 to write action statements describing what you've done in paid or volunteer work, in classes, in extracurricular activities, or in community service.

12.6 Evaluating Career Objective Statements

The following career objective statements are not effective. What is wrong with each statement as it stands? Which statements could be revised to be satisfactory? Which should be dropped?

1. To use my acquired knowledge of accounting to eventually own my own business.
2. A progressively responsible position as a MARKETING MANAGER where education and ability would have valuable application and lead to advancement.
3. To work with people responsibly and creatively, helping them develop personal and professional skills.
4. A position in international marketing which makes use of my specialization in marketing and my knowledge of foreign markets.
5. To bring Faith, Hope, and Charity to the American workplace.
6. To succeed in sales.
7. To design and maintain web pages.

12.7 Deciding How Much Detail to Use

In each of the following situations, how detailed should the applicant be? Why?

1. Ron Oliver has been steadily employed for the last six years while getting his college degree, but the jobs have been low-level ones, whose prime benefit was that they paid well and fit around his class schedule.
2. Adrienne Barcus was an assistant department manager at a clothing boutique. As assistant manager, she was authorized to approve checks in the absence of the manager. Her other duties were ringing up sales, cleaning the area, and helping mark items for sales.
3. Lois Heilman has been a clerk-typist in the Alumni Office. As part of her job, she developed a schedule for mailings to alumni, set up a merge system, and wrote two of the letters that go out to alumni. The merge system she set up has cut in half the time needed to produce letters.
4. As a co-op student, Stanley Greene spends every other term in a paid job. He now has six semesters of job experience in television broadcasting. During his last co-op he was the assistant producer for a daily "morning magazine" show.

12.8 Evaluating Web Résumés

Evaluate five résumés you find on the web. Many schools of business have places where students can post résumés online. You may find other résumés on job boards (see the list in Figure 12.2).

As your instructor directs,

a. Share your results with a small group of students.
b. Write an e-mail message analyzing what works and what doesn't. Provide URLs or links to the pages you discuss.
c. Write a memo analyzing what works and what doesn't. Attach printouts of each page you discuss.
d. Join with a small group of students to analyze the pages.
e. Make a short oral presentation to the class discussing the best (or worst) page you found.

12.9 Writing Job Search Goals

Write a list of goals and tasks you need to accomplish for a successful job search. Which ones are crucial? What steps do you need to start taking now to accomplish these goals and tasks? Make a tentative time line for the steps.

12.10   Writing a Job Description

Write a job description for your "dream position."
Include the following:

- Position title
- Position description including tasks, special requirements
- Location
- Work hours
- Working conditions (for example, office space, scheduling, amount of supervision)
- Company culture

- Pay
- Experience and education requirements
- Personal competencies (for example, ability to communicate, work in teams, problem solve, etc.).
- Amount of travel
- Social, political, and ethical issues that may be involved

In small groups, share your descriptions. Did you get some ideas from the dream jobs of other students?

12.11   Performing a Needs Analysis

Identify a specific job posting you are interested in and list its requirements. Analyze the needs of the job and identify your personal strengths and qualifications to obtain it.

As your instructor directs,

a.   Work on incorporating your list into a résumé.

b.   Compose bullet entries for each qualification using action verbs.

c.   Identify areas in which you still need to improve. Brainstorm a list of ways in which you can achieve what you need.

12.12   Researching a Job Ad

For a specific job ad online, list job requirements and key words. Search online for the corporation that has posted the job. Look up the corporation's mission and objectives pages and look for repeating keywords and hot buttons. Find correlations between the job posting and the company's objectives.

As your instructor directs,

a.   Share your findings with a group and discuss how the given job posting correlates to the company's overall mission and needs.

b.   Identify one such case from your group and present it to the class.

12.13   Editing a Résumé

Below are a job ad and a résumé applying for that job. Using the information you have about Jennifer's two jobs (given below the résumé), critique Jennifer's résumé. Her job letter is Exercise 13.18, if you wish to look at it, too. Redo her résumé to improve it. Then write a memo to your instructor discussing the strengths and weaknesses of the résumé and explaining why you made the changes you did.

Account Manager

Location: Aurora, IL
Job Category: Business/Strategic Management
Career Level: Entry-Level Manager (Manager/Supervisor of Staff)

Quantum National is the market leader in providing research, sales and marketing, health care policy consulting, and health information management services to the health care industry. Quantum has more than 20,000 employees worldwide and offices in 15 countries in Central and South America. Medical Innovation Communications, a division of Quantum National, currently has an opportunity for an Account Manager in our Aurora, IL, office. Medical Innovation Communications provides comprehensive product commercialization at all stages of product development: from phase 2, through national and international product launches to ongoing support.

The Account Manager has global responsibility for managing the client's marketing communications programs, assuring that the client's objectives are met in terms of program quality and on-time delivery.

Responsibilities include:

- Day-to-day client contact to identify and translate marketing objectives into strategic medical communications/education programs.
- Develop proposals, budgets, estimates of job cost, and profitability.
- Lead a team of Project Managers and Marketing Associates through guidance, delegation, and follow-up; and significant interaction with the client.
- Work with New Business Development Teams to develop proposals, budgets, and presenting company capabilities/business pitches to clients.
- Schedule the workflow of a 30-person demonstration and marketing team.

Requirements:

- Bachelors degree.
- Ability to define and respond to client needs, working effectively under tight deadlines.
- Proven client management experience.
- Proven team management experience.
- Superior written and spoken communication skills.

E-mail applications and résumés to pattersj@micquant.com, and direct inquiries to J. Pattersen.

Jennifer Stanton	8523 8th Street	125 A S. 27th Ave
wildechilde@gmail.com	Ames, IA 50011	Omaha, NE 68101
cell: 515-668-9011	515-311-8243	402-772-5106

Objective
To get a job as an account manager.

Education
Iowa State University, Ames, IA—Business
May 2012, maybe December 2012
Minor: Botany
Cumulative GPA: 2.63 / 4.0

Mid-Plains Community College, North Platte, NE—Associate of Arts
May 2008

Bryan High School, Omaha, NE
May 2005

Work Experience
May 2011–August 2011—Summer Internship at FirstWest Insurance, Des Moines, IA

- Worked with a senior account manager to oversee some medical and EAP accounts.
- Made her phone calls to customers.

- Organized meetings with customers.
- I had to write some training "how-to's" for the new billing database.

1998–2010—*Worked in family business*
Worked weekends and summers in my parents' used-book store.

Skills
Microsoft Office
Fluent in Spanish

When you ask, Jennifer tells you about her two jobs:

> At her internship this summer, the person she worked with was pretty much an absentee supervisor: Jennifer had to do all the work alone (and she's still a little bitter about that). Her department managed five Employee Assistance Provider accounts with a total of about 36,000 individual policy holders in five midwestern states. She had to set up and maintain work schedules for 12 employees, and manage the expense reports for the entire group. Four of those employees traveled a lot, so there were lots of expense reports to manage; there were so many that Jennifer had to revise the department's budget twice. She spent about four hours of every day returning customer phone calls and linking customers up on conference calls with her department's employees. And those training how-to's? That turned into a 20-page how-to manual, which she wrote up and then had FirstWest's IT department turn into a website for the department to use.
>
> Her parents' family bookstore in Omaha is actually a franchise of a national chain of aftermarket bookstores: Booktopia. The store generates about $450,000 in gross sales per year, and stocks about 100,000 titles (not counting Internet sales and special orders); it employs 5 full-time and 17 part-time employees. In addition to filling in as a floor clerk, stocker, and cashier—all jobs that put her customer-service, cash-handling, and "people skills" to the test—Jennifer has been handling all of the paperwork between the store and the Booktopia corporate office. (Her parents are great salespeople but they're not good at paying attention to details. That's created friction between them and the corporate office.) That paperwork includes all of the store's quarterly and yearly budget, staffing, and marketing reports since 1999.

Note: This exercise was written by Matthew Search.

12.14 Analyzing Job Applicants Based on Their Résumés

Based on your reading of Chapter 12, the following job description and the résumés below, analyze the two applicants for the position. What are their strengths and weaknesses as highlighted by their résumés? Which of the two candidates would you select? Why?

Job description for Cost Accountant

The position of Cost Accountant is responsible for budgeting, reviewing, analyzing, controlling, and forecasting costs involving different cost centers throughout the production process, including raw material procurement, inventory management, manufacturing, warehousing, and shipping. Other responsibilities include analyzing

G/L reports; ensuring compliance with Generally Accepted Accounting Principles (GAAP) and Cost Accounting Standards (CAS); conducting breakeven (BE), contribution margin, and variance analyses; and preparing periodic reports for upper management. The position requires a bachelor's degree in accounting. A certification in management accounting from the Institute of Management Accountants (IMA) will be a plus. The position also requires a minimum of two years of work experience in cost accounting at a manufacturing company.

STAN GOLDBERG

1010, Buck St., Fairfax, VA
Stanberg@bestwebsite.com

OBJECTIVE

Cost Accountant position in which I can effectively utilize my skills in budgeting, accounting, costing, forecasting, reporting, and teamworking

EXPERIENCE

2005–2006   Abacus Engineering   Portland, OR.
Cost Accounting Trainee
- Calculated cost variance for different cost centers.
- Prepared quarterly budget reports
- Coodinated with employees at different levels for data collection

2007–till date   Bourke Winodws   Fairfax, VA
Costing Manager
- Monitored 12 cost centers
- Implemented policies that reduced costs by 25%
- Supervised a staff of three, including one cost accountant.
- I also produced multiple G/L reports for the production department as well as upper management

EDUCATION

2001–2005   Edward Young University, Perry, OH
- B.A., accounting.
- Currently pursuing CMA of Institute of Management Accounting

INTERESTS

Country music, computers, fishing, golf

Jamal Robinson

1212 S. E. Avenue, Earl, PA
(111) 112-1121-jr8@pearlnews.com

Qualification Summary

Skills in **controling** and reucing costs, experience with GAAP and CAS, skills in cost analyses, project management, CMA (IMA), member of the Financial Management Association International, well-versd with ERP software

Education

- Certification in Management Accounting
  Graduation—2007
  Institute of Management Accountants
- True Blue University, Roald, PA
  Graduation—2006
  Degree—Bachelor of Sciences (BS)
  Major—Accounting, G.P.A. 3.55

Experience

Silverstein Windows and Doors, Earl, PA   2007-Till date

Cost Accountant

- Estimate, review, budget, analyze, and forecast direct / indirect and variable and fixed costs for all stages of production
- Work on the ERP system to genrate reports and data sheets giving cost analyses
- Suggested a procedure in a contract that saved the company $35,000
- Worked with the Marketing Department on the costing / pricing of lower-priced vinyl casement windows

Achievements

- Volunteered more than 100 hours for the Habitat for Humnity Award 2005–2006
- Visted door and widow manufacturing plants in Argentina, Belgium, and Japan
- Received the best employee of the month award at Silverstein Windows and Doors
- Wrote articles for *Financial Control Weekly,* a publication of Costing Professionals Association

References

Available upon request

Note: This exercise was written by Anish Dave.

12.15 Preparing a Résumé

Write a résumé that you could use in your job search.

As your instructor directs,

a. Write a résumé for the field in which you hope to find a job.

b. Write two different résumés for two different job paths you are interested in pursuing. Write a memo to your instructor explaining the differences.

c. Adapt your résumé to a specific company you hope to work for. Write a memo to your instructor explaining the specific adaptations you make and why.

d. Write a résumé for the dream job you developed in Exercise 12.10.

12.16 Critiquing Your Résumé, I

Answer the following overview questions for your résumé:

1. Exactly what position are you applying for? How did you choose the position?

2. What are your concerns with applying for this position?

3. What could the concerns of your audience be with your application? How did you try to address these concerns?

4. How do you think the audience will perceive your résumé? Explain.
5. Does your résumé target your employer and position specifically?

Answer the following questions on your design choices:

1. Does the page look balanced?
2. Does the résumé look original or based on a template?
3. Does the length of your résumé fit your situation and position?
4. Does your résumé include clear headings, bullets, and white space?
5. Do you use fonts appropriate for the career level and industry?
6. Do you use consistent font sizes and spacing throughout the document?
7. Does the design reflect your personality and your career ambitions?

Answer the following questions on the content of your résumé.

1. Are the résumé sections clearly, correctly, and consistently labeled?

2. Does the order of the headings highlight your strongest qualifications?
3. Is the work history listed from most recent to past positions?
4. Do you omit high school information? If not, explain your choice.
5. Do you provide details for your best qualifications?
6. Do you use numbers to support your accomplishments?
7. Is the information provided relevant to the position?
8. Does the information support your claim that you are qualified and the best person for this position?
9. Does the information flow logically and easily?
10. Do your bulleted lists use parallel structure?
11. Do you avoid grammar, punctuation, and spelling errors?

Variation: Review a class member's résumé using the same questions.

12.17 Critiquing Your Résumé, II

Rate your résumé using the résumé checklist in the page 392 sidebar. Write a one-page memo to your instructor stating how you believe your résumé rates. Explain and support your position.

12.18 Creating a Web or Paper Portfolio

Create a web or paper portfolio highlighting your professional and academic accomplishments. Include course projects, workplace samples, and other documents that support your professional accomplishments and goals.

12.19 Evaluating Visual Résumés

Working individually, in pairs, or in small groups, as your instructor directs,

a. Look at five of the example student résumés on VisualCV.com. What features do you like? Why? What features would you change or omit? Why? What are the advantages of VisualCV over your own web page? Disadvantages?

b. Discuss strengths and weaknesses of two résumés in a memo to your teacher, a posting on the class website, or an oral presentation.

12.20 Evaluating LinkedIn Profiles

Working individually, in pairs, or in small groups, as your instructor directs, look at six profiles on LinkedIn. You could use those of your classmates, family members, or local businesspeople.

■ Which one has the best résumé? Why?
■ How do the profiles and résumés differ?

■ Which one has the best recommendations? Why?
■ Overall, which one has the best profile? Why?

Discuss your conclusions in a memo to your teacher, a posting on the class website, or an oral presentation.

CHAPTER

13

Writing Job Application Letters

Chapter Outline

Newsworthy Communication

Unconventional Job Tactics

With high U.S. unemployment rates, even the best-qualified candidates may struggle to make an impression in a sea of other job seekers. Some may turn to unconventional methods to get noticed by hiring directors and recruiters.

Nathan Schwagler, for example, chose an innovative way to get past the traditional hiring process at Ingram Micro. He dressed up as a deliveryman, complete with a clipboard, a bouquet of flowers, and a Candygram. He got through security and to the office of Jessica, the company's recruiter. When he finally met her, Schwagler stripped off his coveralls to reveal his business suit underneath and presented Jessica with his résumé, in addition to the flowers and candy.

These kinds of innovative methods to get noticed are on the rise in the United States. One survey of hiring managers conducted by CareerBuilder.com showed that unconventional methods are rising, with 22% of the managers seeing unusual tactics.

"Remember that most innovative methods backfire."

But do these unusual tactics work? In some cases. Only 9% of the hiring managers surveyed reported having hired someone who used an unconventional tactic to get noticed. However, most of the unusual tactics they list benefit the hiring company in some way: one candidate submitted a business plan for one of the company's products; another presented a solution to one of the company's problems. As you ponder your tactics, keep in mind that the other 91% of the people hired used standard techniques, including a strong application letter and a well-designed résumé.

Remember that most innovative methods backfire. Take Nathan Schwagler. After delivering his résumé, he followed up a week later, only to find himself talking with the head of security: Schwagler had been barred from entering the premises or calling again. As one of his professors told him later, "The world is not ready for that type of creativity."

Sources: Rachel Zupek, "Unusual Job Search Tactics," CareerBuilder, accessed April 9, 2011, http://www.careerbuilder.com/article/cb-1076-job-search-unusual-job-search-tactics/; and "More Employers Seeing Unusual Tactics from Job Seekers in 2010, Finds New CareerBuilder Survey," CareerBuilder, June 9, 2010, http://www.careerbuilder.com/share/aboutus/pressreleasesdetail.aspx?id=pr574&sd=6/9/2010&ed=12/31/2010&siteid=cbpr&sc_cmp1=cb_pr574_.

Learning Objectives

After studying this chapter, you will know how to

LO 13-1   Find the information you need to write a good job letter to a specific employer.

LO 13-2   Write a job letter that makes you look attractive to employers.

Multiple Career Changes

You will probably need a cover letter as you change careers during your lifetime. One widely touted figure you may have heard many times is that U.S. workers average seven career changes during their working years.

Unfortunately, that number is a myth. It has been attributed to the U.S. Bureau of Labor Statistics so many times that the bureau now posts a disclaimer on its website.

The bureau does not estimate lifetime career changes for a simple reason: no consensus exists for the definition of a career change. If a worker takes a company promotion to move from being an active engineer to becoming a manager, is that a career change? Just a promotion? The work being done will certainly change. If someone laid off from her financial career takes a landscaping job for six months to pay bills before her next financial job comes along, is that a career change? Will it count as a double career change when she returns to finance?

Adapted from "National Longitudinal Surveys Frequently Asked Questions: Does BLS Have Information on the Number of Times People Change Careers in their Lives?" Bureau of Labor Statistics, last modified September 23, 2010, http://www.bls.gov/nls/nlsfaqs.htm.

The purpose of a job application letter is to get an interview. If you get a job through interviews arranged by your campus placement office or through contacts, you may not need to write a letter. Similarly, if you apply electronically through a company's website, a letter may not be part of the materials you submit. However, if you want to work for an organization that isn't interviewing on campus, or later when you change jobs, you may need a letter. A survey conducted by Robert Half International, the world's largest specialized staffing firm, found 86% of executives said cover letters were still valuable components of job applications in the electronic age.[1]

The co-founder of one software firm says,

> We ignore résumés. . . . Résumés reduce people to bullet points, and most people look pretty good as bullet points.
>
> What we do look at are cover letters. Cover letters say it all. They immediately tell you if someone wants this job or just any job. And cover letters make something else very clear: They tell you who can and who can't write. . . . When in doubt, always hire the better writer.[2]

Job letters can play an important role in your personal branding (p. 371). They can show your personality and, through careful reference to well-chosen details about the organization, interest in a particular job.

Job letters are frequently seen as evidence of your written communication skills, so you want to do your best work in them. Flaws in your letter may well be seen as predicting shoddy job performance in the future.

HOW CONTENT DIFFERS IN JOB LETTERS AND RÉSUMÉS

The job application letter accompanies your résumé and serves as its cover letter. Make the most of your letter; it is your chance to showcase the features that set you apart from the crowd. Here you bring to life the facts presented in your vita; here you can show some personality (don't overdo it). The cover letter is your opportunity to "sell" yourself into an interview.

Although résumés and job letters overlap somewhat, they differ in three important ways:

- The résumé summarizes *all* your qualifications. The letter expands your *best* qualifications to show how you can help the organization meet its needs, how you differ from other applicants, and how much knowledge of the organization you possess.
- The résumé avoids controversial material. The job letter can explain in a positive way situations such as career changes or gaps in employment history.
- The résumé uses short, parallel phrases and sentence fragments. The letter uses complete sentences in well-written paragraphs.

HOW TO FIND OUT ABOUT EMPLOYERS AND JOBS LO 13-1

To adapt your letter to a specific organization, you need information both about the employer and about the job itself. You'll need to know

- **The name and address of the person who should receive the letter.**   To get this information, check the ad, call the organization, check its website, or check with your job search contacts. An advantage of calling is that you can find out what courtesy title (p. 69) the individual prefers and get current information.
- **What the organization does, and some facts about it.**   Knowing the organization's larger goals enables you to show how your specific work will help the company meet its goals. Useful facts can include market share, new products or promotions, the kind of computer or manufacturing equipment it uses, plans for growth or downsizing, competitive position, challenges the organization faces, and the corporate culture (p. 91).
- **What the job itself involves.**   Campus placement offices and web listings often have fuller job descriptions than appear in ads. Talk to friends who have graduated recently to learn what their jobs involve. Conduct information interviews to learn more about opportunities that interest you.

The websites listed in Figure 13.1 provide a wide range of information. For instance, the Forbes and Money sites have good financial news stories; prars. com is a good source for annual reports. As a consumer, you have probably already used the Better Business Bureau (bbb.org) site.

More specific information about companies can be found on their websites. To get specific financial data (and to see how the organization presents itself to the public), get the company's annual report from your library or the web. (Note: Only companies whose stock is publicly traded are required to issue annual reports. In this day of mergers and buyouts, many companies are owned by other companies. The parent company may be the only one to issue an annual report.) Recruiting notebooks at your campus placement office may provide information about training programs and career paths for new hires. To learn about new products, plans for growth, or solutions to industry challenges, read business newspapers such as the *Wall Street Journal*, business magazines such as *Fortune* or *Bloomberg BusinessWeek*, and trade journals.

Figure 13.1   Web Sources for Facts about Companies

Company Facts	http://www.bbb.org/
http://www.jobbankinfo.org/	http://legacy.www.nypl.org/research/sibl/
http://www.wetfeet.com/	company/c2index.htm
http://www.forbes.com/	http://www.lib.berkeley.edu/BUSI/
http://www.irin.com/tf/IRIN/	http://online.wsj.com/public/page/news-
home?path=/&host=irin.com&	career-jobs.html
http://www.corporateinformation.com/	**Salary Calculators**
http://www.vault.com/	http://salaryexpert.com/
http://www.stockmarketyellowpages.com/	http://www.indeed.com/salary
http://www.prars.com/	http://www.payscale.com/
http://money.cnn.com/	http://www.salary.com/mysalary.asp
http://www.inc.com/inc5000/	

412   **Part 4**   The Job Hunt

TAPPING INTO THE HIDDEN JOB MARKET

Many jobs are never advertised—and the number rises the higher on the job ladder you go. In fact, some authorities put the percentage of jobs that are not advertised as high as 80%.[3] Many new jobs come not from responding to an ad but from networking with personal contacts. Some of these jobs are created especially for a specific person. These unadvertised jobs are called the **hidden job market.** Information and referral interviews are two organized methods of networking.

Information Interviews

In an **information interview** you talk to someone who works in the area you hope to enter to find out what the day-to-day work involves and how you can best prepare to enter that field. An information interview can let you know whether or not you'd like the job, give you specific information that you can use to present yourself effectively in your résumé and application letter, and create a good image of you in the mind of the interviewer. If you present yourself positively, the interviewer may remember you when openings arise.

In an information interview, you might ask the following questions:

- How did you get started in this field?
- What have you been working on today?
- How do you spend your typical day?
- Have your duties changed a lot since you first started working here?
- What do you like best about your job? What do you like least?
- What do you think the future holds for this kind of work?
- What courses, activities, or jobs would you recommend as preparation for this kind of work?

To set up an information interview, you can phone or write an e-mail like the one in Figure 13.2. If you do e-mail, phone the following week to set up a specific time.

Referral Interviews

Referral interviews are interviews you schedule to learn about current job opportunities in your field. Sometimes an interview that starts out as an information interview turns into a referral interview.

A referral interview should give you information about the opportunities currently available in the area you're interested in, refer you to other people who can tell you about job opportunities, and enable the interviewer to see that you could make a contribution to his or her organization. Therefore, the goal of a referral interview is to put you face-to-face with someone who has the power to hire you: the president of a small company, the division vice president or branch manager of a big company, the director of the local office of a state or federal agency.

Start by scheduling interviews with people you know who may know something about that field—professors, co-workers, neighbors, friends, former classmates. Use your alumni website to get the names and phone numbers of alumni who now work where you would like to work. Talk to them to get advice about improving your résumé and about general job-hunting strategy, but also to get referrals to other people. In fact, go into the interview with the names of people you'd like to talk to. If the interviewer doesn't suggest anyone, say, "Do you think it would be a good idea for me to talk to——?"

Armed with a referral from someone you both know, you can call people with hiring power, and say, "So-and-so suggested I talk with you about

Figure 13.2   E-mail Requesting an Information Interview

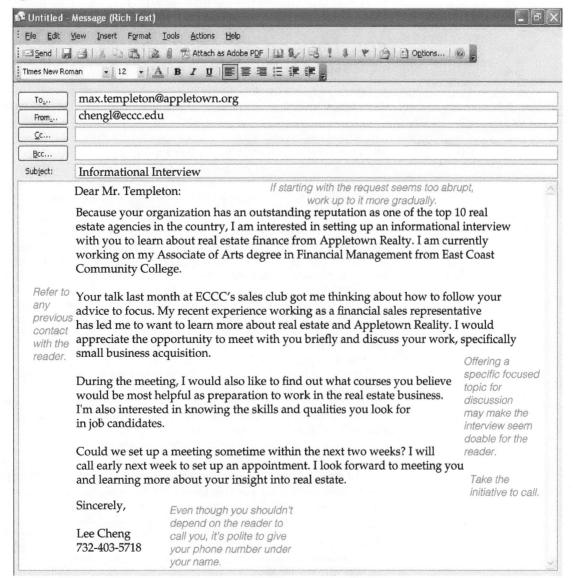

job-hunting strategy." Even when you talk to the person who could create a job for you, you *do not ask for a job.* But to give you advice about your résumé, the person has to look at it. If there's a match between what you can do and what the organization needs, that person has the power to create a position for you.

> ⚠️ **WARNING:** Many businesspeople are cynical about information and referral interviewing; they know the real purpose of such interviews, and they resent the time needed. Therefore you need to prepare carefully for these interviews. Prepare a list of good questions; know something about the general field or industry; research the specific company.

http://www.google
.com/about/corporate

Many websites give
you all the information
you need to write a good job
letter. Google's Corporate
Information page under
Everything Google has links to
jobs, news, company information
and investor relations, where
you will find financial information
and annual reports. Follow the
"Company" link to learn about
topics such as Google's history,
initiatives, and philosophy.

Always follow up information and referral interviews with personal thank-you letters. Use specifics to show that you paid attention during the interview, and enclose a copy of your revised résumé.

CONTENT AND ORGANIZATION FOR JOB APPLICATION LETTERS LO 13-2

Job letters help show employers why they should interview you instead of other—sometimes hundreds of others—qualified applicants. In your letter, focus on

- Your qualifications to meet major requirements of the job.
- Points that separate you from other applicants.
- Points that show your knowledge of the organization.
- Qualities that every employer is likely to value: the ability to write and speak effectively, to solve problems, to work well with people.

Two different hiring situations call for two different kinds of application letters. Write a **solicited letter** when you know that the company is hiring: you've seen an ad, you've been advised to apply by a professor or friend, you've read in a trade publication that the company is expanding. This situation is similar to a direct request in persuasion (p. 321): you can indicate immediately that you are applying for the position. Sometimes, however, the advertised positions may not be what you want, or you may want to work for an organization that has not announced openings in your area. Then you write a **prospecting letter.** (The metaphor is drawn from prospecting for gold.) The prospecting letter is like a problem-solving persuasive message (p. 323).

Prospecting letters help you tap into the hidden job market. In some cases, your prospecting letter may arrive at a company that has decided to hire but has not yet announced the job. In other cases, companies create positions to get a good person who is on the market. Even in a hiring freeze, jobs are sometimes created for specific individuals.

In both solicited and prospecting letters you should

- Address the letter to a specific person (a must for a prospecting letter).
- Indicate the specific position for which you're applying.
- Be specific about your qualifications.
- Show what separates you from other applicants.
- Show a knowledge of the company and the position.
- Refer to your résumé (which you would enclose with the letter).
- Ask for an interview.

The following discussion follows the job letter from beginning to end. The two kinds of letters are discussed separately where they differ and together where they are the same. Letters for internships follow the same patterns: use a solicited letter to apply for an internship that has been advertised and a prospecting letter to create an internship with a company that has not announced one.

How to Organize Solicited Letters

When you know the company is hiring, use the pattern of organization in Figure 13.3. A sample solicited letter for a graduating senior is shown in Figure 13.4. A solicited letter following up from a career fair and requesting an internship is shown in Figure 13.7. The job ad for the letter in Figure 13.4 is printed in Exercise 13.20.

Figure 13.3   How to Organize a Solicited Job Application Letter

1. State that you're applying for the job (phrase the job title as your source phrased it). Tell where you learned about the job (ad, referral, etc.). Include any reference number mentioned in the ad. Briefly show that you have the major qualifications required by the ad: a college degree, professional certification, job experience, etc. Summarize your other qualifications briefly in the same order in which you plan to discuss them in the letter.
2. Develop your major qualifications in detail. Be specific about what you've done; relate your achievements to the work you'd be doing in this new job.
3. Develop your other qualifications, even if the ad doesn't ask for them. Show what separates you from the other applicants who will also answer the ad. Demonstrate your knowledge of the organization.
4. Ask for an interview; tell when you'll be available to be interviewed and to begin work. Thank them for considering your application. End on a positive, forward-looking note.

How to Organize Prospecting Letters

When you don't have any evidence that the company is hiring, you cannot use the pattern for solicited letters. Instead, use the pattern of organization in Figure 13.5. A sample prospecting letter for a student desiring to change fields is shown in Figure 13.6.

First Paragraphs of Solicited Letters

When you know that the firm is hiring, announcing that you are applying for a specific position enables the firm to route your letter to the appropriate person, thus speeding consideration of your application. Identify where you learned about the job: "the position of junior accountant announced in Sunday's *Dispatch*," "William Paquette, our placement director, told me that you are looking for. . . ."

Note how the following paragraph picks up several of the characteristics of the ad:

Ad: Business Education Instructor at Shelby Adult Education. Candidate must possess a Bachelor's degree in Business Education. Will be responsible for providing in-house training to business and government leaders. . . . Candidate should have at least one year teaching experience.

Letter: I am applying for your position in Business Education that is posted on your school website. In December, I will receive a Bachelor of Science degree from North Carolina A & T University in Business Education. My work has given me two years' experience teaching word processing and computer accounting courses to adults plus leadership skills developed in the North Carolina National Guard.

Your **summary sentence** or **paragraph** covers everything you will talk about and serves as an organizing device for your letter.

Through my education, I have a good background in standard accounting principles and procedures and a working knowledge of some of the special accounting practices of the oil industry. This working knowledge is enhanced by practical experience in the oil fields: I have pumped, tailed rods, and worked as a roustabout.

My business experience, familiarity with DeVilbiss equipment, and communication skills qualify me to be an effective part of the sales staff at DeVilbiss.

Passion

[Lucinda B. Watson, career counselor and author of *How They Achieved: Stories of Personal Achievement and Business Success,* transcribes in her book an interview with Ted Bell, the former Vice Chairman and Worldwide Creative Director of Young and Rubicam. An excerpt:]

"My advice to young people is to just be passionate about whatever it is you do. Be the most passionate person in the room. Not the smartest or the cleverest, but the most passionate. Total passion. Say thank you. Say please. Don't take credit, take the blame. Do all that stuff, that's good. But if you are the most passionate person, you'll probably win. Care more about it than anybody and you'll be the one that wins. People love that. People gravitate toward that."

Quoted from Lucinda Watson, *How They Achieved: Stories of Personal Achievement and Business Success* (New York: John Wiley, 2001), 66.

Figure 13.4 A Solicited Letter from a Graduating Senior

Jeff Moeller

831.503.4692
51 Willow Street
San José, CA 95112
jmoeller@csmb.edu

April 4, 2012

Mr. Richard Grove
Telltale Games
P.O. Box 9737
San Rafael, CA 94912

Dear Mr. Grove:

Tell where you learned about the job.
If the job has a reference number, provide it.

In paragraph 1, show you have the qualifications the ad lists.

I am applying for your Game Designer position posted on your website. As an avid player of Telltale games, I believe that I have all the qualifications to do a great job. With my degree in Computer Science and Information Technology and my experience creating game content, I will be able to apply many skills to the Game Designer position. My passion for becoming part of the gaming industry, combined with my oral and written communication skills, makes me a great fit for the Telltale team.

This summary sentence forecasts the structure of the rest of the letter.

Shows enthusiasm for the profession and picks up on the programming experience emphasis in the job ad.

Since I was five, I have had a strong interest in computers and video games, and my interest and knowledge have only increased in recent years. Not only do I play video games, I discuss them with others, read news articles about them online, and consider ways to improve or change a specific game. I have also used game editors to create my own content in games. When it comes to computers, I have a keen interest in staying current with the latest technology, and I apply my knowledge hands-on by building systems. These experiences give me an understanding of how modern computers and video game systems function. I also have experience with several programming languages, from both taking courses and learning them on my own. This has increased my eye for detail, a necessary ability for any game designer.

My passion for creating video games was recognized this year in President Obama's National STEM video game challenge. With a team of students in Professor Kent Olbernath's game development class at California State University, I produced "Parrot Villa," the first level of an immersive game where players solve mysteries on a unique jungle world. The programming quality and detailed story line helped my team earn second place in the nationwide competition. You can see a demo of "Parrot Villa" at www.STEMChallenge.gov/2011_Winners.

Provides evidence for his achievements in the profession.

Relates what he has done to what he could do for the company.

Evidence of communication skills is a plus for almost any job.

Along with my enthusiasm for games, I have strong oral and written communication skills. I am a confident public speaker, and I have an ability to relay information in a clear and concise manner. More importantly, though, I have developed the ability in my creative writing courses to create engaging and coherent narratives, which will be a large component of developing new games. In addition to my coursework and experience, I have honed my skills online by writing articles about games. In covering the video game industry for Point Network, I have reviewed Telltale's own *Tales of Monkey Island*.

Shows familiarity with company's products.

Working in the video game industry is my goal, and I would be a great asset to Telltale Games. I would love to come in for an interview to discuss the position and the contributions I can make. I have always enjoyed playing Telltale's games, and I look forward to the possibility of working on them one day soon.

Sincerely,

Jeff Moeller

Jeff Moeller

Figure 13.5   How to Organize a Prospecting Letter

1. Catch the reader's interest.

2. Create a bridge between the attention-getter and your qualifications. Focus on what you know and can do. Since the employer is not planning to hire, he or she won't be impressed with the fact that you're graduating. Summarize your qualifications briefly in the same order in which you plan to discuss them in the letter. This summary sentence or paragraph then covers everything you will talk about and serves as an organizing device for your letter.

3. Develop your strong points in detail. Be specific. Relate what you've done in the past to what you could do for this company. Show that you know something about the company. Identify the specific niche you want to fill.

4. Ask for an interview and tell when you'll be available for interviews. (Don't tell when you can begin work.) Thank them for considering your application. End on a positive, forward-looking note.

First Paragraphs of Prospecting Letters

In a prospecting letter, asking for a job in the first paragraph is dangerous: unless the company plans to hire but has not yet announced openings, the reader is likely to throw the letter away. Instead, catch the reader's interest. Then in the second paragraph you can shift the focus to your skills and experience, showing how they can be useful to the employer and specifying the job you are seeking.

Here are some effective first and second paragraphs that provide a transition to the writer's discussion of his or her qualifications.

First two paragraphs of a letter to the director of publications at an oil company:

> If scarcity of resources makes us use them more carefully, perhaps it would be a good idea to ration words. If people used them more carefully, internal communications specialists like you would have fewer headaches because communications jobs would be done right the first time.
>
> For the last six years I have worked on improving my communications skills, learning to use words more carefully and effectively. I have taught business communication at a major university, worked for two newspapers, completed a Master's degree in English, and would like to contribute my skills to your internal communications staff.

First two paragraphs of a letter applying to be a computer programmer for an insurance company:

> As you know, merging a poorly written letter with a database of customers just sends out bad letters more quickly. But you also know how hard it is to find people who can both program computers and write well.
>
> My education and training have given me this useful combination. I'd like to put my associate's degree in computer technology and my business experience writing to customers to work in State Farm's service approach to insurance.

Notice how the second paragraph provides a transition to a discussion of qualifications.

Questions work well only if the answers aren't obvious. The computer programmer above should *not* ask this question:

> Do you think that training competent and motivated personnel is a serious concern in the insurance industry?

Jocks Rock in the Workplace

Some employers are seeking athletes to fill jobs because athletes possess qualities which lead to success in the workplace. For example Gretchen Tonnesen, former flying halfback captain for the Princeton University women's rugby team, now works at JP Morgan Chase & Co. where she examines technology, media, and telecommunications companies for the investment bank. JP Morgan chose her because of her passionate involvement in sports.

Recruiters and employers recognize that college athletes provide leadership, competitiveness, and a sharp focus on goals. Athletes also understand team responsibility, time management, and dedication. In addition, athletes from top schools typically have the drive and stamina that matches the 80-hour high pressure workweeks found in many Wall Street jobs.

By the way, Tonnesen got her job through the Alumni Athlete Network, founded by a Harvard basketball captain. The carefully selected students in the Network's program have average GPAs of 3.6 and average SAT scores of 1320.

How can you capitalize on your extracurricular activities to help your job search?

Adapted from John DeBruicker, "If You're A Jock, You Rock," *BusinessWeek*, September 18, 2006, 67.

418   Part 4   The Job Hunt

Figure 13.6   A Prospecting Letter from a Career Changer

Molly Schooner
www.ukansas.edu/~Schoonerm88/home.htm

Molly uses a "letterhead" that hamonizes with her résumé. (see Figure 12.7)

266 Van Buren Drive
Lawrence, KS 66044
schoonerm@ukansas.edu
785-897-1534 (home)
785-842-4242 (cell)

March 29, 2012

Mr. Franklin Kohl
PDF Productions
3232 White Castle Road
Minneapolis, MN 85434

Dear Mr. Kohl:

In a prospecting letter, open with a sentence which (1) will seem interesting and true to the reader and (2) provides a natural bridge to talking about yourself.

The Wall Street Journal says that PDF Productions is expanding operations into Kansas, Minnesota, and Nebraska. My experience in technical writing, design, and computers would be an asset to your expanding organization. *Shows knowledge of the organization.*

Briefly shows a variety of technical writing and computer skills. While working at a local animal shelter, I used my technical writing skills to create a website that allows users to easily access information. To improve the website, I conducted usability tests which provided useful feedback that I incorporated to modify the overall design. In addition, I was also responsible for writing and editing the shelter's monthly newsletter, which was distributed to roughly 1,200 "Friends of the Shelter." I have extensive computer and design skills, which I am anxious to put to use for PDF Productions.

Relates what she's done to what she could do for this company. Course work has also prepared me well for technical writing. I have written technical material on a variety of levels ranging from publicity flyers for the animal shelter to scientific reports for upper-level science courses. My course work in statistics has shown me how to work with data and present it accurately for various audiences. Because of my scientific background, I also have a strong vocabulary in both life sciences and chemistry. This background will help me get up to speed quickly with clients such as ChemPro and Biostage. My background in science has also taught me just how important specific details can be. *Shows how her course-work is an asset.* *Names specific clients, showing more knowledge of company.*

In May, I will complete my degree from the University of Kansas and will be most interested in making a significant contribution to PDF Productions. I am available every Monday, Wednesday, and Friday for an interview (785-897-1534). Thank you for considering my appliction. I look forward to talking with you about technical writing I can do for PDF Productions.

Sincerely,

Molly Schooner

Molly Schooner

Figure 13.7   Letter Following Up from a Career Fair and Requesting an Internship

Lee Cheng
chengl@eccc.edu

Campus Address
1524 Main Street
New Brunswick, NJ 08901
732-403-5718

Letterhead matches his résumé.

Permanent Address
2526 Prairie Lane
Middlesex, NJ 08846
402-442-7793

January 23, 2012

Ms. Deborah Pascel, HR Department
Prime Financial
401 Prime Park Place
New Brunswick, NJ 08901

Dear Ms. Pascel:

Uses his contact immediately.

Mary Randi at the East Coastal Community College Career Fair suggested I send you my résumé for the Sales Advisor internship. My education, combined with my past work experiences, makes me a strong candidate for Prime Financial.

Shows he has been getting full value from his schooling.

While working toward my Associate of Arts degree in Financial Management from East Coastal Community College, I have learned the value of fiscal responsibility. For example, in my social financial planning course, I developed a strategic plan to eliminate credit card debt for a one-income household with two children. Moreover, in my business communication course, I improved my oral communication ability so that I could effectively communicate my plans to potential clients. This ability will be an asset to Prime Financial as the organization works to maintain the strong relationship with the community and small business owners that Ms. Randi informed me about.

Refers to knowledge gained at career fair.

Paragraphs 2 and 3 show he has skills he can use immediately as an intern.

My financial education, combined with my previous work experiences in sales, will allow me to thoroughly analyze investment opportunities and establish a strong client base for Prime Financial. For example, I started the A-Plus T-Shirt Company that sold graphic T-shirts to high school students; it had a routine client base of over 150 customers. From managing this business, I know what it takes to be reliable and responsive to customer needs. I am looking forward to learning new approaches from Prime Financial's internship, particularly new ways to work with small businesses.

Provides details about his sales experience to interest his reader.

With my education and experience, I can provide the innovative and competitive edge necessary to be part of your team. I would welcome an interview to discuss your internship and the contributions I could make at Prime Financial.

Sincerely,

Lee Cheng

Lee Cheng

420   **Part 4** The Job Hunt

Unfortunate Cover Letter Statements

- "Please find my résumé." Did you look under the couch?
- "I have integrity so I will not steal office supplies and take them home." Good to know.
- "Please, please, please hire me for this job. I will be waiting by the phone." Don't wait too long.
- "What interested me about this job is that it's with a prestigious company." Glad to hear it.
- "After perusing my résumé, I am looking forward to hearing from you soon." If you don't mind, we'd appreciate the opportunity to peruse it ourselves before we get back to you.
- "I'm submitting the attached copy of my résumé for your consumption." Yum.
- "I perform my job with effortless efficiency, effectiveness, efficacy, and expertise." And an awful lot of alliteration, apparently.
- "The interview you schedule will undoubtedly reveal my unmatched talent and suitability for the position." Uh, don't count your chickens. . . .
- "But wait . . . there's more. You get all this business knowledge plus a grasp of finance that is second nature." If I act now, will you throw in a set of kitchen knives?

Quoted from "Resumania Archive," Resumania, accessed March 20, 2011, http://www.resumania.com/ ResumaniaArchive.

If the reader says *yes*, the question will seem dumb. If the reader says *no*, the student has destroyed his or her common ground. The computer programmer, however, could pose this question:

> How often do you see a programmer with both strong programming skills and good communication skills?

This question would give him or her an easy transition into paragraphs about his/her programming and communication skills.

Showing a Knowledge of the Position and the Company

If you could substitute another inside address and salutation and send out the letter without any further changes, it isn't specific enough. A job application letter is basically a claim that you could do a specific job for a particular company. Use your knowledge of the position and the company to choose relevant evidence from what you've done to support your claims that you could help the company. (See Figures 13.4 and 13.6.)

The following paragraphs show the writer's knowledge of the company.

A letter to PricewaterhouseCoopers's Minneapolis office uses information the student learned in a referral interview with a partner in an accounting firm. Because the reader will know that Herr Wollner is a partner in the Berlin office, the student does not need to identify him.

> While I was studying in Berlin last spring, I had the opportunity to discuss accounting methods for multinational clients of PricewaterhouseCoopers with Herr Fritz Wollner. We also talked about communication among PricewaterhouseCoopers's international offices.
>
> Herr Wollner mentioned that the increasing flow of accounting information between the European offices—especially those located in Germany, Switzerland, and Austria—and the U.S. offices of PricewaterhouseCoopers makes accurate translations essential. My fluency in German enables me to translate accurately; and my study of communication problems in Speech Communication, Business and Professional Speaking, and Business and Technical Writing will help me see where messages might be misunderstood and choose words which are more likely to communicate clearly.

A letter to KMPG uses information the student learned in a summer job.

> As an assistant accountant for Pacific Bell during this past summer, I worked with its computerized billing and record-keeping system, BARK. I had the opportunity to help the controller revise portions of the system, particularly the procedures for handling delinquent accounts. When the KMPG audit team reviewed Pacific Bell's transactions completed for July, I had the opportunity to observe your System 2170. Several courses in computer science allow me to appreciate the simplicity of your system and its objective of reducing audit work, time, and costs.

One or two specific details about the company usually are enough to demonstrate your knowledge. Be sure to use the knowledge, not just repeat it. Never present the information as though it will be news to the reader. After all, the reader works for the company and presumably knows much more about it than you do.

Showing What Separates You from Other Applicants

Your knowledge of the company can separate you from other applicants. You can also use coursework, an understanding of the field, and experience in jobs and extracurricular events to show that you're unique. Stress your accomplishments, not your job responsibilities. Be specific but concise; usually three to five sentences will enable you to give enough specific supporting details.

This student uses both coursework and summer jobs to set herself apart from other applicants. Her research told her Monsanto had recently adopted new accounting methods for fluctuations in foreign currencies. Therefore, she mentions relevant simulations from her coursework.

> My college courses have taught me the essential accounting skills required to contribute to the growth of Monsanto. In two courses in international accounting, I compiled simulated accounting statements of hypothetical multinational firms in countries experiencing different rates of currency devaluation. Through these classes, I acquired the skills needed to work with the daily fluctuations of exchange rates and at the same time formulate an accurate and favorable representation of Monsanto.
>
> Both my summer jobs and my coursework prepare me to do extensive record keeping as well as numerous internal and external communications. As Office Manager for the steamboat *Julia Belle Swain*, I was in charge of most of the bookkeeping and letter writing for the company. I kept accurate records for each workday, and I often entered over 100 transactions in a single day. In business communication I learned how to write persuasive messages and how to present extensive data in reports in a simplified style that is clear and easy to understand.

In your résumé, you may list activities, offices, and courses. In your letter, give more detail about what you did and show how those experiences will help you contribute to the employer's organization more quickly.

When you discuss your strengths, don't exaggerate. No employer will believe that a new graduate has a "comprehensive" knowledge of a field. Indeed, most employers believe that six months to a year of on-the-job training is necessary before most new hires are really earning their pay. Specifics about what you've done will make your claims about what you can do more believable and ground them in reality.

The Last Paragraph

In the last paragraph, indicate when you'd be available for an interview. If you're free anytime, you can say so. But it's likely that you have responsibilities in class and work. If you'd have to go out of town, there may be only certain days of the week or certain weeks that you could leave town for several days. Use a sentence that fits your situation.

> November 5–10 I'll be attending the Oregon Forestry Association's annual meeting and will be available for interviews then.

> Any Monday or Friday I could come to Memphis for an interview.

Study Abroad and Overseas Work Programs

Have you considered a studies abroad program or international job?

If so, a variety of resources are available. These websites offer assistance for students interested in study abroad programs:

http://www.ciee.org/

http://studyabroad.com/

http://iiepassport.org/

For information regarding full-time overseas opportunities, visit the following websites:

http://www.monster.com/geo/siteselection/

http://www.jobsabroad.com/search.cfm

http://transitionsabroad.com/

Email Horror Story

"I sent a digital resume and cover letter via email to apply for a position as a technical writer. Within a few hours, a message from the director in charge of hiring came via email. Full of anticipation, I opened the email to find a terse message: 'your resume is infected with a virus and has been quarantined.' A person cannot recover from an infected resume. I did not pursue the position further."

Quoted from "Horror Stories," ResumeEdge .com, accessed April 5, 2011, http:// www.resumeedge.com/contentpartners/ interviews13.html.

Should you wait for the employer to call you, or should you call the employer to request an interview? In a solicited letter, it's safe to wait to be contacted: you know the employer wants to hire someone, and if your letter and résumé show that you're one of the top applicants, you'll get an interview. In a prospecting letter, call the employer. Because the employer is not planning to hire, you'll get a higher percentage of interviews if you're assertive.

If you're writing a prospecting letter to a firm that's more than a few hours away by car, say that you'll be in the area the week of such-and-such and could stop by for an interview. Companies pay for follow-up visits, but not for first interviews. A company may be reluctant to ask you to make an expensive trip when it isn't yet sure it wants to hire you.

End the letter on a positive note that suggests you look forward to the interview and that you see yourself as a person who has something to contribute, not as someone who just needs a job.

> I look forward to discussing with you ways in which I could contribute to The Limited's continued growth.

Do not end your letter with a variation of the negative cliché "Please do not hesitate to contact me." Why do you think they would hesitate? Also avoid this other tired cliche: "Thank you for your time." Using an overworked ending dumps you right back in the pool with all the other applicants.

Oh yes, one more thing. Don't forget to sign your letter—with blue or black ink—legibly.

E-MAIL APPLICATION LETTERS

You will probably e-mail most of your applications. If your application is solicited, you can paste your traditional letter into your e-mail. If your application is prospecting, you need a shorter letter that will catch the reader's attention within the first screen (see Figure 13.8). Your first paragraph is crucial; use it to hook the reader.

Some experts are starting to recommend a shorter letter for both situations, but many caution that you need to include enough information to make you, not one of the numerous other applicants, the person for the job. Frequently that is hard to do in one screen.

When you submit an e-mail letter with your résumé,

- Include your name as part of the subject line.
- Put the job number or title for which you're applying in the first paragraph.
- Prepare your letter in a word-processing program. Use a spell checker to make it easier to edit and proof the document; then paste it into the e-mail.
- Use standard business letter features: salutation, standard closing, single-spacing with double-spacing between paragraphs.
- Keep line length to a maximum of 65 characters, including spaces, so receivers won't get a strange mixture of long and short lines.
- Don't put anything in all capital letters.
- Don't use smiley faces or other emotions.
- Put your name at the end of the message.

Figure 13.8   An E-mail with Application Letter and Résumé

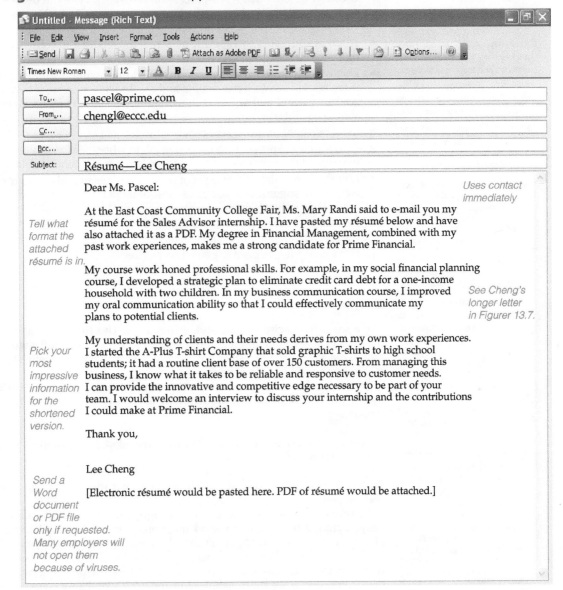

Follow all guidelines posted by the company. Do not add attachments unless you know doing so is OK. Test your e-mail by sending it to a friend; have your friend recheck it for appearance and correctness.

CREATING A PROFESSIONAL IMAGE

Every employer wants businesslike employees who understand professionalism. To make your application letter professional,

You(r) Attitude Matters

If you find getting a job difficult, your attitude may be the reason. Here are four common career-blocking attitudes and responses to them:

Attitude: I deserve a good job because I went to school for four years.

Response: Employers are looking for who is best for a job, not who "deserves" a job.

Attitude: I am open to any job. I have no idea what I want to do.

Response: Employers want workers who are focused.

Attitude: I don't have experience because no one will give me a chance.

Response: Employers do not employ people to give them a "chance." Employers are concerned with what an applicant can do for them.

Attitude: I am so down on myself that it's hard to keep looking for a job.

Response: Get professional help, because this attitude is poisonous to your life as well as your career.

Adapted from Peter Vogt, "Self-Defeating Attitudes Will Stop Your Job Search Cold," Monster.com, accessed April 8, 2011, http://career-advice.monster.com/job-search/getting-started/self-defeating-attitudes-job-search/article.aspx.

- ■ Create your letter in a word-processing program so you can use features such as spell check. Use a standard font such as Times New Roman, Arial, or Helvetica in 12-point type.
- ■ Address your letter to a specific person. If the reader is a woman, call the office to find out what courtesy title she prefers.
- ■ Don't mention relatives' names. It's OK to use names of other people if the reader knows those people and thinks well of them, if they think well of you and will say good things about you, and if you have permission to use their names.
- ■ Omit personal information not related to the job.
- ■ Unless you're applying for a creative job in advertising, use a conservative style: few contractions; no sentence fragments, clichés, or slang.
- ■ Edit the letter carefully and proof it several times to make sure it's perfect. Errors suggest that you're careless or inept. Double-check the spelling of the receiver's name.
- ■ Print on the same paper (both shade and weight) you used for your résumé. Envelopes should match, too.
- ■ Use a computer to print the envelope address.

Writing Style

Use a smooth, concise writing style (Chapter 5). Use the technical jargon of the field to show your training, but avoid businesese and stuffy words like *utilize*, *commence*, and *transpire* (for *happen*). Use a lively, energetic style that makes you sound like a real person.

Avoid words that can be interpreted sexually. A model letter distributed by the placement office at a midwestern university included the following sentence:

> I have been active in campus activities and have enjoyed good relations with my classmates and professors.

Sentences like this get shared for laughs; that's not the kind of attention you want to get!

Be sure your letter uses the exact language of the job ad and addresses all items included in the ad. If the ad mentions teamwork, your letter should give examples of teamwork; don't shift the vocabulary to collaboration. Many readers expect their job ad language in applicants' letters. If the language is not there, they may judge the applicant as not fitting the position. And so may their computer, since the vocabulary of the job ad probably contains crucial key words for the computer to find.

Positive Emphasis

Be positive. Don't plead ("Please give me a chance") or apologize ("I cannot promise that I am substantially different from the lot"). Most negatives should be omitted from the letter.

Avoid word choices with negative connotations (see Chapter 3). Note how the following revisions make the writer sound more confident.

Negative: I have learned an excessive amount about writing through courses in journalism and advertising.

| Positive: | Courses in journalism and advertising have taught me to recognize and to write good copy. My profile of a professor was published in the campus newspaper; I earned an "A +" on my direct mail campaign for the American Dental Association to persuade young adults to see their dentist more often. |

Excessive suggests that you think the courses covered too much—hardly an opinion likely to endear you to an employer.

| Negative: | You can check with my references to verify what I've said. |
| Positive: | Professor Hill can give you more information about my work on his national survey. |

Verify suggests that you expect the employer to distrust what you've said.

You-Attitude

Unsupported claims may sound overconfident, selfish, or arrogant. Create you-attitude (Chapter 3) by describing accomplishments and by showing how they relate to what you could do for this employer.

| Lacks you-attitude: | An inventive and improvising individual like me is a necessity in your business. |
| You-attitude: | Building a summer house-painting business gave me the opportunity to find creative solutions to challenges. At the end of the first summer, for example, I had nearly 10 gallons of exterior latex left, but no more jobs. I contacted the home economics teacher at my high school. She agreed to give course credit to students who were willing to give up two Saturdays to paint a house being renovated by Habitat for Humanity. I donated the paint and supervised the students. I got a charitable deduction for the paint and hired the three best students to work for me the following summer. I could put these skills in problem solving and supervising to work as a personnel manager for Burroughs. |

Show what you can do for them, not what they can do for you.

| Lacks you-attitude: | A company of your standing could offer the challenging and demanding kind of position in which my abilities could flourish. |
| You-attitude: | Omit. |

Remember that the word *you* refers to your reader. Using *you* when you really mean yourself or "all people" can insult your reader by implying that he or she still has a lot to learn about business:

| Lacks you-attitude: | Running my own business taught me that you need to learn to manage your time. |
| You-attitude: | Running my own business taught me to manage my time. |

Beware of telling readers information they already know as though they do not know it. This practice can also be considered insulting.

| Lacks you-attitude: | Your company has just purchased two large manufacturing plants in France. |
| You-attitude: | My three college French courses would help me communicate in your newly acquired French manufacturing facilities. |

Since you're talking about yourself, you'll use *I* in your letter. Reduce the number of *Is* by revising some sentences to use *me* or *my*.

Under my presidency, the Agronomy Club . . .

Courses in media and advertising management gave me a chance to . . .

My responsibilities as a summer intern included . . .

In particular, avoid beginning every paragraph with *I*. Begin sentences with prepositional phrases or introductory clauses:

As my résumé shows, I . . .

In my coursework in media and advertising management, I . . .

As a summer intern, I . . .

While I was in Italy, . . .

Paragraph Length and Unity

Keep your first and last paragraphs fairly short—preferably no more than four or five typed lines. Vary paragraph length within the letter; it's OK to have one long paragraph, but don't use a series of eight-line paragraphs.

When you have a long paragraph, check to be sure that it covers only one subject. If it covers two or more subjects, divide it into two or more paragraphs.

Use topic sentences at the beginning of your paragraphs to make your letter more readable.

Letter Length

Have at least three paragraphs. A short letter throws away an opportunity to be persuasive; it may also suggest that you have little to say for yourself or that you aren't very interested in the job.

Without eliminating content, tighten each sentence (Chapter 5) to be sure that you're using words as efficiently as possible. If your letter is a bit over a page, use slightly smaller margins or a type size that's one point smaller to get more on the page.

If you have excellent material that will not fit on one page, use it—as long as you have at least 6–12 lines of body text on the second page. The extra space gives you room to be more specific about what you've done and to add details about your experience that will separate you from other applicants. Employers don't *want* longer letters, but they will read them *if* the letter is well written and *if* the applicant establishes early in the letter that he or she has the credentials the company needs. Remember, however, that the trend is toward shorter letters.

Editing and Proofreading

Be sure you edit and proofread your cover letter. Failure to do so can undo all the work you put into it. The web abounds with humorous examples of spelling errors making unintended statements (I'm excellent at spelling and grammer). In fact, some companies post the best bloopers on their web sites. For example, Robert Half International maintains Resumania (resumania.com); Killian Branding, an advertising agency, has "Cover Letters from Hell" on their website (www.killianbranding.com/cover-letters-from-hell/): the "poetic" Night-before-Christmas cover letter is amazing.

Check your content one last time to ensure that everything presents you as a hard-working professional. Make sure you are not revealing any frustration with the job search process in your content or diction. Check your tone to see that it is positive about your previous experiences and yourself. Don't beg or show too much gratitude for commonplaces such as reading your letter.

Follow-Up

Follow up with the employer once if you hear nothing after two or three weeks. It is also OK to ask once after one week if e-mail materials were received. If your job letter was prospecting, it is fine to follow up two or three times. Do not make a pest of yourself, however, by calling or e-mailing too often; doing so could eliminate you from further consideration.

APPLICATION ESSAYS

Some jobs and internships, and many scholarship and graduate school applications, ask for an application essay. In a sense, this essay is an extended cover letter, but one written in an essay format rather than letter format. It will detail your strengths for the job/internship/scholarship/graduate school slot and show why you should be chosen instead of other applicants.

The essay offers you a chance to expand on your best points in more detail than does a cover letter. In so doing, you need to capture your readers' attention and show that you are exceptional. Frequently this means you need to put some of your personality into your essay. Here you can spell out with more interesting details skills you have already acquired from previous experiences and will bring to the new job or internship. Here you can elaborate on your academic achievements so you seem worthy of a scholarship or able to thrive in the rigors of graduate school. You can also expand more on general skills such as communication, critical thinking, and teamwork. Show that you are capable, hard working, and interesting.

The essay also gives you room to include content that you would not put in a cover letter. For instance, you might want to include an anecdote that shows something about you as a developing professional (hint: make it interesting but not melodramatic). Or you might talk some about future goals. How did you arrive at these goals? How would this internship advance your career goals? Why do you want to go to graduate school? What do you want to do after the internship, scholarship, or graduate career is over?

> ⚠ **WARNING:** Be careful when giving goals for job application essays. You do not want your goals to make the job seem like a quick steppingstone to better opportunities.

Remember to use the good writing techniques you have learned in this course and your other communication classes.

- Follow the directions, especially word and page limits, precisely. If the essay is to respond to a question, make sure it answers the question.
- Have a focal point for your essay, a unifying theme. This will help prevent you from merely listing accomplishments (your résumé did that).
- Start your essay with an interesting paragraph to catch attention. Do not summarize your essay, or your reader may go no further.
- Remember your audience. Show what you can do for this company, or why you want to go to this particular graduate school. But most of all, show what's in it for them if they accept you.

Fatal Spelling Errors

These spelling errors occurred in actual cover letters:

- "I feel my rigorous education and subsequent internship have prepared me for any obstical I might encounter." Except the challenge of finding misspelled words.

- "I prefer a fast-paste work environment." For life's stickiest situations.

- "I am very interested in the newspaper add for the accounting position." And we're divided on your qualifications.

- "I am extremely detailoriented." I'm afraid we're not convinced.

- Name on letterhead: "Sam Mevlin"; Signature: "Sam Melvin" Would the real Sam please come forward?

Robert Half International, "Cover Letter Statements," accessed March 20, 2011, http://www.resumania.com/Resumania Archive.

- Use vivid details in the body of the essay. They don't have to be wildly creative for a job essay; showing how you cut production time for the department newsletter by 15% will be interesting to your reader if the job is a good fit for you.
- Use some unique details. If your sentence could be used in many other applications, it is not showing why *you* should get the internship/job/scholarship/graduate school slot.
- Avoid unsupported generalities and clichés.
- Use topic sentences at the beginnings of your paragraphs. Remember these essays are frequently read quickly.
- Let your word choice reveal your personal voice. Since the essay is about you, it's fine to use some first person. Avoid thesaurus diction.
- End with a strong concluding paragraph. Remember, this is their last impression of you. Do not waste it on a boring summary of a one-page essay.

SUMMARY OF KEY POINTS

- Résumés differ from letters of application in the following ways:
  - The résumé summarizes all your qualifications. The letter expands your best qualifications to show how you can help the organization meet its needs, how you differ from other applicants, and that you have some knowledge of the organization.
  - The résumé avoids controversial material. The letter can explain in positive ways situations such as gaps in employment history.
  - The résumé uses short, parallel phrases and sentence fragments. The letter uses complete sentences in well-written paragraphs.
- Information and referral interviews can help you tap into the **hidden job market**—jobs that are not advertised. In an **information interview** you find out what the day-to-day work involves and how you can best prepare to enter that field. **Referral interviews** are interviews you schedule to learn about current job opportunities in your field.
- When you know that a company is hiring, send a **solicited job letter.** When you want a job with a company that has not announced openings, send a **prospecting job letter.** In both letters, you should
  - Address the letter to a specific person.
  - Indicate the specific position for which you're applying.
  - Be specific about your qualifications.
  - Show what separates you from other applicants.
  - Show a knowledge of the company and the position.
  - Refer to your résumé (which you would enclose with the letter).
  - Ask for an interview.
- Use your knowledge of the company, your coursework, your understanding of the field, and your experience in jobs and extracurricular activities to show that you're unique.
- Don't repeat information that the reader already knows; don't seem to be lecturing the reader on his or her business.

- Use positive emphasis to sound confident. Use you-attitude by supporting general claims with specific examples and by relating what you've done to what the employer needs.
- Have at least three paragraphs in your letter. Most job letters are only one page.
- Application essays give you a chance to expand on your best points and show your personality.

CHAPTER 13   Exercises and Problems

*Go to www.mhhe.com/locker10e for additional Exercises and Problems.

13.1   Reviewing the Chapter

1. What are three ways that job letters differ from résumés? (LO 13-2)
2. What are some ways to research specific employers? (LO 13-1)
3. What is the difference between information and referral interviews? (LO 13-1)
4. What are the differences between solicited and prospecting letters? (LO 13-2)
5. What are five tips for writing a job letter that makes you look attractive to employers? (LO 13-2)
6. What are 10 ways to create a professional image with your letter? (LO 13-2)

13.2   Reviewing Grammar

As you have read, it is crucial that your job letter be error-free. One common error in job letters, and one that spell-checking programs will not catch, is confusing word pairs like *affect/effect*. Practice choosing the correct word with Exercises B.12, B.13, and B.14 in Appendix B.

13.3   Analyzing First Paragraphs of Prospecting Letters

All of the following are first paragraphs in prospecting letters written by new college graduates. Evaluate the paragraphs on these criteria:

- Is the paragraph likely to interest readers and motivate them to read the rest of the letter?
- Does the paragraph have some content that the student can use to create a transition to talking about his or her qualifications?
- Does the paragraph avoid asking for a job?

1. For the past two and one-half years I have been studying turf management. On August 1, I will graduate from —— University with a BA in Ornamental Horticulture. The type of job I will seek will deal with golf course maintenance as an assistant superintendent.

2. Ann Gibbs suggested that I contact you.

3. Each year, the Christmas shopping rush makes more work for everyone at Nordstrom's, especially for the Credit Department. While working for Nordstrom's Credit Department for three Christmas and summer vacations, the Christmas sales increase is just one of the credit situations I became aware of.

4. Whether to plate a two-inch eyebolt with cadmium for a tough, brilliant shine or with zinc for a rust-resistant, less expensive finish is a tough question. But similar questions must be answered daily by your salespeople. With my experience in the electroplating industry, I can contribute greatly to your constant need of getting customers.

5. What a set of tractors! The new 9430 and 9630 diesels are just what is needed by today's farmer with his ever-increasing acreage. John Deere has truly done it again.

6. Prudential Insurance Company did much to help my college career as the sponsor of my National Merit Scholarship. Now I think I can give something back to Prudential. I'd like to put my education, including a BS degree in finance from —— University, to work in your investment department.

7. Since the beginning of Delta Electric Construction Co. in 1993, the size and profits have grown steadily. My father, being a stockholder and vice president, often discusses company dealings with me. Although the company has prospered, I understand there have been a few problems of mismanagement. I feel with my present and future qualifications, I could help ease these problems.

13.4   Improving You-Attitude and Positive Emphasis in Job Letters

Revise each of these sentences to improve you-attitude and positive emphasis. You may need to add information.

1. I understand that your company has had problems due to the mistranslation of documents during international ad campaigns.
2. Included in my résumé are the courses in Finance that earned me a fairly attractive grade average.
3. I am looking for a position that gives me a chance to advance quickly.
4. Although short on experience, I am long on effort and enthusiasm.
5. I have been with the company from its beginning to its present unfortunate state of bankruptcy.
6. I wish to apply for a job at Austin Electronics. I will graduate from Florida State in May. I offer you a degree in electrical engineering and part-time work at Best Buy.
7. I was so excited to see your opening. This job is perfect for me.
8. You will find me a dedicated worker, because I really need a job.

13.5   Evaluating Letter Content

Improve the content of these passages from job cover letters. You may need to add content.

1. My internship gave me lots of experience for this job.
2. My job duties at Saxon Sport were to create displays, start an employee newsletter, and on weekends I was part of the sales staff.
3. While at San Fernando State, I participated in lots of activities. I played intramurals in baseball, football, basketball, hockey, and volley ball. I was treasurer and then president of the Marketing Club. I was in the Gaffers' Guild, where I made blown-glass creations. I was also in Campus Democrats.
4. I will be in Boston for a family reunion June 23–25 and will drop by your office then for an interview.
5. I feel any of my bosses would tell you that I try hard and pay attention to to detail.
6. I wish to apply for your job as a computer programmer. I have a computer science minor and two summers of sales experience at Best Buy in their computer department.
7. I am a very hard worker. In fact, I have a reputation for finishing the jobs of other workers.

13.6   Evaluating Rough Drafts

Evaluate the following drafts. What parts should be omitted? What needs to be changed or added? What parts would benefit from specific supporting details?

1.
> Dear _____ :
>
> There is more to a buyer's job than buying the merchandise. And a clothing buyer in particular has much to consider.
>
> Even though something may be in style, customers may not want to buy it. Buyers should therefore be aware of what customers want and how much they are willing to pay.
>
> In the buying field, request letters, thank-you letters, and persuasive letters are frequently written.
>
> My interest in the retail field inspired me to read The Gap's annual report. I saw that a new store is being built. An interview would give us a chance to discuss how I could contribute to this new store. Please call me to schedule an interview.
>
> Sincerely,

2.

Dear Sir or Madam:

I am taking the direct approach of a personnel letter. I believe you will under stand my true value in the areas of practical knowledge and promotional capabilities.

I am interested in a staff position with Darden in relation to trying to improve the operations and moral of the Olive Garden Restaurants, which I think that I am capable of doing. Please take a minute not to read my résumé (enclosed) and call to schedule an interview.

Sincerely,

3.

Dear_____:

I would like to apply for the opening you announced for an Assistant Golf Course Superintendent. I have the qualifications you are asking for.

Every year the Superintendent must go before the greens committee to defend its budget requests. To prepare myself to do this, I took courses in accounting, business and administrative writing, and speech.

I have done the operations necessary to maintain the greens properly.

I look forward to talking with you about this position.

Sincerely,

13.7   Gathering Information about an Industry

Use six recent issues of a trade journal to report on three or four trends, developments, or issues that are important in an industry.

As your instructor directs,

a. Share your findings with a small group of other students.

b. Summarize your findings in a memo to your instructor. Include a discussion of how you could use this information in your job letter and résumé.

c. Present your findings to the class.

d. Join with a small group of other students to write a report summarizing the results of this research.

13.8   Gathering Information about Companies in Your Career Field

Use five different websites, such as those listed in Figure 13.1, to investigate three companies in your career field. Look at salary guides for your level of qualifications, product/service information, news articles about the companies, mission/vision statements, main competitors, annual reports, and financial reports.

As your instructor directs,

a. Share your findings with a small group of other students.

b. Summarize your findings in a memo to your instructor. Include a discussion of how you could use this information in your job letter and résumé.

c. Present your findings to the class.

d. Join with a small group of other students to write a report summarizing the results of this research.

13.9   Gathering Information about a Specific Organization

Gather information about a specific organization, using several of the following methods:

■ Check the organization's website.

■ Read the company's annual report.

- Pick up relevant information at the Chamber of Commerce.
- Read articles in trade publications and the *Wall Street Journal* or that mention the organization (check the indexes).
- Read recruiting literature provided by the company.

As your instructor directs,

a. Share your findings with a small group of other students.

b. Summarize your findings in a memo to your instructor. Include a discussion of how you could use this information in your job letter and résumé.

c. Present your findings orally to the class.

d. Write a paragraph for a job letter using (directly or indirectly) the information you found.

13.10 Conducting an Information Interview

Interview someone working in a field you're interested in. Use the questions listed on page 412 or the shorter list here:

- How did you get started in this field?
- What do you like about your job?
- What do you dislike about your job?
- What courses and jobs would you recommend as preparation for this field?

As your instructor directs,

a. Share the results of your interview with a small group of other students.

b. Write up your interview in a memo to your instructor. Include a discussion of how you could use this information in your job letter and résumé.

c. Present the results of your interview orally to the class.

d. Write to the interviewee thanking him or her for taking the time to talk to you.

13.11 Conducting a Referral Interview

a. Write to a friend who is already in the workforce, asking about one or more of the following topics:
   - Are any jobs in your field available in your friend's organization? If so, what?
   - If a job is available, can your friend provide information beyond the job listing that will help you write a more detailed, persuasive letter? (Specify the kind of information you'd like to have.)
   - Can your friend suggest people in other organizations who might be useful to you in your

   job search? (Specify any organizations in which you're especially interested.)

b. List possible networking contacts from your co-workers, classmates, fraternity/sorority members, friends, family friends, former employers and co-workers, neighbors, faculty members, and local business people. Who would be the most valuable source of information for you? Who would you feel most comfortable contacting?

13.12 Writing a Solicited Letter

Write a letter of application in response to an announced opening for a full-time job (not an internship) you would like.

   Turn in a copy of the listing. If you use option (a) below, your listing will be a copy. If you choose option (b), you will write the listing.

a. Respond to an ad in a newspaper, in a professional journal, in the placement office, or on the web. Use an

   ad that specifies the company, not a blind ad. Be sure that you are fully qualified for the job.

b. If you have already worked somewhere, assume that your employer is asking you to apply for full-time work after graduation. Be sure to write a fully persuasive letter.

13.13   Writing a Prospecting Letter

Pick a company you'd like to work for and apply for a specific position that is not being advertised. The position can be one that already exists or one that you would create if you could to match your unique blend of talents.

Address your letter to the person with the power to create a job for you: the president of a small company,

or the area vice president or branch manager of a large company.

Create a job description; give your instructor a copy of it with your letter.

13.14   Critiquing a Job Letter

After you have written your job letter for Exercise 13.12 or 13.13, bring it to class and share it with a classmate.

- Read your cover letter aloud to your classmate noting any changes you would like to make and any areas that may not sound appropriate.

- Have your classmate reread your job letter and make suggestions to enhance it.
- Swap letters and go through the exercise again.

Write a memo to your instructor discussing the changes you will make to your job letter on the basis of this exercise.

13.15   Writing a Rhetorical Analysis of Your Job Letter

a. Examine the job letter you wrote for Exercise 13.12 or 13.13 and answer the following questions in a memo to your instructor:

- Who is your audience? Identify them beyond their name. What will they be looking for?
- How did you consider this audience when selecting information and the level of detail to use? What information did you exclude? How did you shape the information about you to address your audience's needs?
- How did you organize your information for this audience?

- How did you adapt your tone and style for this audience? How did you balance your need to promote yourself without bragging? Where did you use you-attitude, positive tone, and goodwill?
- How did you show knowledge of the company and the position without telling your audience what they already know?

b. Review a class member's cover letter using the same questions.

13.16   Applying Electronically

Write an e-mail application letter with a résumé in the text of the message.

13.17   Applying at Google

Using the Google sidebar on page 414, research possible jobs at Google. Pick the one most appropriate for you and write an electronic job letter to Google.

13.18   Editing a Cover Letter

In Chapter 12, Exercise 12.13, you critiqued the résumé of Jennifer Stanton. Below is her cover letter. Using the information about Jennifer from Exercise 12.13, redo her

letter to improve it. Then write a memo to your instructor discussing the strengths and weaknesses of the letter and explaining why you made the changes you did.

From: wildechilde@gmail.com

To: pattersj@micquant.com

Date: 13 February, 2012

Re: Job!

Dear Ms. Patterson:

My name is Jennifer Stanton and I really want to work with you at Quantum National! Your job looks a whole lot like the one I had at my internship this past summer, so I'm pretty sure I'd be great at it.

I can't start until this Summer, because I'm finishing up my degree at Iowa State. I'm currently working on a degree in Buisness Management, so I'd be a great manager at your business. The one thing I've learned for sure in college is how to balance deadlines to get everything done on time. I've had a few classes where we had to work in teams, and I've been the team leader every time: once I step in, people just want to follow where I lead.

I think my work experience is exactly what you're looking for, too. At my internship last summer, I was basically unsupervised, so I had to learn fast! I managed cliet and department needs, I did the budgets—twice!—and I worked with a sales and marketing team to put together client information packages. I also did the scheduling for the team the whole time, which was my supervisor's job but she delegated it to me, because I am trustworthy. I also worked for years at my family's bookstore, which shows I can hold down a job.

Like I said, I'm really interested in this job. I think that this would be a great place to start my career, and I know I can do the job! Give me a call on my cell when you decide who you're interviewing!

Thanks,

Jennifer Stanton

13.19   Reviewing Cover Letters

All-Weather, Inc., invited applications for the position of Sales Representative (Residential Sales). To be based in Nebraska, this person will be mainly responsible for sales of All-Weather's vinyl windows in local markets, including single- and double-hung windows and casement windows. The job description for the position reads as follows:

The Sales Representative (Residential Sales) will be responsible for successful market penetration of identified market segments. Specifically, the duties include achieving targeted sales, conducting product demonstrations, contacting customers and other stakeholders, gathering market intelligence, preparing market and sales reports, communicating with internal customers, coordinating between customers and the Service and Installation Group, participating in meetings of trade associations and government agencies, attending company training events, and performing other duties assigned by managers. The ideal candidate will be someone with a BS degree, preferably with a technical major. Additionally, the candidate must have at least one year of sales experience, preferably in industrial products. Candidates with experience in brand marketing will also be considered. Among skills for the job, the candidate must possess computer skills, PR and communication skills, teamwork skills, and the ability to perform basic mathematical computations.

Below are two cover letters received from applicants. In a memo to your instructor, discuss the strengths and weaknesses of both. Judging just from their cover letter, which applicant would you prefer to hire? Why?

Figure 1   Antonio Ramirez's Cover Letter

Antonio Ramirez aramirez@bestmail.com 164 Beet St. Houston, TX

October 12, 2012
Ms. Erin Lenhardt
1210 Polaroid Av.
St. Paul, MN

Dear Ms. Lenhardt:

Please consider this letter as my application for the post of Sales Representative (Residential Sales). I learned about your job from the journal *Plastics US* (September issue). I have a bachelor's degree in chemistry from the University of Austin, Texas, and have two years of experience selling PVC resin.

The last two years I have been a Sales Executive in Goodman Petrochemicals in Houston, TX. My responsibilities include selling Goodman's PVC resin to Houston-based PVC processors of rigid and flexible applicatons.

As you suggest in your advertisement, my degree in chemistry will help me explain to customers the important technical attributes of your vinyl windows. My focus during my bachelor's degree was inorganic chemistry, especially hydrocarbons and its practical applications. Apart from my coursework, I also interned at Bright Fenestration Products in Austin, TX.

I look forward to discussing my experience and interst in your organization with you in a face-to-face interview. I'm available for the interview anytime in the next two weeks at a day's notice. I'm confident I will meet—and exceed—all your expetations for this important front line position.

Sincerely,

Antonio Ramirez

Figure 2 Michelle Chang's Cover Letter

Michelle Chang
4334, Sunset Boulevard, Lincoln, NE
mchang@myemail.com

October 14, 2012
Ms. Erin Lenhardt
HR Manager
1210 Polaroid Av.
St. Paul, MN

Dear Ms. Lenhardt:

I wish to apply for the position of Sales Representative (Residential Sales) advertised through Monster.com. After acquiring a bachelor's degree in design, I joined Albatross Advertising in November, 2010, as a trainee in the Accounts Department. Currently, I'm an Account Representative handling three of our most promising brands: *LiteWait* vacuum cleaners, Nebraska Furniture Mart, and Chimney Rock Art Gallery.

My bachelor's degree in design with a major in community and regional planning not only familiarized me with demands of buildings and landscapes in our 21st century living but also acquainted me with concepts of media and design. I joined Albatross because I wanted to see if my education has equipped me to inform, persuade, and help customers with regard to products and brands.

During my nearly two-year tenure at Albatross as Account Representative, I have created and given insightful presentations to clients. As a result of my performance, the agency has entrusted me with three of its most promising accounts, the ones that I mention above.

I would be delighted at an opportunity for a personal interview to further make my case for the job. You can contact me at my e-mail address mentioned above.

Sincerely,

Michelle Chang

13.20 Reviewing a Cover Letter

In the cover letter in Figure 13.4, Jeff Moeller is responding to the following job advertisement from Telltale Games. Using the ad, evaluate Jeff's letter to see how well he shows he is qualified for the job.

Game Designer

Telltale is searching for game designers to work on our growing library of unique episodic games. The game designer will be responsible for generation of detailed concepts covering all aspects of gameplay and story, as well as for prototyping, implementation and polish. Creative writing skills are a plus.

- Responsibilities
  - Work with lead designer to conceive fresh, innovative storytelling games, consistent with company game philosophy and vision

- Design and implement gameplay-related functionality including controls, dialogs, puzzles, and mini-games using Lua
- Implement front end and menu systems, NPC interactions and various other scripted events
- Implement character behaviors in various game scenarios according to story specifications and gameplay needs
- Test and refine gameplay features throughout the development cycle of the project
- Essential Skills and Experience
  - Demonstrated ability to work with artists and other designers
  - Good communication and interpersonal skills
  - Proven experience and proficiency with high level scripting languages (examples: JavaScript, Lua, Python, Perl)
  - Demonstrated ability to write clear, maintainable code
- Preferred Skills and Experience
  - Game industry experience in a design or programming position
  - Experience with Lua
  - Experience with Visual Studio and Source Safe
  - Creative writing skills
  - B.S. in Computer Science, Literature or Creative Writing

Principals only. Sorry, no unsolicited agencies, please!

17

Writing Proposals and Progress Reports

Chapter Outline

Writing Proposals
- Proposal Questions
- Proposal Style
- Proposals for Class Research Projects
- Proposals for Action
- Sales Proposals
- Business Plans and Other Proposals for Funding
- Budget and Costs Sections

Writing Progress Reports
- Chronological Progress Reports
- Task Progress Reports
- Recommendation Progress Reports

Summary of Key Points

NEWSWORTHY COMMUNICATION

Proposals by Corporate Investors

Public companies invite proposals from their shareholders on the company's response to its stakeholders. Corporate investors, led by religious groups and socially responsible investors, have increasingly been bringing forth environmental and social proposals. Often companies work with proponents of these proposals to arrive at mutually agreeable outcomes.

The growth in these proposals has been tremendous—from around 7% to 32% between 2004 and 2007—counting those that garnered at least 15% votes. Among specific issues that these proposals address are companies' sexual orientation policies, pollution policies, labor policies, efforts on climate change, and political contributions. Some of these proposals find mention in the following year's annual or corporate sustainability report, while some others result in specific agreements with the company. Proposals can be resubmitted, so it's in the companies' interest to take proposals seriously.

> *"Corporate investors . . . have increasingly been bringing forth environmental and social proposals."*

Two major examples come from Exxon. The Sisters of St. Dominic were the lead filers on a proposal, which got 31% support, asking for greenhouse gas reduction. A different proposal from an individual investor, which got 27% support, asked for the development of renewable energy sources. Another instance is Domini Social Investments' proposal asking Home Depot to produce a report on its sustainably harvested lumber. Home Depot agreed to publish on its website its wood purchasing policy, including quantitative information.

Adapted from William J. Holstein, "A Bumper Crop of Green Proposals," *BusinessWeek*, June 26, 2008, http://www.businessweek.com/managing/content/jun2008/ca20080626_395541.htm.

Learning Objectives

After studying this chapter, you will know how to

LO 17-1 Write proposals.

LO 17-2 Prepare budget and costs sections.

LO 17-3 Write progress reports.

Proposals and progress reports are two documents that frequently are part of larger, longer projects. **Proposals** argue for the work that needs to be done and who will do it. **Progress reports** let people know how you are coming on the project.

WRITING PROPOSALS **LO 17-1**

In the workplace, much work is routine or specifically assigned by other people. But sometimes you or your organization will want to consider new opportunities, and you will need to write a proposal for that work. Generally, proposals are created for projects that are longer or more expensive than routine work, that differ significantly from routine work, or that create larger changes than does normal work.

Proposals argue for work that needs to be done; they offer a method to find information, evaluate something new, solve a problem, or implement a change. (See Figure 17.1.) Proposals have two major goals: to get the project accepted and to get you or your organization accepted to do the work. To accomplish these goals, proposals must stress benefits for all affected audiences. A proposal for an organization to adopt flex hours would offer benefits for both employees and management, as well as for key departments such as finance.

Proposals may be competitive or noncompetitive. **Competitive proposals** compete against each other for limited resources. Applications for research funding are often highly competitive. Many companies will bid for corporate or government contracts, but only one will be accepted. In FY 2010, the National Science Foundation spent $6.9 billion supporting research. The National Institute of Health supports almost 50,000 research projects at a cost of $31.2 billion annually.[1] These funds are awarded mainly through competitive proposals.

Noncompetitive proposals have no real competition. For example, a company could accept all of the internal proposals it thought would save money or

Figure 17.1   Relationship among Situation, Proposal, and Final Report

Company's current situation	The proposal offers to	The final report will provide
We don't know whether we should change.	Assess whether change is a good idea.	Insight, recommending whether change is desirable.
We need to/want to change, but we don't know exactly what we need to do.	Develop a plan to achieve desired goal.	A plan for achieving the desired change.
We need to/want to change, and we know what to do, but we need help doing it.	Implement the plan, increase (or decrease) measurable outcomes.	A record of the implementation and evaluation process.

Source: Adapted from Richard C. Freed, Shervin Freed, and Joseph D. Romano, *Writing Winning Business Proposals: Your Guide to Landing the Client, Making the Sale, Persuading the Boss,* 3rd ed (New York: McGraw-Hill, 2010).

improve quality. And often a company that is satisfied with a vendor asks for a noncompetitive proposal to renew the contract. Noncompetitive proposals can still be enormous. In 2009 the Census Bureau submitted to Congress a $1 billion proposal for the 2010 census jobs.[2]

Proposal Questions

To write a good proposal, you need to have a clear view of the opportunity you want to fill or the problem you hope to solve and the kind of research or other action needed to solve it. A proposal must answer the following questions convincingly:

- **What problem are you going to solve or what opportunity do you hope to fill?** Show that you understand the problem or the opportunity and the organization's needs. Define the problem or opportunity as the audience sees it, even if you believe it is part of a larger problem that must first be solved. Sometimes you will need to show that the problem or opportunity exists. For instance, management might not be aware of subtle discrimination against women that your proposal will help eliminate.
- **Why does the problem need to be solved now or the opportunity explored immediately?** Show that money, time, health, or social concerns support solving the problem or exploring the opportunity immediately. Provide the predicted consequences if the problem is not solved now or if the opportunity is not explored immediately.
- **How are you going to solve it?** Prove that your methods are feasible. Show that a solution can be found in the time available. Specify the topics you'll investigate. Explain how you'll gather data. Show your approach is effective and desirable.
- **Can you do the work?** Show that you, or your organization, have the knowledge, means, personnel, and experience to do the work well. For larger projects, you will have to show some evidence such as preliminary data, personnel qualifications, or similar projects in the past.
- **Why should you be the one to do it?** Show why you or your company should do the work. For many proposals, various organizations could do the work. Why should the work be given to you? Discuss the benefits—direct and indirect—you and your organization can provide.
- **When will you complete the work?** Provide a detailed schedule showing when each phase of the work will be completed.
- **How much will you charge?** Provide a detailed budget that includes costs for items such as materials, salaries, and overhead. Give careful thought to unique expenses that may be part of the work. Will you need to travel? Pay fees? Pay benefits in addition to salary for part-time workers?
- **What exactly will you provide for us?** Specify the tangible products you'll produce; develop their benefits.

Since proposals to outside organizations are usually considered legally binding documents, get expert legal and financial advice on the last two bullets. Even if the proposal will not be legally binding (perhaps it is an internal proposal), safeguard your professional reputation. Be sure you can deliver the promised products at the specified time using resources and personnel available to you.

MBA Business Plans

Some students working toward MBA degrees participate in business plan contests. Groups of students write a business plan and present it to real-world bankers and venture capitalists. The stakes are high. Major contests have big cash awards and a shot at really starting the business the students have been planning. Even the losers benefit from the writing practice and the feedback they can use to continue improving their plans.

Among the winners is Sarah Takesh, who took first place in the National Social Ventures Competition, earning $25,000 for a fashion company called Tarsian and Blinkley. In Takesh's business, which she has since launched, Afghan workers apply local handicrafts to produce clothing sold in boutiques in New York and San Francisco. Although the items are beautiful, Takesh's fashion sense was less important to the judges than her insights about international trade.

Another contest winner, KidSmart, is a plan for a company offering a new product: a smoke alarm that alerts children with a recording of a parent's voice, rather than the earsplitting beeps of a traditional smoke alarm. The KidSmart business plan won the $100,000 grand prize in Moot Corp, sponsored by the University of Texas. The four-person KidSmart team supported its presentation with video footage showing that its smoke detector is better at waking children than the traditional beeps.

Adapted from Patrick J. Sauer, "How to Win Big Money and Get Ahead in Business," *Inc.* 25, no. 9 (September 2003): 95–96 +.

Proposal Style

Good proposals are clear and easy to read. Remember that some of your audience may not be experts in the subject matter. Highly statistical survey and data analysis projects may be funded by finance people; medical and scientific studies may be approved by bureaucrats. This means you should use the language your readers understand and expect to see. Anticipate and answer questions your readers may have. Support generalizations and inferences with data and other information. Stress benefits throughout the proposal, and make sure you include benefits for all elements of your audience.

Watch your word choice. Avoid diction that shows doubt.

Weak:	"*If* we can obtain X. . . ."
	"We *hope* we can obtain X."
	"We will *try* to obtain X."
Better:	"We plan to obtain X."
	"We expect to obtain X."

Avoid bragging diction: "huge potential," "revolutionary process." Also avoid "believing" diction: "we believe that. . . ." Use facts and figures instead. Be particularly careful to avoid bragging diction about yourself.

Use the expected format for your proposal. Shorter proposals (one to four pages) are generally in letter or memo format; longer proposals are frequently formal reports. Government agencies and companies often issue **requests for proposals,** known as **RFPs.** Follow the RFP's specified format to the letter. Use the exact headings, terminology, and structure of the RFP when responding to one. Competitive proposals are often scored by giving points in each category. Evaluators look only under the headings specified in the RFP. If information isn't there, the proposal may get no points in that category.

Beginnings and endings of proposals are important. If you are not following an RFP, your proposal should begin with a clear statement of what you propose doing, why you propose doing it, and what the implications are of the proposed action, or why the action is important. Proposals should end with a brief but strong summary of major benefits of having you do the work. In some circumstances, an urge to action is appropriate:

> If I get your approval before the end of the month, we can have the procedures in place in time for the new fiscal year.

Allow a generous amount of time before the due date for polishing and finishing your proposal:

- Edit carefully.
- Make a final check that you have included all sections and pieces of information requested in the RFP. Many RFPs call for appendices with items such as résumés and letters of support. Do you have all of yours?
- Ensure that your proposal's appearance will create a good impression. This step includes careful proofreading.
- Allow enough time for production, reproduction, and administrative approvals before the deadline for receipt of the proposal. If multiple signatures are needed, it may take more than a day to get them all. If you are submitting a government grant, the grants.gov server may be clogged with heavy usage on the final due date, or even the day before, so don't wait until the last minute.

Proposals for Class Research Projects

You may be asked to submit a proposal for a report that you will write for a class. Your instructor wants evidence that your problem is meaningful but not too big to complete in the allotted time, that you understand it, that your method will give you the information you need, that you have the knowledge and resources to collect and analyze the data, and that you can produce the report by the deadline.

A proposal for a student report usually has the following sections:

1. In your first paragraph (no heading), summarize in a sentence or two the topic and purposes of your report.
2. **Problem/Opportunity.**   What problem or opportunity exists? Why does it need to be solved or explored? Is there a history or background that is relevant?
3. **Feasibility.**   Are you sure that a solution can be found in the time available? How do you know? (This section may not be appropriate for some class projects.)
4. **Audience.**   Who in the organization would have the power to implement your recommendation? What secondary audiences might be asked to evaluate your report? What audiences would be affected by your recommendation? Will anyone in the organization serve as a gatekeeper, determining whether your report is sent to decision makers? What watchdog audiences might read the report? Will there be other readers?

   For each of these audiences give the person's name and job title and answer the following questions:

   - What is the audience's major concern or priority? What "hot buttons" must you address with care?
   - What will the audience see as advantages of your proposal? What objections, if any, is the audience likely to have?
   - How interested is the audience in the topic of your report?
   - How much does the audience know about the topic of your report?

   List any terms, concepts, or assumptions that one or more of your audiences may need to have explained. Briefly identify ways in which your audiences may affect the content, organization, or style of the report.
5. **Topics to investigate.**   List the questions and subquestions you will answer in your report, the topics or concepts you will explain, the aspects of the problem or opportunity you will discuss. Indicate how deeply you will examine each of the aspects you plan to treat. Explain your rationale for choosing to discuss some aspects of the problem or opportunity and not others.
6. **Methods/procedure.**   How will you get answers to your questions? Whom will you interview or survey? What questions will you ask? What published sources will you use? Give the full bibliographic references. Your methods section should clearly indicate how you will get the information needed to answer questions posed in the other sections of the proposal.
7. **Qualifications/facilities/resources.**   Do you have the knowledge and skills needed to conduct this study? Do you have adequate access to the organization? Is the necessary information available to you? Are you aware of any supplemental information? Where will you turn for help if you hit an unexpected snag?

538   Part 5   Proposals and Reports

Evidence to Support Superlatives in Business Plans

Dave Lavinsky, a cofounder of Growthink, a professional consulting firm, advises small business owners to draft their business plans carefully because investors will evaluate the potential of the business based on the intelligence shown in the plan.

Specifically, Dave advises his clients to provide evidence for superlatives (*best* customer service, *finest* quality) in the plan.

He advises business owners to cite third-party research or offer other concrete evidence when making superlative claims. For instance, if a firm believes that the market for its products is growing exponentially, it should cite some independent research that validates this claim. Similarly, if a firm claims in the business plan that it has the best people working for it, the plan should include details of qualifications and experiences of the personnel to support the claim.

The practice of always supporting superlative claims in the business plan will increase a firm's fundraising chances by making it appear more credible in the eyes of the investors.

Adapted from Dave Lavinsky, "Business Plan Readers No Longer Believe the Hype," in *BusinessWeek: Small Biz: Tips*, March 20, 2009, http://www .businessweek.com/smallbiz/tips/ archives/2009/03/business_plan_r.html.

You'll be more convincing if you have already scheduled an interview, checked out books, or printed online sources.

8. **Work schedule.**   For each activity, list both the total time you plan to spend on it and the date when you expect to finish it. Some possible activities you might include could be gathering information, analyzing information, preparing a progress report, writing the report draft, revising the draft, preparing visuals, and editing and proofreading the report. Think of activities needed to complete your specific project.

These activities frequently overlap. Many writers start analyzing and organizing information as it comes in. They start writing pieces of the final document and preparing visuals early in the process.

Organize your work schedule in either a chart or calendar. A good schedule provides realistic estimates for each activity, allows time for unexpected snags, and shows that you can complete the work on time.

9. **Call to action.**   In your final section, indicate that you'd welcome any suggestions your instructor may have for improving the research plan. Ask your instructor to approve your proposal so that you can begin work on your report.

Figure 17.2 shows a student proposal for a long report.

Proposals for Action

Some proposals call for action or change in your organization. Normally, proposals for action recommend new programs or ways to solve problems. As manager of compensation planning, Catherine Beck had to propose a compensation system when telephone companies Bell Atlantic and Nynex Corporation merged and again a few years later when Bell Atlantic merged with GTE to form Verizon. When two companies merge, each has its own pay scale, bonus policy, and so on; the problem is that the merged companies will need a single, unified system. In these two mergers, Beck had to recommend the system she thought would work best in the new company.[3]

Writing a proposal for action requires considerable research. Beck worked with a team of human resource and other managers plus compensation experts. Together they began by studying the existing policies of the merging organizations. They compared the two systems, looking for their underlying principles. In the first merger, between Bell Atlantic and Nynex, they determined that the two plans were so different that they would have to create a completely new system. In the second merger, of Bell Atlantic and GTE, they concluded that the plans were similar enough to be modified and combined into a single system. After this internal research leading to an initial decision, preparing a proposal and implementing a system for tens of thousands of management employees took months in both mergers.[4]

Often, writing a proposal requires gathering information from outside the organization, too. Basic steps include reading articles in trade and professional journals, looking up data online, and talking to employees or customers.

Remember that all proposals, including in-house ones, need benefits for all levels of audiences. These benefits help ensure buy-in.

Sales Proposals

To sell expensive goods or services, you may be asked to submit a proposal.

To write a good sales proposal, be sure that you understand the buyer's priorities. A phone company lost a $36 million sale to a university because it assumed the university's priority would be cost. Instead, the university wanted a state-of-the-art system. The university accepted a higher bid.

Figure 17.2   Proposal for a Student Team Report

March 24, 2011

To: Professor Christopher Toth

From: JASS LLC (Jordan Koole, Alex Kuczera,
           Shannon Jones, Sean Sterling)

In the subject line ① indicate that this is a proposal ② specify the kind of report ③ specify the topic.

Subject: Proposal to Research and Make Recommendations on the Feasibility
           of Expanding RAC Inc. to South Korea

Summarize topic and purpose of report. RAC Inc. has recently approached our company to determine the possibility of expanding internationally. We believe South Korea could be suitable for this expansion based on our initial investigation of technology in the country. This proposal provides a brief look at South Korea and gives an overview of our research topics and procedures in preparation for the formal research report.

Problem
If the "Problem" section is detailed and well-written, you may be able to use it unchanged in your report.

After establishing a solid consumer base in the U.S., RAC Inc. is looking to expand their business internationally so that they do not fall behind their competitors. They have asked us to research South Korea as a possible alternative site for the manufacturing of their slate tablets.

Country Overview   *This section is a "Background" section for this proposal. Not all proposals include background.*

After some initial research, we believe that South Korea is a suitable country to research for RAC's international manufacturing of new technology. South Korea has a population of 48.3 million, with 27% of the population located in the capital city Seoul and in Busan. They have a labor force of 24.62 million, ranking as the 25th highest workforce in the world (CIA Factbook, 2011). The official language is Korean, but English, Chinese, and Japanese are taught as second languages (U.S. Department of State, 2010). *Proposal uses in-text citations.*

In 1950, North Korea invaded South Korea, beginning the Korean War. After three years of fighting and pushing troops across both borders, North and South Korea signed an armistice and agreed to a demilitarized zone (DMZ), which currently serves as the border between the two countries and is protected by both countries' military (U.S. Department of State, 2010). While relations between the two countries are still tense and a few minor skirmishes along the border have occurred, we are not concerned about South Korea's stability.

In fact, since the devastation of the Korean War, the economy of South Korea has recovered and has joined the ranks of the most economically prosperous nations. They have risen to the 13th highest GDP in the world and have the 45th highest GDP per capita at the equivalent of $30,200. They have a very low unemployment rate that has dropped in the last year to 3.3% (CIA Factbook, 2011).

South Korea is now ranked the 7th largest exporter in the world and the 9th largest importer. Their economic policy has emphasized exporting products, explaining why their exports are so high (U.S. Department of State, 2010). Their main exports include computers and component parts, semiconductors, and wireless telecommunication equipment. South Korea is known for making excellent products in these areas. They export mainly to the U.S., China, and Japan, and import primarily from the same countries. As one of the most economically healthy countries in the world, South Korea is situated as a prime country for RAC Inc.'s possible expansion.

Not all class reports will need a "Feasibility" section.

(Continued)

Figure 17.2   Proposal for a Student Team Report (Continued)

RAC Inc. Proposal
March 24, 2011
Page 2

List your major audiences. Identify their knowledge, interests, and concerns.

Audience

Our formal report will have multiple layers of audiences.

- *Gatekeeper*: Professor Toth has the power to accept or reject our proposal for the formal report before it is passed on to Ms. Katie Nichols from RAC Inc.

- *Primary*: Ms. Katie Nichols, CEO of RAC Inc., and the board of directors are our primary audiences, along with other influential members of RAC Inc. They will decide whether to accept the recommendation found in the formal report.

- *Secondary*: Employees of RAC Inc., the legal department of RAC Inc., as well as current RAC Inc. employees who may be transferred to South Korea may all be affected by the primary audience's decision. In addition, the potential employees in South Korea who would work for RAC Inc. also make up this audience.

- *Auxiliary*: Other employees not involved with the expansion effort into South Korea and any Americans or South Koreans who will read about the expansion in the news serve this role.

- *Watchdog*: Stockholders of RAC Inc., the South Korean government, the Securities and Exchange Commission (SEC), the U.S. Department of Commerce, and other companies that may want to expand internationally to South Korea all have economic, social, and political power. Competitors of RAC Inc. already in South Korea (Samsung and LG) may also pay close attention.

Indicate what you'll discuss briefly and what you'll discuss in more detail. This list should match your audiences' concerns.

Topics to Investigate

We plan to answer the following questions in detail:

1. What information does RAC Inc. need to know about South Korean culture, politics, economy, and workforce to be succesful?

All items in list must be grammatically parallel. Here, all are questions.

- Culture—What differences exist between Korean and American cultures that might influence the move?
- Politics—How will relationships between North and South Korea and relationships between the U.S. and South Korea affect business with South Korea?
- Economics—What is the current economic state of the country? How could free trade between the U.S. and South Korea affect business?
- Workforce—What is the availabe workforce? How will the economy of the country affect the overall workforce?

2. How should RAC Inc. adapt their business practices to successfully expand into the South Korean market?

- Competition—Who is the competition in South Korea? How could they affect the business?
- Location—What city could RAC Inc. expand to for production of the slate tablet? Where should they locate the headquarters? Where should they host the initial product launch?
- Slate Tablet—What changes, if any, are needed to market and sell the product in South Korea?

Figure 17.2 Proposal for a Student Team Report (Continued)

RAC Inc. Proposal
March 24, 2011
Page 3

3. What other issues may RAC Inc. have by introducing their product into South Korea?

If it is well written, "Topics to Investigate" section will become the "Scope" section of the report—with minor revisions.

- Business Culture—How will the differences in business culture influence the expansion to South Korea?
- Technology—To what extent will the advanced state of South Korean technology influence marketing the tablet?
- Marketing—How will competitors' similar products sold in South Korea influence business?
- Integration—How receptive are the people of South Korea to new products from different companies and countries?

If you'll administer a survey or conduct interviews, tell how many subjects you'll have, how you'll choose them, and what you'll ask them. This group does not use a survey.

Methods and Resources

We expect to obtain our information from: (1) various websites, (2) books, and (3) interviews with a native South Korean. The following websites and books appear useful.

Central Intelligence Agency. (2011). *The world factbook: South Korea.* Retrieved March 18, 2011, from https:/ /www.cia.gov/library/publications/the-world-factbook/geos/ks.html#.

If you're using library or web research, list sources you hope to use. Use full bibliographic citations.

Fackler, M. (2011, January 6). Lessons learned, South Korea makes quick economic recovery. *The New York Times.* Retrieved from http:/ /www.nytimes.com/2011/01/07/world/asia/07seoul.html?_r=2.

Jeon, Kyung-Hwan. (2010, September 7). Why your business belongs in South Korea. Retrieved from http:/ /www.openforum.com/articles/why-your-business-belongs-in-south-korea-kyung-hwan-jeon.

This list uses APA format.

Life in Korea. (n.d.). Cultural spotlight. Retrieved March 31, 2011, from http:/ /www.lifeinkorea.com/Culture/spotlight.cfm.

Manyin, M. E. (2004). *South Korea–U.S. economic relations.* Washington, D.C: CRS of Congress.

Manyin, M. E. (2007). *The proposed South Korea–U.S. free trade.* Washington, D.C.: CRS of Congress.

Moon, K. (2004). South Korea–U.S. relations. *The Asian Perspective 28.4.* Retrieved from http:/ /www.asianperspective.org/articles/v28n4-c.pdf.

Ogg, E. (2010, May 28). What makes a tablet a tablet? *CNet News.* Retrieved March 19, 2011, from http:/ /news.cnet.com/8301-31021_3-20006077-260.html?tag=newsLeadStoriesArea.1.

Savada, A.M. & Shaw, W. (1990). South Korea: A country study. *South Korea.* Retrieved March 18, 2011, from http:/ /countrystudies.us/south-korea/.

Settimi, C. (2010, September 1). Asia's 200 best under a billion. *Forbes.* Retrieved from http://www.forbes.com/2010/09/01/ bub-200-intro-asia-under-billion-10-small-companies.html.

Taylor, C. (2006, July 14). The future is in South Korea. *CNN Money.* Retrieved from http:/ /money.cnn.com/2006/06/08/technology/business2_futureboy0608/index.htm.

Your list of sources should convince your instructor that you have made initial progress on the report.

(Continued)

Figure 17.2   Proposal for a Student Team Report (Concluded)

RAC Inc. Proposal
March 24, 2011
Page 4

UK Trade & Investment. (2011). 100 opportunities for UK companies in South Korea. Retrieved
    March 19, 2011, from http:/ /www.ukti.gov.uk/export/countries/asiapacific/fareast/
    koreasouth/item/119500.html.

U.S. Deparment of State. (2010, December 10). Background note: South Korea. Retrieved
    March 18, 2011, from http:/ /www.state.gov/r/pa/ei/bgn/2800.htm.

World Business Culture. (n.d.). Doing business in South Korea. Retrieved March 19, 2011, from
    http:/ /www.worldbusinessculture.com/Business-in-South-Korea.html.

Qualifications   *Cite knowledge and skills from other classes, jobs, and activities that will enable you to conduct the research and interpret your data.*

We are all members of JASS LLC who have backgrounds in finance, accounting, computer science, and technology. These diverse backgrounds in the business and technology world give us a good perspective and insight for this project. In addition, we are all enrolled in a business communication course that provides us with knowledge on producing high-quality documents. We are dedicated to producing a thoroughly researched report that will provide solid evidence on the feasibility of an international expansion for RAC Inc. into South Korea.

Work Schedule

The following schedule will enable us to finish this report on time.

Activity	Total Time	Completion Date
Gathering information	12 hours	March 30
Analyzing information	8 hours	April 2
Organizing information	4 hours	April 7
Writing draft/creating visuals	8 hours	April 10
Revising draft	3 hours	April 12
Preparing presentation slides	3–4 hours	April 14
Editing draft	3 hours	April 17
Proofreading report	3 hours	April 18
Rehearsing presentation	2 hours	April 20
Delivering presentaion	1 hour	April 21

Good reports need good revision, editing, and proofreading as well as good research.

Allow plenty of time

Time will depend on the length and topic of your report, your knowledge of the topic, and your writing skills.

Call to Action

We are confident that JASS LLC can complete the above tasks as scheduled. We would appreciate any suggestions for improving our project plan. Please approve our proposal so that we may begin work on the formal report.   *It's tactful to indicate you'll accept suggestions. End on a positive, forward-looking note.*

Make sure your proposal presents your goods or services as solving the problem your audience perceives. Don't assume that the buyer will understand why your product or system is good. For everything you offer, show the benefits of each feature. Be sure to present the benefits using you-attitude.

Use language appropriate for your audience. Even if the buyers want a state-of-the-art system, they may not want the level of detail that your staff could provide; they may not understand or appreciate technical jargon.

Sales proposals, particularly for complicated systems costing millions of dollars, are often long. Provide a one-page cover letter to present your proposal succinctly. The best organization for this letter is usually a modified version of the sales pattern in Chapter 11:

1. Catch the reader's attention and summarize up to three major benefits you offer.
2. Discuss each of the major benefits in the order in which you mentioned them in the first paragraph.
3. Deal with any objections or concerns the reader may have. In a sales proposal, these objections probably include costs. Connect costs with benefits.
4. Mention other benefits briefly.
5. Ask the reader to approve your proposal and provide a reason for acting promptly.

Business Plans and Other Proposals for Funding

Proposals for funding include both **business plans** (documents written to raise capital for new business ventures) and proposals submitted to foundations, corporations, and government agencies, to seek money for public service projects. In a proposal for funding, stress the needs your project will meet and show how your project helps fulfill the goals of the organization you are asking for funds. Every funding agency has a mission, so be sure to align your idea to fit their needs in obvious ways. Try to weave their mission throughout your proposal's content. Remember effective you-attitude—write for the needs of your audience, not yourself.

Since venture capitalists and other investors are not known for their patience, business plans in particular need to have a concise, compelling beginning describing exactly what you plan to do and what need it will fill. Pay careful attention to the Executive Summary. This overview section is one of the most important places in any proposal. After reading this opening, the reviewer will make initial decisions about you, your writing, your idea, and your logic. Therefore, it must spark enthusiasm for your idea; the reviewer's interest will never increase later on in your proposal. This section should also provide an overview of all of the major topics you will cover in the body.

Your business plan should answer these questions:

- What is your product or service?
- How well developed is it? Is a mock-up or demo available?
- Who is your market? How large is it? Why does this market need your product or service?
- How will you promote your product or service?
- Who are your competitors? How will you be better?
- Who is also providing support for your business?
- Who will be working with you? How many more employees will you need? What will you pay them? What benefits will you give them?

Financial information is important in any proposal, but it is even more crucial in a business plan. You will need to show how much of your own money you are

Writing an Effective Business Plan

How do entrepreneurs raise the capital needed to launch a new business? They write a business plan. When you write one, you need to persuade an investor that your concept for an organization is solid and that you're the best person to carry it out. Venture capitalists and successful entrepreneurs give the following advice about writing a solid business plan:

- Keep it short and simple—a good business plan articulates what the company will do and how it will benefit the customer. Specify the product or service. Begin with an executive summary.

- Introduce the management team—a good business plan explains the people behind the product.

- Anticipate problems and challenges—a good business plan answers the tough questions about your idea. Venture capitalists will already know the problem; they want to be sure you do too.

- Show there is a market—a good business plan identifies a target market and demonstrates that people will use the product or service offered.

- Show a path to profit—a good business plan explains how the business will make money.

- Make it personal—a good business plan is not a template; it shows passion about ideas.

Adapted from Greg Farrell, "Business Plans Should Be Simple, Passionate," *USA Today*, July 31, 2006, 5E.

investing, what investors you already have supporting you, and how you plan to use the money you get. Many investors want to see a five-year financial forecast. Explain with convincing detail how you expect to make money. What is your time frame for financial success? What is your estimated monthly income the first year?

Anticipate problems (investors will already know them; this shows you do, too); show how you plan to solve them. Use details to help convince your audience. Many business plans are too general to convince investors. Details show you have done your homework; they can also show your business acumen.

Proposals are also a major part of nonprofits' fund-raising activity; they write grant proposals to governmental organizations, foundations, and individuals to raise money for their organization. The writing process involves considerable research and planning, and often is preceded by informal conversations and formal presentations to potential funders. The funding process is often seen as a relationship-building process that involves researching, negotiating with, and persuading funders that the proposal not only meets their guidelines, but also is a cause worthy of a grant.

Every funding source has certain priorities; some have detailed lists of the kind of projects they fund. Be sure to do research before applying. Check recent awards to discover foundations that may be interested in your project. See Figure 17.3 for additional resources.

When you write proposals for funding, be sure you follow all format criteria to the letter. Be particularly obedient to specifications about page count, type size, margins, and spacing (single or double spacing). When flooded with applications, many funders use these criteria as preliminary weeding devices. One state Department of Education threw out funding applications from 30 school districts because they were not double-spaced as required.[5]

Finally, be sure to pay close attention to deadlines by reading the fine print. Turn your materials in early. The National Endowment for the Humanities encourages fund seekers to submit drafts six weeks before the deadline to allow time for their staff to review materials.[6]

Budget and Costs Sections LO 17-2

For a class research project, you may not be asked to prepare a budget. However, many proposals do require budgets, and a good budget is crucial to making the winning bid. In fact, your budget may well be the most carefully scrutinized part of your proposal.[7]

Ask for everything you need to do a quality job. Asking for too little may backfire, leading the funder to think that you don't understand the scope of the project. Include less obvious costs, such as overhead. Also include costs that will be paid from other sources. Doing so shows that other sources also have confidence in your work. Pay particular attention to costs that may appear to

Figure 17.3   Additional Resources for Writing Business Plans and Funding Proposals

Organization	URL	Description
U.S. Small Business Administration	http://www.sba.gov/category/navigation-structure/starting-managing-business/starting-business	Offers detailed advice for writing a business plan.
Philanthropic Research Inc.	http://www.guidestar.org	Publishes free information about grants and grantmakers.
U.S. Department of Health and Human Services	http://www.grants.gov	Offers information on grant programs of all federal grant-making agencies, as well as downloadable grant applications.
The Foundation Center	http://foundationcenter.org/	Indexes foundations by state and city as well as by field of interest.

benefit you more than the sponsor such as travel and equipment. Make sure they are fully justified in the proposal.

Do some research. Read the RFP to find out what is and isn't fundable. Talk to the program officer (the person who administers the funding process) and read successful past proposals to find answers to the following questions:

- What size projects will the organization fund in theory?
- Does the funder prefer making a few big grants or many smaller grants?
- Does the funder expect you to provide in-kind or cost-sharing funds from other sources?

Think about exactly what you'll do and who will do it. What will it cost to get that person? What supplies or materials will he or she need? Also think about indirect costs for using office space, about retirement and health benefits as well as salaries, about office supplies, administration, and infrastructure.

Make the basis of your estimates specific.

Weak:	75 hours of transcribing interviews	$1,500
Better:	25 hours of interviews; a skilled transcriber can complete 1 hour of interviews in 3 hours; 75 hours @ $20/hour	$1,500

Figure your numbers conservatively. For example, if the going rate for skilled transcribers is $20 an hour, but you think you might be able to train someone and pay only $12 an hour, use the higher figure. Then, even if your grant is cut, you'll still be able to do the project well.

WRITING PROGRESS REPORTS   LO 17-3

When you're assigned to a single project that will take a month or more, you'll probably be asked to file one or more progress reports. A progress report reassures the funding agency or employer that you're making progress and allows you and the agency or employer to resolve problems as they arise. Different readers may have different concerns. An instructor may want to know whether you'll have your report in by the due date. A client may be more interested in what you're learning about the problem. Adapt your progress report to the needs of the audience.

Christine Barabas's study of the progress reports in a large research and development organization found that poor writers tended to focus on what they had done and said very little about the value of their work. Good writers, in contrast, spent less space writing about the details of what they'd done but much more space explaining the value of their work for the organization.[8]

When you write progress reports, use what you know about emphasis, positive tone, and you-attitude. Don't present every detail as equally important. Use emphasis techniques to stress the major ones. Readers will generally not care that Jones was out of the office when you went to visit him and that you had to return a second time to catch him. Trivial details like this should be omitted.

In your report, try to exceed expectations in at least some small way. Perhaps your research is ahead of schedule or needed equipment arrived earlier than expected. However, do not present the good news by speculating on the reader's feelings; many readers find such statements offensive.

Poor:	You will be happy to hear the software came a week early.
Better:	The software came a week early, so Pat can start programming earlier than expected.

Remember that your audience for your report is usually in a position of power over you, so be careful what you say to them. Generally it is not wise to blame them for project problems even if they are at fault.

Tapping into the Research Experts

Where else can you go besides Google to find the information you need for your next report? You might try your local library. While you can find a wealth of information on Google, libraries subscribe to commercial databases that can give you access to powerful tools for writing your company's business or marketing plan. An added plus is that librarians are experts at navigating those databases.

Small business owners, in particular, can benefit. Many libraries even hold classes for entrepreneurs and provide networking opportunities with other local agencies and organizations geared to help the small business person. So the next time you are working out a business problem, visit your local library.

Adapted from Tara Siegel Bernhard, "Enterprise: Big Help for Small Businesses at the Library; Commercial Databases, Assistance on Research and Classes Are Offered," *Wall Street Journal*, August 29, 2006, B4.

546   **Part 5**   Proposals and Reports

Poor:	We could not proceed with drafting the plans because you did not send us the specifications for the changes you want.
Better:	Chris has prepared the outline for the plan. We are ready to start drafting as soon as we receive the specifications. Meanwhile, we are working on. . . .

Subject lines for progress reports are straightforward. Specify the project on which you are reporting your progress.

> Subject: Progress on Developing a Marketing Plan for Fab Fashions

If you are submitting weekly or monthly progress reports on a long project, number your progress reports or include the time period in your subject line. Include information about the work completed since the last report and work to be completed before the next report.

Make your progress report as positive as you *honestly* can. You'll build a better image of yourself if you show that you can take minor problems in stride and that you're confident of your own abilities.

> The preliminary data sets were two days late because of a server crash. However, Nidex believes they will be back on schedule by next week. Past performance indicates their estimate is correct, and data analysis will be finished in two weeks, as originally scheduled.

Focus on your solutions to problems rather than the problems themselves:

Negative:	Southern data points were corrupted, and that problem set us back three days in our data analysis.
Positive:	Although southern data points were corrupted, the northern team was able to loan us Chris and Lee to fix the data set. Both teams are currently back on schedule.

In the above example the problem with the southern data points is still noted, because readers may want to know about it, but the solution to the problem is emphasized.

Do remember to use judicious restraint with your positive tone. Without details for support, glowing judgments of your own work may strike readers as ill-advised bragging, or maybe even dishonesty.

Overdone positive tone, lack of support	Our data analysis is indicating some great new predictions; you will be very happy to see them.
Supported optimism:	Our data analysis is beginning to show that coastal erosion may not be as extensive as we had feared; in fact, it may be almost 10% less than originally estimated. We should have firm figures by next week.

Progress reports can be organized in three ways: by chronology, by task, and to support a recommendation. Some progress reports may use a combination: they may organize material chronologically within each task section, for instance.

Chronological Progress Reports

The chronological pattern of organization focuses on what you have done and what work remains.

1. **Summarize your progress in terms of your goals and your original schedule.** Use measurable statements.

Poor: Progress has been slow.

Better: Analysis of data sets is about one-third complete.

2. **Under the heading "Work Completed," describe what you have already done.**   Be specific, both to support your claims in the first paragraph and to allow the reader to appreciate your hard work. Acknowledge the people who have helped you. Describe any serious obstacles you've encountered and tell how you've dealt with them.

Poor: I have found many articles about Procter & Gamble on the web. I have had a few problems finding how the company keeps employees safe from chemical fumes.

Better: On the web, I found Procter & Gamble's home page, its annual report, and mission statement. No one whom I interviewed could tell me about safety programs specifically at P&G. I have found seven articles about ways to protect workers against pollution in factories, but none mentions P&G.

3. **Under the heading "Work to Be Completed," describe the work that remains.**   If you're more than three days late (for school projects) or two weeks late (for business projects) submit a new schedule, showing how you will be able to meet the original deadline. You may want to discuss "Observations" or "Preliminary Conclusions" if you want feedback before writing the final report or if your reader has asked for substantive interim reports.

4. **Express your confidence in having the report ready by the due date.**   If you are behind your original schedule, show why you think you can still finish the project on time.

Even in chronological reports you need to do more than merely list work you have done. Show the value of that work and your prowess in achieving it, particularly your ability at solving problems. The student progress report in Figure 17.4 uses the chronological pattern of organization.

Task Progress Reports

In a task progress report, organize information under the various tasks you have worked on during the period. For example, a task progress report for a team report project might use the following headings:

> Finding Background Information on the Web and in Print
> Analyzing Our Survey Data
> Working on the Introduction of the Report and the Appendices

Under each heading, the team could discuss the tasks it has completed and those that remain.

Task progress reports are appropriate for large projects with distinct topics or projects.

Recommendation Progress Reports

Recommendation progress reports recommend action: increasing the funding or allotted time for a project, changing its direction, canceling a project that isn't working out. When the recommendation will be easy for the reader to accept, use the direct request pattern of organization from Chapter 11. If the recommendation is likely to meet strong resistance, the problem-solving pattern may be more effective.

Figure 17.4 A Student Chronological Progress Report

Date: April 11, 2012

To: Ms. Katie Nichols, CEO of RAC. Inc

From: S. Jones   *SJ*

Subject: Progress on JASS LLC's South Korean Feasibility Study

¶ 1:
Summarize results in terms of purpose, schedule.

JASS LLC has collected information on South Korea that will enable us to answer the Topics to Investigate section from our proposal. We are currently analyzing and compiling the information for the formal report that will be submitted on April 21. Although we are slightly behind our original work schedule, we have planned an additional meeting on April 12 and will be back on track.

Work Completed   *Bold headings*

Be very specific about what you've done.

To invesigate the feasibility of RAC Inc. expanding operations into South Korea, JASS LLC submitted a research proposal to Professor Toth that defined our topics to investigate and provided a list of preliminary sources. For this proposal, I wrote part of the problem, country overview, and qualifications sections. I also discovered three sources included in the methods section. These sources will give RAC Inc. important information regarding the competition, the available workforce, and the state of technology in South Korea. Serving as editor for the proposal, I also assisted with improving our writing style and formatting. Since submitting the proposal and getting approval, I have found six additional sources that should prove useful in our formal report.

Show how you've solved minor problems.

Due to scheduling conflicts with our course projects, we were unable to complete the first draft of the report as we had originally planned. However, we scheduled an additional meeting for tomorrow to accomplish this task and to get our group back on schedule. For tomorrow's meeting, I have read and analyzed eight sources and will be ready to compile information into our report draft.   *Specify steps you will take to correct deviations from schedule.*

Work to Be Completed

Specify the work that remains.

During our additional meeting, JASS LLC will write the first full draft of our formal report by organizing information that the four of us have researched. We will also be prepared to conference with Professor Toth about our rough draft by the end of this week. After we receive his feedback, we will move into the revising and editing stages for the formal report. Finally, we still need to assemble our presentation slides and begin rehearsing together.

We will be prepared to submit our formal report and to deliver our presentation for you on April 21.

End on a positive note.

SUMMARY OF KEY POINTS

- Proposals argue for the work that needs to be done and who will do it.
- A proposal must answer the following questions:
  - What problem are you going to solve?
  - Why does the problem need to be solved now?
  - How are you going to solve it?
  - Can you do the work?
  - Why should you be the one to do it?
  - When will you complete the work?
  - How much will you charge?
  - What exactly will you provide for us?
- In a proposal for a class research project, prove that your problem is the right size, that you understand it, that your method will give you the information you need to solve the problem, that you have the knowledge and resources, and that you can produce the report by the deadline.
- In a project budget, ask for everything you will need to do a good job. Research current cost figures so yours are in line.
- Business plans need to pay particular attention to market potential and financial forecasts.
- In a proposal for funding, stress the needs your project will meet. Show how your project will help fulfill the goals of the organization you are asking for funds.
- Progress reports let people know how you are coming on a project.
- Progress reports may be organized by chronology, by task, or to support a recommendation.
- Use positive emphasis in progress reports to create an image of yourself as a capable, confident worker.

CHAPTER 17   Exercises and Problems

Go to www.mhhe.com/locker10e for additional Exercises and Problems.

17.1   Reviewing the Chapter

1. What are six questions a good proposal should answer? (LO 17-1)

2. What are some guidelines for preparing a budget for a proposal? (LO 17-2)

3. What are the differences between chronological and task progress reports? (LO 17-3)

17.2   Writing a Proposal for a Student Report

Write a proposal to your instructor to do the research for a formal or informal report.

The headings and the questions in the section titled "Proposals for Class Research Projects" are your RFP; be sure to answer every question and to use the headings exactly as stated in the RFP. Exception: where alternate heads are listed, you may choose one, combine the two ("Qualifications and Facilities"), or treat them as separate headings in separate categories.

17.3   Proposing a Change

No organization is perfect, especially when it comes to communication. Propose a change that would improve communication within your organization. The change can be specific to your unit or can apply to the whole organization; it can relate to how important information is distributed, who has access to important information, how information is accessed, or any other change in communication practices that you see as having a benefit. Direct your proposal to the person or committee with the power to authorize the change.

17.4   Proposing to Undertake a Research Project

Pick a project you would like to study whose results could be used by your organization. Write a proposal to your supervisor requesting time away from other duties to do the research. Show how your research (whatever its outcome) will be useful to the organization.

17.5   Writing a Proposal for Funding for a Nonprofit Group

Pick a nonprofit group you care about. Examples include professional organizations, a charitable group, a community organization, or your own college or university.

As your instructor directs,

a. Check the web or a directory of foundations to find one that makes grants to groups like yours. Brainstorm a list of businesses that might be willing to give money for specific projects. Check to see whether state or national levels of your organization make grants to local chapters.

b. Write a proposal to obtain funds for a special project your group could undertake if it had the money. Address your proposal to a specific organization.

c. Write a proposal to obtain operating funds or money to buy something your group would like to have. Address your proposal to a specific organization.

17.6   Writing a Sales Proposal

Pick a project that you could do for a local company or government office. Examples include

- Creating a brochure or web page.
- Revising form letters.
- Conducting a training program.
- Writing a newsletter or an annual report.
- Developing a marketing plan.
- Providing plant care, catering, or janitorial services.

Write a proposal specifying what you could do and providing a detailed budget and work schedule.

As your instructor directs,

a. Phone someone in the organization to talk about its needs and what you could offer.

b. Write an individual proposal.

c. Join with other students in the class to create a team proposal.

d. Present your proposal orally.

17.7   Presenting a Stockholder Proposal

Visit the websites of the following companies and locate their latest proxy statements or reports. These are generally linked from the "about us/company information–investor relations" or "investors" pages. Find shareholder proposals under the heading "proposals requiring your vote," "stockholder proposals," or "shareholder proposals."

- Ford Motor Company
- Citigroup
- AT&T
- J. P. Morgan Chase & Co.
- Southwest Airlines
- Home Depot
- Procter & Gamble
- Boeing
- Google
- Dow Chemical

As a team, select one proposal, and the management response following it, and give an oral presentation answering these questions:

1. What is the problem discussed in the proposal?
2. What is the rationale given for the urgency to solve the problem?
3. How does the proposal seek to solve it?
4. What benefits does the proposal mention that will accrue from the solution?
5. What is the management response to the proposal and what are the reasons given for the response? Does the management response strike you as justified? Why or why not?

Hint: it may help you to do some research on the topic of the proposal.

17.8   Writing a Progress Report to Your Superior

Describe the progress you have made this week or this month on projects you have been assigned. You may describe progress you have made individually, or progress your unit has made as a team.

17.9   Writing a Progress Report

Write a memo to your instructor summarizing your progress on your report.

In the introductory paragraph, summarize your progress in terms of your schedule and your goals. Under a heading titled *Work Completed*, list what you have already done. (This is a chance to toot your own horn: if you have solved problems creatively, say so. You can also describe obstacles you've encountered that you have not yet solved.) Under *Work to Be Completed*, list what you still have to do. If you are more than two days behind the schedule you submitted with your proposal, include a revised schedule, listing the completion dates for the activities that remain.

17.10   Writing a Progress Report for a Team Report

Write a memo to your instructor summarizing your team's progress.

In the introductory paragraph, summarize the team's progress in terms of its goals and its schedule, your own progress on the tasks for which you are responsible, and your feelings about the team's work thus far.

Under a heading titled *Work Completed*, list what has already been done. Be most specific about what you yourself have done. Describe briefly the chronology of team activities: number, time, and length of meetings; topics discussed and decisions made at meetings.

If you have solved problems creatively, say so. You can also describe obstacles you've encountered that you have not yet solved. In this section, you can also comment on problems that the team has faced and whether or not they've been solved. You can comment on things that have gone well and have contributed to the smooth functioning of the team.

Under *Work to Be Completed*, list what you personally and other team members still have to do. Indicate the schedule for completing the work.

CHAPTER

18

Analyzing Information and Writing Reports

Chapter Outline

Newsworthy Communication

Reporting on Life

Each year, most publicly held companies produce annual reports. Because the reports can affect stock prices and credit ratings, companies take great care to produce detailed, attractive, and persuasive reports that fit within government guidelines.

Nicholas Felton, a graphic designer in New York City, has taken the idea of an annual report one step farther. Each year since 2005, he has produced a personal annual report, filled with the minute details of his life—encounters with other individuals, places he traveled, restaurants and shops he visited, and so on. With custom-designed charts and graphs, Felton tells his own story of the previous year in "The Feltron Annual Report," which

"Like Nicholas Felton, companies then compile the data into charts, graphs, and text that will help their readers understand and interpret the data."

he produces as a printed brochure and sells on his website.

Felton's creative approach to cataloging his life in an annual report has caught the attention of others. A 2010 *New York Times* profile of him reported that other people have begun similar personal data collections. In fact, Felton got so many requests that he started a website to help people track their movements and record their personal data.

Companies gather data for months or even years to produce reports. They analyze the data, looking for patterns that will shape the narratives of their final documents. And, like Nicholas Felton, companies then compile the data into charts, graphs, and text that will help their readers understand and interpret the data.

Sources: "Feltron," Nicholas Felton, accessed June 16, 2011, http://feltron.com/; and "An Annual Report on One Man's Life," *Bits* (blog), *New York Times*, February 9, 2010, http://bits.blogs.nytimes.com/2010/02/09/an-annual-report-on-one-mans-life/.

Learning Objectives

After studying this chapter, you will know

LO 18-1 Ways to analyze data, information, and logic.

LO 18-2 How to choose information for reports.

LO 18-3 Different ways to organize reports.

LO 18-4 How to present information effectively in reports.

LO 18-5 How to prepare the different components of formal reports.

Careful analysis, smooth writing, and effective document design work together to make effective reports, whether you're writing a 2½-page memo report or a 250-page formal report complete with all the report components.

Chapter 15 covered the first two steps in writing a report:

1. Define the problem.
2. Gather the necessary data and information.

This chapter covers the last three steps:

3. Analyze the data and information.
4. Organize the information.
5. Write the report.

USING YOUR TIME EFFICIENTLY

To use your time efficiently, think about the parts of the report before you begin writing. Much of the introduction can come from your proposal (see Chapter 17), with only minor revisions. You can write six sections even before you've finished your research: Purpose, Scope, Assumptions, Methods, Criteria, and Definitions. Mock up tables and figures early using the guidelines in Chapter 16.

The background reading for your proposal can form the first draft of your list of references. Save a copy of your questionnaire or interview questions to use as an appendix. You can print appendixes before the final report is ready if you number their pages separately. Appendix A pages would be A-1, A-2, and so forth; Appendix B pages would be B-1, B-2, and so forth.

You can write the title page and the transmittal as soon as you know what your recommendation will be.

After you've analyzed your data, write the body, the conclusions and recommendations, and the executive summary. Prepare a draft of the table of contents and the list of illustrations.

When you write a long report, list all the sections (headings) that your report will have. Mark those that are most important to your reader and your logic, and spend most of your time on them. Write the important sections early. That way, you won't spend all your time on Background or History of the Problem. Instead, you'll get to the heart of your report.

ANALYZING DATA AND INFORMATION FOR REPORTS LO 18-1

Good reports begin with good data. Analyzing the data you have gathered is essential to produce the tight logic needed for a good report. Analyze your data with healthy skepticism. Check to see that they correspond with expectations or other existing data. If they don't, check for well-supported explanations of the difference.

Be suspicious of all data, even from reputable sources. Ask yourself "How do they know?" or "What could prevent that data from being right?"

- If you read in the paper that 300,000 people attended a demonstration at the National Mall in Washington, D.C., ask yourself how they know. Unless they were able to get a photo from a satellite, they are estimating, and such estimates have been known to vary by 100,000 or more, depending on whether the estimator wants a larger or smaller crowd.

- Want to know how many centenarians live in the United States? Surely the Census Bureau knows? Well, not exactly. An accurate count is obscured by lack of birth records, low literacy levels, cognitive disabilities, and the human desire to hit a milestone number.

- Did you read in a job-hunt article that U.S. workers average seven career changes during their working years? That number is a myth. It has been attributed to the U.S. Bureau of Labor Statistics so many times that the bureau now posts a disclaimer on its website. The bureau does not estimate lifetime career changes for a simple reason: no consensus exists for the definition of a career change. Is a promotion a career change? Is a layoff, a temporary subsistence job, and a return to work 0, 1, or 2 career changes?

- Have you heard that Thanksgiving is the busiest travel day of the year? Actually, no day in November has made the top 35 busiest airline days for years, according to the U.S. Department of Transportation (busiest days occur in the summer, when school is out). Even for those traveling by car, July 4, Labor Day, and Christmas are busier holidays.[1]

- Sometimes the discrepancies are not fun facts. Some states are meeting No Child Left Behind federal mandates for continued funding by lowering grade-level proficiency standards (see sidebar on this page).[2]

Spreadsheets can be particularly troublesome. Cell results derived by formulas can be subtly, or grossly, wrong by incorrectly defining ranges, for example. It is easy to generate results that are impossible, such as sums that exceed known totals. Always have an estimate of the result of a calculation. Using spreadsheets, you can easily be wrong by a factor of 10, 100, or even 1,000. Studies have found up to 80% of spreadsheets have errors, such as misplaced decimal points, transposed digits, and wrong signs. Some of these errors are enormous. Fidelity's Magellan fund's dividend estimate spreadsheet was $2.6 billion off when a sign was wrongly transposed from minus to plus. Fannie Mae, the financer of home mortgages, once discovered a $1.136 billion error in total shareholder equity, again from a spreadsheet mistake.[3]

Try to keep ballpark figures, estimates of what the numbers should be, in mind as you look at numerical data. Question surprises before accepting them.

Analyzing data can be hard even for experts. Numerous studies exist in scholarly journals challenging the data-based conclusions of earlier articles. One example is the fate of unmarried, college-educated women over 30. A famous *Newsweek* cover story, "Too Late for Prince Charming?" reported the Yale and Harvard study that suggested such women had only a 20% chance of finding husbands, and only a 2.6% chance by the time they reached 40. Twenty years later an economist at the University of Washington examined 30 years of census data. Her figures for the decade of the original study showed that women aged 40–44 with advanced degrees were only 25% less likely to be married than comparably aged women with just high school diplomas. By 2000, those women with postcollege education were slightly more likely to be married than those who had finished only high school.[4]

Changing Standards

Under the No Child Left Behind law, every child in the United States must become proficient in reading and math by 2014. Schools that fail to show consistent improvement risk losing funding from both state and federal education programs.

Some states, according to research by the U.S. Department of Education, have been meeting the goals of NCLB in a unique way: by changing what it means to be proficient. The NCLB law requires states to set standards and measure achievement. As the 2014 goal deadline approaches, however, states are changing those standards to make sure their schools meet the requirements of the law.

Between 2005 and 2007, fifteen states lowered the standards for fourth and eighth graders on at least one subject test. Eight other states raised their standards. The result? *Proficient* means something different in every state. According to these different standards, a proficient math student in Massachusetts would be five or six years more advanced than a student in the same grade in Tennessee.

Do you think it is ethical for states to lower their standards for proficiency? Would your opinion change if the states were doing this so they could continue to receive money badly needed for educating children? Is raising standards fair?

Adapted from John Hechinger, "Some States Drop Testing Bar," *Wall Street Journal*, October 30, 2009, A3.

Measuring Innovation

It is commonly accepted wisdom that one measure of a company's innovation is the number of patents it commands. In recent years, however, research has shown that companies increasingly use patents as a defensive strategy rather than a strategy for innovation.

A Boston University study found that software companies with more patents actually reduced their research and development expenditure vis-à-vis sales. Additionally, with companies vying for patents for the smallest addition to product features, patents may be a dubious measure of innovation.

Recent studies on patents also show a growing trend of acquiring patents on design or form of products rather than their technical aspects. Companies such as Samsung Electronics and Nike have earned a name for themselves for innovation by acquiring patents based on product design.

Compared to patents themselves, patent citations, or the references to a company's patent by patents of other companies, may be a better metric of innovation. A high number of patent citations may show that the company's patent truly represents innovation and may be licensed for a fee or royalties. Companies such as Procter & Gamble have adopted this strategy.

Adapted from Jena McGregor, "Are Patents the Measure of Innovation?" *BusinessWeek*, May 4, 2007, http://www.businessweek.com/innovate/content/may2007/id20070504_323562.htm.

Evaluating the Source of the Data

When evaluating the source of your data, question the authors, objectivity, completeness, and currency of the source.

Identify the **authors.** Which people or organization provided the data? What credentials do they have? If you want national figures on wages and unemployment, the U.S. Bureau of Labor Statistics would be a good source. But if you want the figures for your local town, your local Chamber of Commerce might be a more credible source. Use the strategies outlined in Chapter 15 to evaluate web sources.

Assess the **objectivity** of the source. Does the source give evidence to support claims? Is the surrounding prose professional and unbiased? If the subject supports multiple viewpoints, are other opinions referenced or explained? When the source has a vested interest in the results, scrutinize the data with special care. To analyze a company's financial prospects, use independent information as well as the company's annual report and press releases.

Drug and medical device companies, and the researchers funded by them, keep appearing in the news with reports of undue influence. Duke University researchers checked 746 studies of heart stents published in one year in medical journals. They found that 83% of the papers did not disclose whether authors were paid consultants for companies, even though many journals require that information. Even worse, 72% of the papers did not say who funded the research.[5] A study in the prestigious *New England Journal of Medicine* noted that positive studies of antidepressant trials got published and negative ones did not: "According to the published literature, it appeared that 94% of the trials conducted were positive. By contrast, the FDA analysis showed that 51% were positive."[6]

If your report is based upon secondary data from library and online research, look at the sample, the sample size, and the exact wording of questions to see what the data actually measure. (See Chapter 15 for more information on sampling and surveying.) Does the sample have a built-in bias? A survey of city library users may uncover information about users, but it may not find what keeps other people away from the library.

Try to assess the **completeness** of the data. What are they based on? Two reputable sources can give different figures because they take their data from different places. Suppose you wanted to know employment figures. The Labor Department's monthly estimate of nonfarm payroll jobs is the most popular, but some economists like Automatic Data Processing's monthly estimate, which is based on the roughly 20 million paychecks it processes for clients. Both survey approximately 400,000 workplaces, but the Labor Department selects employers to mirror the U.S. economy, while ADP's sample is skewed, with too many construction firms and too few of the largest employers. On the other hand, the government has trouble counting jobs at businesses that are opening and closing, and some employers do not return the survey. (Both organizations do attempt to adjust their numbers to compensate accurately.)[7]

Also check the **currency** of the data. Population figures should be from the 2010 census, not the 2000 one. Technology figures in particular need to be current. Do remember, however, that some large data sets are one to two years behind in being analyzed. Such is the case for some government figures, also. If you are doing a report in 2012 that requires national education data from the Department of Education, for instance, 2011 data may not even be fully collected. And even the 2010 data may not be fully analyzed, so indeed the 2009 data may be the most current available.

Sharp uses what it calls "academic marketing" to sell air purifiers in Japan. Ads in Japanese newspapers and magazines provide data, diagrams, and charts in support of Sharp's plasmacluster technology.

Source: Daisuke Wakabayashi, "Using 'Academic Marketing' to Sell Air Purifiers," *Wall Street Journal,* December 26, 2008, B4.

Analyzing Numbers

Many reports analyze numbers—either numbers from databases and sources or numbers from a survey you have conducted. The numerical information, properly analyzed, can make a clear case in support of a recommendation.

Recognize that even authorities can differ on the numbers they offer, or on the interpretations of the same data sets. Researchers from the United Nations and Johns Hopkins University differed on their estimates of Iraqi deaths in the war by 500% (see sidebar on this page).[8] The cover story of the January 4, 2008, *National Journal* was an explanation of how the two estimates could vary so wildly (research design and execution flaws; sampling error; lack of transparency with the data).[9] You will be best able to judge the quality of data if you know how it was collected.

In their books, *The Tipping Point* and *Freakonomics,* Malcolm Gladwell and Steven D. Levitt and Stephen J. Dubner reach different conclusions about the data on dropping crime rates for New York City. Gladwell attributes the drop to the crackdown by the new police chief on even minor crimes such as graffiti and public drunkenness. Levitt and Dubner first explain why the cause was not a crackdown on crime (the years don't match well; other cities also experienced the drop) and attribute it to the legalization of abortion (at the time of the crime drop the first wave of children born after Roe v. Wade was hitting late teen years and thus prime crime time; that group was short on the category most likely to become criminal: unwanted children). They also provide corroborating evidence from other countries.[10]

When you have multiple numbers for salaries or other items, an early analysis step is to figure the average (or mean), the median, and the range. The **average** or **mean** is calculated by adding up all the figures and dividing by

Getting the Data Right

A 2006 report by Johns Hopkins University claimed that 655,000 Iraqis had died in the war in Iraq, a figure that diverged wildly from other estimates—sometimes more than 1,000%. The Hopkins figure is 500% more than that of the United Nations. Such a difference from other reports calls into question the accuracy of the Hopkins report.

To understand why the figure is so much higher than other research reports, it is important to consider how the data were gathered. The Hopkins researchers used cluster sampling for interviews, a methodology that makes sense given the country's war-zone status. Researchers randomly selected neighborhoods and then conducted door-to-door interviews with "clusters" of individuals from within those neighborhoods. Such a technique saves time and money and is common in research within developing countries.

But the key to this kind of technique is to use enough cluster points. A lack of cluster points can mean that the population sampled isn't representative of the population in Iraq. The Hopkins researchers did not use enough cluster points. In addition, the Hopkins researchers didn't gather demographic data from their participants for comparison to census data. Doing so would have added to the believability of their results.

Getting the data right is important because numbers can have a significant impact on decisions and policies. In terms of casualties, the decisions made based on the numbers reported have an impact on millions of Iraqis and Americans.

Adapted from Stephen E. Moore, "655,000 War Dead?" *Wall Street Journal,* October 18, 2006, A20.

Sun and Statistics

Recent research suggests that patients with low levels of vitamin D, which can be gained from moderate exposure to the sun, have higher risks of cancer, heart disease, and autoimmune disorders.

The Indoor Tanning Association quickly jumped at this new finding. They used their interpretation of the statistics about low vitamin D levels as a way to promote indoor tanning, suggesting that UV rays can prevent cancer.

The medical community was outraged at the ITA's twisted approach to the statistics. Doctor Lichtenfeld of the American Cancer Society suggested that UV ray promotion was "like recommending smoking to reduce stress." The ITA advertisements failed to suggest there were any downsides to tanning, such as the link between prolonged exposure to UV rays and melanoma. They also omitted that the tanner the skin, the longer it takes to absorb vitamin D.

How ethical is the ITA's use of research statistics? Would you be more likely to tan indoors if you saw one of their advertisements?

Adapted from Pat Wingert, "Teens, Tans, and Truth," *Newsweek*, May 19, 2008, 42–43.

the number of samples. The **mode** is the number that occurs most often. The **median** is the number that is exactly in the middle in a ranked list of observations. When you have an even number, the median will be the average of the two numbers in the center of the list. The **range** is the difference between the high and low figures for that variable.

Averages are particularly susceptible to a single extreme figure. In 2007, three different surveys reported the average cost of a wedding at nearly $30,000. Many articles picked up that figure because weddings are big business. However, the median cost in those three surveys was only about $15,000. And even that is probably on the high side, since the samples were convenience samples for a big wedding website, a bride magazine, and a maker of wedding invitations, and thus probably did not include smaller, less elaborate weddings.[11]

Often it's useful to simplify numerical data: rounding it off, combining similar elements. Then you can see that one number is, for instance, about 2½ times another. Graphing it can also help you see patterns in your data. (See Chapter 16 for a full discussion of tables and graphs as a way of analyzing and presenting numerical data.) Look at the raw data as well as at percentages. For example, a 50% increase in shoplifting incidents sounds alarming. An increase from two to three shoplifting incidents sounds less so but could be the same data, just stated differently.

Analyzing Words

Be sure you are clear about definitions on which data are based. For instance, China and the United States are jockeying for first place in number of Internet users. Different sources give different results, and one reason is that they are defining "Internet user" in different ways: Is a user anyone who has access to the Internet at home, school, or work? What about a four-year-old child who has access to the Internet through her family but does not use it? Is anyone who has used the Internet only once in the past six months a user?[12]

State accurately what your data show. For example, suppose that you've asked people who use computers if they could be as productive without them and the overwhelming majority say *no*. This finding shows that people *believe* that computers make them more productive, but it does not prove that they in fact are more productive.

Also try to measure words against numbers. A study of annual reports in the United Kingdom found a large increase (375%) in narrative information and noted that accounting narratives were being used to manage impressions of annual performance.[13] Numbers require interpretation and context for easy comprehension.

Analyzing Patterns

Patterns can help you draw meaning from your data. If you have library sources, on which points do experts agree? Which disagreements can be explained by early theories or numbers that have now changed? Which disagreements are the result of different interpretations of the same data? Which are the result of having different values and criteria? In your interviews and surveys, what patterns do you see?

- Have things changed over time?
- Does geography account for differences?
- Do demographics such as gender, age, or income account for differences?

- What similarities do you see?
- What differences do you see?
- What confirms your hunches?
- What surprises you?

Many descriptions of sales trends are descriptions of patterns derived from data.

Checking Your Logic

Check that your data actually measure what you want them to. A common belief is that satisfied customers will be repeat customers. But a *Harvard Business Review* study found little relationship between the two groups; customers who said on surveys they were satisfied did not necessarily make repeat purchases. Instead, the best predictor of repeat purchases was that the customer would recommend the company to others.[14]

Another common logic error is confusing causation with correlation. *Causation* means that one thing causes or produces another. *Correlation* means that two things happening at the same time are positively or negatively related. One might cause the other, but both might be caused by a third. For instance, consider a study that shows pulling all-nighters hurts grades: students who pull all-nighters get lower grades than those who do not pull all-nighters. But maybe it is not the all-nighter causing the poor grades; maybe students who need all-nighters are weaker students to begin with.

Correlation and causation are easy to confuse, but the difference is important. The Census Bureau publishes figures showing that greater education levels are associated with greater incomes. A widely held assumption is that more education causes greater earnings. But might people from richer backgrounds seek more education? Or might some third factor, such as intelligence, lead to both greater education and higher income?[15]

Some spurious correlations are amusing. The *Wall Street Journal* reported with tongue in cheek the Tiger Woods phenomenon. During the 11 years of 1997–2008, the April bond market performed positively when Woods won the Masters golf tournament, and negatively when he did not.[16]

Consciously search for at least three possible causes for each phenomenon you've observed and at least three possible solutions for each problem. The more possibilities you brainstorm, the more likely you are to find good options. In your report, discuss in detail only the possibilities that will occur to readers and that you think are the real reasons and the best solutions.

When you have identified causes of the problem or the best solutions, check these ideas against reality. Can you find support in references or in numbers? Can you answer claims of people who interpret the data in other ways?

Make the nature of your evidence clear to your reader. Do you have observations that you yourself have made? Or do you have inferences based on observations or data collected by others? Old data may not be good guides to future action.

If you can't prove the claim you originally hoped to make, modify your conclusions to fit your data. Even when your market test is a failure or your experiment disproves your hypothesis, you can still write a useful report.

- Identify changes that might yield a different result. For example, selling the product at a lower price might enable the company to sell enough units.
- Divide the discussion to show what part of the test succeeded.

Charity Data

Many people believe they "know" "facts" and figures that are not so. When you encounter these false beliefs, you need to be sure you provide reliable data to counteract them. One area subject to common misperceptions is charity donations. Below are some common myths paired with realities.

Myth: Most charitable giving goes to help the needy. Reality: Less than one-third of individually donated money to nonprofits goes to the economically disadvantaged. And only 8% provides basic needs like food and shelter.

Myth: The wealthy look after those in need. Reality: Only about a quarter of their donations go to the poor, and only 4% to basic needs.

Myth: Religious donations go to those in need. Reality: Less than one-fifth of money donated goes to the poor.

Myth: Americans give generously to international causes. Reality: Only 8% of US individual donations support any international cause whatsoever.

Adapted from Sheryl Sandberg [board member of Google.org, Google's philanthropic arm], "The Charity Gap," *Wall Street Journal*, April 4, 2007, A15.

560   **Part 5** Proposals and Reports

As employees become buried in paperwork, it becomes even more important to select carefully and interpret clearly the information to be included in reports.

- Discuss circumstances that may have affected the results.
- Summarize your negative findings in progress reports to let readers down gradually and to give them a chance to modify the research design.
- Remember that negative results aren't always disappointing to the audience. For example, the people who commissioned a feasibility report may be relieved to have an impartial outsider confirm their suspicions that a project isn't feasible.

A common myth associated with numbers is that numbers are more objective than words: "numbers don't lie." But as the above examples show, numbers can be subject to widely varying interpretation.

CHOOSING INFORMATION FOR REPORTS LO 18-2

Don't put information in reports just because you have it or just because it took you a long time to find it. Instead, choose the information that your reader needs to make a decision. NASA received widespread criticism over the way it released results from an $11.3 million federal air safety study. NASA published 16,208 pages of findings with no guide to understanding them. Critics maintain the lapse was deliberate because the data contained hundreds of cases of pilot error.[17]

If you know your readers well, you may already know their priorities. For example, the supervisor of a call center knows that management will be looking for certain kinds of performance data including costs, workload handled, and customer satisfaction. To write regular reports, the supervisor could set up a format in which it is easy to see how well the center is doing in each of these areas. Using the same format month after month simplifies the reader's task.

If you don't know your readers, you may be able to get a sense of what is important by showing them a tentative table of contents (a list of your headings) and asking, "Have I included everything?" When you cannot contact an external audience, show your draft to colleagues and superiors in your organization.

How much information you need to include depends on whether your audience is likely to be supportive, neutral, or skeptical. If your audience is likely to be pleased with your research, you can present your findings directly. If your audience will not be pleased, you will need to explain your thinking in a persuasive way and provide substantial evidence.

You must also decide whether to put information in the body of the report or in appendixes. Put material in the body of the report if it is crucial to your proof, if your most significant readers will want to see it there, or if it is short. (Something less than half a page won't interrupt the reader.) Frequently decision makers want your analysis of the data in the report body rather than the actual data itself. Supporting data that will be examined later by specialists such as accountants, lawyers, and engineers are generally put in an appendix.

Anything that a careful reader will want but that is not crucial to your proof can go in an appendix. Appendixes can include

- A copy of a survey questionnaire or interview questions.
- A tally of responses to each question in a survey.
- A copy of responses to open-ended questions in a survey.
- A transcript of an interview.
- Complex tables and visuals.
- Technical data.
- Previous reports on the same subject.

ORGANIZING INFORMATION IN REPORTS LO 18-3

Most sets of data can be organized in several logical ways. Choose the way that makes your information easiest for the audience to understand and use. If you were compiling a directory of all the employees at your plant, for example, alphabetizing by last name would be far more useful than listing people by height, social security number, or length of service with the company, although those organizing principles might make sense in lists for other purposes.

The following three guidelines will help you choose the arrangement that will be the most useful for your audience:

1. **Process your information before you present it to your audience.** The order in which you became aware of information usually is not the best order to present it to your audience.
2. **When you have lots of information, group it into three to seven categories.** The average person's short-term memory can hold only seven chunks, though the chunks can be of any size.[18] By grouping your information into seven categories (or fewer), you make your report easier to comprehend.
3. **Work with the audience's expectations, not against them.** Introduce ideas in the overview in the order in which you will discuss them.

Basic Patterns for Organizing Information

Organize information in a way that will work best for your audience. Here are basic patterns for organizing information that are particularly useful in reports:

- Comparison/contrast.
- Problem-solution.
- Elimination of alternatives.
- SWOT analysis.
- General to particular or particular to general.
- Geographic or spatial.
- Functional.
- Chronological.

Tell Them a Story

To persuade people, tell them a story or anecdote that proves your point.

Experiments show that people are more likely to believe a point and more likely to be committed to it when points were made by examples, stories, and case studies. Stories alone were more effective than a combination of stories and statistics; the combination was more effective than statistics alone. In another experiment, attitude changes lasted longer when the audience had read stories than when they had only read numbers. Research suggests that stories are more persuasive because people remember them.

In many cases, you'll need to provide statistics or numbers to convince the careful reader that your anecdote is a representative example. But give the story first. It's more persuasive.

Adapted from Dean C. Kazoleas, "A Comparison of the Persuasive Effectiveness of Qualitative versus Quantitative Evidence," *Communication Quarterly* 41, no. 1 (Winter 1993): 40–50; and Joanne Martin and Melanie E. Powers, "Truth of Corporate Propaganda," in *Organizational Symbolism*, ed. Louis R. Pondy, et al. (Greenwich, CT: JAI Press, 1983), 97–107.

Any of these patterns can be used for a whole report or for only part of it.

Comparison/contrast   Many reports use comparison/contrast sections within a larger report pattern. Comparison/contrast can also be the purpose of the whole report. Recommendation studies usually use this pattern. You can focus either on the alternatives you are evaluating or on the criteria you use. See Figure 18.1 for ways to organize these two patterns in a report.

Focus on the alternatives when

- One alternative is clearly superior.
- The criteria are hard to separate.
- The audience will intuitively grasp the alternative as a whole rather than as the sum of its parts.

Focus on the criteria when

- The superiority of one alternative to another depends on the relative weight assigned to various criteria. Perhaps Alternative A is best if we are most concerned about Criterion 1, cost, but worst if we are most concerned about Criterion 2, proximity to target market.
- The criteria are easy to separate.
- The audience wants to compare and contrast the options independently of your recommendation.

Figure 18.1   Two Ways to Organize a Comparison/Contrast Report

Focus on alternatives	
Alternative A	Opening a New Store on Campus
Criterion 1	Cost of Renting Space
Criterion 2	Proximity to Target Market
Criterion 3	Competition from Similar Stores
Alternative B	Opening a New Store in the Suburban Mall
Criterion 1	Cost of Renting Space
Criterion 2	Proximity to Target Market
Criterion 3	Competition from Similar Stores

Focus on criteria	
Criterion 1	Cost of Renting Space for the New Store
Alternative A	Cost of Campus Locations
Alternative B	Cost of Locations in the Suburban Mall
Criterion 2	Proximity to Target Market
Alternative A	Proximity on Campus
Alternative B	Proximity in the Suburban Mall
Criterion 3	Competition from Similar Stores
Alternative A	Competing Stores on Campus
Alternative B	Competing Stores in the Suburban Mall

Chapter 18   Analyzing Information and Writing Reports   563

A variation of the comparison/contrast pattern is the **pro-and-con pattern.** In this pattern, under each specific heading, give the arguments for and against that alternative. A report recommending new plantings for a university quadrangle uses the pro-and-con pattern:

> Advantages of Monocropping
>   High Productivity
>   Visual Symmetry
> Disadvantages of Monocropping
>   Danger of Pest Exploitation
>   Visual Monotony

This pattern is least effective when you want to de-emphasize the disadvantages of a proposed solution, for it does not permit you to bury the disadvantages between neutral or positive material.

Problem-solution   Identify the problem; explain its background or history; discuss its extent and seriousness; identify its causes. Discuss the factors (criteria) that affect the decision. Analyze the advantages and disadvantages of possible solutions. Conclusions and recommendation can go either first or last, depending on the preferences of your audience. This pattern works well when the audience is neutral.

A report recommending ways to eliminate solidification of a granular bleach during production uses the problem–solution pattern:

> Recommended Reformulation for Vibe Bleach
> Problems in Maintaining Vibe's Granular Structure
>   Solidification during Storage and Transportation
>   Customer Complaints about "Blocks" of Vibe in Boxes
> Why Vibe Bleach "Cakes"
>   Vibe's Formula
>   The Manufacturing Process
>   The Chemical Process of Solidification
> Modifications Needed to Keep Vibe Flowing Freely

Elimination of alternatives   After discussing the problem and its causes, discuss the *impractical* solutions first, showing why they will not work. End with the most practical solution. This pattern works well when the solutions the audience is likely to favor will not work, while the solution you recommend is likely to be perceived as expensive, intrusive, or radical.

A report on toy commercials, "The Effect of TV Ads on Children," eliminates alternatives:

> Alternative Solutions to Problems in TV Toy Ads
>   Leave Ads Unchanged
>   Mandate School Units on Advertising
>   Ask the Industry to Regulate Itself
>   Give FCC Authority to Regulate TV Ads Directed at Children

SWOT Analysis   A SWOT analysis is frequently used to evaluate a proposed project, expansion, or new venture. The analysis discusses **S**trengths, **W**eaknesses, **O**pportunities, and **T**hreats of the proposed action. Strengths and weaknesses are usually factors within the organization; opportunities and threats are usually factors external to the organization.

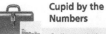

Cupid by the Numbers

Online dating sites collect mountains of data about their users—interests, hobbies, demographics, and characteristics—all of which are used to match users with potential partners. One site, however, is using all of that data to do more.

OkCupid, founded by four Harvard-educated mathematicians, maintains a blog called OkTrends, which mines user data to note interesting, amusing, and controversial trends. By running computer calculations and comparisons, the blog has compiled features like "Rape Fantasies and Hygiene by State," and "How Your Race Affects the Messages You Get."

While some of the data presented on OkTrends is useful to OkCupid's users (like how to pose for a profile picture and what greetings to use), much of it is posted simply to show trends and interesting facts (like iPhone users have more sex than other smartphone users). It also serves to drive traffic to the OkCupid site—visits have doubled since the OkTrends blog was introduced.

Adapted from Jason Del Ray, "In Love with Numbers: Getting the Most Out of Your Data," *Inc.*, October 2010, 105–6.

564   Part 5 Proposals and Reports

A report recommending an in-house training department uses a SWOT analysis to support its recommendation:

> Advantages of In-House Training
> Disadvantages of In-House Training
> Competitor Training Businesses
> Opportunities for Training Expansion

This report switches the order of threats (Competitor Training Businesses) and opportunities to end with positive information.

General to particular or particular to general General to particular starts with the problem as it affects the organization or as it manifests itself in general and then moves to a discussion of the parts of the problem and solutions to each of these parts. Particular to general starts with the problem as the audience defines it and moves to larger issues of which the problem is a part. Both are good patterns when you need to redefine the audience's perception of the problem to solve it effectively.

The directors of a student volunteer organization, VIP, have defined their problem as "not enough volunteers." After studying the subject, the writer is convinced that problems in training, supervision, and campus awareness are responsible for both a high dropout rate and a low recruitment rate. The general-to-particular pattern helps the audience see the problem in a new way:

> Why VIP Needs More Volunteers
> Why Some VIP Volunteers Drop Out
>   Inadequate Training
>   Inadequate Supervision
>   Feeling That VIP Requires Too Much Time
>   Feeling That the Work Is Too Emotionally Demanding
> Why Some Students Do Not Volunteer
>   Feeling That VIP Requires Too Much Time
>   Feeling That the Work Is Too Emotionally Demanding
>   Preference for Volunteering with Another Organization
>   Lack of Knowledge about VIP Opportunities
> How VIP Volunteers Are Currently Trained and Supervised
> Time Demands on VIP Volunteers
> Emotional Demands on VIP Volunteers
> Ways to Increase Volunteer Commitment and Motivation
>   Improving Training and Supervision
>   Improving the Flexibility of Volunteers' Hours
>   Providing Emotional Support to Volunteers
>   Providing More Information about Community Needs and VIP Services

Geographic or spatial In a geographic or spatial pattern, you discuss problems and solutions by units according to their physical arrangement. Move from office to office, building to building, factory to factory, state to state, region to region, etc.

A sales report uses a geographic pattern of organization:

> Sales Have Risen in the European Community
> Sales Are Flat in Eastern Europe
> Sales Have Fallen Sharply in the Middle East

Sales Are Off to a Strong Start in Africa
Sales Have Risen Slightly in Asia
Sales Have Fallen Slightly in South America
Sales Are Steady in North America

Functional   In functional patterns, discuss the problems and solutions of each functional unit. For example, a small business might organize a report to its venture capitalists by the categories of research, production, and marketing. A government report might divide data into the different functions an agency performed, taking each in turn:

Major Accomplishments FY 12
   Regulation
   Education
   Research
   International coordination

Chronological   A chronological report records events in the order in which they happened or are planned to happen. Many progress reports are organized chronologically:

Work Completed in October
Work Planned for November

If you choose this pattern, be sure you do not let the chronology obscure significant points or trends.

Specific Varieties of Reports

Informative, recommendation, and justification reports will be more successful when you work with the audience's expectations for that kind of report.

Informative and closure reports   **Informative** and **closure reports** summarize completed work or research that does not result in action or recommendation.

Informative reports often include the following elements:

- Introductory paragraph summarizing the problems or successes of the project.
- Purpose and scope section(s) giving the purpose of the report and indicating what aspects of the topic it covers.
- Chronological account of how the problem was discovered, what was done, and what the results were.
- Concluding paragraph with suggestions for later action. In a recommendation report, the recommendations would be based on proof. In contrast, the suggestions in a closure or informative report are not proved in detail.

Figure 18.2 presents this kind of informative closure report.

Closure reports also allow a firm to document the alternatives it has considered before choosing a final design.

566   Part 5   Proposals and Reports

Figure 18.2   An Informative Memo Report Describing How a Company Solved a Problem

March 14, 2012

To: Donna S. Kienzler

From: Sara A. Ratterman *GAR*   *Informal short reports use*
                                          letter or memo format.

First   Subject: Recycling at Bike Nashbar
paragraph
summarizes
main   Two months ago, Bike Nashbar began recycling its corrugated cardboard boxes. The program
points.   was easy to implement and actually saves the company a little money compared to our previous
                garbage pickup.

Purpose   In this report, I will explain how and why Bike Nashbar's program was initiated, how the
and scope   program works and what it costs, and why other businesses should consider similar programs.
of report.

                                    Bold headings.

The Problem of Too Many Boxes and Not Enough Space in Bike Nashbar

                Every week, Bike Nashbar receives about 40 large cardboard boxes containing bicycles and other
                merchandise. As many boxes as possible would be stuffed into the trash bin behind the building,
Cause of   which also had to accommodate all the other solid waste the shop produces. Boxes that didn't fit
problem.   in the trash bin ended up lying around the shop, blocking doorways, and taking up space needed
                for customers' bikes. The trash bin was emptied only once a week, and by that time, even more
                boxes would have arrived.

                    Triple space before
                        heading.
The Importance of Recycling Cardboard Rather than Throwing It Away
                        Double space after heading.
                Arranging for more trash bins or more frequent pickups would have solved the immediate
                problem at Bike Nashbar but would have done nothing to solve the problem created by throwing
                away so much trash in the first place.
                        Double space between paragraphs within heading.
                According to David Crogen, sales representative for Waste Management, Inc., 75% of all solid
                waste in Columbus goes to landfills. The amount of trash the city collects has increased 150% in
Further   the last five years. Columbus's landfill is almost full. In an effort to encourage people and
seriousness   businesses to recycle, the cost of dumping trash in the landfill is doubling from $4.90 a cubic yard
of problem.   to $9.90 a cubic yard next week. Next January, the price will increase again, to $12.95 a cubic
                yard. Crogen believes that the amount of trash can be reduced by cooperation between the
                landfill and the power plant and by recycling.

                                                        Capitalize first letter of
How Bike Nashbar Started Recycling Cardboard   *major words in heading.*

                Waste Management, Inc., is the country's largest waste processor. After reading an article about
                how committed Waste Management, Inc., is to waste reduction and recycling, I decided to see
Solution.   whether Waste Management could recycle our boxes. Corrugated cardboard (which is what Bike
                Nashbar's boxes are made of) is almost 100% recyclable, so we seemed to be a good candidate for
                recycling.

Figure 18.2   An Informative Memo Report Describing How a Company Solved a Problem *(Continued)*

Donna S. Kienzler   *Reader's name,*
March 14, 2012   *date,*
Page 2   *page number.*

To get the service started, I met with a friendly sales rep, David Crogen, that same afternoon to discuss the service.

Waste Management, Inc., took care of all the details. Two days later, Bike Nashbar was recycling its cardboard.

How the Service Works and What It Costs   *Talking heads tell reader what to expect in each section.*

Details of solution. Waste Management took away our existing 8-cubic-yard garbage bin and replaced it with two 4-yard bins. One of these bins is white and has "cardboard only" printed on the outside; the other is brown and is for all other solid waste. The bins are emptied once a week, with the cardboard going to the recycling plant and the solid waste going to the landfill or power plant.

Double space between paragraphs. Since Bike Nashbar was already paying more than $60 a week for garbage pickup, our basic cost stayed the same. (Waste Management can absorb the extra overhead only if the current charge is at least $60 a week.) The cost is divided 80/20 between the two bins: 80% of the cost pays for the bin that goes to the landfill and power plant; 20% covers the cardboard pickup. Bike Nashbar actually receives $5.00 for each ton of cardboard it recycles.

Each employee at Bike Nashbar is responsible for putting all the boxes he or she opens in the recycling bin. Employees must follow these rules:

- The cardboard must have the word "corrugated" printed on it, along with the universal recycling symbol.

Indented lists provide visual variety.

- The boxes must be broken down to their flattest form. If they aren't, they won't all fit in the bin and Waste Management would be picking up air when it could pick up solid cardboard. The more boxes that are picked up, the more money that will be made.

- No other waste except corrugated cardboard can be put in the recycling bin. Other materials could break the recycling machinery or contaminate the new cardboard.

- The recycling bin is to be kept locked with a padlock provided by Waste Management so that vagrants don't steal the cardboard and lose money for Waste Management and Bike Nashbar.

(Continued)

Figure 18.2   An Informative Memo Report Describing How a Company Solved a Problem
(Concluded)

Donna S. Kienzler
March 14, 2012
Page 3

*Dis-
advantages
of
solution.*

Minor Problems with Running the Recycling Program

The only problems we've encountered have been minor ones of violating the rules. Sometimes employees at the shop forget to flatten boxes, and air instead of cardboard gets picked up. Sometimes people forget to lock the recycling bin. When the bin is left unlocked, people do steal the cardboard, and plastic cups and other solid waste get dumped in the cardboard bin. I've posted signs where the key to the bin hangs, reminding employees to empty and fold boxes and relock the bin after putting cardboard in it. I hope this will turn things around and these problems will be solved.

Advantages of the Recycling Program

*Advantages
of
solution.*

The program is a great success. Now when boxes arrive, they are unloaded, broken down, and disposed of quickly. It is a great relief to get the boxes out of our way, and knowing that we are making a contribution to saving our environment builds pride in ourselves and Bike Nashbar.

Our company depends on a clean, safe environment for people to ride their bikes in. Now we have become part of the solution. By choosing to recycle and reduce the amount of solid waste our company generates, we can save money while gaining a reputation as a socially responsible business.

Why Other Companies Should Adopt Similar Programs

*Argues
that her
company's
experience
is relevant
to other
companies.*

Businesses and institutions in Franklin County currently recycle less than 4% of the solid waste they produce. David Crogen tells me he has over 8,000 clients in Columbus alone, and he acquires new ones every day. Many of these businesses can recycle a large portion of their solid waste at no additional cost. Depending on what they recycle, they may even get a little money back.

The environmental and economic benefits of recycling as part of a comprehensive waste reduction program are numerous. Recycling helps preserve our environment. We can use the same materials over and over again, saving natural resources such as trees, fuel, and metals and decreasing the amount of solid waste in landfills. By conserving natural resources, recycling helps the U.S. become less dependent on imported raw materials. Crogen predicts that Columbus will be on a 100% recycling system by the year 2020. I strongly hope that his prediction will come true.

Recommendation reports   Recommendation reports evaluate two or more alternatives and recommend one of them. (Doing nothing or delaying action can be one of the alternatives.)

Recommendation reports normally open by explaining the decision to be made, listing the alternatives, and explaining the criteria. In the body of the report, each alternative will be evaluated according to the criteria using one of the two comparison/contrast patterns. Discussing each alternative separately is better when one alternative is clearly superior, when the criteria interact, or when each alternative is indivisible. If the choice depends on the weight given to each criterion, you may want to discuss each alternative under each criterion.

Whether your recommendation should come at the beginning or the end of the report depends on your audience and the culture of your organization. Most audiences want the "bottom line" up front. However, if the audience will find your recommendation hard to accept, you may want to delay your recommendation until the end of the report when you have given all your evidence.

Justification reports   **Justification reports** justify a purchase, investment, hiring, or change in policy. If your organization has a standard format for justification reports, follow that format. If you can choose your headings and organization, use this pattern when your proposal will be easy for your audience to accept:

1. **Indicate what you're asking for and why it's needed.**   Since the audience has not asked for the report, you must link your request to the organization's goals.
2. **Briefly give the background of the problem or need.**
3. **Explain each of the possible solutions.**   For each, give the cost and the advantages and disadvantages.
4. **Summarize the action needed to implement your recommendation.**   If several people will be involved, indicate who will do what and how long each step will take.
5. **Ask for the action you want.**

If the reader will be reluctant to grant your request, use this variation of the problem-solving pattern described in Chapter 11:

1. **Describe the organizational problem (which your request will solve).** Use specific examples to prove the seriousness of the problem.
2. **Show why easier or less expensive solutions will not solve the problem.**
3. **Present your solution impersonally.**
4. **Show that the disadvantages of your solution are outweighed by the advantages.**
5. **Summarize the action needed to implement your recommendation.**   If several people will be involved, indicate who will do what and how long each step will take.
6. **Ask for the action you want.**

How much detail you need to give in a justification report depends on the corporate culture and on your audience's knowledge of and attitude toward your recommendation. Many organizations expect justification reports to be short—only one or two pages. Other organizations may expect longer reports with much more detailed budgets and a full discussion of the problem and each possible solution.

PRESENTING INFORMATION EFFECTIVELY IN REPORTS LO 18-4

The advice about style in Chapter 5 also applies to reports, with three exceptions:

1. **Use a fairly formal style, without contractions or slang.**
2. **Avoid the word** *you.*   In a document with multiple audiences, it will not be clear who *you* is. Instead, use the company's name.

The Importance of Annual Reports

A survey, conducted by WithumSmith & Brown and MGT Design Inc., found that the annual report is the most important publication that a company produces. To understand the value of annual reports, the survey asked individual investors, portfolio managers, and securities analysts (the primary audiences for annual reports) about the ways that they read and use the reports to make decisions.

Here are some of their findings:

- 75% said the annual report is the most important publication that a company produces.
- 79% said the annual report is an important tool for investment decisions.
- 66% prefer photos and/or illustrations in annual reports.
- 90% said that important concerns facing the industry, such as environment issues and corporate governance, should be addressed in the report.
- 81% prefer a print version over electronic versions. Respondents said the print documents were easier to read, highlight, annotate, and file.

Taken together, these findings suggest that the annual report is an important communication for organizations and well worth the time spent creating it.

Adapted from Kirk Holderbaum, "Survey Reveals Importance of Corporate Annual Reports," Commerce & Industry Association of New Jersey, accessed May 29, 2011, 66, http://www.withum.com/fileSave/Commerce_Kirk_0207.pdf.

Who Did What?

The passive verbs and impersonal constructions in U.S. reports of coal mine disasters ("coal dust was permitted to accumulate" and "an accident occurred") suggest that accidents are inevitable. Who permitted the coal dust to accumulate? What could have been done to prevent the accumulation? Mine disaster reports contain sentences like the following: "The . . . fatality occurred when the victim proceeded into an area . . . before the roof was supported." *Why* did the man who was killed go into the area? Had a supervisor checked to see that the roof was supported? Who ordered what?

British reports of mine disasters, in contrast, focus on people and what they did to limit the damage from the disaster. Perhaps as a result, British mines have a much lower incidence of disasters than do U.S. coal mines.

Adapted from Beverly A. Sauer, "Sense and Sensibility in Technical Documentation: How Feminist Interpretation Strategies Can Save Lives in the Nation's Mines," *Journal of Business and Technical Communication* 7 (January 1993): 63–83.

3. **Include in the report all the definitions and documents needed to understand the recommendations.**   The multiple audiences for reports include readers who may consult the document months or years from now; they will not share your special knowledge. Explain acronyms and abbreviations the first time they appear. Explain as much of the history or background of the problem as necessary. Add as appendixes previous documents on which you are building.

The following points apply to any kind of writing, but they are particularly important in reports:

1. Use clear, engaging writing.
2. Keep repetition to a minimum.
3. Introduce sources and visuals.
4. Use forecasting, transitions, topic sentences, and headings to make your organization clear to your reader.

Let's look at each of these principles as they apply to reports.

1. Use Clear, Engaging Writing.

Most people want to be able to read a report quickly while still absorbing its important points. You can help them do this by using accurate diction. Not-quite-right word choices are particularly damaging in reports, which may be skimmed by readers who know little about the subject. Occasionally you can simply substitute a word:

Incorrect:	With these recommendations, we can overcome the solutions to our problem.
Correct:	With these recommendations, we can overcome our problem.
Also correct:	With these recommendations, we can solve our problem.

Sometimes you'll need to completely recast the sentence.

Incorrect:	The first problem with the incentive program is that middle managers do not use good interpersonal skills in implementing it. For example, the hotel chef openly ridicules the program. As a result, the kitchen staff fear being mocked if they participate in the program.
Better:	The first problem with the incentive program is that some middle managers undercut it. For example, the hotel chef openly ridicules the program. As a result, the kitchen staff fear being mocked if they participate in the program.

A strong writing style is especially important when you are preparing a report that relies on a wealth of statistics. Most people have difficulty absorbing number after number. To help your audiences, use text to highlight the message you want the statistics to convey. Examples and action-oriented details keep the audience engaged.

Warren Buffett says this about clear, engaging writing in annual reports, which can certainly present a wealth of statistics:

I really have a mental picture of my sisters in mind and it's Dear Doris and Birdie. And I envision them as people who have a very significant part of their net worth in the company, who are bright but who have been away for a year and who are not business specialists.

And once a year I tell them what's going on. . . . I think that should be the mental approach.[19]

2. Keep Repetition to a Minimum.

Some repetition in reports is legitimate. The conclusion restates points made in the body of the report; the recommendations appear in the transmittal, the abstract or executive summary, and in the recommendations sections of the report. However, repetitive references to earlier material ("As we have already seen") may indicate that the document needs to be reorganized. Read the document through at a single sitting to make sure that any repetition serves a useful purpose.

3. Introduce Sources and Visuals.

The first time you cite an author's work, use his or her full name as it appears on the work: "Thomas L. Friedman points out. . . ." In subsequent citations, use only the last name: "Friedman shows. . . ." Use active rather than passive verbs.

The verb you use indicates your attitude toward the source. *Says* and *writes* are neutral. *Points out, shows, suggests, discovers,* and *notes* suggest that you agree with the source. Words such as *claims, argues, contends, believes,* and *alleges* distance you from the source. At a minimum, they suggest that you know that not everyone agrees with the source; they are also appropriate to report the views of someone with whom you disagree.

The report text should refer to all visuals:

As Table 1 shows, . . .
See Figure 4.

4. Use Forecasting, Transitions, Topic Sentences, and Headings.

Forecasts are overviews that tell the audience what you will discuss in a section or in the entire report. Make your forecast easy to read by telling the audience how many points there are and using bullets or numbers (either words or figures). In the following example, the first sentence in the revised paragraph tells the reader to look for four points; the numbers separate the four points clearly. This overview paragraph also makes a contract with readers, who now expect to read about tax benefits first and employee benefits last.

Paragraph without numbers:	Employee stock ownership programs (ESOPs) have several advantages. They provide tax benefits for the company. ESOPs also create tax benefits for employees and for lenders. They provide a defense against takeovers. In some organizations, productivity increases because workers now have a financial stake in the company's profits. ESOPs are an attractive employee benefit and help the company hire and retain good employees.
Revised paragraph with numbers:	Employee stock ownership programs (ESOPs) provide four benefits. First, ESOPs provide tax benefits for the company, its employees, and lenders to the plan. Second, ESOPs help create a defense against takeovers. Third, ESOPs may increase productivity by giving workers a financial stake in the company's profits. Fourth, as an attractive employee benefit, ESOPs help the company hire and retain good employees.

Legal Liability and Report Drafts

During civil litigation (such as a tort case charging that a product has injured a user), rough drafts may be important to establish the state of mind and intent of a document's drafters.

To protect the company, one lawyer recommends labeling all but the final draft "Preliminary Draft: Subject to Change." That way, if there's ever a lawsuit, the company will be able to argue that only the final report, not the drafts, should be used as evidence.

Adapted from Elizabeth McCord, "'But What You Really Meant Was . . . Multiple Drafts and Legal Liability," paper presented at the Association for Business Communication Midwest Regional Conference, Akron, OH, April 3–5, 1991.

Transitions are words, phrases, or sentences that tell audiences whether the discussion is continuing on the same point or shifting points.

There are economic advantages, too.

(Tells audience that we are still discussing advantages but that we have now moved to economic advantages.)

An alternative to this plan is . . .

(Tells audience that a second option follows.)

The second factor . . .

(Tells audience that the discussion of the first factor is finished.)

These advantages, however, are found only in A, not in B or C.

(Prepares audience for a shift from A to B and C.)

A **topic sentence** introduces or summarizes the main idea of a paragraph. Audiences who skim reports can follow your ideas more easily if each paragraph begins with a topic sentence.

Hard to read (no topic sentence):	Another main use of ice is to keep the fish fresh. Each of the seven kinds of fish served at the restaurant requires one gallon twice a day, for a total of 14 gallons. An additional 6 gallons a day are required for the salad bar.
Better (begins with topic sentence):	Twenty gallons of ice a day are needed to keep food fresh. Of this, the biggest portion (14 gallons) is used to keep the fish fresh. Each of the seven kinds of fish served at the restaurant requires one gallon twice a day. An additional 6 gallons a day are required for the salad bar.

Headings (see Chapter 6) are single words, short phrases, or complete sentences that indicate the topic in each section. A heading must cover all of the material under it until the next heading. For example, *Cost of Tuition* cannot include the cost of books or of room and board; *College Costs* could include all costs. You can have just one paragraph under a heading or several pages. If you do have several pages between headings you may want to consider using subheadings. Use subheadings only when you have two or more divisions within a main heading.

Topic headings focus on the structure of the report. As you can see from the following example, topic headings are vague and give little information.

```
Recommendation
Problem
    Situation 1
    Situation 2
Causes of the Problem
    Background
    Cause 1
    Cause 2
Recommended Solution
```

Talking heads, in contrast, tell the audience what to expect. Talking heads, like those in the examples in this chapter, provide a specific overview of each section and of the entire report.

Recommended Reformulation for Vibe Bleach
  Problems in Maintaining Vibe's Granular Structure
    Solidification during Storage and Transportation
    Customer Complaints about "Blocks" of Vibe in Boxes
Why Vibe Bleach "Cakes"
  Vibe's Formula
  The Manufacturing Process
  The Chemical Process of Solidification
Modifications Needed to Keep Vibe Flowing Freely

Headings must be parallel (see Chapter 5); that is, they must use the same grammatical structure. Subheads must be parallel to each other but do not necessarily have to be parallel to subheads under other headings.

Not parallel:	Are Students Aware of VIP?
	Current Awareness among Undergraduate Students
	Graduate Students
	Ways to Increase Volunteer Commitment and Motivation
	We Must Improve Training and Supervision
	Can We Make Volunteers' Hours More Flexible?
	Providing Emotional Support to Volunteers
	Provide More Information about Community Needs and VIP Services
Parallel:	Campus Awareness of VIP
	Current Awareness among Undergraduate Students
	Current Awareness among Graduate Students
	Ways to Increase Volunteer Commitment and Motivation
	Improving Training and Supervision
	Improving the Flexibility of Volunteers' Hours
	Providing Emotional Support to Volunteers
	Providing More Information about Community Needs and VIP Services

In a complicated report, you may need up to three levels of headings. Figure 18.3 illustrates one way to set up headings. Follow these standard conventions for headings:

- Although the figure shows only one example of each level of headings, in an actual report you would use a subheading only when you had at least two subsections under the next higher heading.
- Avoid having a subhead come immediately after a heading. Instead, some text should follow the main heading before the subheading. (If you have nothing else to say, give an overview of the division.)
- Avoid having a heading or subheading all by itself at the bottom of the page. Instead, have at least one line (preferably two) of type. If there isn't room for a line of type under it, put the heading on the next page.
- Don't use a heading as the antecedent for a pronoun. Instead, repeat the noun.

574   **Part 5**   Proposals and Reports

Figure 18.3   Setting Up Headings in a Single-Spaced Document

Center the title; use bold and a bigger font.   **Typing Titles and Headings for Reports**   *14-point type.*

For the title of a report, use a bold font two point sizes bigger than the largest size in the body of the report. You may want to use an even bigger size or a different font to create an attractive title page. Capitalize the first word and all major words of the title.

Heading for main divisions   *Two empty spaces (triple space)*

Typing Headings for Reports   *12-point type.*
One empty space (double space)

12-point type for body text   Center main headings, capitalize the first and all major words, and use bold. In single-spaced text, leave two empty spaces before main headings and one after. Also leave an extra space between paragraphs. You may also want to use main headings that are one point size bigger than the body text.

This example provides just one example of each level of heading. However, in a real document, use headings only when you have at least two of them in the document. In a report, you'll have several.

Two empty spaces (triple space)

Typing Subheadings   *Bold; left margin*
One empty space

Most reports use subheadings under some main headings. Use subheadings only if you have at least two of them under a given heading. It is OK to use subheadings in some sections and not in others. Normally you'll have several paragraphs under a subheading, but it's OK to have just one paragraph under some subheadings.

12-point type   Subheadings in a report use the same format as headings in letters and memos. Bold subheadings and set them at the left margin. Capitalize the first word and major words. Leave two empty spaces before the subheading and one empty space after it, before the first paragraph under the subheading. Use the same size font as the body paragraphs.

Period after heading   *One empty space (normal paragraph spacing)*

Typing Further Subdivisions. For a very long report, you may need further subdivisions under a subheading. Bold the further subdivision, capitalizing the first word and major words, and end the phrase with a period. Begin the text on the same line. Use normal spacing between paragraphs. Further subdivide a subheading only if you have at least two such subdivisions under a given subheading. It is OK to use divisions under some subheadings and not under others.

WRITING FORMAL REPORTS   LO 18-5

Formal reports are distinguished from informal letter and memo reports by their length and by their components. A full formal report may contain the following components (see Figures 18.4 and 18.5):

- Cover
- Title Page
- Letter or Memo of Transmittal
- Table of Contents
- List of Illustrations
- Executive Summary

Figure 18.4   The Components in a Report Can Vary

More formal ←		→ Less formal
Cover	Title Page	Introduction
Title Page	Table of Contents	Body
Transmittal	Executive Summary	Conclusions
Table of Contents	Body	Recommendations
List of Illustrations	Introduction	
Executive Summary	Body	
Body	Conclusions	
Introduction	Recommendations	
Body		
Conclusions		
Recommendations		
References/Works Cited		
Appendixes		
Questionnaires		
Interviews		
Computer Printouts		
Related Documents		

**http://www
.pewinternet.org/**

To see examples of the ways in which reports are written and disseminated, visit the Pew Internet & American Life Project at the above website.

The project produces reports on the impact of the Internet on American lives, collecting and analyzing data on real-world developments as they intersect with the virtual world. Following data collection, the results are written into the reports and posted as PDFs to the website.

Visit the Project's web pages to see examples of the ways in which reports are first presented and then rewritten by the press for their audience and purpose.

- **Report Body**
  - Introduction (Orients the reader to the report. Usually has subheadings for Purpose and Scope; depending on the situation, may also have Limitations, Assumptions, Methods, Criteria, and Definitions.)
  - Background or History of the Problem (Orients the reader to the topic of the report. Serves as a record for later readers of the report.)
  - Body (Presents and interprets data in words and visuals. Analyzes causes of the problem and evaluates possible solutions. Specific headings will depend on the topic of the report.)
  - Conclusions (Summarizes main points of report.)
  - Recommendations (Recommends actions to solve the problem. May be combined with Conclusions; may be put at beginning of body rather than at the end.)
- Notes, References, or Works Cited (Documents sources cited in the report.)
- Appendixes (Provides additional materials that the careful reader may want: transcripts of interviews, copies of questionnaires, tallies of all the questions, complex tables, computer printouts, previous reports.)

As Figure 18.4 shows, not every formal report necessarily has all these components. In addition, some organizations call for additional components or arrange these components in a different order. As you read each section below, you may want to turn to the corresponding pages of the long report in Figure 18.5 to see how the component is set up and how it relates to the total report.

576   **Part 5**   Proposals and Reports

Figure 18.5   A Formal Report

Center all text on the title page.

Slated for Success

Use a large font size for the main title.

RAC Inc. Expanding to South Korea

Use a slightly smaller font size for the subheading.

Prepared for   — No punctuation.

Name of audience, job title, organization, city, state, and zip code.

Ms. Katie Nichols
CEO of RAC Inc.
Grand Rapids, Michigan, 49503

Prepared by   — No punctuation.

JASS LLC
Jordan Koole
Alex Kuczera
Shannon Jones
Sean Sterling
Allendale, MI 49401

Name of writer(s), organization, city, state, and zip code.

April 21, 2011   Date report is released.

Figure 18.5   A Formal Report *(Continued)*

This student group designed their own letterhead, assuming they were doing this report as consultants.

This letter uses block format.

JASS LLC
1 Campus Drive
Allendale, MI 49401

April 21, 2011

Ms. Katie Nichols, CEO
RAC Inc.
1253 W. Main Street
Grand Rapids, MI 49504

In paragraph 1, release the report. Note when and by whom the report was authorized. Note the report's purpose.

Dear Ms. Nichols:

In this document you will find the report that you requested in March. We have provided key information and made recommendations on a plan of action for the expansion of a RAC Inc. slate tablet manufacturing plant into South Korea.

Give recommendations or thesis of report.

Our analysis of expansion into South Korea covered several important areas that will help you decide whether or not RAC Inc. should expand and build a manufacturing plant in South Korea. To help us make our decision, we looked at the government, economy, culture, and most important the competition. South Korea is a technologically advanced country and its economy is on the rise. Our research has led us to recommend expansion into South Korea. We strongly believe that RAC Inc. can be profitable in the long run and become a successful business in South Korea.

Note sources that were helpful.

JASS LLC used several resources in forming our analysis. The Central Intelligence Agency's *World Factbook*, the U.S. Department of State, World Business Culture, and Kwintessential were all helpful in answering our research questions.

Thank the audience for the opportunity to do the research.

Thank you for choosing JASS to conduct the research into South Korea. If you have any further questions about the research or recommendation please contact us (616-331-1100, info@jass.com) and we will be happy to answer any questions referring to your possible expansion into South Korea at no charge. JASS would be happy to conduct any further research on this issue or any other projects that RAC Inc. is considering. We look forward to building on our relationship with you in the future.

Sincerely,

Jordan Koole

Jordan Koole
JASS Team Member

Offer to answer questions about the report.

Center initial page numbers at the bottom of the page. Use a lowercase roman numeral for initial pages of report.

i

(Continued)

578   **Part 5**   Proposals and Reports

Figure 18.5   A Formal Report *(Continued)*

Main headings are parallel, as are subheadings within a section.

Table of Contents does not list itself.

Table of Contents

Use lowercase roman numerals for initial pages.

Introduction begins on page 1.

Capitalize first letter of each major word in headings.

Indentions show level of heading at a glance.

Line up right margin (justify).

List of Illustrations

Add a "List of Illustrations" at the bottom of the page or on a separate page if the report has many visuals.

Figures and tables are numbered independently.

ii

Figure 18.5   A Formal Report *(Continued)*

Report title.
Slated for Success

Many audiences read only the Executive Summary, not the report. Include enough information to give audiences the key points you make.

RAC Inc. Expanding to South Korea

Executive Summary

Start with recommendation or thesis.

To continue growth and remain competitive on a global scale, RAC Inc. should expand its business operations into South Korea. The country is a technologically advanced nation and would provide a strong base for future expansion. Slate tablet competitors of RAC Inc. in South Korea are doing quite well. Since RAC Inc. can compete with them in the United States, we are confident that RAC can remain on par with them in this foreign market.

Provide brief support for recommendations.

The research we have done for this project indicates that this expansion will be profitable, primarily because the South Korean economy is flourishing. The workforce in South Korea is large, and finding talented employees to help set up and run the facility will be easy. In addition, the regulations and business structure are similar to those in the United States and will provide an easy transition into this foreign nation. The competition will be fierce; however, we believe that RAC Inc. will be profitable because of its track record with the Notion Tab in the United States.

To ensure a successful expansion, JASS LLC recommends the following:

1. **RAC Inc. should establish its headquarters and manufacturing plant in Busan.**
   - Purchase a building to have a place to begin manufacturing the Notion Tab.
   - Educate RAC employees about South Korean culture and business practices before they begin working directly with South Koreans to avoid being disrespectful.
   - Explore hiring South Koreans; the available workforce is large.
   - Ensure that the Notion name is appropriate when translated into Korean. If not, change the name to better market the product.
   - Market and sell the product in both Busan and Seoul.

2. **After one year RAC should determine the acceptance and profitability of the expansion.**
   - Conduct a customer satisfaction survey with people who purchased the Notion Tab living in Seoul and Busan to determine the acceptance of the product.
   - Compare and contrast first-year sales with a competitor's similar product.

3. **If the tablet is competitive and profitable, RAC Inc. should expand its product line into all large cities in South Korea.**
   - To gain an edge on the competition, create a marketing plan that will offer the Notion Tab at some discount in the new cities.
   - Explore integrating other RAC Inc. products into South Korea. These products could also be manufactured at the new manufacturing plant in Busan.

Language in the Executive Summary can come from the report. Make sure any repeated language is well-written!

The Abstract or Executive Summary contains the logical skeleton of the report: the recommendation(s) and supporting evidence.

iii

(Continued)

Figure 18.5 A Formal Report *(Continued)*

A running header is optional.

Slated for Success   1

Introduction *Center main headings.*

To avoid getting left behind by competition in global expansion, RAC Inc. has contacted JASS LLC to perform an analysis about expanding into South Korea. JASS has researched South Korea to determine if RAC Inc. will be successful in expanding into this foreign market.

"Purpose" and "Scope" can be separate sections if either is long.

Purpose and Scope

RAC Inc. is a successful business in the United States and has had substantial growth over the last five years. With their competitors beginning to venture into foreign markets to gain more global market share, RAC Inc. is looking to expand into the international market as well. The purpose of our research is to decide whether or not RAC Inc. should expand its business into South Korea.

Give topics in the order you'll discuss them.

Tell what you discuss and how thoroughly you discuss each topic.

Topics in "Scope" section should match those in the report.

This report will cover several topics about South Korea including their government, economy, culture, technology market competition, and possible locations. Our research will not include any on-site research in South Korea. We are also not dealing directly with the South Korean people.

List any relevant topics you do not discuss.

Assumptions *Assumptions cannot be proved. But if they are wrong, the report's recommendation may no longer be valid.*

The recommendations that we make are based on the assumption that the relationship between North and South Korea will remain the same as of the first part of 2011. We are also assuming that the technological state of South Korea will remain constant and not suffer from a natural disaster or an economic crash. In addition, we assume that the process of expansion into South Korea is the same with RAC Inc. as it has been with other American companies. Another assumption that we are making is that RAC Inc. has a good name brand and is competitive in the United States with Apple, Samsung, LG and other electronic companies.

If you collected original data (surveys, interviews, and observations), tell how you chose your subjects, what kind of sample you used, and when you collected the information. This report does not use original data; it just provides a brief discussion of significant sources.

Methods

The information in our report comes from online sources and reference books. We found several good sources, but the best information that we obtained came from The Central Intelligence Agency's *World Factbook*, the U.S. Department of State, World Business Culture, and Kwintessential. These resources have given us much useful information on which we have based our recommendation.

These limitations are listed because the students correctly assumed their teacher would want to know them. Limitations such as these would never be listed in a real consulting report, since they would disqualify the firm.

Limitations *If your report has limitations, state them.*

The information in the report was limited to what we retrieved from our sources. We were not able to travel to South Korea to conduct on-site research. JASS was also limited by the language barrier that exists between the United States and South Korea. Other limitations exist because we have not been immersed in the Korean culture and have not gotten input from South Koreans on the expansion of companies into their country.

Definitions

Define key terms your audience will need to read your report.

There are a few terms that we use throughout the report that we would like to explain beforehand. The first term is slate tablet, an industry term, which from this point on is referred to as a tablet. Another term we would like to clarify is the city Busan. Some sources referred to it as Pusan. From this point forward, we use only Busan. An abbreviation we use is GDP, which stands for gross domestic product. The South Korean and United States Free Trade Agreement signed in 2007 is abbreviated as KORUS FTA, its official name in the United States government.

Figure 18.5 A Formal Report *(Continued)*

Slated for Success   2

This section outlines the criteria used to make the overall recommendation.

Criteria

JASS LLC has established criteria that need to be favorable before we give a positive recommendation about South Korea. The criteria include the government, economy, culture, and market competition. We have weighted our criteria by percentages:

- Government = 20%
- Economy = 20%
- South Korean culture = 20%
- Market possibilities and competitors = 40%

We will examine each separately and give each criterion a favorable or not favorable recommendation. Market competition is weighted the heaviest and must be favorable or somewhat favorable for us to give a positive recommendation. Market competition can be given a favorable, nonfavorable, or somewhat favorable recommendation based on various external factors in the marketplace. We need a minimum of a 70% total to give a positive recommendation overall.

Triple-space before major headings and double-space after them.

Government

Begin most paragraphs with topic sentences.

South Korea is recognized as a republic government by the rest of the world. A republic government is a democracy where the people have supreme control over the government (South Korea: Political structure, 2009). This foundation makes it similar to the United States' democracy. There is a national government as well as provincial-level governments (similar to state-level governments) with different branches. Larger cities, like Seoul and Busan, have their own city government as well. The government is considered multipartied and has multiple parties vying for positions (South Korea: Political structure, 2009). The Republic of South Korea shares its power among three branches of government, thus providing checks and balances inside the government. The three branches of the government are the presidential, legislative, and judicial (U.S. Department of State, 2010). In this section, we will discuss government control, business regulations, taxes, free trade, and concerns about North Korea.

List subtopics in the order in which they are discussed.

Government Control

It's OK to have subheadings under some headings and not others.

The Grand National Party (GNP) controls the major policy-making branches of the government. President Lee Myung-Bak and Prime Minister Kim Hwang-Sik are both members of the GNP. Winning control of the National Assembly in April 2008 (South Korea: Political structure, 2009), the GNP is considered the conservative party in South Korea and is similar to the Republican Party in the United States. Their policies favor conservatism and are considered pro-business (Grand National Party, 2011). RAC Inc. should not expect much interference from the government with their business venture into South Korea, unless the GNP loses control of the government in the next election.

Use subheadings only when you have two or more sections.

Business Regulations

South Korea ranks 16th on the ease of doing business index (World Bank Group, 2011a). This index measures the regulations that a government imposes on businesses and how easy it is to start and run a business in a given country. Factors this index measures include the ease of starting a business, doing taxes, and enforcing contracts. For comparison, the United States is ranked fifth on this list (World Bank Group, 2011b). While there are more regulations on business in South Korea, they are still near the top of the list. The relatively low rating on regulation can be due in part to the Grand National Party controlling the government. There are a few general regulations that RAC Inc. should know before going into South Korea. For more specific business regulations, RAC Inc. may need to do further research before expanding.

(Continued)

Figure 18.5   A Formal Report *(Continued)*

Slated for Success   3

South Korea has been known for having long workweeks and long working days. South Korea leads the world in hours worked with an average of 2,357 hours per worker per year (Olson, 2008). However, the government has recently passed laws regulating the workweek. In 2003, they shortened their workweek from six days down to the traditional five-day workweek within the public sector. They also shortened the workweek for the public sector down to 40 hours a week (Kirk, 2001). The private sector, however, continues to work long hours because it has not yet been regulated. But the government hinted at regulating the private sector in the future when the public sector law was passed (Kirk, 2001). Nonetheless, no legislation has come through the National Assembly, and South Koreans continue to be the hardest-working people in the world.

Period goes outside of parenthesis.

The South Korean government has also been known to have strong import restrictions placed on companies (Central Intelligence Agency, 2011). As a result, companies have been forced to gather resources from South Korea instead of importing them. This approach helped South Korea grow its GDP and other economic health measures. It has also influenced the South Korean consumers' view of foreign products.

RAC Inc. may need to be concerned about these regulations when expanding to South Korea. In general, however, regulations on business in South Korea are similar to those of the United States because of the closeness in government structures. While the conservative Grand National Party is in control of the major branches of the government, they are likely to shoot down any attempts at business regulations. The result is that future regulations on business in South Korea will remain low.

Taxes

The total tax rate in South Korea is lower than that of the United States. (The total tax rate measures all of the mandatory taxes that a company has to pay on their operations in a given country.) The United States has a 46% tax rate, while South Korea has only a 29% tax rate (World Bank Group, 2011a, 2011b). This lower rate means that a company is able to keep more of their profits in South Korea than in the United States. Lower taxes are a positive factor for RAC Inc. to consider.

Free Trade

In June 2007, South Korea and the United States announced that they had drafted a free trade agreement with each other known as the KORUS FTA (Manyin, 2007). Even though it has been agreed upon since that date, neither nation's legislature has ratified the agreement. Ratification stalled in 2007 because of concerns by a Democratic-controlled congress in the United States and opposition lead by current President Barack Obama. In 2010, President Obama got both sides back together and drafted a new agreement that is pending the approval of both nations' legislatures (AFP, 2010). The highlights of the agreement are an immediate reduction of tariffs and duty-free trade on 95% of all goods exchanged between the countries in three years. In 10 years, all tariffs will be eliminated between the two nations. There would be access between the two countries' service sectors, allowing for faster international deliveries between the two nations (Office of the U.S. Trade Representative, 2011).

The KORUS FTA will be a positive for potential companies expanding into the region by creating a stable political and economic relationship between the United States and South Korea. KORUS FTA will give companies an open door into the region and an ability to conduct business with little to no interference between the governments. However, both nations' legislatures need to ratify the agreement before this trade agreement can make positive impacts for RAC Inc.

Concerns about North Korea

North and South Korea have been separated since 1945. These two countries were at war between 1950 and 1953. Since this conflict, there have been moments of tension, including some moments in 2010. Currently there is no escalation of hostilities (U.S. Department of State, 2010). We are assuming this state of conflict will not change in the near future. Improved relations would be ideal for the region, the world, and RAC Inc.

Figure 18.5   A Formal Report *(Continued)*

Slated for Success   4

Summary   *This team provides a "summary" section at the end of each major section to highlight important points.*

JASS LLC believes that South Korea's politics favor RAC Inc. expanding into the country. The Grand National Party allows for a favorable government for all businesses. South Korea has low regulations by the government, and they have lower taxes. The restrictions on importing and future workweek regulations are factors that need to be researched more by RAC Inc. if they decide to expand their operations. The KORUS FTA shows the stable relations between the United States and South Korea. The situation with North Korea is as stable as can be at this time. These factors allow JASS to give the government criterion a favorable rating.

Economy   *Headings must cover everything under that heading until the next one.*

South Korea's economy is considered one of the largest in the world. According to the CIA's *World Factbook*, the country recently became part of the top 20 economies in the world. They are considered a high-tech industrialized country (2011). Major industries in South Korea's economy include electronics, telecommunications, automobile production, chemicals, ship building, and the steel industries. Natural resources from South Korea include coal, tungsten, graphite, molybdenum, lead, and hydropower (U.S. Department of State, 2010). Not only is South Korea one of the largest economies in the world, it is one of the fastest growing. Economic growth, along with the GDP, imports and exports, and currency will be addressed in this section.

Economic Growth   *Capitalize all main words of headings and subheadings.*

World War II and the Korean War ravished the country and its economic base, and the country has had to rebuild its entire economy. Their GDP was among the poorest in the world in 1960. Since then, South Korea has had record growth in economic measures such as GDP and GDP per capita (South Korea's GDP Growth, 2010). According to the CIA's *World Factbook*, "a system of close *Refer to figure* government and business ties, including directed credit and import restrictions, made this success *in text.* possible. The government promoted the import of raw materials and technology at the expense *Tell what point* of consumer goods, and encouraged savings and investment over consumption" (2011). *it makes.* Figure 1 shows how the economy of South Korea has grown over time using GDP as a measure.

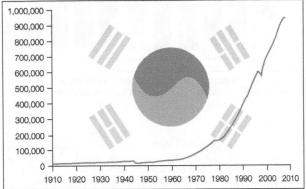

Figure 1: South Korea's GDP (PPP) Growth from 1911 to 2008 (Source: South Korea's GDP Growth, 2010)

Number figures and tables independently.   *Cite source of data.*

(Continued)

Figure 18.5 A Formal Report *(Continued)*

Slated for Success   5

Since the 1960s, the GDP has had only one dip, a result of the Asian Economic crisis in the late 1990s that affected most Asian countries. In 2004, South Korea became a part of the trillion-dollar economy club, making them one of the world's top economies (Central Intelligence Agency, 2011).

However the economy faces challenges in maintaining steady growth in the future. These challenges include an aging population, inflexible workforce, and an overdependence on exports. Right now, though, South Korea's economy continues to grow. Their industrial production growth rate was 12.1% in 2010, making them the 11th fastest-growing nation in the production industry. In 2010, their GDP grew by 6.8%, the 28th largest growth of GDP in the world (Central Intelligence Agency, 2011). This growth makes South Korea a viable place of expansion.

GDP and Other Important Economic Measures

The official GDP of South Korea was $1.467 trillion in 2010 (Central Intelligence Agency, 2011). This GDP is the 13th highest in the world. GDP measures the total value of goods produced by a country's economy. Figure 2 shows a comparison of GDP growth rates for top countries. GDP per capita in South Korea is $30,200, which is the 44th largest in the world. This measures the output of goods and services per person in the country. It is also an indicator of the average worker's

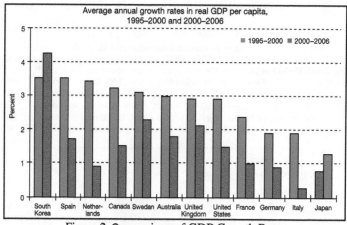

Label both axes of graphs. See chapter 16 for more information on creating data displays.

Figure 2: Comparison of GDP Growth Rates
(Source: U.S. Bureau of Labor Statistics, 2008)

Number figures consecutively throughout the report.

Figure captions need to be descriptive.

salary in the country. South Korea only has 15% of their population living in poverty. They have a labor force of 24.62 million which is the 25th largest labor force in the world, with an unemployment rate of 3.3% (Central Intelligence Agency, 2011). These numbers need to be considered when starting operations in South Korea. South Korea also has a service-driven economy with 57.6% of the country's GDP output in the service industry and 68.4% of the labor force employed in the service industry (Central Intelligence Agency, 2011). All of these numbers and high world rankings of the economic measures show that South Korea has a stable and healthy economy where a business could prosper.

Figure 18.5 A Formal Report *(Continued)*

Slated for Success   6

Imports and Exports

The South Korean economy has grown exponentially because of the government's policy on exporting products instead of importing them. As a result, South Korea has traditionally had more exports than imports. They are the world's seventh largest exporter: $466.3 billion dollars' worth of goods in 2010. The countries they export to are China, the United States, Japan, and Hong Kong (Central Intelligence Agency, 2011). Exporting has helped the South Korean economy grow into what it is today and has made it an important economy in the global marketplace.

With the world becoming more globalized, South Korea now also imports a large amount of goods. South Korea is practically on an island because the only land border is with North Korea, which is not connected to the global marketplace. These factors have made it more important over time for South Korea to import products and relax the government's stance on limiting imports. South Korea is the ninth largest importer in the world. The total dollar amount of imports was $417.9 billion in 2010. Major import partners are China, Japan, the United States, Saudi Arabia, and Australia (Central Intelligence Agency, 2011).

South Korea exports were $48.4 billion greater than its imports while trading with its partners throughout the world (Central Intelligence Agency, 2011). This balance has stayed positive helping the South Korean economy grow. This balance can also be taken as a sign that South Korea's economy is healthy and has useful products and services for their people and consumers worldwide.

Dollars and Cents

South Korea's currency is the won. Asian currencies are traditionally inflated compared to the United States dollar and other currencies around the world. The won is no exception. According to *MSN Money,* the exchange rate as of April 10, 2011, was 1090.513 won to 1 American dollar (KRWUS, 2011).

Summary

With all of these economic factors, JASS LLC believes that the economy is strong enough to support expansion. South Korea has been one of the world's fastest-growing economic markets and has become a major player in today's global economy. All measures and statistics of the economy lead JASS to give a favorable rating to the economy of South Korea.

South Korean Culture

For RAC Inc. to be successful in South Korea, they need to understand its people and culture. Unlike the United States with its numerous cultures, South Korea is primarily made up of South Koreans. Their family heritage and customs are extremely important to them, passing down through generations (Life, n.d.). South Korean society is a class system primarily based on economic status, but also partly based on education. Major status symbols are the size of one's residence, whether it is a house or a condominium, having a chauffeur, and the style and quality of one's clothes (Advameg, Inc., 2011).

Outlines subsections for this part of report

Not only is South Korean society based on a class system, but there is also a long tradition of male superiority, in public, though not private, situations. In this section, we will report findings about the business culture, honor and respect, and religion as it relates to RAC's interests.

(Continued)

Figure 18.5 A Formal Report *(Continued)*

Slated for Success   7

Business Culture

Division of labor by gender is something that RAC Inc. should be extremely aware of, because of its impact on the workforce and social patterns. In public, men are the household head (*boju*) making decisions for their wives and daughters, and women are expected to be submissive. However in private settings, husbands tend to leave the decision making to their wives (Kwintessential, 2010).

Many South Koreans, however, believe that women's work is to take care of the home and house work, even if they work outside the home. Women doing the same job as men are paid only 63.4% of what their male counterparts earn (Advameg, Inc., 2011). RAC Inc. may see this as being sexist, but for many South Koreans, it is an integral part of their culture.

When hiring, many South Koreans rely on social connections for new employees, especially in small companies. Larger companies tend to hire headhunters for finding candidates in upper-level management. South Korean job advancement reflects a strong tradition of seniority, and sometimes will bypass qualified women for a man with higher seniority. New or empty job positions that need to be filled will first be filled by the most senior of employees before someone from the outside is brought in. Only in more recent times is this tradition being challenged (World Business Culture, n.d.).

Use "n.d." for a source with no date.

In the United States, many important meeting and business deals happen in an office, whereas in South Korea these happen in bars and restaurants. Entertainment is as much a part of their culture as it is of their business (Kwintessential, 2010). If RAC employees are invited for dinner, they should accept the invitation. While out, many South Koreans are apt to decide if RAC employees are trustworthy and honorable, thus deciding if they will do business with them or not. Although it may be considered taboo to drink while doing business in America, the Koreans enjoy their alcohol and want to share it with people with whom they wish to do business. They will not look poorly on RAC employees if they don't but joining South Koreans could help build goodwill (World Business Culture, n.d.).

Honor and Respect

Honor and respect work hand-in-hand with Korean culture. Their values stem from their ancestors, elders, and belief in Confucianism (see Religion). These follow them into the workplace where they value collective group harmony and respect for authority, as well as embracing the importance of family, clan, and friendship (World Business Culture, n.d.). When American companies come to South Korea, the traditional values can cause tension between the two styles of management. Being on time, knowing facts (especially technical details), having patience, presenting gifts with both hands, and thanking Koreans with small gifts are things to keep in mind to be both honorable and respectful (Kwintessential, 2010). Something as small as a business card holds a great deal of honor to many Koreans; it is taboo to either write on or fold them (World Business Culture, n.d.).

South Korean managers have a primary goal of encouraging their employees to work together as a unit. They spend most of their day ensuring that the team has a good working relationship. Managers also take a holistic interest in their employees, including their personal lives (World Business Culture, n.d.). This approach contrasts to how American companies may work.

Religion

South Korea has a wide range of religious beliefs, including Shamanism, Confucianism, Buddhism, Christianity, and Islam. Shamanism has evolved from indigenous folk; they believe in the existence of a myriad of gods (such as mountain, house, and fire) and spirits of the dead, all of which influence people's fortunes. Korean Buddhists believe that human suffering is caused mainly by desire; therefore, they try to reach enlightenment by cultivating an attitude of detachment. Others try to seek fulfillment by offering prayers to Kwanum, the Bodhisattva of Compassion. Within Christianity, Catholicism and Protestantism have became the two most popular (Advameg, Inc., 2011).

Figure 18.5   A Formal Report *(Continued)*

Slated for Success   8

Confucianism emphasizes propriety in the five sets of human relationships between sovereign and subject, father and son, husband and wife, senior and junior, and friend and friend. It is also a political and social philosophy that emphasizes the values of *in* (translated as "human-heartedness"). Death and the afterlife are other areas of strong involvement from South Koreans. They believe in ancestral spirits and observe Confucian rituals concerning funerals, mourning practices, and memorial services (Advameg, Inc., 2011).

Summary
Although the culture of South Korean can be vastly different from that of the United Stares, RAC Inc. can overcome these differences. JASS recommends that additional education in Korean culture and business practices be given to any RAC employee that would be directly doing business with them to prevent disrespect. As for religious practices, they are similar to what exists in the United States, though RAC may have to allow special days off work for religious ceremonies. Being honorable and respectful is at the heart of Korean culture and should not be difficult for RAC to adapt. JASS finds the culture favorable for expanding into South Korea.

Market Possibilities and Competitors

Use author's name in parentheses when it isn't introduced in the sentence.

Tablets are one of the newest products to emerge in the last few years and are growing in popularity. The tablet is marketed as a computer that is more mobile than a laptop, with the ease of use of a smartphone (Ogg, 2010). With app development supported by several companies, tablets constantly offer new features.

Currently, the most popular product around the world, with millions of products sold, is Apple's iPad and iPad 2 (iPad 2, 2011). This product, along with products from Samsung, LG, Motorola, and other companies, will create a tough foreign market for RAC to enter. However, since RAC Inc. is competing with these companies and their products in the United States, a successful integration of RAC's Notion Tab is definitely possible. In this section, we will cover information on technology use in South Korea, competition—LG and Samsung—and integration of the Notion Tab.

Technology Use
Tablets are one of the fastest-growing devices in the technology field worldwide; South Koreans have been quick to embrace this technology. In general, the country is on the cutting edge with new technologies such as tablets and NFC (near field communication). Earlier this decade, a greater number of South Korean homes had faster Internet connections than United States homes (Borland & Kanellos, 2004). As of 2009, the year with the latest data, South Korea has the 11th most Internet users worldwide, with 39.4 million (Central Intelligence Agency, 2011).

About 90% of South Koreans own a cellular phone (Koreans love, 2009). Along with the normal calling and texting, they also have Digital Multimedia Broadcasting (DMB), which is used for watching videos, listening to radio, and datacasting (Cho, 2006). The country is set up nicely for technology companies like RAC Inc. to produce and sell their products.

(Continued)

Figure 18.5   A Formal Report *(Continued)*

Slated for Success   9

Competition

Since RAC Inc. has decided what specifications their Notion Tab will have, they should understand what the competition offers with their tablets. Currently, LG and Samsung are the leading competition for RAC Inc. in South Korea. The current specs for LG's G-Slate, Samsung's Galaxy Tab and Apple's iPad 2 are as outlined in Table 1.

Refer to figure or table before it appears in text.

Specs	G-Slate	Galaxy Tab	iPad 2	Notion Tab
Processor	1 Ghz NVidia Terga 2 Dual-Core	1 Ghz NVidia Terga 2 Dual-Core	1 Ghz Dual-Core A5	1 Ghz NVidia Terga 2 Dual-Core
Memory	1 GB	1 GB	512 MB	1 GB
Hard Drive	32 GB	16 GB or 32 GB	16 GB, 32 GB, 64 GB	32 GB or 64 GB
Screen Resolution	1280 × 768	1280 × 800	1024 × 768	1024 × 768
Camera	Front and Rear	Front and Rear	Front and Rear	Front and Rear
Display Size	8.9" LCD	8.9" or 10.1" LCD	9.7" LED	9.0" LCD
Operation System	Android 3.0 (Honeycomb)	Android 3.0 (Honeycomb)	iOS 4.3	Android 3.0 (Honeycomb)
Price	$699.99	$469.99–$599.99	$499.99	$499.99

Table 1: Comparsion of Specifications for Existing Tablets
(Sources: LG Slate, 2011; Samsung Galaxy Tab, 2011; iPad 2, 2011)

Because tables are numbered separately from other visuals, reports can have both a Figure 1 and a Table 1

LG

The LG Corporation is the second largest company in South Korea behind Samsung (see below). Their revenues, as of 2009, were $78.89 billion (in U.S. dollars). LG is not as diversified as Samsung, but they do produce products in the fields of electronics, telecommunications, and chemicals (LG Corp, 2011). LG will be one of the main rivals for RAC Inc. in South Korea. LG released their version of a tablet, the G-Slate, as it is called in the United States, in March 2011. The specifications of this tablet are outlined in Table 1 (LG Slate, 2011). LG is relatively new to the field of tablets, so JASS believes RAC Inc. will not have to worry as much about LG as it does about Samsung.

Samsung

Samsung is the largest company in the world, and in South Korea, based upon revenue. As of 2009, their revenue was $172.5 billion (in U.S. dollars). Samsung is part of a larger group of corporations that comprise a diverse set of areas; technology is the biggest (Samsung, 2011). Samsung would be RAC Inc.'s largest competitor in South Korea. Samsung has a tablet, called the Galaxy Tab, launched at the end of 2010. They have a newer version hitting retail stores sometime late 2011. The specifications of this tablet are outlined in Table 1 (Samsung Galaxy, 2011). The Galaxy Tab is actually the second version of their tablet that they have released, with updated technology and software. As a hometown Seoul business, Samsung will present a challenge for RAC Inc. to win the loyalties of the South Korean people and increase market share.

Integration

One way RAC Inc. could improve receptiveness from the South Korean people, and possibly cut costs for their Notion Tab, is to partner with a South Korean company to more readily manufacture their product. Some of these companies are Digitech Systems, Nextchip, and Partron. Digitech Systems has an emphasis on touch screens for phones and other devices, which is a major component of tablets. Nextchip deals with the sensors that are used in touch screens, which is another important element of the device. And finally, Partron deals with basic parts for mobile phones and telecommunication devices (Settimi, 2010).

Figure 18.5   A Formal Report *(Continued)*

Slated for Success   10

If RAC Inc. does expand to South Korea, they will need to have a telecommunications company to carry the service, at least the data service for their Notion Tab. The best option JASS has researched is SK Telecom. SK Telecom, part of the SK group, is South Korea's largest telecommunications group for cellular phone service in the region. They have 50.5% of the market share (SK Telecom, 2011). The other two options are LG Telecom and KT, formally Korea Telecom. LG Telecom would not be a good choice since they are a subsidiary of a competitor, LG (LG Telecom, 2010). KT would also not be the best choice because they are not the largest provider in the country and all of the competitors use SK Telecom as their data service (KT, 2011).

Summary

The people of South Korea are in sync with the latest technology trends such as NFC and DMB. Their affinity with technology has led JASS to choose South Korea as a viable option. However, there are disadvantages as well. The main competitors of RAC Inc. in South Korea, LG and Samsung, are major hurdles. They are the top two companies in South Korea, with Samsung being the largest in the world. Because of these factors, we have determined this criterion is only somewhat favorable for expansion. This criterion could go either way; therefore, JASS cannot give it a full favorable recommendation for expansion into South Korea.

Location, Location, Location

South Korea offers many suitable cities for RAC's expansion. We researched many before picking a city that will generate the most benefits for RAC Inc. Our research covered possible locations for RAC's headquarters, operations, and Notion Tab product launches. We researched the cities of Seoul, Busan, Incheon, Daegu and Cheongju. We picked these cities to research based on size and location. The factors we used in determining the right cities are economic status, population, proximity to North Korea, proximity to shipping ports (coastline), and direct competition to Samsung and LG, whose headquarters are in Seoul. The entire country of South Korea is technologically advanced, so any of these cities could be a possibility for expansion.

JASS has decided that the city with the highest potential to expand business operations is the centrally located Busan. Busan is the second largest city in South Korea with population of 3.4 million. Busan is also the largest port city in South Korea and the fifth largest port city in the world (Park, 2009). Because Busan is a port city, it will allow easy importation of raw materials, as well as easier exportation of finished product to other countries and back to the United States. If manufacturing is cheaper in South Korea, RAC Inc. may decide to create more products in South Korea and ship them back to the United States.

JASS also recommends that the headquarters be in Busan, allowing close proximity to the manufacturing plant, if any issues arise. RAC Inc. should initially launch the Notion Tab in Seoul and Busan. These are the two largest cities in South Korea and have a high-density population. Launching the Notion Tab in these cities will result in the greatest benefit for RAC Inc.

(Continued)

Figure 18.5   A Formal Report *(Continued)*

Slated for Success   11

Conclusions repeat points made in the report. Recommendations are actions the audience should take.

Some companies ask for Conclusions and Recommendations at the beginning of the report.

Conclusions and Recommendations

All of the research that we have done supports the decision to expand into South Korea. The government, economy, and culture criteria all received favorable recommendations for a total of 60%. Market possibilities and competition received half support for an additional 20%. Together, South Korea has earned 80% based on our criteria.

Therefore, we believe that RAC Inc. could profitably expand into South Korea. The Notion Tab is a high-quality product, and it will be easily integrated into this technologically advanced county. In conclusion, we recommend that RAC Inc. should expand into South Korea.

To ensure a successful expansion, JASS LLC recommends the following:

1. **RAC Inc. should establish its headquarters and manufacturing plant in Busan.**
   - Purchase a building to have a place to begin manufacturing the Notion Tab.
   - Educate RAC employees about South Korean culture and business practices before they begin working directly with South Koreans to avoid being disrespectful.
   - Explore hiring South Koreans; the available workforce is large.
   - Ensure that the Notion name is appropriate when translated into Korean. If not, change the name to better market the product.
   - Market and sell the product in both Busan and Seoul.

Numbering points makes it easier for the audience to follow and discuss them.

2. **After one year RAC should determine the acceptance and profitability of the expansion.**
   - Conduct a customer satisfaction survey with people who purchased the Notion Tab living
   - in Seoul and Busan to determine the acceptance of the product.
   Compare and contrast first-year sales with a competitor's similar product.

Make sure all items in a list are parallel.

3. **If the tablet is competitive and profitable, RAC Inc. should expand its product line into all large cities in South Korea.**
   - To gain an edge on the competition, create a marketing plan that will offer the Notion Tab
   - at some discount in the new cities.
   Explore integrating other RAC Inc. products into South Korea. These products could also be manufactured at the new manufacturing plant in Busan.

Because many readers turn to the "Recommendations" first, provide enough information so that the reason is clear all by itself. The ideas in this section must be logical extensions of the points made and supported in the body of the report.

Copy + Paste from beginning.

4-5 Sources
6 pages minimum.

Figure 18.5   A Formal Report *(Continued)*

Slated for Success   12

References

This report uses APA citation style.

Advameg, Inc. (2011). Culture of South Korea. *Countries and Their Cultures.*
    Retrieved April 2, 2011, from http://www.everyculture.com/Ja-Ma/South-Korea.html.

AFP. (2010, December 5). U.S., South Korea sign sweeping free-trade agreement. *Taipei Times.*
    Retrieved from http://www.taipeitimes.com/News/front/archives/2010/12/05/200349014.

Borland, J., & Kanellos, M. (2004, July 28). South Korea leads the way. *CNET News.*
    Retrieved from http://news.cnet.com/South-Korea-leads-the-way/2009-1034_3-5261393.html.

Central Intelligence Agency. (2011). *The world factbook: South Korea.* Retrieved March 18, 2011,
    from https://www.cia.gov/library/publications/the-world-factbook/geos/ks.html#.

Cho, J. (2006, February 12). Korea: Terrestrial-DMB adds color to Korean lifestyle. *Asia Media
    Archives.* Retrieved from http://www.asiamedia.ucla.edu/article-eastasia.asp?parentid=38998.

Grand National Party. (2011, April 1). In *Wikipedia.* Retrieved April 6, 2011, from
    http://en.wikipedia.org/wiki/Grand_National_Party.

iPad 2 specs. (2011). *OS X Daily.* Retrieved from http://osxdaily.com/2011/03/02/ipad-2-specs.

Kirk, D. (2001, July 26). World business briefing: Asia: South Korea: Shorter workweek. *New York
    Times.* Retrieved from http://www.nytimes.com/2001/07/26/business/world-business-
    briefing-asia-south-korea-shorter-workweek.html.

Koreans love their mobile phones. (2009, January 28). *Korean JoongAng Daily.* Retrieved from
    http://joongangdaily.joins.com/article/view.asp?aid=2900275.

KRWUS. (2011). *MSN Money.* Retrieved April 10, 2011, from
    http://investing.money.msn.com/investments/currency-exchange-rates/?symbol=%2fKRWUS.

KT. (2011, April 1). In *Wikipedia.* Retrieved April 2, 2011, from
    http://en.wikipedia.org/wiki/KT_%28telecommunication_company%29.

Kwintessential. (2010). *South Korea: Language, culture, customers and etiquette.* Retrieved from
    http://www.kwintessential.co.uk/resources/global-etiquette/south-korea-country-profile.html.

LG Corp. (2011, April 1). In *Wikipedia.* Retrieved April 2, 2011, from http://en.wikipedia.org/wiki/LG.

LG Slate full specifications and product details. (2011, February 2). *Gadgetian.* Retrieved
    April 3, 2011, from http: //gadgetian.com/7069/lg-g-slate-t-mobile-specs-price/.

LG Telecom. (2010, November 29). In *Wikipedia.* Retrieved April 2, 2011, from
    http://en.wikipedia.org/wiki/LG_Telecom.

Life in Korea. (n.d.). *Cultural spotlight.* Retrieved March 31, 2011, from
    http://www.lifeinkorea.com/Culture/spotlight.cfm.

Compare this list of sources with those in the proposal. Notice how the authors had to adjust the list as they completed research.

*List all the printed and online sources cited in your report.
Do not list sources you used for background but did not cite.*

(Continued)

Figure 18.5   A Formal Report *(Concluded)*

Slated for Success   13

Manyin, M. E. (2007). *The proposed South Korea–U.S. free trade agreement.* Washington, DC:
    CRS of Congress.

Office of the U.S. Trade Representative. (2011, February 10). Korea–U.S. free trade agreement. *Executive
    Office of the President: Office of the United States Trade Representative.* Retrieved April 3,
    2011, from http://www.ustr.gov/trade-agreements/free-trade-agreements/korus-fta.

Ogg, E. (2010, May 28). What makes a tablet a tablet? *CNet News.* Retrieved March 23, 2011, from
    http://news.cnet.com/8301-31021_3-20006077-260.html?tag=newsLeadStoriesArea.1.

Olson, P. (2008, May 21). The world's hardest-working countries. *Forbes.* Retrieved from
    http://www.forbes.com/2008/05/21/labor-market-workforce-lead-citizen-cx_po_0521
    countries.html.

Park, K. (2009, March 3). Empty containers clog Busan port as trade slumps. *Bloomberg.* Retrieved
    from http://www.bloomberg.com/apps/news?pid=newsarchive&sid=ah2Znx0vQ580.

Samsung. (2011, April 5). In *Wikipedia.* Retrieved April 8, 2011, from http://en.wikipedia.org/
    wiki/Samsung

Samsung Galaxy Tab. (2011, March 22). Retrieved from
    http://www.phonearena.com/phones/Samsung-GALAXY-Tab-8.9_id5333.

Settimi, C. (2010, September 1). Asia's 200 best under a billion. *Forbes.* Retrieved from
    http://www.forbes.com/2010/09/01/bub-200-intro-asia-under-billion-10-small-companies.html.

SK Telecom. (2011, April 8). In *Wikipedia.* Retrieved April 10, 2011, from
    http://en.wikipedia.org/wiki/SK_Telecom.

South Korea: Political structure. (2009, June 11). *The Economist.* Retrieved from
    http://www.economist.com/node/13805244.

South Korea's GDP Growth. (2010, May 28). In *Wikipedia.* Retrieved April 10, 2011, from
    http://en.wikipedia.org/wiki/File:South_Korea's_GDP_(PPP)_growth_from_1911_to_2008.png.

U.S. Bureau of Labor of Statistics. (2008, March). "Around the world in eight charts." Retrieved
    from http://www.bls.gov/spotlight/2008/around_the_world/.

U.S. Department of State. (2010, December 10). *Background note: South Korea.* Retrieved March
    21, 2011, from http://www.state.gov/r/pa/ei/bgn/2800.htm.

World Bank Group. (2011a). Ease of doing business in Korea, Rep. *Doing Business: Measuring
    Business Regulations.* Retrieved from http://www.doingbusiness.org/data/
    exploreeconomies/korea/.

World Bank Group (2011b). Ease of doing business in United States. *Doing Business: Measuring
    Business Regulations.*Retrieved from http://www.doingbusiness.org/data/
    exploreeconomies/united-states/.

World Business Culture. (n.d.). *Doing business in South Korea.* Retrieved March 22, 2011, from
    http://www.worldbusinessculture.com/Business-in-South-Korea.html.

Title Page

The title page of a report usually contains four items: the title of the report, the person or organization for whom the report is prepared, the person or group who prepared the report, and the release date. Some title pages also contain a brief summary or abstract of the contents of the report; some title pages contain decorative artwork.

The title of the report should be as informative as possible. Like subject lines, report titles are straightforward.

Poor title: New Plant Site

Better title: Eugene, Oregon, Site for the New Kemco Plant

Large organizations that issue many reports may use two-part titles to make it easier to search for reports electronically. For example, U.S. government report titles first give the agency sponsoring the report, then the title of that particular report.

> Small Business Administration: Management Practices Have Improved for the Women's Business Center Program

In many cases, the title will state the recommendation in the report: "Why the United Nations Should Establish a Seed Bank." However, the title should omit recommendations when

- The reader will find the recommendations hard to accept.
- Putting all the recommendations in the title would make it too long.
- The report does not offer recommendations.

If the title does not contain the recommendation, it normally indicates what problem the report tries to solve or the topic the report discusses.
Eliminate any unnecessary words:

Wordy: Report of a Study on Ways to Market Life Insurance to Urban Professional People Who Are in Their Mid-40s

Better: Marketing Life Insurance to the Mid-40s Urban Professional

The identification of the receiver of the report normally includes the name of the person who will make a decision based on the report, his or her job title, the organization's name, and its location (city, state, and zip code). Government reports often omit the person's name and simply give the organization that authorized the report.

If the report is prepared primarily by one person, the *Prepared by* section will have that person's name, his or her title, the organization, and its location (city, state, and zip code). In internal reports, the organization and location are usually omitted if the report writer works at the headquarters office.

If several people write the report, government reports normally list all their names, using a separate sheet of paper if the group working on the report is large. Practices in business differ. In some organizations, all the names are listed; in others, the division to which they belong is listed; in still others, the name of the chair of the group appears.

The **release date,** the date the report will be released to the public, is usually the date the report is scheduled for discussion by the decision makers. The report is frequently due four to six weeks before the release date so that the decision makers can review the report before the meeting.

If you have the facilities and the time, try using type variations, color, and artwork to create a visually attractive and impressive title page. However, a plain typed page is acceptable. The format in Figure 18.5 will enable you to create an acceptable typed title page.

Letter or Memo of Transmittal

Use a letter of transmittal if you are not a regular employee of the organization for which you prepare the report; use a memo if you are a regular employee.

The transmittal has several purposes: to transmit the report, to orient the reader to the report, and to build a good image of the report and of the writer. An informal writing style is appropriate for a transmittal even when the style in the report is more formal. A professional transmittal helps you create a good image of yourself and enhances your credibility. Personal statements are appropriate in the transmittal, even though they would not be acceptable in the report itself.

Organize the transmittal in this way:

1. **Transmit the report.**   Tell when and by whom it was authorized and the purpose it was to fulfill.
2. **Summarize your conclusions and recommendations.**   If the recommendations will be easy for the audience to accept, put them early in the transmittal. If they will be difficult, summarize the findings and conclusions before the recommendations.
3. **Mention any points of special interest in the report. Show how you surmounted minor problems you encountered in your investigation. Thank people who helped you.**   These optional items can build goodwill and enhance your credibility.
4. **Point out additional research that is necessary, if any.**   Sometimes your recommendation cannot be implemented until further work is done. If you'd be interested in doing that research, or if you'd like to implement the recommendations, say so.
5. **Thank the audience for the opportunity to do the work and offer to answer questions.**   Provide contact information. Even if the report has not been fun to do, expressing satisfaction in doing the project is expected. Saying that you'll answer questions about the report is a way of saying that you won't charge the audience your normal hourly fee to answer questions (one more reason to make the report clear!).

The letter of transmittal on page i of Figure 18.5 uses this pattern of organization.

Table of Contents

In the table of contents, list the headings exactly as they appear in the body of the report. If the report is less than 25 pages, you'll probably list all the levels of headings. In a long report, pick a level and put all the headings at that level and above in the table of contents.

Page ii of Figure 18.5 shows the table of contents.

List of Illustrations

A list of illustrations enables audiences to refer to your visuals.

Report visuals comprise both tables and figures. *Tables* are words or numbers arranged in rows and columns. *Figures* are everything else: bar graphs, pie charts, flow charts, maps, drawings, photographs, computer printouts, and so on. Tables and figures may be numbered independently, so you may have both a Table 1 and a Figure 1. In a report with maps and graphs but no other visuals, the visuals are sometimes called Map 1 and Graph 1. Whatever you call the illustrations, list them in the order in which they appear in the report; give the name of each visual as well as its number.

See Chapter 16 for information about how to design and label visuals.

Executive Summary

An **executive summary** or **abstract** tells the audience what the document is about. It summarizes the recommendation of the report and the reasons for the recommendation or describes the topics the report discusses and indicates the depth of the discussion. It should be clear even to people who will read only the abstract.

A good abstract is easy to read, concise, and clear. Edit your abstract carefully to tighten your writing and eliminate any unnecessary words.

Wordy: The report describes two types of business jargon, *businessese* and *reverse gobbledygook*. It gives many examples of each of these and points out how their use can be harmful.

Tight: The report describes and illustrates two harmful types of business jargon, *businessese* and *reverse gobbledygook*.

Abstracts generally use a more formal style than other forms of business writing. Avoid contractions and colloquialisms. Try to avoid using the second-person *you*. Because reports may have many different audiences, *you* may become inaccurate. It's OK to use exactly the same words in the abstract and the report.

Summary abstracts present the logic skeleton of the report: the thesis or recommendation and its proof. Use a summary abstract to give the most useful information in the shortest space.

> To market life insurance to mid-40s urban professionals, Interstate Fidelity Insurance should advertise in upscale publications and use direct mail.
>
> Network TV and radio are not cost-efficient for reaching this market. This group comprises a small percentage of the prime-time network TV audience and a minority of most radio station listeners. They tend to discard newspapers and general-interest magazines quickly, but many of them keep upscale periodicals for months or years. Magazines with high percentages of readers in this group include *Architectural Digest*, *Bon Appetit*, *Forbes*, *Golf Digest*, *Metropolitan Home*, *Southern Living*, and *Smithsonian*.
>
> Any advertising campaign needs to overcome this group's feeling that they already have the insurance they need. One way to do this would be to encourage them to check the coverage their employers provide and to calculate the cost of their children's expenses through college graduation. Insurance plans that provide savings and tax benefits as well as death benefits might also be appealing.

One way to start composing an abstract is to write a sentence outline. A **sentence outline** not only uses complete sentences rather than words or phrases but also contains the thesis sentence or recommendation and the evidence that proves that point. Combine the sentences into paragraphs, adding transitions if necessary, and you'll have your abstract.

Descriptive abstracts indicate what topics the report covers and how deeply it goes into each topic, but they do not summarize what the report says about each topic. Phrases that describe the report ("this report covers," "it includes,"

Executive Summary of a Government Plan

On February 18, 2009, the Obama administration announced a "Homeowner Affordability and Stability" plan to counter the home mortgage crisis. The executive summary of the plan—given to the press—included the following:

- First, a statement of background, which included bullet points listing the effects of the crisis (for example, that nearly 6 million households will face foreclosure), and ending with the purpose of the plan (that the plan will help nearly 7 to 9 million families to "restructure" their mortgages to avoid foreclosure).

- Then, the two main components of the plan ("affordability" and "stability") together with their subcomponents (a few subcomponents are given below as examples):

- "Affordability"
  - "Enabling refinancing"
  - "Reducing monthly payments"

- "Stability"
  - "Helping homeowners stay in their homes"
  - "Not aiding speculators"
  - "Protecting neighborhoods"

The summary provided numbers and, where appropriate, examples to inform and explain the plan. A busy reader—or one who wanted to know the broad contours of the plan without going through its nuts and bolts—would likely benefit from reading the summary before deciding whether to read the whole plan.

Adapted from "Homeowner Affordability and Stability Plan Executive Summary," *BusinessWeek*, February 18, 2009, http://www.businessweek.com/bwdaily/dnflash/content/feb2009/db20090218_403370.htm.

596   **Part 5**   Proposals and Reports

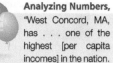

"it summarizes," "it concludes") are marks of a descriptive abstract. An additional mark of a descriptive abstract is that the audience can't tell what the report says about the topics it covers.

> This report recommends ways Interstate Fidelity Insurance could market insurance to mid-40s urban professionals. It examines demographic and psychographic profiles of the target market. Survey results are used to show attitudes toward insurance. The report suggests some appeals that might be successful with this market.

Introduction

The **Introduction** of the report always contains a statement of purpose and scope and may include all the parts in the following list.

- **Purpose.** The purpose statement identifies the problem the report addresses, the technical investigations it summarizes, and the rhetorical purpose (to explain, to recommend).
- **Scope.** The scope statement identifies how broad an area the report surveys. For example, Company XYZ is losing money on its line of computers. Does the report investigate the quality of the computers? The advertising campaign? The cost of manufacturing? The demand for computers? A scope statement allows the reader to evaluate the report on appropriate grounds.
- **Assumptions.** Assumptions in a report are like assumptions in geometry: statements whose truth you assume, and which you use to prove your final point. If they are wrong, the conclusion will be wrong too.

  For example, to plan cars that will be built five years from now, an automobile manufacturer commissions a report on young adults' attitudes toward cars. The recommendations would be based on assumptions both about gas prices and about the economy. If gas prices radically rose or fell, the kinds of cars young adults wanted would change. If there were a major recession, people wouldn't be able to buy new cars.

  Almost all reports require assumptions. A good report spells out its assumptions so that audiences can make decisions more confidently.
- **Methods.** If you conducted surveys, focus groups, or interviews, you need to tell how you chose your subjects, and how, when, and where they were interviewed. If the discussion of your methodology is more than a paragraph or two, you should probably make it a separate section in the body of the report rather than including it in the introduction. Reports based on scientific experiments usually put the methods section in the body of the report, not in the Introduction.

  If your report is based solely on library or online research, provide a brief description of significant sources. See Appendix C on how to cite and document sources.
- **Limitations.** Limitations make your recommendations less valid or valid only under certain conditions. Limitations usually arise because time or money constraints haven't permitted full research. For example, a campus pizza restaurant considering expanding its menu may ask for a report but not have enough money to take a random sample of students and townspeople. Without a random sample, the writer cannot generalize from the sample to the larger population.

  Many recommendations are valid only for a limited time. For instance, a campus store wants to know what kinds of clothing will appeal to college men. The recommendations will remain valid for only a short time: three years from now, styles and tastes may have changed, and the clothes that would sell best now may no longer be in demand.

■ **Criteria.** The criteria section outlines the factors or standards that you are considering and the relative importance of each. If a company is choosing a city for a new office, is the cost of office space more or less important than the availability of skilled workers? Check with your audience before you write the draft to make sure that your criteria match those of your audiences.

■ **Definitions.** Many reports define key terms in the introduction. For instance, a report on unauthorized Internet use by employees might define what is meant by "unauthorized use." A report on the corporate dress code might define such codes broadly to include general appearance, so it could include items such as tattoos, facial piercings, and general cleanliness. Also, if you know that some members of your primary, or secondary audience will not understand technical terms, define them. If you have only a few definitions, you can put them in the Introduction. If you have many terms to define, put a **glossary** in an appendix. Refer to it in the Introduction so that audiences know that you've provided it.

Background or History

Formal reports usually have a section that gives the background of the situation or the history of the problem. Even though the current audience for the report probably knows the situation, reports are filed and consulted years later. These later audiences will probably not know the background, although it may be crucial for understanding the options that are possible.

In some cases, the history section may cover many years. For example, a report recommending that a U.S. hotel chain open hotels in Romania may give the history of that country for at least several decades. In other cases, the background section is much briefer, covering only a few years or even just the immediate situation.

The purpose of most reports is rarely to provide a history of the problem. Do not let the background section achieve undue length.

Body

The body of the report is usually its longest section. Analyze causes of the problem and offer possible solutions. Present your argument with all its evidence and data. Data that are necessary to follow the argument are included with appropriate visuals and explanatory text. Extended data sets, such as large tables and long questionnaires, are generally placed in appendixes. It is particularly important in the body that you use headings, forecasting statements, and topic sentences to help lead your audience through the text. Audiences will also appreciate clear, concise, and engaging prose. Remember to cite your sources (see Appendix C) and to refer in the text to all visuals and appendixes.

Conclusions and Recommendations

Conclusions summarize points you have made in the body of the report; **Recommendations** are action items that would solve or ameliorate the problem. These sections are often combined if they are short: *Conclusions and Recommendations*. No new information should be included in this section.

Many audiences turn to the recommendations section first; some organizations ask that recommendations be presented early in the report. Number the recommendations to make it easy for people to discuss them. If the recommendations will seem difficult or controversial, give a brief paragraph of rationale after each recommendation. If they'll be easy for the audience to accept, you can simply list them without comments or reasons. The recommendations will also be in the executive summary and perhaps in the title and the transmittal.

SUMMARY OF KEY POINTS

- Good reports begin with good data. Make sure your data come from reliable sources.
- Analyze report numbers and text for accuracy and logic.
- Choose an appropriate organizational pattern for your information and purposes. The most common patterns are comparison/contrast, problem-solving, elimination of alternatives, SWOT analysis, general to particular, particular to general, geographic or spatial, functional, and chronological.
- Reports use the same style as other business documents, with three exceptions:
  1. Reports use a more formal style, without contractions or slang, than do many letters and memos.
  2. Reports rarely use the word *you*.
  3. Reports should include all the definitions and documents needed to understand the recommendations.
- To create good report style,
  1. Use clear, engaging writing.
  2. Keep repetition to a minimum.
  3. Introduce all sources and visuals.
  4. Use forecasting, transitions, topic sentences, and headings.
- **Headings** are single words short phrases, or complete sentences that describe all of the material under them until the next heading. **Talking heads** tell the audience what to expect in each section.
- Headings must use the same grammatical structure. Subheads under a heading must be parallel to each other but do not necessarily have to be parallel to subheads under other headings.
- The title page of a report usually contains four items: the title of the report, whom the report is prepared for, whom it is prepared by, and the date.
- If the report is 25 pages or less, list all the headings in the table of contents. In a long report, pick a level and put all the headings at that level and above in the contents.
- Organize the transmittal in this way:
  1. Release the report.
  2. Summarize your conclusions and recommendations.
  3. Mention any points of special interest in the report. Show how you surmounted minor problems you encountered in your investigation. Thank people who helped you.
  4. Point out additional research that is necessary, if any.
  5. Thank the reader for the opportunity to do the work and offer to answer questions.

- **Summary abstracts** present the logic skeleton of the article: the thesis or recommendation and its proof. **Descriptive abstracts** indicate what topics the article covers and how deeply it goes into each topic, but do not summarize what the article says about each topic.

- A good abstract or executive summary is easy to read, concise, and clear. A good abstract can be understood by itself, without the report or references.

- The **Introduction** of the report always contains a statement of purpose and scope. The **Purpose** statement identifies the organizational problem the report addresses, the technical investigations it summarizes, and the rhetorical purpose (to explain, to recommend). The **Scope** statement identifies how broad an area the report surveys. The introduction may also include **Limitations,** problems or factors that limit the validity of your recommendations; **Assumptions,** statements whose truth you assume, and which you use to prove your final point; **Methods,** an explanation of how you gathered your data; **Criteria** used to weigh the factors in the decision; and **Definitions** of terms audiences may not know.

- A **Background** or **History** section is usually included because reports are filed and may be consulted years later by people who no longer remember the original circumstances.

- The **Body** of the report, usually the longest section, analyzes causes of the problem and offers possible solutions. It presents your argument with all evidence and data.

- **Conclusions** summarize points made in the body of the report; **Recommendations** are action items that would solve or ameliorate the problem. These sections are often combined if they are short.

CHAPTER 18   Exercises and Problems

Go to www.mhhe.com/locker10e for additional Exercises and Problems.

18.1   Reviewing the Chapter

1. What are some criteria to check to ensure you have quality data? (LO 18-1)

2. What kinds of patterns should you look for in your data and text? (LO 18-1)

3. What are some guidelines for choosing information for reports? (LO 18-2)

4. Name seven basic patterns for organizing reports. For four of them, explain when they would be particularly effective or ineffective. (LO 18-3)

5. What are three ways that style in reports differs from conventional business communication style? (LO 18-4)

6. Name four good writing principles that are particularly important in reports. (LO 18-4)

7. How do you introduce sources in the text of the report? (LO 18-4)

8. Why should reports try to have a topic sentence at the beginning of each paragraph? (LO 18-4)

9. What are the characteristics of an effective report title? (LO 18-5)

10. What goes in the letter of transmittal? (LO 18-5)

11. What is the difference between summary and descriptive abstracts? (LO 18-5)

12. What goes in the introduction of a report? (LO 18-5)

13. What is the difference between conclusions and recommendations? (LO 18-5)

18.2   Identifying Assumptions and Limitations

Indicate whether each of the following would be an assumption or a limitation in a formal report.

a. Report on Ways to Encourage More Students to Join XYZ Organization

   1. I surveyed a judgment sample rather than a random sample.

   2. These recommendations are based on the attitudes of current students. Presumably, students in the next several years will have the same attitudes and interests.

b. Report on the Feasibility of Building Hilton Hotels in Romania

1. This report is based on the expectation that the country will be politically stable.
2. All of my information is based on library research. The most recent articles were published two months ago; much of the information was published a year ago or more. Therefore some of my information may be out of date.
c. Report on Car-Buying Preferences of Young Adults

1. These recommendations may change if the cost of gasoline increases dramatically or if there is another deep recession.
2. This report is based on a survey of adults ages 20 to 24 in California, Texas, Illinois, Ontario, and Massachusetts.
3. These preferences are based on the cars now available. If a major technical or styling innovation occurs, preferences may change.

18.3   Revising an Executive Summary

The following Executive Summary is poorly organized and too long. Rearrange information to make it more effective. Cut information that does not belong in the summary. You may use different words as you revise.

In this report I will discuss the communication problems which exist at Rolling Meadows Golf Club. The problems discussed will deal with channels of communication. The areas which are causing problems are internal. Radios would solve these internal problems.

Taking a 15-minute drive on a golf cart in order to find the superintendent is a common occurrence. Starters and rangers need to keep in touch with the clubhouse to maintain a smooth flow of players around the course. The rangers have expressed an interest in being able to call the clubhouse for advice and support.

Purchasing two-channel FM radios with private channels would provide three advantages. First, radios would make the golf course safer by providing a means of notifying someone in the event of an emergency. Second, radios would make the staff more efficient by providing a faster channel of communication. Third, radios would enable clubhouse personnel to keep in touch with the superintendent, the rangers, and the starters.

During the week, radios can be carried by the superintendent, the golf pro, and another course worker. On weekends and during tournaments, one radio will be used by the golf professional. The other two will be used by one starter and one ranger. Three radios is the minimum needed to meet basic communication needs. A fourth radio would provide more flexibility for busy weekends and during tournaments.

Tekk T-20 radios can be purchased from Page-Com for $129 each. These radios have the range and options needed for use on the golf course. Radios are durable and easy to service. It is possible that another brand might be even less expensive.

Rolling Meadows Golf Club should purchase four radios. They will cost under $600 and can be paid for from the current equipment budget.

18.4   Comparing Report Formats

Locate five business or organizational reports (or white papers as they're sometimes called) on the Internet. A good online collection of organizational reports is the website of the Council on Library and Information Resources (CLIR) accessible at http://www.clir.org/pubs/reports/. Additionally, you can find reports linked from the websites of the Fortune 500 organizations, or you can search for them on Google using keywords such as "reports," "business reports," "company reports," or "organizational reports."

The reports you find could be about the organizations' environmental sustainability efforts, their products, or any other aspect of their operations.

Compare the organization (the reports' contents or the way they're structured) of the five reports you select. What similarities and differences do you see in the formatting of all these reports? Make a table of your findings. Discuss your findings in small groups.

18.5   Comparing Style in Annual Reports

Locate two annual reports on the Internet. A good source is Report Watch, http://www.reportwatch.net/ Compare the style of the two reports. Here are some questions to get you started:

1. How do they use visuals to keep attention?
2. What differences do you see in the letters from the CEOs?
3. How do they present number-heavy information? Do they rely mainly on tables and graphs? Do they give prose summaries?
4. Is the writing easy to understand?
5. Do you see places where negative information is given a positive spin?
6. Is one report easier to understand than the other? Why?
7. Is one report more interesting than the other? Why?
8. Is one report more convincing than the other? Why?

As your instructor directs,

a. Work in small groups to do your comparison. Share your findings in a five-minute oral presentation to the class.
b. Work in small groups to do your comparison. Share your findings in a memo posted on the class website.
c. Work individually to do your comparison. Share your findings in a memo to your instructor.

18.6   Evaluating a Report from Your Workplace

Consider the following aspects of a report from your workplace:

■ Content. How much information is included? How is it presented?
■ Emphasis. What points are emphasized? What points are deemphasized? What verbal and visual techniques are used to highlight or minimize information?
■ Visuals and layout. Are visuals used effectively? Are they accurate and free from chartjunk? What image do the pictures and visuals create? Are color and white space used effectively? (See Chapter 16 on visuals.)

As your instructor directs,

a. Write a memo to your instructor analyzing the report.
b. Join with a small group of students to compare and contrast several reports. Present your evaluation in an informal group report.
c. Present your evaluation orally to the class.

18.7   Analyzing and Writing Reports

Reread the sidebar about the Pew Internet and American Life Project at http://www.pewinternet.org/ on page 575. Go to the website and browse through the reports. Select a report and answer the following questions:

■ Who is the report's audience?
■ What is its purpose?
■ How were the data collected?
■ What did the data collection measure?
■ Why was the data collection important?

Given your analysis of the report's audience, purpose, and data collection, consider the strategies used in the report to convey the information. Answer these questions:

■ What tone did the writer adopt?
■ How was the report organized and designed to meet the needs of the audience?
■ What language choices did the writer make?

Finally, examine the press releases that are written about the report (the press releases for each report are included as links) for the ways the information in the report is adapted for a different audience and purpose. How do the content, organization, tone, and language choices differ from those of the original report? Do you see any ethical issues involved in condensing the report into a press release?

As your instructor directs,

■ Write a report of your findings to your instructor.
■ Present your findings to the class using presentation software.

18.8   Preparing an Information Report

Visit the website of the Global Reporting Initiative (http://www.globalreporting.org/Home), a group of analysts from various industries and professions that is committed to advancing the cause of socially responsible reporting by organizations. Prepare an information report, either as a memo to your instructor or as a PowerPoint presentation for the class, describing the organization, the people behind it, their guidelines, their work, and their impact on the corporate world.

18.9   Recommending Action

Write a report recommending an action that your unit or organization should take. Possibilities include

- Buying more equipment for your department.
- Hiring an additional worker for your department.
- Making your organization more family-friendly.
- Making a change that will make the organization more efficient.
- Making changes to improve accessibility for customers or employees with disabilities.

Address your report to the person who would have the power to approve your recommendation.

As your instructor directs,

a. Create a document or presentation to achieve the goal.

b. Write a memo to your instructor describing the situation at your workplace and explaining your rhetorical choices (medium, strategy, tone, wording, graphics or document design, and so forth).

18.10   Writing a Recommendation Report

Write a report evaluating two or more alternatives. Possible topics include the following:

1. Should students in your major start a monthly newsletter?

2. Should your student organization write an annual report? Would doing so help the next year's officers?

3. Should your student organization create a wiki, blog, or newsletter to facilitate communication with a constituency?

4. Should your workplace create a newsletter to communicate internally?

5. Should a local restaurant open another branch? Where should it be?

In designing your study, identify the alternatives, define your criteria for selecting one option over others, carefully evaluate each alternative, and recommend the best course of action.

18.11   Writing an Informative or Closure Report

Write an informative report on one of the following topics.

1. What should a U.S. manager know about dealing with workers from _____ [you fill in the country or culture]? What factors do and do not motivate people in this group? How do they show respect and deference? Are they used to a strong hierarchy or to an egalitarian setting? Do they normally do one thing at once or many things? How important is clock time and being on time? What factors lead them to respect someone? Age? Experience? Education? Technical knowledge? Wealth? Or what? What conflicts or miscommunications may arise between workers from this culture and other workers due to cultural differences? Are people from this culture similar in these beliefs and behaviors, or is there lots of variation?

2. What benefits do companies offer? To get information, check the web pages of three companies in the same industry. Information about benefits is usually on the page about working for the company.

3. Describe an ethical dilemma encountered by workers in a specific organization. What is the

background of the situation? What competing loyalties exist? In the past, how have workers responded? How has the organization responded? Have whistle-blowers been rewarded or punished? What could the organization do to foster ethical behavior?

4. Describe a problem or challenge encountered by an organization where you've worked. Describe the problem, show why it needed to be solved, tell who did what to try to solve it, and tell how successful the efforts were. Possibilities include

- How the organization is implementing work teams, downsizing, or changing organizational culture.
- How the organization uses e-mail or voice mail.
- How the organization uses telecommuting.
- How managers deal with stress, make ethical choices, or evaluate subordinates.
- How the organization is responding to changing U.S. demographics, the Americans with Disabilities Act, or international competition and opportunities.

18.12   Writing a Consultant's Report—Restaurant Tipping

Your consulting company has been asked to conduct a report for Diamond Enterprises, which runs three national chains: FishStix, The Bar-B-Q Pit, and Morrie's.

All are medium-priced, family-friendly restaurants. The CEO is thinking of replacing optional tips with a 15% service fee automatically added to bills.

You read articles in trade journals, surveyed a random sample of 200 workers in each of the chains, and conducted an e-mail survey of the 136 restaurant managers. Here are your findings:

1. Trade journals point out that the Internal Revenue Service (IRS) audits restaurants if it thinks that servers underreport tips. Dealing with an audit is time-consuming and often results in the restaurant's having to pay penalties and interest.

2. Only one Morrie's restaurant has actually been audited by the IRS. Management was able to convince the IRS that servers were reporting tips accurately. No penalty was assessed. Management spent $1,000 on CPA and legal fees and spent over 80 hours of management time gathering data and participating in the audit.

3. Restaurants in Europe already add a service fee (usually 15%) to the bill. Patrons can add more if they choose. Local custom determines whether tips are expected and how much they should be. In Germany, for example, it is more usual to round up the bill (from 27 € to 30 €, for example) than to figure a percentage.

4. If the restaurant collected a service fee, it could use the income to raise wages for cooks and hosts and pay for other benefits, such as health insurance, rather than giving all the money to servers and bussers.

5. Morrie's servers tend to be under 25 years of age. FishStix employs more servers over 25, who are doing this for a living. The Bar-B-Q Pit servers are students in college towns.

6. In all three chains, servers oppose the idea. Employees other than servers generally support it.

	Retain tips	Change to service fee added to bill	Don't care
FishStix servers ($n = 115$)	90%	7%	3%
Bar-B-Q servers ($n = 73$)	95%	0%	5%
Morrie's servers ($n = 93$)	85%	15%	0%
Morrie's nonservers ($n = 65$)	25%	70%	5%
FishStix nonservers ($n = 46$)	32%	32%	37%
Bar-B-Q nonservers ($n = 43$)	56%	20%	25%

(Numbers do not add up to 100% due to rounding.)

7. Servers said that it was important to go home with money in their pockets (92%), that their expertise increased food sales and should be rewarded (67%), and that if a service fee replaced tips they would be likely to look for another job (45%). Some (17%) thought that if the manager distributed service-fee income, favoritism rather than the quality of work would govern how much tip income they got. Most (72%) thought that customers would not add anything beyond the 15% service fee, and many (66%) thought that total tip income would decrease and their own portion of that income would decrease (90%).

8. Managers generally support the change.

	Retain tips	Change to service fee added to bill	Don't care
FishStix managers ($n = 44$)	20%	80%	0%
Bar-B-Q managers ($n = 13$)	33%	67%	0%
Morrie's managers ($n = 58$)	55%	45%	0%

9. Comments from managers include: "It isn't fair for a cook with eight years of experience to make only $12 an hour while a server can make $25 an hour in just a couple of months," and "I could have my pick of employees if I offered health insurance."

10. Morale at Bar-B-Q seems low. This is seen in part in the low response rate to the survey.

11. In a tight employment market, some restaurants might lose good servers if they made the change. However, hiring cooks and other nonservers would be easier.

12. The current computer systems in place can handle figuring and recording the service fee. Since bills are printed by computer, an additional line could be added. Allocating the service-fee income could take extra managerial time, especially at first.

Write the report.

18.13   Writing a Library Research Report

Write a library research report.

As your instructor directs,

Turn in the following documents:

a. The approved proposal.

b. Two copies of the report, including

Cover.

Title Page.

Letter or Memo of Transmittal.

Table of Contents.

List of Illustrations.

Executive Summary or Abstract.

Body (Introduction, all information, recommendations). Your instructor may specify a minimum length, a minimum number or kind of sources, and a minimum number of visuals.

References or Works Cited.

c. Your notes and at least one preliminary draft.

Choose one of the following topics.

1. **Selling to College Students.** Your car dealership is located in a university town, but the manager doubts that selling cars to college students will be profitable. You agree that college incomes are low to nonexistent, but you see some students driving late-model cars. Recommend to the dealership's manager whether to begin marketing to college students, suggesting some tactics that would be effective.

2. **Advertising on the Internet.** You work on a team developing a marketing plan to sell high-end sunglasses. Your boss is reluctant to spend money for online advertising because she has heard that the money is mostly wasted. Also, she associates the ads with spam, which she detests. Recommend whether the company should devote some of its advertising budget to online ads. Include samples of online advertising that supports your recommendation.

3. **Improving Job Interview Questions.** Turnover among the sales force has been high, and your boss believes the problem is that your company has been hiring the wrong people. You are part of a team investigating the problem, and your assignment is to evaluate the questions used in job interviews. Human resource personnel use tried-and-true questions like "What is your greatest strength?" and "What is your greatest weakness?" The sales manager has some creative alternatives, such as asking candidates to solve logic puzzles and seeing how they perform under stress by taking frequent phone calls during the interview. You are to evaluate the current interviewing approaches and propose changes that would improve hiring decisions.

4. **Selling to Walmart.** Your company has a reputation for making high-quality lamps and ceiling fans sold in specialty stores. Although the company has been profitable, it could grow much faster if it sold through Walmart. Your boss is excited about her recent discussions with that retailer, but she has heard from associates that Walmart can be a demanding customer. She asked you to find out if there is a downside to selling through Walmart and, if so, whether manufacturers can afford to say no to a business deal with the retail giant.

5. **Making College Affordable.** The senator you work for is concerned about fast-rising costs of a college education. Students say they cannot afford their tuition bills. Colleges say they are making all the cuts they can without compromising the quality of education. In order to propose a bill that would help make college affordable for those who are qualified to attend, the senator has asked you to research alternatives for easing the problem. Recommend one or two measures the senator could include in a bill for the Senate to vote on.

6. With your instructor's permission, investigate a topic of your choice.

18.14 Writing a Recommendation Report

Write an individual or a team report.

As your instructor directs,

Turn in the following documents:

1. The approved proposal.
2. Two copies of the report, including
   Cover.
   Title Page.
   Letter or Memo of Transmittal.
   Table of Contents.
   List of Illustrations.
   Executive Summary or Abstract.
   Body (Introduction, all information, recommendations). Your instructor may specify a minimum length, a minimum number or kind of sources, and a minimum number of visuals.
   Appendixes if useful or relevant.
3. Your notes and at least one preliminary draft.

Pick one of the following topics.

1. **Improving Customer Service.** Many customers find that service is getting poorer and workers are getting ruder. Evaluate the service in a local store, restaurant, or other organization. Are customers made to feel comfortable? Is workers' communication helpful, friendly, and respectful? Are workers knowledgeable about products and services? Do they sell them effectively? Write a report analyzing the quality of service and recommending what the organization should do to improve.

2. **Recommending Courses for the Local Community College.** Businesses want to be able to send workers to local community colleges to upgrade their skills; community colleges want to prepare students to enter the local workforce. What skills are in demand in your community? What courses at what levels should the local community college offer?

3. **Improving Sales and Profits.** Recommend ways a small business in your community can increase sales and profits. Focus on one or more of the following: the products or services it offers, its advertising, its decor, its location, its accounting methods, its cash management, or any other aspect that may be keeping the company from achieving its potential. Address your report to the owner of the business.

4. **Increasing Student Involvement.** How could an organization on campus persuade more of the

students who are eligible to join or to become active in its programs? Do students know that it exists? Is it offering programs that interest students? Is it retaining current members? What changes should the organization make? Address your report to the officers of the organization.

5. **Evaluating a Potential Employer.**   What training is available to new employees? How soon is the average entry-level person promoted? How much travel and weekend work are expected? Is there a "busy season," or is the workload consistent year-round?

What fringe benefits are offered? What is the corporate culture? Is the climate nonracist and nonsexist? How strong is the company economically? How is it likely to be affected by current economic, demographic, and political trends? Address your report to the Placement Office on campus; recommend whether it should encourage students to work at this company.

6. With your instructor's permission, choose your own topic.

APPENDIX

A

Formatting Letters, Memos, and E-Mail Messages

Appendix Outline

Formats for Letters

Formats for Envelopes

Formats for Memos

Formats for E-Mail Messages

State and Province Abbreviations

Learning objective

After studying this appendix, you will know

LO A-1 Formats for letters.

LO A-2 Formats for envelopes.

LO A-3 Formats for memos.

LO A-4 Formats for e-mail messages.

Letters normally go to people outside your organization; **memos** go to other people in your organization. E-mails go to both audiences. Letters, memos, and e-mails do not necessarily differ in length, formality, writing style, or pattern of organization. However, letters, memos, and e-mails do differ in format. **Format** means the parts of a document and the way they are arranged on the page.

FORMATS FOR LETTERS   **LO A-1**

If your organization has a standard format for letters, use it.

Many organizations and writers choose one of three letter formats: **block format** (see Figure A.2), **modified block format** (see Figure A.3), or the **simplified format** (see Figure A.4). Your organization may make minor changes from the diagrams in margins or spacing.

Figure A.1 shows how the three formats differ.

Use the same level of formality in the **salutation**, or greeting, as you would in talking to someone on the phone: *Dear Glenn* if you're on a first-name basis, *Dear Mr. Helms* if you don't know the reader well enough to use the first name.

Some writers feel that the simplified format is better since the reader is not *Dear*. Omitting the salutation is particularly good when you do not know the reader's name or do not know which courtesy title to use. (For a full discussion on nonsexist salutations and salutations when you don't know the reader's name, see Chapter 3.) However, readers like to see their names. Since the simplified format omits the reader's name in the salutation, writers who use this format but who also want to be friendly often try to use the reader's name early in the body of the letter.

The simplified letter format is good in business-to-business mail, or in letters where you are writing to anyone who holds a job (admissions officer, customer service representative) rather than to a specific person. It is too cold and distancing for cultures that place a premium on relationships.

Sincerely and *Yours truly* are standard **complimentary closes**. When you are writing to people in special groups or to someone who is a friend as well as a business acquaintance, you may want to use a less formal close. Depending on the circumstances, the following informal closes might be acceptable: *Cordially, Thank you,* or even *Ciao*.

In **mixed punctuation**, a colon follows the salutation and a comma follows the close.

A **subject line** tells what the message is about. Subject lines are required in memos and e-mails; they are optional in letters. Good subject lines are specific, concise, and appropriate for your purposes and the response you expect from your reader:

Figure A.1   Comparing and Contrasting Letter Formats

	Block	**Modified block**	**Simplified**
Date and signature block	Lined up at left margin	Lined up $1/2$ or $2/3$ of the way over to the right	Lined up at left margin
Paragraph indentation	None	Optional	None
Salutation and complimentary close	Yes	Yes	None
Subject line	Optional	Rare	Yes
Lists, if any	Indented	Indented	At left margin
Writer's typed name	Upper- and lowercase	Upper- and lowercase	Full capital letters
Paragraph spacing	Single-spaced, double-space between	Single-spaced, double-space between	Single-spaced, double-space between

- When you have good news, put it in the subject line.
- When your information is neutral, summarize it concisely in the subject line.
- When your information is negative, use a negative subject line if the reader may not read the message or needs the information to act. Otherwise, use a neutral subject line.
- When you have a request that will be easy for the reader to grant, put either the subject of the request or a direct question in the subject line.
- When you must persuade a reluctant reader, use a common ground, a benefit, or a neutral subject line.

For examples of subject lines in each of these situations, see Chapters 9, 10, and 11.

A **reference line** refers the reader to the number used on the previous correspondence this letter replies to, or the order or invoice number this letter is about. Very large organizations use numbers on every piece of correspondence they send out so that it is possible to find quickly the earlier document to which an incoming letter refers.

All three formats can use headings, lists, and indented sections for emphasis.

Each of the three formats has advantages. Both block and simplified can be typed quickly since everything is lined up at the left margin. Block format is the format most frequently used for business letters; readers expect it. Modified block format creates a visually attractive page by moving the date and signature block over into what would otherwise be empty white space. Modified block is also a traditional format; readers are comfortable with it.

The examples of the three formats in Figures A.2–A.4 show one-page letters on company letterhead. **Letterhead** is preprinted stationery with the organization's name, logo, address, phone number, and frequently e-mail. Figure A.5 shows how to set up modified block format when you do not have letterhead. (It is also acceptable to use block format without letterhead.)

When your letter runs two or more pages, use a heading on the second page to identify it. Using the reader's name helps the writer, who may be printing out many letters at a time, to make sure the right second page gets in the envelope. The two most common formats are shown in Figures A.6, A.7, A.8, and

Figure A.2   Block Format on Letterhead

Northwest Hardware Warehouse

100 Freeway Exchange   Provo, UT 84610   (801) 555-4683   www.northwesthardware.com

Line up everything at left margin

3–6 spaces depending on length of letter

June 20, 2012

2–4 spaces

Mr. James E. Murphy, Accounts Payable   *Title could be on a separate line*
Salt Lake Equipment Rentals
5600 Wasatch Boulevard
Salt Lake City, Utah 84121   *zip code on same line*

1″–1½″

Use first name in salutation if you'd use it on the phone

Dear Jim: *Colon in mixed punctuation*

The following items totaling $393.09 are still open on your account.   ¶ *1 never has a heading*

Invoice #01R-784391 *Bold heading*

After the bill for this invoice arrived on May 14, you wrote saying that the material had not been delivered to you. On May 29, our Claims Department sent you a copy of the delivery receipt signed by an employee of Salt Lake Equipment. You have had proof of delivery for over three weeks, but your payment has not yet arrived.

1″, because right margin is justified

Please send a check for $78.42.

Single-space paragraphs
Double-space between paragraphs (one blank space)

Voucher #59351

Triple-space before a heading (2 blank spaces); double-space after the heading

Do not indent paragraphs

The reference line on your voucher #59351, dated June 16, indicates that it is the gross payment for invoice #01G-002345. However, the voucher was only for $1171.25, while the invoice amount was $1246.37. Please send a check for $75.12 to clear this item.

Voucher #55032

Voucher #55032, dated June 16, subtracts a credit for $239.55 from the amount due. Our records do not show that any credit is due on this voucher. Please send either an explanation or a check to cover the $239.55 immediately.

Total Amount Due   *Headings are optional in letters*

Please send a check for $393.09 to cover these three items and to bring your account up to date.

1–2 spaces

Sincerely,

2–4 spaces

Neil Hutchinson
Credit Representative

cc: Joan Stottlemyer, Credit Manager

Leave bottom margin of 6 spaces— more if letter is short

Figure A.3   Modified Block Format on Letterhead

Bay City Information Systems
151 Bayview Road • San Francisco, CA 81153 • (650) 405-7849 • www.baycity.com

3–6 spaces

September 15, 2012
Line up date with signature block
½ or ⅔ of the way over to the right

2–4 spaces

Ms. Mary E. Arcas
Personnel Director
Cyclops Communication Technologies
1050 South Sierra Bonita Avenue
Los Angeles, CA 90019 *Zip code on same line*

1"–1½"

Dear Ms. Arcas: *Colon in mixed punctuation*

Indenting ¶ is optional in modified block

Let me respond to your request for an evaluation of Colleen Kangas. Colleen was hired as a clerk-typist by Bay City Information Systems on April 4, 2010, and was promoted to Administrative Assistant on August 1, 2011. At her review in June, I recommended that she be promoted again. She is an intelligent young woman with good work habits and a good knowledge of computer software.

1", because right margin is justified

Single-space paragraphs

As an Adminstrative Assistant, Colleen not only handles routine duties such as processing time cards, ordering supplies, and entering data, but also screens calls for two marketing specialists, answers basic questions about Bay City Information Systems, compiles the statistics I need for my monthly reports, and investigates special assignments for me. In the past eight months, she has investigated freight charges, inventoried department hardware, and transferred files to archives. I need only to give her general directions: she has a knack for tracking down information quickly and summarizing it accurately.

Double-space between paragraphs (one blank line)

Although the department's workload has increased during the year, Colleen manages her time so that everything gets done on schedule. She is consistently poised and friendly under pressure. Her willingness to work overtime on occasion is particularly remarkable considering that she has been going to college part-time ever since she joined our firm.

At Bay City Information Systems, Colleen uses Microsoft Word, Excel, and Access software. She tells me that she also uses PowerPoint in her college classes.

If Colleen were staying in San Francisco, we would want to keep her. She has the potential either to become an Executive Secretary or to move into line or staff work, especially once she completes her degree. I recommend her highly.

1–2 spaces

Sincerely, *Comma in mixed punctuation*

Headings are optional in letters

2–4 spaces

Jeanne Cederlind

Jeanne Cederlind
Vice President, Marketing
jeanne_c@baycity.com

Line up signature block with date

1–4 spaces

Encl.: Evaluation Form for Colleen Kangas

Leave at least 6 spaces at bottom of page—more if letter is short

Figure A.4   Simplified Format on Letterhead

1500 Main Street   Iowa City, IA 52232   (319) 555-3113

↕ 3–6 spaces

Line up everything at left margin

August 24, 2012

↕ 2–4 spaces

←— 1"–1½"

Melinda Hamilton
Medical Services Division
Health Management Services, Inc.
4333 Edgewood Road, NE
Cedar Rapids, IA 52401

Triple-space (two blank spaces)   *Subject line in full capital letters*

REQUEST FOR INFORMATION ABOUT COMPUTER SYSTEMS

←— No salutation

We're interested in upgrading our computer system and would like to talk to one of your marketing representatives to see what would best meet our needs. We will use the following criteria to choose a system:

1.   Ability to use our current software and data files.

Double-space (one blank space) between items in list if any items are more than one line long

2.   Price, prorated on a three-year expected life.

3.   Ability to provide auxiliary services, e.g., controlling inventory of drugs and supplies, monitoring patients' vital signs, and processing insurance forms more quickly.

4.   Freedom from downtime.

Triple-space (two blank spaces) between list, next paragraph

Do not indent paragraphs

McFarlane Memorial Hospital has 50 beds for acute care and 75 beds for long-term care. In the next five years, we expect the number of beds to remain the same while outpatient care and emergency room care increase.

←— ¾"–1" when right margin is not justified →

Could we meet the first or the third week in September? We are eager to have the new system installed by Christmas if possible.

Please call me to schedule an appointment.

Headings are optional in letters

No close.

HUGH PORTERFIELD   *Writer's name in full capital letters*
Controller

↕ 1–4 spaces

Encl.:   Specifications of Current System
        Databases Currently in Use

cc: Rene Seaburg

↕ Leave 6 spaces at bottom of page—more if letter is short

Figure A.5   Modified Block Format without Letterhead

6–12 spaces

Single-space 11408 Brussels Avenue NE
Albuquerque, NM 87111
November 5, 2012

1"–1½"

2–6 spaces

Mr. Tom Miller, President
Miller Construction
P.O. Box 2900
Lincolnshire, IL 60197-2900

Subject: Invoice No. 664907, 10/29/12   *Subject line is optional in block & modified block*

Indenting paragraphs is optional in modified block   Dear Mr. Miller:

As part of our kitchen remodeling, your crew installed beautiful Sanchez cabinets. The next day they varnished them, but the varnish was not even. It had bubbles and drip marks, and in some places looked and felt rough. My wife complained to the foreman, and he had the crew revarnish the cabinets. If anything, they looked even worse. At that point, the foreman said he could not do any better and if we wanted a better job, we would have to see to it ourselves. So we did. We called Mr. Sancehz, who sent some of his men over, and now the cabinets are lovely.

1", because right margin is justifed

Because a professional-looking finish on the cabinets is part of what we expected in the remodeling, we ask you to cover Mr. Sanchez's $1050 fee as part of your contract, and to remove it from our bill. The entire kitchen now looks lovely; we love your granite-top counters.

Please send us a new invoice showing Mr. Sanchez's fee removed and our balance paid in full.

Sincerely,

2–4 spaces

William T. Mozing

1–4 spaces

Encl.: Check #7587

Line up signature block with date

below. Note even when the signature block is on the second page, it is still lined up with the date.

Reader's Name
Date
Page Number

or

| Reader's Name | Page Number | Date |

When a letter runs two or more pages, use letterhead only for page 1. (See Figures A.6, A.7, and A.8.) For the remaining pages, use plain paper that matches the letterhead in weight, texture, and color.

Set side margins of 1 inch to 1½ inches on the left and ¾ inch to 1 inch on the right. If you are right justifying, use the 1 inch margin. If your letterhead extends all the way across the top of the page, set your margins even with the ends of the letterhead for the most visually pleasing page. The top margin should be three to six lines under the letterhead, or 1 to 2 inches down from the top of the page if you aren't using letterhead. If your letter is very short, you may want to use bigger side and top margins so that the letter is centered on the page.

The **inside address** gives the reader's name, title (if appropriate), and address: always double check to see the name is spelled correctly. To eliminate typing the reader's name and address on an envelope, some organizations use envelopes with cutouts or windows so that the inside address on the letter shows through and can be used for delivery. If your organization does this, adjust your margins, if necessary, so that the whole inside address is visible.

Many letters are accompanied by other documents. Whatever these documents may be—a multipage report or a two-line note—they are called **enclosures,** since they are enclosed in the envelope. The writer should refer to the enclosures in the body of the letter: "As you can see from my résumé, . . . " The enclosure notation (Encl.:) at the bottom of the letter lists the enclosures. (See Figures A.3, A.4, and A.5.)

Sometimes you write to one person but send copies of your letter to other people. If you want the reader to know that other people are getting copies, list their names on the last page. The abbreviation *cc* originally meant *carbon copy* but now means *computer copy.* Other acceptable abbreviations include *pc* for *photocopy* or simply *c* for *copy.* You can also send copies to other people without telling the reader. Such copies are called **blind copies.** Blind copies are not mentioned on the original; they are listed on the copy saved for the file with the abbreviation *bcc* preceding the names of people getting these copies.

FORMATS FOR ENVELOPES   LO A-2

Business envelopes need to put the reader's name and address in the area that is picked up by the Post Office's Optical Character Readers (OCRs). Use side margins of at least 1 inch. Your bottom margin must be at least $5/8$ inch but no bigger than 2¼ inches.

Most businesses use envelopes that already have the return address printed in the upper left-hand corner. When you don't have printed envelopes, type

Figure A.6   Second Page of a Two-Page Letter, Block Format

State
University

4300 Gateway Boulevard
Midland, TX 78603

August 11, 2012

↕ 2–4 spaces

1"–1½" →

Ms. Stephanie Voght
Stephen F. Austin High School
1200 Southwest Blvd.
San Antonio, TX 78214

Dear Ms. Voght: *Colon in mixed punctuation.*

Enclosed are 100 brochures about State University to distribute to your students. The   *1"*
brochures describe the academic programs and financial aid available. When you need
additional brochures, just let me know.

Further information about State University

You may also want your students to learn more about life at State University. You

---

*Plain paper
for page 2.*

↕ ½"–1"

Stephanie Voght ← *Reader's name*   **2**   August 11, 2012
                                        Center
                                        *Also OK to line up page number and
                                        date at left under reader's name.*

campus life, including football and basketball games, fraternities and sororities, clubs and
organizations, and opportunities for volunteer work. It stresses the diversity of the student
body and the very different lifestyles that are available at State.

*Triple-space before
each new heading (two blank spaces).*

Scheduling a State Squad Speaker   *Bold or underline headings.*

*Same
margins
as p 1.*

To schedule one of the these dynamic speakers for your students, just fill out the
enclosed card with your first, second, and third choices for dates, and return it in the
stamped, self-addressed envelope. Dates are reserved in the order that requests arrive.
Send in your request early to increase the chances of getting the date you want.

Any one of our State Squad speakers will give your high school students a colorful
preview of the college experience. They are also great at answering questions.

1–2 spaces ↕

Sincerely,   *Comma in mixed punctuation.*

*2–4
spaces* ↕

Michael L. Mahler   *Headings are
Director of Admissions   optional in
                                                      letters.*

↕ 1–4 spaces

Encl.: Brochures, Reservation Form

cc: R. J. Holland, School Superintendent
    Jose Lavilla, President, PTS Association

Figure A.7   Second Page of a Two-Page Letter, Modified Block Format

1500 Summit Avenue   (612) 555-1002
Minneapolis, MN   Fax (612) 555-4032
                www.glenarvon.biz

↕ 2–4 spaces

November 5, 2012

*Line up date with
signature block.*

Mr. Roger B. Castino
Castino Floors and Carpets
418 E. North Street
Brockton, MA 02410

*Indenting
paragraphs
is optional
in modified
block.*

Dear Mr. Castino:

Welcome to the team of Glenarvon Carpet dealers!

Your first shipment of Glenarvon samples should reach you within ten days. The samples include

---

*Plain paper
for page 2*

↕ ½"–1"

Mr. Roger B. Castino ← *Reader's
                           name*

Center

2

November 5, 2012

territory . In addition, as a dealer you receive

- Sales kit highlighting product features
- Samples to distribute to customers
- Advertising copy to run in local newspapers
- Display units to place in your store.

*Indent or center list
to emphasize it.*

The Annual Sales Meeting each January keeps you up-to-date on new products while you get to know other dealers and Glenarvon executives and relax at a resort hotel.

*Use
same
margins
as p 1.*

Make your reservations now for Monterey January 10–13 for your first Glenarvon Sales Meeting!

Cordially,

*2–4
spaces ↕*

Barbara S. Charbonneau

Barbara S. Charbonneau
Vice President, Marketing

*Line up signature block with
date in heading and on p1.*

↕ 1–4 spaces

Encl.: Organization Chart
          Product List
          National Advertising Campaigns in 2011

1–4 spaces

cc: Nancy Magill, Northeast Sales Manager
       Edward Spaulding, Sales Representative

*↕ 6 spaces—more if
   second page isn't a full page.*

Figure A.8   Second Page of a Two-Page Letter, Simplified Format

for Living

115 State Street
Ames, IA 50014
515-292-8756
www.optionsforliving.org

⇕ 2–4 spaces

January 20, 2012
⇕ 2–4 spaces
Gary Sammons, Editor
Southeastern Home Magazine
253 North Lake Street
Newport News, VA 23612

Triple-space (two blank spaces)   *Subject line in full caps*

MATERIAL FOR YOUR STORY ON HOMES FOR PEOPLE WITH DISABILITIES

No salutation

Apartments and houses can easily be designed to accommodate people with disabilities. From the outside, the building is indistinguishable from conventional housing. But the modifications inside permit people who use wheelchairs or whose sight or hearing is impaired to do everyday

⇕ ½″–1″   *Plain paper for page 2*

Gary Sammons   *← Reader's*
January 20, 2012   *name*
Page 2

Everything   in hallways and showers and adjustable cabinets that can be raised or lowered. Cardinal says
lined up   that the adaptations can run from a few dollars to $5000, depending on what the customer
at left   selects.
margin

Same   The Builders Association of Virginia will install many features at no extra cost: 36-inch
margins   doorways—8 inches wider than standard—to accommodate wheelchairs and extra wiring for
as page 1   electronic items for people whose sight or hearing is impaired.

If you'd like pictures to accompany your story, just let me know.

No close   MARILYN TILLOTSON   *Writer's name in full caps*
Executive Director

Encl.: Blueprints for Housing for People with Disabilities

cc: Douglas Stringfellow, President, BASF
      Thomas R. Galliher, President, Cardinal Industries

⇕ at least 6 spaces—more if page 2 is not a full page

your name (optional), your street address, and your city, state, and zip code in the upper left-hand corner. Since the OCR doesn't need this information to route your letter, exact margins don't matter. Use whatever is convenient and looks good to you.

FORMATS FOR MEMOS LO A-3

Memos omit both the salutation and the close entirely. Memos rarely use indented paragraphs. Subject lines are required; headings are optional but useful in memos a full page or longer. Each heading must cover all the information until the next heading. Never use a separate heading for the first paragraph.

Figure A.9 illustrates the standard memo format typed on a plain sheet of paper. Note that the first letters of the date, reader's name, writer's name, and subject phrase are lined up vertically. Note also that memos are usually initialed by the To/From block. Initialing tells the reader that you have proofread the memo and prevents someone sending out your name on a memo you did not in fact write.

Some organizations have special letterhead for memos. (See Figure A.10.)

Some organizations alter the order of items in the Date/To/From/Subject block. Some organizations ask employees to sign memos rather than simply initialing them. The signature goes below the last line of the memo and prevents anyone from adding unauthorized information.

If the memo runs two pages or more, set up the second and subsequent pages in one of the following ways (see Figure A.11):

Brief Subject Line
Date
Page Number

or

Brief Subject Line	Page Number	Date

FORMATS FOR E-MAIL MESSAGES LO A-4

E-mail programs prompt you to supply the various parts of the memo format. See Chapters 9, 10, and 11 for information about designing e-mail subject lines. "Cc:" denotes computer copies; the recipient will see that these people are getting the message. "Bcc:" denotes blind computer copies; the recipient does not see the names of these people. Most e-mail programs also allow you to attach documents from other programs, thus e-mails have attachments rather than enclosures. The computer program supplies the date and time automatically.

Some aspects of e-mail format are still evolving. In particular, some writers treat e-mail messages as if they were informal letters; some treat them as memos. Even though the e-mail screen has a "To" line (as do memos), some writers still use an informal salutation, as in Figure A.12. The writer in Figure A.12 ends the message with a signature block. Signature blocks are particularly useful for e-mail recipients outside the organization who may not know your title or contact information. You can store a signature block in the e-mail program and set the program to insert the signature block automatically.

Figure A.9   Memo Format (on plain paper)

Everything lined up at left   *Plain paper*

Line up

Date: October 7, 2012

Double-space (one blank space)   To: Annette T. Califero

1"–1½"   From: Kyle B. Abrams **KBA**   *Writer's initials added in ink*

Subject: A Low-Cost Way to Reduce Energy Use   *Capitalize first letter of each major word in subject line*

No heading for ¶ 1   As you requested, I've investigated low-cost ways to reduce our energy use. Reducing the building temperature on weekends is a change that we could make immediately, that would cost nothing, and that would cut our energy use by about 6%.   *¾"–1"*

Triple-space before each new heading (two blank spaces)

The Energy Savings from a Lower Weekend Temperature   *Bold or underline headings*

Single-space paragraphs; double-space between paragraphs (one blank space)   Lowering the temperature from 68° to 60° from 8 P.M. Friday evening to 4 A.M. Monday morning could cut our total consumption by 6%. It is not feasible to lower the temperature on weeknights because a great many staff members work late; the cleaning crew also is on duty from 6 P.M. to midnight. Turning the temperature down for only four hours would not result in a significant heat saving.

Turning the heat back up at 4 A.M. will allow the building temperature to be back to 68° by 9 A.M. Our furnace already has computerized controls which can be set to automatically lower and raise the temperature.

Triple-space (two blank spaces)

How a Lower Temperature Would Affect Employees   *Capitalize first letter of each major word of heading*

Do not indent paragraphs   A survey of employees shows that only 7 people use the building every weekend or almost every weekend. Eighteen percent of our staff have worked at least one weekend day in the last two months; 52% say they "occasionally" come in on weekends.

People who come in for an hour or less on weekends could cope with the lower temperature just by wearing warm clothes. However, most people would find 60° too cool for extended work. Employees who work regularly on weekends might want to install space heaters.

Action Needed to Implement the Change

Would you also like me to check into the cost of buying a dozen portable space heaters? Providing them would allow us to choose units that our wiring can handle and would be a nice gesture towards employees who give up their weekends to work. I could have a report to you in two weeks.

We can begin saving energy immediately. Just authorize the lower temperature, and I'll see that the controls are reset for this weekend.

Memos are initialed by To/From/Subject block—no signature usually   *Headings are optional in memos*

Figure A.10   Memo Format (on memo letterhead)

Kimball, Walls, and Morganstern

aligned vertically

Date: March 15, 2012   *Line up horizontally with printed Date/To/From/Subject*

To: Annette T. Califero

From: Kyle B. Abrams **KBA**   *Writer's initials added in ink*   *Capitalize first letter of each major word in subject line*

Subject: The Effectiveness of Reducing Building Temperatures on Weekends
         Triple-space (two blank spaces)

Reducing the building temperature to 60° on weekends has cut energy use by 4% compared to last year's use from December to February and has saved our firm $22,000.

This savings is particularly remarkable when you consider that this winter has been colder than last year's, so that more heat would be needed to maintain the same temperature.   *$\frac{3}{4}"-1"$*

Fewer people have worked weekends during the past three months than during the preceding three months, but snow and bad driving conditions may have had more to do with keeping people home than the fear of being cold. Five of the 12 space heaters we bought have been checked out on an average weekend. On one weekend, all 12 were in use and some people shared their offices so that everyone could be in a room with a space heater.

Fully 92% of our employees support the lower temperature. I recommend that we continue turning down the heat on weekends through the remainder of the heating season and that we resume the practice when the heat is turned on next fall.

Headings are optional in memos

In contrast, the writer in Figure A.13 omits both the salutation and his name. When you send a message to an individual or a group you have set up, the "From:" line will have your name and e-mail address.

If you post a message to a listserv, be sure to give at least your name and e-mail address at the end of your message, as some list-servs strip out identifying information when they process messages.

When you hit "reply," the e-mail program automatically uses "Re:" (Latin for *about*) and the previous subject line. The original message is set off, usually with one or more vertical lines in the left margin or with carats (see Figure A.14). You may want to change the subject line to make it more appropriate for your message.

Use short line lengths in your e-mail message. If the line lengths are too long, they'll produce awkward line breaks, as in Figure A.14.

Appendix A   Formatting Letters, Memos, and E-Mail Messages   645

Figure A.11   Second Page of Two-Page Memo

1"–1½"

February 18, 2012

To: Dorothy N. Blasingham

Double-space (one blank space) From: Roger L. Trout **R.L.T.** *Writer's initials added in ink*

Subject: Request for Third-Quarter Computer Training Sessions *Capitalize first letter of all major words in subject line*

Triple-space (two blank spaces)

¶ 1 never has a heading Could you please run advanced training sessions on using Excel in April and May and basic training sessions for new hires in June? *¾"–1"*

Triple-space before a heading (two blank spaces)

Advanced Sessions on Excel
   Bold headings

Double-space between paragraphs (one blank space) Once the tax season is over, Jose Cisneros wants to have his first- and second-year people take your advanced course on Excel. Plan on about 45–50 people in three sessions. The people in the course already use Excel for basic spreadsheets but need to learn the fine points of macros and charting.

If possible, it would be most convenient to have the sessions run for four afternoons rather

Plain paper for page 2 *½"–1"*

Brief subject line or reader's name
Dorothy N. Blasingham ←   2 *Page number*   February 18, 2012

Also OK to line up page number, date at left under reader's name

Same margins as p 1. before the summer vacation season begins.

Orientation for New Hires *Capitalize first letter of all major words in heading*

With a total of 16 full-time and 34 part-time people being hired either for summer or permanent work, we'll need at least two and perhaps three orientation sessions. We'd like to hold these the first, second, and third weeks in June. By May 1, we should know how many people will be in each training session.

Would you be free to conduct training sessions on how to use our computers on June 9, June 16, and June 23? If we need only two dates, we'll use June 9 and June 16, but please block off the 23rd too in case we need a third session.

Triple-space before a heading (two blank spaces)

Request for Confirmation

Let me know whether you're free on these dates in June, and which dates you'd prefer. If you'll let me know by February 25, we can get information out to participants in plenty of time for the sessions.

Thanks! *Headings are optional in memos*

Memos are initialed by To/From/Subject block

Figure A.12   A Basic E-Mail Message (direct request)

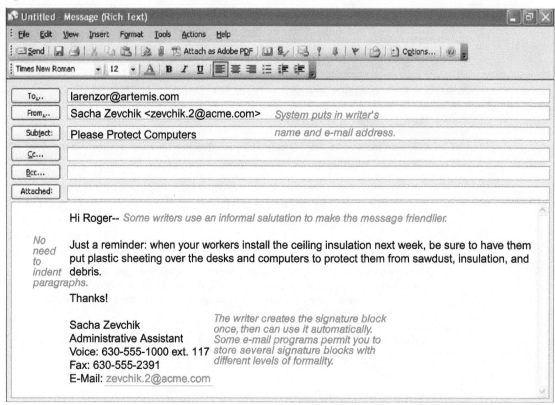

Figure A.13   An E-Mail Message with an Attachment (direct request)

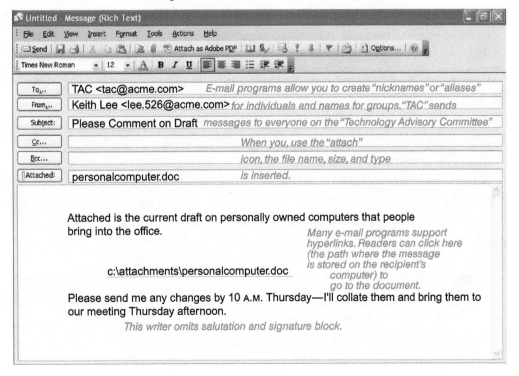

648   Appendix A   Formatting Letters, Memos, and E-Mail Messages

Figure A.14 An E-Mail Reply with Copies (response to a complaint)

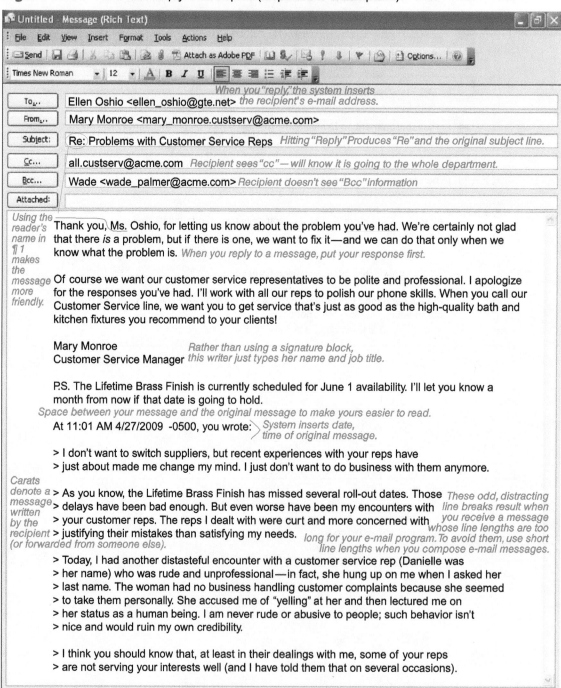

STATE AND PROVINCE ABBREVIATIONS

States with names of more than five letters are frequently abbreviated in letters and memos. The post office abbreviations use two capital letters with no punctuation. See Figure A.15.

Figure A.15   Post Office Abbreviations for States, Territories, and Provinces

State name	Post office abbreviation	State name	Post office abbreviation
Alabama	AL	Missouri	MO
Alaska	AK	Montana	MT
Arizona	AZ	Nebraska	NE
Arkansas	AR	Nevada	NV
California	CA	New Hampshire	NH
Colorado	CO	New Jersey	NJ
Connecticut	CT	New Mexico	NM
Delaware	DE	New York	NY
District of Columbia	DC	North Carolina	NC
Florida	FL	North Dakota	ND
Georgia	GA	Ohio	OH
Hawaii	HI	Oklahoma	OK
Idaho	ID	Oregon	OR
Illinois	IL	Pennsylvania	PA
Indiana	IN	Rhode Island	RI
Iowa	IA	South Carolina	SC
Kansas	KS	South Dakota	SD
Kentucky	KY	Tennessee	TN
Louisiana	LA	Texas	TX
Maine	ME	Utah	UT
Maryland	MD	Vermont	VT
Massachusetts	MA	Virginia	VA
Michigan	MI	Washington	WA
Minnesota	MN	West Virginia	WV
Mississippi	MS	Wisconsin	WI
		Wyoming	WY

Territory name	Post office abbreviation	Province name	Post office abbreviation
Guam	GU	Alberta	AB
Puerto Rico	PR	British Columbia	BC
Virgin Islands	VI	Manitoba	MB
		New Brunswick	NB
		Newfoundland and Labrador	NL
		Northwest Territories	NT
		Nova Scotia	NS
		Nunavut	NU
		Ontario	ON
		Prince Edward Island	PE
		Quebec	QC
		Saskatchewan	SK
		Yukon Territory	YT

APPENDIX

C

Citing and Documenting Sources

Appendix Outline

American Psychological Association (APA) Format

Modern Language Association (MLA) Format

Learning Objectives

After studying this appendix, you will know how to

LO C-1   Use APA format for citing and documenting sources.

LO C-2   Use MLA format for citing and documenting sources.

Citing and documenting sources is an important part of any research process. In effective business proposals and reports, sources are cited and documented smoothly and unobtrusively. **Citation** means attributing an idea or fact to its source in the body of the text: "Bill Gates argues that . . ." "According to the John Deere annual report. . . ." **Documentation** means providing the bibliographic information readers would need to go back to the original source. The usual means of documentation are notes (endnotes or footnotes) and lists of references.

Failure to cite and document sources is **plagiarism,** the passing off of the words or ideas of others as one's own. Plagiarism can lead to serious consequences. The news regularly showcases examples of people who have been fired or sued for plagiarism. Now that curious people can type sentences into Google and other search engines and find the sources, plagiarism is easier than ever to catch.

Note that citation and documentation are used in addition to quotation marks. If you use the source's exact words, you'll use the name of the person you're citing and quotation marks in the body of the proposal or report; you'll indicate the source in parentheses and a list of references or in a footnote or endnote. If you put the source's idea into your own words (paraphrasing), or if you condense or synthesize information, you don't need quotation marks, but you still need to tell whose idea it is and where you found it.

Long quotations (four typed lines or more) are used sparingly in business proposals and reports. Since many readers skip quotes, always summarize the main point of the quotation in a single sentence before the quotation itself. End the sentence with a colon, not a period, because it introduces the quote. Indent long quotations on the left to set them off from your text. Indented quotations do not need quotation marks; the indentation shows the reader that the passage is a quote.

To make a quotation fit the grammar of your report, you may need to change one or two words. Sometimes you may want to add a few words to explain something in the longer original. In both cases, use square brackets to indicate words that are your replacements or additions. Omit any words in the original source that are not essential for your purposes. Use ellipses (spaced dots) to indicate your omissions.

Document every fact and idea that you take from a source except facts that are common knowledge. Historical dates and facts are considered common knowledge (e.g., Barack Obama is the 44th president of the United States or the Twin Towers came down on September 11, 2001). Generalizations are considered common knowledge ("More and more women are entering the workforce") even though specific statements about the same topic (such as the percentage of women in the workforce in 1975 and in 2010) would require documentation.

Two widely used formats for citing and documenting sources in proposals and reports are those of the American Psychological Association (APA) and the Modern Language Association (MLA). Each will be discussed in this appendix.

AMERICAN PSYCHOLOGICAL ASSOCIATION (APA) FORMAT LO C-1

The APA format is a widely used documentation style, most notably in the natural and human sciences. *Publication Manual of the American Psychological Association*, 6th edition, second printing, 2009, is the official source for this type of documentation.

For APA in-text citations, the source is indicated by the author's last name and the date of the work in parentheses, unless those items are already in the text. A comma separates the author's name from the date: (Salt, 2009). Page numbers are only given for direct quotations or in cases where the reader may need help to find the location: (Salt, 2009, p. 20). If you have a source with two authors, use an ampersand in the citation: (Locker & Kienzler, 2012). If the author's name is used in the sentence, only the date is given in parentheses. Sec Figure C.1 for a portion of a report that uses APA format.

At the end of your document, include a **References** list that provides the full bibliographic citation for each source used. Arrange the entries alphabetically by the first author's last name. Use only initials for first and middle names. Figure C.2 shows APA format examples of the most often used sources in proposals and reports.

MODERN LANGUAGE ASSOCIATION (MLA) FORMAT LO C-2

The MLA format is another widely used documentation style, most notably in the arts and humanities. *MLA Style Manual and Guide to Scholarly Publishing*, 3rd edition, 2008, is the official source for this type of documentation.

For MLA in-text citations, the source is indicated by the author's last name and page number in parentheses in the text for paraphrases and direct quotations. Unlike APA, the year is not given, unless you're using two or more works by the same author or if the dates are important. No comma separates the name and page number, and the abbreviation "p." is not used: (Salt 20). If you have a source with two authors, use "and" in the citation: (Locker and Kienzler 222). If the author's name is used in the sentence, only the page number is given in parentheses. See Figure C.3 for a portion of a report that uses MLA format and includes a Works Cited section.

At the end of your document, include a **Works Cited** list that provides the full bibliographic citation for each source you have cited. Arrange the entries alphabetically by the first author's last name. Use authors' names as they appear on the source. Note that the Works Cited list gives the medium (e.g., Web, Print, DVD). URLs for web sources are given only when the item may be otherwise hard to find. Figure C.4 shows MLA format examples of the most often used sources in proposals and reports.

Figure C.1   Report Paragraphs with APA Documentation

Headings and paragraph numbers help readers find material in a website without page numbers. If the source does not number the paragraphs, number the paragraphs yourself under each heading.

Social media can be defined as "technology facilitated dialogue among individuals or groups, such as blogs, microblogs, forums, wikis," and other unofficial forms of electronic communication (Cone, 2008, What is social media? ¶. 1). In a 2008 study on social media, Cone found that 39% of Americans reported using social media websites at least once a week; 30% reported using them two or more times a week. Additionally, the study found that 34% believed that companies should have a presence on social media websites and use their presence to interact with their customers. Fifty-one percent of users believed that companies should be present on these websites but interact only if customers ask them to do so (Cone). "While the ultimate measure [of most companies' marketing efforts] is sales, social media expands that because of its focus on influencers," says Simon Salt (2009, p. 20), the CEO of Inc-Slingers, a marketing communication firm. For example, he says "cable provider Comcast utilizes social media to monitor existing customer issues. . . . Known on Twitter as @comcastcares, it quickly developed a reputation for engaging its customer base" (p. 20).   *Use page number for direct quote. Author's name already in text, so not repeated here.*

Numbers at the beginning of sentences must be written out.

This citation for a direct quote uses only year and page number ("p." before number) since author is identified in sentence.

Square brackets indicate a change from the original to make the quote fit into the structure of your sentence.

An ellipsis (three spaced dots) indicates some material has been omitted. An extra dot serves as the period of the sentence.

The Cone study also found that 25% of users of social media websites reported interacting with companies at least once a week. When asked what kind of role companies should play on these Web sites, 43% said giving virtual customer service, 41% said soliciting customer feedback. Among some of the most popular social media websites are Facebook, My Space, Twitter, Blogger, and Digg.

No need to provide a citation for facts that are general or common knowledge.

Because source is adequately identified in text, no parenthetical source citation is needed.

Twitter, a microblogging website, asks its users a simple question: "What are you doing?" Users can post their own updates and follow others' updates. Twitter has grown at a breathtaking pace in the last few months. It registered a whopping 600% increase in traffic in the 12 months leading up to November 2008. It is estimated that the microblogging website has approximately 3 million registered account holders from across the globe (Salt, 2009). A message or post on Twitter, known as a "tweet," cannot be more than 140 characters long. Companies and organizations are increasingly taking to Twitter.

Basic APA citation: Place author and date in parentheses; separate with a comma. Use page numbers only for a direct quote.

Visible Technologies, a Seattle-based market research firm, helps companies search for valuable market information from a virtual pool of millions of tweets. Some of the firm's clients include Hormel Foods and Panasonic. The computer manufacturer Dell, another customer, asks its customer representatives to interact with customers on Twitter. Recently, the company announced that it increased its sales by $500,000 through the use of Twitter (Baker, 2008, Promotional Tweets, para. 1). Zappos.com, an online shoe seller, encourages its employees to use Twitter to communicate about subjects as wide-ranging as politics to marketing plans (Vascellaro, 2008).

Article titles use sentence capitalization and no quotation marks.

References

List all works (but only those works) cited in the text. List sources alphabetically.

Date of publication (year, month day) for a weekly source.

Baker, S. (2008, May 15). Why Twitter matters. *BusinessWeek.* Retrieved April 15, 2009, from http://www.businessweek.com/technology/content/may2008/tc20080514_269697.htm

Retrieval date is month day, year.

Use URL of a specific web page; do not put period after URL. Break long URLs after a /.

Cone. (2008). 2008 business in social media study [Fact sheet]. Retrieved April 15, 2009 from http://www.coneinc.com /stuff /contentmgr/ files/0/26ff8eb1d1a9371210502558013fe2a6/files / 2008_business_in_social_media_fact_sheet.pdf

Source by a corporate author.

Salt, S. (2009, February 15). Track your success. *Marketing News, 43,* 20.

Italicize volume number.

Only initials for all names except last.

Vascellaro, J. (2008, October 27). Twitter goes mainstream. *Wall Street Journal,* p. R3.

Don't abbreviate month.

Figure C.2   APA Format for Sources Used Most Often in Proposals and Reports *(Continued)*

In the examples below, headings in green identify the kind of work being referenced. The green headings are not part of the actual citation.

Put authors' last names first. Use only initials for first and middle names.

In titles of articles and books capitalize only (1) first word, (2) first word of subtitle, (3) proper nouns.

Note comma after initial, use of ampersand, period after parenthesis.

No quotation marks around title of article.

Article in a Periodical

Stowers, R. H., & Hummel, J. Y. (2011, June). The use of technology to combat plagiarism

Ampersands join names of coauthors, coeditors.

in business communication classes. *Business Communication Quarterly, 74,*

Use a DOI (Digital Object Identifier) when available because it is more stable than a URL.

164–169. doi:10.1177//1080569911404406

Give complete page numbers.
No "pp." when journal has a volume number

Volume number is italicized. Provide issue number in parentheses only if each issue begins with page 1.

Date is year, month day

Article in a Newspaper

Trottman, M. (2011, February 8). Facebook firing case is settled. *The Wall Street*

Capitalize all major words in title of journal, magazine, or newspaper.

Journal, p. B3.

Use "p." for single page, "pp." for multiple pages.

Chapter in an Edited book

Author and editor names use initials for first and middle names.

Blakeslee, A. M. (2010). Addressing audiences in a digital age. In R. Spilka (Ed.), *Digital*

Put editor before book title.

literacy for technical communication: 21st century theory and practice (pp. 199–229).

Editor names have last names last.

Give state abbreviation

New York, NY: Routledge.

Use full page numbers for article.

Publication date: year, month day.

Article from a Publication on the Web

Lowery, A. (2011, May 20). LinkedIn is worth $9 billion? How the year's hottest IPO is

fueling speculation about a new tech bubble. *Slate*. Retrieved from http://

Only list retrieval date if the source is likely to change (i.e., wikis, blogs); the date would be inserted between "Retrieved" and "from".

www.slate.com/id/2295189/

No punctuation after URL

Book

Baker, A. C. (2010). *Catalytic conversations: Organizational communication and*

innovation. New York, NY: M. E. Sharpe.

Appendix C   Citing and Documenting Sources   681

Figure C.2   APA Format for Sources Used Most Often in Proposals and Reports *(Concluded)*

Book or Pamphlet with a Corporate Author
American Cancer Society. (2011). *Cancer facts & figures 2010.* [Atlanta, GA:] Author.

Put in brackets information known to you but not printed in document.

Indicates organization authoring document also published it.

E-mail Message
[Identify e-mail messages in the text as personal communication. Give name of author

and specific date. Do not list in References.]

Government Document Available on the Web from the GPO Access Database
U.S. Government Accountability Office. (2011, May 19). *Banking regulation: Enhanced*

Abbreviate and use periods.

guidance on commerical real estate risks needed. (Publication No. GAO-11-489).

Retrieved from Government Accountability Office Reports Online via GPO Access:

Abbreviate Government Printing Office

http://www.gao.gov/htext/d11477r.html

Interview Conducted by the Researcher
[Identify interview in the text as personal communication. Give name of interviewee

and specific date. Do not list in References.]

n.d. if no date is given

Website
Berry, T. (n.d.). *Getting started on your business plan.* Retrieved May 25, 2011, from

Retrieval dates: Month day, year

http://articles.bplans.com/writing-a-business-plan/getting-started-on-your-

business-plan/26

Break long URLs after a slash. No period after URL.

Italicize titles of stand-alone works. An article that is part of a larger work is put in Roman type and quotation marks.

Figure C.3   Report Paragraphs with MLA Documentation

Do not list page or paragraph numbers if the source is unnumbered.

Square brackets indicate a change from the original to make the quote fit into the structure of your sentence.

An ellipsis (three spaced dots) indicates some material has been omitted. An extra dot serves as the period of the sentence.

Because source is identified in text and has no page numbers, no citation is needed.

Basic MLA citation: author and page number. Give page number for facts as well as quotes. No comma or "p." between author and number.

Social media can be defined as "technology facilitated dialogue among individuals or groups, such as blogs, microblogs, forums, wikis" and other unofficial forms of electronic communication (Cone). In a 2008 study on social media, Cone found that 39% of Americans reported using social media websites at least once a week; 30% reported using them two or more times a week. Additionally, the study found that 34% believed that companies should have a presence on social media websites and use their presence to interact with their customers. Fifty-one percent of users believed that companies should be present on these websites but interact only if customers ask them to do so (Cone). "While the ultimate measure [of most companies' marketing efforts] is sales, social media expands that because of its focus on influencers," says Simon Salt, the CEO of Inc-Slingers, a marketing communication firm (20). For example, he says "cable provider Comcast utilizes social media to monitor existing customer issues. . . . Known on Twitter as @comcastcares, it quickly developed a reputation for engaging its customer base" (20).

Numbers at the beginnings of sentences must be written out.

No "p." before page number; use only page number since author identified in sentence.

Use page number (no "p.") for direct quote. Author's name is already in text, so is not repeated here.

The Cone study also found that 25% of users of social media websites reported interacting with companies at least once a week. When asked what kind of role companies should play on these websites, 43% said giving virtual customer service, 41% said soliciting customer feedback. Among some of the most popular social media websites are Facebook, MySpace, Twitter, Blogger, and Digg.

No need to provide a citation for facts that are general or common knowledge.

Twitter, a microblogging website, asks its users a simple question: "What are you doing?" Users can post their own updates and follow others' updates. Twitter has grown at a breathtaking pace in the last few months. It registered a whopping 600% increase in traffic in the 12 months leading up to November 2008. It is estimated that the micro-blogging website has approximately 3 million registered account holders from across the globe (Salt 20). A message or post on Twitter, known as a "tweet," cannot be more than 140 characters long. Companies and organizations are increasingly taking to Twitter.

Visible Technologies, a Seattle-based market research firm, helps companies search for valuable market information from a virtual pool of millions of tweets. Some of the firm's clients include Hormel Foods and Panasonic. The computer manufacturer Dell, another customer, asks its customer representatives to interact with customers on Twitter. Recently, the company announced that it increased its sales by $500,000 through the use of Twitter (Baker). Zappos.com, an online shoe seller, encourages its employees to use Twitter to communicate, about subjects as wide-ranging as politics to marketing plans (Vascellaro R3).

Do not list headings or paragraph numbers if the source is unnumbered.

Article titles use title capitalization and quotation marks.

Date of publication: day month (abbreviated) year.

Source by a corporate author.

All names typed as they appear in the source.

Abbreviate months with five of more letters.

Works Cited

List all works (but only those works) cited in the text. List sources alphabetically.

Baker, Stephen. "Why Twitter Matters." *BusinessWeek.* 15 May 2008. Web. 2 Apr. 2009.

Date you visited site: day month year. Abbreviate months.

Type of source (Print or Web).

Cone. "2008 Business in Social Media Study." 2008. Web. 2 Apr. 2009 <http://www.coneinc.com/stuff/contentmgr/files/ 0/26ff8eb1d1a9371210502558013fe2a6/files/ 2008_business_in_social_media_fact_sheet.pdf>.

Salt, Simon. "Track Your Success." *Marketing News.* 2 Apr. 2009: 20. Print.

Vascellaro, Jessica. "Twitter Goes Mainstream." *Wall Street Journal.* 27 Oct. 2008: R3. Print.

URL in angle brackets; period after angle brackets. Break long URLs after a slash. URLs are only given for sites that may be difficult to find otherwise.

Volume and issue number not listed for weekly magazines.

Figure C.4   MLA Format for Sources Used Most Often in Proposals and Reports *(Continued)*

In the examples below, headings in green identify the kind of work being referenced. The green headings are not part of the actual citation.

Use authors' full names as printed in source. First name first for second author

Join authors' names with "and"

Put quotation marks around title of article

Capitalize all major words in titles of articles, books, journals, magazines, and newspapers

Article in a Periodical

Stowers, Robert H., and Julie Y. Hummel. "The Use of Technology to Combat Plagiarism in

Busniness Communication Classes." *Business Communication Quarterly 74.2* (2011):

Use both volume and issue number; do not italicize

Omit "1" in "169" — 164–69. Print.

Entries designated as Print or Web

Omit introductory articles (e.g. "The") for newspapers and journals.

Article in a Newspaper

Trottman, Melanie. "Facebook Firing Case Is Settled." *Wall Street Journal* 8 Feb. 2011: B3.

Print.

Date given as day month (abbreviated) year

Give author's or editor's full name as printed in the source.

Chapter in an Edited Book

Blakeslee, Ann M. "Addressing Audiences in a Digital Age." *Digital Literacy for Technical*

Communication: 21st Century Theory and Practice. Ed. Rachel Spilka.

Editor's first name goes first

New York: Routlege, 2010. 199–229. Print.

Put book title before editor's name.

City of publication but not state

Article from a Publication on the Web

Lowery, Annie. "LinkedIn Is Worth $9 Billion? How the Year's Hottest IPO Is Fueling

Speculation about a New Tech Bubble." *Slate.* Washington Post Co. 20 May 2011. Web.

Publication date

Access date 25 May 2011.

Publisher or sponsor of site.

URLS are given only for sites that may be difficult to find.

Book

Baker, Ann C. *Catalytic Conversations: Organizational Communication and Innovation.* New

Date after city and publisher

York: M. E. Sharpe, 2010. Print.

(Continued)

684   **Appendix C**   Citing and Documenting Sources

Figure C.4   MLA Format for Sources Used Most Often in Proposals and Reports *(Concluded)*

Book or Pamphlet with a Corporate Author
American Cancer Society. *Cancer Facts & Figures 2010*. [Atlanta, GA:] ACS Publishing,

    2011. Print.

Put in brackets information known to you but not printed in source.

E-mail Message
Kienzler, Donna S. "Re: Project Guidelines and New Criteria." Message to Abhijit Rao.

    15 July 2011. E-mail.

Name of government, not abbreviated, then name of agency

Government Document Available on the Web from the GPO Access Database
United States. U.S. Government Accountability Office. *Banking Regulation: Enhanced*

    Guidance on Commerical Real Estate Risks Needed. Rep GAO-11-489. Wahington:

    GPO, 19 May 2011. Web. 25 May 2011. <http://www.gao.gov/htext/d11477r.html>.

Abbreviate Government Printing Office

URL in angle brackets; period after angle brackets. Separate long URLs after a slash. URLs are given only for site that may be difficult to find.

Interview Conducted by the Researcher
Drysdale, Marissa. Telephone interview. 12 July 2011.

Italicize titles of stand-alone works. An article that is part of a larger work is put in Roman type and quotation marks.

Website
Berry, Tim. "Getting Started on Your Business Plan." *Bplans* Palo Alto Software,

Publisher or sponsor of site

n.d. if no date is given

    Inc., n.d. Web. 25 May 2011. <http://articles.bplans.com/writing-a-business-plan/

    getting-started-on-your-busines-plan/26>.

Give URL if source is difficult to find.

GLOSSARY

A

abstract A summary of a report, specifying the recommendations and the reasons for them. Also called an executive summary.

acknowledgment responses Nods, smiles, frowns, and words that let a speaker know you are listening.

active listening Feeding back the literal meaning or the emotional content or both so that the speaker knows that the listener has heard and understood.

active voice A verb that describes the action done by the grammatical subject of the sentence.

adjustment A positive response to a claim letter. If the company agrees to grant a refund, the amount due will be adjusted.

agenda A list of items to be considered or acted upon at a meeting.

alliteration A sound pattern occurring when several words begin with the same sound.

alternating pattern (of organization) Discussing the alternatives first as they relate to the first criterion, then as they relate to the second criterion, and so on: ABC, ABC, ABC. Compare *divided pattern*.

analytical report A report that interprets information.

argument The reasons or logic offered to persuade the audience.

assumptions Statements that are not proved in a report, but on which the recommendations are based.

audience benefits Benefits or advantages that the audience gets by using the communicator's services, buying the communicator's products, following the communicator's policies, or adopting the communicator's ideas. Audience benefits can exist for policies and ideas as well as for goods and services.

auxiliary audience People who may encounter your message but will not have to interact with it. This audience includes "read only" people.

average See *mean*.

B

bar chart A visual consisting of parallel bars or rectangles that represent specific sets of data.

behavioral economics A branch of economics that uses social and psychological factors in understanding decision making. It is particularly concerned with the limits of rationality in those decisions.

behavioral interviews Job interviews that ask candidates to describe actual behaviors they have used in the past in specific situations.

bias-free language Language that does not discriminate against people on the basis of sex, physical condition, race, age, or any other category.

blind ads Job listings that do not list the company's name.

blind copies Copies sent to other recipients that are not listed on the original letter, memo or e-mail.

block format In letters, a format in which inside address, date, and signature block are lined up at the left margin; paragraphs are not indented. In résumés, a format in which dates are listed in one column and job titles and descriptions in another.

blocking Disagreeing with every idea that is proposed.

body language Nonverbal communication conveyed by posture and movement, eye contact, facial expressions, and gestures.

boilerplate Language from a previous document that a writer includes in a new document. Writers use boilerplate both to save time and energy and to use language that has already been approved by the organization's legal staff.

boxhead Used in tables, the boxhead is the variable whose label is at the top.

brainstorming A method of generating ideas by recording everything people in a group think of, without judging or evaluating the ideas.

branching question Question that sends respondents who answer differently to different parts of the questionnaire. Allows respondents to answer only those questions that are relevant to their experience.

bridge (in prospecting job letters) A sentence that connects the attention-getter to the body of a letter.

brochure Leaflet (often part of a direct mailing) that gives more information about a product or organization.

buffer A neutral or positive statement designed to allow the writer to delay, or buffer, the negative message.

build goodwill To create a good image of yourself and of your organization–the kind of image that makes people want to do business with you.

bullets Small circles (filled or open) or squares that set off items in a list. When you are giving examples, but the number is not exact and the order does not matter, use bullets to set off items.

business plan A document written to raise capital for a new business venture or to outline future actions for an established business.

businessese A kind of jargon including unnecessary words. Some words were common 200–300 years ago but are no longer part of spoken English. Some have never been used outside of business writing. All of these terms should be omitted.

buying time with limited agreement Agreeing with the small part of a criticism that one does accept as true.

bypassing Miscommunication that occurs when two people use the same language to mean different things.

C

case The grammatical role a noun or pronoun plays in a sentence. The nominative case is used for the subject of a clause, the possessive to show who or what something belongs to, the objective case for the object of a verb or a preposition.

central selling point A strong audience benefit, big enough to motivate people by itself, but also serving as an umbrella to cover other benefits and to unify the message.

channel The physical means by which a message is sent. Written channels include e-mails memos, letters, and billboards.

Oral channels include phone calls, speeches, and face-to-face conversations.

channel overload   The inability of a channel to carry effectively all the messages that are being sent.

chartjunk   Decoration that is irrelevant to a visual and that may be misleading.

checking for feelings   Identifying the emotions that the previous speaker seemed to be expressing verbally or nonverbally.

checking for inferences   Trying to identify the unspoken content or feelings implied by what the previous speaker has actually said.

chronological résumé   A résumé that lists what you did in a dated order, starting with the most recent events and going backward in reverse chronology.

citation   Attributing a quotation or other idea to a source in the body of the report.

claim   The part of an argument that the speaker or writer wants the audience to agree with.

claim letter   A letter seeking a replacement or refund.

clip art   Predrawn images that you can import into your documents.

close   The ending of a communication.

closed body position   Includes keeping the arms and legs crossed and close to the body. Suggests physical and psychological discomfort, defending oneself, and shutting the other person out. Also called a defensive body position.

closed question   Question with a limited number of possible responses.

closure report   A report summarizing completed work that does not result in new action or a recommendation.

clowning   Making unproductive jokes and diverting the group from its task.

cluster sample   A sample of subjects at each of a random sample of locations. This method is usually faster and cheaper than random sampling when face-to-face interviews are required.

clustering   A method of thinking up ideas by writing the central topic in the middle of the page, circling it, writing down the ideas that topic suggests, and circling them.

cognitive dissonance   A theory which posits that it is psychologically uncomfortable to hold two ideas that are dissonant or conflicting. The theory of cognitive dissonance explains that people will resolve dissonance by deciding that one of the ideas is less important, by rejecting one of the ideas, or by constructing a third idea that has room for both of the conflicting ideas.

cold list   A list used in marketing of people with no prior connection to your group.

collaborative writing   Working with other writers to produce a single document.

collection letter   A letter asking a customer to pay for goods and services received.

collection series   A series of letters asking customers to pay for goods and services they have already received. Early letters in the series assume that the reader intends to pay but final letters threaten legal action if the bill is not paid.

comma splice or **comma fault**   Using a comma to join two independent clauses. To correct, use a semicolon, use a comma with a conjunction, subordinate one of the clauses, or use a period and start a new sentence.

common ground   Values and goals that the communicator and audience share.

communication channel   The means by which you convey your message.

communication theory   A theory explaining what happens when we communicate and where miscommunication can occur.

competitive proposal   A proposal that has to compete for limited resources.

complaint letter   A letter that challenges a policy or tries to get a decision changed.

complex sentence   Sentence with one main clause and one or more subordinate clauses.

complimentary close   The words after the body of the letter and before the signature. *Sincerely* and *Yours truly* are the most commonly used complimentary closes in business letters.

compound sentence   Sentence with two main clauses joined by a comma and conjunction.

conclusions   Section of a report or other communication that restates the main points.

conflict resolution   Strategies for getting at the real issue, keeping discussion open, and minimizing hurt feelings so that people can find a solution that seems good to everyone involved.

connotations   The emotional colorings or associations that accompany a word.

consensus   Group solidarity supporting a decision.

contact letter   Letter written to keep in touch with a customer or donor.

convenience sample   A group of subjects to whom the researcher has easy access; not a random sample.

conventions   Widely accepted practices.

conversational style   Conversational patterns such as speed and volume of speaking, pauses between speakers, whether questions are direct or indirect. When different speakers assign different meanings to a specific pattern, miscommunication results.

coordination   The second stage in the life of a task group, when the group finds, organizes, and interprets information and examines alternatives and assumptions. This is the longest of the stages.

corporate culture   The values, beliefs, norms, history, and assumptions of an organization that shape behaviors and decisions of individual employees.

counterclaim   A statement whose truth would negate the truth of the main claim.

credibility   Ability to come across to the audience as believable.

criteria   The standards used to evaluate or weigh the factors in a decision.

critical activities (in a schedule)   Activities that must be done on time if a project is to be completed by its due date.

critical incident   An important event that illustrates behavior or a history.

crop   To trim a photograph to fit a specific space, typically to delete visual information that is unnecessary or unwanted.

culture   The patterns of behavior and beliefs that are common to a people, nation, or organization.

cutaway drawings   Line drawings that depict the hidden or interior portions of an object.

cycling   The process of sending a document from writer to superior to writer to yet another superior for several rounds of revisions before the document is approved.

D

dangling modifier   A phrase that modifies the wrong word or a word that is not actually in a sentence. To correct a dangling modifier, recast the modifier as a subordinate clause or revise the sentence so its subject or object can be modified by the dangling phrase.

decode   To extract meaning from symbols.

decorative visual   A visual that makes the speaker's points more memorable but that does not convey numerical data.

defensive body position   See *closed body position.*

demographic characteristics   Measurable features of an audience that can be counted objectively: age, education level, income, etc.

denotation   A word's literal or "dictionary" meaning. Most common words in English have more than one denotation. Context usually makes it clear which of several meanings is appropriate.

dependent clause   See *subordinate clause.*

descriptive abstract   A listing of the topics an article or report covers that does not summarize what is said about each topic.

deviation bar charts   Bar charts that identify positive and negative values, or winners and losers.

devil's advocate   Person who defends a less popular viewpoint so that it receives fuller consideration.

dingbats   Small symbols such as arrows, pointing fingers, and so forth that are part of a typeface.

direct mail   A form of direct marketing that asks for an order, inquiry, or contribution directly from the reader.

direct mail package   The outer envelope of a direct mail letter and everything that goes in it: the letter, brochures, samples, secondary letters, reply card, and reply envelope.

direct marketing   All advertisements that ask for an order, inquiry, or contribution directly from the audience. Includes direct mail, catalogs, telemarketing (telephone sales), and newspaper and TV ads with 800 numbers to place an order.

direct request pattern   A pattern of organization that makes the request directly in the first paragraph.

discourse community   A group of people who share assumptions about what channels, formats, and styles to use for communication, what topics to discuss and how to discuss them, and what constitutes evidence.

divided pattern (of organization)   Discussing each alternative completely, through all criteria, before going on to the next alternative: AAA, BBB, CCC. Compare *alternating pattern.*

document design   The process of writing, organizing, and laying out a document so that it can be easily used by the intended audience.

documentation   Full bibliographic information so that interested readers can go to the original source of material used in a report.

dominating (in groups)   Trying to run a group by ordering, shutting out others, and insisting on one's own way.

dot chart   A chart that shows correlations or other large data sets. Dot charts have labeled horizontal and vertical axes.

dot planning   A way for large groups to set priorities; involves assigning colored dots to ideas.

E

editing   Checking the draft to see that it satisfies the requirements of good English and the principles of business writing. Unlike revision, which can produce major changes in meaning, editing focuses on the surface of writing.

ego-involvement   The emotional commitment that people have to their positions.

elimination of alternatives   A pattern of organization for reports that discusses the problem and its causes, the impractical solutions and their weaknesses, and finally the solution the writer favors.

ellipsis   Spaced dots used in reports to indicate that words have been omitted from quoted material and in direct mail to give the effect of pauses in speech.

emotional appeal   A persuasive technique that uses the audience's emotions to make them want to do what the writer or speaker asks.

empathy   The ability to put oneself in someone else's shoes, to feel with that person.

enclosure   A document that accompanies a letter.

enunciate   To voice all the sounds of each word while speaking.

evaluating   Measuring something, such as a document draft or a group decision, against your goals and the requirements of the situation and audience.

evidence   Data the audience already accepts.

exaggeration   Making something sound bigger or more important than it really is.

executive summary   See *abstract.*

expectancy theory   A theory that argues that motivation is based on the expectation of being rewarded for performance and the importance of the reward.

external audiences   Audiences who are not part of the writer's organization.

external documents   Documents that go to people in another organization.

external report   Report written by a consultant for an organization of which he or she is not a permanent employee.

extranets   Web pages for customers and suppliers.

extrinsic motivators   Benefits that are "added on"; they are not a necessary part of the product or action.

eye contact   Looking another person directly in the eye.

F

fallacies   Common errors in logic that weaken arguments.

feasibility report   A report that evaluates a proposed action and shows whether or not it will work.

feedback   The receiver's response to a message.

figure   Any visual that is not a table.

filler sounds   Syllables, such as *um* and *uh*, which some speakers use to fill silence as they mentally search for their next words.

five Ws and H   Questions that must be answered early in a press release: who, what, when, where, why, and how.

fixed font   A typeface in which each letter has the same width on the page. Sometimes called *typewriter typeface*.

flaming   Sending out an angry e-mail message before thinking about the implications of venting one's anger.

focus groups   Small groups who come in to talk with a skilled leader about a potential product or process.

font   A unified style of type. Fonts come in various sizes.

forecast   An overview statement that tells the audience what you will discuss in a section or an entire report.

form letter   A prewritten, fill-in-the-blank letter designed to fit standard situations.

formal meetings   Meetings run under strict rules, like the rules of parliamentary procedure summarized in *Robert's Rules of Order*.

formal report   A report containing formal elements such as a title page, a transmittal, a table of contents, and an abstract.

formalization   The third and last stage in the life of a task group, when the group makes its decision and seeks consensus.

format   The parts of a document and the way they are arranged on a page.

formation   The first stage in the life of a task group, when members choose a leader and define the problem they must solve.

freewriting   A kind of writing uninhibited by any constraints. Freewriting may be useful in overcoming writer's block, among other things.

frozen evaluation   An assessment that does not take into account the possibility of change.

full justification   Making both right and left margins of a text even, as opposed to having a ragged right margin.

fused sentence   The result when two or more sentences are joined without punctuation or conjunctions.

G

Gantt charts   Bar charts used to show schedules. Gantt charts are most commonly used in proposals.

gatekeeper   The audience with the power to decide whether your message is sent on to other audiences.

gathering data   Physically getting the background data you need. It can include informal and formal research or simply getting the letter to which you're responding.

general semantics   The study of the ways behavior is influenced by the words and other symbols used to communicate.

gerund   The *-ing* form of a verb; grammatically, it is a verb used as a noun.

getting feedback   Asking someone else to evaluate your work. Feedback is useful at every stage of the writing process, not just during composition of the final draft.

glossary   A list of terms used in a document with their definitions.

good appeal   An appeal in direct marketing that offers believable descriptions of benefits, links the benefits of the product or service to a need or desire that motivates the audience and makes the audience act.

goodwill   The value of a business beyond its tangible assets, including its reputation and patronage. Also, a favorable condition and overall atmosphere of trust that can be fostered between parties conducting business.

goodwill ending   Shift of emphasis away from the message to the reader. A goodwill ending is positive, personal, and forward-looking and suggests that serving the reader is the real concern.

goodwill presentation   A presentation that entertains and validates the audience.

grammar checker   Software program that flags errors or doubtful usage.

grapevine   An organization's informal informational network that carries gossip and rumors as well as accurate information.

grid system   A means of designing layout by imposing columns on a page and lining up graphic elements within the columns.

ground rules   Procedural rules adopted by groups to make meetings and processes run smoothly.

grouped bar chart   A bar chart that allows the viewer to compare several aspects of each item or several items over time.

groupthink   The tendency for a group to reward agreement and directly or indirectly punish dissent.

guided discussion   A presentation in which the speaker presents the questions or issues that both speaker and audience have agreed on in advance. Instead of functioning as an expert with all the answers, the speaker serves as a facilitator to help the audience tap its own knowledge.

H

headings   Words or short phrases that group points and divide your letter, memo, e-mail or report into sections.

hearing   Perceiving sounds. (Not the same thing as listening.)

hidden job market   Jobs that are never advertised but that may be available or may be created for the right candidate.

hidden negatives   Words that are not negative in themselves, but become negative in context.

high-context culture   A culture in which most information is inferred from the context, rather than being spelled out explicitly in words.

histogram   A bar chart using pictures, asterisks, or points to represent a unit of the data.

hypothetical interview question A questions that asks what a person would do in an imaginary situation

I

impersonal expression A sentence that attributes actions to inanimate objects, designed to avoid placing blame on a reader.

indented format A format for résumés in which items that are logically equivalent begin at the same horizontal space, with carryover lines indented.

independent clause See *main clause.*

infinitive The form of the verb that is preceded by *to.*

informal meetings Loosely run meetings in which votes are not taken on every point.

informal report A report using letter or memo format.

information interview An interview in which you talk to someone who works in the area you hope to enter to find out what the day-to-day work involves and how you can best prepare to enter that field.

information overload A condition in which a person cannot process all the messages he or she receives.

information report A report that collects data for the reader but does not recommend action.

informational dimensions Dimensions of group work focusing on the problem, data, and possible solutions.

informative message Message giving information to which the reader's basic reaction will be neutral.

informative presentation A presentation that informs or teaches the audience.

informative report A report that provides information.

inside address The reader's name and address; put below the date and above the salutation in most letter formats.

interactive presentation A presentation that is a conversation between the speaker and the audience.

intercultural competence The ability to communicate sensitively with people from other cultures and countries, based on an understanding of cultural differences.

internal audiences Audiences in the communicator's organization.

internal document Document written for other employees in the same organization.

internal documentation Providing information about a source in the text itself rather than in footnotes or endnotes.

internal report Reports written by employees for use only in their organization.

interpersonal communication Communication between people.

interpersonal dimensions In a group, efforts promoting friendliness, cooperation, and group loyalty.

interview Structured conversation with someone who is able to give you useful information.

intranet A web page just for employees.

intrapreneurs Innovators who work within organizations.

intrinsic motivators Benefits that come automatically from using a product or doing something.

introduction The part of a report that states the purpose and scope of the report. The introduction may also include limitations, assumptions, methods, criteria, and definitions.

J

jargon There are two kinds of jargon. The first kind is the specialized terminology of a technical field. The second is businessese, outdated words that do not have technical meanings and are not used in other forms of English.

judgment See *opinion.*

judgment sample A group of subjects whose views seem useful.

justification report Report that justifies the need for a purchase, an investment, a new personnel line, or a change in procedure.

justified margins Margins that end evenly on both sides of the page.

K

key words Words used in (1) a résumé to summarize areas of expertise, qualifications, and (2) an article or report to describe the content. Key words facilitate computer searches.

L

letter Short document using block, modified, or simplified letter format that goes to readers outside your organization.

letterhead Stationery with the organization's name, logo, address, and telephone number printed on the page.

limitations Problems or factors that constrain the validity of the recommendations of a report.

line graph A visual consisting of lines that show trends or allow the viewer to interpolate values between the observed values.

logical fallacies See *fallacies.*

low-context culture A culture in which most information is conveyed explicitly in words rather than being inferred from context.

M

main clause A group of words that can stand by itself as a complete sentence. Also called an independent clause.

Maslow's hierarchy of needs Five levels of human need posited by Abraham H. Maslow. They include physical needs, the need for safety and security, for love and belonging, for esteem and recognition, and for self-actualization.

mean The average of a group of numbers. Found by dividing the sum of a set of figures by the number of figures.

median The middle number in a ranked set of numbers.

memo Document using memo format sent to readers in your organization.

methods section The section of a report or survey describing how the data were gathered.

minutes Records of a meeting, listing the items discussed, the results of votes, and the persons responsible for carrying out follow-up steps.

mirror question   Question that paraphrases the content of the answer an interviewee gave to the last question.

misplaced modifier   A word or phrase that appears to modify another element of the sentence than the writer intended.

mixed punctuation   Using a colon after the salutation and a comma after the complimentary close in a letter.

mode   The most frequent number in a set of numbers.

modified block format   A letter format in which the inside address, date, and signature block are lined up with each other one-half or two-thirds of the way over on the page.

modifier   A word or phrase giving more information about another word in a sentence.

monochronic culture   Culture in which people do only one important activity at a time.

monologue presentation   A presentation in which the speaker talks without interruption. The presentation is planned and is delivered without deviation.

multiple graphs   Three or more simple stories told by graphs juxtaposed to create a more powerful story.

Myers-Briggs Type Indicator   A scale that categorizes people on four dimensions: introvert-extravert; sensing-intuitive; thinking-feeling; and perceiving-judging.

N

negative message   A message in which basic information conveyed is negative; the reader is expected to be disappointed or angry.

networking   Using your connections with other people to help you achieve a goal.

neutral subject line   A subject line that does not give away the writer's stance on an issue.

noise   Any physical or psychological interference in a message.

nominative case   The grammatical form used for the subject of a clause. *I, we, he, she,* and *they* are nominative pronouns.

nonageist   Refers to words, images, or behaviors that do not discriminate against people on the basis of age.

noncompetitive proposal   A proposal with no real competition and hence a high probability of acceptance.

nonracist   Refers to words, images, or behaviors that do not discriminate against people on the basis of race.

nonrestrictive clause   A clause giving extra but unessential information about a noun or pronoun. Because the information is extra, commas separate the clause from the word it modifies.

nonsexist language   Language that treats both sexes neutrally, that does not make assumptions about the proper gender for a job, and that does not imply that one sex is superior to or takes precedence over the other.

nonverbal communication   Communication that does not use words.

normal interview   A job interview with mostly expected questions.

noun–pronoun agreement   Having a pronoun be the same number (singular or plural) and the same person (first, second, or third) as the noun it refers to.

O

objective case   The grammatical form used for the object of a verb or preposition. *Me, us, him, her,* and *them* are objective pronouns.

omnibus motion   A motion that allows a group to vote on several related items in a single vote. Saves time in formal meetings with long agendas.

open body position   Includes keeping the arms and legs uncrossed and away from the body. Suggests physical and psychological comfort and openness.

open punctuation   Using no punctuation after the salutation and the complimentary close.

open question   Question with an unlimited number of possible responses.

opinion   A statement that can never be verified, since it includes terms that cannot be measured objectively. Also called a judgment.

organization (in messages)   The order in which ideas are arranged.

organizational culture   The values, attitudes, and philosophies shared by people in an organization that shape its behaviors and reward structure.

outsourcing   Going outside the company for products and services that once were made by the company's employees.

P

package   The outer envelope and everything that goes in it in a direct mailing.

paired bar chart   A bar chart that shows the correlation between two items.

parallel structure   Using the same grammatical and logical form for words, phrases, clauses, and ideas in a series.

paraphrase   To repeat in your own words the verbal content of another communication.

passive verb   A verb that describes action done to the grammatical subject of the sentence.

people-first language   Language that names the person first, then the condition: "people with mental retardation." Used to avoid implying that the condition defines the person's potential.

performance appraisals   Supervisors' written evaluations of their subordinates' work.

persona   The "author" or character who allegedly writes a document; the voice that a communicator assumes in creating a message.

personal brandings   A pop term for marketing yourself, including job searching. It includes an expectation that you will use various options, including social media such as LinkedIn, to market yourself.

personal space   The distance someone wants between him- or herself and other people in ordinary, nonintimate interchanges.

personalized   A message that is adapted to the individual reader by including the reader's name and address and perhaps other information.

persuade   To motivate and convince the audience to act or change a belief.

persuasive presentation   A presentation that motivates the audience to act or to believe.

phishing e-mails   E-mails that look like messages from official business but actually connect to private sites seeking to acquire data for fraud or identity theft.

pictogram   A bar chart using pictures or symbols to represent a unit of data.

pie chart   A circular chart whose sections represent percentages of a given quantity.

pitch   The highness or lowness of a sound.

plagiarism   Passing off the words or ideas of others as one's own.

planning   All the thinking done about a subject and the means of achieving your purposes. Planning takes place not only when devising strategies for the document as a whole, but also when generating "miniplans" that govern sentences or paragraphs.

polarization   A logical fallacy that argues there are only two possible positions, one of which is clearly unacceptable.

polychronic culture   Culture in which people do several things at once.

population   The group a researcher wants to make statements about.

positive emphasis   Focusing on the positive rather than the negative aspects of a situation.

positive or good news message   Message to which the reader's reaction will be positive.

possessive case   The grammatical form used to indicate possession or ownership. *My, our, his, hers, its,* and *their* are possessive pronouns.

post office abbreviations   Two-letter abbreviations for states and provinces.

prepositions   Words that indicate relationships, for example, *with, in, under, at.*

presenting problem   The problem that surfaces as the subject of discord. The presenting problem is often not the real problem.

primary audience   The audience who will make a decision or act on the basis of a message.

primary research   Research that gathers new information.

pro-and-con pattern   A pattern of organization that presents all the arguments for an alternative and then all the arguments against it.

probe question   A follow-up question designed to get more information about an answer or to get at specific aspects of a topic.

problem-solving pattern   A pattern of organization that describes a problem before offering a solution to the problem.

procedural dimensions   Dimensions of group work focusing on methods: how the group makes decisions, who does what, when assignments are due.

process of writing   What people actually do when they write: planning, gathering, writing, evaluating, getting feedback, revising, editing, and proofreading.

progress report   A statement of the work done during a period of time and the work proposed for the next period.

proofreading   Checking the final copy to see that it's free from typographical errors.

proportional font   A font in which some letters are wider than other letters (for example, *w* is wider than *i*).

proposal   Document that suggests a method and personnel for finding information or solving a problem.

prospecting letter   A job application letter written to a company that has not announced openings but where you'd like to work.

psychographic characteristics   Human characteristics that are qualitative rather than quantitative: values, beliefs, goals, and lifestyles.

psychological description   Description of a product or service in terms of audience benefits.

psychological reactance   Phenomenon occurring when a person reacts to a negative message by asserting freedom in some other arena.

purpose statement   The statement in a proposal or a report specifying the organizational problem, the technical questions that must be answered to solve the problem, and the rhetorical purpose of the report (to explain, to recommend, to request, to propose).

Q

questionnaire   List of questions for people to answer in a survey.

R

ragged right margins   Margins that do not end evenly on the right side of the page.

random sample   A sample for which each member of the population has an equal chance of being chosen.

range   The difference between the highest and lowest numbers in a set of figures.

recommendation report   A report that evaluates two or more possible alternatives and recommends one of them. Doing nothing is always one alternative.

recommendations   Section of a report that specifies items for action.

reference line   A *subject line* that refers the reader to another document (usually a numbered one, such as an invoice).

referral interview   Interviews you schedule to learn about current job opportunities in your field and to get referrals to other people who may have the power to create a job for you. Useful for tapping into unadvertised jobs and the hidden job market.

reflexive pronoun   Refers to or emphasizes a noun or pronoun that has already appeared in the sentence. *Myself, herself,* and *themselves* are reflexive pronouns.

release date Date a report will be made available to the public.

reply card A card or form designed to make it easy for the reader to respond to a direct mail letter. A good reply card repeats the central selling point, basic product information, and price.

request for proposal (RFP) A statement of the service or product that an agency wants; an invitation for proposals to provide that service or product.

respondents The people who fill out a questionnaire; also called *subjects.*

response rate The percentage of subjects receiving a questionnaire who answer the questions.

restrictive clause A clause limiting or restricting the meaning of a noun or pronoun. Because its information is essential, no commas separate the clause from the word it restricts.

résumé A persuasive summary of your qualifications for employment.

résumé blasting Posting your résumé widely—usually by the hundreds—on the web.

reverse chronology Starting with the most recent events, such as job or degree, and going backward in time. Pattern of organization used for chronological résumés.

revising Making changes in the draft: adding, deleting, substituting, or rearranging. Revision can be changes in single words, but more often it means major additions, deletions, or substitutions, as the writer measures the draft against purpose and audience and reshapes the document to make it more effective.

RFP See *request for proposal.*

rhetorical purpose The effect the writer or speaker hopes to have on the audience (to inform, to persuade, to build goodwill).

rhythm The repetition of a pattern of accented and unaccented syllables.

rival hypotheses Alternate explanations for observed results.

rule of three The rule noting a preference for three short parallel examples and explaining that the last will receive the most emphasis.

run-on sentence A sentence containing two or more main clauses strung together with *and, but, or, so,* or *for.*

S

sales pattern A pattern of persuasion that consists of an attention getting opener, a body with reasons and details, and an action close.

salutation The greeting in a letter: "Dear Ms. Smith:"

sample (in marketing) A product provided to the audience to whet their appetite for more.

sample (in research) The portion of the population a researcher actually studies.

sampling frame The list of all possible sampling units.

sampling units Those items/people actually sampled.

sans serif Literally, *without serifs.* Typeface whose letters lack bases or flicks. Helvetica and Geneva are examples of sans serif typefaces.

saves the reader's time The result of a message whose style, organization, and visual impact help the reader to read, understand, and act on the information as quickly as possible.

schematic diagrams Line drawings of objects and their parts.

scope statement A statement in a proposal or report specifying the subjects the report covers and how broadly or deeply it covers them.

secondary audience The audience who may be asked by the primary audience to comment on a message or to implement ideas after they've been approved.

secondary research Research retrieving data someone else gathered. Includes library research.

segmented, subdivided, or stacked bars Bars in a bar chart that sum components of an item.

semantics or general semantics The study of the ways behavior is influenced by the words and other symbols used to communicate.

sentence fragment Words that are not a complete sentence but that are punctuated as if they were a complete sentence.

sentence outline An outline using complete sentences. It contains the thesis or recommendation plus all supporting points.

serif The little extensions from the main strokes on letters. Times Roman and Courier are examples of serif typefaces.

signpost An explicit statement of the place that a speaker or writer has reached: "Now we come to the third point."

simple sentence Sentence with one main clause.

simplified format A letter format that omits the salutation and complimentary close and lines everything up at the left margin.

situational interviews Job interviews in which candidates are asked to describe what they would do in specific hypothetical situations.

skills résumé A résumé organized around the skills you've used, rather than the date or the job in which you used them.

social signals Nonverbal communications such as gestures, facial expressions, voice tone, and proximity.

solicited letter A job letter written when you know that the company is hiring.

spot visuals Informal visuals that are inserted directly into text. Spot visuals do not have numbers or titles.

stereotyping Putting similar people or events into a single category, even though significant differences exist.

storyboard A visual representation of the structure of a document, with a rectangle representing each page or unit. An alternative to outlining as a method of organizing material.

strategy   A plan for reaching your specific goals with a specific audience.

stratified random sample   A sample generated by first dividing the sample into subgroups in the population and then taking a random sample for each subgroup.

stress (in a communication)   Emphasis given to one or more words in a sentence, or one or more ideas in a message.

stress interview   A job interview that deliberately puts the applicant under stress, physical or psychological. Here it's important to change the conditions that create physical stress and to meet psychological stress by rephrasing questions in less inflammatory terms and treating them as requests for information.

structured interview   An interview that follows a detailed list of questions prepared in advance.

stub   The variable listed on the side in a table.

subject line   The title of the document, used to file and retrieve the document. A subject line tells readers why they need to read the document and provides a framework in which to set what you're about to say.

subordinate clause   A group of words containing a subject and a verb but that cannot stand by itself as a complete sentence. Also called a dependent clause.

summarizing   Restating and relating major points, pulling ideas together.

summary abstract   The logic skeleton of an article or report, containing the thesis or recommendation and its proof.

summary sentence or paragraph   A sentence or paragraph listing in order the topics that following sentences or paragraphs will discuss.

survey   A method of getting information from a group of people.

SWOT analysis   A method of evaluating a proposed action that examines both internal factors (Strengths, Weaknesses) and external factors (Opportunities, Threats).

T

table   Numbers or words arrayed in rows and columns.

talking heads   Headings that are detailed enough to provide an overview of the material in the sections they introduce.

template   A design or format that serves as a pattern.

10-K report   A report filed with the Securities and Exchange Commission summarizing the firm's financial performance.

thank-you note   A note thanking someone for helping you.

threat   A statement, explicit or implied, that someone will be punished if he or she does or doesn't do something.

360-degree feedback   A form of assessment in which an employee receives feedback from peers, managers, subordinates, customers, and suppliers.

tone   The implied attitude of the author toward the reader and the subject.

tone of voice   The rising or falling inflection that indicates whether a group of words is a question or a statement, whether

the speaker is uncertain or confident, whether a statement is sincere or sarcastic.

topic heading   A heading that focuses on the structure of a report. Topic headings give little information.

topic outline   An outline listing the main points and the subpoints under each main point. A topic outline is the basis for the table of contents of a report.

topic sentence   A sentence that introduces or summarizes the main idea in a paragraph.

transitions   Words, phrases, or sentences that show the connections between ideas.

transmit   To send a message.

transmittal   A message explaining why something is being sent.

truncated code   Symbols such as asterisks that turn up other forms of a keyword in a computer search.

truncated graphs   Graphs with part of the scale missing.

two-margin format   A format for résumés in which dates are listed in one column and job titles and descriptions in another. This format emphasizes work history.

U

umbrella sentence or paragraph   A sentence or paragraph listing in order the topics that following sentences or paragraphs will discuss.

understatement   Downplaying or minimizing the size or features of something.

unity   Using only one idea or topic in a paragraph or other piece of writing.

unjustified margins   Margins that do not end evenly on the right side of the page.

unstructured interview   An interview based on three or four main questions prepared in advance and other questions that build on what the interviewee says.

usability testing   Testing a document with users to see that it functions as desired.

V

venting   Expressing pent-up negative emotions.

verbal communication   Communication that uses words; may be either oral or written.

vested interest   The emotional stake readers have in something if they benefit from maintaining or influencing conditions or actions.

vicarious participation   An emotional strategy in fundraising letters based on the idea that by donating money, readers participate in work they are not able to do personally.

visual impact   The visual "first impression" you get when you look at a page.

volume   The loudness or softness of a voice or other sound.

W

watchdog audience   An audience that has political, social, or economic power and that may base future actions on its evaluation of your message.

white space The empty space on the page. White space emphasizes material that it separates from the rest of the text.

widget A software program that can be dropped into social networking sites and other places.

wild card Symbols such as asterisks that turn up other forms of a keyword in a computer search. See also *truncated code.*

withdrawing Being silent, not contributing, not helping with the work, not attending meetings.

wordiness Taking more words than necessary to express an idea.

works cited The sources specifically referred to in a report.

works consulted Sources read during the research for a report but not mentioned specifically in the report.

Y

you-attitude A style of communicating that looks at things from the audience's point of view, emphasizes what the audience wants to know, respects the audience's intelligence, and protects the audience's ego. Using *you* generally increases you-attitude in positive situations. In negative situations or conflict, avoid *you* since that word will attack the audience.

NOTES

Chapter 1

1. United States Postal Service, "Postal Facts 2010," news release, accessed April 18, 2011, http://www.usps.com/communications/newsroom/postalfacts.htm; Jennifer Valentino-DeVries, "With Catalogs, Opt-Out Policies Vary," *Wall Street Journal,* April 13, 2011, B7; Brian Dunn, "Hard Choices," *Bloomberg Businessweek,* December 6, 2010, 104; and "Internet 2010 in Numbers," *Pingdom* (blog), January 12, 2011, http://royal.pingdom.com/2011/01/12/internet-2010-in-numbers.

2. National Association of Colleges and Employers, "Top Skills for Job Candidates," press release, December 2, 2010, http://www.naceweb.org/Press/Releases/Top_Skills_for_Job_Candidates.aspx.

3. Alex Crippen, "Warren Buffett's $100,000 Offer and $500,000 Advice for Columbia Business School Students," CNBC, November 12, 2009, http://www.cnbc.com/id/33891448/Warren_Buffett_s_100_000_Offer_and_500_000_Advice_for_Columbia_Business_School_Students.

4. Peter Coy, "The Future of Work," *BusinessWeek,* March 22, 2004, 50.

5. The National Commission on Writing for America's Families, Schools, and Colleges, "Writing: A Ticket to Work. . .or a Ticket Out: A Survey of Business Leaders," *College Board* (2004), 7–8.

6. Anne Fisher, "The High Cost of Living and Not Writing Well," *Fortune,* December 7, 1998, 244.

7. Jeffrey Gitomer, *Jeffrey Gitomer's Little Black Book of Connections: 6.5 Assets for Networking Your Way to Rich Relationships* (Austin, TX: Bard Press, 2006), 128–31.

8. Peter D. Hart Research Associate, Inc., *How Should Colleges Assess and Improve Student Learning? Employers' Views on the Accountability Challenge: A Survey of Employers Conducted on Behalf of the Association of American Colleges and Universities* (Washington, DC: The Association of American Colleges and Universities, 2008), 3.

9. The Conference Board et al., *Are They Really Ready To Work? Employers' Perspectives on the Basic Knowledge and Applied Skills of New Entrants to the 21st Century U.S. Workforce,* accessed April 18, 2011, http://www.conference-board.org/pdf_free/BED-06-workforce.pdf.

10. Tom DeMint, "So You Want to be Promoted," *Fire Engineering* 159, no. 7 (2006); Karen M. Kroll, "Mapping Your Career," *PM Network* 19, no. 11 (2005): 28; and Jeff Snyder, "Recruiter: What It Takes," *Security* 43, no. 11 (2006): 70.

11. ". . . Lost Mail," *News & Observer* (Raleigh, NC), April 12, 2011, 8A.

12. "Case Studies," Xerox Corporation, accessed April 19, 2011, http://www.consulting.xerox.com/case-studies/enus.html; and Xerox, *The Optimum Office: How to Achieve Immediate and Guaranteed Cost Savings via a Managed Print Service,* April 2009, http://www.xerox.com/downloads/usa/en/xgs/casestudies/xgs_whitepaper_Optimum_Office_US.pdf.

13. Eric Krell, "The Unintended Word," *HRMagazine* 51, no. 8 (2006): 52.

14. Pui-Wing Tam, "Cutting Files Down to Size: New Approaches Tackle Surplus of Data," *Wall Street Journal,* May 8, 2007, B4.

15. Manuel E. Sosa, Steven D. Eppinger, and Craig M. Rowles, "Are Your Engineers Talking to One Another When They Should?" *Harvard Business Review* 85, no. 11 (2007): 133–42.

16. Peter Sanders, "Boeing Has New Delay for Dreamliner," *Wall Street Journal,* August 28, 2010, B6.

17. The National Commission on Writing for America's Families, Schools, and Colleges, "Writing: A Ticket to Work. . .or a Ticket Out: A Survey of Business Leaders," *College Board* (2004), 29.

18. Michael Lewis, "The End of Wall Street's Boom," Portfolio.com, November 11, 2008, http://www.portfolio.com/news-markets/national-news/portfolio/2008/11/11/The-End-of-Wall-Streets-Boom; and Jean Eaglesham, "Banks Near Deal with SEC: Wall Street Is Keen to Settle Fraud Charges Involving Toxic Mortgage Bonds," *Wall Street Journal,* April 15, 2011, A1.

19. U.S. House of Representatives, *A Failure of Initiative: Final Report of the Select Bipartisan Committee to Investigate the Preparation for and Response to Hurricane Katrina,* 109th Cong., 2d sess. (Washington, DC, February 15, 2006), http://www.gpoaccess.gov/katrinareport/mainreport.pdf; Stephen Power and Ben Casselman, "White House Probe Blames BP, Industry in Gulf Blast," *Wall Street Journal,* January 6, 2011, A2.

20. Janet Adamy, "Advertising: Will a Twist on an Old Vow Deliver for Domino's Pizza?" *Wall Street Journal,* December 17, 2007, B1.

21. Stephen Baker, "A Painful Lesson: E-mail Is Forever," *BusinessWeek,* March 21, 2005, 36; Gary McWilliams, "Wal-Mart Details Roehm Firing," *Wall Street Journal,* March 21, 2007, B11; Peter Waldman and Don Clark, "California Charges Dunn, 4 Others in H-P Scandal; Action Sends Strong Message to Business about Privacy; Precedents for the Web Age?" *Wall Street Journal,* October 5, 2006, A1; and "Will 'Love Factor' Help Make S. C.'s Sanford More Forgivable?" *Des Moines Register,* June 29, 2009, 12A.

22. Elizabeth A. McCord, "The Business Writer, the Law, and Routine Business Communication: A Legal and Rhetorical Analysis," *Journal of Business and Technical Communication* 5, no. 3 (1991): 173–99.

23. The Nielsen Company, "Television, Internet and Mobile Usage in the U.S." Three Screen Report 8, 1st Quarter 2010, http://www.nielsen.com/content/dam/corporate/us/en/reports-downloads/3%20Screen/2010/Three%20Screen%20Report%20%28Q1%202010%29.pdf; Bureau of Labor Statistics, "American Time Use Survey Summary," news release, June 22, 2010, http://www.bls.gov/news.release/atus.nr0.htm; Kristen Purcell, Lee Rainie, Amy Mitchell, Tom Rosenstiel, and Kenny Olmstead, "Understanding the Participatory News Customer," Pew Internet & American Life Project, March 1, 2010, http://www.pewinternet.org/Reports/2010/Online-News.aspx?r=1; and The Nielsen Company, "What Americans Do Online: Social Media and Games Dominate Activity," *Nielsenwire* (blog), August 2, 2010, http://blog.nielsen.com/nielsenwire/online_mobile/what-americans-do-online-social-media-and-games-dominate-activity/.

Chapter 2

1. Isabel Briggs Myers, *Introduction to Type* (Palo Alto, CA: Consulting Psychologists Press, 1980). The material in this section follows Myers's paper.

2. Isabel Briggs Myers and Mary H. McCaulley, *Manual: A Guide to the Development and Use of the Myers-Briggs Type Indicator* (Palo Alto, CA: Consulting Psychologists Press, 1985), 248–51.

3. Eleanor Laise, "Fund Firms Lower Bar for Younger Investors: Wall Street Unveils Slew of Products with 20-Something Slant; 'My Whatever Plan' Cuts Minimums but Limits Choices," *Wall Street Journal,* July 17, 2007, D1.

4. Miguel Bustillo, "Wal-Mart Adds Guns alongside Butter," *Wall Street Journal,* April 28, 2011, B1.

5. Doug Henschen, "Social Media Shapes Up as Next Analytic Frontier," *InformationWeek*, May 2, 2011, http://www.informationweek.com/news/software/bi/229402598; and Emily Steel, "Exploring Ways to Build a Better Consumer Profile: Nielsen, Digital-Marketing Firm eXelate Form Alliance to Merge Online and Offline Data in Bid to Improve Ad Targeting," *Wall Street Journal*, March 15, 2010, B4.

6. Doug Henschen, "Social Media Shapes Up as Next Analytic Frontier."

7. Ellen Byron, "Big Diaper Makers Square Off," *Wall Street Journal*, April 13, 2009, B7; and Suzanne Vranica, "Tweeting to Sell Cars: Auto Makers Turn to Social Media 'Influencers' for Buzz," *Wall Street Journal*, November 15, 2010, B12.

8. Marc Gunther, "Hard News," *Fortune*, August 6, 2007, 82.

9. "The State of the News Media 2011: An Annual Report on American Journalism: Key Findings," Pew Research Center's Project for Excellence in Journalism, March 14, 2011, http://stateofthemedia.org/2011/overview-2/key-findings/.

10. "The State of the News Media 2011: An Annual Report on American Journalism: Key Findings," Pew Research Center's Project for Excellence in Journalism; and "Peggy Sue Got Old," *Economist*, April 7, 2011, http://www.economist.com/node/18527255?story_id=18527255.

11. "Intel Taps 'Minority Report' for Ad Idea," *Wall Street Journal*, December 13, 2010, B6.

12. John Jurgensen, "How to Make It in the Music Business Today," *Wall Street Journal*, December 17, 2010, D2.

13. Elizabeth Olson, "The Ken Doll Turns 50, and Wins a New Face," *New York Times*, March 21, 2011, http://www.nytimes.com/2011/03/22/business/media/22adco.html.

14. Ben Paynter, "Five Steps to Social Currency," *Fast Company*, May 1, 2010, 45.

15. Emily Steel, "Marketers Test Ads in E-Books," *Wall Street Journal*, December 13, 2010, B1.

16. Stephanie Kang, "Magic of Clorox Sells for a Song," *Wall Street Journal*, March 28, 2008, B4; and "Meet the Newest Rap Recording Artist," *Des Moines Register*, April 16, 2008, 2A.

17. "Steamy Hot Line Raises Pulses, Library Funds," *Des Moines Register*, May 9, 2007, 4A.

18. Suzanne Vranica, "Hanger Ads Ensure Message Gets Home," *Wall Street Journal*, March 12, 2007, B4.

19. Jeffery F. Rayport, "Where Is Advertising Going? Into 'Stitials,'" *Harvard Business Review* 86, no. 5 (2008): 18–19.

20. Lev Grossman, "A Game for All Ages," *Time*, May 15, 2006, 39.

21. Miguel Bustillo and Christopher Lawton, "Best Buy Expands Private-Label Brands," *Wall Street Journal*, April 29, 2009, B1.

22. Cecilie Rohwedder, "Store of Knowledge: No. 1 Retailer in Britain Uses 'Clubcard' to Thwart Wal-Mart: Data from Loyalty Program Help Tesco Tailor Products as It Resists U.S. Invader," *Wall Street Journal*, June 6, 2006, A1.

23. Frederick Herzberg, "One More Time: How Do You Motivate Employees?" *Harvard Business Review* 65, no. 5 (1987): 109–20.

24. John Ketzenberger, "Respect, Not Money, Priceless in Cutting Turnover," *Des Moines Register*, November 20, 2006, 3D.

25. Teri Agins, "Over-40 Finds a Muse," *Wall Street Journal*, December 6, 2008, W4.

26. Ellen Byron, "How P&G Led Also-Ran to Sweet Smell of Success: By Focusing on Fragrance, Gain Detergent Developed a Billion-Dollar Following," *Wall Street Journal*, September 4, 2007, B2.

27. Ryan Chittum, "Price Points: Good Customer Service Costs Money. Some Expenses Are Worth It—and Some Aren't," *Wall Street Journal*, October 30, 2006, R7.

28. David Wessel, "Paper Chase: South Africa's Sun Targets New Class: Tabloid Melds Sex, Soccer with Tales from Townships; Report on Flying Tortoise," *Wall Street Journal*, August 17, 2007, A1.

29. Jeff Eckhoff, "Less Huffing, More Fitness in Meredith's Workout Plan," *Des Moines Register*, June 14, 2009, 1D.

30. Stephen W. Brown, Aners Gustafsson, and Lars Witell, "Beyond Products," *Wall Street Journal*, June 22, 2009, R7.

31. Richard M. Smith, "Stay True to Your Brand: Ad Guru Rance Crain Says the Rules Are Eternal," *Newsweek*, May 5, 2008, E18.

32. James Surowiecki, "The Financial Page Feature Presentation," *The New Yorker*, May 28, 2007, 28.

33. Reuters, "Scientist: Complexity Causes 50% of Product Returns," *Computer World*, May 6, 2006, http://www.computerworld.com/s/article/109254/Scientist_Complexity_causes_50_of_product_returns.

34. Rachael Spilka, "Orality and Literacy in the Workplace: Process- and Text-Based Strategies for Multiple Audience Adaptation," *Journal of Business and Technical Communication* 4, no. 1 (1990): 44–67.

Chapter 3

1. "Amazon Investor Relations," Amazon.com, March 25, 2011, http://phx.corporate-ir.net/phoenix.zhtml?p=irol-irhome&c=97664; and "Video from Jeff Bezos about Amazon and Zappos," YouTube video, 8:10, posted by "07272009july," July 22, 2009, http://www.youtube.com/watch?v=-hxX_Q5CnaA.

2. Linda Kaplan Thaler and Robin Koval, *The Power of Nice: How to Conquer the Business World with Kindness* (New York: Currency, 2006), 3.

3. Aaron Pressman, "When Service Means Survival," *BusinessWeek*, March 2, 2009, 62.

4. John A. Byrne, "How to Lead Now: Getting Extraordinary Performance When You Can't Pay for It," *Fast Company*, August 2003, 65.

5. Timothy Aeppel, "Too Good for Lowe's and Home Depot?" *Wall Street Journal*, July 24, 2006, B1, B6.

6. Annette N. Shelby and N. Lamar Reinsch, "Positive Emphasis and You-Attitude: An Empirical Study," *Journal of Business Communication* 32, no. 4 (1995): 303–27.

7. Martin E. P. Seligman, *Learned Optimism: How to Change Your Mind and Your Life*, 2nd ed. (New York: Pocket Books, 1998), 96–107.

8. Mark A. Sherman, "Adjectival Negation and Comprehension of Multiply Negated Sentences," *Journal of Verbal Learning and Verbal Behavior* 15 (1976): 143–57.

9. Jeffrey Zaslow, "In Praise of Less Praise," *Wall Street Journal*, May 3, 2007, D1.

10. Associated Press, "Florida Police Chief Ousted after 'Jelly Bellies' Memo Telling Cops to Get Fit," *Fox News*, November 2, 2006, http://www.foxnews.com/story/0,2933,226808,00.html.

11. Stephen C. Dillard, "Litigation Nation," *Wall Street Journal*, November 25, 2006, A9.

12. Margaret Baker Graham and Carol David, "Power and Politeness: Administrative Writing in an 'Organized Anarchy,'" *Journal of Business and Technical Communication* 10, no. 1 (1996): 5–27.

13. "Women's History Month: March 2011," U.S. Census Bureau Newsroom, January 26, 2011, http://www.census.gov/newsroom/releases/archives/facts_for_features_

special_editions/cb11-ff04.html; "2010 Census Shows America's Diversity," U.S. Census Bureau Newsroom, March 23, 2011, http://www.census.gov/newsroom/releases/archives/2010_census/cb11-cn125.html; and "Older Americans Month: May 2011," U.S. Census Bureau Newsroom, March 23, 2011, http://www.census.gov/newsroom/releases/archives/facts_for_features_special_editions/cb11-ff08.html.

14. Laura Stevens, "German CEO's Remark on Women Draws Fire," *Wall Street Journal*, February 8, 2011, A9.

15. Frank Newport, "Black or African American?" Gallup, September 28, 2007, http://www.gallup.com/poll/28816/black-african-american.aspx.

16. "20th Anniversary of Americans with Disabilities Act: July 26," U.S. Census Bureau Newsroom, May 26, 2010, http://www.census.gov/newsroom/releases/archives/facts_for_features_special_editions/cb10-ff13.html.

17. M. P. McQueen, "Workplace Disabilities Are on the Rise: Employers Devise Strategies to Accommodate Growing Ranks of Employees Impaired by Age, Obesity, and Disease," *Wall Street Journal*, May 1, 2007, D1.

18. Clark Ansberry, "Erasing a Hurtful Label from the Books," *Wall Street Journal*, November 30, 2010, A6.

Chapter 4

1. Peter Loftus and Jon Kamp, "Glaxo to Pay $750 Million in Pact; Whistleblower Due Big Payment," *Wall Street Journal*, November 27, 2010, B3.

2. Michael Rothfeld, Susan Pulliam, and Chad Bray, " Fund Titan Found Guilty," *Wall Street Journal*, May 12, 2011, A1.

3. Ethics Resource Center, *2009 National Business Ethics Survey* 9, no. 33, accessed May 24, 2011, http://www.ethics.org/nbes/files/nbes-final.pdf.

4. Mary C. Gentile, "Keeping Your Colleagues Honest," *Harvard Business Review* 88, no. 2 (2010): 114–15.

5. "United Nations Global Compact Participants," United Nations Global Compact, accessed May 26, 2011, http://www.unglobalcompact.org/ParticipantsAndStakeholders/index.html.

6. "About Us," Clinton Global Initiative, accessed May 26, 2011, http://www.clintonglobalinitiative.org/aboutus/default.asp.

7. "About Us," Google, accessed May 26, 2011, http://www.google.org/about.html.

8. "Robin Hood: Targeting Poverty in New York City," Robin Hood Foundation, accessed May 26, 2011, http://www.robinhood.org; and Andy Serwer, "The Legend of Robin Hood," *Fortune*, September 18, 2006, 103–14.

9. "Grameen Bank at a Glance," Grameen Bank, last updated March 2011, http://www.grameen-info.org/index.php?option=com_content&task=view&id=26&Itemid=175; and Social Finance.org, "Social Finance Launches First Social Impact Bond," news release, March 18, 2010, http://www.socialfinance.org.uk/sites/default/files/SIB_March18_PR.pdf.

10. Quoted from Tony Hsieh, *Delivering Happiness: A Path to Profits, Passion, and Purpose* (New York: Business Plus, 2010), 243.

11. Leigh Buchanan, "Learning from the Best: Smart Strategies from the Top Small Company Workplaces," *Inc.*, June 2010, 92.

12. Ellen Byron, "Merger Challenge: Unite Toothbrush, Toothpaste: P&G and Gillette Find Creating Synergy Can Be Harder than It Looks," *Wall Street Journal*, April 24, 2007, A1.

13. Phred Dvorak, "Hotelier Finds Happiness Keeps Staff Checked In," *Wall Street Journal*, December 17, 2007, B3.

14. Tony Hsieh, *Delivering Happiness: A Path to Profits, Passion, and Purpose* (New York: Business Plus, 2010), 150–65.

15. Tony Hsieh, *Delivering Happiness: A Path to Profits, Passion, and Purpose*, 148.

16. Daniel Goleman, *Emotional Intelligence: The Tenth Anniversary Edition* (New York: Bantam, 2005), xiv–xv.

17. Deborah Tannen, *That's Not What I Meant!* (New York: William Morrow, 1986).

18. Daniel N. Maltz and Ruth A. Borker, "A Cultural Approach to Male–Female Miscommunication," in *Language and Social Identity*, ed. John J. Gumperz (Cambridge: Cambridge University Press, 1982), 202.

19. Marie Helweg-Larson et al., "To Nod or Not to Nod: An Observational Study of Nonverbal Communication and Status in Female and Male College Students," *Psychology of Women Quarterly* 28, no. 4 (2004): 358–61.

20. Carol Kinsey Goman, "10 Common Body Language Traps for Women in the Workplace," *On Leadership* (blog), *Washington Post*, March 3, 2011, http://www.washingtonpost.com/blogs/on-leadership/post/10-common-body-language-traps-for-women-in-the-workplace/2011/03/03/AFl0GFbF_blog.html.

21. Alex Pentland, "We Can Measure the Power of Charisma," *Business Review*, January 2010, 34.

22. Alex "Sandy" Pentland, "The Power of Nonverbal Communication," *Wall Street Journal*, October 20, 2008, R2.

23. Daniel Goleman, *Emotional Intelligence: The Tenth Anniversary Edition* (New York: Bantam, 2005), 161–62.

24. Daniel Goleman, *Emotional Intelligence: The Tenth Anniversary Edition*, 162.

25. "Social Studies," *Businessweek*, June 14, 2010, 72–3.

26. Jessica Hodgins, "'You Can't Make More Time': Randy Pausch's Heart-felt Views on Using Time to the Fullest," *BusinessWeek*, September 1, 2008, 71.

27. Stephen R. Covey, *The 7 Habits of Highly Effective People: Restoring the Character* (New York: Free Press, 2004), 150–54.

28. Jared Sandberg, "Yes, Sell All My Stocks. No, the 3:15 from JFK. and Get Me Mr. Sister," *Wall Street Journal*, September 12, 2006, B1.

29. Toddi Gutner, "Beat the Clock: E-mails, Faxes, Phone Calls, Oh My. Here's How to Get It All Done," *BusinessWeek SmallBiz*, February/March 2008, 58.

30. Adam Gorlick, "Media Multitaskers Pay Mental Price, Stanford Study Shows," *Stanford Report*, August 24, 2009, http://news.stanford.edu/news/2009/august24/multi-task-research-study-082409.html.

31. Maggie Jackson, "May We Have Your Attention, Please?" *BusinessWeek*, June 23, 2008, 56.

32. Sharon Begley, "Will the BlackBerry Sink the Presidency?" *Newsweek*, February 16, 2009, 37.

33. Nick Wingfield, Ian Sherr, and Ben Worthen, "Hacker Raids Sony Videogame Network," *Wall Street Journal*, April 27, 2011, A1.

34. Stephanie Armour, "Employers Look Closely at What Workers Do on Job: Companies Get More Vigilant as Technology Increases their Risks," *USA Today*, November 8, 2006, 2B; and M. P. McQueen, "Laptop Lockdown: Companies Start Holding Employees Responsible for Security of Portable Devices They Use for Work," *Wall Street Journal*, June 28, 2006, D1.

35. "Electronic Monitoring and Surveillance 2007 Survey," American Management Association, February 28, 2008, http://www.amanet.org/training/whitepapers/2007-Electronic-Monitoring-and-Surveillance-Survey-41.aspx.\.

700   Notes

36. Andie Coller, "Grassley Launches Porn Inquiry," Capitol News Company, January 28, 2009, http://dyn.politico.com/members/forums/thread.cfm?catid=1&subcatid=1&threadid=1970273.

37. Chris Newmarker, "On the Off-Ramp to Adultery, There's No Fooling EZ-Pass," *Des Moines Register*, August 12, 2007, 8A.

38. Stephanie Armour, "Employers Look Closely at What Workers Do on Job: Companies Get More Vigilant as Technology Increases their Risks," *USA Today*, November 8, 2006, 2B; M. P. McQueen, "Workers' Terminations for Computer Misuse Rise," *Wall Street Journal*, July 15, 2006, B4; and "Burger King Fires Workers over Blogs," *Wall Street Journal*, May 14, 2008, A18.

39. Dalia Fahmy, "Can You Be Fired for Sending Personal E-Mails at Work?" *ABC News*, December 17, 2009, http://abcnews.go.com/Business/GadgetGuide/supreme-court-employee-rights-privacy-workplace-emails/story?id=9345057.

40. John Markoff, "Armies of Expensive Lawyers, Replaced by Cheaper Software," *New York Times*, March 4, 2011, http://www.nytimes.com/2011/03/05/science/05legal.html.

41. "Twitter Tirades Test Free-Speech Limits," *Des Moines Register*, November 25, 2010, 4A.

42. Lauren A.E. Schuker, "Secret Texting . . . Pass It On," *Wall Street Journal*, February 4, 2011, B11.

43. Nick Wingfield and Julia Angwin, "Microsoft Adds Privacy Tool," *Wall Street Journal*, March 15, 2011, B1.

44. Emily Steel and Jessica E. Vascellaro, "FTC Backs Web-Ad Self-Regulation: Agency Lays Out Principles for Protecting the Privacy of 'Targeted' Users," *Wall Street Journal*, February 13, 2009, B7.

45. Julia Angwin and Tom McGinty, "Sites Feed Personal Details to New Tracking Industry," *Wall Street Journal*, July 31, 2010, A1; Scott Thurm and Yukari Iwatani Kane, "Your Apps Are Watching You," *Wall Street Journal*, December 18, 2010, C1.

46. Christopher W. Hart, "Beating the Market with Customer Satisfaction," *Harvard Business Review* 85, no. 3 (2007): 30–32.

47. "Frequently Asked Questions: What Can ACSI Tell Us," American Customer Satisfaction Index, http://www.theacsi.org/index.php?option=com_content&view=article&id=46&Itemid=124#what_can.

48. Dana Mattioli, "Customer Service as a Growth Engine," *Wall Street Journal*, June 7, 2010, B6.

49. "2010 Working Mother 100 Best Companies: Cisco," Working Mother, accessed May 27, 2011, http://www.workingmother.com/best-companies/cisco-2; and "2010 Working Mother 100 Best Companies: Microsoft," Working Mother, accessed May 27, 2011, http://www.workingmother.com/best-companies/microsoft-0.

50. Scott Adams, "Work–Life Integration," *Dilbert*, March 23, 2011.

51. Betsy McKay and Suzanne Vranica, "Firms Use Earth Day to Show Their Green Side," *Wall Street Journal*, April 22, 2008, B7.

52. Gwendolyn Bounds, "Misleading Claims on 'Green' Labeling," *Wall Street Journal*, October 26, 2010, D4.

53. Ann Zimmerman, "Wal-Mart Boosts Local Produce: Retailer to Expand Purchases from Small Farmers, Monitor Fertilizer, Water Use," *Wall Street Journal*, November 15, 2010, B2; and General Electric Company, "GE Surpassed $5 Billion in Research & Development Investment in Ecomagination Technology," news release, June 24, 2010, http://www.genewscenter.com/Press-Releases/GE-Surpassed-5-Billion-in-Research-Development-Investment-in-Ecomagination-Technology-2902.aspx.

54. "McDonald's Canada: FAQs," McDonald's Corporation, accessed May 27, 2011, http://www.mcdonalds.ca/en/aboutus/faq.aspx.

55. "3M Facts: Year-end 2010," 3M, accessed May 27, 2011, http://multimedia.mmm.com/mws/mediawebserver.dyn?6666660Zjcf6lVs6EVs66S592COrrrrQ-.

56. "Worldwide Facts," United Parcel Service of America, Inc., accessed May 27, 2011, http://www.ups.com/content/us/en/about/facts/worldwide.html.

57. "Growth, Leadership, Sustainability," Coca-Cola Company, accessed May 27, 2011, http://www.thecoca-cola-company.com/ourcompany/index.html.

58. "International," Walmart Corporate, accessed May 27, 2011, http://walmartstores.com/aboutus/246.aspx.

59. Thomas L. Friedman, *The World Is Flat: A Brief History of the Twenty-First Century*, updated and expanded ed. (New York: Farrar, Straus, and Giroux, 2006), 14.

60. Thomas L. Friedman, *The World Is Flat: A Brief History of the Twenty-First Century*, 86.

61. Christine Uber Grosse, "Managing Communication within Virtual Intercultural Teams," *Business Communication Quarterly* (2002): 22; and Linda H. Heuring, "Patients First," *HRMagazine*, July 2003, 67–68.

62. Sue Shellenbarger, "Some Companies Rethink the Telecommuting Trend," *Wall Street Journal*, February 28, 2008, D1.

63. Linda H. Heuring, "Patients First," *HRMagazine*, July 2003, 67–68.

64. Jörgen Sandberg, "Understanding Competence at Work," *Harvard Business Review*, 79, no. 3 (2001): 24–28.

65. L. D. DeSimone et al., "How Can Big Companies Keep the Entrepreneurial Spirit Alive?" *Harvard Business Review* 73, no. 6 (1995): 183–92.

66. Anne Fisher, "America's Most Admired Companies," *Fortune*, March 17, 2008, 65–67.

67. "How Google Fuels Its Idea Factory," *BusinessWeek*, May 12, 2008, 54–55.

68. U.S. Census Bureau, "Census Bureau Reports Nation Has Nearly 350,000 Fewer Nonemployer Business Locations," press release, June 24, 2010, http://www.census.gov/newsroom/releases/archives/business_ownership/cb10-93.html.

69. Max Messmer, "Soft Skills Are Key to Advancing Your Career," *Business Credit* 109, no. 4 (2007): 34.

Chapter 5

1. See especially Linda Flower and John R. Hayes, "The Cognition of Discovery: Defining a Rhetorical Problem," *College Composition and Communication* 31, no. 1 (February 1980): 21–32; Mike Rose, *Writer's Block: The Cognitive Dimension*, published for Conference on College Composition and Communication, 1984.; and essays in two collections: Charles R. Cooper and Lee Odell, *Research on Composing: Points of Departure* (Urbana, IL: National Council of Teachers of English, 1978); Mike Rose, ed., *When a Writer Can't Write: Studies in Writer's Block and Other Composing-Process Problems* (New York: Guilford Press, 1985).

2. Peter Elbow, *Writing with Power: Techniques for Mastering the Writing Process* (New York: Oxford University Press, 1981), 15–20.

3. See Gabriela Lusser Rico, *Writing the Natural Way* (Los Angeles: J. P. Tarcher, 1983), 10.

4. Rachel Spilka, "Orality and Literacy in the Workplace: Process- and Text-Based Strategies for Multiple Audience

Adaptation," *Journal of Business and Technical Communication* 4, no. 1 (January 1990): 44–67.

5. Robert L. Brown, Jr., and Carl G. Herndl, "An Ethnographic Study of Corporate Writing: Job Status as Reflected in Written Text," in *Functional Approaches to Writing: A Research Perspective*, ed. Barbara Couture (Norwood, NJ: Ablex, 1986), 16–19, 22–23.

6. U.S. Securities and Exchange Commission Office of Investor Education and Assistance, *A Plain English Handbook: How to Create Clear SEC Disclosure Documents* (Washington, D.C.: 1998).

7. Eleanor Laise, "Some Consumers Say Wall Street Failed Them," *Wall Street Journal*, November 28, 2008, B1.

8. Gerard Braud, "What Does That Mean?" *Communication World* 24, no. 1 (2007): 34.

9. Warren Buffett, "Letters 2010," Berkshire Hathaway Inc., accessed May 24, 2011, http://www.berkshirehathaway.com/letters/2010ltr.pdf.

10. Richard Lederer and Richard Dowis, *Sleeping Dogs Don't Lay: Practical Advice for the Grammatically Challenged*, (New York: St. Martin's Press, 1999), 91–92.

11. James Suchan and Robert Colucci, "An Analysis of Communication Efficiency between High-Impact and Bureaucratic Written Communication," *Management Communication Quarterly* 2, no. 4 (1989): 464–73.

12. Hilvard G. Rogers and F. William Brown, "The Impact of Writing Style on Compliance with Instructions," *Journal of Technical Writing and Communication* 23, no. 1 (1993): 53–71.

13. Richard Lederer, "The Terrible Ten," *Toastmaster*, July 2003, 28–29.

14. Robert Frank, "The Wealth Report: Millionaires Need Not Apply; SEC and Others Rewrite the Definition of 'Rich'; The Haves and Have-Mores," *Wall Street Journal*, March 16, 2007, W2.

15. Geoff Mullins, "With Wetlands, Words Matter," *Ames Tribune*, April 3, 2008, A4.

16. Arlene Weintraub, "Revenge of the Overworked Nerds," *BusinessWeek*, December 8, 2003, 41.

17. Peter Conrad, *The Medicalization of Society: On the Transformation of Human Conditions into Treatable Disorders* (Baltimore: The Johns Hopkins University Press, 2007).

18. Chad Bray and Anjali Cordeiro, "Tobacco Firms Score Victory as Class-Action Suit Is Denied," *Wall Street Journal*, April 4, 2008, B3; "FDA May Rephrase Pacemaker Warnings," *Wall Street Journal*, September 29, 2006, A8.

19. Melinda Beck, "Getting an Earful: Testing a Tiny, Pricey Hearing Aid," *Wall Street Journal*, January 29, 2008, D1.

20. Jaguar ad, *Wall Street Journal*, September 29, 2000, A20.

21. Betsy Taylor, "Experts: Flood Terms Can Deceive," *Des Moines Register*, July 1, 2008, 9A.

22. Evan Perez, "Mukasey Cites Risk in Using Term 'Torture,'" *Wall Street Journal*, January 17, 2009, A2.

23. Richard C. Anderson, "Concretization and Sentence Learning," *Journal of Educational Psychology* 66, no. 2 (1974): 179–83.

24. Ben Worthen, "Oracle's Hot New Offering: Corporate Technobabble," *Wall Street Journal*, February 12, 2008, B4.

25. Pamela Layton and Adrian J. Simpson, "Deep Structure in Sentence Comprehension," *Journal of Verbal Learning and Verbal Behavior* 14 (1975); Harris B. Savin and Ellen Perchonock, "Grammatical Structure and the Immediate Recall of English Sentences," *Journal of Verbal Learning and Verbal Behavior* 4 (1965): 348–53.

26. Federal Aviation Administration, "Document Checklist for Plain Language," PlainLanguage.gov, accessed May 24, 2011, http://www.plainlanguage.gov/howto/quickreference/checklist.cfm.

27. Bill Walsh, *The Elephants of Style: A Trunkload of Tips on the Big Issues and Gray Areas of Contemporary American English* (New York: McGraw-Hill, 2004), 68.

28. Lloyd Bostian and Ann C. Thering, "Scientists: Can They Read What They Write?" *Journal of Technical Writing and Communication* 17 (1987): 417–27; E. B. Coleman, "The Comprehensibility of Several Grammatical Transformations," *Journal of Applied Psychology* 48, no. 3 (1964): 186–90; Keith Rayner, "Visual Attention in Reading: Eye Movements Reflect Cognitive Processes," *Memory and Cognition* 5 (1977): 443–48.

29. Don Bush, "The Most Obvious Fault in Technical Writing," *Intercom*, July/August 2003, 50.

30. Adam Freedman, "And the Winners Are...," The Party of the First Part (blog), last updated September 21, 2007, http://thepartyofthefirstpart.blogspot.com/2007/09/and-winners-are.html.

31. Thomas N. Huckin, "A Cognitive Approach to Readability," in *New Essays in Technical and Scientific Communication: Research, Theory, Practice*, eds. Paul V. Anderson, R. John Brockmann, and Carolyn R. Miller (Farmingdale, NY: Baywood, 1983), 93–98.

32. James Suchan and Ronald Dulek, "A Reassessment of Clarity in Written Managerial Communications," *Management Communication Quarterly* 4, no. 1 (1990): 93–97.

33. Doris Kearns Goodwin, *Team of Rivals: The Political Genius of Abraham Lincoln* (New York: Simon & Schuster, 2005), 583–87.

34. "Law Typo Allows Children to Marry," *Des Moines Register*, August 18, 2007, 8A.

35. Carol Hymowitz, "Diebold's New Chief Shows How to Lead after a Sudden Rise," *Wall Street Journal*, May 8, 2006, B1.

36. Lynne Truss, *Eats, Shoots & Leaves: The Zero Tolerance Approach to Punctuation* (New York: Gotham Books, 2003), 9–10.

37. Bill Walsh, *Lapsing into a Comma: A Curmudgeon's Guide to the Many Things That Can Go Wrong in Print—and How to Avoid Them* (Lincolnwood (Chicago): Contemporary Books, 2000), 1.

38. Dianna Booher, "Cutting Paperwork in the Corporate Culture," *New York: Facts on File Publications* (1986): 23.

39. Susan D. Kleimann, "The Complexity of Workplace Review," *Technical Communication* 38, no. 4 (1991): 520–26.

40. Glenn J. Broadhead and Richard C. Freed, *The Variables of Composition: Process and Product in a Business Setting*, Conference on College Composition and Communication Studies in Writing and Rhetoric (Carbondale, IL: Southern Illinois University Press, 1986), 57.

41. Janice C. Redish and Jack Selzer, "The Place of Readability Formulas in Technical Communication," *Technical Communication* 32, no. 4 (1985): 46–52.

Chapter 6

1. Edward Tufte, *Beautiful Evidence* (Cheshire, CT: Graphics Press, 2006), 153–55.

2. Charles Kostelnick and Michael Hassett, *Shaping Information: The Rhetoric of Visual Conventions* (Carbondale, IL: Southern Illinois University Press, 2003), 92, 94.

3. Kostelnick and Hassett, *Shaping Information*, 206–07.

4. Charles Kostelnick and David Roberts, *Designing Visual Language*, 2nd ed. (Boston: Allyn & Bacon, 2011), 81–83.

5. George A. Miller, "The Magical Number Seven, Plus or Minus Two: Some Limits on Our Capacity for Processing Information," *Psychological Review* 63, no. 2 (1956): 81–97.

6. Marlee M. Spafford, Catherine F. Schryer, Lorelei Lingard, and Marcellina Mian, "Accessibility and Order: Crossing

702　　　　　　　　Notes

Borders in Child Abuse Forensic Reports," *Technical Communication Quarterly* 19, no. 2 (2010): 118–43.

7. Jerry E. Bishop, "Word Processing: Research on Stroke Victims Yields Clues to the Brain's Capacity to Create Language," *Wall Street Journal*, October 12, 1993, A6; Anne Meyer and David H. Rose, "Learning to Read in the Computer Age," in *Reading Research to Practice* ed. Jeanne S. Chall, (Cambridge, MA: Brookline Books, 1998), 4–6.

8. Karen A. Schriver, *Dynamics in Document Design* (New York: Wiley, 1997), 274.

9. Jo Mackiewicz, "What Technical Writing Students Should Know about Typeface Personality," *Journal of Technical Writing and Communication* 34, no. 1–2 (2004): 113–31.

10. Miles A. Kimball and Ann R. Hawkins, *Document Design: A Guide for Technical Communicators* (Boston: Bedford/St. Martin's, 2008), 49, 125.

11. Harald Weinreich et al., "Not Quite the Average: An Empirical Study of Web Use," *ACM Transactions on the Web* 2, no. 1 (2008): 18.

12. Jakob Nielsen, "F-Shaped Pattern for Reading Web Content," Jakob Nielsen's Alertbox, April 17, 2006, http://www.useit.com/alertbox/reading_pattern.html.

13. Jakob Nielsen, "Website Response Time," Jakob Nielsen's Alertbox, June 21, 2010, http://www.useit.com/alertbox/response-times.html.

14. Geoffrey A. Fowler and Scott Morrison, "Ebay Attempts to Clean Up the Clutter," *Wall Street Journal*, November 1, 2010, B3; and Lee Gomes, "Good Site, Bad Site: Evolving Web Design," *Wall Street Journal*, June 12, 2007, B3.

15. Jakob Nielsen, "Top Ten Mistakes in Web Design," Jakob Nielsen's Alertbox, accessed May 23, 2011, http://www.useit.com/alertbox/9605.html; and Emily Steel, "Neglected Banner Ads Get a Second Life," *Wall Street Journal*, June 20, 2007, B4.

16. "Corporate News: Target Settles with Blind Group on Web Access," *Wall Street Journal*, August 28, 2008, B4; and Lauren Pollock, "iTunes Eases Access for Blind," *Wall Street Journal*, September 29, 2008, B5.

17. Stephanie Clifford and Claire Cain Miller, "Retailers Retool Sites to Ease Mobile Shopping," *New York Times*, April 17, 2011, http://www.nytimes.com/2011/04/18/technology/18mobile.html.

18. Jakob Nielsen, "Why You Only Need to Test with 5 Users," Jakob Nielsen's Alertbox, March 19, 2000, www.useit.com/alertbox/20000319.html.

19. Jakob Nielsen "Usability 101: Introduction to Usability," Jakob Nielsen's Alertbox, accessed May 23, 2011, http://www.useiticom/alertbox/20030825.html.

Chapter 7

1. Sharon Begley, "Studies Take Measure of How Stereotyping Alters Performance," *Wall Street Journal*, February 23, 2007, B1; and Claude Steele and Joshua Aronson, "Stereotype Threat and Intellectual Test Performance of African Americans," *Journal of Personality and Social Psychology* 69, no. 5 (1995): 797–811.

2. McDonald's Corporation, *McDonald's 2010 Annual Report*, 9, February 25, 2011, http://www.aboutmcdonalds.com/etc/medialib/aboutMcDonalds/investor_relations3.Par.56096.File.dat/2010%20Annual%20Report%20%28print%29.pdf; "3M at a Glance," 3M Corporation, accessed May 30, 2011, http://solutions.3m.com/wps/portal/3M/en_US/careers/home/about/3M/; "Global Structure & Governance," Proctor and Gamble, accessed May 30, 2011, http://www.pg.com/en_US/company/global_structure_operations/index.shtml; "Unilever Facts," Unilever, accessed May 30, 2011, http://www.unilever.com/aboutus/introductiontounilever/unileverataglance/index.aspx; Walmart Corporation, Walmart's *2011 Annual Report*, 2, http://walmartstores.com/sites/annualreport/2011/financials/Walmart_2011_Annual_Report.pdf.

3. Lauren A. E. Schuker, "Plot Change: Foreign Forces Transform Hollywood Films," *Wall Street Journal*, July 31, 2010, A1.

4. Emily Maltby, "Expanding Abroad? Avoid Cultural Gaffes," *Wall Street Journal*, January 19, 2010, B5.

5. William W. Maddux, Adam D. Galinshky, and Carmit T. Tadmor, "Be a Better Manager: Live Abroad," *Harvard Business Review* 88, no. 9 (2010): 24.

6. Joann S. Lublin, "Hunt Is On for Fresh Executive Talent: Recruiters List Hot Prospects, Cultural Flexibility in Demand," *Wall Street Journal*, April 11, 2011, B1.

7. Diana Middleton, "Schools Set Global Track, for Students and Programs," *Wall Street Journal*, April 7, 2011, B7.

8. Jason DeParle, "Global Migration: A World Ever More on the Move," *New York Times*, June 26, 2010, http://www.nytimes.com/2010/06/27/weekinreview/27deparle.html?pagewanted=2.

9. Jason DeParle, "Global Migration: A World Ever More on the Move."

10. Thomas L. Friedman, *The World Is Flat: A Brief History of the Twenty-first Century*, Updated and Expanded ed. (New York: Farrar, Straus and Giroux, 2006), 8.

11. U.S. Census Bureau, "Statistical Abstract of the United States, Table 9: Resident Population by Race, Hispanic Origin, and Age: 2000 and 2009," accessed May 30, 2011, http://www.census.gov/compendia/statab/2011/tables/11s0009.pdf.

12. U.S. Census Bureau, "Statistical Abstract of the United States, Table 50: Persons Obtaining Legal Permanent Resident Status by Country of Birth: 1981 to 2009," accessed May 30, 2011, http://www.census.gov/compendia/statab/2011/tables/11s0050.pdf.

13. Conor Dougherty, "Whites to Lose Majority Status in U.S. by 2042," *Wall Street Journal*, August 14, 2008, A3.

14. U.S. Census Bureau, "2010 Census Shows America's Diversity," news release, March 24, 2011, http://www.census.gov/newsroom/releases/archives/2010_census/cb11-cn125.html.

15. "About Us," CHIN Radio, accessed May 30, 2011, http://chinradio.com/chin-radio/.

16. U.S. Census Bureau, "2010 Census Shows America's Diversity," news release, March 24, 2011, http://www.census.gov/newsroom/releases/archives/2010_census/cb11-cn125.html.

17. U.S. Census Bureau, "Statistical Abstract of the United States, Table 54: Language Spoken at Home by State: 2008," accessed May 30, 2011, http://www.census.gov/compendia/statab/2011/tables/11s0054.pdf.

18. U.S. Census Bureau, "Statistical Abstract of the United States, Table 54.

19. "Employee Resource Groups and Networks at Microsoft," Microsoft Corporation, accessed May 30, 2011, http://www.microsoft.com/about/diversity/en/us/programs/ergen/default.aspx.

20. Cedric Herring, "Does Diversity Pay?: Race, Gender, and the Business Case for Diversity," *American Sociological Review* 74 (April 2009): 208–224.

21. Abhijit Rao, e-mail message to author, February 15, 2009.

22. "Geert Hofstede™ Cultural Dimensions: United States," ITIM International, last updated 2009, accessed May 30, 2011,

http://www.geert-hofstede.com/hofstede_united_states.shtml.

23. John Webb and Michael Keene, "The Impact of Discourse Communities on International Professional Communication," in *Exploring the Rhetoric of International Professional Communication: An Agenda for Teachers and Researchers*, ed. Carl R. Lovitt and Dixie Goswami (Amityville, NY: Baywood, 1999), 81–109.

24. Richard M. Steers, Carlos J. Sanchez-Runde, Luciara Nardon, *Management across Cultures: Challenges and Strategies* (New York: Cambridge University Press, 2010), 205–6.

25. "Business Cards," *BusinessWeek SmallBiz*, June/July 2008, 28.; and Roy A. Cook and Gwen O. Cook, *Guide to Business Etiquette* (New York: Prentice Hall, 2011), 113.

26. Kathryn King-Metters and Ricard Metters, "Misunderstanding the Chinese Worker: Western Impressions Are Dated—And Probably Wrong," *Wall Street Journal*, July 7, 2008, R11; Jason Leow, "Chinese Bigwigs Are Quick to Reach for the Hair Color: Politicians and Executives Look for Youth in a Bottle of Black Dye on the Sly," *Wall Street Journal*, December 11, 2007, A1, A24.

27. Robert T. Moran, Philip R. Harris, and Sarah V. Moran, *Managing Cultural Differences: Global Leadership Strategies for the 21st Century*, 7th ed. (Boston: Elsevier, 2007), 341–42.

28. Robert T. Moran, Philip R. Harris, and Sarah V. Moran, *Managing Cultural Differences*, 64.

29. Richard M. Steers, Carlos J. Sanchez-Runde, Luciara Nardon, *Management across Cultures: Challenges and Strategies* (New York: Cambridge University Press, 2010), 219.

30. Robert T. Moran, Philip R. Harris, and Sarah V. Moran, *Managing Cultural Differences*, 579.

31. Mike Kilen, "Watch Your Language: Rude or Polite? Gestures Vary with Cultures," *Des Moines Register*, May 30, 2006, E1–2.

32. Martin J. Gannon, *Understanding Global Cultures: Metaphorical Journeys through 23 Nations*, 2nd ed. (Thousand Oaks, CA: Sage, 2001), 13.

33. Edward Twitchell Hall, *Hidden Differences: Doing Business with the Japanese* (Garden City, NY: Anchor-Doubleday, 1987), 25.

34. Robert T. Moran, Philip R. Harris, and Sarah V. Moran, *Managing Cultural Differences: Global Leadership Strategies for the 21st Century*, 7th ed. (Boston: Elsevier, 2007), 445, 78.

35. Malcolm Fleschner, "Worldwide Winner," *Selling Power*, November–December 2001, 54–61.

36. Ira Carnahan, "Presidential Timber Tends to Be Tall," *Forbes*, May 19, 2004, http://www.forbes.com/2004/05/19/cz_ic_0519beltway.html.

37. Craig Storti, *Old World, New World: Bridging Cultural Differences: Britain, France, Germany, and the U.S.* (Yarmouth, ME: Intercultural Press, 2001), 209.

38. Nick Easen, "Don't Send the Wrong Message," *Business 2.0*, August 2005, 102.

Chapter 8

1. Kevin S. Groves, "Leader Emotional Expressivity, Visionary Leadership, and Organizational Change," *Leadership & Organizational Development Journal* 27, no. 7 (2006): 566–83; Ajay Mehra et al., "Distributed Leadership in Teams: The Network of Leadership Perceptions and Team Performance," *The Leadership Quarterly* 17, no. 3 (2006): 232–45; Kenneth David Stand, "Examining Effective and Ineffective Transformational Project Leadership," *Team Performance Management* 11, no. 3/4 (2005): 68–103.

2. Jeswald W. Salacuse, *The Global Negotiator: Making, Managing, and Mending Deals around the World in the Twenty-First Century* (New York: Palgrave Macmillan, 2003), 92.

3. Bob Frisch, "When Teams Can't Decide," *Harvard Business Review* 86, no. 11 (2008): 121–26.

4. Sue Shellenbarger, "Work & Family Mailbox," *Wall Street Journal*, February 9, 2011, D3.

5. Caroline Bailey and Michelle Austin, "360 Degree Feedback and Developmental Outcomes: The Role of Feedback Characteristics, Self-Efficacy and Importance of Feedback Dimensions to Focal Managers' Current Role," *International Journal of Selection and Assessment* 14, no. 1 (2006): 51–66.

6. Kimberly Merriman, "Low-Trust Teams Prefer Individualized Pay," *Harvard Business Review* 86, no. 11 (2008): 32.

7. Sari Lindblom-Ylanne, Heikki Pihlajamaki, and Toomas Kotkas, "What Makes a Student Group Successful? Student-Student and Student–Teacher Interaction in a Problem–Based Learning Environment," *Learning Environments Research* 6, no. 1 (2003): 59–76.

8. Rebecca E. Burnett, "Conflict in Collaborative Decision-Making," in *Professional Communication: The Social Perspective*, ed. Nancy Roundy Blyler and Charlotte Thralls (Newbury Park, CA: Sage, 1993), 144–62; Rebecca E. Burnett, "Productive and Unproductive Conflict in Collaboration," in *Making Thinking Visible: Writing, Collaborative Planning, and Classroom Inquiry*, ed. Linda Flower et al. (Urbana, IL: NCTE, 1994), 239–44.

9. Sue Dyer, "The Root Causes of Poor Communication," *Cost Engineering* 48, no. 6 (2006): 8–10.

10. Solomon F. Asch, "Opinions and Social Pressure," *Scientific American* 193, no. 5 (1955): 31–35. For a review of recent literature on groupthink, see Marc D. Street, "Groupthink: An Examination of Theoretical Issues, Implications, and Future Research Suggestions," *Small Group Research* 28, no. 1 (1997): 72–93.

11. Jared Diamond, *Collapse: How Societies Choose to Fail or Succeed* (New York: Penguin Books, 2005), 439.

12. Francesca Bariela-Chiappini et al., "Five Perspectives on Intercultural Business Communication," *Business Communication Quarterly* 66, no. 3 (2003): 73–96.

13. Ursula Hess and Pierre Philippot, *Group Dynamics and Emotional Expression* (New York: Cambridge University Press, 2007).

14. Kristina B. Dahlin, Laurie R. Weingart, and Pamela J. Hinds, "Team Diversity and Information Use," *Academy of Management Journal* 68, no. 6 (2005): 1107–23; Susannah B. F. Paletz et al., "Ethnic Composition and Its Differential Impact on Group Processes in Diverse Teams," *Small Group Research* 35, no. 2 (2004): 128–57; Leisa D. Sargent and Christina Sue-Chan, "Does Diversity Affect Efficacy? The Intervening Role of Cohesion and Task Interdependence," *Small Group Research* 32, no. 4 (2001): 426–50.

15. Jeswald W. Salacuse, *The Global Negotiator: Making, Managing, and Mending Deals around the World in the Twenty-First Century* (New York: Palgrave Macmillan, 2003), 96–97.

16. Jeanne Brett, Kristin Behfar, and Mary C. Kern, "Managing Multicultural Teams," *Harvard Business Review* 84, no. 11 (2006): 84–91.

17. John E. Tropman, *Making Meetings Work*, 2nd ed. (Thousand Oaks, CA: Sage, 2003), 28.

18. Rebecca E. Burnett, "Productive and Unproductive Conflict in Collaboration," in *Making Thinking Visible: Writing, Collaborative Planning, and Classroom Inquiry*, ed. Linda Flower et al. (Urbana, IL: NCTE, 1994), 239–44.

704   Notes

19. Kitty O. Locker, "What Makes a Collaborative Writing Team Successful? A Case Study of Lawyers and Social Service Workers in a State Agency," in *New Visions in Collaborative Writing*, ed. Janis Forman (Portsmouth, NJ: Boynton, 1991), 37–52.

20. Lisa Ede and Andrea Lunsford, *Singular Texts/Plural Authors: Perspectives on Collaborative Writing* (Carbondale, IL: Southern Illinois Press, 1990), 66.

Chapter 9

1. Drake Bennett, "I'll Have My Robots Talk to Your Robots," *Bloomberg Businessweek*, February 21, 2011, 51–61.

2. Jonathan B. Spira, "The Knowledge Worker's Day: Our Findings," *Basex* (blog), November 4, 2010, http://www.basexblog.com/2010/11/04/our-findings/.

3. Xerox Newsroom, "For Government Workers: Easing Information Overload Will Save," news release, February 19, 2009, http://news.xerox.com/pr/xerox/NR_2009Feb19_Xerox_and_Harris_Interactive_Public_Sector_Survey.aspx

4. Symantec.cloud, "Death to PST Files: The Hidden Costs of Email," *White Paper: Email Management*, Symantec Corporation, March 2011, http://www.radicati.com/?page_id=46.

5. "Internet 2010 in Numbers," *Pingdom* (blog), January 12, 2011, http://royal.pingdom.com/2011/01/12/internet-2010-in-numbers.

6. Jonathan B. Spira and Cody Burke, "Intel's War on Information Overload: A Case Study," *Basex*, August 2009, http://bsx.stores.yahoo.net/inwaroninov.html.

7. Gail Fann Thomas and Cynthia L. King, "Reconceptualizing E-Mail Overload," *Journal of Business and Technical Communication* 20, no. 3 (2006): 252–87.

8. Geoffrey A. Fowler, "Are You Talking to Me?" *Wall Street Journal*, April 25, 2011, R5.

9. Soumitra Dutta, "What's Your Personal Social Media Strategy?" *Harvard Business Review* 88, no. 11 (November 2010): 127; and Emily Glazer, "Fund Firms Cautiously Tweet Their Way into a New World," *Wall Street Journal*, February 7, 2011, R1.

10. Jennifer Saba, "Facebook Tops Google as Most Visited Site in U.S.," Reuters, December 30, 2010, http://www.reuters.com/article/2010/12/30/us-facebook-google-idUSTRE6BT40320101230.

11. Geoffrey A. Fowler, "Are You Talking to Me?" *Wall Street Journal*, April 25, 2011, R5.

12. "11 Career Ending Facebook Faux Pas," *Forbes*, April 13, 2010, http://www.forbes.com/2010/04/13/how-facebook-ruined-my-career-entrepreneurs-human-resources-facebook_slide.html.

13. Serena Dai, "Tweeting Diners Get Quick Response," *Des Moines Register*, September 25, 2010, 3E.

14. William M. Bulkeley, "Playing Well with Others: How IBM's Employees Have Taken Social Networking to an Unusual Level," *Wall Street Journal*, June 18, 2007, R10.

15. Catherine Arnst, "Can Patients Cure Health Care?" *BusinessWeek*, December 15, 2008, 58–61.

16. "Social Networking Rules Vary among Businesses," *Des Moines Register*, October 19, 2009, 6E.

17. Kristin Byron, "Carrying Too Heavy a Load? The Communication and Miscommunication of Emotion by E-Mail," *Academy of Management Review* 33, no. 2 (2008): 309–27.

18. Jane Larson, "Be Careful with Business E-Mail Content," *Des Moines Register*, January 21, 2008, 2D.

19. Dinesh Ramde, "Anti-War E-Mail to Soldier Stirs Furor," *Des Moines Register*, January 24, 2007, 5A.

20. Dalia Fahmy, "Can You Be Fired for Sending Personal E-Mails at Work?" *ABC News*, December 17, 2009, http://abcnews.go.com/Business/GadgetGuide/supreme-court-employee-rights-privacy-workplace-emails/story?id=9345057.

21. MailerMailer LLC, *Email Marketing Metrics Report*, July 2010, http://www.mailermailer.com/resources/metrics/index.rwp.

22. Gilbert Ross, "Black Box Backfire," *Wall Street Journal*, April 21, 2007, A8.

23. Jeanne Whalen, "Shareholders Sue Glaxo over Avandia Disclosure," *Wall Street Journal*, June 13, 2007, D7.

24. Mike Spector, "New IRS Rules Help Donors Vet Charities: Revised Tax Form Will Make Nonprofits Reveal More about How They Spend," *Wall Street Journal*, May 29, 2008, D1.

25. Bob Mills, e-mail message to author.

26. "Lighting a Fire under Campbell," *BusinessWeek*, December 4, 2006, 96; and Lee Smith, "Linden Lab's Love Machine," *Talking Internal Communication* (blog), June 15, 2008, http://talkingic.typepad.com/foureightys_lee_smith_tal/2008/06/linden-labs-love-machine.html.

27. Kenneth Blanchard and Spencer Johnson, *The One Minute Manager* (New York: William Morrow, 1982), 19.

Chapter 10

1. Ben Levisohn, "Getting More Workers to Whistle," *BusinessWeek*, January 28, 2008, 18.

2. Robert I. Sutton, *The No Asshole Rule: Building a Civilized Workplace and Surviving One That Isn't* (New York: Warner Business Books, 2007), 45–48.

3. William Ury, *The Power of a Positive No: How to Say No and Still Get to Yes* (New York: Bantam Books, 2007), 41–42.

4. L. Gordon Crovitz, "The Business of Restoring Trust," *Wall Street Journal*, January 31, 2011, A13.

5. Peter D. Timmerman and Wayne Harrison, "The Discretionary Use of Electronic Media: Four Considerations for Bad News Bearers," *Journal of Business Communication* 42, no. 4 (2005): 379–89.

6. Jack Ewing, "Nokia: Bring on the Employee Rants," *BusinessWeek*, June 22, 2009, 50.

7. Kitty O. Locker, "Factors in Reader Responses to Negative Letters: Experimental Evidence for Changing What We Teach," *Journal of Business and Technical Communication* 13, no. 1 (January 1999): 21.

8. Locker, "Factors in Reader Responses to Negative Letters: Experimental Evidence for Changing What We Teach," 25–26.

9. Sharon S. Brehm and Jack W. Brehm, *Psychological Reactance: A Theory of Freedom and Control* (New York: Academic Press, 1981), 3.

10. Elizabeth Bernstein, "I'm Very, Very, Very Sorry. . .Really?" *Wall Street Journal*, October 19, 2010, D1, D2.

11. Melanie Trottman and Andy Pasztor, "Southwest Airlines CEO Apologizes for Lapses," *Wall Street Journal*, March 14, 2008, B1.

12. Norihiko Shirouzu and Yoshio Takahashi, "Toyota Apologizes for Massive Recall," *Wall Street Journal*, February 6, 2010, B1, B5; and Alex Taylor III, "Toyota's No-Show Leadership," *CNNMoney*, February 4, 2010, http://money.cnn.com/2010/02/04/autos/toyota.fortune/index.htm.

13. hallmark@update.hallmark.com, e-mail message to author, May 8, 2007.

14. Scott McCartney, "What Airlines Do When You Complain," *Wall Street Journal*, March 20, 2007, D1; Nick Wingfield,

"Steve Jobs Offers Rare Apology Credit for iPhone," *Wall Street Journal*, September 7, 2007, B1.

15. Laura Landro, "The Informed Patient: Hospitals Own Up to Errors," *Wall Street Journal*, August 25, 2009, D1.

16. Ury, *The Power of a Positive No: How to Say No and Still Get to Yes*, 19.

17. Nathan Becker, "Taco Bell Plans Spin as Critic Drops Beef," *Wall Street Journal*, April 20, 2011, B7.

18. "United Airlines to Unplug Number of Complaints," *Wall Street Journal*, February 11, 2009, D6.

19. Scott McCartney, "The Airlines' Squeaky Wheels Turn to Twitter," *Wall Street Journal*, October 28, 2010, D1, D5.

20. Crovitz, "The Business of Restoring Trust," A13.

21. Stephen W. Gilliland et al., "Improving Applicants' Reactions to Rejection Letters: An Application of Fairness Theory," *Personnel Psychology* 54, no. 3 (2001): 669–704; Robert E. Ployhart, Karen Holcombe Ehrhart, and Seth C. Hayes, "Using Attributions to Understand the Effects of Explanations on Applicant Reactions: Are Reactions Consistent with the Covariation Principle?" *Journal of Applied Social Psychology* 35, no. 2 (2005): 259–96.

22. John P. Hausknecht, David V. Day, and Scott C. Thomas, "Applicant Reactions to Selection Procedures: An Updated Model and Meta-Analysis," *Personnel Psychology* 57, no. 3 (2004): 639–84.

23. Kenneth Blanchard and Spencer Johnson, *The One Minute Manager* (New York: William Morrow, 1982), 59.

24. Carol Hymowitz, "Though Now Routine, Bosses Still Stumble During Layoff Process," *Wall Street Journal*, June 25, 2007, B1.

25. Carol Hymowitz, "Personal Boundaries Shrink as Companies Punish Bad Behavior," *Wall Street Journal*, June 18, 2007, B1.

Chapter 11

1. Jay Heinrichs, "Spot Fallacies," in *Thank You for Arguing: What Aristotle, Lincoln, and Homer Simpson Can Teach Us about the Art of Persuasion* (New York: Three Rivers Press, 2007), chap. 14.

2. Jay A. Conger, "The Necessary Art of Persuasion," *Harvard Business Review* 76, no. 3 (May–June 1998): 88.

3. John Kotter and Holger Rathgeber, *Our Iceberg Is Melting: Changing and Succeeding under Any Conditions* (New York: St. Martin's Press, 2005), 140.

4. Jonah Lehrer, *How We Decide* (New York: Houghton Mifflin Harcourt, 2009), 26, 235.

5. EACA Promotional Marketing Council, "Cyriel (84) Needs a Job," accessed June 22, 2011, http://www.adforum.com/creative_archive/award/reel_detail.asp?tb=1&awy=2006&ID=16&AD=6684218&TDA=VD1tK1qetl.

6. Michael Sanserino, "Peer Pressure and Other Pitches," *Wall Street Journal*, September 14, 2009, B6.

7. Vanessa Fuhrmans, "Training the Brain to Choose Wisely," *Wall Street Journal*, April 28, 2009, D1.

8. Daniel H. Pink, *Drive: The Surprising Truth about What Motivates Us* (New York: Riverhead Books, 2009), 145.

9. Chip Heath and Dan Heath, *Made to Stick: Why Some Ideas Survive and Others Die* (New York: Random House, 2007), 195–98; and Mark Schoofs, "Novel Police Tactic Puts Drug Markets out of Business: Confronted by the Evidence, Dealers in High Point, N.C., Succumb to Pressure," *Wall Street Journal*, September 27, 2006, A1, A16.

10. "'Don't Mess with Texas' Anti-Litter Ad Features Strait," *Des Moines Register*, May 11, 2010, 2A.

11. National Science Foundation, "Why 'Scientific Consensus' Fails to Persuade," news release, September 13, 2010, http://www.nsf.gov/news/news_summ.jsp?cntn_id=117697.

12. Min-Sun Kim and Steven R. Wilson, "A Cross-Cultural Comparison of Implicit Theories of Requesting," *Communication Monographs* 61, no. 3 (September 1994): 210–35; and K. Yoon, C. H. Kim, and M. S. Kim, "A Cross-Cultural Comparison of the Effects of Source Creditability on Attitudes and Behavior Intentions," *Mass Communication and Society* 1, nos. 3 and 4 (1998): 153–73.

13. Daniel D. Ding, "An Indirect Style in Business Communication," *Journal of Business and Technical Communication* 20, no. 1 (2006): 87–100.

14. Peggy E. Chaudhry and Stephen A. Stumpf, "Getting Real about Fakes," *Wall Street Journal*, August 17, 2009, R4.

15. E. L. Fink et al., "The Semantics of Social Influence: Threats vs. Persuasion," *Communication Monographs* 70, no. 4 (2003): 295–316.

16. Malcolm Gladwell, *The Tipping Point: How Little Things Can Make a Big Difference* (New York: Little, Brown and Company, 2002), 96–98.

17. David Wessel, "Inside Dr. Bernanke's E.R." *Wall Street Journal*, July 18, 2009, W3.

18. Judge Baker Children's Center and Campaign for a Commercial-Free Childhood, "Tell Toy Companies: Target Parents, Not Kids, with Holiday Ads," accessed June 22, 2011, http://www.commercialfreechildhood.org/pressreleases/holidaymarketer.htm.

19. Ray Considine and Murray Raphael, *The Great Brain Robbery* (Los Angeles: Rosebud Books, 1980), 95–96.

20. Phred Dvorak, "How Understanding the 'Why' of Decisions Matters," *Wall Street Journal*, March 19, 2007, B3.

21. Chip Heath and Dan Heath, *Made to Stick: Why Some Ideas Survive and Others Die* (New York: Random House, 2007), 165–68.

22. Scott Robinette, "Get Emotional," *Harvard Business Review* 79, no. 5 (May 2001): 24–25.

23. Martin Lindstrom, *Buyology: Truth and Lies about Why We Buy* (New York: Doubleday, 2008), 133–34.

24. "Around the World," *Washington Post*, March 27, 2009, A14.

25. Susan Linn and Alvin Poussaint, "Campaign for a Commercial-Free Childhood," accessed June 22, 2011, http://commercialfreechildhood.org/actions/lettertoceo.pdf.

26. "Fort Hood Suspect's Personnel File Filled with Praise, Despite Problems," *Des Moines Register*, January 20, 2010, 5A.

27. Samuel A. Culbert, "Get Rid of the Performance Review! It Destroys Morale, Kills Teamwork, and Hurts the Bottom Line. And That's Just for Starters," *Wall Street Journal*, October 20, 2008, R4; and Jared Sandberg, "Performance Reviews Need Some Work, Don't Meet Potential," *Wall Street Journal*, November 20, 2007, B1.

28. Jeffrey Zaslow, "The Most-Praised Generation Goes to Work," *Wall Street Journal*, April 20, 2007, W1, W7.

29. Joe Light, "Performance Reviews by the Numbers," *Wall Street Journal*, June 29, 2010, D4.

30. Steve Salerno, "As Seen on TV: But Wait. . . There's More!" *Wall Street Journal*, March 25, 2009, A11.

31. "How to Launch a Direct-Mail Campaign," *BusinessWeek SmallBiz*, August/September 2008, 28.

32. Barbara Kiviat, "Why We Buy: Consumers Tend to Go with What (Little) They Know," *Time*, August 27, 2007, 50–51.

706   Notes

33. Jeffrey Gitomer, *Little Red Book of Sales Answers: 99.5 Real World Answers That Make Sense, Make Sales, and Make Money* (Upper Saddle River, NJ: Prentice Hall, 2005), 112.

34. Beth Negus Viveiros, "Gifts for Life," *Direct*, July (2004): 9.

35. Charity: water homepage, accessed June 22, 2011, http://www.charitywater.org.

36. Lee Rood, "Little Raised over Phone Goes to Charity," *Des Moines Register*, December 14, 2008, 1A.

37. Fund-raising letter from Kevin M Ryan. Undated correspondence.

38. Maxwell Sackheim, *My First Sixty-Five Years in Advertising* (Blue Ridge Summit, PA: Tab Books, 1975), 97–100.

Chapter 12

1. U.S. Department of Labor Bureau of Labor Statistics, "Number of Jobs Held, Labor Market Activity, and Earnings Growth among the Youngest Baby Boomers: Results from a Longitudinal Survey," news release, September 10, 2010, USDL-10-1243, http://www.bls.gov/news.release/pdf/nlsoy.pdf.

2. Richard Nelson Bolles, *What Color Is Your Parachute? A Practical Manual for Job-Hunters and Career-Changers* (Berkeley: Ten Speed Press, 2007), 209.

3. Sarah E. Needleman, "It Isn't Always a Job behind an Online Job Posting: Employment Ads on the Web Can Lead You to Marketing Pitches, or Worse: Ways to See Which Ones Are Sincere," *Wall Street Journal*, February 17, 2009, B14.

4. Anne Fisher, "10 Ways to Use Social Media in Your Job Hunt," CNNMoney, May 20, 2011, http://management.fortune.cnn.com/2011/01/13/10-ways-to-use-social-media-in-your-job-hunt/.

5. Cross-Tab, *Online Reputation in a Connected World*, 2010, accessed April 2, 2011, http://go.microsoft.com/?linkid=9709510.

6. Teri Evans, "Penn State, Texas A&M Top the List: Recruiters Like One-Stop Shopping for Grads with Solid Academics, Job Skills, Record of Success," *Wall Street Journal*, September 13, 2010, B1; and Alexandra Cheney, "Firms Assess Young Interns' Potential: Businesses Look to Pools for Full-Time Hires, Tracking Future Employees as Early as Freshman Year," *Wall Street Journal*, September 13, 2010, B10.

7. Accountemps: A Robert Half Company, "Résumés Inching Up: Survey Shows Longer Résumés Now More Acceptable," news release, March 20, 2010, http://accountemps.rhi.mediaroom.com/index.php?s=189&item=210.

8. Elizabeth Blackburn-Brockman and Kelly Belanger, "One Page or Two? A National Study of CPA Recruiters' Preferences for Résumé Length," *The Journal of Business Communication* 38 (2001): 29–45.

9. CareerBuilder.com, "Nearly Half of Employers Have Caught a Lie on a Résumé, CareerBuilder.com Survey Shows," press release, July 30, 2008, http://www.careerbuilder.com/share/aboutus/pressreleasesdetail.aspx?id=pr448&sd=7%2f30%2f2008&ed=12%2f31%2f2008.

10. National Association of Colleges and Employers, "Job Outlook: What Do Employers Look for in Candidates? Spotlight Online for Career Services Professionals," news release, January 6, 2010, http://www.naceweb.org/Publications/Spotlight_Online/2010/0106/Job_Outlook_What_do_employers_look_for_in_candidates_.aspx.

11. Roni Noland, "It's Not a Disaster if Your Old Boss Won't Provide a Reference," *Boston Globe*, March 8, 2009, 5.

12. Phil Elder, "The Trade Secrets of Employment Interviews," paper presented at the Association for Business Communication Midwest Convention, Kansas City, MO, May 2, 1987.

13. "For Job Seekers, Company Sites Beat Online Boards, Social Media," *Wall Street Journal*, April 4, 2011, B8.

14. John B. Killoran, "Self-Published Web Résumés: Their Purposes and Their Genre Systems," *Journal of Business and Technical Communication* 20, no. 4 (2006): 425–59.

15. Keith J. Winstein and Daniel Golden, "MIT Admissions Dean Lied on Résumé in 1979, Quits," *Wall Street Journal*, April 27, 2007, B1.

16. Jon Weinbach, "The Admissions Police," *Wall Street Journal*, April 6, 2007, W1, W10.

17. ". . . And I Invented Velcro," *BusinessWeek*, August 4, 2008; "Nearly Half of Employers Have Caught a Lie on a Résumé, CareerBuilder.com Survey Shows"; and Cari Tuna and Keith J Winstein, "Economy Promises to Fuel Résumé Fraud: Practices Vary for Vetting Prospective Employees, but Executives Usually Face Tougher Background Checks," *Wall Street Journal*, November 17, 2008, B4.

Chapter 13

1. Max Messmer, "Cover Letter Still Important in Online Age," *Pittsburgh Post–Gazette*, August 10, 2008, J1.

2. Jason Fried, "Never Read Another Résumé," *Inc.*, June 2010, 37.

3. Katharine Hansen and Randall Hansen, "The Basics of a Dynamic Cover Letter," in *Cover Letter Resources for Job-Seekers*, accessed April 9, 2011, http://www.quintcareers.com/cover_letter_basics.html.

Chapter 14

1. Robert Half Finance and Accounting, "Tell Me about Yourself," news release, November 8, 2005, http://rhfa.mediaroom.com/index.php?s=305&item=560; and Accountemps, "Hiring Manager to Applicant: 'What Is Your Greatest Weakness?': Accountemps Survey Finds Job Seekers Make Most Mistakes During Interview," news release, September 23, 2010, http://accountemps.rhi.mediaroom.com/interview_mistakes.

2. Accountemps, "The Personal Connection: Survey Shows That in Hiring Process, There's No Substitute for Being There," news release, September 11, 2008, http://accountemps.rhi.mediaroom.com/PersonalConnection.

3. Rachel Emma Silverman, "Choosing the Appropriate Clothes Adds to Stress of the Job Interview," *Wall Street Journal*, April 17, 2001, http://online.wsj.com/article/SB987460110121095208.html.

4. Victoria Knight, "Personality Tests as Hiring Tools," *Wall Street Journal*, March 15, 2006, http://online.wsj.com/article/SB114237811535098217.html.

5. Dana Mattioli, "Sober Thought: How to Mix Work, Alcohol: Taking Cues from Bosses and Clients Can Keep Parties or Meals under Control," *Wall Street Journal*, December 5, 2006, B10.

6. Geoff Smart and Randy Street, *Who: The A Method for Hiring* (New York: Ballantine, 2008).

7. U.S. Department of Commerce Economics and Statistics Administration and Executive Office of the President, Office of Management and Budget, White House Council on Women and Girls, *Women in America: Indicators of Social and Economic Well-Being*, March 2011, 32, http://www.whitehouse.gov/sites/default/files/rss_viewer/Women_in_America.pdf.

Chapter 15

1. "Wikipedia," *Wikipedia*, last modified June 11, 2011, http://en.wikipedia.org/wiki/Wikipedia.

2. Katie Hafner, "Seeing Corporate Fingerprints in Wikipedia Edits," *New York Times,* August 19, 2007, http://www.nytimes.com/2007/08/19/technology/19wikipedia.html?_r=1; and Jonathan Zittrain, Robert McHenry, Benjamin Mako Hill, and Mike Schroepfer, "Ten Years of ~~Inaccuracy and~~ Remarkable Detail: Wikipedia," *Bloomberg Businessweek,* January 10, 2011, 57–61.

3. Julia Angwin and Geoffrey A. Fowler, "Volunteers Log Off as Wikipedia Ages," *Wall Street Journal,* November 23, 2009, A1, A17.

4. "United States: The Ladder of Fame; College Education," *The Economist,* August 26, 2006, 35.

5. Sharon L. Lohr, *Sampling: Design and Analysis* (Pacific Grove, CA: Duxbury Press, 1999), 3.

6. "Television Measurement," The Nielsen Company, accessed June 11, 2011, http://www.nielsen.com/us/en/measurement/television-measurement.html.

7. Cynthia Crossen, "Fiasco in 1936 Survey Brought 'Science' to Election Polling," *Wall Street Journal,* October 2, 2006, B1.

8. Carl Bialik, "Which Is Epidemic—Sexting or Worrying about It? Cyberpolls, Relying on Skewed Samples of Techno-Teen, Aren't Always Worth the Paper They're Not Printed On," *Wall Street Journal,* April 8, 2009, A9.

9. Ann Zimmerman, "Revenge of the Nerds: How Barbie Got Her Geek On," *Wall Street Journal,* April 9, 2010, A1.

10. Andrew O'Connell, "Reading the Public Mind," *Harvard Business Review* 88, no. 10 (October 2010): 28.

11. Carl Bialik, "Online Polling, Once Easily Dismissed, Burnishes Its Image," *Wall Street Journal,* August 7, 2010, A2.

12. Lean Christian, Scott Keeter, Kristen Purcell, and Aaron Smith, "Assessing the Cell Phone Challenge," Pew Research Center, May 20, 2010, http://pewresearch.org/pubs/1601/assessing-cell-phone-challenge-in-public-opinion-surveys.

13. Paul J. Lavrakas, "Nonresponse Issues in U.S. Cell Phone and Landline Telephone Surveys," National Research Council, February 17, 2011, http://www7.nationalacademies.org/cnstat/Lavakas%20Pres.pdf.

14. Carl Bialik, "Making It Count: Alternative Ways to Gather Census Data," *Wall Street Journal,* July 31, 2010, A2; and Paul J. Lavrakas, "Nonresponse Issues in U.S. Cell Phone and Landline Telephone Surveys," National Research Council, February 17, 2011, http://www7.nationalacademies.org/cnstat/Lavakas%20Pres.pdf.

15. Palmer Morrel-Samuels, "Getting the Truth into Workplace Surveys," *Harvard Business Review* 80, no. 2 (February 2002): 111–18.

16. See, for example, "Many Who Say Homosexual Relations Should Be Illegal Change Their Minds When Told It Could Mean That Consenting Adults Could Be Prosecuted for Activities in Their Own Homes," Public Agenda, accessed June 12, 2011, http://www.publicagenda.org/charts/many-who-say-homosexual-relations-should-be-illegal-change-their-minds-when-told-it-could-mean-consenting-adults; Public Agenda, "Now Online—Just the Facts on Gay Rights," news release, February 5, 2002, http://www.publicagenda.org/press-releases/now-online-just-facts-gay-rights; Pew Forum on Religion and Public Life, "Religious Beliefs Underpin Opposition to Homosexuality," November 18, 2003, http://pewforum.org/Gay-Marriage-and-Homosexuality/Religious-Beliefs-Underpin-Opposition-to-Homosexuality.aspx.

17. "20 Questions Journalists Should Ask about Poll Results," Public Agenda, accessed June 12, 2011, http://www.publicagenda.org/pages/20-questions-journalists-should-ask-about-poll-results.

18. Palmer Morrel-Samuels, "Getting the Truth into Workplace Surveys," *Harvard Business Review* 80, no. 2 (February 2002): 116.

19. Carl Bialik, "When Wording Skews Results in Polls," *Wall Street Journal,* September 25, 2010, A2.

20. Earl E. McDowell, Bridget Mrolza, and Emmy Reppe, "An Investigation of the Interviewing Practices of Technical Writers in Their World of Work," in *Interviewing Practices for Technical Writers,* ed. Earl E. McDowell (Amityville, NY: Baywood Publishing, 1991), 207.

21. Thomas Hunter, "Pulitzer Winner Discusses Interviewing," *IABC Communication World,* April 1985, 13–14.

22. Julie Jargon, "Kiwi Goes Beyond Shine in Effort to Step Up Sales," *Wall Street Journal,* December 20, 2007, B1.

23. Peter Noel Murray, "Focus Groups Are Valid When Done Right," *Marketing News,* September 1, 2006, 21, 25.

24. Emily Steel, "The New Focus Groups: Online Networks: Proprietary Panels Help Consumer Companies Shape Products, Ads," *Wall Street Journal,* January 14, 2008, B6.

25. Kelly K. Spors, "The Customer Knows Best," *Wall Street Journal,* July 13, 2009, R5.

26. Andrew O'Connell, "Reading the Public Mind," *Harvard Business Review* 88, no. 10 (October 2010): 28.

27. Louise Witt, "Inside Intent," *American Demographics* 26, no. 2 (2004): 34.

28. The Nielsen Company, "DVR Viewing of Programs and Commercials Varies Based on Time Elapsed between Original Airing and Playback, Nielsen Says," news release, February 15, 2007, http://www.nielsen.com/us/en/insights/press-room/2007/DVR_Viewing_of_Programs_and_Commercials_Varies_Based_on_Time_Elapsed_Between_Original_Airing_and_Playback_Nielsen_Says.html.

29. Emily Steel, "TV Networks Launch Big Campus Push; New Nielsen System Makes College Students Coveted Ratings Draw," *Wall Street Journal,* March 5, 2007, B3.

30. Christopher Meyer and Andre Schwager, "Understanding Customer Experience," *Harvard Business Review* 85, no. 2 (February 2007): 116–26.

31. Daniel Kruger, "You Want Data with That?" *Forbes* 173, no. 6 (2004): 58.

Chapter 16

1. Monica M. Clark, "Nielsen's 'People Meters' Go Top 10: Atlanta Debut Is Milestone for Device That's Redefining Local TV Audiences' Image," *Wall Street Journal,* June 30, 2006, B2.

2. Gerald J. Alred, Charles T. Brusaw, and Walter E. Oliu, *The Business Writer's Handbook,* 8th ed. (New York: St. Martin's Press, 2006), 248–50; William Horton, "The Almost Universal Language: Graphics for International Documents," *Technical Communication* 40, no. 4 (1993): 687; Thyra Rauch, "IBM Visual Interface Design," *The STC Usability PIC Newsletter,* January, 1996, 3; L. G. Thorell and W. J. Smith, *Using Computer Color Effectively: An Illustrated Reference* (Englewood Cliffs, NJ: Prentice Hall, 1990), 12–13.

3. Eric Kenly and Mark Beach, *Getting It Printed: How to Work with Printers & Graphic Imaging Services to Assure Quality, Stay on Schedule, and Control Costs,* 4th ed. (Cincinnati, OH: HOW Design Books, 2004), 68.

4. Miles A. Kimball and Ann R. Hawkins, *Document Design: A Guide for Technical Communicators* (Boston: Bedford/St. Martins, 2008), 253.

5. Edward R. Tufte, *The Visual Display of Quantitative Information,* 2nd ed. (Cheshire, CT: Graphics Press, 2001), 107–21.

708   Notes

6. Charles Kostelnick, "The Visual Rhetoric of Data Displays: The Conundrum of Clarity," *IEEE Transactions on Professional Communication* 51, no. 1 (2008): 116–30.

7. Jerry Bowyer, "In Defense of the Unemployment Rate," *National Review Online*, March 5, 2004, http://article .nationalreview.com/?q=YzNiZGJjYTZlZDNlYzQzZjUxN zFlMWJkNjBiODIzMmI; Mark Gongloff, "Payroll Growth Disappoints," *CNN Money*, December 5, 2003, http:// money.cnn.com; and Joint Economic Committee, "Charts: Economy," last updated August 27, 2004 http://jec.senate .gov.

8. Tufte, *The Visual Display of Quantitative Information*, 74–75.

9. Brett Michael Dykes, "British Airways Red-Faced over Faux Image of Bin Laden Boarding Pass," in *Yahoo! News*, June 2, 2010, http://news.yahoo.com/s/ynews/ ynews_ts2359/print.

10. Richard B. Woodward, "Debatable 'Evidence,'" *Wall Street Journal*, May 4, 2011, D5.

11. Steven Mufson, "Altered BP Photo Comes into Question," *Washington Post*, July 20, 2010, http://www.wash- ingtonpost.com/wp-dyn/content/article/2010/07/19/ AR2010071905256.html.

12. Laura T. Coffey, "Gasp! Babies' Fat Rolls Being Airbrushed Away?" in TodayHealth.com, November 24, 2009, http:// today.msnbc.msn.com/id/34046700/ns/today-today_ health/t/gasp-babies-fat-rolls-being-airbrushed-away/.

13. John Long, "Ethics in the Age of Digital Photography," in *National Press Photographers Association: Educational Workshops*, accessed June 1, 2011, http://www.nppa .org/professional_development/self-training_resources/ eadp_report/index.html.

14. Accenture Advertisement, *Fortune*, August 16, 2010, 17.

15. Lon Tweeten, "Seek & Find," *Time*, June 25, 2007, 64.

Chapter 17

1. "NSF at a Glance," in *About*, accessed May 24, 2011, http://www.nsf.gov/about/glance.jsp; and "NIH Budget," in *About NIH*, accessed May 23, 2011, http://www .nih.gov/about/budget.htm.

2. Julianne Pepitone, "Census Bureau Submits $1B Job Creation Proposal: Agency Received Funds through the Stimulus Measure," *CNNMoney.com*, accessed May 24, 2011, http://money.cnn.com/2009/04/10/news/economy/ census_stimulus/index.htm.

3. Susan J. Wells, "Merging Compensation Strategies," *HRMagazine* 49, no. 5 (May 2004): 66.

4. Wells, "Merging Compensation Strategies," 66.

5. Todd Dorman, "No Double-Space? No Grant for You: Preschool Grants Tossed for Failing to Double-Space on Application," *Ames Tribune*, September 12, 2007, B1.

6. "Grant Programs and Details," in *National Endowment for the Humanities*, accessed May 28, 2011, http://www.neh .gov/grants/grants.html.

7. Laura K. Grove, "Finding Funding: Writing Winning Proposals for Research Funds," *Technical Communication* 51 (2004): 25–33.

8. Christine Peterson Barabas, *Technical Writing in a Corporate Culture: A Study of the Nature of Information* (Norwood, NJ: Ablex Publishing, 1990), 327.

Chapter 18

1. Carl Bialik, "Sizing Up Crowds Pushes Limits of Technology," *Wall Street Journal*, February 5, 2011, A4; Constance A. Krach and Victoria A. Velkoff, "Centenarians in the United States," *Current Population Reports*, Series P23-199RV, U.S. Bureau of the Census (Washington, DC: Government Printing Office, 1999), 14; "National Longitudinal Surveys Frequently Asked Questions: Does BLS Have Information on the Number of Times People Change Careers in Their Lives?" Bureau of Labor Statistics, last modified September 23, 2010, http://www.bls.gov/nls/ nlsfaqs.htm; and Carl Bialik, "Claims of Thanksgiving Excess Fueled by Feast of Fuzzy Data," *Wall Street Journal*, November 25, 2009, A20.

2. John Hechinger, "Some States Drop Testing Bar," *Wall Street Journal*, October 30, 2009, A3.

3. Thomas Wailgum, "Eight of the Worst Spreadsheet Blunders," *CIO*, August 17, 2007, http://www.cio.com/ article/131500/Eight_of_the_Worst_Spreadsheet_Blunders.

4. Jeffrey Zaslow, "An Iconic Report 20 Years Later: Many of Those Women Married After All," *Wall Street Journal*, May 25, 2006, D1.

5. Arlene Weintraub, "What the Doctors Aren't Disclosing: A New Study Shows How Authors of Medical Journal Articles Flout Rules on Revealing Conflicts of Interest," *BusinessWeek*, May 26, 2008, 32.

6. Erick H. Turner et al., "Selective Publication of Antidepressant Trials and Its Influence on Apparent Efficacy," *New England Journal of Medicine* 358, no. 3 (2008): 252.

7. Scott Thurm, "Mind the Gap: Employment Figures Tell Different Stories," *Wall Street Journal*, October 2, 2010, A2.

8. Stephen E. Moore, "655,000 War Dead?" *Wall Street Journal*, October 18, 2006, A20.

9. Neil Munro and Carl M. Cannon, "Data Bomb," *National Journal*, January 4, 2008, http://www.freerepublic.com/ focus/f-news/1948378/posts.

10. Malcolm Gladwell, *The Tipping Point: How Little Things Can Make a Big Difference* (New York: Little, Brown and Company, 2002), 146; Steven D. Levitt and Stephen J. Dubner, *Freakonomics: A Rogue Economist Explores the Hidden Side of Everything* (New York: William Morrow, 2005), 119–41.

11. Carl Bialik, "Weddings Are Not the Budget Drains Some Surveys Suggest," *Wall Street Journal*, August 24, 2007, B1.

12. Carl Bialik, "Numbers Show China Beats U.S. in Net Use, but Which Numbers?" *Wall Street Journal*, March 28, 2008, B1.

13. Vivien Beattie, Alpa Dhanani, and Michael John Jones, "Longitudinal Perspective Investigating Presentational Change in U.K. Annual Reports," *Journal of Business Communication* 45, no. 2 (April 2008): 186–95.

14. Frederick F. Reichheld, "The One Number You Need to Grow," *Harvard Business Review* 81, no. 12 (December 2003): 46–54.

15. Jakob Nielsen, "Risks of Quantitative Studies," *Alertbox*, March 1, 2004, http://www.useit.com/alertbox/20040301 .html; and Dan Seligman, "The Story They All Got Wrong," *Forbes*, November 25, 2002, 124.

16. "Tiger Effect? Not This Year," *Wall Street Journal*, April 15, 2008, B6.

17. "NASA Releases Information on Federal Survey of Pilots," *Des Moines Register*, January 1, 2008, 2A.

18. George A. Miller, "The Magical Number Seven, Plus or Minus Two: Some Limits on Our Capacity for Processing Information," *Psychological Review* 63, no. 2 (1956): 81–97.

19. Richard J. Connors, ed., *Warren Buffett on Business: Principles from the Sage of Omaha* (Hoboken, NJ: Wiley, 2010), 125.

Chapter 19

1. Sara Silver, "With Its Future Now Uncertain, Bell Labs Turns to Commerce: Storied Font of Basic Research Gets More Practical Focus Amid Worry over a Merger," *Wall Street Journal*, August 21, 2006, A1.
2. Julie Hill, "The Attention Deficit," *Presentations* 17, no. 10 (2003): 26.
3. Patricia Fripp, "Want Your Audiences to Remember What You Say? Learn the Importance of Clear Structure," Fripp and Associates, accessed June 25, 2011, http://www.fripp.com/art.clearstructure.html.
4. Jon Birger et al., "The Best Advice I Ever Got," *Fortune*, May 12, 2008, 70.
5. Chip Heath and Dan Heath, *Made to Stick: Why Some Ideas Survive and Others Die* (New York: Random House, 2007), 7.
6. Heath and Heath, *Made to Stick*, 16–18.
7. Ann Burnett and Diane M. Badzinski, "Judge Nonverbal Communication on Trial: Do Mock Trial Jurors Notice?" *Journal of Communication* 55, no. 2 (2005): 209–24.
8. "Executives' Remarks Annoy Coastal Residents," *Des Moines Register*, June 17, 2010, 4A.
9. Michael Waldholz, "Lab Notes," *Wall Street Journal*, March 19, 1991, B1; and Dave Zielinski, "Perfect Practice," *Presentations* 17, no. 5 (2003): 30–36.
10. G. Michael Campbell, *Bulletproof Presentations* (Franklin Lakes, NJ: Career Press, 2003), 66–67.

SUBJECT INDEX

Online Supplements

ConnectPlus Business Communications One-Semester Online Access for Business and Administrative Communication, 10th Edition

McGraw-Hill ConnectPlus® provides an online eBook and immediate feedback on online assignments, quizzes, and practice tests, providing a learning experience that is personalized for YOU. Study more efficiently and engage with your learning process – Connect with future success!

HOW TO REGISTER

Using a <u>Print Book</u>?
To register and activate your ConnectPlus account, simply follow these easy steps:
1. **Go to the ConnectPlus course web address provided by your instructor or visit the Connect link set up on your instructor's course within your campus learning management system.**
2. **Click on the link to register.**
3. **When prompted, enter the ConnectPlus code found on the inside back cover of your book and click Submit. Complete the brief registration form that follows to begin using Connect.**

Using an <u>eBook</u>?
To register and activate your ConnectPlus account, simply follow these easy steps:
1. **Upon purchase of your eBook, you will be granted automatic access to ConnectPlus.**
2. **Go to the ConnectPlus course web address provided by your instructor or visit the Connect link set up on your instructor's course within your campus learning management system.**
3. **Sign in using the same email address and password you used to register on the eBookstore. Complete your registration and begin using Connect.**

Note: Access Code is for one use only. If you did not purchase this book new, the access code included in this book is no longer valid.

Need help? Visit mhhe.com/support